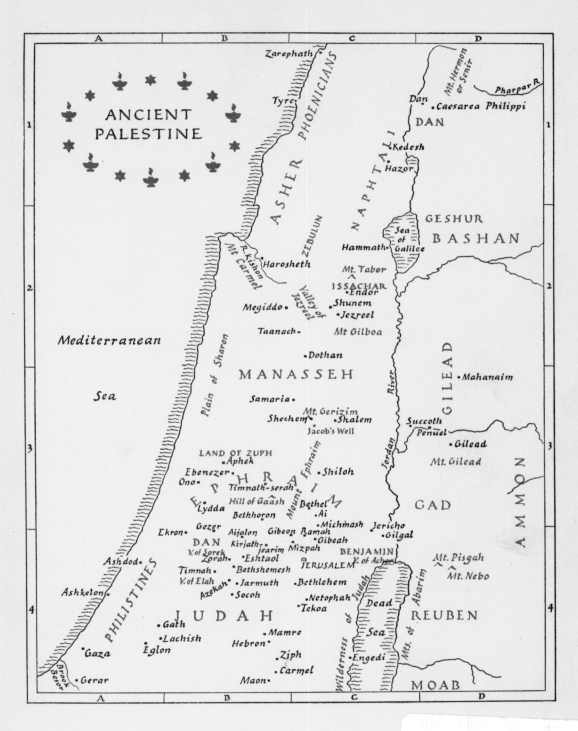

# ANCIENT PALESTINE

Zarephath

Tyre

ASHER PHOENICIANS

NAPHTALI

Mt. Hermon or Senir

Pharpar R.

Dan

Caesarea Philippi

DAN

Kedesh

Hazor

GESHUR

BASHAN

ZEBULUN

R. Kishon

Mt. Carmel

Harosheth

Hammath

Sea of Galilee

Mt. Tabor

Valley of Jezreel

ISSACHAR

Endor

Shunem

Jezreel

Mt Gilboa

Megiddo

Taanach

Mediterranean

Plain of Sharon

Dothan

MANASSEH

Samaria

Shechem

Mt. Gerizim

Shalem

Jacob's Well

GILEAD

Mahanaim

Jordan River

Succoth

Penuel

Gilead

Mt. Gilead

Sea

LAND OF ZUPH

Aphek

Ebenezer

Ono

Mount Ephraim

Shiloh

Timnath-serah

Hill of Gaâsh

Bethel

Ai

Lydda

Bethhoron

Michmash

Jericho

Ekron

Gezer

Aijalon

Gibeon

Ramah

Gilgal

GAD

AMMON

DAN

Kirjath-jearim

Mizpah

Gibeah

V. of Sorek

Zorah

Eshtaol

BENJAMIN

V. of Achor

Mt. Pisgah

Ashdod

Timnah

Bethshemesh

JERUSALEM

Mt. Nebo

V. of Elah

Jarmuth

Bethlehem

Mts. of Abarim

Azekah

Socoh

Netophah

Dead

Ashkelon

Tekoa

Sea

REUBEN

JUDAH

Gath

Mamre

Lachish

Hebron

Wilderness of Judah

Gaza

Eglon

Ziph

Engedi

Brook Besor

Gerar

Maon

Carmel

MOAB

PHILISTINES

# THE HOME BIBLE

# THE HOME BIBLE
## ARRANGED FOR FAMILY READING
### *from the King James Version*

BY

RUTH HORNBLOWER GREENOUGH

*With illustrations from designs by*
WILLIAM BLAKE

DECORATIONS BY RUDOLPH RUZICKA

*HARPER & BROTHERS · PUBLISHERS · NEW YORK*

*Printed in the United States of America*

TO MY MOTHER
AND TO THE MEMORY OF
MY FATHER

# PREFACE

*I also came out as a brook from a river,*
*And as a conduit into a garden.*
*I said, I will water my best Garden,*
*And will water abundantly my garden bed:*
*And, lo, my brook became a river,*
*And my river became a sea.*

*THUS sang the poet more than two thousand years ago. And so it has been with this volume whose first purpose was to fulfill the expressed desire of my children that I gather together for their children those passages from the Bible which they were accustomed to hear read aloud. My husband, Chester Noyes Greenough, had also suggested that I write a book on religious education. From working with him I learned his reverence for sources and like to think that this would have met with his approval. The search for the familiar revealed seas which we had never before sighted. Truly, in the words of the ancient poet "my brook became a river and my river became a sea", as the projected little manual for family reading became ever more comprehensive.*

*The Bible is a difficult study, and many are bewildered, and turn aside for lack of guidance. Here I have endeavored to select those parts which might properly become a sacred book designed to be read by young and old.*

*In Part One, the story of the Creation and verses describing and praising its wonders are followed by the lives of great heroes of old who sought to know God and to do his will. Here also are the clear ringing words of the prophets to a wayward people, and their promises of the coming of a Messiah to redeem the world.*

*Part Two opens with The Life of Jesus, made one account from the four gospels that he may be seen more vividly. I would have him pictured as he went about with his friends in Galilee and Judæa, spending himself in teaching and healing, with increasing awareness that he must steadfastly set his face to Jerusalem, there to die.*

[ vii ]

# PREFACE

*The parables and the discourse of Jesus at the Last Supper are printed in italics to set them apart from the narrative.*

*After The Life of Jesus comes Paul the Apostle, the mentor of youth for all succeeding generations, of whom Schweitzer says, "the followers of Paul, believing in the spirit, walk secure and undismayed." I have taken many liberties with the Letters of Paul, selecting those passages which to me seem timeless, and arranging them by subject. This, it is hoped, will lead to a closer study of the epistles themselves.*

*Many of the Psalms are here, arranged as hymns of praise and worship, psalms of reflection and personal confession of faith.*

*Placed together are the more philosophical and preceptual books, including Job, that magnificent universal character, and Jonah, often called our first internationalist. The commandments of Moses and of Jesus are repeated, as are God's covenants with his people.*

*All is here that one may find the way to make "the spirit of man the candle of the Lord"; and transfiguring all is a sense of the mystery and the majesty which daily surround our lives.*

RUTH HORNBLOWER GREENOUGH

*Belmont*
*Massachusetts*

# ACKNOWLEDGMENTS

GRATITUDE is not easily expressed. To Robert H. Pfeiffer I shall always be deeply indebted for the encouragement which he gave me from the beginning, and for the time which he generously took from his own work to read the manuscript. He gave me confidence, and his judgments are sure. My friends, James Buell Munn and Ruth Hanford Munn, have often lent an attentive ear and given me helpful suggestions.

In the making of this book I am happy to have been associated with Rudolph Ruzicka and John Bianchi, each a master in his field. Mr. Ruzicka has made searching and scholarly study for each drawing, always having in mind its close association with Blake. In the design and typography Mr. Bianchi carries on here the high excellence which Mr. Updike gave to The Merrymount Press; without his wise counsel and years of experience it is doubtful if I could have finished this work. Mr. Ruzicka's daughter, Veronica Ruzicka, in preparing the maps, has added imagination and charm to her great skill as a cartographer. The exacting work of preparing the indices and of proof reading has been done by Ralph Lazzaro of the Harvard Divinity School.

There is one whose work began with the first page of the manuscript and who has been steadfast throughout. It would be impossible adequately to express my appreciation to Phyllis C. MacLean, who has done all of the typing. More than that, she has been the gentle reader; her advice has been valuable, her patience endless, and her enthusiasm has never failed.

The assembling of the illustrations, all by William Blake with the exception of the mosaic in Hagia Sophia, has been a pleasant task. Everywhere, I have met very real interest and have been given generous assistance.

Mrs. William Emerson has assured me that nothing would please her more than to have a part in my book and has permitted me to reproduce the "Act of Creation" from her copy of *Europe* and "Father, Son and Holy Ghost" from *Blake's Notebook*, formerly known as "The Rossetti Notebook".

With Mr. Kerrison Preston, literary executor of the Estate of Graham Robertson, I have enjoyed a delightful correspondence. He gave me permission to use eight of the Blakes and provided photographs from the originals.

Professor Chauncey B. Tinker of Yale kindly offered "The Book of My Remembrance", and Mr. and Mrs. Philip Hofer "The Wise and Foolish Virgins".

In addition, I should like to express my appreciation for permission gener-

[ ix ]

## ACKNOWLEDGMENTS

ously granted to reproduce pictures, in England: the Fitzwilliam Museum (Cambridge), the Tate Gallery, The Whitworth Art Gallery (Manchester); and in this country: the Fogg Museum of Art, the Museum of Fine Arts (Boston), the Metropolitan Museum of Art, the Museum of Art at the Rhode Island School of Design, the Yale University Art Gallery, the Huntington Library, and the Houghton Library.

R. H. G.

# CONTENTS

## PART I

## PART II

# CONTENTS

# ILLUSTRATIONS

## PART I

# ILLUSTRATIONS

# PART II

# ILLUSTRATIONS

PART  I

# I

# THE CREATION

I N the beginning God created the heaven and the earth. And the *The first days* earth was without form, and void; and darkness was upon the face of the deep. And the Spirit of God moved upon the face of the waters. And God said, "Let there be light": and there was light. And God saw the light, that it was good: and God divided the light from the darkness. And God called the light Day, and the darkness he called Night. And the evening and the morning were the first day.

And God said, "Let there be a firmament in the midst of the waters, and let it divide the waters from the waters." And God made the firmament, and divided the waters which were under the firmament from the waters which were above the firmament: and it was so. And God called the firmament Heaven. And the evening and the morning were the second day.

And God said, "Let the waters under the heaven be gathered together unto one place, and let the dry land appear": and it was so. And God called the dry land Earth; and the gathering together of the waters called he Seas: and God saw that it was good. And God said, "Let the earth bring forth grass, the herb yielding seed, and the fruit tree yielding fruit after his kind, whose seed is in itself, upon the earth": and it was so. And the earth brought forth grass, and herb yielding seed after his kind, and the tree yielding fruit, whose seed was in itself, after his kind: and God saw that it was good. And the evening and the morning were the third day.

And God said, "Let there be lights in the firmament of the heaven to divide the day from the night; and let them be for signs, and for seasons, and for days, and years: and let them be for lights in the firmament of the heaven to give light upon the earth": and it was so. And God made two great lights; the greater light to rule the day, and the lesser light to rule the night: he made the stars also. And God set them in the firmament of the heaven to give light upon the earth, and to rule over the day and over the night, and to divide the light from the darkness: and God saw that it was good. And the evening and the morning were the fourth day.

*The earth made fruitful* And God said, "Let the waters bring forth abundantly the moving creature that hath life, and fowl that may fly above the earth in the open firmament of heaven." And God created great whales, and every living creature that moveth, which the waters brought forth abundantly, after their kind, and every winged fowl after his kind: and God saw that it was good. And God blessed them, saying, "Be fruitful, and multiply, and fill the waters in the seas, and let fowl multiply in the earth." And the evening and the morning were the fifth day.

And God said, "Let the earth bring forth the living creature after his kind, cattle, and creeping thing, and beast of the earth after his kind": and it was so. And God made the beast of the earth after his kind, and cattle after their kind, and every thing that creepeth upon the earth after his kind: and God saw that it was good. And God said, "Let us make man in our image, after our likeness: and let them have dominion over the fish of the sea, and over the fowl of the air, and over the cattle, and over all the earth, and over every creeping thing that creepeth upon the earth." So God created man in his own image, in the image of God created he him; male and female created he them. And God blessed them, and God said unto them, "Be fruitful, and multiply, and replenish the earth, and subdue it: and have dominion over the fish of the sea, and over the fowl of the air, and over every living thing that moveth upon the earth."

And God said, "Behold, I have given you every herb bearing seed, which is upon the face of all the earth, and every tree, in the which is the fruit of a tree yielding seed; to you it shall be for meat. And to every beast of the earth, and to every fowl of the air, and to every thing that creepeth upon the earth, wherein there is life, I have given every green herb for meat": and it was so. And God saw every thing that he had made, and, behold, it was very good. And the evening and the morning were the sixth day.

*The first sabbath* Thus the heavens and the earth were finished, and all the host of them. And on the seventh day God ended his work which he had made; and he rested on the seventh day from all his work which he had made. And God blessed the seventh day, and sanctified it: because that in it he had rested from all his work which God created and made.

These are the generations of the heavens and of the earth when they were created, in the day that the LORD God made the earth and the

*ADAM NAMING THE BEASTS*

heavens, and every plant of the field before it was in the earth, and every *The Garden of Eden* herb of the field before it grew: for the Lord God had not caused it to rain upon the earth, and there was not a man to till the ground. But there went up a mist from the earth, and watered the whole face of the ground. And the Lord God formed man of the dust of the ground, and breathed into his nostrils the breath of life; and man became a living soul.

And the Lord God planted a garden eastward in Eden; and there he put the man whom he had formed. And out of the ground made the Lord God to grow every tree that is pleasant to the sight, and good for food; the tree of life also in the midst of the garden; and the tree of knowledge of good and evil. And a river went out of Eden to water the garden.

And the Lord God took the man, and put him into the garden of Eden to dress it and to keep it. And the Lord God commanded the man, saying, "Of every tree of the garden thou mayest freely eat: but of the tree of the knowledge of good and evil, thou shalt not eat of it: for in the day that thou eatest thereof thou shalt surely die."

And the Lord God said, "It is not good that the man should be alone; *Creation of Eve* I will make him an help meet for him." And out of the ground the Lord God formed every beast of the field, and every fowl of the air; and brought them unto Adam to see what he would call them: and whatsoever Adam called every living creature, that was the name thereof. And Adam gave names to all cattle, and to the fowl of the air, and to every beast of the field; but for Adam there was not found an help meet for him. And the Lord God caused a deep sleep to fall upon Adam, and he slept: and he took one of his ribs, and closed up the flesh instead thereof; and the rib, which the Lord God had taken from man, made he a woman, and brought her unto the man. And Adam said,

> This is now bone of my bones,
> And flesh of my flesh:
> She shall be called Woman,
> Because she was taken out of Man.

Therefore shall a man leave his father and his mother, and shall cleave unto his wife: and they shall be one flesh.

[ 3 ]

## THE CREATION

*The works of God throughout nature*

THE pride of the height, the clear firmament,
The beauty of heaven, with his glorious shew;
The sun when it appeareth, declaring at his rising a marvellous
    instrument,
The work of the most High:
At noon it parcheth the country,
And who can abide the burning heat thereof?
A man blowing a furnace is in works of heat,
But the sun burneth the mountains three times more;
Breathing out fiery vapours, and sending forth bright beams,
It dimmeth the eyes.
Great is the Lord that made it;
And at his commandment it runneth hastily.

He made the moon also to serve in her season
For a declaration of times, and a sign of the world.
From the moon is the sign of feasts,
A light that decreaseth in her perfection.
The month is called after her name,
Increasing wonderfully in her changing,
Being an instrument of the armies above,
Shining in the firmament of heaven;

The beauty of heaven, the glory of the stars,
An ornament giving light in the highest places of the Lord.
At the commandment of the Holy One they will stand in their order,
And never faint in their watches.
Look upon the rainbow, and praise him that made it;
Very beautiful it is in the brightness thereof.
It compasseth the heaven about with a glorious circle,
And the hands of the most High have bended it.

By his commandment he maketh the snow to fall apace,
And sendeth swiftly the lightnings of his judgment.
Through this the treasures are opened:
And clouds fly forth as fowls.

[ 4 ]

*THE CREATION OF EVE*

## THE CREATION

By his great power he maketh the clouds firm,
And the hailstones are broken small.
At his sight the mountains are shaken,
And at his will the south wind bloweth.
The noise of the thunder maketh the earth to tremble:
So doth the northern storm and the whirlwind:
As birds flying he scattereth the snow,
And the falling down thereof is as the lighting of grasshoppers:
The eye marvelleth at the beauty of the whiteness thereof,
And the heart is astonished at the raining of it.

The hoarfrost also as salt he poureth on the earth,
And being congealed, it lieth on the top of sharp stakes.
When the cold north wind bloweth,
And the water is congealed into ice,
It abideth upon every gathering together of water,
And clotheth the water as with a breastplate.
It devoureth the mountains,
And burneth the wilderness, and consumeth the grass as fire.
A present remedy of all is a mist coming speedily:
A dew coming after heat refresheth.

By his counsel he appeaseth the deep,
And planteth islands therein.
They that sail on the sea tell of the danger thereof;
And when we hear it with our ears, we marvel thereat.
For therein be strange and wondrous works,
Variety of all kinds of beasts and whales created.
By him the end of them hath prosperous success,
And by his word all things consist.

We may speak much, and yet come short:
Wherefore in sum, he is all.
How shall we be able to magnify him?
For he is great above all his works.
The Lord is terrible and very great,

*God is terrible and
very great*

[ 5 ]

*Marvellous is the power
of God*

And marvellous in his power.
When ye glorify the Lord, exalt him as much as ye can;
For even yet will he far exceed:
And when ye exalt him, put forth all your strength,
And be not weary; for ye can never go far enough.

Who hath seen him, that he might tell us?
And who can magnify him as he is?
There are yet hid greater things than these be,
For we have seen but a few of his works.
For the LORD hath made all things;
And to the godly hath he given wisdom.

*Meditations on his
mighty power*

BLESS the Lord, O my soul.
O LORD my God, thou art very great;
Thou art clothed with honour and majesty.
Who coverest thyself with light as with a garment:
Who stretchest out the heavens like a curtain:
Who layeth the beams of his chambers in the waters:
Who maketh the clouds his chariot:
Who walketh upon the wings of the wind:
Who maketh his angels spirits;
His ministers a flaming fire:
Who laid the foundations of the earth,
That it should not be removed for ever.
Thou coveredst it with the deep as with a garment:
The waters stood above the mountains.
At thy rebuke they fled;
At the voice of thy thunder they hasted away.
They go up by the mountains; they go down by the valleys
Unto the place which thou hast founded for them.
Thou hast set a bound that they may not pass over;
That they turn not again to cover the earth.
He sendeth the springs into the valleys,
Which run among the hills.
They give drink to every beast of the field:

## THE CREATION

The wild asses quench their thirst.
By them shall the fowls of the heaven have their habitation,
Which sing among the branches.
He watereth the hills from his chambers:
The earth is satisfied with the fruit of thy works.
He causeth the grass to grow for the cattle,
And herb for the service of man:
That he may bring forth food out of the earth;
And wine that maketh glad the heart of man,
And oil to make his face to shine,
And bread which strengtheneth man's heart.
The trees of the Lord are full of sap;
The cedars of Lebanon, which he hath planted;
Where the birds make their nests:
As for the stork, the fir trees are her house.
The high hills are a refuge for the wild goats;
And the rocks for the conies.
He appointed the moon for seasons:
The sun knoweth his going down.
Thou makest darkness, and it is night:
Wherein all the beasts of the forest do creep forth.
The young lions roar after their prey,
And seek their meat from God.
The sun ariseth, they gather themselves together,
And lay them down in their dens.
Man goeth forth unto his work
And to his labour until the evening.
O Lord, how manifold are thy works!
In wisdom hast thou made them all:
The earth is full of thy riches.
So is this great and wide sea,
Wherein are things creeping innumerable,
Both small and great beasts.
There go the ships:
There is that leviathan, whom thou hast made to play therein.
These wait all upon thee;

*Eternity of God's glory*

That thou mayest give them their meat in due season.
That thou givest them they gather:
Thou openest thine hand, they are filled with good.
Thou hidest thy face, they are troubled:
Thou takest away their breath, they die,
And return to their dust.
Thou sendest forth thy spirit, they are created:
And thou renewest the face of the earth.
The glory of the Lord shall endure for ever:
The Lord shall rejoice in his works.
He looketh on the earth, and it trembleth:
He toucheth the hills, and they smoke.
I will sing unto the Lord as long as I live:
I will sing praise to my God while I have my being.
My meditation of him shall be sweet:
I will be glad in the Lord.
Bless thou the Lord, O my soul.
Praise ye the Lord.

*Deception of Eve*

Now the serpent was more subtil than any beast of the field which the Lord God had made. And he said unto the woman, "Yea, hath God said, 'Ye shall not eat of every tree of the garden'?"

And the woman said unto the serpent, "We may eat of the fruit of the trees of the garden: but of the fruit of the tree which is in the midst of the garden, God hath said, 'Ye shall not eat of it, neither shall ye touch it, lest ye die.'"

And the serpent said unto the woman, "Ye shall not surely die: for God doth know that in the day ye eat thereof, then your eyes shall be opened, and ye shall be as gods, knowing good and evil."

And when the woman saw that the tree was good for food, and that it was pleasant to the eyes, and a tree to be desired to make one wise, she took of the fruit thereof, and did eat, and gave also unto her husband with her; and he did eat. And the eyes of them both were opened. And they heard the voice of the Lord God walking in the garden in the cool of the day: and Adam and his wife hid themselves from the presence of the Lord God amongst the trees of the garden.

And the Lord God called unto Adam, and said unto him, "Where art *The fall of man* thou?"

And he said, "I heard thy voice in the garden, and I was afraid, and I hid myself."

And he said, "Hast thou eaten of the tree, whereof I commanded thee that thou shouldest not eat?"

And the man said, "The woman whom thou gavest to be with me, she gave me of the tree, and I did eat."

And the Lord God said unto the woman, "What is this that thou hast done?"

And the woman said, "The serpent beguiled me, and I did eat."

And the Lord God said unto the serpent,

> Because thou hast done this,
> Thou art cursed above all cattle,
> And above every beast of the field;
> And upon thy belly shalt thou go,
> And dust shalt thou eat all the days of thy life.

Unto the woman he said,

> In sorrow thou shalt bring forth children;
> Thy husband shall rule over thee.

And unto Adam he said, "Because thou hast hearkened unto the voice of thy wife, and hast eaten of the tree, of which I commanded thee, saying, ' Thou shalt not eat of it':

> Cursed is the ground for thy sake;
> In sorrow shalt thou eat of it all the days of thy life;
> Thorns also and thistles shall it bring forth to thee;
> And thou shalt eat the herb of the field;
> In the sweat of thy face shalt thou eat bread,
> Till thou return unto the ground;
> For out of it wast thou taken:
> For dust thou art, and unto dust shalt thou return."

Unto Adam also and to his wife did the Lord God make coats of

*Expulsion from the garden* skins, and clothed them. And Adam called his wife's name Eve; because she was the mother of all living.

And the LORD God said, "Behold, the man is become as one of us, to know good and evil: and now, lest he put forth his hand, and take also of the tree of life, and eat, and live for ever": therefore the LORD God sent him forth from the garden of Eden, to till the ground from whence he was taken. So he drove out the man; and he placed at the east of the garden of Eden Cherubims, and a flaming sword which turned every way, to keep the way of the tree of life.

# II

# EARLY MAN

AND Adam knew Eve his wife; and she conceived, and bare Cain, and said, "I have gotten a man from the LORD." And she again bare his brother Abel. And Abel was a keeper of sheep, but Cain was a tiller of the ground. And in process of time it came to pass, that Cain brought of the fruit of the ground an offering unto the LORD. And Abel, he also brought of the firstlings of his flock and of the fat thereof. And the LORD had respect unto Abel and to his offering; but unto Cain and to his offering he had not respect. And Cain was very wroth, and his countenance fell.

And the LORD said unto Cain, "Why art thou wroth? and why is thy countenance fallen? If thou doest well, shalt thou not be accepted? and if thou doest not well, sin lieth at the door."

And Cain talked with Abel his brother: and it came to pass, when they were in the field, that Cain rose up against Abel his brother, and slew him.

And the LORD said unto Cain, "Where is Abel thy brother?"

And he said, "I know not: Am I my brother's keeper?"

And he said, "What hast thou done? the voice of thy brother's blood crieth unto me from the ground. When thou tillest the ground, it shall not henceforth yield unto thee her strength; a fugitive and a vagabond shalt thou be in the earth."

And Cain said unto the LORD, "My punishment is greater than I can bear."

And Cain went out from the presence of the LORD, and dwelt in the land of Nod, on the east of Eden. And Cain knew his wife; and she conceived, and bare Enoch: and he builded a city, and called the name of the city, after the name of his son, Enoch. And Enoch walked with God: and he was not; for God took him.

And Jabal was the father of such as dwell in tents, and of such as have cattle. And his brother's name was Jubal: he was the father of all such as handle the harp and organ. And Tubal-cain was an instructer of every artificer in brass and iron.

*Noah instructed
to build the ark*

And it came to pass, when men began to multiply on the face of the earth, and daughters were born unto them, that the sons of God saw the daughters of men that they were fair; and they took them wives of all which they chose.

And the LORD said, "My spirit shall not always strive with man, for that he also is flesh."

There were giants in the earth in those days; and also after that, the same became mighty men which were of old, men of renown. And God saw that the wickedness of man was great in the earth, and that every imagination of the thoughts of his heart was only evil continually. And it repented the LORD that he had made man on the earth, and it grieved him at his heart.

And the LORD said, "I will destroy man whom I have created from the face of the earth; both man, and beast, and the creeping thing, and the fowls of the air; for it repenteth me that I have made them."

But Noah found grace in the eyes of the LORD. These are the generations of Noah: Noah was a just man and perfect in his generations, and Noah walked with God. And Noah begat three sons, Shem, Ham, and Japheth.

And God said unto Noah, "Make thee an ark of gopher wood: rooms shalt thou make in the ark, and shalt pitch it within and without with pitch. A window shalt thou make to the ark; and the door of the ark shalt thou set in the side thereof. And, behold, I, even I, do bring a flood of waters upon the earth, to destroy all flesh, wherein is the breath of life, from under heaven; and every thing that is in the earth shall die. But with thee will I establish my covenant; and thou shalt come into the ark, thou, and thy sons, and thy wife, and thy sons' wives with thee. And of every living thing of all flesh, two of every sort shalt thou bring into the ark, to keep them alive with thee; they shall be male and female. Of fowls after their kind, and of cattle after their kind, of every creeping thing of the earth after his kind, two of every sort shall come unto thee, to keep them alive. And take thou unto thee of all food that is eaten, and thou shalt gather it to thee; and it shall be for food for thee, and for them."

Thus did Noah; according to all that God commanded him, so did he.

And the LORD said unto Noah, "Come thou and all thy house into the ark; for thee have I seen righteous before me in this generation. I *The flood* will cause it to rain upon the earth forty days and forty nights; and every living substance that I have made will I destroy from off the face of the earth."

And Noah did according unto all that the LORD commanded him. In the selfsame day entered Noah, and Shem, and Ham, and Japheth, the sons of Noah, and Noah's wife, and the three wives of his sons with them, into the ark; they, and every beast after his kind, and all the cattle after their kind, and every creeping thing that creepeth upon the earth after his kind, and every fowl after his kind, every bird of every sort. And they went in unto Noah into the ark, two and two of all flesh, wherein is the breath of life. And they that went in, went in male and female of all flesh, as God had commanded him: and the LORD shut him in.

And it came to pass, after seven days, that the waters of the flood were upon the earth. In the six hundredth year of Noah's life, in the second month, the seventeenth day of the month, the same day were all the fountains of the great deep broken up, and the windows of heaven were opened. And the rain was upon the earth forty days and forty nights; and the waters increased, and bare up the ark, and it was lift up above the earth. And the waters prevailed, and were increased greatly upon the earth; and the ark went upon the face of the waters. And the waters prevailed exceedingly upon the earth; and all the high hills, that were under the whole heaven, were covered. And every living substance was destroyed which was upon the face of the ground. All in whose nostrils was the breath of life, of all that was in the dry land, died, both man, and cattle, and the creeping things, and the fowl of the heaven; and they were destroyed from the earth: and Noah only remained alive, and they that were with him in the ark. And God remembered Noah, and every living thing, and all the cattle that was with him in the ark: and God made a wind to pass over the earth, and the waters asswaged: the fountains also of the deep and the windows of heaven were stopped, and the rain from heaven was restrained; and the waters returned from off the earth continually: and after the end of the hundred and fifty days the waters were abated. And the ark rested in the seventh month, on the seventeenth day of the month, upon the mountains of Ararat. And the

*The ark rests* waters decreased continually until the tenth month: in the tenth month, on the first day of the month, were the tops of the mountains seen.

And it came to pass at the end of forty days, that Noah opened the window of the ark which he had made: and he sent forth a raven, which went forth to and fro, until the waters were dried up from off the earth. Also he sent forth a dove from him, to see if the waters were abated from off the face of the ground; but the dove found no rest for the sole of her foot, and she returned unto him into the ark, for the waters were on the face of the whole earth: then he put forth his hand, and took her, and pulled her in unto him into the ark. And he stayed yet other seven days; and again he sent forth the dove out of the ark; and the dove came in to him in the evening; and, lo, in her mouth was an olive leaf pluckt off: so Noah knew that the waters were abated from off the earth. And he stayed yet other seven days; and sent forth the dove; which returned not again unto him any more. And it came to pass in the six hundredth and first year, in the first month, the first day of the month, the waters were dried up from off the earth: and Noah removed the covering of the ark, and looked, and, behold, the face of the ground was dry. And in the second month, on the seven and twentieth day of the month, was the earth dried.

And God spake unto Noah, saying, "Go forth of the ark, thou, and thy wife, and thy sons, and thy sons' wives with thee. Bring forth with thee every living thing that is with thee, of all flesh, both of fowl, and of cattle, and of every creeping thing that creepeth upon the earth; that they may breed abundantly in the earth, and be fruitful, and multiply upon the earth."

And Noah went forth, and his sons, and his wife, and his sons' wives with him: every beast, every creeping thing, and every fowl, and whatsoever creepeth upon the earth, after their kinds, went forth out of the ark. And Noah builded an altar unto the LORD, and offered burnt offerings on the altar. And the LORD smelled a sweet savour; and the LORD said in his heart, "I will not again curse the ground any more for man's sake; neither will I again smite any more every thing living, as I have done. While the earth remaineth, seedtime and harvest, and cold and heat, and summer and winter, and day and night shall not cease."

And God blessed Noah and his sons, and said unto them, "Be fruit-

ful, and multiply, and replenish the earth. Every moving thing that liveth *The covenant*
shall be meat for you; even as the green herb have I given you all things. *established*
Whoso sheddeth man's blood, by man shall his blood be shed": for in the
image of God made he man.

And God said, "This is the token of the covenant which I make between me and you and every living creature that is with you, for perpetual generations: I do set my bow in the cloud, and it shall be for a
token of a covenant between me and the earth. And it shall come to pass,
when I bring a cloud over the earth, that the bow shall be seen in the
cloud: and I will remember my covenant, which is between me and you
and every living creature of all flesh; and the waters shall no more become a flood to destroy all flesh. And the bow shall be in the cloud; and
I will look upon it, that I may remember the everlasting covenant between God and every living creature of all flesh that is upon the earth."

And God said unto Noah, "This is the token of the covenant, which
I have established between me and all flesh that is upon the earth."

And the whole earth was of one language, and of one speech. And *One language*
it came to pass, as they journeyed from the east, that they found a plain
in the land of Shinar; and they dwelt there. And they said one to another, "Go to, let us make brick, and burn them throughly." And they
had brick for stone, and slime had they for morter. And they said, "Go
to, let us build us a city and a tower, whose top may reach unto heaven;
and let us make us a name, lest we be scattered abroad upon the face of
the whole earth."

And the LORD came down to see the city and the tower, which the
children of men builded. And the LORD said, "Behold, the people is one,
and they have all one language; and this they begin to do: and now
nothing will be restrained from them, which they have imagined to do.
Go to, let us go down, and there confound their language, that they may
not understand one another's speech."

So the LORD scattered them abroad from thence upon the face of all
the earth: and they left off to build the city. Therefore is the name of it
called Babel; because the LORD did there confound the language of all
the earth: and from thence did the LORD scatter them abroad upon the
face of all the earth.

Let us now praise famous men.
  The Lord hath wrought great glory by them
Through his great power from the beginning.
Such as did bear rule in their kingdoms,
Men renowned for their power,
Giving counsel by their understanding,
And declaring prophecies:
Leaders of the people by their counsels,
And by their knowledge of learning meet for the people,
Wise and eloquent in their instructions:
Such as found out musical tunes,
And recited verses in writing:
Rich men furnished with ability,
Living peaceably in their habitations:
All these were honoured in their generations,
And were the glory of their times.
There be of them, that have left a name behind them,
That their praises might be reported.
And some there be, which have no memorial.
These were merciful men,
Whose righteousness hath not been forgotten.
With their seed shall continually remain a good inheritance.
Their seed standeth fast,
And their children for their sakes.
Their seed shall remain for ever,
And their glory shall not be blotted out.
Their bodies are buried in peace;
But their name liveth for evermore.
The people will tell of their wisdom,
And the congregation will shew forth their praise.

Enoch pleased the Lord, and was translated,
Being an example of repentance to all generations.
Noah was found perfect and righteous;
Therefore was he left as a remnant unto the earth,

## EARLY MAN

When the flood came.
An everlasting covenant was made with him,
That all flesh should perish no more by the flood.
Abraham was a great father of many people:
In glory was there none like unto him;
Who kept the law of the most High,
And was in covenant with him:
He established the covenant in his flesh;
And when he was proved, he was found faithful.
Therefore he assured him by an oath,
That he would bless the nations,
And that he would multiply him as the dust of the earth,
And exalt his seed as the stars,
And cause them to inherit from sea to sea,
And from the river unto the utmost part of the land.
With Isaac did he establish likewise
[For Abraham his father's sake]
The blessing of all men, and the covenant,
And made it rest upon the head of Jacob.
He acknowledged him in his blessing,
And gave him an heritage,
And divided his portions;
Among the twelve tribes did he part them.
And he brought out of him a merciful man,
Which found favour in the sight of all flesh,
Even Moses, beloved of God and men,
Whose memorial is blessed.
He made him like to the glorious saints,
And magnified him.
By his words he caused the wonders to cease,
And he made him glorious in the sight of kings,
And gave him a commandment for his people,
And shewed him part of his glory.
He sanctified him in his faithfulness and meekness,
And chose him out of all men.

*Of Aaron*

He made him to hear his voice,
And brought him into the dark cloud,
And gave him commandments before his face,
Even the law of life and knowledge,
That he might teach Jacob his covenants,
And Israel his judgments.

He exalted Aaron, an holy man like unto him,
Even his brother, of the tribe of Levi.
An everlasting covenant he made with him,
And gave him the priesthood among the people;
He beautified him with comely ornaments,
And clothed him with a robe of glory.
He put upon him perfect glory;
And strengthened him with rich garments,
With breeches, with a long robe, and the ephod.
And he compassed him with pomegranates,
And with many golden bells round about,
That as he went there might be a sound,
And a noise made that might be heard in the temple,
For a memorial to the children of his people;
With an holy garment, with gold, and blue silk,
And purple, the work of the embroiderer,
With a breastplate of judgment,
With twisted scarlet, the work of the cunning workman,
With precious stones graven like seals,
And set in gold, the work of the jeweller,
With a writing engraved for a memorial,
After the number of the tribes of Israel.
He set a crown of gold upon the mitre,
Wherein was engraved Holiness,
An ornament of honour, a costly work,
The desires of the eyes, goodly and beautiful.
Before him there were none such,
Neither did ever any stranger put them on,
But only his children and his children's children perpetually.

Moses consecrated him,
And anointed him with holy oil:
This was appointed unto him by an everlasting covenant,
And to his seed, so long as the heavens should remain,
That they should minister unto him, and execute the office of the
　　priesthood,
And bless the people in his name.
He chose him out of all men living
To offer sacrifices to the Lord, incense,
And a sweet savour, for a memorial,
To make reconciliation for his people.
He gave unto him his commandments,
And authority in the statutes of judgments,
That he should teach Jacob the testimonies, and inform Israel in his
　　laws.
Strangers conspired together against him,
And maligned him in the wilderness.
This the Lord saw, and it displeased him.
But he made Aaron more honourable,
And gave him an heritage,
And divided unto him the firstfruits of the increase;
Especially he prepared bread in abundance.
Howbeit in the land of the people he had no inheritance,
Neither had he any portion among the people:
For the Lord himself is his portion and inheritance.

The third in glory is Phinees the son of Eleazar,
Because he had zeal in the fear of the Lord,
And stood up with good courage of heart
When the people were turned back,
And made reconciliation for Israel.
Therefore was there a covenant of peace made with him,
That he should be the chief of the sanctuary and of his people,
And that he and his posterity should have the dignity of the priesthood
　　for ever.
God give you wisdom in your heart

*Of Caleb*   To judge his people in righteousness,
That their good things be not abolished,
And that their glory may endure for ever.

The Lord gave strength also unto Caleb,
Which remained with him unto his old age:
So that he entered upon the high places of the land,
And his seed obtained it for an heritage:
That all the children of Israel might see
That it is good to follow the Lord.
And concerning the judges, every one by name,
Who departed not from the Lord,
Let their memory be blessed,
And let the name of them that were honoured be continued upon their
        children.

*Of Samuel*   Samuel, the prophet of the Lord, beloved of his Lord,
Established a kingdom,
And anointed princes over his people.
By the law of the Lord he judged the congregation.
By his faithfulness he was found a true prophet,
And by his word he was known to be faithful in vision.
He called upon the mighty Lord,
When his enemies pressed upon him on every side.
And the Lord thundered from heaven,
And with a great noise made his voice to be heard.
And he destroyed the rulers of the Tyrians,
And all the princes of the Philistines.
And before his long sleep
He made protestations in the sight of the Lord and his anointed,
"I have not taken any man's goods, so much as a shoe":
And no man did accuse him.
And after his death he prophesied,
And shewed the king his end,
And lifted up his voice from the earth in prophecy.
The remembrance of Josias is like the composition of the perfume

# EARLY MAN

That is made by the art of the apothecary: *Of Josias*
It is sweet as honey in all mouths,
And as musick at a banquet of wine.
He behaved himself uprightly in the conversion of the people,
And took away the abominations of iniquity.
He directed his heart unto the Lord,
And in the time of the ungodly he established the worship of God.

Simon the high priest, the son of Onias, *Of Simon*
Who in his life repaired the house again,
And in his days fortified the temple:
And by him was built from the foundation the double height,
The high fortress of the wall about the temple:
In his days the cistern to receive water,
Being in compass as the sea, was covered with plates of brass:
He took care of the temple that it should not fall,
And fortified the city against besieging:
How was he honoured in the midst of the people
In his coming out of the sanctuary!
He was as the morning star in the midst of a cloud,
And as the moon at the full:
As the sun shining upon the temple of the most High,
And as the rainbow giving light in the bright clouds:
And as the flower of roses in the spring of the year,
As lilies by the rivers of waters,
And as the branches of the frankincense tree in the time of summer:
As fire and incense in the censer,
And as a vessel of beaten gold
Set with all manner of precious stones:
And as a fair olive tree budding forth fruit,
And as a cypress tree which groweth up to the clouds.
When he put on the robe of honour,
And was clothed with the perfection of glory,
When he went up to the holy altar,
He made the garment of holiness honourable.
When he took the portions out of the priests' hands,

He himself stood by the hearth of the altar,
Compassed with his brethren round about,
As a young cedar in Libanus;
And as palm trees compassed they him round about.

So were all the sons of Aaron in their glory,
And the oblations of the Lord in their hands,
Before all the congregation of Israel.
And finishing the service at the altar,
That he might adorn the offering of the most high Almighty,
He stretched out his hand to the cup,
And poured of the blood of the grape,
He poured out at the foot of the altar
A sweetsmelling savour unto the most high King of all.
Then shouted the sons of Aaron,
And sounded the silver trumpets,
And make a great noise to be heard,
For a remembrance before the most High.
Then all the people together hasted,
And fell down to the earth upon their faces
To worship their Lord God Almighty,
The most High.
The singers also sang praises with their voices,
With great variety of sounds was there made sweet melody.
And the people besought the Lord, the most High,
By prayer before him that is merciful,
Till the solemnity of the Lord was ended,
And they had finished his service.
Then he went down, and lifted up his hands
Over the whole congregation of the children of Israel,
To give the blessing of the Lord with his lips,
And to rejoice in his name.
And they bowed themselves down to worship the second time,
That they might receive a blessing from the most High.

## EARLY MAN

Now therefore bless ye the God of all, *The people pray*
Which only doeth wondrous things every where,
Which exalteth our days from the womb,
And dealeth with us according to his mercy.
He grant us joyfulness of heart,
And that peace may be in our days in Israel for ever:
That he would confirm his mercy with us,
And deliver us at his time!
Blessed is he that shall be exercised in these things;
And he that layeth them up in his heart shall become wise.
For if he do them, he shall be strong to all things:
For the light of the Lord leadeth him,
Who giveth wisdom to the godly.
Blessed be the Lord for ever. Amen, Amen.

# III

# HISTORY OF ISRAEL

TERAH lived seventy years, and begat Abram in the land of his nativity, in Ur of the Chaldees. And Terah took Abram his son, and Lot the son of Haran, and Sarai his daughter in law, his son Abram's wife; and they went forth with them from Ur of the Chaldees, to go into the land of Canaan; and they came unto Haran, and dwelt there.

Now the LORD had said unto Abram, "Get thee out of thy country, and from thy kindred, and from thy father's house, unto a land that I will shew thee: and I will make of thee a great nation, and I will bless thee, and make thy name great."

So Abram departed, as the LORD had spoken unto him; and Lot went with him: and Abram was seventy and five years old when he departed out of Haran. And Abram took Sarai his wife, and Lot his brother's son, and all their substance that they had gathered, and the souls that they had gotten in Haran; and they went forth to go into the land of Canaan; and into the land of Canaan they came.

And the LORD appeared unto Abram, and said, "Unto thy seed will I give this land": and there builded he an altar unto the LORD, who appeared unto him. And he removed from thence unto a mountain on the east of Beth-el, and pitched his tent, having Beth-el on the west, and Hai on the east: and there he builded an altar unto the LORD, and called upon the name of the LORD. And Abram journeyed, going on still toward the south. And there was a famine in the land: and Abram went down into Egypt to sojourn there; for the famine was grievous in the land.

And Abram went up out of Egypt, he, and his wife, and all that he had, and Lot with him, into the south. And Abram was very rich in cattle, in silver, and in gold. And he went on his journeys from the south even to Beth-el, unto the place where his tent had been at the beginning, between Beth-el and Hai; unto the place of the altar, which he had made there at the first: and there Abram called on the name of the LORD. And Lot also, which went with Abram, had flocks, and herds, and tents. And the land was not able to bear them, that they might dwell together: for *Abram and Lot part* their substance was great, so that they could not dwell together. And there was a strife between the herdmen of Abram's cattle and the herdmen of Lot's cattle.

And Abram said unto Lot, "Let there be no strife, I pray thee, between me and thee, and between my herdmen and thy herdmen; for we be brethren. Is not the whole land before thee? separate thyself, I pray thee, from me: if thou wilt take the left hand, then I will go to the right; or if thou depart to the right hand, then I will go to the left."

And Lot lifted up his eyes, and beheld all the plain of Jordan, that it was well watered every where, even as the garden of the LORD, like the land of Egypt. Then Lot chose him all the plain of Jordan; and Lot journeyed east: and they separated themselves the one from the other. Abram dwelled in the land of Canaan, and Lot dwelled in the cities of the plain, and pitched his tent toward Sodom.

And the LORD said unto Abram, after that Lot was separated from him, "Lift up now thine eyes, and look from the place where thou art northward, and southward, and eastward, and westward: for all the land which thou seest, to thee will I give it, and to thy seed for ever. And I will make thy seed as the dust of the earth: so that if a man can number the dust of the earth, then shall thy seed also be numbered. Arise, walk through the land in the length of it and in the breadth of it; for I will give it unto thee."

Then Abram removed his tent, and came and dwelt in the plain of Mamre, which is in Hebron, and built there an altar unto the LORD. And he blessed him, and said, "Blessed be Abram of the most high God, possessor of heaven and earth."

The word of the LORD came unto Abram in a vision, saying, "Fear not, Abram: I am thy shield, and thy exceeding great reward."

And Abram said, "Lord GOD, what wilt thou give me, seeing I go childless? To me thou hast given no seed."

And, behold, the LORD came unto him and brought him forth abroad, and said, "Look now toward heaven, and tell the stars, if thou be able to number them": and he said unto him, "So shall thy seed be." And he believed in the LORD; and he counted it to him for righteousness.

And he said unto him, "I am the LORD that brought thee out of Ur of the Chaldees, to give thee this land to inherit it. And thou shalt go to thy fathers in peace; thou shalt be buried in a good old age."

In that same day the LORD made a covenant with Abram, saying, "Unto thy seed have I given this land, from the river of Egypt unto the great river, the river Euphrates."

And when Abram was ninety years old and nine, the LORD appeared to Abram, and said unto him, "I am the Almighty God; walk before me, and be thou perfect. And I will make my covenant between me and thee, and will multiply thee exceedingly."

And Abram fell on his face: and God talked with him, saying, "As for me, behold, my covenant is with thee for an everlasting covenant, to be a God unto thee, and thy seed after thee. Neither shall thy name any more be called Abram, but thy name shall be Abraham; for a father of many nations have I made thee."

And God said unto Abraham, "As for Sarai thy wife, thou shalt not call her name Sarai, but Sarah shall her name be. And I will bless her, and give thee a son also of her: yea, I will bless her, and she shall be a mother of nations; kings of people shall be of her." And he left off talking with him, and God went up from Abraham.

And the LORD appeared unto him in the plains of Mamre: and he sat in the tent door in the heat of the day; and he lift up his eyes and looked, and, lo, three men stood by him: and when he saw them, he ran to meet them from the tent door, and bowed himself toward the ground, and said, "My Lord, if now I have found favour in thy sight, pass not away, I pray thee, from thy servant: let a little water, I pray you, be fetched, and wash your feet, and rest yourselves under the tree: and I will fetch a morsel of bread, and comfort ye your hearts; after that ye shall pass on: for therefore are ye come to your servant."

And they said, "So do, as thou hast said."

And Abraham hastened into the tent unto Sarah, and said, "Make ready quickly three measures of fine meal, knead it, and make cakes upon the hearth." And Abraham ran unto the herd, and fetcht a calf tender and good, and gave it unto a young man; and he hasted to dress it. And he took butter, and milk, and the calf which he had dressed, and set it before them; and he stood by them under the tree, and they did eat.

And the men rose up from thence, and looked toward Sodom: and *Abraham pleads for Sodom* Abraham went with them to bring them on the way.

And the LORD said, "Shall I hide from Abraham that thing which I do; seeing that Abraham shall surely become a great and mighty nation, and all the nations of the earth shall be blessed in him? For I know him, that he will command his children and his household after him and they shall keep the way of the LORD, to do justice and judgment; that the LORD may bring upon Abraham that which he hath spoken of him."

And the LORD said, "Because the cry of Sodom and Gomorrah is great, and because their sin is very grievous; I will go down now, and see whether they have done altogether according to the cry of it, which is come unto me; and if not, I will know."

And the men turned their faces from thence, and went toward Sodom: but Abraham stood yet before the LORD.

And Abraham drew near, and said, "Wilt thou also destroy the righteous with the wicked? Peradventure there be fifty righteous within the city: wilt thou also destroy and not spare the place for the fifty righteous that are therein? That be far from thee to do after this manner, to slay the righteous with the wicked: and that the righteous should be as the wicked, that be far from thee: Shall not the Judge of all the earth do right?"

And the LORD said, "If I find in Sodom fifty righteous within the city, then I will spare all the place for their sakes."

And Abraham answered and said, "Behold now, I have taken upon me to speak unto the Lord, which am but dust and ashes: Peradventure there shall lack five of the fifty righteous: wilt thou destroy all the city for lack of five?"

And he said, "If I find there forty and five, I will not destroy it."

And he spake unto him yet again, and said, "Peradventure there shall be forty found there."

And he said, "I will not do it for forty's sake."

And he said unto him, "Oh let not the Lord be angry, and I will speak: Peradventure there shall be thirty found there."

And he said, "I will not do it, if I find thirty there."

And he said, "Behold now, I have taken upon me to speak unto the Lord: Peradventure there shall be twenty found there."

And he said, "I will not destroy it for twenty's sake."

And he said, "Oh let not the Lord be angry, and I will speak yet but this once: Peradventure ten shall be found there."

And he said, "I will not destroy it for ten's sake." And the LORD went his way, as soon as he had left communing with Abraham: and Abraham returned unto his place.

And Abraham gat up early in the morning to the place where he stood before the LORD: and he looked toward Sodom and Gomorrah, and toward all the land of the plain, and beheld, and, lo, the smoke of the country went up as the smoke of a furnace. And it came to pass, when God destroyed the cities of the plain, that God remembered Abraham, and sent Lot out of the midst of the overthrow, when he overthrew the cities in the which Lot dwelt.

And Abraham journeyed from thence toward the south country, and dwelled between Kadesh and Shur, and sojourned in Gerar. And Abimelech king of Gerar took sheep, and oxen, and menservants, and women-servants, and gave them unto Abraham.

And Abimelech said, "Behold, my land is before thee: dwell where it pleaseth thee."

And the LORD visited Sarah as he had said, and the LORD did unto Sarah as he had spoken. For Sarah conceived, and bare Abraham a son in his old age, at the set time of which God had spoken to him. And Abraham called the name of his son that was born unto him, whom Sarah bare to him, Isaac.

And Sarah said, "God hath made me to laugh, so that all that hear will laugh with me." And the child grew, and was weaned: and Abraham made a great feast the same day that Isaac was weaned.

And Abraham sojourned in the Philistines' land many days. And the angel of the LORD called unto him out of heaven, and said, "Abraham, Abraham": And he said, "Here am I."

"In blessing I will bless thee, and in multiplying I will multiply thy seed as the stars of the heaven, and as the sand which is upon the sea-shore."

And Abraham was old, and well stricken in age: and the LORD had blessed Abraham in all things. And Abraham said unto his eldest servant of his house, that ruled over all that he had, "Put, I pray thee, thy hand

under my thigh: and I will make thee swear by the Lord, the God of *Abraham seeks a wife*
heaven, and the God of the earth, that thou shalt not take a wife unto *for Isaac*
my son of the daughters of the Canaanites, among whom I dwell: but
thou shalt go unto my country, and to my kindred, and take a wife unto
my son Isaac."

And the servant said unto him, "Peradventure the woman will not
be willing to follow me unto this land: must I needs bring thy son again
unto the land from whence thou camest?"

And Abraham said unto him, "Beware thou that thou bring not my
son thither again. The Lord God of heaven, which took me from my
father's house, and from the land of my kindred, and which spake unto
me, and that sware unto me, saying, 'Unto thy seed will I give this land';
he shall send his angel before thee, and thou shalt take a wife unto my
son from thence. And if the woman will not be willing to follow thee,
then thou shalt be clear from this my oath: only bring not my son thither
again."

And the servant put his hand under the thigh of Abraham his master,
and sware to him concerning that matter. And the servant took ten camels of the camels of his master, and departed; for all the goods of his
master were in his hand: and he arose, and went to Mesopotamia, unto
the city of Nahor. And he made his camels to kneel down without the city
by a well of water at the time of the evening, even the time that women
go out to draw water.

And he said, "O Lord God of my master Abraham, I pray thee, send
me good speed this day, and shew kindness unto my master Abraham.
Behold, I stand here by the well of water; and the daughters of the
men of the city come out to draw water: and let it come to pass, that the
damsel to whom I shall say, 'Let down thy pitcher, I pray thee, that I
may drink'; and she shall say, 'Drink, and I will give thy camels drink
also': let the same be she that thou hast appointed for thy servant Isaac;
and thereby shall I know that thou hast shewed kindness unto my
master."

And it came to pass, before he had done speaking, that, behold,
Rebekah came out with her pitcher upon her shoulder. And the damsel
was very fair to look upon: and she went down to the well, and filled her
pitcher and came up.

*Abraham's servant
meets Rebekah*

And the servant ran to meet her, and said, "Let me, I pray thee, drink a little water of thy pitcher."

And she said, "Drink, my lord": and she hasted, and let down her pitcher upon her hand, and gave him drink. And when she had done giving him drink, she said, "I will draw water for thy camels also, until they have done drinking." And she hasted, and emptied her pitcher into the trough, and ran again unto the well to draw water, and drew for all his camels. And the man wondering at her held his peace, to wit whether the LORD had made his journey prosperous or not.

And it came to pass, as the camels had done drinking, that the man took a golden earring of half a shekel weight, and two bracelets for her hands of ten shekels weight of gold; and said, "Whose daughter art thou? tell me, I pray thee: is there room in thy father's house for us to lodge in?"

And she said unto him, "I am the daughter of Bethuel the son of Milcah, which she bare unto Nahor." She said moreover unto him, "We have both straw and provender enough, and room to lodge in."

And the man bowed down his head, and worshipped the LORD. And he said, "Blessed be the LORD God of my master Abraham, who hath not left destitute my master of his mercy and his truth: I being in the way, the LORD led me to the house of my master's brethren."

And the damsel ran, and told them of her mother's house these things.

And Rebekah had a brother, and his name was Laban: and Laban ran out unto the man, unto the well. And it came to pass, when he saw the earring and bracelets upon his sister's hands, and when he heard the words of Rebekah his sister, saying, "Thus spake the man unto me"; that he came unto the man; and, behold, he stood by the camels at the well. And he said, "Come in, thou blessed of the LORD; wherefore standest thou without? for I have prepared the house, and room for the camels."

And the man came into the house: and he ungirded his camels, and gave straw and provender for the camels, and water to wash his feet, and the men's feet that were with him. And there was set meat before him to eat: but he said, "I will not eat, until I have told mine errand."

And he said, "Speak on."

And he said, "I am Abraham's servant. And the LORD hath blessed my master greatly; and he is become great: and he hath given him flocks, and herds, and silver, and gold, and menservants, and maidservants, and camels, and asses. And Sarah my master's wife bare a son to my master when she was old: and unto him hath he given all that he hath. And my master made me swear, saying, 'Thou shalt not take a wife to my son of the daughters of the Canaanites, in whose land I dwell: but thou shalt go unto my father's house, and to my kindred, and take a wife unto my son.' And I said unto my master, 'Peradventure the woman will not follow me.' And he said unto me, 'The LORD before whom I walk, will send his angel with thee, and prosper thy way; and thou shalt take a wife for my son of my kindred, and of my father's house: then shalt thou be clear from this my oath, when thou comest to my kindred; and if they give not thee one, thou shalt be clear from my oath.' And I came this day unto the well, and said, 'O LORD God of my master Abraham, if now thou do prosper my way which I go: behold, I stand by the well of water; and it shall come to pass, that when the virgin cometh forth to draw water, and I say to her, "Give me, I pray thee, a little water of thy pitcher to drink"; and she say to me, "Both drink thou, and I will also draw for thy camels": let the same be the woman whom the LORD hath appointed out for my master's son.' And before I had done speaking in mine heart, behold, Rebekah came forth with her pitcher on her shoulder; and she went down unto the well, and drew water: and I said unto her, 'Let me drink, I pray thee.' And she made haste, and let down her pitcher from her shoulder, and said, 'Drink, and I will give thy camels drink also': so I drank, and she made the camels drink also. And I asked her, and said, 'Whose daughter art thou?' And she said, 'The daughter of Bethuel, Nahor's son, whom Milcah bare unto him': and I put the earring upon her face, and the bracelets upon her hands. And I bowed down my head, and worshipped the LORD, and blessed the LORD God of my master Abraham, which had led me in the right way to take my master's brother's daughter unto his son. And now if ye will deal kindly and truly with my master, tell me: and if not, tell me; that I may turn to the right hand, or to the left."

Then Laban and Bethuel answered and said, "The thing proceedeth from the LORD: we cannot speak unto thee bad or good. Behold, Rebekah is before thee, take her, and go, and let her be thy master's son's wife, as the LORD hath spoken."

[ 31 ]

*Rebekah chosen* And it came to pass, that, when Abraham's servant heard their words, he worshipped the LORD, bowing himself to the earth. And the servant brought forth jewels of silver, and jewels of gold, and raiment, and gave them to Rebekah: he gave also to her brother and to her mother precious things. And they did eat and drink, he and the men that were with him, and tarried all night; and they rose up in the morning, and he said, "Send me away unto my master."

And her brother and her mother said, "Let the damsel abide with us a few days, at the least ten; after that she shall go."

And he said unto them, "Hinder me not, seeing the LORD hath prospered my way; send me away that I may go to my master."

And they said, "We will call the damsel, and enquire at her mouth." And they called Rebekah, and said unto her, "Wilt thou go with this man?"

And she said, "I will go." And they sent away Rebekah their sister, and her nurse, and Abraham's servant, and his men. And they blessed Rebekah, and said unto her, "Thou art our sister, be thou the mother of thousands of millions."

And Rebekah arose, and her damsels, and they rode upon the camels, and followed the man: and the servant took Rebekah, and went his way.

And Isaac came from the way of the well Lahai-roi; for he dwelt in the south country. And Isaac went out to meditate in the field at the eventide: and he lifted up his eyes, and saw, and, behold, the camels were coming. And Rebekah lifted up her eyes, and when she saw Isaac, she lighted off the camel. For she had said unto the servant, "What man is this that walketh in the field to meet us?" And the servant had said, "It is my master": therefore she took a vail, and covered herself. And the servant told Isaac all things that he had done. And Isaac brought her into his mother Sarah's tent, and took Rebekah, and she became his wife; and he loved her: and Isaac was comforted after his mother's death.

Then Abraham gave up the ghost, and died in a good old age, an old man, and full of years; and was gathered to his people. And it came to pass after the death of Abraham, that God blessed his son Isaac; and Isaac dwelt by the well Lahai-roi. And Isaac was forty years old when he took Rebekah to wife, the daughter of Bethuel the Syrian of Padan-aram,

the sister to Laban the Syrian. And Isaac intreated the LORD for his wife, *Death of Abraham*
because she was barren: and the LORD was intreated of him, and Rebekah
his wife conceived. And when her days to be delivered were fulfilled, behold, there were twins in her womb. And the boys grew: and Esau was
a cunning hunter, a man of the field; and Jacob was a plain man, dwelling
in tents.

And Isaac called Jacob, and blessed him, and charged him, and said
unto him, "Thou shalt not take a wife of the daughters of Canaan. Arise,
go to Padan-aram, to the house of Bethuel thy mother's father; and take
thee a wife from thence of the daughters of Laban thy mother's brother.
And God Almighty bless thee, and make thee fruitful, and multiply thee,
and give thee the blessing of Abraham, to thee, and to thy seed with
thee; that thou mayest inherit the land wherein thou art a stranger, which
God gave unto Abraham." And Isaac sent away Jacob: and he went to
Padan-aram unto Laban, son of Bethuel the Syrian, the brother of Rebekah, Jacob's and Esau's mother. And Jacob obeyed his father and his
mother, and was gone to Padan-aram.

And Jacob went out from Beer-sheba, and went toward Haran. And
he lighted upon a certain place, and tarried there all night, because the
sun was set; and he took of the stones of that place, and put them for his
pillows, and lay down in that place to sleep. And he dreamed, and behold
a ladder set up on the earth, and the top of it reached to heaven: and behold the angels of God ascending and descending on it. And, behold,
the LORD stood above it, and said, "I am the LORD God of Abraham thy
father, and the God of Isaac: the land whereon thou liest, to thee will I
give it, and to thy seed; and thy seed shall be as the dust of the earth,
and thou shalt spread abroad to the west, and to the east, and to the
north, and to the south: and in thee and in thy seed shall all the families
of the earth be blessed. And, behold, I am with thee, and will keep thee
in all places whither thou goest, and will bring thee again into this land;
for I will not leave thee, until I have done that which I have spoken to
thee of."

And Jacob awaked out of his sleep, and he said, "Surely the LORD is
in this place; and I knew it not." And he was afraid, and said, "How
dreadful is this place! this is none other but the house of God, and this
is the gate of heaven."

[ 33 ]

*Jacob's vow*    And Jacob rose up early in the morning, and took the stone that he had put for his pillows, and set it up for a pillar, and poured oil upon the top of it. And he called the name of that place Beth-el. And Jacob vowed a vow, saying, "If God will be with me, and will keep me in this way that I go, and will give me bread to eat, and raiment to put on, so that I come again to my father's house in peace; then shall the LORD be my God: and this stone, which I have set for a pillar, shall be God's house: and of all that thou shalt give me I will surely give the tenth unto thee."

Then Jacob went on his journey, and came into the land of the people of the east. And he looked, and behold a well in the field, and, lo, there were three flocks of sheep lying by it; for out of that well they watered the flocks: and a great stone was upon the well's mouth. And thither were all the flocks gathered: and they rolled the stone from the well's mouth, and watered the sheep, and put the stone again upon the well's mouth in his place.

And Jacob said unto them, "My brethren, whence be ye?"

And they said, "Of Haran are we."

And he said unto them, "Know ye Laban the son of Nahor?"

And they said, "We know him."

And he said unto them, "Is he well?"

And they said, "He is well: and, behold, Rachel his daughter cometh with the sheep."

And he said, "Lo, it is yet high day, neither is it time that the cattle should be gathered together: water ye the sheep, and go and feed them."

And they said, "We cannot, until all the flocks be gathered together, and till they roll the stone from the well's mouth; then we water the sheep."

And while he yet spake with them, Rachel came with her father's sheep: for she kept them. And it came to pass, when Jacob saw Rachel the daughter of Laban his mother's brother, and the sheep of Laban his mother's brother, that Jacob went near, and rolled the stone from the well's mouth, and watered the flock of Laban his mother's brother. And Jacob kissed Rachel, and lifted up his voice, and wept. And Jacob told Rachel that he was her father's brother, and that he was Rebekah's son: and she ran and told her father. And it came to pass, when Laban heard

*THE VISION OF JACOB'S LADDER*

the tidings of Jacob his sister's son, that he ran to meet him, and em- *Jacob serves Laban*
braced him and kissed him, and brought him to his house. And he told
Laban all these things. And Laban said to him, "Surely thou art my bone
and my flesh." And he abode with him the space of a month.

And Laban said unto Jacob, "Because thou art my brother, shouldest
thou therefore serve me for nought? tell me, what shall thy wages
be?"

And Laban had two daughters: the name of the elder was Leah, and
the name of the younger was Rachel. Leah was tender eyed; but Rachel
was beautiful and well favoured. And Jacob loved Rachel; and said, "I
will serve thee seven years for Rachel thy younger daughter."

And Laban said, "It is better that I give her to thee, than that I
should give her to another man: abide with me."

And Jacob served seven years for Rachel; and they seemed unto him
but a few days, for the love he had to her.

And Jacob said unto Laban, "Give me my wife, for my days are fulfilled."

And Laban gathered together all the men of the place, and made a
feast. And it came to pass in the evening, that he took Leah his daughter,
and brought her to him. And he said to Laban, "What is this thou hast
done unto me? did not I serve with thee for Rachel?"

And Laban said, "It must not be so done in our country, to give the
younger before the firstborn."

And he gave him Rachel his daughter to wife also. And Jacob loved
also Rachel more than Leah, and served with him yet seven other years.
And Leah conceived, and bare a son, and she called his name Reuben.
And God remembered Rachel, and God hearkened to her. And she con-
ceived, and bare a son; and she called his name Joseph; and said, "The
LORD shall add to me another son."

And the LORD said unto Jacob, "Return unto the land of thy fathers,
and to thy kindred; and I will be with thee."

Then Jacob rose up, and set his sons and his wives upon camels; and
he carried away all his cattle, and all his goods which he had gotten, the
cattle of his getting, which he had gotten in Padan-aram, for to go to
Isaac his father in the land of Canaan. Then Laban overtook Jacob. And
Laban said to Jacob, "What hast thou done, that thou hast stolen away

[ 35 ]

*Covenant between Jacob and Laban*

unawares to me, and carried away my daughters, as captives? Wherefore didst thou flee away secretly, and steal away from me; and didst not tell me, that I might have sent thee away with mirth, and with songs, with tabret, and with harp? And hast not suffered me to kiss my sons and my daughters? thou hast now done foolishly in so doing."

And Jacob was wroth, and chode with Laban: and Jacob answered and said to Laban, "What is my trespass? what is my sin, that thou hast so hotly pursued after me? Thus have I been twenty years in thy house; I served thee fourteen years for thy two daughters, and six years for thy cattle: and thou hast changed my wages ten times."

And Laban answered and said unto Jacob, "These daughters are my daughters, and these children are my children, and these cattle are my cattle, and all that thou seest is mine: and what can I do this day unto these my daughters, or unto their children which they have borne? Now therefore come thou, let us make a covenant, I and thou; and let it be for a witness between me and thee."

And Jacob took a stone, and set it up for a pillar. And Jacob said unto his brethren, "Gather stones"; and they took stones, and made an heap: and they did eat there upon the heap.

And Laban said, "This heap is a witness between me and thee this day." Therefore was the name of it called Galeed; and Mizpah; for he said, "The LORD watch between me and thee, when we are absent one from another. This heap be witness, and this pillar be witness, that I will not pass over this heap to thee, and that thou shalt not pass over this heap and this pillar unto me, for harm. God is witness betwixt me and thee."

And Jacob went on his way, and the angels of God met him. And when Jacob saw them, he said, "This is God's host": and he called the name of that place Mahanaim.

And Jacob sent messengers before him to Esau his brother unto the land of Seir, the country of Edom. And he commanded them, saying, "Thus shall ye speak unto my lord Esau; 'Thy servant Jacob saith thus, "I have sojourned with Laban, and stayed there until now: And I have oxen, and asses, flocks, and menservants, and womenservants: and I have sent to tell my lord, that I may find grace in thy sight." ' "

And the messengers returned to Jacob, saying, "We came to thy brother Esau, and also he cometh to meet thee, and four hundred men with him."

And Jacob lodged there that same night; and took of that which came to his hand a present for Esau his brother; two hundred she goats, and twenty he goats, two hundred ewes, and twenty rams, thirty milch camels with their colts, forty kine, and ten bulls, twenty she asses, and ten foals. And he delivered them into the hand of his servants, every drove by themselves; and said unto his servants, "Pass over before me, and put a space betwixt drove and drove." And he commanded the foremost, saying, "When Esau my brother meeteth thee, and asketh thee, saying, 'Whose art thou? and whither goest thou? and whose are these before thee?' Then thou shalt say, 'They be thy servant Jacob's; it is a present sent unto my lord Esau: and, behold, also he is behind us.' "

So went the present over before him: and himself lodged that night in the company. And he rose up that night, and took his two wives, and his two womenservants, and his eleven sons, and passed over the ford Jabbok. And he took them, and sent them over the brook, and sent over that he had.

And Jacob was left alone; and there wrestled a man with him until the breaking of the day. And when he saw that he prevailed not against him, he touched the hollow of his thigh; and the hollow of Jacob's thigh was out of joint, as he wrestled with him. And he said, "Let me go, for the day breaketh." And he said, "I will not let thee go, except thou bless me."

And he said unto him, "What is thy name?"

And he said, "Jacob."

And he said, "Thy name shall be called no more Jacob, but Israel: for as a prince hast thou power with God and with men, and hast prevailed."

And Jacob asked him, and said, "Tell me, I pray thee, thy name." And he said, "Wherefore is it that thou dost ask after my name?" And he blessed him there. And Jacob called the name of the place Peniel: "For I have seen God face to face, and my life is preserved." And as he passed over Penuel the sun rose upon him, and he halted upon his thigh.

And Jacob lifted up his eyes, and looked, and, behold, Esau came, and with him four hundred men. And he divided the children unto Leah, and unto Rachel, and unto the two handmaids. And he put the handmaids and their children foremost, and Leah and her children after, and Rachel and Joseph hindermost. And he passed over before them, and bowed himself to the ground seven times, until he came near to his brother. And Esau ran to meet him, and embraced him, and fell on his neck, and kissed him: and they wept. And he lifted up his eyes, and saw the women and the children; and said, "Who are those with thee?"

And he said, "The children which God hath graciously given thy servant."

Then the handmaidens came near, they and their children, and they bowed themselves. And Leah also with her children came near, and bowed themselves: and after came Joseph near and Rachel, and they bowed themselves. And he said, "What meanest thou by all this drove which I met?"

And he said, "These are to find grace in the sight of my lord."

And Esau said, "I have enough, my brother; keep that thou hast unto thyself."

And Jacob said, "Nay, I pray thee, if now I have found grace in thy sight, then receive my present at my hand: for therefore I have seen thy face, as though I had seen the face of God, and thou wast pleased with me. Take, I pray thee, my blessing that is brought to thee; because God hath dealt graciously with me, and because I have enough." And he urged him, and he took it.

And he said, "Let us take our journey, and let us go, and I will go before thee."

And he said unto him, "My lord knoweth that the children are tender, and the flocks and herds with young are with me: and if men should over-drive them one day, all the flock will die. Let my lord, I pray thee, pass over before his servant: and I will lead on softly, according as the cattle that goeth before me and the children be able to endure, until I come unto my lord unto Seir."

And Esau said, "Let me now leave with thee some of the folk that are with me."

And he said, "What needeth it? let me find grace in the sight of my lord."

So Esau returned that day on his way unto Seir. And Jacob journeyed to Succoth, and built him an house, and made booths for his cattle. And

[ 38 ]

Jacob came to Shalem, a city of Shechem, which is in the land of Canaan, *Benjamin is born*
when he came from Padan-aram; and pitched his tent before the city.
And he bought a parcel of a field, where he had spread his tent, for an
hundred pieces of money. And God appeared unto Jacob again, when
he came out of Padan-aram, and blessed him.

And God said unto him, "Thy name is Jacob: thy name shall not be
called any more Jacob, but Israel shall be thy name": and he called his
name Israel. And Jacob called the name of the place where God spake
with him, Beth-el.

And they journeyed from Beth-el; and there was but a little way to
come to Ephrath: and Rachel travailed, and she had hard labour. And
it came to pass, when she was in hard labour, that the midwife said unto
her, "Fear not; thou shalt have this son also." And it came to pass, as
her soul was in departing, (for she died) that she called his name Ben-oni:
but his father called him Benjamin. And Rachel died, and was buried in
the way to Ephrath, which is Beth-lehem. And Jacob set a pillar upon
her grave: that is the pillar of Rachel's grave unto this day. And Israel
journeyed, and spread his tent beyond the tower of Edar.

Now the sons of Jacob were twelve, which were born to him in Padan-
aram. And Jacob came unto Isaac his father unto Mamre, unto the city of
Arbah, which is Hebron, where Abraham and Isaac sojourned. And the
days of Isaac were an hundred and fourscore years. And Isaac gave up
the ghost, and died, and was gathered unto his people, being old and full
of days: and his sons Esau and Jacob buried him. And Jacob dwelt in the
land wherein his father was a stranger, in the land of Canaan.

Joseph, being seventeen years old, was feeding the flock with his
brethren. Now Israel loved Joseph more than all his children, because
he was the son of his old age: and he made him a coat of many colours.
And when his brethren saw that their father loved him more than all his
brethren, they hated him, and could not speak peaceably unto him. And
Joseph dreamed a dream, and he told it his brethren: and they hated him
yet the more. And he said unto them, "Hear, I pray you, this dream
which I have dreamed: for, behold, we were binding sheaves in the field,
and, lo, my sheaf arose, and also stood upright; and, behold, your sheaves
stood round about, and made obeisance to my sheaf."

[ 39 ]

*Joseph's dreams*   And his brethren said to him, "Shalt thou indeed reign over us? or shalt thou indeed have dominion over us?"

And they hated him yet the more for his dreams, and for his words. And he dreamed yet another dream, and told it his brethren, and said, "Behold, I have dreamed a dream more; and, behold, the sun and the moon and the eleven stars made obeisance to me."

And he told it to his father, and to his brethren: and his father rebuked him, and said unto him, "What is this dream that thou hast dreamed? Shall I and thy mother and thy brethren indeed come to bow down ourselves to thee to the earth?"

And his brethren envied him; but his father observed the saying. And his brethren went to feed their father's flock in Shechem.

And Israel said unto Joseph, "Do not thy brethren feed the flock in Shechem? Come, and I will send thee unto them."

And he said to him, "Here am I."

And he said to him, "Go, I pray thee, see whether it be well with thy brethren, and well with the flocks; and bring me word again."

So he sent him out of the vale of Hebron, and he came to Shechem. And a certain man found him, and, behold, he was wandering in the field: and the man asked him, saying, "What seekest thou?"

And he said, "I seek my brethren: tell me, I pray thee, where they feed their flocks."

And the man said, "They are departed hence; for I heard them say, 'Let us go to Dothan.' "

And Joseph went after his brethren, and found them in Dothan.

And when they saw him afar off, even before he came near unto them, they conspired against him to slay him. And they said one to another, "Behold, this dreamer cometh. Come now therefore, and let us slay him, and cast him into some pit, and we will say, 'Some evil beast hath devoured him': and we shall see what will become of his dreams."

And Reuben heard it, and he delivered him out of their hands; and said, "Let us not kill him." And Reuben said unto them, "Shed no blood, but cast him into this pit that is in the wilderness, and lay no hand upon him"; that he might rid him out of their hands, to deliver him to his father again.

And it came to pass when Joseph was come unto his brethren, that they stript Joseph out of his coat, his coat of many colours that was on him; and they took him, and cast him into a pit: and the pit was empty, there was no water in it. And they sat down to eat bread: and they lifted up their eyes and looked, and, behold, a company of Ishmeelites came from Gilead with their camels bearing spicery and balm and myrrh, going to carry it down to Egypt. And Judah said unto his brethren, "What profit is it if we slay our brother, and conceal his blood? Come, and let us sell him to the Ishmeelites, and let not our hand be upon him; for he is our brother and our flesh." And his brethren were content. Then there passed by Midianites merchantmen; and they drew and lifted up Joseph out of the pit, and sold Joseph to the Ishmeelites for twenty pieces of silver: and they brought Joseph into Egypt. And Reuben returned unto the pit; and, behold, Joseph was not in the pit; and he rent his clothes. And he returned unto his brethren, and said, "The child is not; and I, whither shall I go?"

*Joseph sold to the Ishmeelites*

And they took Joseph's coat, and killed a kid of the goats, and dipped the coat in the blood; and they sent the coat of many colours, and they brought it to their father; and said, "This have we found: know now whether it be thy son's coat or no."

And he knew it, and said, "It is my son's coat; an evil beast hath devoured him; Joseph is without doubt rent in pieces."

And Jacob rent his clothes, and put sackcloth upon his loins, and mourned for his son many days. And all his sons and all his daughters rose up to comfort him; but he refused to be comforted; and he said, "For I will go down into the grave unto my son mourning." Thus his father wept for him.

And Joseph was brought down to Egypt; and Potiphar, an officer of Pharaoh, captain of the guard, an Egyptian, bought him of the hands of the Ishmeelites, which had brought him down thither. And the LORD was with Joseph, and he was a prosperous man; and he was in the house of his master the Egyptian. And his master saw that the LORD was with him, and that the LORD made all that he did to prosper in his hand. And Joseph found grace in his sight, and he served him: and he made him overseer over his house, and all that he had he put into his hand. And it came to pass from the time that he had made him overseer in his house, and over all that he had, that the LORD blessed the Egyptian's house for

Joseph's sake; and the blessing of the LORD was upon all that he had in the house, and in the field. And he left all that he had in Joseph's hand; and he knew not ought he had, save the bread which he did eat. And Joseph was a goodly person, and well favoured.

Pharaoh sent and called Joseph, and they brought him hastily: and he shaved himself, and changed his raiment, and came in unto Pharaoh. And Pharaoh said unto Joseph, "I have dreamed a dream, and there is none that can interpret it: and I have heard say of thee, that thou canst understand a dream to interpret it."

And Joseph answered Pharaoh, saying, "It is not in me: God shall give Pharaoh an answer of peace."

And Pharaoh said unto Joseph, "In my dream, behold, I stood upon the bank of the river: and, behold, there came up out of the river seven kine, fatfleshed and well favoured; and they fed in a meadow: and, behold, seven other kine came up after them, poor and very ill favoured and leanfleshed, such as I never saw in all the land of Egypt for badness: and the lean and the ill favoured kine did eat up the first seven fat kine: and when they had eaten them up, it could not be known that they had eaten them; but they were still ill favoured, as at the beginning. So I awoke. And I saw in my dream, and, behold, seven ears came up in one stalk, full and good: and, behold, seven ears, withered, thin, and blasted with the east wind, sprung up after them: and the thin ears devoured the seven good ears: and I told this unto the magicians; but there was none that could declare it to me."

And Joseph said unto Pharaoh, "The dream of Pharaoh is one: God hath shewed Pharaoh what he is about to do. The seven good kine are seven years; and the seven good ears are seven years: the dream is one. And the seven thin and ill favoured kine that came up after them are seven years; and the seven empty ears blasted with the east wind shall be seven years of famine. This is the thing which I have spoken unto Pharaoh: what God is about to do he sheweth unto Pharaoh. Behold, there come seven years of great plenty throughout all the land of Egypt: and there shall arise after them seven years of famine; and all the plenty shall be forgotten in the land of Egypt; and the famine shall consume the land; and the plenty shall not be known in the land by reason of that famine following; for it shall be very grievous. And for that the dream was doubled unto Pharaoh twice; it is because the thing is established *Joseph made ruler* by God, and God will shortly bring it to pass. Now therefore let Pharaoh look out a man discreet and wise, and set him over the land of Egypt. Let Pharaoh do this, and let him appoint officers over the land, and take up the fifth part of the land of Egypt in the seven plenteous years. And let them gather all the food of those good years that come, and lay up corn under the hand of Pharaoh, and let them keep food in the cities. And that food shall be for store to the land against the seven years of famine, which shall be in the land of Egypt; that the land perish not through the famine."

And the thing was good in the eyes of Pharaoh, and in the eyes of all his servants. And Pharaoh said unto his servants, "Can we find such a one as this is, a man in whom the Spirit of God is?"

And Pharaoh said unto Joseph, "Forasmuch as God hath shewed thee all this, there is none so discreet and wise as thou art: thou shalt be over my house, and according unto thy word shall all my people be ruled: only in the throne will I be greater than thou." And Pharaoh said unto Joseph, "See, I have set thee over all the land of Egypt."

And Pharaoh took off his ring from his hand, and put it upon Joseph's hand, and arrayed him in vestures of fine linen, and put a gold chain about his neck; and he made him to ride in the second chariot which he had; and they cried before him, "Bow the knee": and he made him ruler over all the land of Egypt.

And Pharaoh said unto Joseph, "I am Pharaoh, and without thee shall no man lift up his hand or foot in all the land of Egypt."

And Joseph was thirty years old when he stood before Pharaoh king of Egypt. And Joseph went out from the presence of Pharaoh, and went throughout all the land of Egypt. And in the seven plenteous years the earth brought forth by handfuls. And he gathered up all the food of the seven years, which were in the land of Egypt, and laid up the food in the cities: the food of the field, which was round about every city, laid he up in the same. And Joseph gathered corn as the sand of the sea, very much, until he left numbering; for it was without number.

And unto Joseph were born two sons before the years of famine came, which Asenath the daughter of Poti-pherah, priest of On, bare unto him. And Joseph called the name of the first born Manasseh: "For God," said

*The famine* he, "hath made me forget all my toil, and all my father's house." And the name of the second called he Ephraim: "For God hath caused me to be fruitful in the land of my affliction."

And the seven years of plenteousness, that was in the land of Egypt, were ended. And the seven years of dearth began to come, according as Joseph had said: and the dearth was in all lands; but in all the land of Egypt there was bread. And when all the land of Egypt was famished, the people cried to Pharaoh for bread: and Pharaoh said unto all the Egyptians, "Go unto Joseph; what he saith to you, do." And the famine was over all the face of the earth: and Joseph opened all the storehouses, and sold unto the Egyptians; and the famine waxed sore in the land of Egypt. And all countries came into Egypt to Joseph for to buy corn; because that the famine was so sore in all lands.

Now when Jacob saw that there was corn in Egypt, Jacob said unto his sons, "Why do ye look one upon another?" And he said, "Behold, I have heard that there is corn in Egypt: get you down thither, and buy for us from thence; that we may live, and not die."

And Joseph's ten brethren went down to buy corn in Egypt. But Benjamin, Joseph's brother, Jacob sent not with his brethren; for he said, "Lest peradventure mischief befall him." And the sons of Israel came to buy corn among those that came: for the famine was in the land of Canaan. And Joseph was the governor over the land, and he it was that sold to all the people of the land: and Joseph's brethren came, and bowed down themselves before him with their faces to the earth. And Joseph saw his brethren, and he knew them, but made himself strange unto them, and spake roughly unto them; and he said unto them, "Whence come ye?"

And they said, "From the land of Canaan to buy food."

And Joseph knew his brethren, but they knew not him. And Joseph remembered the dreams which he dreamed of them, and said unto them, "Ye are spies; to see the nakedness of the land ye are come."

And they said, "Thy servants are twelve brethren, the sons of one man in the land of Canaan; and, behold, the youngest is this day with our father, and one is not."

And Joseph said unto them, "Send one of you, and let him fetch your brother, and ye shall be kept in prison, that your words may be proved, whether there be any truth in you: or else, by the life of Pharaoh surely *Joseph's treatment* ye are spies." And he put them all together into ward three days. *of his brethren*

And Joseph said unto them the third day, "This do, and live; for I fear God. If ye be true men, let one of your brethren be bound in the house of your prison: go ye, carry corn for the famine of your houses: but bring your youngest brother unto me; so shall your words be verified, and ye shall not die." And they did so.

And they said one to another, "We are verily guilty concerning our brother, in that we saw the anguish of his soul, when he besought us, and we would not hear; therefore is this distress come upon us."

And Reuben answered them, saying, "Spake I not unto you, saying 'Do not sin against the child'; and ye would not hear? therefore, behold, also his blood is required." And they knew not that Joseph understood them; for he spake unto them by an interpreter. And he turned himself about from them, and wept; and returned to them again, and communed with them, and took from them Simeon, and bound him before their eyes.

Then Joseph commanded to fill their sacks with corn, and to restore every man's money into his sack, and to give them provision for the way: and thus did he unto them. And they laded their asses with the corn, and departed thence. And as one of them opened his sack to give his ass provender in the inn, he espied his money; for, behold, it was in his sack's mouth. And he said unto his brethren, "My money is restored; and, lo, it is even in my sack": and their heart failed them, and they were afraid, saying one to another, "What is this that God hath done unto us?"

And they came unto Jacob their father unto the land of Canaan, and told him all that befell unto them; saying, "The man, who is the lord of the land, spake roughly to us, and took us for spies of the country. And we said unto him, 'We are true men; we are no spies: we be twelve brethren, sons of our father; one is not, and the youngest is this day with our father in the land of Canaan.' And the man, the lord of the country, said unto us, 'Hereby shall I know that ye are true men; leave one of your brethren here with me, and take food for the famine of your households, and be gone: and bring your youngest brother unto me: then shall I know that ye are no spies, but that ye are true men: so will I deliver you your brother, and ye shall traffick in the land.' " And it came to pass as they emptied their sacks, that, behold, every man's bundle of money was in his sack: and when both they and their father saw the bundles of money, they were afraid.

And Jacob their father said unto them, "Me have ye bereaved of my children: Joseph is not, and Simeon is not, and ye will take Benjamin away: all these things are against me."

And Reuben spake unto his father, saying, "Slay my two sons, if I bring him not to thee: deliver him into my hand, and I will bring him to thee again."

And he said, "My son shall not go down with you; for his brother is dead, and he is left alone: if mischief befall him by the way in the which ye go, then shall ye bring down my gray hairs with sorrow to the grave."

And the famine was sore in the land. And it came to pass, when they had eaten up the corn which they had brought out of Egypt, their father said unto them, "Go again, buy us a little food."

And Judah spake unto him, saying, "The man did solemnly protest unto us, saying, 'Ye shall not see my face, except your brother be with you.' If thou wilt send our brother with us, we will go down and buy thee food: but if thou wilt not send him, we will not go down: for the man said unto us, 'Ye shall not see my face, except your brother be with you.'"

And Israel said, "Wherefore dealt ye so ill with me, as to tell the man whether ye had yet a brother?"

And they said, "The man asked us straitly of our state, and of our kindred, saying, 'Is your father yet alive? have ye another brother?' and we told him according to the tenor of these words: could we certainly know that he would say, 'Bring your brother down'?"

And Judah said unto Israel his father, "Send the lad with me, and we will arise and go; that we may live, and not die, both we, and thou, and also our little ones. I will be surety for him; of my hand shalt thou require him: if I bring him not unto thee, and set him before thee, then let me bear the blame for ever: for except we had lingered, surely now we had returned this second time."

And their father Israel said unto them, "If it must be so now, do this; take of the best fruits in the land in your vessels, and carry down the man a present, a little balm, and a little honey, spices, and myrrh, nuts and

[ 46 ]

*HIS BRETHREN BOWING BEFORE JOSEPH*

almonds: and take double money in your hand; and the money that was brought again in the mouth of your sacks, carry it again in your hand; peradventure it was an oversight: take also your brother, and arise, go again unto the man: and God Almighty give you mercy before the man, that he may send away your other brother, and Benjamin. If I be bereaved of my children, I am bereaved."

And the men took that present, and they took double money in their hand, and Benjamin; and rose up, and went down to Egypt, and stood before Joseph. And when Joseph saw Benjamin with them, he said to the ruler of his house, "Bring these men home, and slay, and make ready; for these men shall dine with me at noon."

And the man did as Joseph bade; and the man brought the men into Joseph's house. And the men were afraid, because they were brought into Joseph's house; and they said, "Because of the money that was returned in our sacks at the first time are we brought in; that he may seek occasion against us, and fall upon us, and take us for bondmen, and our asses."

And they came near to the steward of Joseph's house, and they communed with him at the door of the house, and said, "O sir, we came indeed down at the first time to buy food: and it came to pass, when we came to the inn, that we opened our sacks, and, behold, every man's money was in the mouth of his sack, our money in full weight: and we have brought it again in our hand. And other money have we brought down in our hands to buy food: we cannot tell who put our money in our sacks."

And he said, "Peace be to you, fear not: your God, and the God of your father, hath given you treasure in your sacks: I had your money." And he brought Simeon out unto them. And the man brought the men into Joseph's house, and gave them water, and they washed their feet; and he gave their asses provender. And they made ready the present against Joseph came at noon: for they heard that they should eat bread there. And when Joseph came home, they brought him the present which was in their hand into the house, and bowed themselves to him to the earth.

And he asked them of their welfare and said, "Is your father well, the old man of whom ye spake? Is he yet alive?"

*Joseph stays his
brethren*

And they answered, "Thy servant our father is in good health, he is yet alive." And they bowed down their heads, and made obeisance.

And he lifted up his eyes, and saw his brother Benjamin, his mother's son, and said, "Is this your younger brother, of whom ye spake unto me?" And he said, "God be gracious unto thee, my son."

And Joseph made haste; for his bowels did yearn upon his brother: and he sought where to weep; and he entered into his chamber, and wept there. And he washed his face, and went out, and refrained himself, and said, "Set on bread." And they set on for him by himself, and for them by themselves, and for the Egyptians, which did eat with him, by themselves: because the Egyptians might not eat bread with the Hebrews; for that is an abomination unto the Egyptians. And they sat before him, the firstborn according to his birthright, and the youngest according to his youth: and the men marvelled one at another. And he took and sent messes unto them from before him: but Benjamin's mess was five times so much as any of their's. And they drank, and were merry with him.

And he commanded the steward of his house, saying, "Fill the men's sacks with food, as much as they can carry, and put every man's money in his sack's mouth. And put my cup, the silver cup, in the sack's mouth of the youngest, and his corn money." And he did according to the word that Joseph had spoken.

As soon as the morning was light, the men were sent away, they and their asses. And when they were gone out of the city, and not yet far off, Joseph said unto his steward, "Up, follow after the men; and when thou dost overtake them, say unto them, 'Wherefore have ye rewarded evil for good? Is not this it in which my lord drinketh, and whereby indeed he divineth? ye have done evil in so doing.' "

And he overtook them, and he spake unto them these same words.

And they said unto him, "Wherefore saith my lord these words? God forbid that thy servants should do according to this thing: behold, the money, which we found in our sacks' mouths, we brought again unto thee out of the land of Canaan: how then should we steal out of thy lord's house silver or gold? With whomsoever of thy servants it be found, both let him die, and we also will be my lord's bondmen."

And he said, "Now also let it be according unto your words: he with whom it is found shall be my servant; and ye shall be blameless."

## HISTORY OF ISRAEL

Then they speedily took down every man his sack to the ground, and opened every man his sack. And he searched, and began at the eldest, and left at the youngest: and the cup was found in Benjamin's sack. Then they rent their clothes, and laded every man his ass, and returned to the city. And Judah and his brethren came to Joseph's house; for he was yet there: and they fell before him on the ground.

*Judah's plea for Benjamin*

And Joseph said unto them, "What deed is this that ye have done? wot ye not that such a man as I can certainly divine?"

And Judah said, "What shall we say unto my lord? what shall we speak? or how shall we clear ourselves? God hath found out the iniquity of thy servants: behold, we are my lord's servants, both we, and he also with whom the cup is found."

And he said, "God forbid that I should do so: but the man in whose hand the cup is found, he shall be my servant; and as for you, get you up in peace unto your father."

Then Judah came near unto him, and said, "O my lord, let thy servant, I pray thee, speak a word in my lord's ears, and let not thine anger burn against thy servant: for thou art even as Pharaoh. My lord asked his servants, saying, 'Have ye a father, or a brother?' And we said unto my lord, 'We have a father, an old man, and a child of his old age, a little one; and his brother is dead, and he alone is left of his mother, and his father loveth him.' And thou saidst unto thy servants, 'Bring him down unto me, that I may set mine eyes upon him.' And we said unto my lord, 'The lad cannot leave his father: for if he should leave his father, his father would die.' And thou saidst unto thy servants, 'Except your youngest brother come down with you, ye shall see my face no more.' And it came to pass when we came up unto thy servant my father, we told him the words of my lord. And our father said, 'Go again, and buy us a little food.' And we said, 'We cannot go down: if our youngest brother be with us, then will we go down: for we may not see the man's face, except our youngest brother be with us.' And thy servant my father said unto us, 'Ye know that my wife bare me two sons: and the one went out from me, and I said, "Surely he is torn in pieces"; and I saw him not since: and if ye take this also from me, and mischief befall him, ye shall bring down my gray hairs with sorrow to the grave.' Now therefore when I come to thy servant my father, and the lad be not with us; seeing that

*Joseph makes himself known*

his life is bound up in the lad's life; it shall come to pass, when he seeth that the lad is not with us, that he will die: and thy servants shall bring down the gray hairs of thy servant our father with sorrow to the grave. For thy servant became surety for the lad unto my father, saying, 'If I bring him not unto thee, then I shall bear the blame to my father for ever.' Now therefore, I pray thee, let thy servant abide instead of the lad a bondman to my lord; and let the lad go up with his brethren. For how shall I go up to my father, and the lad be not with me? lest peradventure I see the evil that shall come on my father."

Then Joseph could not refrain himself before all them that stood by him; and he cried, "Cause every man to go out from me." And there stood no man with him, while Joseph made himself known unto his brethren. And he wept aloud: and the Egyptians and the house of Pharaoh heard.

And Joseph said unto his brethren, "I am Joseph; doth my father yet live?" And his brethren could not answer him; for they were troubled at his presence.

And Joseph said unto his brethren, "Come near to me, I pray you." And they came near. And he said, "I am Joseph your brother, whom ye sold into Egypt. Now therefore be not grieved, nor angry with yourselves, that ye sold me hither: for God did send me before you to preserve life. For these two years hath the famine been in the land: and yet there are five years, in the which there shall neither be earing nor harvest. And God sent me before you to preserve you a posterity in the earth, and to save your lives by a great deliverance. So now it was not you that sent me hither, but God: and he hath made me a father to Pharaoh, and lord of all his house, and a ruler throughout all the land of Egypt. Haste ye, and go up to my father, and say unto him, 'Thus saith thy son Joseph, "God hath made me lord of all Egypt: come down unto me, tarry not: and thou shalt dwell in the land of Goshen, and thou shalt be near unto me, thou, and thy children, and thy children's children, and thy flocks, and thy herds, and all that thou hast: and there will I nourish thee; for yet there are five years of famine; lest thou, and thy household, and all that thou hast, come to poverty."' And, behold, your eyes see, and the eyes of my brother Benjamin, that it is my mouth that speaketh unto you. And

*JOSEPH MAKING HIMSELF KNOWN*

ye shall tell my father of all my glory in Egypt, and of all that ye have seen; and ye shall haste and bring down my father hither."

And he fell upon his brother Benjamin's neck, and wept; and Benjamin wept upon his neck. Moreover he kissed all his brethren, and wept upon them: and after that his brethren talked with him. And the fame thereof was heard in Pharaoh's house, saying, "Joseph's brethren are come": and it pleased Pharaoh well, and his servants.

And Pharaoh said unto Joseph, "Say unto thy brethren, 'This do ye; lade your beasts, and go, get you unto the land of Canaan; and take your father and your households, and come unto me: and I will give you the good of the land of Egypt, and ye shall eat the fat of the land. Now thou art commanded, this do ye; take you wagons out of the land of Egypt for your little ones, and for your wives, and bring your father, and come. Also regard not your stuff; for the good of all the land of Egypt is your's.' "

And the children of Israel did so: and Joseph gave them wagons, according to the commandment of Pharaoh, and gave them provision for the way. To all of them he gave each man changes of raiment; but to Benjamin he gave three hundred pieces of silver, and five changes of raiment. And to his father he sent after this manner; ten asses laden with the good things of Egypt, and ten she asses laden with corn and bread and meat for his father by the way. So he sent his brethren away, and they departed: and he said unto them, "See that ye fall not out by the way."

And they went up out of Egypt, and came into the land of Canaan unto Jacob their father, and told him, saying, "Joseph is yet alive, and he is governor over all the land of Egypt." And Jacob's heart fainted, for he believed them not. And they told him all the words of Joseph, which he had said unto them: and when he saw the wagons which Joseph had sent to carry him, the spirit of Jacob their father revived. And Israel said, "It is enough; Joseph my son is yet alive: I will go and see him before I die."

And Israel took his journey with all that he had, and came to Beersheba, and offered sacrifices unto the God of his father Isaac. And God spake unto Israel in the visions of the night, and said, "Jacob, Jacob."

And he said, "Here am I."

*Jacob moves to Egypt*      And he said, "I am God, the God of thy father: fear not to go down into Egypt; for I will there make of thee a great nation: I will go down with thee into Egypt; and I will also surely bring thee up again: and Joseph shall put his hand upon thine eyes." And Jacob rose up from Beer-sheba: and the sons of Israel carried Jacob their father, and their little ones, and their wives, in the wagons which Pharaoh had sent to carry him. And they took their cattle, and their goods, which they had gotten in the land of Canaan, and came into Egypt, Jacob, and all his seed with him: his sons, and his sons' sons with him, his daughters, and his sons' daughters, and all his seed brought he with him into Egypt. And he sent Judah before him unto Joseph, to direct his face unto Goshen.

And Joseph made ready his chariot, and went up to meet Israel his father, to Goshen, and presented himself unto him; and he fell on his neck, and wept on his neck a good while. And Israel said unto Joseph, "Now let me die, since I have seen thy face, because thou art yet alive."

And Joseph said unto his brethren, and unto his father's house, "I will go up, and shew Pharaoh, and say unto him, 'My brethren, and my father's house, which were in the land of Canaan, are come unto me; and the men are shepherds, for their trade hath been to feed cattle; and they have brought their flocks, and their herds, and all that they have.' And it shall come to pass, when Pharaoh shall call you, and shall say, 'What is your occupation?' that ye shall say, 'Thy servants' trade hath been about cattle from our youth even until now, both we, and also our fathers: that ye may dwell in the land of Goshen; for every shepherd is an abomination unto the Egyptians."

And he took some of his brethren, even five men, and presented them unto Pharaoh. And Pharaoh spake unto Joseph, saying, "Thy father and thy brethren are come unto thee: the land of Egypt is before thee; in the best of the land make thy father and brethren to dwell; in the land of Goshen let them dwell: and if thou knowest any men of activity among them, then make them rulers over my cattle." And Joseph brought in Jacob his father, and set him before Pharaoh: and Jacob blessed Pharaoh. And Pharaoh said unto Jacob, "How old art thou?"

And Jacob said unto Pharaoh, "The days of the years of my pilgrimage are an hundred and thirty years: few and evil have the days of the years of my life been, and have not attained unto the days of the years of the life of my fathers in the days of their pilgrimage." And Jacob blessed Pharaoh, and went out from before Pharaoh.

And Joseph placed his father and his brethren, and gave them a possession in the land of Egypt, in the best of the land, in the land of Rameses, as Pharaoh had commanded. And Joseph nourished his father, and his brethren, and all his father's household, with bread, according to their families. And there was no bread in all the land; for the famine was very sore, so that the land of Egypt and all the land of Canaan fainted by reason of the famine. And Joseph bought all the land of Egypt for Pharaoh; for the Egyptians sold every man his field, because the famine prevailed over them: so the land became Pharaoh's. And as for the people, he removed them to cities from one end of the borders of Egypt even to the other end thereof.

And it came to pass after these things, that one told Joseph, "Behold, thy father is sick": and he took with him his two sons, Manasseh and Ephraim. And one told Jacob, and said, "Behold, thy son Joseph cometh unto thee": and Israel strengthened himself, and sat upon the bed.

And Jacob said unto Joseph, "God Almighty appeared unto me at Luz in the land of Canaan, and blessed me, and said unto me, 'Behold, I will make thee fruitful, and multiply thee, and I will make of thee a multitude of people; and will give this land to thy seed after thee for an everlasting possession.' And as for me, when I came from Padan, Rachel died by me in the land of Canaan in the way, when yet there was but a little way to come unto Ephrath: and I buried her there in the way of Ephrath; the same is Beth-lehem."

And Israel beheld Joseph's sons, and said, "Who are these?"

And Joseph said unto his father, "They are my sons, whom God hath given me in this place."

And he said, "Bring them, I pray thee, unto me, and I will bless them."

Now the eyes of Israel were dim for age, so that he could not see. And he brought them near unto him; and he kissed them, and embraced them. And Israel said unto Joseph, "I had not thought to see thy face: and, lo, God hath shewed me also thy seed."

And Joseph brought them out from between his knees, and he bowed

*Jacob's dying blessing* himself with his face to the earth. And Joseph took them both, Ephraim in his right hand toward Israel's left hand, and Manasseh in his left hand toward Israel's right hand, and brought them near unto him. And Israel stretched out his right hand, and laid it upon Ephraim's head, who was the younger, and his left hand upon Manasseh's head, guiding his hand wittingly; for Manasseh was the firstborn. And he blessed Joseph, and said, "God, before whom my fathers Abraham and Isaac did walk, the God which fed me all my life long unto this day, the Angel which redeemed me from all evil, bless the lads; and let my name be named on them, and the name of my fathers Abraham and Isaac; and let them grow into a multitude in the midst of the earth."

And when Joseph saw that his father laid his right hand upon the head of Ephraim, it displeased him: and he held up his father's hand, to remove it from Ephraim's head unto Manasseh's head. And Joseph said unto his father, "Not so, my father: for this is the firstborn; put thy right hand upon his head."

And his father refused, and said, "I know it, my son, I know it: he also shall become a people, and he also shall be great: but truly his younger brother shall be greater than he, and his seed shall become a multitude of nations." And Israel said unto Joseph, "Behold, I die: but God shall be with you, and bring you again unto the land of your fathers."

And Jacob called unto his sons, and said, "Gather yourselves together, that I may tell you that which shall befall you in the last days.

"Gather yourselves together, and hear, ye sons of Jacob;
And hearken unto Israel your father.
Joseph is a fruitful bough,
Even a fruitful bough by a well;
Whose branches run over the wall:
The archers have sorely grieved him,
And shot at him, and hated him:
But his bow abode in strength,
And the arms of his hands were made strong
By the hands of the mighty God of Jacob; (From thence is the shepherd, the stone of Israel:)
Even by the God of thy father, who shall help thee;

And by the Almighty, who shall bless thee
With blessings of heaven above,
Blessings of the deep that lieth under:
The blessings of thy father have prevailed
Above the blessings of my progenitors
Unto the utmost bound of the everlasting hills:
They shall be on the head of Joseph,
And on the crown of the head of him that was separate from his
　　brethren."

And when Jacob had made an end of commanding his sons, he gathered up his feet into the bed, and yielded up the ghost, and was gathered unto his people. And Joseph fell upon his father's face, and wept upon him, and kissed him. And Joseph commanded his servants the physicians to embalm his father: and the physicians embalmed Israel. And Joseph went up to bury his father: and with him went up all the servants of Pharaoh, the elders of his house, and all the elders of the land of Egypt, and all the house of Joseph, and his brethren, and his father's house: only their little ones, and their flocks, and their herds, they left in the land of Goshen. And there went up with him both chariots and horsemen: and it was a very great company. And his sons did unto him according as he commanded them: for his sons carried him into the land of Canaan, and buried him in the cave of the field of Machpelah, which Abraham bought with the field for a possession of a buryingplace. And Joseph returned into Egypt, he, and his brethren, and all that went up with him to bury his father. And when Joseph's brethren saw that their father was dead, they said, "Joseph will peradventure hate us, and will certainly requite us all the evil which we did unto him."

And they sent a messenger unto Joseph, saying, "Thy father did command before he died, saying, 'So shall ye say unto Joseph, "Forgive, I pray thee now, the trespass of thy brethren, and their sin; for they did unto thee evil" ': and now, we pray thee, forgive the trespass of the servants of the God of thy father."

And Joseph wept when they spake unto him. And his brethren also went and fell down before his face; and they said, "Behold, we be thy servants."

*Growth of Israel* And Joseph said unto them, "Fear not: for am I in the place of God? But as for you, ye thought evil against me: but God meant it unto good, to bring to pass, as it is this day, to save much people alive. Now therefore fear ye not: I will nourish you, and your little ones." And he comforted them, and spake kindly unto them.

And Joseph dwelt in Egypt, he, and his father's house: and Joseph lived an hundred and ten years. And Joseph said unto his brethren, "I die: and God will surely visit you, and bring you out of this land unto the land which he sware to Abraham, to Isaac, and to Jacob." So Joseph died, being an hundred and ten years old: and they embalmed him, and he was put in a coffin in Egypt. And all his brethren died, and all that generation. And the children of Israel were fruitful, and increased abundantly, and multiplied, and waxed exceeding mighty; and the land was filled with them.

*Birth of Moses* Now there arose up a new king over Egypt, which knew not Joseph. And he said unto his people, "Behold, the people of the children of Israel are more and mightier than we: come on, let us deal wisely with them; lest they multiply, and it come to pass, that, when there falleth out any war, they join also unto our enemies, and fight against us, and so get them up out of the land."

Therefore they did set over them taskmasters to afflict them with their burdens. And they built for Pharaoh treasure cities, Pithom and Raamses. But the more they afflicted them, the more they multiplied and grew. And the Egyptians made the children of Israel to serve with rigour: and they made their lives bitter with hard bondage, in morter, and in brick, and in all manner of service in the field: and Pharaoh charged all his people, saying, "Every son that is born ye shall cast into the river, and every daughter ye shall save alive."

And there went a man of the house of Levi, and took to wife a daughter of Levi. And the woman conceived, and bare a son: and when she saw him that he was a goodly child, she hid him three months. And when she could not longer hide him, she took for him an ark of bulrushes, and daubed it with slime and with pitch, and put the child therein; and she laid it in the flags by the river's brink. And his sister stood afar off, to wit what would be done to him.

PHARAOH'S DAUGHTER AND THE INFANT MOSES

And the daughter of Pharaoh came down to wash herself at the river; and her maidens walked along by the river's side; and when she saw the ark among the flags, she sent her maid to fetch it. And when she had opened it, she saw the child: and, behold, the babe wept. And she had compassion on him, and said, "This is one of the Hebrews' children."

Then said his sister to Pharaoh's daughter, "Shall I go and call to thee a nurse of the Hebrew women, that she may nurse the child for thee?"

And Pharaoh's daughter said to her, "Go." And the maid went and called the child's mother.

And Pharaoh's daughter said unto her, "Take this child away, and nurse it for me, and I will give thee thy wages."

And the woman took the child, and nursed it. And the child grew, and she brought him unto Pharaoh's daughter, and he became her son. And she called his name Moses: and she said, "Because I drew him out of the water."

And it came to pass in those days, when Moses was grown, that he went out unto his brethren, and looked on their burdens: and he spied an Egyptian smiting an Hebrew, one of his brethren. And he looked this way and that way, and when he saw that there was no man, he slew the Egyptian, and hid him in the sand. And when he went out the second day, behold, two men of the Hebrews strove together: and he said to him that did the wrong, "Wherefore smitest thou thy fellow?"

And he said, "Who made thee a prince and a judge over us? intendest thou to kill me, as thou killedst the Egyptian?" And Moses feared, and said, "Surely this thing is known."

Now when Pharaoh heard this thing, he sought to slay Moses. But Moses fled from the face of Pharaoh, and dwelt in the land of Midian: and he sat down by a well. Now the priest of Midian had seven daughters: and they came and drew water, and filled the troughs to water their father's flock. And the shepherds came and drove them away: but Moses stood up and helped them, and watered their flock. And when they came to Reuel their father, he said, "How is it that ye are come so soon today?"

And they said, "An Egyptian delivered us out of the hand of the shepherds, and also drew water enough for us, and watered the flock."

And he said unto his daughters, "And where is he? why is it that ye have left the man? call him, that he may eat bread."

And Moses was content to dwell with the man: and he gave Moses Zipporah his daughter. And she bare him a son, and he called his name Gershom: for he said, "I have been a stranger in a strange land."

And it came to pass in process of time, that the king of Egypt died: and the children of Israel sighed by reason of the bondage, and they cried, and their cry came up unto God by reason of the bondage. And God heard their groaning, and God remembered his covenant with Abraham, with Isaac, and with Jacob.

Now Moses kept the flock of Jethro his father in law, the priest of Midian: and he led the flock to the backside of the desert, and came to the mountain of God, even to Horeb. And the angel of the LORD appeared unto him in a flame of fire out of the midst of a bush: and he looked, and, behold, the bush burned with fire, and the bush was not consumed. And Moses said, "I will now turn aside, and see this great sight, why the bush is not burnt."

And when the LORD saw that he turned aside to see, God called unto him out of the midst of the bush, and said, "Moses, Moses."

And he said, "Here am I."

And he said, "Draw not nigh hither: put off thy shoes from off thy feet, for the place whereon thou standest is holy ground." Moreover he said, "I am the God of thy father, the God of Abraham, the God of Isaac, and the God of Jacob." And Moses hid his face; for he was afraid to look upon God.

And the LORD said, "I have surely seen the affliction of my people which are in Egypt, and have heard their cry by reason of their taskmasters; for I know their sorrows; and I am come down to deliver them out of the hand of the Egyptians, and to bring them up out of that land unto a good land and a large, unto a land flowing with milk and honey. Come now therefore, and I will send thee unto Pharaoh, that thou mayest bring forth my people the children of Israel out of Egypt."

And Moses said unto God, "Who am I, that I should go unto Pharaoh, and that I should bring forth the children of Israel out of Egypt?"

And he said, "Certainly I will be with thee; and this shall be a token

*Rod of Moses*

unto thee, that I have sent thee: When thou hast brought forth the people out of Egypt, ye shall serve God upon this mountain."

And Moses said unto God, "Behold, when I come unto the children of Israel, and shall say unto them, 'The God of your fathers hath sent me unto you'; and they shall say to me, 'What is his name?' what shall I say unto them?"

And God said unto Moses, "I AM THAT I AM": and he said, "Thus shalt thou say unto the children of Israel, 'I AM hath sent me unto you.' " And God said moreover unto Moses, "Thus shalt thou say unto the children of Israel, 'The Lord God of your fathers, the God of Abraham, the God of Isaac, and the God of Jacob, hath sent me unto you: this is my name for ever, and this is my memorial unto all generations.' "

And Moses answered and said unto the Lord, "But, behold, they will not believe me, nor hearken unto my voice: for they will say, 'The Lord hath not appeared unto thee.' "

And the Lord said unto him, "What is that in thine hand?"

And he said, "A rod."

And he said, "Cast it on the ground." And he cast it on the ground, and it became a serpent; and Moses fled from before it.

And the Lord said unto Moses, "Put forth thine hand, and take it by the tail." And he put forth his hand, and caught it, and it became a rod in his hand: "That they may believe that the Lord God of their fathers, the God of Abraham, the God of Isaac, and the God of Jacob, hath appeared unto thee."

And Moses said unto the Lord, "O my Lord, I am not eloquent, neither heretofore, nor since thou hast spoken unto thy servant: but I am slow of speech, and of a slow tongue."

And the Lord said unto him, "Who hath made man's mouth? or who maketh the dumb, or deaf, or the seeing, or the blind? have not I the Lord? Now therefore go, and I will be with thy mouth, and teach thee what thou shalt say."

And he said, "O my Lord, send, I pray thee, by the hand of him whom thou wilt send."

And the anger of the Lord was kindled against Moses, and he said, "Is not Aaron the Levite thy brother? I know that he can speak well.

And also, behold, he cometh forth to meet thee: and when he seeth thee, he will be glad in his heart. And thou shalt speak unto him, and put words in his mouth, and I will be with thy mouth, and with his mouth, and will teach you what ye shall do. And he shall be thy spokesman unto the people: and he shall be, even he shall be to thee instead of a mouth, and thou shalt be to him instead of God. And thou shalt take this rod in thine hand, wherewith thou shalt do signs."

And Moses went and returned to Jethro his father in law, and said unto him, "Let me go, I pray thee, and return unto my brethren which are in Egypt, and see whether they be yet alive."

And Jethro said to Moses, "Go in peace."

And the LORD said unto Moses in Midian, "Go, return into Egypt: for all the men are dead which sought thy life."

And Moses took his wife and his sons, and set them upon an ass, and he returned to the land of Egypt: and Moses took the rod of God in his hand. And Moses and Aaron went and gathered together all the elders of the children of Israel: and Aaron spake all the words which the LORD had spoken unto Moses, and did the signs in the sight of the people. And the people believed: and when they heard that the LORD had visited the children of Israel, and that he had looked upon their affliction, then they bowed their heads and worshipped.

And God spake unto Moses, "Wherefore say unto the children of Israel, 'I am the LORD, and I will bring you out from under the burdens of the Egyptians, and I will rid you out of their bondage, and I will redeem you with a stretched out arm, and with great judgments: and I will take you to me for a people, and I will be to you a God: and ye shall know that I am the LORD your God, which bringeth you out from under the burdens of the Egyptians.' "

And he called for Moses and Aaron by night, and said, "Rise up, and get you forth from among my people, both ye and the children of Israel; and go, serve the LORD, as ye have said. Also take your flocks and your herds, as ye have said, and be gone; and bless me also."

And the Egyptians were urgent upon the people, that they might send them out of the land in haste; for they said, "We be all dead men."

And the people took their dough before it was leavened, their kneadingtroughs being bound up in their clothes upon their shoulders.

And the children of Israel did according to the word of Moses; and they *The exodus begun* borrowed of the Egyptians jewels of silver, and jewels of gold, and raiment: and the LORD gave the people favour in the sight of the Egyptians, so that they lent unto them such things as they required. And they spoiled the Egyptians.

And the children of Israel journeyed from Rameses to Succoth, about six hundred thousand on foot that were men, beside children. And a mixed multitude went up also with them; and flocks, and herds, even very much cattle. And they baked unleavened cakes of the dough which they brought forth out of Egypt, for it was not leavened; because they were thrust out of Egypt, and could not tarry, neither had they prepared for themselves any victual.

And Moses said unto the people, "Remember this day, in which ye came out from Egypt, out of the house of bondage; for by strength of hand the LORD brought you out from this place: there shall no leavened bread be eaten."

And it came to pass, when Pharaoh had let the people go, that God led them not through the way of the land of the Philistines, although that was near; for God said, "Lest peradventure the people repent when they see war, and they return to Egypt": but God led the people about, through the way of the wilderness of the Red sea: and the children of Israel went up harnessed out of the land of Egypt.

And Moses took the bones of Joseph with him: for he had straitly sworn the children of Israel, saying, "God will surely visit you; and ye shall carry up my bones away hence with you."

And they took their journey from Succoth, and encamped in Etham, in the edge of the wilderness. And the LORD went before them by day in a pillar of a cloud, to lead them the way; and by night in a pillar of fire, to give them light; to go by day and night: he took not away the pillar of the cloud by day, nor the pillar of fire by night, from before the people. And the LORD spake unto Moses, saying, "Speak unto the children of Israel, that they turn and encamp."

And it was told the king of Egypt that the people fled: and the heart of Pharaoh and of his servants was turned against the people, and they said, "Why have we done this, that we have let Israel go from serving us?"

And he made ready his chariot, and took his people with him: and he took six hundred chosen chariots, and all the chariots of Egypt, and captains over every one of them. And he pursued after the children of Israel, and overtook them encamping by the sea. And when Pharaoh drew nigh, the children of Israel lifted up their eyes, and, behold, the Egyptians marched after them; and they were sore afraid: and the children of Israel cried out unto the LORD.

And they said unto Moses, "Hast thou taken us away to die in the wilderness? wherefore hast thou dealt thus with us, to carry us forth out of Egypt? Is not this the word that we did tell thee in Egypt, saying, 'Let us alone, that we may serve the Egyptians'? For it had been better for us to serve the Egyptians, than that we should die in the wilderness."

And Moses said unto the people, "Fear ye not, stand still, and see the salvation of the LORD, which he will shew to you to day: for the Egyptians whom ye have seen to day, ye shall see them again no more for ever. The LORD shall fight for you, and ye shall hold your peace."

And the LORD said unto Moses, "Wherefore criest thou unto me? speak unto the children of Israel, that they go forward: but lift thou up thy rod, and stretch out thine hand over the sea, and divide it: and the children of Israel shall go on dry ground through the midst of the sea." And the angel of God, which went before the camp of Israel, removed and went behind them; and the pillar of the cloud went from before their face, and stood behind them: and it came between the camp of the Egyptians and the camp of Israel; and it was a cloud and darkness to them, but it gave light by night to these: so that the one came not near the other all the night.

And Moses stretched out his hand over the sea; and the LORD caused the sea to go back by a strong east wind all that night, and made the sea dry land, and the waters were divided. And the children of Israel went into the midst of the sea upon the dry ground: and the waters were a wall unto them on their right hand, and on their left. And the Egyptians pursued, and went in after them to the midst of the sea, even all Pharaoh's horses, his chariots, and his horsemen. And it came to pass, that in the morning watch the LORD looked unto the host of the Egyptians through the pillar of fire and of the cloud, and troubled the host of the

Egyptians, and took off their chariot wheels, that they drave them heavily: so that the Egyptians said, "Let us flee from the face of Israel; for the Lord fighteth for them against the Egyptians."

And the Lord said unto Moses, "Stretch out thine hand over the sea, that the waters may come again upon the Egyptians, upon their chariots, and upon their horsemen."

And Moses stretched forth his hand over the sea, and the sea returned to his strength when the morning appeared; and the Egyptians fled against it; and the Lord overthrew the Egyptians in the midst of the sea. And the waters returned, and covered the chariots, and the horsemen, and all the host of Pharaoh that came into the sea after them; there remained not so much as one of them. But the children of Israel walked upon dry land in the midst of the sea; and the waters were a wall unto them on their right hand, and on their left. Thus the Lord saved Israel that day out of the hand of the Egyptians. And Israel saw that great work which the Lord did upon the Egyptians: and the people feared the Lord, and believed the Lord, and his servant Moses.

Then sang Moses and the children of Israel this song unto the Lord, and spake, saying,

I will sing unto the Lord, for he hath triumphed gloriously:
The horse and his rider hath he thrown into the sea.
The Lord is my strength and song,
And he is become my salvation:
He is my God, and I will prepare him an habitation;
My father's God, and I will exalt him.
The Lord is his name.
Pharaoh's chariots and his host hath he cast into the sea:
The depths have covered them:
They sank into the bottom as a stone.
Thy right hand, O Lord, is become glorious in power:
And with the blast of thy nostrils the waters were gathered together,
The floods stood upright as an heap,
And the depths were congealed in the heart of the sea.
Thou didst blow with thy wind, the sea covered them:
They sank as lead in the mighty waters.

*Sending of quails and manna*

Who is like unto thee, O Lord, among the gods?
Who is like thee, glorious in holiness,
Fearful in praises, doing wonders?
Thou in thy mercy hast led forth the people which thou hast re-
deemed:
Thou hast guided them in thy strength unto thy holy habitation.
Thou shalt bring them in, and plant them in the mountain of thine
inheritance,
In the place, O Lord, which thou hast made for thee to dwell in,
In the Sanctuary, O Lord, which thy hands have established.
The Lord shall reign for ever and ever.

So Moses brought Israel from the Red sea, and they went out into the wilderness of Shur; and they went three days in the wilderness, and found no water. And they came to Elim, where were twelve wells of water, and threescore and ten palm trees: and they encamped there by the waters. And they took their journey from Elim, and all the congregation of the children of Israel came unto the wilderness of Sin, which is between Elim and Sinai. And the whole congregation of the children of Israel murmured against Moses and Aaron in the wilderness, and said, "Who shall give us flesh to eat? We remember the fish, which we did eat in Egypt freely; the cucumbers, and the melons, and the leeks, and the onions, and the garlick."

And the Lord spake unto Moses, saying, "I have heard the murmurings of the children of Israel: speak unto them, saying, 'At even ye shall eat flesh, and in the morning ye shall be filled with bread; and ye shall know that I am the Lord your God.'" And it came to pass, that at even there went forth a wind from the Lord, and brought quails from the sea, and let them fall by the camp, as it were a day's journey on this side, and as it were a day's journey on the other side, round about the camp, and as it were two cubits high upon the face of the earth. And the people stood up all that day, and all that night, and they gathered the quails. And in the morning the dew lay round about the host. And when the dew that lay was gone up, behold, upon the face of the wilderness there lay a small round thing, as small as the hoar frost on the ground.

And when the children of Israel saw it, they said one to another, "It *Visit of Jethro* is manna": for they wist not what it was.

And Moses said unto them, "This is the bread which the LORD hath given you to eat." It was like coriander seed, white; and the taste of it was like wafers made with honey. And the people went about, and gathered it, and ground it in mills, or beat it in a mortar, and baked it in pans, and made cakes of it. And when the dew fell upon the camp in the night, the manna fell upon it. And the children of Israel did eat manna forty years, until they came to a land inhabited; they did eat manna, until they came unto the borders of the land of Canaan.

When Jethro, the priest of Midian, Moses' father in law, heard of all that God had done for Moses, and for Israel his people, and that the LORD had brought Israel out of Egypt; then Jethro, Moses' father in law, took Zipporah, Moses' wife, and her two sons, and came unto Moses into the wilderness where he encamped at the mount of God: and Moses went out to meet his father in law, and did obeisance, and kissed him; and they asked each other of their welfare; and they came into the tent. And Moses told his father in law all that the LORD had done unto Pharaoh and to the Egyptians for Israel's sake, and all the travail that had come upon them by the way, and how the LORD delivered them. And Jethro said, "Blessed be the LORD, who hath delivered you out of the hand of the Egyptians, and out of the hand of Pharaoh, who hath delivered the people from under the hand of the Egyptians. Now I know that the LORD is greater than all gods: for in the thing wherein they dealt proudly he was above them."

And Jethro, Moses' father in law, took a burnt offering and sacrifices for God: and Aaron came, and all the elders of Israel, to eat bread with Moses' father in law before God.

And it came to pass on the morrow, that Moses sat to judge the people; and the people stood by Moses from the morning unto the evening. And when Moses' father in law saw all that he did to the people, he said, "What is this thing that thou doest to the people? why sittest thou thyself alone, and all the people stand by thee from morning unto even?"

And Moses said unto his father in law, "Because the people come unto me to enquire of God: when they have a matter, they come unto

*Jethro counsels Moses* me; and I judge between one and another, and I do make them know the statutes of God, and his laws."

And Moses' father in law said unto him, "The thing that thou doest is not good. Thou wilt surely wear away, both thou, and this people that is with thee: for this thing is too heavy for thee; thou art not able to perform it thyself alone. Hearken now unto my voice, I will give thee counsel, and God shall be with thee: Be thou for the people to Godward, that thou mayest bring the causes unto God: and thou shalt teach them ordinances and laws, and shalt shew them the way wherein they must walk, and the work that they must do. Moreover thou shalt provide out of all the people able men, such as fear God, men of truth, hating covetousness; and place such over them, to be rulers of thousands, and rulers of hundreds, rulers of fifties, and rulers of tens: and let them judge the people at all seasons: and it shall be, that every great matter they shall bring unto thee, but every small matter they shall judge: so shall it be easier for thyself, and they shall bear the burden with thee. If thou shalt do this thing, and God command thee so, then thou shalt be able to endure, and all this people shall also go to their place in peace."

So Moses hearkened to the voice of his father in law, and did all that he had said. And Moses chose able men out of all Israel, and made them heads over the people, rulers of thousands, rulers of hundreds, rulers of fifties, and rulers of tens. And they judged the people at all seasons: the hard causes they brought unto Moses, but every small matter they judged themselves. And Moses let his father in law depart; and he went his way into his own land.

In the third month, when the children of Israel were gone forth out of the land of Egypt, the same day came they into the wilderness of Sinai, and camped before the mount. And Moses went up unto God, and the LORD called unto him out of the mountain, saying, "Thus shalt thou say to the house of Jacob, and tell the children of Israel; 'Ye have seen what I did unto the Egyptians, and how I bare you on eagles' wings, and brought you unto myself. Now therefore, if ye will obey my voice indeed, and keep my covenant, then ye shall be a peculiar treasure unto me above all people: for all the earth is mine: and ye shall be unto me a kingdom of priests, and an holy nation.' These are the words which thou shalt speak unto the children of Israel."

And Moses came and called for the elders of the people, and laid before their faces all these words which the LORD commanded him. And all the people answered together, and said, "All that the LORD hath spoken we will do."

And Moses returned the words of the people unto the LORD. And the LORD said unto Moses, "Lo, I come unto thee in a thick cloud, that the people may hear when I speak with thee, and believe thee for ever."

And Moses told the words of the people unto the LORD. And the LORD said unto Moses, "Go unto the people, and sanctify them to day and to morrow, and let them wash their clothes, and be ready against the third day: for the third day the LORD will come down in the sight of all the people upon mount Sinai."

And Moses went down from the mount unto the people, and sanctified the people; and they washed their clothes.

And it came to pass on the third day in the morning, that there were thunders and lightnings, and a thick cloud upon the mount, and the voice of the trumpet exceeding loud; so that all the people that was in the camp trembled. And Moses brought forth the people out of the camp to meet with God; and they stood at the nether part of the mount. And mount Sinai was altogether on a smoke, because the LORD descended upon it in fire: and the smoke thereof ascended as the smoke of a furnace, and the whole mount quaked greatly. And when the voice of the trumpet sounded long, and waxed louder and louder, Moses spake, and God answered him by a voice. And the LORD came down upon mount Sinai, on the top of the mount: and the LORD called Moses up to the top of the mount; and Moses went up.

And the LORD said unto Moses, "Go down, charge the people, lest they break through unto the LORD to gaze."

And Moses said unto the LORD, "The people cannot come up to mount Sinai: for thou chargedst us, saying, 'Set bounds about the mount, and sanctify it.'"

And the LORD said unto him, "Away, get thee down, and thou shalt come up, thou, and Aaron with thee: but let not the priests and the people break through to come up unto the LORD."

So Moses went down unto the people, and spake unto them.

*The ten Commandments*

And God spake all these words, saying, "I am the LORD thy God, which have brought thee out of the land of Egypt, out of the house of bondage.

"Thou shalt have no other gods before me.

"Thou shalt not make unto thee any graven image, or any likeness of any thing that is in heaven above, or that is in the earth beneath, or that is in the water under the earth: thou shalt not bow down thyself to them, nor serve them: for I the LORD thy God am a jealous God, visiting the iniquity of the fathers upon the children unto the third and fourth generation of them that hate me; and shewing mercy unto thousands of them that love me, and keep my commandments.

"Thou shalt not take the name of the LORD thy God in vain; for the LORD will not hold him guiltless that taketh his name in vain.

"Remember the sabbath day, to keep it holy. Six days shalt thou labour, and do all thy work: but the seventh day is the sabbath of the LORD thy God: in it thou shalt not do any work, thou, nor thy son, nor thy daughter, thy manservant, nor thy maidservant, nor thy cattle, nor thy stranger that is within thy gates: for in six days the LORD made heaven and earth, the sea, and all that in them is, and rested the seventh day: wherefore the LORD blessed the sabbath day, and hallowed it.

"Honour thy father and thy mother: that thy days may be long upon the land which the LORD thy God giveth thee.

"Thou shalt not kill.

"Thou shalt not commit adultery.

"Thou shalt not steal.

"Thou shalt not bear false witness against thy neighbour.

"Thou shalt not covet thy neighbour's house, thou shalt not covet thy neighbour's wife, nor his manservant, nor his maidservant, nor his ox, nor his ass, nor any thing that is thy neighbour's."

And all the people saw the thunderings, and the lightnings, and the noise of the trumpet, and the mountain smoking: and when the people saw it, they removed, and stood afar off. And they said unto Moses, "Speak thou with us, and we will hear: but let not God speak with us, lest we die."

And Moses said unto the people, "Fear not: for God is come to prove you, and that his fear may be before your faces, that ye sin not."

And the people stood afar off, and Moses drew near unto the thick darkness where God was.

And the LORD said unto Moses, "Thus thou shalt say unto the children of Israel, 'Ye have seen that I have talked with you from heaven. Ye shall not make with me gods of silver, neither shall ye make unto you gods of gold. An altar of earth thou shalt make unto me, and shalt sacrifice thereon thy burnt offerings, and thy peace offerings, thy sheep, and thine oxen: in all places where I record my name I will come unto thee, and I will bless thee. And if thou wilt make me an altar of stone, thou shalt not build it of hewn stone: for if thou lift up thy tool upon it, thou hast polluted it. Neither shalt thou go up by steps unto mine altar, that thy nakedness be not discovered thereon.'

"Now these are the judgments which thou shalt set before them.

" 'Thou shalt not see thy brother's ox or his sheep go astray, and hide thyself from them: thou shalt in any case bring them again unto thy brother. And if thy brother be not nigh unto thee, or if thou know him not, then thou shalt bring it unto thine own house, and it shall be with thee until thy brother seek after it, and thou shalt restore it to him again. In like manner shalt thou do with his ass; and so shalt thou do with his raiment; and with all lost thing of thy brother's, which he hath lost, and thou hast found, shalt thou do likewise: thou mayest not hide thyself. Thou shalt not see thy brother's ass or his ox fall down by the way, and hide thyself from them: thou shalt surely help him to lift them up again.

" 'If a bird's nest chance to be before thee in the way in any tree, or on the ground, whether they be young ones, or eggs, and the dam sitting upon the young, or upon the eggs, thou shalt not take the dam with the young: but thou shalt in any wise let the dam go, and take the young to thee; that it may be well with thee, and that thou mayest prolong thy days.

" 'When thou dost lend thy brother any thing, thou shalt not go into his house to fetch his pledge. Thou shalt stand abroad, and the man to whom thou dost lend shall bring out the pledge abroad unto thee. And if the man be poor, thou shalt not sleep with his pledge: in any case thou shalt deliver him the pledge again when the sun goeth down, that he may sleep in his own raiment, and bless thee: and it shall be righteousness unto thee before the Lord thy God.

" 'Thou shalt not oppress an hired servant that is poor and needy, whether he be of thy brethren, or of thy strangers that are in thy land within thy gates: at his day thou shalt give him his hire, neither shall the sun go down upon it; for he is poor, and setteth his heart upon it: lest he cry against thee unto the LORD, and it be sin unto thee.

" 'When thou cuttest down thine harvest in thy field, and hast forgot a sheaf in the field, thou shalt not go again to fetch it: it shall be for the stranger, for the fatherless, and for the widow: that the LORD thy God may bless thee in all the work of thine hands. When thou beatest thine olive tree, thou shalt not go over the boughs again: it shall be for the stranger, for the fatherless, and for the widow. When thou gatherest the grapes of thy vineyard, thou shalt not glean it afterward: it shall be for the stranger, for the fatherless, and for the widow. And six years thou shalt sow thy land, and shalt gather in the fruits thereof: but the seventh year thou shalt let it rest and lie still; that the poor of thy people may eat: and what they leave the beasts of the field shall eat. In like manner thou shalt deal with thy vineyard, and with thy oliveyard.

" 'And thou shalt take no gift: for the gift blindeth the wise, and perverteth the words of the righteous.

" 'And ye shall serve the LORD your God, and he shall bless thy bread, and thy water; and I will take sickness away from the midst of thee.

" 'Thou shalt not have in thy bag divers weights, a great and a small. Thou shalt not have in thine house divers measures, a great and a small. But thou shalt have a perfect and just weight, a perfect and just measure shalt thou have: that thy days may be lengthened in the land which the LORD thy God giveth thee.

" 'And it shall be, when thou art come in unto the land which the LORD thy God giveth thee for an inheritance, and possessest it, and dwellest therein; that thou shalt take of the first of all the fruit of the earth, which thou shalt bring of thy land that the LORD thy God giveth thee, and shalt put it in a basket, and shalt go unto the place which the LORD thy God shall choose to place his name there. And thou shalt go unto the priest that shall be in those days, and say unto him, "The LORD brought us forth out of Egypt with a mighty hand, and with an outstretched arm, and with great terribleness, and with signs, and with wonders: and he hath brought us into this place, and hath given us this land, even a land that floweth with milk and honey. And now, behold, I have brought the firstfruits of the land, which thou, O LORD, hast given me." And thou shalt set it before the LORD thy God, and worship before the LORD thy God: and thou shalt rejoice in every good thing which the LORD thy God hath given unto thee, and unto thine house, thou, and the Levite, and the stranger that is among you.

" 'Thou shalt not hate thy brother in thine heart: thou shalt in any wise rebuke thy neighbour, and not suffer sin upon him. But thou shalt love thy neighbour as thyself: I am the LORD.

" 'If there be among you a poor man of one of thy brethren within any of thy gates in thy land which the LORD thy God giveth thee, thou shalt not harden thine heart, nor shut thine hand from thy poor brother: but thou shalt open thine hand wide unto him, and shalt surely lend him sufficient for his need, in that which he wanteth. Thou shalt surely give him, and thine heart shall not be grieved when thou givest unto him: because that for this thing the LORD thy God shall bless thee in all thy works, and in all that thou puttest thine hand unto. For the poor shall never cease out of the land: therefore I command thee, saying, "Thou shalt open thine hand wide unto thy brother, to thy poor, and to thy needy, in thy land."

" 'Thou shalt rise up before the hoary head, and honour the face of the old man, and fear thy God: I am the LORD.' "

And Moses came and told the people all the words of the LORD, and all the judgments: and all the people answered with one voice, and said, "All the words which the LORD hath said will we do."

And Moses wrote all the words of the LORD, and rose up early in the morning, and builded an altar under the hill. And he sent young men of the children of Israel, which offered burnt offerings, and sacrificed peace offerings of oxen unto the LORD. And he took the book of the covenant, and read in the audience of the people: and they said, "All that the LORD hath said will we do, and be obedient."

And the LORD said unto Moses, "Come up to me into the mount, and be there: and I will give thee tables of stone, and a law, and commandments which I have written; that thou mayest teach them."

And Moses went up into the mount, and a cloud covered the mount. And the glory of the LORD abode upon mount Sinai, and the cloud covered it six days: and the seventh day he called unto Moses out of the midst of the cloud. And the sight of the glory of the LORD was like devouring fire on the top of the mount in the eyes of the children of Israel. And Moses went into the midst of the cloud, and gat him up into the mount: and Moses was in the mount forty days and forty nights.

And the LORD spake unto Moses, saying, "Speak unto the children of Israel, that they bring me an offering: of every man that giveth it willingly with his heart ye shall take my offering. And let them make me a sanctuary; that I may dwell among them. According to all that I shew thee, after the pattern of the tabernacle, and the pattern of all the instruments thereof, even so shall ye make it. And they shall make an ark of shittim wood: and thou shalt overlay it with pure gold, within and without shalt thou overlay it, and shalt make upon it a crown of gold round about. And thou shalt make staves of shittim wood, and overlay them with gold. And thou shalt put the staves into the rings by the sides of the ark, that the ark may be borne with them. The staves shall be in the rings of the ark: they shall not be taken from it.

"And thou shalt make a mercy seat of pure gold: and thou shalt make two cherubims of gold, of beaten work shalt thou make them, in the two ends of the mercy seat. And the cherubims shall stretch forth their wings on high, covering the mercy seat with their wings, and their faces shall look one to another; toward the mercy seat shall the faces of the cherubims be. And thou shalt put the mercy seat above upon the ark; and in the ark thou shalt put the testimony that I shall give thee. And there I will meet with thee, and I will commune with thee from above the mercy seat, from between the two cherubims which are upon the ark of the testimony, of all things which I will give thee in commandment unto the children of Israel.

"And take thou unto thee Aaron thy brother, and his sons with him, from among the children of Israel, that he may minister unto me in the priest's office, even Aaron, Nadab and Abihu, Eleazar and Ithamar, Aaron's sons. And thou shalt make holy garments for Aaron thy brother for glory and for beauty. And thou shalt speak unto all that are wise hearted, whom I have filled with the spirit of wisdom, that they may make Aaron's garments to consecrate him, that he may minister unto me in the priest's office."

And the Lord spake unto Moses, saying, "See, I have called by name Bezaleel the son of Uri: and I have filled him with the spirit of God, in wisdom, and in understanding, and in knowledge, and in all manner of workmanship, to devise cunning works, to work in gold, and in silver, and in brass, and in cutting of stones, to set them, and in carving of timber, to work in all manner of workmanship. And I, behold, I have given with him Aholiab, the son of Ahisamach: and in the hearts of all that are wise hearted I have put wisdom, that they may make all that I have commanded thee; the tabernacle of the congregation, and the ark of the testimony, and the mercy seat that is thereupon, and all the furniture of the tabernacle, and the table and his furniture, and the pure candlestick with all his furniture, and the altar of incense, and the altar of burnt offering with all his furniture, and the laver and his foot, and the cloths of service, and the holy garments for Aaron the priest, and the garments of his sons, to minister in the priest's office, and the anointing oil, and sweet incense for the holy place: according to all that I have commanded thee shall they do."

And the Lord spake unto Moses, saying, "Speak thou also unto the children of Israel, saying, 'Verily my sabbaths ye shall keep: for it is a sign between me and you throughout your generations; that ye may know that I am the Lord that doth sanctify you. Ye shall keep the sabbath therefore; for it is holy unto you. Six days may work be done; but in the seventh is the sabbath of rest, holy to the Lord. Wherefore the children of Israel shall keep the sabbath, to observe the sabbath throughout their generations, for a perpetual covenant. It is a sign between me and the children of Israel for ever: for in six days the Lord made heaven and earth, and on the seventh day he rested, and was refreshed.' "

And he gave unto Moses, when he had made an end of communing with him upon mount Sinai, two tables of testimony, tables of stone, written with the finger of God.

And when the people saw that Moses delayed to come down out of the mount, the people gathered themselves together unto Aaron, and said unto him, "Up, make us gods, which shall go before us; for as for this Moses, the man that brought us up out of the land of Egypt, we wot not what is become of him."

And Aaron said unto them, "Break off the golden earrings, which

*Moses breaks the tables* are in the ears of your wives, of your sons, and of your daughters, and bring them unto me."

And all the people brake off the golden earrings which were in their ears, and brought them unto Aaron. And he received them at their hand, and fashioned it with a graving tool, after he had made it a molten calf: and they said, "These be thy gods, O Israel, which brought thee up out of the land of Egypt."

And when Aaron saw it, he built an altar before it; and Aaron made proclamation, and said, "To morrow is a feast to the LORD."

And they rose up early on the morrow, and offered burnt offerings, and brought peace offerings; and the people sat down to eat and to drink, and rose up to play.

And Moses turned, and went down from the mount, and the two tables of the testimony were in his hand: the tables were written on both their sides; on the one side and on the other were they written. And the tables were the work of God, and the writing was the writing of God, graven upon the tables. And when Joshua heard the noise of the people as they shouted, he said unto Moses, "There is a noise of war in the camp."

And he said, "It is not the voice of them that shout for mastery, neither is it the voice of them that cry for being overcome: but the noise of them that sing do I hear."

And it came to pass, as soon as he came nigh unto the camp, that he saw the calf, and the dancing: and Moses' anger waxed hot, and he cast the tables out of his hands, and brake them beneath the mount. And he took the calf which they had made, and burnt it in the fire, and ground it to powder, and strawed it upon the water, and made the children of Israel drink of it.

And Moses said unto Aaron, "What did this people unto thee, that thou hast brought so great a sin upon them?"

And Aaron said, "Let not the anger of my lord wax hot: thou knowest the people, that they are set on mischief. For they said unto me, 'Make us gods, which shall go before us: for as for this Moses, the man that brought us up out of the land of Egypt, we wot not what is become of him.' And I said unto them, 'Whosoever hath any gold, let them break it off.' So they gave it me: then I cast it into the fire, and there came out this calf."

And it came to pass on the morrow, that Moses said unto the people,
"Ye have sinned a great sin: and now I will go up unto the LORD; peradventure I shall make an atonement for your sin."

And Moses returned unto the LORD, and said, "Oh, this people have
sinned a great sin, and have made them gods of gold. Yet now, if thou
wilt forgive their sin —; and if not, blot me, I pray thee, out of thy book
which thou hast written."

And the LORD said unto Moses, "Whosoever hath sinned against me,
him will I blot out of my book. Therefore now go, lead the people unto
the place of which I have spoken unto thee."

And the LORD spake unto Moses, saying, "Send thou men, that they
may search the land of Canaan, which I give unto the children of Israel:
of every tribe of their fathers shall ye send a man, every one a ruler among
them."

And Moses by the commandment of the LORD sent them from the
wilderness of Paran: all those men were heads of the children of Israel.
And Moses sent them to spy out the land of Canaan, and said unto them,
"Get you up this way southward, and go up into the mountain: and see
the land, what it is; and the people that dwelleth therein, whether they
be strong or weak, few or many; and what the land is that they dwell in,
whether it be good or bad; and what cities there be that they dwell in,
whether in tents, or in strong holds; and what the land is, whether it be
fat or lean, whether there be wood therein, or not. And be ye of good
courage, and bring of the fruit of the land."

Now the time was the time of the firstripe grapes. So they went up,
and searched the land. And they came unto the brook of Eshcol, and cut
down from thence a branch with one cluster of grapes, and they bare it
between two upon a staff; and they brought of the pomegranates, and
of the figs. The place was called the brook Eshcol, because of the cluster
of grapes which the children of Israel cut down from thence. And they
returned from searching of the land after forty days.

Then Israel sang this song,

Spring up, O well;
Sing ye unto it:
The princes digged the well,

*God talks with Moses*

The nobles of the people digged it,
By the direction of the lawgiver,
With their staves.

And from the wilderness they went to Mattanah.

And the LORD said unto Moses, "Depart, and go up hence, thou and the people which thou hast brought up out of the land of Egypt, unto the land which I sware unto Abraham, to Isaac, and to Jacob, saying, 'Unto thy seed will I give it.' "

And Moses took the tabernacle, and pitched it without the camp, afar off from the camp, and called it the Tabernacle of the congregation. And it came to pass, that every one which sought the LORD went out unto the tabernacle of the congregation, which was without the camp. And it came to pass, when Moses went out unto the tabernacle, that all the people rose up, and stood every man at his tent door, and looked after Moses, until he was gone into the tabernacle. And it came to pass, as Moses entered into the tabernacle, the cloudy pillar descended, and stood at the door of the tabernacle, and the LORD talked with Moses. And all the people saw the cloudy pillar stand at the tabernacle door: and all the people rose up and worshipped, every man in his tent door. And the LORD spake unto Moses face to face, as a man speaketh unto his friend.

And Moses said unto the LORD, "See, thou sayest unto me, 'Bring up this people': and thou hast not let me know whom thou wilt send with me. Yet thou hast said, 'I know thee by name, and thou hast also found grace in my sight.' Now therefore, I pray thee, if I have found grace in thy sight, shew me now thy way, that I may know thee, that I may find grace in thy sight: and consider that this nation is thy people."

And he said, "My presence shall go with thee, and I will give thee rest."

And he said unto him, "If thy presence go not with me, carry us not up hence. For wherein shall it be known here that I and thy people have found grace in thy sight? is it not in that thou goest with us?"

And the LORD said unto Moses, "I will do this thing also that thou hast spoken: for thou hast found grace in my sight, and I know thee by name."

And he said, "I beseech thee, shew me thy glory."

And he said, "I will make all my goodness pass before thee, and I *The tables of the law* will proclaim the name of the LORD before thee." And he said, "Thou *renewed* canst not see my face: for there shall no man see me, and live."

And the LORD said, "Behold, there is a place by me, and thou shalt stand upon a rock: and it shall come to pass, while my glory passeth by, that I will put thee in a clift of the rock, and will cover thee with my hand while I pass by: and I will take away mine hand, and thou shalt see my back parts: but my face shall not be seen."

And the LORD said unto Moses, "Hew thee two tables of stone like unto the first: and I will write upon these tables the words that were in the first tables, which thou brakest. And be ready in the morning, and come up in the morning unto mount Sinai, and present thyself there to me in the top of the mount. And no man shall come up with thee, neither let any man be seen throughout all the mount; neither let the flocks nor herds feed before that mount."

And he hewed two tables of stone like unto the first; and Moses rose up early in the morning, and went up unto mount Sinai, as the LORD had commanded him, and took in his hand the two tables of stone. And the LORD descended in the cloud, and stood with him there. And the LORD passed by before him, and proclaimed, "The LORD, the LORD God, merciful and gracious, longsuffering, and abundant in goodness and truth, keeping mercy for thousands, forgiving iniquity and transgression and sin."

And Moses made haste, and bowed his head toward the earth, and worshipped. And he said, "If now I have found grace in thy sight, O Lord, let my Lord, I pray thee, go among us; for it is a stiffnecked people; and pardon our iniquity and our sin, and take us for thine inheritance."

And it came to pass, when Moses came down from mount Sinai with the two tables of testimony in Moses' hand, when he came down from the mount, that Moses wist not that the skin of his face shone while he talked with him. And Moses spake unto all the congregation of the children of Israel, saying, "This is the thing which the LORD commanded, saying, 'Take ye from among you an offering unto the LORD: whosoever is of a willing heart, let him bring it, an offering of the LORD; gold, and silver, and brass, and blue, and purple, and scarlet, and fine linen, and goats' hair, and rams' skins dyed red, and badgers' skins, and shittim wood, and oil for the light, and spices for anointing oil, and for the sweet incense, and onyx stones, and stones to be set for the ephod, and for the breastplate. And every wise hearted among you shall come, and make all that the LORD hath commanded; the altar of burnt offering, with his brasen grate, his staves, and all his vessels, the laver and his foot.' "

And all the congregation of the children of Israel departed from the presence of Moses. And they came, every one whose heart stirred him up, and every one whom his spirit made willing, and they brought the LORD's offering to the work of the tabernacle of the congregation, and for all his service, and for the holy garments. And they came, both men and women, as many as were willing hearted, and brought bracelets, and earrings, and rings, and tablets, all jewels of gold. And every man, with whom was found blue, and purple, and scarlet, and fine linen, and goats' hair, and red skins of rams, and badgers' skins, brought them. Every one that did offer an offering of silver and brass brought the LORD's offering: and every man, with whom was found shittim wood for any work of the service, brought it. And all the women that were wise hearted did spin with their hands, and brought that which they had spun, both of blue, and of purple, and of scarlet, and of fine linen. And all the women whose heart stirred them up in wisdom spun goats' hair. And the rulers brought onyx stones, and stones to be set, for the ephod, and for the breastplate; and spice, and oil for the light, and for the anointing oil, and for the sweet incense. The children of Israel brought a willing offering unto the LORD, every man and woman, whose heart made them willing to bring for all manner of work, which the LORD had commanded to be made by the hand of Moses.

And Moses said unto the children of Israel, "See, the LORD hath called by name Bezaleel the son of Uri; and he hath filled him with the spirit of God, in wisdom, in understanding, and in knowledge, and in all manner of workmanship; and to devise curious works, to work in gold, and in silver, and in brass, and in the cutting of stones, to set them, and in carving of wood, to make any manner of cunning work. And he hath put in his heart that he may teach, both he, and Aholiab, the son of Ahisamach, of the tribe of Dan. Them hath he filled with wisdom of heart, to work all manner of work, of the engraver, and of the cunning workman, and of the embroiderer, in blue, and in purple, in scarlet, and

in fine linen, and of the weaver, even of them that do any work, and of
those that devise cunning work."

And they brought yet unto him free offerings every morning. And all the wise men, that wrought all the work of the sanctuary, came every man from his work which they made; and they spake unto Moses, saying, "The people bring much more than enough for the service of the work, which the LORD commanded to make." And Moses gave commandment, and they caused it to be proclaimed throughout the camp, saying, "Let neither man nor woman make any more work for the offering of the sanctuary."

So the people were restrained from bringing. For the stuff they had was sufficient for all the work to make it, and too much. Thus was all the work of the tabernacle of the tent of the congregation finished. And Moses did look upon all the work, and, behold, they had done it as the LORD had commanded, even so had they done it: and Moses blessed them.

And the LORD spake unto Moses, saying, "Speak unto Aaron and unto his sons, saying, 'On this wise ye shall bless the children of Israel, saying unto them,

The LORD bless thee, and keep thee:
The LORD make his face shine upon thee, and be gracious unto thee:
The LORD lift up his countenance upon thee, and give thee peace.

And they shall put my name upon the children of Israel; and I will bless them.' "

These be the words which Moses spake unto all Israel on this side Jordan in the wilderness, in the plain over against the Red sea, between Paran, and Tophel, and Laban, and Hazeroth, and Dizahab.

"The LORD our God spake unto us in Horeb, saying, 'Ye have dwelt long enough in this mount: turn you, and take your journey, and go to the mount of the Amorites, and unto all the places nigh thereunto, in the plain, in the hills, and in the vale, and in the south, and by the sea side, to the land of the Canaanites, and unto Lebanon, unto the great river, the river Euphrates. Behold, I have set the land before you: go in and possess the land which the LORD sware unto your fathers, Abraham,

*Speech of Moses in the
end of the fortieth year*

Isaac, and Jacob, to give unto them and to their seed after them. And I spake unto you at that time, saying, "I am not able to bear you myself alone: the LORD your God hath multiplied you, and, behold, ye are this day as the stars of heaven for multitude. How can I myself alone bear your cumbrance, and your burden, and your strife? Take you wise men, and understanding, and known among your tribes, and I will make them rulers over you." And ye answered me, and said, "The thing which thou hast spoken is good for us to do." So I took the chief of your tribes, wise men, and known, and made them heads over you, captains over thousands, and captains over hundreds, and captains over fifties, and captains over tens, and officers among your tribes. And I charged your judges at that time, saying, "Hear the causes between your brethren, and judge righteously between every man and his brother, and the stranger that is with him. Ye shall not respect persons in judgment; but ye shall hear the small as well as the great; ye shall not be afraid of the face of man; for the judgment is God's: and the cause that is too hard for you, bring it unto me, and I will hear it." And I commanded you at that time all the things which ye should do.' When we departed from Horeb, we went through all that great and terrible wilderness, which ye saw by the way of the mountain of the Amorites, as the LORD our God commanded us; and we came to Kadesh-barnea. And I said unto you, 'Ye are come unto the mountain of the Amorites, which the LORD our God doth give unto us. Behold, the LORD thy God hath set the land before thee: go up and possess it, as the LORD God of thy fathers hath said unto thee; fear not, neither be discouraged.' And ye came near unto me every one of you, and said, 'We will send men before us, and they shall search us out the land, and bring us word again by what way we must go up, and into what cities we shall come.' And the saying pleased me well: and I took twelve men of you: and they turned and went up into the mountain, and came unto the valley of Eshcol, and searched it out. And they took of the fruit of the land in their hands, and brought it down unto us, and brought us word again, and said, 'It is a good land which the LORD our God doth give us.' Notwithstanding ye would not go up, but rebelled against the commandment of the LORD your God: and ye murmured in your tents, and said, 'Because the LORD hated us, he hath brought us forth out of the land of Egypt, to deliver us into the hand of the Amorites,

[ 80 ]

to destroy us. Whither shall we go up? our brethren have discouraged *Speech of Moses* our heart, saying, "The people is greater and taller than we; the cities are great and walled up to heaven"; and moreover we have seen the sons of the Anakims there.' Then I said unto you, 'Dread not, neither be afraid of them. The LORD your God which goeth before you, he shall fight for you, according to all that he did for you in Egypt before your eyes; and in the wilderness, where thou hast seen how that the LORD thy God bare thee, as a man doth bear his son, in all the way that ye went, until ye came into this place.' Yet in this thing ye did not believe the LORD your God.

"Behold, I have taught you statutes and judgments, even as the LORD my God commanded me, that ye should do so in the land whither ye go to possess it. Keep therefore and do them; for this is your wisdom and your understanding in the sight of the nations, which shall hear all these statutes, and say, 'Surely this great nation is a wise and understanding people.' For what nation is there so great, who hath God so nigh unto them, as the LORD our God is in all things that we call upon him for? And what nation is there so great, that hath statutes and judgments so righteous as all this law, which I set before you this day? Only take heed to thyself, and keep thy soul diligently, lest thou forget the things which thine eyes have seen, and lest they depart from thy heart all the days of thy life: but teach them thy sons, and thy sons' sons; specially the day that thou stoodest before the LORD thy God in Horeb, when the LORD said unto me, 'Gather me the people together, and I will make them hear my words, that they may learn to fear me all the days that they shall live upon the earth, and that they may teach their children.' And ye came near and stood under the mountain; and the mountain burned with fire unto the midst of heaven, with darkness, clouds, and thick darkness. And the LORD spake unto you out of the midst of the fire: ye heard the voice of the words, but saw no similitude; only ye heard a voice. And he declared unto you his covenant, which he commanded you to perform, even ten commandments; and he wrote them upon two tables of stone.

"Furthermore the LORD was angry with me for your sakes, and sware that I should not go over Jordan, and that I should not go in unto that good land, which the LORD thy God giveth thee for an inheritance: but I must die in this land, I must not go over Jordan: but ye shall go over, and possess that good land. Take heed unto yourselves, lest ye forget the covenant of the LORD your God, which he made with you, and make you a graven image, or the likeness of any thing, which the LORD thy God hath forbidden thee. For the LORD thy God is a consuming fire, even a jealous God. But if from thence thou shalt seek the LORD thy God, thou shalt find him, if thou seek him with all thy heart and with all thy soul. When thou art in tribulation, and all these things are come upon thee, even in the latter days, if thou turn to the LORD thy God, and shalt be obedient unto his voice; (for the LORD thy God is a merciful God;) he will not forsake thee, neither destroy thee, nor forget the covenant of thy fathers which he sware unto them.

"Know therefore that the LORD thy God, he is God, the faithful God, which keepeth covenant and mercy with them that love him and keep his commandments to a thousand generations. For ask now of the days that are past, which were before thee, since the day that God created man upon the earth, and ask from the one side of heaven unto the other, whether there hath been any such thing as this great thing is, or hath been heard like it? Did ever people hear the voice of God speaking out of the midst of the fire, as thou hast heard, and live? Unto thee it was shewed, that thou mightest know that the LORD he is God; there is none else beside him. Out of heaven he made thee to hear his voice, that he might instruct thee. Know therefore this day, and consider it in thine heart, that the LORD he is God in heaven above, and upon the earth beneath: there is none else. And ye said, 'Behold, the LORD our God hath shewed us his glory and his greatness, and we have heard his voice out of the midst of the fire: we have seen this day that God doth talk with man, and he liveth.' Ye shall walk in all the ways which the LORD your God hath commanded you, that ye may live, and that it may be well with you, and that ye may prolong your days in the land which ye shall possess.

"Hear, O Israel: The LORD our God is one LORD: and thou shalt love the LORD thy God with all thine heart, and with all thy soul, and with all thy might. And these words, which I command thee this day, shall be in thine heart: and thou shalt teach them diligently unto thy children, and shalt talk of them when thou sittest in thine house, and when thou walkest by the way, and when thou liest down, and when thou risest up.

Therefore shall ye lay up these my words in your heart and in your soul, and thou shalt bind them for a sign upon thine hand, that they may be as frontlets between thine eyes. And thou shalt write them upon the posts of thy house, and on thy gates. And now, Israel, what doth the LORD thy God require of thee, but to fear the LORD thy God, to walk in all his ways, and to love him, and to serve the LORD thy God with all thy heart and with all thy soul, to keep the commandments of the LORD, and his statutes, which I command thee this day for thy good? Behold, the heaven and the heaven of heavens is the LORD's thy God, the earth also, with all that therein is. For the LORD your God is God of gods, and Lord of lords, a great God, a mighty, and a terrible, which regardeth not persons, nor taketh reward: he doth execute the judgment of the fatherless and widow, and loveth the stranger, in giving him food and raiment. Love ye therefore the stranger: for ye were strangers in the land of Egypt. Thou shalt fear the LORD thy God; him shalt thou serve, and to him shalt thou cleave, and swear by his name. He is thy praise, and he is thy God.

*Moses views the promised land*

"And I besought the LORD at that time, saying, 'O Lord GOD, thou hast begun to shew thy servant thy greatness, and thy mighty hand: for what God is there in heaven or in earth, that can do according to thy works, and according to thy might? I pray thee, let me go over, and see the good land that is beyond Jordan, that goodly mountain, and Lebanon.' But the LORD was wroth with me for your sakes, and would not hear me: and the LORD said unto me, 'Let it suffice thee; speak no more unto me of this matter. Get thee up into the top of Pisgah, and lift up thine eyes westward, and northward, and southward, and eastward, and behold it with thine eyes: for thou shalt not go over this Jordan. But charge Joshua, and encourage him, and strengthen him: for he shall go over before this people, and he shall cause them to inherit the land which thou shalt see.' So we abode in the valley over against Beth-peor. And thou shalt remember all the way which the LORD thy God led thee these forty years in the wilderness, to humble thee, and to prove thee, to know what was in thine heart, whether thou wouldest keep his commandments, or no. And he humbled thee, and suffered thee to hunger, and fed thee with manna, which thou knewest not, neither did thy fathers know; that he might make thee know that man doth not live by bread only, but by every word that proceedeth out of the mouth of the LORD doth man live.

[ 83 ]

*Exhortation to obedience* Thy raiment waxed not old upon thee, neither did thy foot swell, these forty years.

"Thou shalt also consider in thine heart, that, as a man chasteneth his son, so the LORD thy God chasteneth thee. Therefore thou shalt keep the commandments of the LORD thy God, to walk in his ways, and to fear him. And it shall be, when the LORD thy God shall have brought thee into the land which he sware unto thy fathers, to Abraham, to Isaac, and to Jacob, to give thee great and goodly cities, which thou buildedst not, and houses full of all good things, which thou filledst not, and wells digged, which thou diggedst not, vineyards and olive trees, which thou plantedst not; then beware lest thou forget the LORD, which brought thee forth out of the land of Egypt, from the house of bondage.

"The LORD said unto me, 'The land, whither thou goest in to possess it, is a land of hills and valleys, and drinketh water of the rain of heaven: a land which the LORD thy God careth for: the eyes of the LORD thy God are always upon it, from the beginning of the year even unto the end of the year. And it shall come to pass, if ye shall hearken diligently unto my commandments which I command you this day, to love the LORD your God, and to serve him with all your heart and with all your soul,

that I will give you the rain of your land in his due season, the first rain and the latter rain, that thou mayest gather in thy corn, and thy wine, and thine oil. And I will send grass in thy fields for thy cattle, that thou mayest eat and be full.' For the LORD thy God bringeth thee into a good land, a land of brooks of water, of fountains and depths that spring out of valleys and hills; a land of wheat, and barley, and vines, and fig trees, and pomegranates; a land of oil olive, and honey; a land wherein thou shalt eat bread without scarceness, thou shalt not lack any thing in it; a land whose stones are iron, and out of whose hills thou mayest dig brass. When thou hast eaten and art full, then thou shalt bless the LORD thy God for the good land which he hath given thee. Beware that thou forget not the LORD thy God, in not keeping his commandments, and his judgments, and his statutes, which I command thee this day: lest when thou hast eaten and art full, and hast built goodly houses, and dwelt therein; and when thy herds and thy flocks multiply, and thy silver and thy gold is multiplied, and all that thou hast is multiplied; then thine heart be lifted up, and thou forget the LORD thy God, which brought thee forth out of the land of Egypt, from the house of bondage; and thou say in thine heart, My power and the might of mine hand hath gotten me this wealth. But thou shalt remember the LORD thy God: for it is he that giveth thee power to get wealth, that he may establish his covenant which he sware unto thy fathers, as it is this day. And it shall be, if thou do at all forget the LORD thy God, and walk after other gods, and serve them, and worship them, I testify against you this day that ye shall surely perish.

"Observe the month Abib, and keep the passover unto the LORD thy God: for in the month of Abib the LORD thy God brought thee forth out of Egypt by night. Thou shalt therefore sacrifice the passover unto the LORD thy God, of the flock and the herd, in the place which the LORD shall choose to place his name there. Thou shalt eat no leavened bread with it; seven days shalt thou eat unleavened bread therewith, even the bread of affliction; for thou camest forth out of the land of Egypt in haste: that thou mayest remember the day when thou camest forth out of the land of Egypt all the days of thy life. Thou mayest not sacrifice the passover within any of thy gates, which the LORD thy God giveth thee: but at the place which the LORD thy God shall choose to place his name in, there thou shalt sacrifice the passover at even, at the going down of the sun, at the season that thou camest forth out of Egypt. And it shall come to pass, when your children shall say unto you 'What mean ye by this service?' that ye shall say, 'It is the sacrifice of the LORD's passover, who passed over the houses of the children of Israel in Egypt, when he smote the Egyptians, and delivered our houses.'

"Seven weeks shalt thou number unto thee: begin to number the seven weeks from such time as thou beginnest to put the sickle to the corn. And thou shalt keep the feast of weeks unto the LORD thy God with a tribute of a freewill offering of thine hand, which thou shalt give unto the LORD thy God, according as the LORD thy God hath blessed thee: and thou shalt rejoice before the LORD thy God, thou, and thy son, and thy daughter, and thy manservant, and thy maidservant, and the Levite that is within thy gates, and the stranger, and the fatherless, and the widow, that are among you, in the place which the LORD thy God hath chosen to place his name there. And thou shalt remember that thou wast a bondman in Egypt: and thou shalt observe and do these statutes.

"Thou shalt observe the feast of tabernacles seven days, after that thou hast gathered in thy corn and thy wine: and thou shalt rejoice in thy feast, thou, and thy son, and thy daughter, and thy manservant, and thy maidservant, and the Levite, the stranger, and the fatherless, and the widow, that are within thy gates. Seven days shalt thou keep a solemn feast unto the LORD thy God in the place which the LORD shall choose: because the LORD thy God shall bless thee in all thine increase, and in all the works of thine hands, therefore thou shalt surely rejoice.

"Three times in a year shall all thy males appear before the LORD thy God in the place which he shall choose; in the feast of unleavened bread, and in the feast of weeks, and in the feast of tabernacles: and they shall not appear before the LORD empty: every man shall give as he is able, according to the blessing of the LORD thy God which he hath given thee. Judges and officers shalt thou make thee in all thy gates, which the LORD thy God giveth thee, throughout thy tribes: and they shall judge the people with just judgment. Thou shalt not wrest judgment; thou shalt not respect persons, neither take a gift: for a gift doth blind the eyes of the wise, and pervert the words of the righteous. That which is altogether just shalt thou follow, that thou mayest live, and inherit the land which the LORD thy God giveth thee. And this shall be the priest's due from the people, from them that offer a sacrifice, whether it be ox or sheep; and they shall give unto the priest the shoulder, and the two cheeks, and the maw. The firstfruit also of thy corn, of thy wine, and of thine oil, and the first of the fleece of thy sheep, shalt thou give him. For the LORD thy God hath chosen him out of all thy tribes, to stand to minister in the name of the LORD, him and his sons for ever.

"Thou shalt be perfect with the LORD thy God. The LORD thy God will raise up unto thee a Prophet from the midst of thee, of thy brethren, like unto me; unto him ye shall hearken; and he shall speak unto them all that I shall command him. And it shall come to pass, if thou shalt hearken diligently unto the voice of the LORD thy God, to observe and to do all his commandments which I command thee this day, that the LORD thy God will set thee on high above all nations of the earth: and all these blessings shall come on thee, and overtake thee, if thou shalt hearken unto the voice of the LORD thy God. Blessed shalt thou be in the city, and blessed shalt thou be in the field. Blessed shall be the fruit of thy body, and the fruit of thy ground, and the fruit of thy cattle, the increase of thy kine, and the flocks of thy sheep. Blessed shall be thy basket and thy store. Blessed shalt thou be when thou comest in, and blessed shalt thou be when thou goest out. The LORD shall command the blessing upon thee in thy storehouses, and in all that thou settest thine hand unto; and he shall bless thee in the land which the LORD thy God giveth thee. And all the people of the earth shall see that thou art called by the name of the LORD. The LORD shall open unto thee his good treasure, the heaven to give the rain unto thy land in his season, and to bless all the work of thine hand: and thou shalt lend unto many nations, and thou shalt not borrow. And the LORD shall make thee the head, and not the tail; and thou shalt be above only, and thou shalt not be beneath; if that thou hearken unto the commandments of the LORD thy God, which I command thee this day, to observe and to do them: and thou shalt not go aside from any of the words which I command thee this day, to the right hand, or to the left, to go after other gods to serve them. Then thou shalt say before the LORD thy God, 'I have hearkened to the voice of the LORD my God, and have done according to all that thou hast commanded me. Look down from thy holy habitation, from heaven, and bless thy people Israel, and the land which thou hast given us, as thou swarest unto our fathers, a land that floweth with milk and honey.'

"This day the LORD thy God hath commanded thee to do these statutes and judgments: thou shalt therefore keep and do them with all thine heart, and with all thy soul. Thou hast avouched the LORD this day to be thy God, and to walk in his ways, and to keep his statutes, and his commandments, and his judgments, and to hearken unto his voice. Ye stand this day all of you before the LORD your God; your captains of your tribes, your elders, and your officers, with all the men of Israel, your little ones, your wives, and thy stranger that is in thy camp, from the hewer of thy wood unto the drawer of thy water: that thou shouldest enter into covenant with the LORD thy God, and into his oath, which the LORD thy God maketh with thee this day: that he may establish thee to day for a people unto himself, and that he may be unto thee a God, as he hath said unto thee, and as he hath sworn unto thy fathers, to Abraham, to Isaac, and to Jacob. And the LORD thy God will make thee plenteous in every work of thine hand. For this commandment which I command thee this day, it is not hidden from thee, neither is it far off. It is not in heaven, that thou shouldest say, 'Who shall go up for us to heaven, and bring it unto us, that we may hear it, and do it?' Neither is it beyond the sea, that thou shouldest say, 'Who shall go over the sea for us, and bring it unto us, that we may hear it, and do it?' But the word is very nigh unto thee, in thy mouth, and in thy heart, that thou mayest do it.

"See, I have set before thee this day life and good, and death and evil; in that I command thee this day to love the LORD thy God, to walk in his ways, and to keep his commandments and his statutes and his judgments. I call heaven and earth to record this day against you, that I have set before you life and death, blessing and cursing: therefore choose life, that both thou and thy seed may live: that thou mayest love the LORD thy God, and that thou mayest obey his voice, and that thou mayest cleave unto him: for he is thy life, and the length of thy days: that thou mayest dwell in the land which the LORD sware unto thy fathers, to Abraham, to Isaac, and to Jacob, to give them."

And the LORD said unto Moses, "Take thee Joshua the son of Nun, a man in whom is the spirit, and lay thine hand upon him."

Now the children of Reuben and the children of Gad had a very great multitude of cattle: and when they saw the land of Jazer, and the land of Gilead, that, behold, the place was a place for cattle; the children of Gad and the children of Reuben came and spake unto Moses, and to Eleazar the priest, and unto the princes of the congregation, saying, "If we have found grace in thy sight, let this land be given unto thy servants for a possession, and bring us not over Jordan."

And Moses said unto the children of Gad and to the children of Reuben, "Shall your brethren go to war, and shall ye sit here? And wherefore discourage ye the heart of the children of Israel from going over into the land which the LORD hath given them? Thus did your fathers, when I sent them from Kadesh-barnea to see the land. For when they went up unto the valley of Eshcol, and saw the land, they discouraged the heart of the children of Israel, that they should not go into the land which the LORD had given them. For if ye turn away from after him, he will yet again leave them in the wilderness; and ye shall destroy all this people."

And they came near unto him, and said, "We will build sheepfolds here for our cattle, and cities for our little ones: but we ourselves will go ready armed before the children of Israel, until we have brought them unto their place: and our little ones shall dwell in the fenced cities, because of the inhabitants of the land. We will not return unto our houses, until the children of Israel have inherited every man his inheritance."

And Moses said unto them, "If ye will do this thing, if ye will go armed before the LORD to war, and will go all of you armed over Jordan before the LORD, until he hath driven out his enemies from before him, and the land be subdued before the LORD: then afterward ye shall return, and be guiltless before the LORD, and before Israel; and this land shall be your possession before the LORD. But if ye will not do so, behold, ye have sinned against the LORD: and be sure your sin will find you out. Build you cities for your little ones, and folds for your sheep; and do that which hath proceeded out of your mouth." And the children of Gad and the children of Reuben spake unto Moses, saying, "Thy servants will do as my lord commandeth. Our little ones, our wives, our flocks, and all our cattle, shall be there in the cities of Gilead: but thy servants will pass over, every man armed for war, before the LORD to battle, as my lord saith."

And it came to pass, when Moses had made an end of writing the words of this law in a book, until they were finished, that Moses commanded the Levites, which bare the ark of the covenant of the LORD, saying, "Take this book of the law, and put it in the side of the ark of the covenant of the LORD your God, that it may be there for a witness against thee. Now therefore write ye this song for you, and teach it the children of Israel: put it in their mouths, that this song may be a witness for me against the children of Israel."

Moses therefore wrote this song the same day, and taught it the children of Israel. And Moses spake in the ears of all the congregation of Israel the words of this song, until they were ended.

> Give ear, O ye heavens, and I will speak;
> And hear, O earth, the words of my mouth.
> My doctrine shall drop as the rain,
> My speech shall distil as the dew,
> As the small rain upon the tender herb,

And as the showers upon the grass:
Because I will publish the name of the LORD:
Ascribe ye greatness unto our God.
He is the Rock, his work is perfect:
For all his ways are judgment:
A God of truth and without iniquity,
Just and right is he.
Remember the days of old,
Consider the years of many generations:
Ask thy father, and he will shew thee;
Thy elders, and they will tell thee.
For the LORD's portion is his people;
Jacob is the lot of his inheritance.
He found him in a desert land,
And in the waste howling wilderness;
He led him about, he instructed him,
He kept him as the apple of his eye.

As an eagle stirreth up her nest,
Fluttereth over her young,
Spreadeth abroad her wings, taketh them,
Beareth them on her wings:
So the LORD alone did lead him,
And there was no strange god with him.
He made him ride on the high places of the earth,
That he might eat the increase of the fields;
And he made him to suck honey out of the rock,
And oil out of the flinty rock;
But he forsook God which made him,
And lightly esteemed the Rock of his salvation.
The LORD saw it and said,
"I will hide my face from them,
I will see what their end shall be:
For they are a very froward generation,
Children in whom is no faith.
I would scatter them into corners,
I would make the remembrance of them to cease from among men:

# THE EXODUS FROM EGYPT
## AND THE GREAT EMPIRES OF ASIA

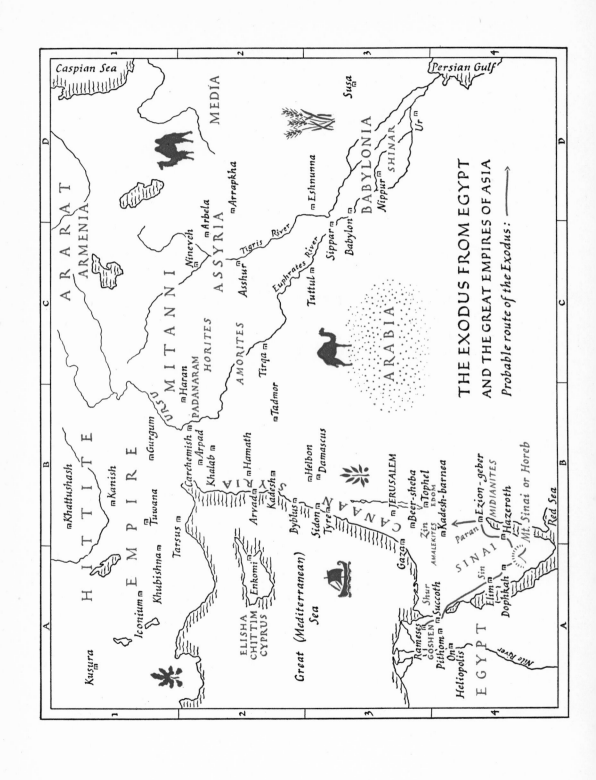

THE EXODUS FROM EGYPT
AND THE GREAT EMPIRES OF ASIA
*Probable route of the Exodus:* ⟶

# KEY TO MAP

| | | | | | |
|---|---|---|---|---|---|
| Amalekites | A-4 | Gaza | B-3 | Padanaram | B-2 |
| Amorites | C-2 | Gebal, *see* Byblus | | Paran, Wilderness of | B-4 |
| Arabia | C-3 | Goshen | A-3 | Persian Gulf | D-4 |
| Ararat | C-1 | Great Sea, *see also* Mediterranean Sea | A-2 | Pithom | A-4 |
| Arbela | C-2 | Gurgum | B-1 | Rameses | A-3 |
| Armenia | C-1 | Hamath | B-2 | Red Sea | B-4 |
| Arpad | B-2 | Haran | C-1 | Shinar | D-3 |
| Arrapkha | D-2 | Hazeroth | B-4 | Shur, Wilderness of | A-3 |
| Arvad | B-2 | Helbon | B-2 | Sidon | B-3 |
| Asshur | C-2 | Heliopolis, *see also* On | A-4 | Sin, Wilderness of | A-4 |
| Assyria | C-2 | Hittite Empire | B-1 | Sinai | A-4 |
| Babylon | D-3 | Horeb, Mount, *see also* Sinai | A-4 | Sinai, Mount, *see also* Horeb | A-4 |
| Babylonia | D-3 | Horites | C-2 | Sippar | C-3 |
| Beer-sheba | B-3 | Iconium | A-1 | Succoth | A-4 |
| Byblus | B-2 | Jerusalem | B-3 | Susa | D-3 |
| Canaan | B-3 | Kadesh | B-2 | Syria | B-2 |
| Carchemish | B-2 | Kadesh-barnea | B-4 | Tadmor | B-2 |
| Caspian Sea | D-1 | Kanish | B-1 | Tarsus | B-1 |
| Chittim, *see also* Cyprus, Elisha | A-2 | Khalab | B-2 | Tigris River | B-2 |
| Cyprus, *see also* Chittim, Elisha | A-2 | Khattushash | B-1 | Tirqa | B-1 |
| Damascus | B-3 | Khubishna | A-1 | Tophel | A-1 |
| Dophkah | A-4 | Kusura | A-1 | Tuttul | B-3 |
| Edom | B-4 | Media | D-2 | Tuwana | C-3 |
| Egypt | A-4 | Mediterranean Sea, *see also* Great Sea | A-2 | Tyre | B-1 |
| Elim | A-4 | Midianites | B-4 | Ur | D-3 |
| Elisha, *see also* Chittim, Cyprus | A-2 | Mitanni | C-1 | Ursu | B-1 |
| Enkomi | A-2 | Nile River | A-4 | Zidon, *see* Sidon | |
| Eshnunna | D-3 | Nineveh | C-2 | Zin, Wilderness of | B-3 |
| Euphrates River | C-2 | Nippur | D-3 | | |
| Ezion-geber | B-4 | On, *see also* Heliopolis | A-4 | | |

Were it not that I feared the wrath of the enemy,
Lest their adversaries should behave themselves strangely,
And lest they should say, 'Our hand is high,
And the LORD hath not done all this.'
For they are a nation void of counsel,
Neither is there any understanding in them.
O that they were wise, that they understood this,
That they would consider their latter end!"
For the LORD shall judge his people,
And repent himself for his servants,
When he seeth that their power is gone.
And he shall say, "Where are their gods,
Their rock in whom they trusted,
Which did eat the fat of their sacrifices,
And drank the wine of their drink offerings?
Let them rise up and help you,
And be your protection.
See now that I, even I, am he,
And there is no god with me:
I kill, and I make alive;
I wound, and I heal:
Neither is there any that can deliver out of my hand.
For I lift up my hand to heaven,
And say, 'I live for ever.' "

And Moses made an end of speaking all these words to all Israel: and he said unto them, "Set your hearts unto all the words which I testify among you this day, which ye shall command your children to observe to do, all the words of this law. For it is not a vain thing for you; because it is your life: and through this thing ye shall prolong your days in the land, whither ye go over Jordan to possess it."

And the LORD spake unto Moses that selfsame day, saying, "Get thee up into this mountain Abarim, unto mount Nebo, which is in the land of Moab, that is over against Jericho; and behold the land of Canaan, which I give unto the children of Israel for a possession: and die in the mount whither thou goest up, and be gathered unto thy people; as Aaron thy

[ 91 ]

*The people encouraged* brother died in mount Hor, and was gathered unto his people: because ye trespassed against me among the children of Israel at the waters of Meribah-Kadesh, in the wilderness of Zin; because ye sanctified me not in the midst of the children of Israel. Yet thou shalt see the land before thee; but thou shalt not go thither unto the land which I give the children of Israel."

And Moses went and spake these words unto all Israel. And he said unto them, "I am an hundred and twenty years old this day; I can no more go out and come in: also the Lord hath said unto me, 'Thou shalt not go over this Jordan.' The Lord thy God, he will go over before thee, and he will destroy these nations from before thee, and thou shalt possess them: and Joshua, he shall go over before thee, as the Lord hath said. Be strong and of a good courage, fear not, nor be afraid of them: for the Lord thy God, he it is that doth go with thee; he will not fail thee, nor forsake thee."

And Moses commanded them, saying, "At the end of every seven years, in the solemnity of the year of release, in the feast of tabernacles, when all Israel is come to appear before the Lord thy God in the place which he shall choose, thou shalt read this law before all Israel in their hearing. Gather the people together, men, and women, and children, and thy stranger that is within thy gates, that they may hear, and that they may learn, and fear the Lord your God, and observe to do all the words of this law: and that their children, which have not known any thing, may hear, and learn to fear the Lord your God, as long as ye live in the land whither ye go over Jordan to possess it."

And Moses called unto Joshua, and said unto him in the sight of all Israel, "Be strong and of a good courage: for thou must go with this people unto the land which the Lord hath sworn unto their fathers to give them; and thou shalt cause them to inherit it. And the Lord, he it is that doth go before thee; he will be with thee, he will not fail thee, neither forsake thee: fear not, neither be dismayed."

And the Lord said unto Moses, "Behold, thy days approach that thou must die: call Joshua, and present yourselves in the tabernacle of the congregation, that I may give him a charge."

And Moses and Joshua went, and presented themselves in the tabernacle of the congregation. And the Lord appeared in the tabernacle in a pillar of a cloud: and the pillar of the cloud stood over the door of the *Moses blesses the tribes* tabernacle.

And the LORD said unto Moses, "Behold, thou shalt sleep with thy fathers."

And Moses gave Joshua the son of Nun a charge, and said, "Be strong and of a good courage: for thou shalt bring the children of Israel into the land which I sware unto them: and I will be with thee."

And this is the blessing, wherewith Moses the man of God blessed the children of Israel before his death. And he said,

> The LORD came from Sinai,
> And rose up from Seir unto them;
> He shined forth from mount Paran,
> And he came with ten thousands of saints:
> From his right hand went a fiery law for them.
> Yea, he loved the people;
> All his saints are in thy hand;
> And they sat down at thy feet;
> Every one shall receive of thy words.
> Moses commanded us a law,
> Even the inheritance of the congregation of Jacob.
> And he was king in Jeshurun,
> When the heads of the people
> And the tribes of Israel were gathered together.
>
> "Let Reuben live, and not die;
> And let not his men be few."

And this is the blessing of Judah: and he said,

> "Hear, LORD, the voice of Judah,
> And bring him unto his people:
> Let his hands be sufficient for him;
> And be thou an help to him from his enemies."

And of Levi he said,

> "Bless, LORD, his substance,

And accept the work of his hands:
Smite through the loins of them that rise against him,
And of them that hate him, that they rise not again."

Of Benjamin he said,

"The beloved of the LORD shall dwell in safety by him;
And the LORD shall cover him all the day long,
And he shall dwell between his shoulders."

And of Joseph he said,

"Blessed of the LORD be his land,
For the precious things of heaven, for the dew,
And for the deep that coucheth beneath,
And for the precious fruits brought forth by the sun,
And for the precious things put forth by the moon,
And for the chief things of the ancient mountains,
And for the precious things of the lasting hills,
And for the precious things of the earth and fulness thereof,
And for the good will of him that dwelt in the bush:
Let the blessing come upon the head of Joseph."

And of Zebulun he said,

"Rejoice, Zebulun, in thy going out;
And, Issachar, in thy tents.
They shall call the people unto the mountain;
There they shall offer sacrifices of righteousness:
For they shall suck of the abundance of the seas,
And of treasures hid in the sand."

And of Gad he said,

"Blessed be he that enlargeth Gad:
He dwelleth as a lion,
And teareth the arm with the crown of the head.
And he provided the first part for himself,
Because there, in a portion of the lawgiver, was he seated;
And he came with the heads of the people,

[ 94 ]

He executed the justice of the LORD,
And his judgments with Israel."

And of Dan, he said,

"Dan is a lion's whelp:
He shall leap from Bashan."

And of Naphtali he said,

"O Naphtali, satisfied with favour,
And full with the blessing of the LORD,
Possess thou the west and the south."

And of Asher he said,

"Let Asher be blessed with children;
And as thy days, so shall thy strength be."

There is none like unto the God of Jeshurun,
Who rideth upon the heaven in thy help,
And in his excellency on the sky.
The eternal God is thy refuge,
And underneath are the everlasting arms:
Israel then shall dwell in safety alone:
The fountain of Jacob shall be
Upon a land of corn and wine;
Also his heavens shall drop down dew.

And Moses went up from the plains of Moab unto the mountain of
Nebo, to the top of Pisgah, that is over against Jericho. And the LORD
shewed him all the land of Gilead, unto Dan, and all Naphtali, and the
land of Ephraim, and Manasseh, and all the land of Judah, unto the utmost sea, and the south, and the plain of the valley of Jericho, the city
of palm trees, unto Zoar. And the LORD said unto him, "This is the land
which I sware unto Abraham, unto Isaac, and unto Jacob, saying, 'I will
give it unto thy seed: I have caused thee to see it with thine eyes, but
thou shalt not go over thither.'" So Moses the servant of the LORD died
there in the land of Moab, according to the word of the LORD. And he

[ 95 ]

*Moses dies*   buried him in a valley in the land of Moab, over against Beth-peor: but no man knoweth of his sepulchre unto this day. And Moses was an hundred and twenty years old when he died: his eye was not dim, nor his natural force abated. And the children of Israel wept for Moses in the plains of Moab thirty days: so the days of weeping and mourning for Moses were ended. And there arose not a prophet since in Israel like unto Moses, whom the LORD knew face to face.

And Joshua the son of Nun was full of the spirit of wisdom; for Moses had laid his hands upon him: and the children of Israel hearkened unto him, and did as the LORD commanded Moses. Now after the death of Moses the servant of the LORD it came to pass, that the LORD spake unto Joshua the son of Nun, Moses' minister, saying, "Moses my servant is dead; now therefore arise, go over this Jordan, thou, and all this people, unto the land which I do give to them, even to the children of Israel. Every place that the sole of your foot shall tread upon, that have I given unto you, as I said unto Moses. From the wilderness and this Lebanon even unto the great river, the river Euphrates, all the land of the Hittites, and unto the great sea toward the going down of the sun, shall be your coast. There shall not any man be able to stand before thee all the days of thy life: as I was with Moses, so I will be with thee: I will not fail thee, nor forsake thee. Be strong and of a good courage: for unto this people shalt thou divide for an inheritance the land, which I sware unto their fathers to give them. Only be thou strong and very courageous, that thou mayest observe to do according to all the law, which Moses my servant commanded thee: turn not from it to the right hand or to the left, that thou mayest prosper whithersoever thou goest. This book of the law shall not depart out of thy mouth; but thou shalt meditate therein day and night, that thou mayest observe to do according to all that is written therein: for then thou shalt make thy way prosperous, and then thou shalt have good success. Have not I commanded thee? Be strong and of a good courage; be not afraid, neither be thou dismayed: for the LORD thy God is with thee whithersoever thou goest."

Then Joshua commanded the officers of the people, saying, "Pass through the host, and command the people, saying, 'Prepare you victuals; for within three days ye shall pass over this Jordan, to go in to possess the land, which the LORD your God giveth you to possess it.' "

And they answered Joshua, saying, "All that thou commandest us we will do, and whithersoever thou sendest us, we will go. According as we hearkened unto Moses in all things, so will we hearken unto thee: only the LORD thy God be with thee, as he was with Moses."

And Joshua the son of Nun sent out of Shittim two men to spy secretly, saying, "Go view the land, even Jericho."

And they went, and came into an harlot's house, named Rahab, and lodged there. And it was told the king of Jericho, saying, "Behold, there came men in hither to night of the children of Israel to search out the country."

And the king of Jericho sent unto Rahab, saying, "Bring forth the men that are come to thee, which are entered into thine house: for they be come to search out all the country."

And the woman took the two men, and hid them, and said thus, "There came men unto me, but I wist not whence they were: and it came to pass about the time of shutting of the gate, when it was dark, that the men went out: whither the men went, I wot not: pursue after them quickly; for ye shall overtake them."

But she had brought them up to the roof of the house, and hid them with the stalks of flax, which she had laid in order upon the roof. And the men pursued after them the way to Jordan unto the fords: and as soon as they which pursued after them were gone out, they shut the gate. And before they were laid down, she came up unto them upon the roof; and she said unto the men, "I know that the LORD hath given you the land, and that your terror is fallen upon us, and that all the inhabitants of the land faint because of you. For we have heard how the LORD dried up the water of the Red sea for you, when ye came out of Egypt. And as soon as we had heard these things, our hearts did melt, neither did there remain any more courage in any man, because of you: for the LORD your God, he is God in heaven above, and in earth beneath. Now therefore, I pray you, swear unto me by the LORD, since I have shewed you kindness, that ye will also shew kindness unto my father's house, and give me a true token: and that ye will save alive my father, and my mother, and my brethren, and my sisters, and all that they have, and deliver our lives from death."

And the men answered her, "Our life for your's, if ye utter not this our

[ 97 ]

*At the Jordan* business. And it shall be, when the LORD hath given us the land, that we will deal kindly and truly with thee."

Then she let them down by a cord through the window: for her house was upon the town wall, and she dwelt upon the wall. And she said unto them, "Get you to the mountain, lest the pursuers meet you; and hide yourselves there three days, until the pursuers be returned: and afterward may ye go your way."

And the men said unto her, "We will be blameless of this thine oath which thou hast made us swear. Behold, when we come into the land, thou shalt bind this line of scarlet thread in the window which thou didst let us down by: and thou shalt bring thy father, and thy mother, and thy brethren, and all thy father's household, home unto thee. And if thou utter this our business, then we will be quit of thine oath which thou hast made us to swear."

And she said, "According unto your words, so be it."

And she sent them away, and they departed: and she bound the scarlet line in the window. And they went, and came unto the mountain, and abode there three days, until the pursuers were returned: and the pursuers sought them throughout all the way, but found them not. So the two men returned, and descended from the mountain, and passed over, and came to Joshua the son of Nun, and told him all things that befell them: and they said unto Joshua, "Truly the LORD hath delivered into our hands all the land; for even all the inhabitants of the country do faint because of us."

And Joshua rose early in the morning, and they came to Jordan, he and all the children of Israel, and lodged there before they passed over. And it came to pass after three days, that the officers went through the host; and they commanded the people, saying, "When ye see the ark of the covenant of the LORD your God, and the priests the Levites bearing it, then ye shall remove from your place, and go after it. Yet there shall be a space between you and it, about two thousand cubits by measure: come not near unto it, that ye may know the way by which ye must go: for ye have not passed this way heretofore."

And Joshua said unto the people, "Sanctify yourselves: for to morrow the LORD will do wonders among you."

And Joshua spake unto the priests, saying, "Take up the ark of the covenant, and pass over before the people."

*The Israelites cross the Jordan*

And they took up the ark of the covenant, and went before the people.

And the LORD said unto Joshua, "This day will I begin to magnify thee in the sight of all Israel, that they may know that, as I was with Moses, so I will be with thee. And thou shalt command the priests that bear the ark of the covenant, saying, 'When ye are come to the brink of the water of Jordan, ye shall stand still in Jordan.' "

And it came to pass, when the people removed from their tents, to pass over Jordan, and the priests bearing the ark of the covenant before the people; and as they that bare the ark were come unto Jordan, and the feet of the priests that bare the ark were dipped in the brim of the water, (for Jordan overfloweth all his banks all the time of harvest,) that the waters which came down from above stood and rose up upon an heap; and those that came down toward the sea of the plain, even the salt sea, failed, and were cut off: and the people passed over right against Jericho. And the priests that bare the ark of the covenant of the LORD stood firm on dry ground in the midst of Jordan, and all the Israelites passed over on dry ground, until all the people were passed clean over Jordan. And it came to pass, when all the people were clean passed over Jordan, that the LORD spake unto Joshua, saying, "Take you twelve men out of the people, out of every tribe a man, and command ye them, saying, 'Take you hence out of the midst of Jordan, out of the place where the priests' feet stood firm, twelve stones, and ye shall carry them over with you, and leave them in the lodging place, where ye shall lodge this night.' "

For the priests which bare the ark stood in the midst of Jordan, until every thing was finished that the LORD commanded Joshua to speak unto the people, according to all that Moses commanded Joshua: and the people hasted and passed over. And it came to pass, when all the people were clean passed over, that the ark of the LORD passed over, and the priests, in the presence of the people. And it came to pass, when the priests that bare the ark of the LORD were come up out of the midst of Jordan, and the soles of the priests' feet were lifted up unto the dry land, that the waters of Jordan returned unto their place, and flowed over all

*The camp at Gilgal* his banks, as they did before. And the people came up out of Jordan on the tenth day of the first month, and encamped in Gilgal, in the east border of Jericho. And those twelve stones, which they took out of Jordan, did Joshua pitch in Gilgal. And he spake unto the children of Israel, saying, "When your children shall ask their fathers in time to come, saying, 'What mean these stones?' Then ye shall let your children know, saying, 'Israel came over this Jordan on dry land.' For the LORD your God dried up the waters of Jordan from before you, until ye were passed over, as the LORD your God did to the Red sea, which he dried up from before us, until we were gone over: that all the people of the earth might know the hand of the LORD, that it is mighty: that ye might fear the LORD your God for ever."

And it came to pass, when all the kings of the Amorites, which were on the side of Jordan westward, and all the kings of the Canaanites, which were by the sea, heard that the LORD had dried up the waters of Jordan from before the children of Israel, until we were passed over, that their heart melted, neither was there spirit in them any more, because of the children of Israel. And the children of Israel encamped in Gilgal, and kept the passover on the fourteenth day of the month at even in the plains of Jericho. And they did eat of the old corn of the land on the morrow after the passover, unleavened cakes, and parched corn in the selfsame day. And the manna ceased on the morrow after they had eaten of the old corn of the land; neither had the children of Israel manna any more; but they did eat of the fruit of the land of Canaan that year.

And it came to pass, when Joshua was by Jericho, that he lifted up his eyes and looked, and, behold, there stood a man over against him with his sword drawn in his hand: and Joshua went unto him, and said unto him, "Art thou for us, or for our adversaries?"

And he said, "Nay; but as captain of the host of the LORD am I now come."

And Joshua fell on his face to the earth, and did worship, and said unto him, "What saith my lord unto his servant?"

And the captain of the LORD's host said unto Joshua, "Loose thy shoe from off thy foot; for the place whereon thou standest is holy." And Joshua did so. Now Jericho was straitly shut up because of the children of Israel: none went out, and none came in. And the LORD said unto Joshua,

"See, I have given into thine hand Jericho, and the king thereof, and the *Siege of Jericho* mighty men of valour. And ye shall compass the city, all ye men of war, and go round about the city once. Thus shalt thou do six days. And seven priests shall bear before the ark seven trumpets of rams' horns: and the seventh day ye shall compass the city seven times, and the priests shall blow with the trumpets. And it shall come to pass, that when they make a long blast with the ram's horn, and when ye hear the sound of the trumpet, all the people shall shout with a great shout; and the wall of the city shall fall down flat, and the people shall ascend up every man straight before him."

And Joshua the son of Nun called the priests, and said unto them, "Take up the ark of the covenant, and let seven priests bear seven trumpets of rams' horns before the ark of the Lord." And he said unto the people, "Pass on, and compass the city, and let him that is armed pass on before the ark of the Lord."

And it came to pass, when Joshua had spoken unto the people, that the seven priests bearing the seven trumpets of rams' horns passed on before the Lord, and blew with the trumpets: and the ark of the covenant of the Lord followed them. And the armed men went before the priests that blew with the trumpets, and the rereward came after the ark, the priests going on, and blowing with the trumpets. And Joshua had commanded the people, saying, "Ye shall not shout, nor make any noise with your voice, neither shall any word proceed out of your mouth, until the day I bid you shout; then shall ye shout."

So the ark of the Lord compassed the city, going about it once: and they came into the camp, and lodged in the camp. And Joshua rose early in the morning, and the priests took up the ark of the Lord. And seven priests bearing seven trumpets of rams' horns before the ark of the Lord went on continually, and blew with the trumpets: and the armed men went before them; but the rereward came after the ark of the Lord, the priests going on, and blowing with the trumpets. And the second day they compassed the city once, and returned into the camp. So they did six days. And it came to pass on the seventh day, that they rose early about the dawning of the day, and compassed the city after the same manner seven times: only on that day they compassed the city seven times. And it came to pass at the seventh time, when the priests blew with the trumpets, Joshua said unto the people, "Shout; for the LORD hath given you the city."

So the people shouted when the priests blew with the trumpets: and it came to pass, when the people heard the sound of the trumpet, and the people shouted with a great shout, that the wall fell down flat, so that the people went up into the city, every man straight before him, and they took the city. But Joshua had said unto the two men that had spied out the country, "Go into the harlot's house, and bring out thence the woman, and all that she hath, as ye sware unto her."

And the young men that were spies went in, and brought out Rahab, and her father, and her mother, and her brethren, and all that she had; and they brought out all her kindred, and left them without the camp of Israel. So the LORD was with Joshua; and his fame was noised throughout all the country.

Now it came to pass when Adoni-zedec king of Jerusalem had heard how Joshua had taken Ai, and had utterly destroyed it; as he had done to Jericho and her king, so he had done to Ai and her king; and how the inhabitants of Gibeon had made peace with Israel, and were among them; that they feared greatly, because Gibeon was a great city, as one of the royal cities, and because it was greater than Ai, and all the men thereof were mighty. Wherefore Adoni-zedec king of Jerusalem sent unto Hoham king of Hebron, and unto Piram king of Jarmuth, and unto Japhia king of Lachish, and unto Debir king of Eglon, saying, "Come up unto me, and help me, that we may smite Gibeon: for it hath made peace with Joshua and with the children of Israel."

Therefore the five kings of the Amorites, the king of Jerusalem, the king of Hebron, the king of Jarmuth, the king of Lachish, the king of Eglon, gathered themselves together, and went up, they and all their hosts, and encamped before Gibeon, and made war against it. And the men of Gibeon sent unto Joshua to the camp to Gilgal, saying, "Slack not thy hand from thy servants; come up to us quickly, and save us, and help us: for all the kings of the Amorites that dwell in the mountains are gathered together against us."

So Joshua ascended from Gilgal, he, and all the people of war with him, and all the mighty men of valour. And the LORD said unto Joshua,

"Fear them not: for I have delivered them into thine hand; there shall not a man of them stand before thee."

Joshua therefore came unto them suddenly, and went up from Gilgal all night. And the LORD discomfited them before Israel, and slew them with a great slaughter at Gibeon, and chased them along the way that goeth up to Beth-horon, and smote them to Azekah, and unto Makkedah. And it came to pass, as they fled from before Israel, and were in the going down to Beth-horon, that the LORD cast down great stones from heaven upon them unto Azekah, and they died: they were more which died with hailstones than they whom the children of Israel slew with the sword. Then spake Joshua to the LORD in the day when the LORD delivered up the Amorites before the children of Israel, and he said in the sight of Israel,

> Sun, stand thou still upon Gibeon;
> And thou, Moon, in the valley of Ajalon.

And there was no day like that before it or after it, that the LORD hearkened unto the voice of a man: for the LORD fought for Israel. And Joshua returned, and all Israel with him, unto the camp to Gilgal. But these five kings fled, and hid themselves in a cave at Makkedah.

Joshua waxed old and stricken in age. And he gathered all the tribes of Israel to Shechem, and called for the elders of Israel, and for their heads, and for their judges, and for their officers; and they presented themselves before God. And Joshua said unto all the people, "Thus saith the LORD God of Israel, 'Your fathers dwelt on the other side of the flood in old time, even Terah, the father of Abraham, and the father of Nachor: and they served other gods. And I took your father Abraham from the other side of the flood, and led him throughout all the land of Canaan, and multiplied his seed, and gave him Isaac. And I gave unto Isaac Jacob and Esau. Jacob and his children went down into Egypt. I sent Moses also and Aaron. And I brought your fathers out of Egypt: and ye came unto the sea; and the Egyptians pursued after your fathers with chariots and horsemen unto the Red sea. And when they cried unto the LORD, he put darkness between you and the Egyptians, and brought the sea upon them, and covered them; and your eyes have seen what I have

*Joshua's dying
exhortation*

done in Egypt: and ye dwelt in the wilderness a long season. And I brought you into the land of the Amorites, which dwelt on the other side Jordan; and they fought with you: and I gave them into your hand. And ye went over Jordan, and came unto Jericho: and the men of Jericho fought against you; and I delivered them into your hand. And I have given you a land for which ye did not labour, and cities which ye built not, and ye dwell in them; of the vineyards and oliveyards which ye planted not do ye eat.' Now therefore fear the LORD, and serve him in sincerity and in truth: and put away the gods which your fathers served on the other side of the flood, and in Egypt; and serve ye the LORD.

"And if it seem evil unto you to serve the LORD, choose you this day whom ye will serve; whether the gods which your fathers served that were on the other side of the flood, or the gods of the Amorites, in whose land ye dwell: but as for me and my house, we will serve the LORD."

And the people answered and said, "God forbid that we should forsake the LORD, to serve other gods; for the LORD our God, he it is that brought us up and our fathers out of the land of Egypt, from the house of bondage, and which did those great signs in our sight, and preserved us in all the way wherein we went, and among all the people through whom we passed: therefore will we also serve the LORD; for he is our God."

And Joshua said unto the people, "Ye are witnesses against yourselves that ye have chosen you the LORD, to serve him."

And they said, "We are witnesses."

"Now therefore put away," said he, "the strange gods which are among you, and incline your heart unto the LORD God of Israel."

And the people said unto Joshua, "The LORD our God will we serve, and his voice will we obey."

So Joshua made a covenant with the people that day, and set them a statute and an ordinance in Shechem. And Joshua wrote these words in the book of the law of God, and took a great stone, and set it up there under an oak, that was by the sanctuary of the LORD. And Joshua said unto all the people, "Behold, this stone shall be a witness unto us; for it hath heard all the words of the LORD which he spake unto us: it shall be therefore a witness unto you, lest ye deny your God." So Joshua let the people depart, every man unto his inheritance. And it came to pass after these things, that Joshua the son of Nun, the servant of the LORD, died, *His death and burial* being an hundred and ten years old. And they buried him in the border of his inheritance in Timnath-serah, which is in mount Ephraim, on the north side of the hill of Gaash. And Israel served the LORD all the days of Joshua, and all the days of the elders that overlived Joshua, and which had known all the works of the LORD, that he had done for Israel. And the bones of Joseph, which the children of Israel brought up out of Egypt, buried they in Shechem, in a parcel of ground which Jacob bought of the sons of Hamor the father of Shechem for an hundred pieces of silver: and it became the inheritance of the children of Joseph.

Also all that generation were gathered unto their fathers: and there arose another generation after them, which knew not the LORD, nor yet the works which he had done for Israel. And the children of Israel did evil in the sight of the LORD, and served Baalim: and they forsook the LORD God of their fathers, which brought them out of the land of Egypt, and followed other gods, of the gods of the people that were round about them, and bowed themselves unto them, and provoked the LORD to anger. Nevertheless the LORD raised up judges, which delivered them out of the hand of those that spoiled them. And yet they would not hearken unto their judges: they turned quickly out of the way which their fathers walked in, obeying the commandments of the LORD; but they did not so.

And the children of Israel again did evil in the sight of the LORD. And the LORD sold them into the hand of Jabin king of Canaan, that reigned in Hazor; the captain of whose host was Sisera, which dwelt in Harosheth of the Gentiles. And the children of Israel cried unto the LORD: for he had nine hundred chariots of iron; and twenty years he mightily oppressed the children of Israel. And Deborah, a prophetess, the wife of Lapidoth, she judged Israel at that time. And she dwelt under the palm tree of Deborah between Ramah and Beth-el in mount Ephraim: and the children of Israel came up to her for judgment. And she sent and called Barak the son of Abinoam out of Kedesh-naphtali, and said unto him, "Hath not the LORD God of Israel commanded, saying, 'Go and draw toward mount Tabor, and take with thee ten thousand men of the children of Naphtali and of the children of Zebulun? And I will draw unto thee to the river Kishon Sisera, the captain of Jabin's army, with his chariots and his multitude; and I will deliver him into thine hand.' "

And Barak said unto her, "If thou wilt go with me, then I will go: but if thou wilt not go with me, then I will not go."

And she said, "I will surely go with thee: notwithstanding the journey that thou takest shall not be for thine honour; for the LORD shall sell Sisera into the hand of a woman."

And Deborah arose, and went with Barak to Kedesh. And Barak called Zebulun and Naphtali to Kedesh; and he went up with ten thousand men at his feet: and Deborah went up with him.

Now Heber the Kenite, which was of the children of Hobab the father in law of Moses, had severed himself from the Kenites, and pitched his tent unto the plain of Zaanaim, which is by Kedesh. And they shewed Sisera that Barak the son of Abinoam was gone up to mount Tabor. And Sisera gathered together all his chariots, even nine hundred chariots of iron, and all the people that were with him, from Harosheth of the Gentiles unto the river of Kishon.

And Deborah said unto Barak, "Up; for this is the day in which the LORD hath delivered Sisera into thine hand: is not the LORD gone out before thee?"

So Barak went down from mount Tabor, and ten thousand men after him. And the LORD discomfited Sisera, and all his chariots, and all his host, with the edge of the sword before Barak; so that Sisera lighted down off his chariot, and fled away on his feet. But Barak pursued after the chariots, and after the host, unto Harosheth of the Gentiles: and all the host of Sisera fell upon the edge of the sword; and there was not a man left. Howbeit Sisera fled away on his feet to the tent of Jael the wife of Heber the Kenite: for there was peace between Jabin the king of Hazor and the house of Heber the Kenite. And Jael went out to meet Sisera, and said unto him, "Turn in, my lord, turn in to me; fear not."

And when he had turned in unto her into the tent, she covered him with a mantle. And he said unto her, "Give me, I pray thee, a little water to drink; for I am thirsty."

And she opened a bottle of milk, and gave him drink, and covered him.

Again he said unto her, "Stand in the door of the tent, and it shall be, when any man doth come and inquire of thee, and say, 'Is there any man here?' that thou shalt say, 'No.'"

Then Jael Heber's wife took an hammer, and went softly unto him, *Song of Deborah and* and smote a nail into his temples; for he was fast asleep and weary. So *Barak* he died. And, behold, as Barak pursued Sisera, Jael came out to meet him, and said unto him, "Come, and I will shew thee the man whom thou seekest." And when he came into her tent, behold, Sisera lay dead, and the nail was in his temples.

So God subdued on that day Jabin the king of Canaan before the children of Israel. And the hand of the children of Israel prospered, and prevailed against Jabin the king of Canaan.

Then sang Deborah and Barak on that day, saying,

> Praise ye the LORD for the avenging of Israel,
> When the people willingly offered themselves.
> Hear, O ye kings; give ear, O ye princes;
> I, even I, will sing unto the LORD;
> I will sing praise to the LORD God of Israel.
> LORD, when thou wentest out of Seir,
> When thou marchedst out of the field of Edom,
> The earth trembled, and the heavens dropped,
> The clouds also dropped water.
> The mountains melted from before the LORD,
> Even that Sinai from before the LORD God of Israel.
> In the days of Shamgar the son of Anath,
> In the days of Jael, the highways were unoccupied,
> And the travellers walked through byways.
> The inhabitants of the villages ceased, they ceased in Israel,
> Until that I Deborah arose,
> That I arose a mother in Israel.
> Was there a shield or spear seen
> Among forty thousand in Israel?
> My heart is toward the governors of Israel,
> That offered themselves willingly among the people.
> Bless ye the LORD.
> Speak, ye that ride on white asses,
> Ye that sit in judgment, and walk by the way.
> They that are delivered from the noise of archers

In the places of drawing water,
There shall they rehearse the righteous acts of the LORD,
Even the righteous acts toward the inhabitants of his villages in
    Israel:
Then shall the people of the LORD go down to the gates.
Awake, awake, Deborah:
Awake, awake, utter a song:
Arise, Barak, and lead thy captivity captive, thou son of Abinoam.
Then he made him that remaineth have dominion over the nobles
    among the people:
The LORD made me have dominion over the mighty.
And the princes of Issachar were with Deborah;
Even Issachar, and also Barak:
He was sent on foot into the valley.
For the divisions of Reuben
There were great thoughts of heart.
Why abodest thou among the sheepfolds,
To hear the bleatings of the flocks?
For the divisions of Reuben
There were great searchings of heart.
Gilead abode beyond Jordan:
And why did Dan remain in ships?
Asher continued on the seashore,
And abode in his breaches.
Zebulun and Naphtali were a people that jeoparded their lives unto
    the death
In the high places of the field.
The kings came and fought,
Then fought the kings of Canaan
In Taanach by the waters of Megiddo;
They took no gain of money.
They fought from heaven;
The stars in their courses fought against Sisera.
The river of Kishon swept them away,
That ancient river, the river Kishon.
O my soul, thou hast trodden down strength.

Then were the horsehoofs broken
By the means of the pransings, the pransings of their mighty
    ones.
"Curse ye Meroz," said the angel of the LORD,
"Curse ye bitterly the inhabitants thereof;
Because they came not to the help of the LORD,
To the help of the LORD against the mighty."
Blessed above women shall Jael
The wife of Heber the Kenite be,
Blessed shall she be above women in the tent.
He asked water, and she gave him milk;
She brought forth butter in a lordly dish.
She put her hand to the nail,
And her right hand to the workmen's hammer;
And with the hammer she smote Sisera,
At her feet he bowed, he fell, he lay down:
At her feet he bowed, he fell:
Where he bowed, there he fell down dead.
The mother of Sisera looked out at a window,
And cried through the lattice,
"Why is his chariot so long in coming?
Why tarry the wheels of his chariots?"
Her wise ladies answered her,
Yea, she returned answer to herself,
"Have they not sped? have they not divided the prey;
To Sisera a prey of divers colours,
A prey of divers colours of needlework,
Of divers colours of needlework on both sides,
Meet for the necks of them that take the spoil?"
So let all thine enemies perish, O LORD:
But let them that love him be as the sun when he goeth forth in his
    might.

And the land had rest forty years.
And the children of Israel did evil in the sight of the LORD: and the
LORD delivered them into the hand of Midian seven years. And the hand

of Midian prevailed against Israel: and because of the Midianites the children of Israel made them the dens which are in the mountains, and caves, and strong holds. And so it was, when Israel had sown, that the Midianites came up, and the Amalekites, and the children of the east, even they came up against them; and they encamped against them, and destroyed the increase of the earth, till thou come unto Gaza, and left no sustenance for Israel, neither sheep, nor ox, nor ass. For they came up with their cattle and their tents, and they came as grasshoppers for multitude; for both they and their camels were without number: and they entered into the land to destroy it. And Israel was greatly impoverished because of the Midianites; and the children of Israel cried unto the LORD. And it came to pass, when the children of Israel cried unto the LORD because of the Midianites, that the LORD sent a prophet unto the children of Israel, which said unto them, "Thus saith the LORD God of Israel, 'I brought you up from Egypt, and brought you forth out of the house of bondage; and I delivered you out of the hand of the Egyptians, and out of the hand of all that oppressed you, and drave them out from before you, and gave you their land; and I said unto you, "I am the LORD your God; fear not the gods of the Amorites, in whose land ye dwell:" but ye have not obeyed my voice.' "

And there came an angel of the LORD, and sat under an oak which was in Ophrah, that pertained unto Joash: and his son Gideon threshed wheat by the winepress, to hide it from the Midianites. And the angel of the LORD appeared unto him, and said unto him, "The LORD is with thee, thou mighty man of valour."

And Gideon said unto him, "O my Lord, if the LORD be with us, why then is all this befallen us? and where be all his miracles which our fathers told us of, saying, 'Did not the LORD bring us up from Egypt?' but now the LORD hath forsaken us, and delivered us into the hands of the Midianites."

And the LORD looked upon him, and said, "Go in this thy might, and thou shalt save Israel from the hand of the Midianites: have not I sent thee?"

And he said unto him, "O my Lord, wherewith shall I save Israel? behold, my family is poor in Manasseh, and I am the least in my father's house."

And the LORD said unto him, "Surely I will be with thee, and thou *Gideon and the angel* shalt smite the Midianites as one man."

And he said unto him, "If now I have found grace in thy sight, then shew me a sign that thou talkest with me. Depart not hence, I pray thee, until I come unto thee, and bring forth my present, and set it before thee."

And he said, "I will tarry until thou come again."

And Gideon went in, and made ready a kid, and unleavened cakes of an ephah of flour: the flesh he put in a basket, and he put the broth in a pot, and brought it out unto him under the oak, and presented it. And the angel of God said unto him, "Take the flesh and the unleavened cakes, and lay them upon this rock, and pour out the broth." And he did so.

Then the angel of the LORD put forth the end of the staff that was in his hand, and touched the flesh and the unleavened cakes; and there rose up fire out of the rock, and consumed the flesh and the unleavened cakes. Then the angel of the LORD departed out of his sight. And when Gideon perceived that he was an angel of the LORD, Gideon said, "Alas, O Lord GOD! for because I have seen an angel of the LORD face to face."

And the LORD said unto him, "Peace be unto thee; fear not: thou shalt not die."

Then all the Midianites and the Amalekites and the children of the east were gathered together, and went over, and pitched in the valley of Jezreel. But the Spirit of the LORD came upon Gideon, and he blew a trumpet; and Abi-ezer was gathered after him. And he sent messengers throughout all Manasseh; who also was gathered after him: and he sent messengers unto Asher, and unto Zebulun, and unto Naphtali; and they came up to meet them. And Gideon said unto God, "If thou wilt save Israel by mine hand, as thou hast said, behold, I will put a fleece of wool in the floor; and if the dew be on the fleece only, and it be dry upon all the earth beside, then shall I know that thou wilt save Israel by mine hand, as thou hast said." And it was so: for he rose up early on the morrow, and thrust the fleece together, and wringed the dew out of the fleece, a bowl full of water.

And Gideon said unto God, "Let not thine anger be hot against me, and I will speak but this once: let me prove, I pray thee, but this once

[ 111 ]

*Gideon's three hundred* with the fleece; let it now be dry only upon the fleece, and upon all the ground let there be dew."

And God did so that night: for it was dry upon the fleece only, and there was dew on all the ground. And the LORD said unto Gideon, "The people that are with thee are too many for me to give the Midianites into their hands, lest Israel vaunt themselves against me, saying, 'Mine own hand hath saved me.' Now therefore go to, proclaim in the ears of the people, saying, 'Whosoever is fearful and afraid, let him return and depart early from mount Gilead.' "

And there returned of the people twenty and two thousand; and there remained ten thousand. So the people took victuals in their hand, and their trumpets: and he sent all the rest of Israel every man unto his tent, and retained three hundred men: and the host of Midian was beneath him in the valley. And the Midianites and the Amalekites and all the children of the east lay along in the valley like grasshoppers for multitude; and their camels were without number, as the sand by the sea side for multitude.

And when Gideon was come, behold, there was a man that told a dream unto his fellow, and said, "Behold, I dreamed a dream, and, lo, a cake of barley bread tumbled into the host of Midian, and came unto a tent, and smote it that it fell, and overturned it, that the tent lay along."

And his fellow answered and said, "This is nothing else save the sword of Gideon the son of Joash, a man of Israel: for into his hand hath God delivered Midian, and all the host."

And it was so, when Gideon heard the telling of the dream, and the interpretation thereof, that he worshipped, and returned into the host of Israel, and said, "Arise; for the LORD hath delivered into your hand the host of Midian."

And he divided the three hundred men into three companies, and he put a trumpet in every man's hand, with empty pitchers, and lamps within the pitchers. And he said unto them, "Look on me, and do likewise: and, behold, when I come to the outside of the camp, it shall be that, as I do, so shall ye do. When I blow with a trumpet, I and all that are with me, then blow ye the trumpets also on every side of all the camp, and say, 'The sword of the LORD, and of Gideon.' "

So Gideon, and the hundred men that were with him, came unto the *An angel visits Manoah* outside of the camp in the beginning of the middle watch; and they had but newly set the watch: and they blew the trumpets, and brake the pitchers that were in their hands. And the three companies blew the trumpets, and brake the pitchers, and held the lamps in their left hands, and the trumpets in their right hands to blow withal: and they cried, "The sword of the LORD, and of Gideon." And they stood every man in his place round about the camp: and all the host ran, and cried, and fled. And Gideon the son of Joash returned from battle before the sun was up. Then the men of Israel said unto Gideon, "Rule thou over us, both thou, and thy son, and thy son's son also: for thou hast delivered us from the hand of Midian."

And Gideon said unto them, "I will not rule over you, neither shall my son rule over you: the LORD shall rule over you."

And the children of Israel did evil again in the sight of the LORD; and the LORD delivered them into the hand of the Philistines forty years. And there was a certain man of Zorah whose name was Manoah; and his wife was barren. And the angel of the LORD appeared unto the woman, and said unto her, "Lo, thou shalt conceive, and bear a son; and no razor shall come on his head: and he shall begin to deliver Israel out of the hand of the Philistines."

Then the woman came and told her husband, saying, "A man of God came unto me, and his countenance was like the countenance of an angel of God, very terrible: but I asked him not whence he was, neither told he me his name: but he said unto me, 'Behold, thou shalt conceive, and bear a son; and now drink no wine nor strong drink, neither eat any unclean thing.' "

Then Manoah intreated the LORD, and said, "O my Lord, let the man of God which thou didst send come again unto us, and teach us what we shall do unto the child that shall be born. And God hearkened to the voice of Manoah; and the angel of God came again unto the woman as she sat in the field: but Manoah her husband was not with her. And the woman made haste, and ran, and shewed her husband, and said unto him, "Behold, the man hath appeared unto me, that came unto me the other day."

*Birth of Samson* And Manoah arose, and went after his wife, and came to the man, and said unto him, "Art thou the man that spakest unto the woman?"

And he said, "I am."

And Manoah said, "Now let thy words come to pass. How shall we order the child, and how shall we do unto him?"

And the angel of the LORD said unto Manoah, "Of all that I said unto the woman let her beware." And Manoah said unto the angel of the LORD, "I pray thee, let us detain thee, until we shall have made ready a kid for thee."

And the angel of the LORD said unto Manoah, "Though thou detain me, I will not eat of thy bread: and if thou wilt offer a burnt offering, thou must offer it unto the LORD." For Manoah knew not that he was an angel of the LORD. And Manoah said unto the angel of the LORD, "What is thy name, that when thy sayings come to pass we may do thee honour?"

And the angel of the LORD said unto him, "Why askest thou thus after my name, seeing it is secret?"

So Manoah took a kid with a meat offering, and offered it upon a rock unto the LORD: and the angel did wonderously; and Manoah and his wife looked on. For it came to pass, when the flame went up toward heaven from off the altar, that the angel of the LORD ascended in the flame of the altar. And Manoah and his wife looked on it, and fell on their faces to the ground. But the angel of the LORD did no more appear to Manoah and to his wife. Then Manoah knew that he was an angel of the LORD. And Manoah said unto his wife, "We shall surely die, because we have seen God."

But his wife said unto him, "If the LORD were pleased to kill us, he would not have received a burnt offering and a meat offering at our hands, neither would he have shewed us all these things, nor would as at this time have told us such things as these."

And the woman bare a son, and called his name Samson: and the child grew, and the LORD blessed him.

And Samson went down to Timnath, and saw a woman in Timnath of the daughters of the Philistines. And he came up, and told his father and his mother, and said, "I have seen a woman in Timnath of the daughters of the Philistines: now therefore get her for me to wife."

Then his father and his mother said unto him, "Is there never a woman among the daughters of thy brethren, or among all my people, *Samson's feast and* that thou goest to take a wife of the uncircumcised Philistines?" *riddle*

And Samson said unto his father, "Get her for me; for she pleaseth me well." But his father and his mother knew not that it was of the LORD, that he sought an occasion against the Philistines: for at that time the Philistines had dominion over Israel.

Then went Samson down, and his father and his mother, to Timnath, and came to the vineyards of Timnath: and, behold, a young lion roared against him. And the Spirit of the LORD came mightily upon him, and he rent him as he would have rent a kid, and he had nothing in his hand: but he told not his father or his mother what he had done. And he went down, and talked with the woman; and she pleased Samson well. And after a time he returned to take her, and he turned aside to see the carcase of the lion: and, behold, there was a swarm of bees and honey in the carcase of the lion. And he took thereof in his hands, and went on eating, and came to his father and mother, and he gave them, and they did eat: but he told not them that he had taken the honey out of the carcase of the lion. So his father went down unto the woman: and Samson made there a feast; for so used the young men to do. And it came to pass, when they saw him, that they brought thirty companions to be with him. And Samson said unto them, "I will now put forth a riddle unto you: if ye can certainly declare it me within the seven days of the feast, and find it out, then I will give you thirty sheets and thirty change of garments: but if ye cannot declare it me, then shall ye give me thirty sheets and thirty change of garments."

And they said unto him, "Put forth thy riddle, that we may hear it."

And he said unto them,

> Out of the eater came forth meat,
> And out of the strong came forth sweetness.

And they could not in three days expound the riddle. And it came to pass on the seventh day, that they said unto Samson's wife, "Entice thy husband, that he may declare unto us the riddle, lest we burn thee and thy father's house with fire: have ye called us to take that we have? is it not so?"

And Samson's wife wept before him, and said, "Thou dost but hate

*Other feasts of Samson* me, and lovest me not: thou hast put forth a riddle unto the children of my people, and hast not told it me."

And he said unto her, "Behold, I have not told it my father nor my mother, and shall I tell it thee?"

And she wept before him the seven days, while their feast lasted: and it came to pass on the seventh day, that he told her: and she told the riddle to the children of her people. And the men of the city said unto him on the seventh day before the sun went down,

> What is sweeter than honey?
> And what is stronger than a lion?

And he said unto them, "If ye had not plowed with my heifer, ye had not found out my riddle."

And the Spirit of the LORD came upon him, and he went down to Ashkelon, and slew thirty men of them, and took their spoil, and gave change of garments unto them which expounded the riddle. And his anger was kindled, and he went up to his father's house. He went down and dwelt in the top of the rock Etam.

Then the Philistines went up, and pitched in Judah, and spread themselves in Lehi. And the men of Judah said, "Why are ye come up against us?"

And they answered, "To bind Samson are we come up, to do to him as he hath done to us."

Then three thousand men of Judah went to the top of the rock Etam, and said to Samson, "Knowest thou not that the Philistines are rulers over us? what is this that thou hast done unto us?" And he said unto them, "As they did unto me, so have I done unto them."

And they said unto him, "We are come down to bind thee, that we may deliver thee into the hand of the Philistines."

And Samson said unto them, "Swear unto me, that ye will not fall upon me yourselves."

And they spake unto him, saying, "No; but we will bind thee fast, and deliver thee into their hand: but surely we will not kill thee."

And they bound him with two new cords, and brought him up from the rock. And when he came unto Lehi, the Philistines shouted against him: and the Spirit of the LORD came mightily upon him, and

the cords that were upon his arms became as flax that was burnt with  Samson slays a thousand
fire, and his bands loosed from off his hands. And he found a new jaw-
bone of an ass, and put forth his hand, and took it, and slew a thousand
men therewith. And Samson said,

> With the jawbone of an ass, heaps upon heaps,
> With the jaw of an ass have I slain a thousand men.

And it came to pass, when he had made an end of speaking, that he cast
away the jawbone out of his hand, and called that place Ramath-lehi.
And he was sore athirst, and called on the LORD, and said, "Thou hast
given this great deliverance into the hand of thy servant: and now shall
I die for thirst, and fall into the hand of the uncircumcised?" But God
clave an hollow place that was in the jaw, and there came water thereout;
and when he had drunk, his spirit came again, and he revived: wherefore
he called the name thereof En-hakkore, which is in Lehi unto this day.
And he judged Israel in the days of the Philistines twenty years.

And it came to pass afterward, that he loved a woman in the valley
of Sorek, whose name was Delilah. And the lords of the Philistines came
up unto her, and said unto her, "Entice him, and see wherein his great
strength lieth, and by what means we may prevail against him, that we
may bind him to afflict him: and we will give thee every one of us eleven
hundred pieces of silver."

And Delilah said to Samson, "Tell me, I pray thee, wherein thy
great strength lieth, and wherewith thou mightest be bound to afflict
thee."

And Samson said unto her, "If they bind me with seven green withs
that were never dried, then shall I be weak, and be as another man."

Then the lords of the Philistines brought up to her seven green withs
which had not been dried, and she bound him with them. Now there
were men lying in wait, abiding with her in the chamber. And she said
unto him, "The Philistines be upon thee, Samson."

And he brake the withs, as a thread of tow is broken when it toucheth
the fire. So his strength was not known.

And Delilah said unto Samson, "Behold, thou hast mocked me, and
told me lies: now tell me, I pray thee, wherewith thou mightest be
bound."

And he said unto her, "If they bind me fast with new ropes that never were occupied, then shall I be weak, and be as another man."

Delilah therefore took new ropes, and bound him therewith, and said unto him, "The Philistines be upon thee, Samson."

And there were liers in wait abiding in the chamber. And he brake them from off his arms like a thread.

And Delilah said unto Samson, "Hitherto thou hast mocked me, and told me lies: tell me wherewith thou mightest be bound."

And he said unto her, "If thou weavest the seven locks of my head with the web."

And she fastened it with the pin, and said unto him, "The Philistines be upon thee, Samson."

And he awaked out of his sleep, and went away with the pin of the beam, and with the web. And she said unto him, "How canst thou say, 'I love thee,' when thine heart is not with me? thou hast mocked me these three times, and hast not told me wherein thy great strength lieth."

And it came to pass, when she pressed him daily with her words, and urged him, so that his soul was vexed unto death; that he told her all his heart, and said unto her, "There hath not come a razor upon mine head; if I be shaven, then my strength will go from me, and I shall become weak, and be like any other man."

And when Delilah saw that he had told her all his heart, she sent and called for the lords of the Philistines, saying, "Come up this once, for he hath shewed me all his heart."

Then the lords of the Philistines came up unto her, and brought money in their hand. And she made him sleep upon her knees; and she called for a man, and she caused him to shave off the seven locks of his head; and she began to afflict him, and his strength went from him. And she said, "The Philistines be upon thee, Samson."

And he awoke out of his sleep, and said, "I will go out as at other times before, and shake myself." And he wist not that the LORD was departed from him.

But the Philistines took him, and put out his eyes, and brought him down to Gaza, and bound him with fetters of brass; and he did grind in the prison house. Howbeit the hair of his head began to grow again after he was shaven.

Then the lords of the Philistines gathered them together for to offer *Samson's tragic death* a great sacrifice unto Dagon their god, and to rejoice: for they said, "Our god hath delivered Samson our enemy into our hand."

And when the people saw him, they praised their god: for they said, "Our god hath delivered into our hands our enemy, and the destroyer of our country, which slew many of us."

And it came to pass, when their hearts were merry, that they said, "Call for Samson, that he may make us sport."

And they called for Samson out of the prison house; and he made them sport: and they set him between the pillars. And Samson said unto the lad that held him by the hand, "Suffer me that I may feel the pillars whereupon the house standeth, that I may lean upon them."

Now the house was full of men and women; and all the lords of the Philistines were there; and there were upon the roof about three thousand men and women, that beheld while Samson made sport. And Samson called unto the LORD, and said, "O Lord GOD, remember me, I pray thee, and strengthen me, I pray thee, only this once, O God, that I may be at once avenged of the Philistines for my two eyes."

And Samson took hold of the two middle pillars upon which the house stood, and on which it was borne up, of the one with his right hand, and of the other with his left. And Samson said, "Let me die with the Philistines."

And he bowed himself with all his might; and the house fell upon the lords, and upon all the people that were therein. So the dead which he slew at his death were more than they which he slew in his life.

Now it came to pass in the days when the judges ruled, that there was a famine in the land. And a certain man of Beth-lehem-judah went to sojourn in the country of Moab, he, and his wife, and his two sons. And the name of the man was Elimelech, and the name of his wife Naomi, and the name of his two sons Mahlon and Chilion, Ephrathites of Beth-lehem-judah. And they came into the country of Moab, and continued there. And Elimelech Naomi's husband died; and she was left, and her two sons. And they took them wives of the women of Moab; the name of the one was Orpah, and the name of the other Ruth: and they dwelled there about ten years. And Mahlon and Chilion died also both of them;

and the woman was left of her two sons and her husband. Then she arose with her daughters in law, that she might return from the country of Moab: for she had heard in the country of Moab how that the LORD had visited his people in giving them bread. Wherefore she went forth out of the place where she was, and her two daughters in law with her; and they went on the way to return unto the land of Judah.

And Naomi said unto her two daughters in law, "Go, return each to her mother's house: the LORD deal kindly with you, as ye have dealt with the dead, and with me. The LORD grant you that ye may find rest, each of you in the house of her husband."

Then she kissed them; and they lifted up their voice, and wept. And they said unto her, "Surely we will return with thee unto thy people."

And Naomi said, "Turn again, my daughters: why will ye go with me? Turn again, my daughters, go your way; for it grieveth me much for your sakes that the hand of the LORD is gone out against me."

And they lifted up their voice, and wept again: and Orpah kissed her mother in law; but Ruth clave unto her.

And she said, "Behold, thy sister in law is gone back unto her people, and unto her gods: return thou after thy sister in law."

And Ruth said, "Intreat me not to leave thee, or to return from following after thee: for whither thou goest, I will go; and where thou lodgest, I will lodge: thy people shall be my people, and thy God my God: where thou diest, will I die, and there will I be buried: the LORD do so to me, and more also, if ought but death part thee and me."

When she saw that she was stedfastly minded to go with her, then she left speaking unto her. So they two went until they came to Beth-lehem. And it came to pass, when they were come to Beth-lehem, that all the city was moved about them, and they said, "Is this Naomi?"

So Naomi returned, and Ruth the Moabitess, her daughter in law, with her, which returned out of the country of Moab: and they came to Beth-lehem in the beginning of barley harvest.

And Naomi had a kinsman of her husband's, a mighty man of wealth, of the family of Elimelech; and his name was Boaz.

And Ruth the Moabitess said unto Naomi, "Let me now go to the field, and glean ears of corn after him in whose sight I shall find grace."

And she said unto her, "Go, my daughter."

And she went, and came, and gleaned in the field after the reapers: *Boaz sees Ruth* and her hap was to light on a part of the field belonging unto Boaz.

And, behold, Boaz came from Beth-lehem, and said unto the reapers, "The Lord be with you."

And they answered him, "The Lord bless thee."

Then said Boaz unto his servant that was set over the reapers, "Whose damsel is this?" And the servant that was set over the reapers answered and said, "It is the Moabitish damsel that came back with Naomi out of the country of Moab. And she said, 'I pray you, let me glean and gather after the reapers among the sheaves': so she came, and hath continued even from the morning until now, that she tarried a little in the house."

Then said Boaz unto Ruth, "Hearest thou not, my daughter? Go not to glean in another field, neither go from hence, but abide here fast by my maidens: let thine eyes be on the field that they do reap, and go thou after them: have I not charged the young men that they shall not touch thee? and when thou art athirst, go unto the vessels, and drink of that which the young men have drawn."

Then she fell on her face, and bowed herself to the ground, and said unto him, "Why have I found grace in thine eyes, that thou shouldest take knowledge of me, seeing I am a stranger?"

And Boaz answered and said unto her, "It hath fully been shewed me, all that thou hast done unto thy mother in law since the death of thine husband: and how thou hast left thy father and thy mother, and the land of thy nativity, and art come unto a people which thou knewest not heretofore. The Lord recompense thy work, and a full reward be given thee of the Lord God of Israel, under whose wings thou art come to trust."

Then she said, "Let me find favour in thy sight, my lord; for that thou hast comforted me, and for that thou hast spoken friendly unto thine handmaid, though I be not like unto one of thine handmaidens."

And Boaz said unto her, "At mealtime come thou hither, and eat of the bread, and dip thy morsel in the vinegar."

And she sat beside the reapers: and he reached her parched corn, and she did eat, and was sufficed, and left. And when she was risen up to glean, Boaz commanded his young men, saying, "Let her glean even among the sheaves, and reproach her not: and let fall also some of the handfuls of purpose for her, and leave them, that she may glean them, and rebuke her not."

So she gleaned in the field until even, and beat out that she had gleaned: and it was about an ephah of barley. And she took it up, and went into the city: and her mother in law saw what she had gleaned: and she brought forth, and gave to her that she had reserved after she was sufficed.

And her mother in law said unto her, "Where hast thou gleaned to day? and where wroughtest thou? blessed be he that did take knowledge of thee."

And she shewed her mother in law with whom she had wrought, and said, "The man's name with whom I wrought to day is Boaz."

And Naomi said unto her daughter in law, "Blessed be he of the LORD, who hath not left off his kindness to the living and to the dead." And Naomi said unto her, "The man is near of kin unto us, one of our next kinsmen."

And Ruth the Moabitess said, "He said unto me also, 'Thou shalt keep fast by my young men, until they have ended all my harvest.' " And she said, "These six measures of barley gave he me; for he said to me, 'Go not empty unto thy mother in law.' "

And Naomi said unto Ruth her daughter in law, "It is good, my daughter, that thou go out with his maidens, that they meet thee not in any other field."

So she kept fast by the maidens of Boaz to glean unto the end of barley harvest and of wheat harvest; and dwelt with her mother in law.

Then Naomi her mother in law said unto her, "My daughter, shall I not seek rest for thee, that it may be well with thee? And now is not Boaz of our kindred, with whose maidens thou wast? Behold, he winnoweth barley to night in the threshingfloor."

And Ruth went down unto the floor.

And Boaz said, "Who art thou?"

And she answered, "I am Ruth thine handmaid: spread therefore thy skirt over thine handmaid; for thou art a near kinsman."

And he said, "Blessed be thou of the LORD, my daughter: for thou hast shewed more kindness in the latter end than at the beginning, inasmuch as thou followedst not young men, whether poor or rich. And now,

my daughter, fear not; I will do to thee all that thou requirest: for all
the city of my people doth know that thou art a virtuous woman. And
now it is true that I am thy near kinsman: howbeit there is a kinsman
nearer than I. Tarry this night, and it shall be in the morning, that if
he will perform unto thee the part of a kinsman, well; let him do the
kinsman's part: but if he will not do the part of a kinsman to thee, then
will I do the part of a kinsman to thee, as the LORD liveth."

Also he said, "Bring the vail that thou hast upon thee, and hold it."
And when she held it, he measured six measures of barley, and laid it on
her: and she went into the city.

And when she came to her mother in law, she said, "Who art thou,
my daughter?"

And she told her all that the man had done to her. And she said,
"These six measures of barley gave he me; for he said to me, 'Go not
empty unto thy mother in law.' "

Then said she, "Sit still, my daughter, until thou know how the matter will fall: for the man will not be in rest, until he have finished the
thing this day."

Then went Boaz up to the gate, and sat him down there: and, behold,
the kinsman of whom Boaz spake came by; unto whom he said, "Ho,
such a one! turn aside, sit down here."

And he turned aside, and sat down. And he took ten men of the elders
of the city, and said, "Sit ye down here." And they sat down.

And he said unto the kinsman, "Naomi, that is come again out of the
country of Moab, selleth a parcel of land, which was our brother Elimelech's: and I thought to advertise thee, saying, 'Buy it before the inhabitants, and before the elders of my people.' If thou wilt redeem it,
redeem it: but if thou wilt not redeem it, then tell me, that I may know:
for there is none to redeem it besides thee; and I am after thee."

And he said, "I will redeem it."

Then said Boaz, "What day thou buyest the field of the hand of
Naomi, thou must buy it also of Ruth the Moabitess, the wife of the dead,
to raise up the name of the dead upon his inheritance."

And the kinsman said, "I cannot redeem it for myself, lest I mar mine
own inheritance: redeem thou my right to thyself; for I cannot redeem
it."

Now this was the manner in former time in Israel concerning redeeming and concerning changing, for to confirm all things; a man plucked off his shoe, and gave it to his neighbour: and this was a testimony in Israel. Therefore the kinsman said unto Boaz, "Buy it for thee." So he drew off his shoe.

And Boaz said unto the elders, and unto all the people, "Ye are witnesses this day, that I have bought all that was Elimelech's, and all that was Chilion's and Mahlon's, of the hand of Naomi. Moreover Ruth the Moabitess, the wife of Mahlon, have I purchased to be my wife, to raise up the name of the dead upon his inheritance, that the name of the dead be not cut off from among his brethren, and from the gate of his place: ye are witnesses this day."

And all the people that were in the gate, and the elders, said, "We are witnesses. The LORD make the woman that is come into thine house like Rachel and like Leah, which two did build the house of Israel: and do thou worthily in Ephratah, and be famous in Beth-lehem."

So Boaz took Ruth, and she was his wife, and she bare a son.

And the women said unto Naomi, "Blessed be the LORD, which hath not left thee this day without a kinsman, that his name may be famous in Israel. And he shall be unto thee a restorer of thy life, and a nourisher of thine old age: for thy daughter in law, which loveth thee, which is better to thee than seven sons, hath born him."

And Naomi took the child, and laid it in her bosom, and became nurse unto it. And the women her neighbours gave it a name, saying, "There is a son born to Naomi; and they called his name Obed: he is the father of Jesse, the father of David."

Now there was a certain man of mount Ephraim, and his name was Elkanah: and he had two wives; the name of the one was Hannah, and he loved Hannah, but Hannah had no children. And this man went up out of his city yearly to worship and to sacrifice unto the LORD of hosts in Shiloh. And the two sons of Eli, Hophni and Phinehas, the priests of the LORD, were there.

Then said Elkanah her husband to her, "Hannah, why weepest thou? and why eatest thou not? and why is thy heart grieved? am not I better to thee than ten sons?"

And she was in bitterness of soul, and prayed unto the Lord, and wept sore. And she vowed a vow, and said, "O Lord of hosts, if thou wilt indeed look on the affliction of thine handmaid, and remember me, and not forget thine handmaid, but wilt give unto thine handmaid a man child, then I will give him unto the Lord all the days of his life."

Now Eli the priest sat upon a seat by a post of the temple of the Lord. And it came to pass, as she continued praying before the Lord, that Eli marked her mouth. Now Hannah, she spake in her heart; only her lips moved, but her voice was not heard: therefore Eli thought she had been drunken.

And Eli said unto her, "How long wilt thou be drunken? put away thy wine from thee."

And Hannah answered and said, "No, my lord, I am a woman of a sorrowful spirit: I have drunk neither wine nor strong drink, but have poured out my soul before the Lord, for out of the abundance of my complaint and grief have I spoken hitherto."

Then Eli answered and said, "Go in peace: and the God of Israel grant thee thy petition that thou hast asked of him."

And she said, "Let thine handmaid find grace in thy sight."

So the woman went her way, and did eat, and her countenance was no more sad. And they rose up in the morning early, and worshipped before the Lord, and returned, and came to their house to Ramah: wherefore it came to pass, she bare a son, and called his name Samuel, saying, "Because I have asked him of the Lord."

And the man Elkanah, and all his house, went up to offer unto the Lord the yearly sacrifice, and his vow. But Hannah went not up; for she said unto her husband, "I will not go up until the child be weaned, and then I will bring him, that he may appear before the Lord, and there abide for ever."

And Elkanah her husband said unto her, "Do what seemeth thee good; tarry until thou have weaned him; only the Lord establish his word."

So the woman abode, and gave her son suck until she weaned him. And when she had weaned him, she took him up with her, and brought him unto the house of the Lord in Shiloh: and the child was young. And she said, "O my lord, as thy soul liveth, my lord, I am the woman

*Hannah's song* that stood by thee here, praying unto the LORD. For this child I prayed; and the LORD hath given me my petition which I asked of him: therefore also I have lent him to the LORD; as long as he liveth he shall be lent to the LORD."

And Hannah prayed, and said,

> My heart rejoiceth in the LORD.
> There is none holy as the LORD:
> For there is none beside thee:
> Neither is there any rock like our God.
> Talk no more so exceeding proudly;
> Let not arrogancy come out of your mouth:
> For the LORD is a God of knowledge,
> And by him actions are weighed.
> The bows of the mighty men are broken,
> And they that stumbled are girded with strength.
> The LORD maketh poor, and maketh rich:
> He bringeth low, and lifteth up;
> For the pillars of the earth are the LORD's,
> And he hath set the world upon them.
> He will keep the feet of his saints,
> And the wicked shall be silent in darkness;
> For by strength shall no man prevail.
> The LORD shall judge the ends of the earth;
> And he shall give strength unto his king,
> And exalt the horn of his anointed.

And Elkanah went to Ramah to his house.

And the child did minister unto the LORD before Eli the priest. Now the sons of Eli knew not the LORD. But Samuel ministered before the LORD, being a child, girded with a linen ephod. Moreover his mother made him a little coat, and brought it to him from year to year, when she came up with her husband to offer the yearly sacrifice. And the child Samuel grew before the LORD.

Now Eli was very old, and heard all that his sons did unto all Israel. And he said unto them, "Nay, my sons; for it is no good report that I hear: ye make the LORD's people to transgress. If one man sin against another, the judge shall judge him: but if a man sin against the LORD, who shall intreat for him?" Notwithstanding they hearkened not unto the voice of their father.

And there came a man of God unto Eli, and said unto him, "Thus saith the LORD, 'Did I plainly appear unto the house of thy father, when they were in Egypt in Pharaoh's house?' Wherefore the LORD God of Israel saith, 'I said indeed that thy house, and the house of thy father, should walk before me for ever: but now,' the LORD saith, 'be it far from me; for them that honour me I will honour, and they that despise me shall be lightly esteemed. And I will raise me up a faithful priest, that shall do according to that which is in mine heart and in my mind: and I will build him a sure house; and he shall walk before mine anointed for ever.' "

And the child Samuel grew on, and was in favour both with the LORD, and also with men. And the child Samuel ministered unto the LORD before Eli. And the word of the LORD was precious in those days; there was no open vision.

And it came to pass at that time, when Eli was laid down in his place, and his eyes began to wax dim, that he could not see; and ere the lamp of God went out in the temple of the LORD, where the ark of God was, and Samuel was laid down to sleep; that the LORD called Samuel: and he answered, "Here am I."

And he ran unto Eli, and said, "Here am I; for thou calledst me."

And he said, "I called not; lie down again." And he went and lay down.

And the LORD called yet again, "Samuel." And Samuel arose and went to Eli, and said, "Here am I; for thou didst call me."

And he answered, "I called not, my son; lie down again."

Now Samuel did not yet know the LORD, neither was the word of the LORD yet revealed unto him. And the LORD called Samuel again the third time. And he arose and went to Eli, and said, "Here am I; for thou didst call me."

And Eli perceived that the LORD had called the child. Therefore Eli said unto Samuel, "Go, lie down: and it shall be, if he call thee, that thou shalt say, 'Speak, LORD; for thy servant heareth.' " So Samuel went and

*Israel smitten* lay down in his place. And the LORD came, and stood, and called as at other times, "Samuel, Samuel."

Then Samuel answered, "Speak; for thy servant heareth."

And the LORD said to Samuel, "Behold, I will do a thing in Israel, at which both the ears of every one that heareth it shall tingle. In that day I will perform against Eli all things which I have spoken concerning his house: when I begin, I will also make an end. For I have told him that I will judge his house for ever for the iniquity which he knoweth; because his sons made themselves vile, and he restrained them not. And therefore I have sworn unto the house of Eli, that the iniquity of Eli's house shall not be purged with sacrifice nor offering for ever."

And Samuel lay until the morning, and opened the doors of the house of the LORD. And Samuel feared to shew Eli the vision.

Then Eli called Samuel, and said, "Samuel, my son."

And he answered, "Here am I."

And he said, "What is the thing that the LORD hath said unto thee? I pray thee hide it not from me: God do so to thee, and more also, if thou hide any thing from me of all the things that he said unto thee."

And Samuel told him every whit, and hid nothing from him.

And he said, "It is the LORD: let him do what seemeth him good."

And Samuel grew, and the LORD was with him, and did let none of his words fall to the ground. And all Israel from Dan even to Beer-sheba knew that Samuel was established to be a prophet of the LORD. And the LORD appeared again in Shiloh: for the LORD revealed himself to Samuel in Shiloh by the word of the LORD. And the word of Samuel came to all Israel.

Now Israel went out against the Philistines to battle, and pitched beside Eben-ezer: and the Philistines pitched in Aphek. And the Philistines put themselves in array against Israel: and when they joined battle, Israel was smitten before the Philistines: and they slew of the army in the field about four thousand men. And when the people were come into the camp, the elders of Israel said, "Wherefore hath the LORD smitten us to day before the Philistines? Let us fetch the ark of the covenant of the LORD out of Shiloh unto us, that, when it cometh among us, it may save us out of the hand of our enemies."

So the people sent to Shiloh, that they might bring from thence the *Death of Eli* ark of the covenant of the LORD of hosts, which dwelleth between the cherubims: and the two sons of Eli, Hophni and Phinehas, were there with the ark of the covenant of God. And when the ark of the covenant of the LORD came into the camp, all Israel shouted with a great shout, so that the earth rang again.

And when the Philistines heard the noise of the shout, they said, "What meaneth the noise of this great shout in the camp of the Hebrews?" And they understood that the ark of the LORD was come into the camp. And the Philistines were afraid, for they said, "God is come into the camp. Woe unto us! who shall deliver us out of the hand of these mighty Gods? Be strong, and quit yourselves like men, O ye Philistines, that ye be not servants unto the Hebrews, as they have been to you: quit yourselves like men, and fight."

And the Philistines fought, and Israel was smitten, and they fled every man into his tent: there fell of Israel thirty thousand footmen. And the ark of God was taken; and the two sons of Eli, Hophni and Phinehas, were slain. And there ran a man of Benjamin out of the army, and came to Shiloh the same day with his clothes rent, and with earth upon his head. And when he came, lo, Eli sat upon a seat by the wayside watching: for his heart trembled for the ark of God. And when the man came into the city, and told it, all the city cried out.

And when Eli heard the noise of the crying, he said, "What meaneth the noise of this tumult?"

And the man came in hastily, and told Eli. Now Eli was ninety and eight years old; and his eyes were dim, that he could not see. And the man said unto Eli, "I am he that fled to day out of the army."

And he said, "What is there done, my son?"

And the messenger answered and said, "Israel is fled before the Philistines, and there hath been also a great slaughter among the people, and thy two sons also, Hophni and Phinehas, are dead, and the ark of God is taken."

And it came to pass, when he made mention of the ark of God, that he fell from off the seat backward by the side of the gate, and he died: for he was an old man, and heavy. And he had judged Israel forty years.

And his daughter in law, Phinehas' wife, was with child, near to be delivered: and when she heard the tidings that the ark of God was taken, and that her father in law and her husband were dead, she bowed herself and travailed; for her pains came upon her. And about the time of her death the women that stood by her said unto her, "Fear not; for thou hast born a son."

But she answered not, neither did she regard it. And she named the child I-chabod, saying, "The glory is departed from Israel": because the ark of God was taken, and because of her father in law and her husband. And she said, "The glory is departed from Israel: for the ark of God is taken." And the ark of the LORD was in the country of the Philistines seven months. And the Philistines called for the priests and the diviners, saying, "What shall we do to the ark of the LORD? tell us wherewith we shall send it to his place. Now therefore make a new cart, and take two milch kine, on which there hath come no yoke, and tie the kine to the cart, and bring their calves home from them: and take the ark of the LORD, and lay it upon the cart; and put the jewels of gold, which ye return him for a trespass offering, in a coffer by the side thereof; and send it away, that it may go. And see, if it goeth up by the way of his own coast to Beth-shemesh, then he hath done us this great evil: but if not, then we shall know that it is not his hand that smote us: it was a chance that happened to us."

And the men did so; and took two milch kine, and tied them to the cart, and shut up their calves at home: and they laid the ark of the LORD upon the cart, and the coffer with the mice of gold and the images of their emerods. And the kine took the straight way to the way of Beth-shemesh, and went along the highway, lowing as they went, and turned not aside to the right hand or to the left; and the lords of the Philistines went after them unto the border of Beth-shemesh. And they of Beth-shemesh were reaping their wheat harvest in the valley: and they lifted up their eyes, and saw the ark, and rejoiced to see it. The five lords of the Philistines returned to Ekron the same day. And they sent messengers to the inhabitants of Kirjath-jearim, saying, "The Philistines have brought again the ark of the LORD; come ye down, and fetch it up to you."

And the men of Kirjath-jearim came, and fetched up the ark of the LORD, and brought it into the house of Abinadab in the hill, and sancti-

fied Eleazar his son to keep the ark of the LORD. And it came to pass,
while the ark abode in Kirjath-jearim, that the time was long; for it was
twenty years: and all the house of Israel lamented after the LORD.

And Samuel spake unto all the house of Israel, saying, "If ye do return unto the LORD with all your hearts, then put away the strange gods
from among you, and prepare your hearts unto the LORD, and serve him
only: and he will deliver you out of the hand of the Philistines."

Then the children of Israel served the LORD only.

And Samuel said, "Gather all Israel to Mizpeh, and I will pray for
you unto the LORD."

And they gathered together to Mizpeh, and drew water, and poured
it out before the LORD, and fasted on that day, and said there, "We have
sinned against the LORD."

And when the Philistines heard that the children of Israel were
gathered together to Mizpeh, the lords of the Philistines went up against
Israel. And when the children of Israel heard it, they were afraid of the
Philistines. And Samuel took a sucking lamb, and offered it for a burnt
offering wholly unto the LORD: and Samuel cried unto the LORD for
Israel; and the LORD heard him. And as Samuel was offering up the burnt
offering, the Philistines drew near to battle against Israel: but the LORD
thundered with a great thunder on that day upon the Philistines, and
discomfited them; and they were smitten before Israel. And the men of
Israel went out of Mizpeh, and pursued the Philistines, and smote them,
until they came under Beth-car. Then Samuel took a stone, and set it
between Mizpeh and Shen, and called the name of it Eben-ezer, saying,
"Hitherto hath the LORD helped us." So the Philistines were subdued,
and they came no more into the coast of Israel.

And Samuel judged Israel all the days of his life. And he went from
year to year in circuit to Beth-el, and Gilgal, and Mizpeh, and judged
Israel in all those places. And his return was to Ramah; for there was
his house; and there he judged Israel; and there he built an altar unto
the LORD.

And it came to pass, when Samuel was old, that he made his sons
judges over Israel. And his sons walked not in his ways, but turned aside
after lucre, and took bribes, and perverted judgment. Then all the elders
of Israel gathered themselves together, and came to Samuel unto Ramah,

and said unto him, "Behold, thou art old, and thy sons walk not in thy ways: now make us a king to judge us like all the nations."

But the thing displeased Samuel, when they said, "Give us a king to judge us." And Samuel prayed unto the LORD. And the LORD said unto Samuel, "Hearken unto the voice of the people in all that they say unto thee: for they have not rejected thee, but they have rejected me, that I should not reign over them. Now therefore hearken unto their voice: howbeit yet protest solemnly unto them, and shew them the manner of the king that shall reign over them."

And Samuel told all the words of the LORD unto the people that asked of him a king. And he said, "This will be the manner of the king that shall reign over you: He will take your sons, and appoint them for himself, for his chariots, and to be his horsemen; and some shall run before his chariots. And he will appoint him captains over thousands, and captains over fifties; and will set them to ear his ground, and to reap his harvest, and to make his instruments of war, and instruments of his chariots. And he will take your daughters to be confectionaries, and to be cooks, and to be bakers. And he will take your fields, and your vineyards, and your oliveyards, even the best of them, and give them to his servants. And he will take the tenth of your seed, and of your vineyards, and give to his officers, and to his servants. And he will take your menservants, and your maidservants, and your goodliest young men, and your asses, and put them to his work. He will take the tenth of your sheep: and ye shall be his servants. And ye shall cry out in that day because of your king which ye shall have chosen you; and the LORD will not hear you in that day."

Nevertheless the people refused to obey the voice of Samuel; and they said, "Nay; but we will have a king over us; that we also may be like all the nations; and that our king may judge us, and go out before us, and fight our battles."

And Samuel heard all the words of the people, and he rehearsed them in the ears of the LORD.

And the LORD said to Samuel, "Hearken unto their voice, and make them a king."

And Samuel said unto the men of Israel, "Go ye every man unto his city."

Now there was a man whose name was Kish, a mighty man of power. *Saul meets Samuel* And he had a son, whose name was Saul, a choice young man, and a goodly: and there was not among the children of Israel a goodlier person than he: from his shoulders and upward he was higher than any of the people.

And the asses of Kish Saul's father were lost. And Kish said to Saul his son, "Take now one of the servants with thee, and arise, go seek the asses."

And he passed through mount Ephraim, and passed through the land of Shalisha, but they found them not: then they passed through the land of Shalim, and there they were not: and he passed through the land of the Benjamites, but they found them not. And when they were come to the land of Zuph, Saul said to his servant that was with him, "Come, and let us return; lest my father leave caring for the asses, and take thought for us."

And he said unto him, "Behold now, there is in this city a man of God, and he is an honourable man; all that he saith cometh surely to pass: now let us go thither; peradventure he can shew us our way that we should go."

Then said Saul to his servant, "But, behold, if we go, what shall we bring the man? for the bread is spent in our vessels, and there is not a present to bring to the man of God: what have we?"

And the servant answered Saul again, and said, "Behold, I have here at hand the fourth part of a shekel of silver: that will I give to the man of God, to tell us our way."

(Beforetime in Israel, when a man went to enquire of God, thus he spake, "Come, and let us go to the seer": for he that is now called a Prophet was beforetime called a Seer.)

Then said Saul to his servant, "Well said; come, let us go." So they went unto the city where the man of God was. And as they went up the hill to the city, they found young maidens going out to draw water, and said unto them, "Is the seer here?"

And they answered them, and said, "He is; behold, he is before you: make haste now, for he came to day to the city; for there is a sacrifice of the people to day in the high place: as soon as ye be come into the city, ye shall straightway find him, before he go up to the high place to eat:

*Samuel's entertainment* for the people will not eat until he come, because he doth bless the sacrifice; and afterward they eat that be bidden. Now therefore get you up; for about this time ye shall find him."

And they went up into the city: and when they were come into the city, behold, Samuel came out against them, for to go up to the high place.

Now the LORD had told Samuel in his ear a day before Saul came, saying, "To morrow about this time I will send thee a man out of the land of Benjamin, and thou shalt anoint him to be captain over my people Israel, that he may save my people out of the hand of the Philistines: for I have looked upon my people, because their cry is come unto me."

And when Samuel saw Saul, the LORD said unto him, "Behold the man whom I spake to thee of! this same shall reign over my people."

Then Saul drew near to Samuel in the gate, and said, "Tell me, I pray thee, where the seer's house is."

And Samuel answered Saul, and said, "I am the seer: go up before me unto the high place; for ye shall eat with me to day, and to morrow I will let thee go, and will tell thee all that is in thine heart. And as for thine asses that were lost three days ago, set not thy mind on them; for they are found. And on whom is all the desire of Israel? Is it not on thee, and on all thy father's house?"

And Saul answered and said, "Am not I a Benjamite, of the smallest of the tribes of Israel? and my family the least of all the families of the tribe of Benjamin? wherefore then speakest thou so to me?"

And Samuel took Saul and his servant, and brought them into the parlour, and made them sit in the chiefest place among them that were bidden, which were about thirty persons. And Samuel said unto the cook, "Bring the portion which I gave thee, of which I said unto thee, 'Set it by thee.'"

And the cook took up the shoulder, and that which was upon it, and set it before Saul. And Samuel said, "Behold that which is left! set it before thee, and eat: for unto this time hath it been kept for thee since I said, 'I have invited the people.'"

So Saul did eat with Samuel that day. And when they were come down from the high place into the city, Samuel communed with Saul upon the top of the house. And they arose early: and it came to pass about the

spring of the day, that Samuel called Saul to the top of the house, saying,
"Up, that I may send thee away."

And Saul arose, and they went out both of them, he and Samuel, abroad. And as they were going down to the end of the city, Samuel said to Saul, "Bid the servant pass on before us," (and he passed on,) "but stand thou still a while, that I may shew thee the word of God."

Then Samuel took a vial of oil, and poured it upon his head, and kissed him, and said, "Is it not because the LORD hath anointed thee to be captain over his inheritance? When thou art departed from me to day, then thou shalt find two men by Rachel's sepulchre; and they will say unto thee, 'The asses which thou wentest to seek are found: and, lo, thy father hath left the care of the asses, and sorroweth for you, saying, "What shall I do for my son?" ' Then shalt thou go on forward from thence, and thou shalt come to the plain of Tabor, and there shall meet thee three men going up to God to Beth-el, one carrying three kids, and another carrying three loaves of bread, and another carrying a bottle of wine: and they will salute thee, and give thee two loaves of bread; which thou shalt receive of their hands. After that thou shalt come to the hill of God, where is the garrison of the Philistines: and it shall come to pass, when thou art come thither to the city, that thou shalt meet a company of prophets coming down from the high place with a psaltery, and a tabret, and a pipe, and a harp, before them; and they shall prophesy: and the Spirit of the LORD will come upon thee, and thou shalt prophesy with them, and shalt be turned into another man. And let it be, when these signs are come unto thee, that thou do as occasion serve thee; for God is with thee. And thou shalt go down before me to Gilgal; and, behold, I will come down unto thee, to offer burnt offerings, and to sacrifice sacrifices of peace offerings: seven days shalt thou tarry, till I come to thee, and shew thee what thou shalt do."

And it was so, that when he had turned his back to go from Samuel, God gave him another heart: and all those signs came to pass that day.

And Samuel called the people together unto the LORD to Mizpeh; and said unto the children of Israel, "Thus saith the LORD God of Israel, 'I brought up Israel out of Egypt, and delivered you out of the hand of the Egyptians, and out of the hand of all kingdoms, and of them that oppressed you': and ye have this day rejected your God, who himself saved you out of all your adversities and your tribulations; and ye have said unto him, 'Nay, but set a king over us.' Now therefore present yourselves before the LORD by your tribes, and by your thousands."

And when they sought Saul the son of Kish, he could not be found. Therefore they enquired of the LORD further, if the man should yet come thither. And the LORD answered, "Behold, he hath hid himself among the stuff."

And they ran and fetched him thence: and when he stood among the people, he was higher than any of the people from his shoulders and upward. And Samuel said to all the people, "See ye him whom the LORD hath chosen, that there is none like him among all the people?"

And all the people shouted, and said, "God save the king."

Then Samuel told the people the manner of the kingdom, and wrote it in a book, and laid it up before the LORD. And Samuel sent all the people away, every man to his house. And Saul also went home to Gibeah; and there went with him a band of men, whose hearts God had touched. But the children of Belial said, "How shall this man save us?"

And they despised him, and brought him no presents. But he held his peace.

Then said Samuel to the people, "Come, and let us go to Gilgal, and renew the kingdom there."

And all the people went to Gilgal; and there they made Saul king before the LORD in Gilgal; and there they sacrificed sacrifices of peace offerings before the LORD; and there Saul and all the men of Israel rejoiced greatly. And Samuel said unto all Israel, "Behold, I have hearkened unto your voice in all that ye said unto me, and have made a king over you. And now, behold, the king walketh before you: and I am old and grayheaded; and, behold, my sons are with you: and I have walked before you from my childhood unto this day. Behold, here I am: witness against me before the LORD, and before his anointed: whose ox have I taken? or whose ass have I taken? or whom have I defrauded? whom have I oppressed? or of whose hand have I received any bribe to blind mine eyes therewith? and I will restore it you."

And they said, "Thou hast not defrauded us, nor oppressed us, neither hast thou taken ought of any man's hand."

And he said unto them, "The LORD is witness against you, and his anointed is witness this day, that ye have not found ought in my hand."

And they answered, "He is witness."

And Samuel said unto the people, "It is the LORD that advanced Moses and Aaron, and that brought your fathers up out of the land of Egypt. Now therefore stand still, that I may reason with you before the LORD of all the righteous acts of the LORD, which he did to you and to your fathers. When Jacob was come into Egypt, and your fathers cried unto the LORD, then the LORD sent Moses and Aaron, which brought forth your fathers out of Egypt, and made them dwell in this place. And when they forgat the LORD their God, he sold them into the hand of Sisera, captain of the host of Hazor, and into the hand of the Philistines, and into the hand of the king of Moab, and they fought against them. And they cried unto the LORD, and said, 'We have sinned, because we have forsaken the LORD, and have served Baalim and Ashtaroth: but now deliver us out of the hand of our enemies, and we will serve thee.' And the LORD sent Jerubbaal, and Bedan, and Jephthah, and Samuel, and delivered you out of the hand of your enemies on every side, and ye dwelled safe. And when ye saw that Nahash the king of the children of Ammon came against you, ye said unto me, 'Nay; but a king shall reign over us': when the LORD your God was king. Now therefore behold the LORD hath set a king over you. If ye will fear the LORD, and serve him, and obey his voice, and not rebel against the commandment of the LORD, then shall both ye and also the king that reigneth over you continue following the LORD your God: but if ye will not obey the voice of the LORD, but rebel against the commandment of the LORD, then shall the hand of the LORD be against you, as it was against your fathers. And turn ye not aside: for then should ye go after vain things, which cannot profit nor deliver; for they are vain. For the LORD will not forsake his people for his great name's sake: because it hath pleased the LORD to make you his people. Moreover as for me, God forbid that I should sin against the LORD in ceasing to pray for you: but I will teach you the good and the right way: only fear the LORD, and serve him in truth with all your heart: for consider how great things he hath done for you."

Now it came to pass upon a day, that Jonathan the son of Saul said unto the young man that bare his armour, "Come, and let us go over to

*Jonathan's exploit* the Philistines' garrison, that is on the other side." But he told not his father.

And Saul tarried in the uttermost part of Gibeah under a pomegranate tree which is in Migron: and the people that were with him were about six hundred men; and the people knew not that Jonathan was gone. And between the passages, by which Jonathan sought to go over unto the Philistines' garrison, there was a sharp rock on the one side, and a sharp rock on the other side: the forefront of the one was situate northward over against Michmash, and the other southward over against Gibeah. And Jonathan said to the young man that bare his armour, "Come, and let us go over unto the garrison: it may be that the LORD will work for us: for there is no restraint to the LORD to save by many or by few."

And his armourbearer said unto him, "Do all that is in thine heart: turn thee; behold, I am with thee according to thy heart."

Then said Jonathan, "Behold, we will pass over unto these men, and we will discover ourselves unto them. If they say thus unto us, 'Tarry until we come to you'; then we will stand still in our place, and will not go up unto them. But if they say thus, 'Come up unto us'; then we will go up: for the LORD hath delivered them into our hand: and this shall be a sign unto us."

And both of them discovered themselves unto the garrison of the Philistines: and the Philistines said, "Behold, the Hebrews come forth out of the holes where they had hid themselves."

And the men of the garrison answered Jonathan and his armourbearer, and said, "Come up to us, and we will shew you a thing."

And Jonathan said unto his armourbearer, "Come up after me: for the LORD hath delivered them into the hand of Israel."

And Jonathan climbed up upon his hands and upon his feet, and his armourbearer after him: and they fell before Jonathan; and his armourbearer slew after him. And that first slaughter, which Jonathan and his armourbearer made, was about twenty men, within as it were an half acre of land, which a yoke of oxen might plow. And there was trembling in the host, in the field, and among all the people: the garrison, and the spoilers, they also trembled, and the earth quaked: so it was a very great trembling.

And the watchmen of Saul in Gibeah of Benjamin looked; and, behold, the multitude melted away, and they went on beating down one another.

*He eats forbidden food*

Then said Saul unto the people that were with him, "Number now, and see who is gone from us." And when they had numbered, behold, Jonathan and his armourbearer were not there.

And Saul said unto Ahiah, "Bring hither the ark of God." For the ark of God was at that time with the children of Israel.

And it came to pass, while Saul talked unto the priest, that the noise that was in the host of the Philistines went on and increased: and Saul said unto the priest, "Withdraw thine hand."

And Saul and all the people that were with him assembled themselves, and they came to the battle: and, behold, every man's sword was against his fellow, and there was a very great discomfiture. Moreover the Hebrews that were with the Philistines before that time, which went up with them into the camp from the country round about, even they also turned to be with the Israelites that were with Saul and Jonathan. Likewise all the men of Israel which had hid themselves in mount Ephraim, when they heard that the Philistines fled, even they also followed hard after them in the battle. So the Lord saved Israel that day: and the battle passed over unto Beth-aven.

And the men of Israel were distressed that day: for Saul had adjured the people, saying, "Cursed be the man that eateth any food until evening, that I may be avenged on mine enemies." So none of the people tasted any food. And all they of the land came to a wood; and there was honey upon the ground. And when the people were come into the wood, behold, the honey dropped; but no man put his hand to his mouth: for the people feared the oath. But Jonathan heard not when his father charged the people with the oath: wherefore he put forth the end of the rod that was in his hand, and dipped it in an honeycomb, and put his hand to his mouth; and his eyes were enlightened.

Then answered one of the people, and said, "Thy father straitly charged the people with an oath, saying, 'Cursed be the man that eateth any food this day.'" And the people were faint.

Then said Jonathan, "My father hath troubled the land: see, I pray you, how mine eyes have been enlightened, because I tasted a little of

*The people save Jonathan*

this honey. How much more, if haply the people had eaten freely to day of the spoil of their enemies which they found?"

And Saul said, "Let us go down after the Philistines by night, and spoil them until the morning light, and let us not leave a man of them."

And they said, "Do whatsoever seemeth good unto thee."

Then said the priest, "Let us draw near hither unto God."

And Saul asked counsel of God, "Shall I go down after the Philistines? wilt thou deliver them into the hand of Israel?"

But he answered him not that day.

And Saul said, "Draw ye near hither, all the chief of the people: and know and see wherein this sin hath been this day. For, as the LORD liveth, which saveth Israel, though it be in Jonathan my son, he shall surely die."

But there was not a man among all the people that answered him.

Then said he unto all Israel, "Be ye on one side, and I and Jonathan my son will be on the other side."

And the people said unto Saul, "Do what seemeth good unto thee."

Therefore Saul said unto the LORD God of Israel, "Give a perfect lot." And Saul and Jonathan were taken: but the people escaped.

And Saul said, "Cast lots between me and Jonathan my son." And Jonathan was taken.

Then Saul said to Jonathan, "Tell me what thou hast done."

And Jonathan told him, and said, "I did but taste a little honey with the end of the rod that was in mine hand, and, lo, I must die."

And Saul answered, "God do so and more also: for thou shalt surely die, Jonathan."

And the people said unto Saul, "Shall Jonathan die, who hath wrought this great salvation in Israel? God forbid: as the LORD liveth, there shall not one hair of his head fall to the ground; for he hath wrought with God this day."

So the people rescued Jonathan, that he died not.

Then Saul went up from following the Philistines: and the Philistines went to their own place.

So Saul took the kingdom over Israel, and fought against all his enemies on every side, against Moab, and against the children of Ammon, and against Edom, and against the kings of Zobah, and against the Philistines: and whithersoever he turned himself, he vexed them. And he *Samuel denounces Saul* gathered an host, and smote the Amalekites, and delivered Israel out of the hands of them that spoiled them.

Now the sons of Saul were Jonathan, and Ishui, and Melchishua: and the names of his two daughters were these; the name of the firstborn Merab, and the name of the younger Michal: and the name of Saul's wife was Ahinoam, the daughter of Ahimaaz: and the name of the captain of his host was Abner, the son of Ner, Saul's uncle. And Kish was the father of Saul; and Ner the father of Abner was the son of Abiel. And there was sore war against the Philistines all the days of Saul: and when Saul saw any strong man, or any valiant man, he took him unto him. And Saul, and Jonathan his son, and the people that were present with them, abode in Gibeah of Benjamin.

Then came the word of the LORD unto Samuel, saying, "It repenteth me that I have set up Saul to be king: for he is turned back from following me, and hath not performed my commandments."

And it grieved Samuel; and he cried unto the LORD all night. And when Samuel rose early to meet Saul in the morning, it was told Samuel, saying, "Saul came to Carmel, and, behold, he set him up a place, and is gone about, and passed on, and gone down to Gilgal."

And Samuel came to Saul. Then Samuel said unto Saul, "Stay, and I will tell thee what the LORD hath said to me this night."

And he said unto him, "Say on."

And Samuel said, "When thou wast little in thine own sight, wast thou not made the head of the tribes of Israel, and the LORD anointed thee king over Israel? And the LORD sent thee on a journey, and said, 'Go and utterly destroy the sinners the Amalekites, and fight against them until they be consumed.' Wherefore then didst thou not obey the voice of the LORD, but didst fly upon the spoil, and didst evil in the sight of the LORD?"

And Saul said unto Samuel, "Yea, I have obeyed the voice of the LORD, and have gone the way which the LORD sent me, and have brought Agag the king of Amalek, and have utterly destroyed the Amalekites. But the people took of the spoil, sheep and oxen, the chief of the things which should have been utterly destroyed, to sacrifice unto the LORD thy God in Gilgal."

And Samuel said, "Hath the Lord as great delight in burnt offerings and sacrifices, as in obeying the voice of the Lord? Behold, to obey is better than sacrifice, and to hearken than the fat of rams. For rebellion is as the sin of witchcraft, and stubbornness is as iniquity and idolatry. Because thou hast rejected the word of the Lord, he hath also rejected thee from being king."

And Saul said unto Samuel, "I have sinned: for I have transgressed the commandment of the Lord, and thy words: because I feared the people, and obeyed their voice. Now therefore, I pray thee, pardon my sin, and turn again with me, that I may worship the Lord."

And Samuel said unto Saul, "I will not return with thee: for thou hast rejected the word of the Lord, and the Lord hath rejected thee from being king over Israel."

And as Samuel turned about to go away, he laid hold upon the skirt of his mantle, and it rent. And Samuel said unto him, "The Lord hath rent the kingdom of Israel from thee this day, and hath given it to a neighbour of thine, that is better than thou. And also the Strength of Israel will not lie nor repent: for he is not a man, that he should repent."

Then he said, "I have sinned: yet honour me now, I pray thee, before the elders of my people, and before Israel, and turn again with me, that I may worship the Lord thy God."

So Samuel turned again after Saul; and Saul worshipped the Lord. And Samuel came no more to see Saul until the day of his death: nevertheless Samuel mourned for Saul: and the Lord repented that he had made Saul king over Israel.

And the Lord said unto Samuel, "How long wilt thou mourn for Saul, seeing I have rejected him from reigning over Israel? fill thine horn with oil, and go, I will send thee to Jesse the Beth-lehemite: for I have provided me a king among his sons."

And Samuel did that which the Lord spake, and came to Beth-lehem. And the elders of the town trembled at his coming, and said, "Comest thou peaceably?"

And he said, "Peaceably: I am come to sacrifice unto the Lord: sanctify yourselves, and come with me to the sacrifice."

And he sanctified Jesse and his sons, and called them to the sacrifice.

And it came to pass, when they were come, that he looked on Eliab, and *Samuel anoints David* said, "Surely the LORD's anointed is before him."

But the LORD said unto Samuel, "Look not on his countenance, or on the height of his stature; because I have refused him: for the LORD seeth not as man seeth; for man looketh on the outward appearance, but the LORD looketh on the heart."

Jesse made his sons to pass before Samuel. And Samuel said unto Jesse, "The LORD hath not chosen these."

And Samuel said unto Jesse, "Are here all thy children?"

And he said, "There remaineth yet the youngest, and, behold, he keepeth the sheep."

And Samuel said unto Jesse, "Send and fetch him: for we will not sit down till he come hither."

And he sent, and brought him in. Now he was ruddy, and withal of a beautiful countenance, and goodly to look to.

And the LORD said, "Arise, anoint him: for this is he."

Then Samuel took the horn of oil, and anointed him in the midst of his brethren: and the Spirit of the LORD came upon David from that day forward. So Samuel rose up, and went to Ramah.

But the Spirit of the LORD departed from Saul, and an evil spirit from the LORD troubled him. And Saul's servants said unto him, "Behold now, an evil spirit from God troubleth thee. Let our lord now command thy servants, which are before thee, to seek out a man, who is a cunning player on an harp: and it shall come to pass, when the evil spirit from God is upon thee, that he shall play with his hand, and thou shalt be well."

And Saul said unto his servants, "Provide me now a man that can play well, and bring him to me."

Then answered one of the servants, and said, "Behold, I have seen a son of Jesse the Beth-lehemite, that is cunning in playing, and a mighty valiant man, and a man of war, and prudent in matters, and a comely person, and the LORD is with him."

Wherefore Saul sent messengers unto Jesse, and said, "Send me David thy son, which is with the sheep."

And Jesse took an ass laden with bread, and a bottle of wine, and a kid, and sent them by David his son unto Saul. And David came to Saul,

*Goliath's challenge* and stood before him: and he loved him greatly; and he became his armourbearer.

And Saul sent to Jesse, saying, "Let David, I pray thee, stand before me; for he hath found favour in my sight."

And it came to pass, when the evil spirit from God was upon Saul, that David took an harp, and played with his hand: so Saul was refreshed, and was well, and the evil spirit departed from him.

Now the Philistines gathered together their armies to battle, and were gathered together at Shochoh. And Saul and the men of Israel were gathered together, and pitched by the valley of Elah, and set the battle in array against the Philistines. And the Philistines stood on a mountain on the one side, and Israel stood on a mountain on the other side: and there was a valley between them.

And there went out a champion out of the camp of the Philistines, named Goliath, of Gath, whose height was six cubits and a span. And he had an helmet of brass upon his head, and he was armed with a coat of mail; and the weight of the coat was five thousand shekels of brass. And he had greaves of brass upon his legs, and a target of brass between his shoulders. And the staff of his spear was like a weaver's beam; and his spear's head weighed six hundred shekels of iron: and one bearing a shield went before him. And he stood and cried unto the armies of Israel, and said unto them, "Why are ye come out to set your battle in array? am not I a Philistine, and ye servants to Saul? choose you a man for you, and let him come down to me. If he be able to fight with me, and to kill me, then will we be your servants: but if I prevail against him, and kill him, then shall ye be our servants, and serve us."

And the Philistine said, "I defy the armies of Israel this day; give me a man, that we may fight together."

When Saul and all Israel heard those words of the Philistine, they were dismayed, and greatly afraid. The three eldest sons of Jesse went and followed Saul to the battle. But David went and returned from Saul to feed his father's sheep at Beth-lehem.

And Jesse said unto David his son, "Take now for thy brethren an ephah of this parched corn, and these ten loaves, and run to the camp to thy brethren; and carry these ten cheeses unto the captain of their thousand, and look how thy brethren fare, and take their pledge."

And David rose up early in the morning, and left the sheep with a *Goliath's challenge* keeper, and took, and went, as Jesse had commanded him; and he came to the trench, as the host was going forth to the fight, and shouted for the battle. For Israel and the Philistines had put the battle in array, army against army. And David left his carriage in the hand of the keeper of the carriage, and ran into the army, and came and saluted his brethren. And as he talked with them, behold, there came up the champion, the Philistine of Gath, Goliath by name, out of the armies of the Philistines, and spake according to the same words: and David heard them. And all the men of Israel, when they saw the man, fled from him, and were sore afraid.

And the men of Israel said, "Have ye seen this man that is come up? surely to defy Israel is he come up: and it shall be, that the man who killeth him, the king will enrich him with great riches, and will give him his daughter, and make his father's house free in Israel."

And David spake to the men that stood by him, saying, "What shall be done to the man that killeth this Philistine, and taketh away the reproach from Israel? for who is this Philistine, that he should defy the armies of the living God?"

And the people answered him after this manner, saying, "So shall it be done to the man that killeth him."

And Eliab his eldest brother heard when he spake unto the men; and Eliab's anger was kindled against David, and he said, "Why camest thou down hither? and with whom hast thou left those few sheep in the wilderness? I know thy pride, and the naughtiness of thine heart; for thou art come down that thou mightest see the battle."

And David said, "What have I now done? Is there not a cause?"

And he turned from him toward another, and spake after the same manner: and the people answered him again after the former manner. And when the words were heard which David spake, they rehearsed them before Saul: and he sent for him.

And David said to Saul, "Let no man's heart fail because of him; thy servant will go and fight with this Philistine."

And Saul said to David, "Thou art not able to go against this Philistine to fight with him: for thou art but a youth, and he a man of war from his youth."

*Goliath's challenge*  And David said unto Saul, "Thy servant kept his father's sheep, and there came a lion, and a bear, and took a lamb out of the flock: and I went out after him, and smote him, and delivered it out of his mouth: and when he arose against me, I caught him by his beard, and smote him, and slew him. Thy servant slew both the lion and the bear: and this Philistine shall be as one of them, seeing he hath defied the armies of the living God."

David said moreover, "The LORD that delivered me out of the paw of the lion, and out of the paw of the bear, he will deliver me out of the hand of this Philistine."

And Saul said unto David, "Go, and the LORD be with thee."

And Saul armed David with his armour, and he put an helmet of brass upon his head; also he armed him with a coat of mail. And David girded his sword upon his armour, and he assayed to go; for he had not proved it. And David said unto Saul, "I cannot go with these; for I have not proved them."

And David put them off him. And he took his staff in his hand, and chose him five smooth stones out of the brook, and put them in a shepherd's bag which he had, even in a scrip; and his sling was in his hand: and he drew near to the Philistine. And the Philistine came on and drew near unto David; and the man that bare the shield went before him. And when the Philistine looked about, and saw David, he disdained him: for he was but a youth, and ruddy, and of a fair countenance. And the Philistine said unto David, "Am I a dog, that thou comest to me with staves? Come to me, and I will give thy flesh unto the fowls of the air, and to the beasts of the field."

Then said David to the Philistine, "Thou comest to me with a sword, and with a spear, and with a shield: but I come to thee in the name of the LORD of hosts, the God of the armies of Israel, whom thou hast defied. This day will the LORD deliver thee into mine hand. The LORD saveth not with sword and spear: for the battle is the LORD's, and he will give you into our hands."

And it came to pass, when the Philistine arose, and came and drew nigh to meet David, that David hasted, and ran toward the army to meet the Philistine. And David put his hand in his bag, and took thence a stone, and slang it, and smote the Philistine in his forehead, that the

stone sunk into his forehead; and he fell upon his face to the earth. So  *David slays Goliath*
David prevailed over the Philistine with a sling and with a stone. And
when Saul saw David go forth against the Philistine, he said unto Abner,
the captain of the host, "Abner, whose son is this youth?"

And Abner said, "As thy soul liveth, O king, I cannot tell."

And the king said, "Enquire thou whose son the stripling is."

And as David returned from the slaughter of the Philistine, Abner
took him, and brought him before Saul.

And Saul said to him, "Whose son art thou, thou young man?"

And David answered, "I am the son of thy servant Jesse the Beth-
lehemite."

And it came to pass, when he had made an end of speaking unto
Saul, that the soul of Jonathan the son of Saul was knit with the soul of
David, and Jonathan loved him as his own soul. And Saul took him that
day, and would let him go no more home to his father's house. Then
Jonathan and David made a covenant, because he loved him as his own
soul. And Jonathan stripped himself of the robe that was upon him, and
gave it to David, and his garments, even to his sword, and to his bow,
and to his girdle.

And David went out whithersoever Saul sent him, and behaved himself wisely: and Saul set him over the men of war, and he was accepted
in the sight of all the people, and also in the sight of Saul's servants. And
it came to pass as they came, when David was returned from the slaughter
of the Philistine, that the women came out of all cities of Israel, singing
and dancing, to meet king Saul, with tabrets, with joy, and with instruments of musick. And the women answered one another as they played,
and said,

> Saul hath slain his thousands,
> And David his ten thousands.

And Saul was very wroth, and the saying displeased him; and he said,
"They have ascribed unto David ten thousands, and to me they have
ascribed but thousands: and what can he have more but the kingdom?"
And Saul eyed David from that day and forward. And it came to pass on
the morrow, that the evil spirit from God came upon Saul, and he prophesied in the midst of the house: and David played with his hand, as at

other times: and there was a javelin in Saul's hand. And Saul cast the javelin; for he said, "I will smite David even to the wall with it." And David avoided out of his presence twice. And Saul was afraid of David, because the LORD was with him, and was departed from Saul. Therefore Saul removed him from him, and made him his captain over a thousand; and he went out and came in before the people. And David behaved himself wisely in all his ways; and the LORD was with him. Wherefore when Saul saw that he behaved himself very wisely, he was afraid of him. But all Israel and Judah loved David, because he went out and came in before them. And Saul saw and knew that the LORD was with David, and that Michal Saul's daughter loved him. And Saul was yet the more afraid of David; and Saul became David's enemy continually.

Then the princes of the Philistines went forth: and it came to pass, after they went forth, that David behaved himself more wisely than all the servants of Saul; so that his name was much set by. And Saul spake to Jonathan his son, and to all his servants, that they should kill David.

But Jonathan Saul's son delighted much in David: and Jonathan told David, saying, "Saul my father seeketh to kill thee: now therefore, I pray thee, take heed to thyself until the morning, and abide in a secret place, and hide thyself: and I will go out and stand beside my father in the field where thou art, and I will commune with my father of thee; and what I see, that I will tell thee."

And Jonathan spake good of David unto Saul his father, and said unto him, "Let not the king sin against his servant, against David; because he hath not sinned against thee, and because his works have been to thee-ward very good: for he did put his life in his hand, and slew the Philistine, and the LORD wrought a great salvation for all Israel: thou sawest it, and didst rejoice: wherefore then wilt thou sin against innocent blood, to slay David without a cause?"

And Saul hearkened unto the voice of Jonathan: and Saul sware, "As the LORD liveth, he shall not be slain."

And Jonathan called David, and Jonathan shewed him all those things. And Jonathan brought David to Saul, and he was in his presence, as in times past. And the evil spirit from the LORD was upon Saul, as he sat in his house with his javelin in his hand: and David played with his hand. And Saul sought to smite David even to the wall with the javelin;

but he slipped away out of Saul's presence, and he smote the javelin into the wall: and David fled, and escaped that night.

Saul also sent messengers unto David's house, to watch him, and to slay him in the morning: and Michal David's wife told him, saying, "If thou save not thy life to night, to morrow thou shalt be slain."

So Michal let David down through a window: and he went, and fled, and escaped. And Michal took an image, and laid it in the bed, and put a pillow of goats' hair for his bolster, and covered it with a cloth. And when Saul sent messengers to take David, she said, "He is sick."

And Saul sent the messengers again to see David, saying, "Bring him up to me in the bed, that I may slay him."

And when the messengers were come in, behold, there was an image in the bed, with a pillow of goats' hair for his bolster.

And Saul said unto Michal, "Why hast thou deceived me so, and sent away mine enemy, that he is escaped?"

And Michal answered Saul, "He said unto me, 'Let me go; why should I kill thee?'"

So David fled, and escaped, and came to Samuel to Ramah, and told him all that Saul had done to him.

And David fled from Ramah, and came and said before Jonathan, "What have I done? what is mine iniquity? and what is my sin before thy father, that he seeketh my life?" And David sware moreover, and said, "Thy father certainly knoweth that I have found grace in thine eyes; and he saith, 'Let not Jonathan know this, lest he be grieved': but truly, as the LORD liveth, and as thy soul liveth, there is but a step between me and death."

Then said Jonathan unto David, "Whatsoever thy soul desireth, I will even do it for thee."

So Jonathan made a covenant with the house of David, saying, "Let the LORD even require it at the hand of David's enemies." And Jonathan caused David to swear again, because he loved him: for he loved him as he loved his own soul.

Then Jonathan said to David, "To morrow is the new moon: and thou shalt be missed, because thy seat will be empty. And when thou hast stayed three days, then thou shalt go down quickly, and come to the place where thou didst hide thyself when the business was in hand, and shalt remain by the stone Ezel. And I will shoot three arrows on the side thereof, as though I shot at a mark. And, behold, I will send a lad, saying, 'Go, find out the arrows.' If I expressly say unto the lad, 'Behold, the arrows are on this side of thee, take them'; then come thou: for there is peace to thee, and no hurt; as the LORD liveth. But if I say thus unto the young man, 'Behold, the arrows are beyond thee'; go thy way: for the LORD hath sent thee away. And as touching the matter which thou and I have spoken of, behold, the LORD be between thee and me for ever."

So David hid himself in the field: and when the new moon was come, the king sat him down to eat meat. And the king sat upon his seat, as at other times, even upon a seat by the wall: and Jonathan arose, and Abner sat by Saul's side, and David's place was empty. Nevertheless Saul spake not any thing that day: and it came to pass on the morrow, which was the second day of the month, that David's place was empty: and Saul said unto Jonathan his son, "Wherefore cometh not the son of Jesse to meat, neither yesterday, nor to day?"

And Jonathan answered Saul, "David earnestly asked leave of me to go to Beth-lehem: and he said, 'Let me go, I pray thee; for our family hath a sacrifice in the city; and my brother, he hath commanded me to be there: and now, if I have found favour in thine eyes, let me get away, I pray thee, and see my brethren.' Therefore he cometh not unto the king's table."

Then Saul's anger was kindled against Jonathan, and he said unto him, "For as long as the son of Jesse liveth upon the ground, thou shalt not be established, nor thy kingdom. Wherefore now send and fetch him unto me, for he shall surely die."

And Jonathan answered Saul his father, and said unto him, "Wherefore shall he be slain? what hath he done?"

And Saul cast a javelin at him to smite him: whereby Jonathan knew that it was determined of his father to slay David. So Jonathan arose from the table in fierce anger, and did eat no meat the second day of the month: for he was grieved for David, because his father had done him shame.

And it came to pass in the morning, that Jonathan went out into the field at the time appointed with David, and a little lad with him. And he said unto his lad, "Run, find out now the arrows which I shoot."

And as the lad ran, he shot an arrow beyond him. And when the lad was come to the place of the arrow which Jonathan had shot, Jonathan cried after the lad, and said, "Is not the arrow beyond thee?" And Jonathan cried after the lad, "Make speed, haste, stay not." *Parting of Jonathan and David*

And Jonathan's lad gathered up the arrows, and came to his master. But the lad knew not any thing: only Jonathan and David knew the matter. And Jonathan gave his artillery unto his lad, and said unto him, "Go, carry them to the city."

And as soon as the lad was gone, David arose out of a place toward the south, and fell on his face to the ground, and bowed himself three times: and they kissed one another, and wept one with another, until David exceeded. And Jonathan said to David, "Go in peace, forasmuch as we have sworn both of us in the name of the LORD, saying, 'The LORD be between me and thee, and between my seed and thy seed for ever.'"

And he arose and departed: and Jonathan went into the city. And David abode in the wilderness in strong holds, and remained in a mountain in the wilderness of Ziph. And Saul sought him every day, but God delivered him not into his hand. And David saw that Saul was come out to seek his life: and David was in the wilderness of Ziph in a wood. And Jonathan Saul's son arose, and went to David into the wood, and strengthened his hand in God. And he said unto him, "Fear not: for the hand of Saul my father shall not find thee; and thou shalt be king over Israel, and I shall be next unto thee; and that also Saul my father knoweth."

And they two made a covenant before the LORD: and David abode in the wood, and Jonathan went to his house.

But there came a messenger unto Saul, saying, "Haste thee, and come; for the Philistines have invaded the land."

Wherefore Saul returned from pursuing after David, and went against the Philistines.

And it came to pass, when Saul was returned from following the Philistines, that it was told him, saying, "Behold, David is in the wilderness of En-gedi."

Then Saul took three thousand chosen men out of all Israel, and went to seek David and his men upon the rocks of the wild goats. And he came to the sheepcotes by the way, where was a cave: and Saul went in to

*David spares Saul's life* cover his feet: and David and his men remained in the sides of the cave.

And the men of David said unto him, "Behold the day of which the LORD said unto thee, 'Behold, I will deliver thine enemy into thine hand, that thou mayest do to him as it shall seem good unto thee.' "

Then David arose, and cut off the skirt of Saul's robe privily. And it came to pass afterward, that David's heart smote him, because he had cut off Saul's skirt. And he said unto his men, "The LORD forbid that I should do this thing unto my master, the LORD's anointed, to stretch forth mine hand against him, seeing he is the anointed of the LORD."

So David stayed his servants with these words, and suffered them not to rise against Saul. But Saul rose up out of the cave, and went on his way. David also arose afterward, and went out of the cave, and cried after Saul, saying, "My lord the king."

And when Saul looked behind him, David stooped with his face to the earth, and bowed himself. And David said to Saul, "Wherefore hearest thou men's words, saying, 'Behold, David seeketh thy hurt?' Behold, this day thine eyes have seen how that the LORD had delivered thee to day into mine hand in the cave: and some bade me kill thee: but mine eye spared thee; and I said, 'I will not put forth mine hand against my lord; for he is the LORD's anointed.' Moreover, my father, see, yea, see the skirt of thy robe in my hand: for in that I cut off the skirt of thy robe, and killed thee not, know thou and see that there is neither evil nor transgression in mine hand, and I have not sinned against thee; yet thou huntest my soul to take it. The LORD judge between me and thee, and the LORD avenge me of thee: but mine hand shall not be upon thee. As saith the proverb of the ancients,

> Wickedness proceedeth from the wicked:
> But mine hand shall not be upon thee.

The LORD therefore be judge, and judge between me and thee, and see, and plead my cause, and deliver me out of thine hand."

And it came to pass, when David had made an end of speaking these words unto Saul, that Saul said, "Is this thy voice, my son David?"

And Saul lifted up his voice, and wept. And he said to David, "Thou art more righteous than I: for thou hast rewarded me good, whereas I have rewarded thee evil. And thou hast shewed this day how that thou hast dealt well with me: forasmuch as when the Lord had delivered me *Death of Samuel* into thine hand, thou killedst me not. For if a man find his enemy, will he let him go well away? wherefore the Lord reward thee good for that thou hast done unto me this day. And now, behold, I know well that thou shalt surely be king, and that the kingdom of Israel shall be established in thine hand. Swear now therefore unto me by the Lord that thou wilt not destroy my name out of my father's house."

And David sware unto Saul. And Saul went home; but David and his men gat them up unto the hold.

And Samuel died; and all the Israelites were gathered together, and lamented him, and buried him in his house at Ramah.

And David arose, and went down to the wilderness of Paran. And there was a man in Maon, whose possessions were in Carmel; and the man was very great, and he had three thousand sheep, and a thousand goats: and he was shearing his sheep in Carmel. Now the name of the man was Nabal, and the name of his wife Abigail: and she was a woman of good understanding, and of a beautiful countenance: but the man was churlish and evil in his doings. And David heard in the wilderness that Nabal did shear his sheep. And David sent out ten young men, and David said unto the young men, "Get you up to Carmel, and go to Nabal, and greet him in my name: and thus shall ye say to him that liveth in prosperity, 'Peace be both to thee, and peace be to thine house, and peace be unto all that thou hast. And now I have heard that thou hast shearers: now thy shepherds which were with us, we hurt them not, neither was there ought missing unto them, all the while they were in Carmel. Ask thy young men, and they will shew thee. Wherefore let the young men find favour in thine eyes: for we come in a good day: give, I pray thee, whatsoever cometh to thine hand unto thy servants, and to thy son David.' "

And when David's young men came, they spake to Nabal according to all those words in the name of David, and ceased. And Nabal answered David's servants, and said, "Who is David? and who is the son of Jesse? there be many servants now a days that break away every man from his master. Shall I then take my bread, and my water, and my flesh that I have killed for my shearers, and give it unto men, whom I know not whence they be?"

So David's young men turned their way, and went again, and came and told him all those sayings. And David said unto his men, "Gird ye on every man his sword."

And they girded on every man his sword; and David also girded on his sword: and there went up after David about four hundred men; and two hundred abode by the stuff.

But one of the young men told Abigail, Nabal's wife, saying, "Behold, David sent messengers out of the wilderness to salute our master; and he railed on them. But the men were very good unto us, and we were not hurt, neither missed we any thing, as long as we were conversant with them, when we were in the fields: they were a wall unto us both by night and day, all the while we were with them keeping the sheep. Now therefore know and consider what thou wilt do; for evil is determined against our master, and against all his household: for he is such a son of Belial, that a man cannot speak to him."

Then Abigail made haste, and took two hundred loaves, and two bottles of wine, and five sheep ready dressed, and five measures of parched corn, and an hundred clusters of raisins, and two hundred cakes of figs, and laid them on asses. And she said unto her servants, "Go on before me; behold, I come after you." But she told not her husband Nabal.

And it was so, as she rode on the ass, that she came down by the covert of the hill, and, behold, David and his men came down against her; and she met them.

Now David had said, "Surely in vain have I kept all that this fellow hath in the wilderness, so that nothing was missed of all that pertained unto him: and he hath requited me evil for good."

And when Abigail saw David, she hasted, and lighted off the ass, and fell before David on her face, and bowed herself to the ground, and fell at his feet, and said, "Upon me, my lord, upon me let this iniquity be: and let thine handmaid, I pray thee, speak in thine audience, and hear the words of thine handmaid. I pray thee, forgive the trespass of thine handmaid: for the LORD will certainly make my lord a sure house; because my lord fighteth the battles of the LORD, and evil hath not been found in thee all thy days. Yet a man is risen to pursue thee, and to seek thy soul: but the soul of my lord shall be bound in the bundle of life with the LORD thy God. And it shall come to pass, when the LORD shall have done to my lord according to all the good that he hath spoken concerning thee, and shall have appointed thee ruler over Israel; that this shall be no grief unto thee, nor offence of heart unto my lord: but when the LORD shall have dealt well with my lord, then remember thine handmaid."

And David said to Abigail, "Blessed be the LORD God of Israel, which sent thee this day to meet me: and blessed be thy advice, and blessed be thou, which hast kept me this day from coming to shed blood, and from avenging myself with mine own hand. For in very deed, as the LORD God of Israel liveth, which hath kept me back from hurting thee, except thou hadst hasted and come to meet me, surely there had not been any left unto Nabal by the morning light."

So David received of her hand that which she had brought him, and said unto her, "Go up in peace to thine house; see, I have hearkened to thy voice, and have accepted thy person."

And Abigail came to Nabal; and, behold, he held a feast in his house, like the feast of a king; and Nabal's heart was merry within him, for he was very drunken: wherefore she told him nothing, less or more, until the morning light. But it came to pass in the morning when his wife had told him these things, that his heart died within him, and he became as a stone. And it came to pass about ten days after, that the LORD smote Nabal, that he died. And when David heard that Nabal was dead, he sent and communed with Abigail, to take her to him to wife. And when the servants of David were come to Abigail to Carmel, they spake unto her, saying, "David sent us unto thee, to take thee to him to wife."

And she arose, and bowed herself on her face to the earth, and said, "Behold, let thine handmaid be a servant to wash the feet of the servants of my lord."

And Abigail hasted, and arose, and rode upon an ass, with five damsels of her's that went after her; and she went after the messengers of David, and became his wife.

And Saul pitched in the hill of Hachilah, which is before Jeshimon, by the way. But David abode in the wilderness, and he saw that Saul came after him into the wilderness. David therefore sent out spies, and understood that Saul was come in very deed. And David arose, and came

*Saul pursues David* to the place, where Saul had pitched: and David beheld the place where Saul lay, and Abner the son of Ner, the captain of his host: and Saul lay in the trench, and the people pitched round about him.

Then answered David, "Who will go down with me to Saul to the camp?"

And Abishai said, "I will go down with thee."

So David and Abishai came to the people by night: and, behold, Saul lay sleeping within the trench, and his spear stuck in the ground at his bolster: but Abner and the people lay round about him.

Then said Abishai to David, "God hath delivered thine enemy into thine hand this day: now therefore let me smite him, I pray thee, with the spear even to the earth at once, and I will not smite him the second time."

And David said to Abishai, "Destroy him not: for who can stretch forth his hand against the LORD's anointed, and be guiltless?"

David said furthermore, "As the LORD liveth, the LORD shall smite him; or his day shall come to die; or he shall descend into battle, and perish. The LORD forbid that I should stretch forth mine hand against the LORD's anointed: but, I pray thee, take thou now the spear that is at his bolster, and the cruse of water, and let us go."

So David took the spear and the cruse of water from Saul's bolster; and they gat them away, and no man saw it, nor knew it, neither awaked: for they were all asleep; because a deep sleep from the LORD was fallen upon them. Then David went over to the other side, and stood on the top of an hill afar off; a great space being between them. And David cried to the people, and to Abner the son of Ner, saying, "Answerest thou not, Abner?"

Then Abner answered and said, "Who art thou that criest to the king?"

And David said to Abner, "Art not thou a valiant man? and who is like to thee in Israel? wherefore then hast thou not kept thy lord the king? for there came one of the people in to destroy the king thy lord. This thing is not good that thou hast done. As the LORD liveth, ye are worthy to die, because ye have not kept your master, the LORD's anointed. And now see where the king's spear is, and the cruse of water that was at his bolster."

And Saul knew David's voice, and said, "Is this thy voice, my son *David dwells at Gath* David?"

And David said, "It is my voice, my lord, O king." And he said, "Wherefore doth my lord thus pursue after his servant? for what have I done? or what evil is in mine hand?"

Then said Saul, "I have sinned: return, my son David: for I will no more do thee harm, because my soul was precious in thine eyes this day: behold, I have played the fool, and have erred exceedingly."

And David answered and said, "Behold the king's spear! and let one of the young men come over and fetch it. The LORD render to every man his righteousness and his faithfulness: for the LORD delivered thee into my hand to day, but I would not stretch forth mine hand against the LORD's anointed. And, behold, as thy life was much set by this day in mine eyes, so let my life be much set by in the eyes of the LORD, and let him deliver me out of all tribulation."

Then Saul said to David, "Blessed be thou, my son David: thou shalt both do great things, and also shalt still prevail."

So David went on his way, and Saul returned to his place.

And David said in his heart, "I shall now perish one day by the hand of Saul: there is nothing better for me than that I should speedily escape into the land of the Philistines; and Saul shall despair of me, to seek me any more in any coast of Israel: so shall I escape out of his hand."

And David arose, and he passed over with the six hundred men that were with him. And it was told Saul that David was fled to Gath: and he sought no more again for him. And the time that David dwelt in the country of the Philistines was a full year and four months.

And it came to pass in those days, that the Philistines gathered their armies together for warfare, to fight with Israel.

And Achish said unto David, "Know thou assuredly, that thou shalt go out with me to battle, thou and thy men."

And David said to Achish, "Surely thou shalt know what thy servant can do."

And Achish said to David, "Therefore will I make thee keeper of mine head for ever."

Now the Philistines gathered together all their armies to Aphek: and the Israelites pitched by a fountain which is in Jezreel. And the lords of the Philistines passed on by hundreds, and by thousands: but David and his men passed on in the rereward with Achish.

Then said the princes of the Philistines, "What do these Hebrews here?"

Then Achish called David, and said unto him, "Surely, as the LORD liveth, thou hast been upright, and thy going out and thy coming in with me in the host is good in my sight: for I have not found evil in thee since the day of thy coming unto me unto this day: nevertheless the lords favour thee not. Wherefore now return, and go in peace, that thou displease not the lords of the Philistines. The princes of the Philistines have said, 'He shall not go up with us to the battle.' Wherefore now rise up early in the morning with thy master's servants that are come with thee: and as soon as ye be up early in the morning, and have light, depart."

So David and his men rose up early to depart in the morning, to return into the land of the Philistines. And the Philistines went up to Jezreel.

And David came to the two hundred men, which were so faint that they could not follow David, whom they had made also to abide at the brook Besor: and they went forth to meet David, and to meet the people that were with him: and when David came near to the people, he saluted them. Then answered all the wicked men and men of Belial, of those that went with David, and said, "Because they went not with us, we will not give them ought of the spoil that we have recovered, save to every man his wife and his children, that they may lead them away, and depart."

Then said David, "Ye shall not do so, my brethren, with that which the LORD hath given us, who hath preserved us, and delivered the company that came against us into our hand. For who will hearken unto you in this matter? but as his part is that goeth down to the battle, so shall his part be that tarrieth by the stuff: they shall part alike."

And it was so from that day forward, that he made it a statute and an ordinance for Israel unto this day.

Now Samuel was dead, and all Israel had lamented him, and buried him in Ramah, even in his own city. And Saul had put away those that had familiar spirits, and the wizards, out of the land. And the Philistines gathered themselves together, and came and pitched in Shunem: and Saul gathered all Israel together, and they pitched in Gilboa. And when

Saul saw the host of the Philistines, he was afraid, and his heart greatly trembled. And when Saul enquired of the LORD, the LORD answered him not, neither by dreams, nor by Urim, nor by prophets.

Then said Saul unto his servants, "Seek me a woman that hath a familiar spirit, that I may go to her, and enquire of her."

And his servants said to him, "Behold, there is a woman that hath a familiar spirit at En-dor."

And Saul disguised himself, and put on other raiment, and he went, and two men with him, and they came to the woman by night: and he said, "I pray thee, divine unto me by the familiar spirit, and bring me him up, whom I shall name unto thee."

And the woman said unto him, "Behold, thou knowest what Saul hath done, how he hath cut off those that have familiar spirits, and the wizards, out of the land: wherefore then layest thou a snare for my life, to cause me to die?"

And Saul sware to her by the LORD saying, "As the LORD liveth, there shall no punishment happen to thee for this thing."

Then said the woman, "Whom shall I bring up unto thee?"

And he said, "Bring me up Samuel."

And when the woman saw Samuel, she cried with a loud voice: and the woman spake to Saul, saying, "Why hast thou deceived me? for thou art Saul."

And the king said unto her, "Be not afraid: for what sawest thou?"

And the woman said unto Saul, "I saw gods ascending out of the earth."

And he said unto her, "What form is he of?"

And she said, "An old man cometh up; and he is covered with a mantle."

And Saul perceived that it was Samuel, and he stooped with his face to the ground, and bowed himself.

And Samuel said to Saul, "Why hast thou disquieted me, to bring me up?"

And Saul answered, "I am sore distressed; for the Philistines make war against me, and God is departed from me, and answereth me no more, neither by prophets, nor by dreams: therefore I have called thee, that thou mayest make known unto me what I shall do."

Then said Samuel, "Wherefore then dost thou ask of me? for the LORD hath rent the kingdom out of thine hand, and given it to thy neighbour, even to David: because thou obeyedst not the voice of the LORD. Moreover the LORD will also deliver Israel with thee into the hand of the Philistines: and to morrow shalt thou and thy sons be with me: the LORD also shall deliver the host of Israel into the hand of the Philistines."

Then Saul fell straightway all along on the earth, and was sore afraid, because of the words of Samuel: and there was no strength in him; for he had eaten no bread all the day, nor all the night.

And the woman came unto Saul, and saw that he was sore troubled, and said unto him, "Behold, thine handmaid hath obeyed thy voice, and I have put my life in my hand, and have hearkened unto thy words which thou spakest unto me. Now therefore, I pray thee, hearken thou also unto the voice of thine handmaid, and let me set a morsel of bread before thee; and eat, that thou mayest have strength, when thou goest on thy way."

But he refused, and said, "I will not eat."

But his servants, together with the woman, compelled him; and he hearkened unto their voice. So he arose from the earth, and sat upon the bed. And the woman had a fat calf in the house; and she hasted, and killed it, and took flour, and kneaded it, and did bake unleavened bread thereof: and she brought it before Saul, and before his servants; and they did eat. Then they rose up, and went away that night. Now the Philistines fought against Israel: and the men of Israel fled from before the Philistines, and fell down slain. And the Philistines followed hard upon Saul and upon his sons; and the Philistines slew Jonathan, and Abinadab, and Melchishua, Saul's sons. And the battle went sore against Saul, and the archers hit him; and he was sore wounded of the archers. Then said Saul unto his armourbearer, "Draw thy sword, and thrust me through therewith."

But his armourbearer would not; for he was sore afraid. Therefore Saul took a sword, and fell upon it. And when his armourbearer saw that Saul was dead, he fell likewise upon his sword, and died with him. So Saul died, and his three sons, and his armourbearer, and all his men, that same day together. And when the men of Israel that were on the other side of the valley, and they that were on the other side Jordan, saw that David's lamentation the men of Israel fled, and that Saul and his sons were dead, they forsook the cities, and fled; and the Philistines came and dwelt in them.

It came even to pass on the third day, that, behold, a man came out of the camp from Saul with his clothes rent, and earth upon his head: and so it was, when he came to David, that he fell to the earth, and did obeisance.

And David said unto him, "From whence comest thou?"

And he said unto him, "Out of the camp of Israel am I escaped."

And David said unto him, "How went the matter? I pray thee, tell me."

And he answered, "The people are fled from the battle, and many of the people also are fallen and dead; and Saul and Jonathan his son are dead also."

And David lamented with this lamentation over Saul and over Jonathan his son:

The beauty of Israel is slain upon thy high places:
How are the mighty fallen!
Tell it not in Gath,
Publish it not in the streets of Askelon;
Lest the daughters of the Philistines rejoice,
Lest the daughters of the uncircumcised triumph.
Ye mountains of Gilboa,
Let there be no dew, neither let there be rain, upon you, nor fields of
　　offerings:
For there the shield of the mighty is vilely cast away.
The shield of Saul, as though he had not been anointed with oil.
From the blood of the slain, from the fat of the mighty,
The bow of Jonathan turned not back,
And the sword of Saul returned not empty.
Saul and Jonathan were lovely and pleasant in their lives,
And in their death they were not divided:
They were swifter than eagles,
They were stronger than lions.

Ye daughters of Israel, weep over Saul,
Who clothed you in scarlet, with other delights,
Who put on ornaments of gold upon your apparel.
How are the mighty fallen in the midst of the battle!
O Jonathan, thou wast slain in thine high places.
I am distressed for thee, my brother Jonathan:
Very pleasant hast thou been unto me:
Thy love to me was wonderful,
Passing the love of women.
How are the mighty fallen,
And the weapons of war perished!

And it came to pass after this, that David enquired of the LORD, saying, "Shall I go up into any of the cities of Judah?"

And the LORD said unto him, "Go up."

And David said, "Whither shall I go up?"

And he said, "Unto Hebron."

So David went up thither. And his men that were with him did David bring up, every man with his household: and they dwelt in the cities of Hebron. And the men of Judah came, and there they anointed David king over the house of Judah.

But Abner the son of Ner, captain of Saul's host, took Ish-bosheth the son of Saul, and brought him over to Mahanaim; and made him king over Gilead. Ish-bosheth Saul's son was forty years old when he began to reign over Israel, and reigned two years. But the house of Judah followed David. And the time that David was king in Hebron over the house of Judah was seven years and six months. Now there was long war between the house of Saul and the house of David: but David waxed stronger and stronger, and the house of Saul waxed weaker and weaker. And unto David were sons born in Hebron: the third, Absalom.

Then came all the tribes of Israel to David unto Hebron, and spake, saying, "Behold, we are thy bone and thy flesh. Also in time past, when Saul was king over us, thou wast he that leddest out and broughtest in Israel: and the LORD said to thee, 'Thou shalt feed my people Israel, and thou shalt be a captain over Israel.' "

So all the elders of Israel came to the king to Hebron; and king David made a league with them in Hebron before the LORD: and they anointed David king over Israel.

*The ark brought to Jerusalem*

David was thirty years old when he began to reign, and he reigned forty years. In Hebron he reigned over Judah seven years and six months: and in Jerusalem he reigned thirty and three years over all Israel and Judah. Nevertheless, David took the strong hold of Zion: the same is the city of David. So David dwelt in the fort, and called it the city of David. And David built round about from Millo and inward. And David went on, and grew great, and the LORD God of hosts was with him. And Hiram king of Tyre sent messengers to David, and cedar trees, and carpenters, and masons: and they built David an house. And David perceived that the LORD had established him king over Israel, and that he had exalted his kingdom for his people Israel's sake.

Again, David gathered together all the chosen men of Israel, thirty thousand. And David arose, and went with all the people that were with him from Baale of Judah, to bring up from thence the ark of God, whose name is called by the name of the LORD of hosts that dwelleth between the cherubims. And they set the ark of God upon a new cart, and brought it out of the house of Abinadab that was in Gibeah: and Uzzah and Ahio, the sons of Abinadab, drave the new cart. And they brought it out of the house of Abinadab which was at Gibeah, accompanying the ark of God: and Ahio went before the ark. And David and all the house of Israel played before the LORD on all manner of instruments made of fir wood, even on harps, and on psalteries, and on timbrels, and on cornets, and on cymbals. So David went and brought up the ark of God into the city of David with gladness.

And it was so, that when they that bare the ark of the LORD had gone six paces, he sacrificed oxen and fatlings. And David danced before the LORD with all his might; and David was girded with a linen ephod. So David and all the house of Israel brought up the ark of the LORD with shouting, and with the sound of the trumpet. And they brought in the ark of the LORD, and set it in his place, in the midst of the tabernacle that David had pitched for it. And as soon as David had made an end of offering burnt offerings, and peace offerings, he blessed the people in the name of the LORD of hosts. And he dealt among all the people, even among the whole multitude of Israel, as well to the women as men, to every

*David forbidden to build
the temple*

one a cake of bread, and a good piece of flesh, and a flagon of wine. So all the people departed every one to his house. Then David returned to bless his household.

And it came to pass, when the king sat in his house, and the LORD had given him rest round about from all his enemies; that the king said unto Nathan the prophet, "See now, I dwell in an house of cedar, but the ark of God dwelleth within curtains."

And Nathan said to the king, "Go, do all that is in thine heart; for the LORD is with thee."

And it came to pass that night, that the word of the LORD came unto Nathan, saying, "Go and tell my servant David, 'Thus saith the LORD, Shalt thou build me an house for me to dwell in? Whereas I have not dwelt in any house since the time that I brought up the children of Israel out of Egypt, even to this day, but have walked in a tent and in a tabernacle. In all the places wherein I have walked with all the children of Israel spake I a word with any of the tribes of Israel, whom I commanded to feed my people Israel, saying, Why build ye not me an house of cedar? Now therefore so shalt thou say unto my servant David, 'Thus saith the LORD of hosts, I took thee from the sheepcote, from following the sheep, to be ruler over my people, over Israel: and I was with thee whithersoever thou wentest, and have cut off all thine enemies out of thy sight, and have made thee a great name, like unto the name of the great men that are in the earth. Moreover I will appoint a place for my people Israel, and will plant them, that they may dwell in a place of their own, and move no more; neither shall the children of wickedness afflict them any more, as beforetime, and as since the time that I commanded judges to be over my people Israel, and have caused thee to rest from all thine enemies.' Also the LORD telleth thee that he will make thee an house. He shall build an house for my name, and I will stablish the throne of his kingdom for ever. I will be his father, and he shall be my son. If he commit iniquity, I will chasten him with the rod of men, and with the stripes of the children of men: but my mercy shall not depart away from him, as I took it from Saul, whom I put away before thee. And thine house and thy kingdom shall be established for ever before thee: thy throne shall be established for ever."

According to all these words, and according to all this vision, so did

Nathan speak unto David. Then went king David in, and sat before the *David's prayerful*
LORD, and he said, "Who am I, O Lord GOD? and what is my house, that *submission*
thou hast brought me hitherto? And this was yet a small thing in thy
sight, O Lord GOD; but thou hast spoken also of thy servant's house for
a great while to come. And is this the manner of man, O Lord GOD? And
what can David say more unto thee? for thou, Lord GOD, knowest thy
servant. For thy word's sake, and according to thine own heart, hast thou
done all these great things, to make thy servant know them. Wherefore
thou art great, O LORD God: for there is none like thee, neither is there
any God beside thee, according to all that we have heard with our ears.
And what one nation in the earth is like thy people, even like Israel, whom
God went to redeem for a people to himself, and to make him a name,
and to do for you great things and terrible, for thy land, before thy people, which thou redeemedst to thee from Egypt, from the nations and
their gods? For thou hast confirmed to thyself thy people Israel to be a
people unto thee for ever: and thou, LORD, art become their God. And
now, O LORD God, the word that thou hast spoken concerning thy servant, and concerning his house, establish it for ever, and do as thou hast
said. And let thy name be magnified for ever, saying, 'The LORD of hosts
is the God over Israel': and let the house of thy servant David be established before thee. For thou, O LORD of hosts, God of Israel, hast revealed to thy servant, saying, 'I will build thee an house': therefore hath
thy servant found in his heart to pray this prayer unto thee. And now,
O Lord GOD, thou art that God, and thy words be true, and thou hast
promised this goodness unto thy servant: therefore now let it please thee
to bless the house of thy servant, that it may continue for ever before
thee: for thou, O Lord GOD, hast spoken it: and with thy blessing let the
house of thy servant be blessed for ever."

And the LORD preserved David whithersoever he went. And David
reigned over all Israel; and David executed judgment and justice unto
all his people.

And David said, "Is there yet any that is left of the house of Saul,
that I may shew him kindness for Jonathan's sake?"

And there was of the house of Saul a servant whose name was Ziba.
And when they had called him unto David, the king said unto him, "Art
thou Ziba?"

And he said, "Thy servant is he."

And the king said, "Is there not yet any of the house of Saul, that I may shew the kindness of God unto him?"

And Ziba said unto the king, "Jonathan hath yet a son, which is lame on his feet."

And the king said unto him, "Where is he?"

And Ziba said unto the king, "Behold, he is in the house of Machir."

Then king David sent, and fetched him out of the house of Machir.

Now when Mephibosheth, the son of Jonathan, the son of Saul, was come unto David, he fell on his face, and did reverence.

And David said, "Mephibosheth."

And he answered, "Behold thy servant!"

And David said unto him, "Fear not: for I will surely shew thee kindness for Jonathan thy father's sake, and will restore thee all the land of Saul thy father; and thou shalt eat bread at my table continually."

And he bowed himself, and said, "What is thy servant, that thou shouldest look upon such a dead dog as I am?"

Then the king called to Ziba, Saul's servant, and said unto him, "I have given unto thy master's son all that pertained to Saul and to all his house. Thou therefore, and thy sons, and thy servants, shall till the land for him, and thou shalt bring in the fruits, that thy master's son may have food to eat: but Mephibosheth thy master's son shall eat bread alway at my table."

Now Ziba had fifteen sons and twenty servants. Then said Ziba unto the king, "According to all that my lord the king hath commanded his servant, so shall thy servant do."

"As for Mephibosheth," said the king, "he shall eat at my table, as one of the king's sons."

And Mephibosheth had a young son, whose name was Micha. And all that dwelt in the house of Ziba were servants unto Mephibosheth. So Mephibosheth dwelt in Jerusalem: for he did eat continually at the king's table; and was lame on both his feet.

When the wife of Uriah the Hittite heard that Uriah her husband was dead, she mourned for her husband. And when the mourning was past, David sent and fetched her to his house, and she became his wife, and bare him a son.

And the LORD sent Nathan unto David. And he came unto him, and *Nathan rebukes David* said unto him, "There were two men in one city; the one rich, and the other poor. The rich man had exceeding many flocks and herds: but the poor man had nothing, save one little ewe lamb, which he had bought and nourished up: and it grew up together with him, and with his children; it did eat of his own meat, and drank of his own cup, and lay in his bosom, and was unto him as a daughter. And there came a traveller unto the rich man, and he spared to take of his own flock and of his own herd, to dress for the wayfaring man that was come unto him; but took the poor man's lamb, and dressed it for the man that was come to him."

And David's anger was greatly kindled against the man; and he said to Nathan, "As the LORD liveth, the man that hath done this thing shall surely die: and he shall restore the lamb fourfold, because he did this thing, and because he had no pity."

And Nathan said to David, "Thou art the man. Thus saith the LORD God of Israel, 'I anointed thee king over Israel, and I delivered thee out of the hand of Saul; wherefore hast thou despised the commandment of the LORD, to do evil in his sight? thou hast killed Uriah the Hittite with the sword, and hast taken his wife to be thy wife, and hast slain him with the sword of the children of Ammon. Now therefore the sword shall never depart from thine house; because thou hast despised me, and hast taken the wife of Uriah the Hittite to be thy wife.' "

And David said unto Nathan, "I have sinned against the LORD."

And Nathan departed unto his house. And the child that Uriah's wife bare unto David was very sick. David therefore besought God for the child; and David fasted, and went in, and lay all night upon the earth. And the elders of his house arose, and went to him, to raise him up from the earth: but he would not, neither did he eat bread with them. And it came to pass on the seventh day, that the child died. And the servants of David feared to tell him that the child was dead: for they said, "Behold, while the child was yet alive, we spake unto him, and he would not hearken unto our voice: how will he then vex himself, if we tell him that the child is dead?"

But when David saw that his servants whispered, David perceived that the child was dead: therefore David said unto his servants, "Is the child dead?"

*Birth of Solomon*    And they said, "He is dead."

Then David arose from the earth, and washed, and anointed himself, and changed his apparel, and came into the house of the LORD, and worshipped: then he came to his own house; and when he required, they set bread before him, and he did eat.

Then said his servants unto him, "What thing is this that thou hast done? thou didst fast and weep for the child, while it was alive; but when the child was dead, thou didst rise and eat bread."

And he said, "While the child was yet alive, I fasted and wept: for I said, 'Who can tell whether GOD will be gracious to me, that the child may live?' But now he is dead, wherefore should I fast? can I bring him back again? I shall go to him, but he shall not return to me."

And David comforted Bath-sheba his wife, and she bare a son, and he called his name Solomon: and the LORD loved him.

But in all Israel there was none to be so much praised as Absalom for his beauty: from the sole of his foot even to the crown of his head there was no blemish in him. And it came to pass, that Absalom prepared him chariots and horses, and fifty men to run before him. And Absalom rose up early, and stood beside the way of the gate: and it was so, that when any man that had a controversy came to the king for judgment, then Absalom called unto him, and said "Of what city art thou?"

And he said, "Thy servant is of one of the tribes of Israel."

And Absalom said unto him, "See, thy matters are good and right; but there is no man deputed of the king to hear thee." Absalom said moreover, "Oh that I were made judge in the land, that every man which hath any suit or cause might come unto me, and I would do him justice!"

And it was so, that when any man came nigh to him to do him obeisance, he put forth his hand, and took him, and kissed him. And on this manner did Absalom to all Israel that came to the king for judgment: so Absalom stole the hearts of the men of Israel.

And it came to pass after forty years, that Absalom said unto the king, "I pray thee, let me go and pay my vow, which I have vowed unto the LORD, in Hebron. For thy servant vowed a vow while I abode at Geshur in Syria, saying, 'If the LORD shall bring me again indeed to Jerusalem, then I will serve the LORD.' "

And the king said unto him, "Go in peace." So he arose, and went to *Return of the ark*
Hebron.

But Absalom sent spies throughout all the tribes of Israel, saying, "As soon as ye hear the sound of the trumpet, then ye shall say, 'Absalom reigneth in Hebron.'"

And with Absalom went two hundred men out of Jerusalem, that were called; and they went in their simplicity, and they knew not any thing. And the conspiracy was strong; for the people increased continually with Absalom.

And David said unto all his servants that were with him at Jerusalem, "Arise, and let us flee; for we shall not else escape from Absalom: make speed to depart, lest he overtake us suddenly, and bring evil upon us, and smite the city with the edge of the sword."

And the king's servants said unto the king, "Behold, thy servants are ready to do whatsoever my lord the king shall appoint."

And the king went forth, and all his household after him. And the king left ten women to keep the house. And the king went forth, and all the people after him, and tarried in a place that was far off. And all the country wept with a loud voice, and all the people passed over: the king also himself passed over the brook Kidron, and all the people passed over, toward the way of the wilderness. And all the Levites were with him, bearing the ark of the covenant of God: and they set down the ark of God.

And the king said, "Carry back the ark of God into the city: if I shall find favour in the eyes of the LORD, he will bring me again, and shew me both it, and his habitation: but if he thus say, 'I have no delight in thee'; behold, here am I, let him do to me as seemeth good unto him. See, I will tarry in the plain of the wilderness, until there come word from you to certify me."

They carried the ark of God again to Jerusalem: and they tarried there. And David went up by the ascent of mount Olivet, and wept as he went up, and had his head covered, and he went barefoot: and all the people that was with him covered every man his head, and they went up, weeping as they went up. And when David was a little past the top of the hill, behold, Ziba the servant of Mephibosheth met him with a couple of

*Absalom is slain* asses saddled, and upon them two hundred loaves of bread, and an hundred bunches of raisins, and an hundred of summer fruits, and a bottle of wine.

And the king said unto Ziba, "What meanest thou by these?"

And Ziba said, "The asses be for the king's household to ride on; and the bread and summer fruit for the young men to eat; and the wine, that such as be faint in the wilderness may drink."

And the king said, "And where is thy master's son?"

And Ziba said unto the king, "Behold, he abideth at Jerusalem: for he said, 'To day shall the house of Israel restore me the kingdom of my father.'"

And the king, and all the people that were with him, came weary, and refreshed themselves there.

So Israel and Absalom pitched in the land of Gilead. And it came to pass, when David was come to Mahanaim, that they brought beds, and basons, and earthen vessels, and wheat, and barley, and flour, and parched corn, and beans, and lentiles, and parched pulse, and honey, and butter, and sheep, and cheese of kine, for David, and for the people that were with him, to eat: for they said, "The people is hungry, and weary, and thirsty, in the wilderness."

And the king stood by the gate side, and all the people came out by hundreds and by thousands. And the king commanded Joab and Abishai and Ittai, saying, "Deal gently for my sake with the young man, even with Absalom."

And all the people heard when the king gave all the captains charge concerning Absalom. So the people went out into the field against Israel: and the battle was in the wood of Ephraim. And Absalom met the servants of David. And Absalom rode upon a mule, and the mule went under the thick boughs of a great oak, and his head caught hold of the oak, and he was taken up between the heaven and the earth; and the mule that was under him went away. And a certain man saw it, and told Joab, and said, "Behold, I saw Absalom hanged in an oak."

And Joab blew the trumpet, and the people returned from pursuing after Israel: for Joab held back the people.

Then said Ahimaaz the son of Zadok, "Let me now run, and bear the king tidings, how that the LORD hath avenged him of his enemies."

And Joab said unto him, "Thou shalt not bear tidings this day, but *Absalom is slain* thou shalt bear tidings another day: but this day thou shalt bear no tidings, because the king's son is dead."

Then said Joab to Cushi, "Go tell the king what thou hast seen."

And Cushi bowed himself unto Joab, and ran.

Then said Ahimaaz the son of Zadok yet again to Joab, "But howsoever, let me, I pray thee, also run after Cushi."

And Joab said, "Wherefore wilt thou run, my son, seeing that thou hast no tidings ready?"

"But howsoever," said he, "let me run."

And he said unto him, "Run." Then Ahimaaz ran by the way of the plain, and overran Cushi.

And David sat between the two gates: and the watchman went up to the roof over the gate unto the wall, and lifted up his eyes, and looked, and behold a man running alone. And the watchman cried, and told the king.

And the king said, "If he be alone, there is tidings in his mouth."

And he came apace, and drew near. And the watchman saw another man running: and the watchman called unto the porter, and said, "Behold another man running alone."

And the king said, "He also bringeth tidings."

And the watchman said, "Me thinketh the running of the foremost is like the running of Ahimaaz the son of Zadok."

And the king said, "He is a good man, and cometh with good tidings."

And Ahimaaz called, and said unto the king, "All is well."

And he fell down to the earth upon his face before the king, and said, "Blessed be the Lord thy God, which hath delivered up the men that lifted up their hand against my lord the king."

And the king said, "Is the young man Absalom safe?"

And Ahimaaz answered, "When Joab sent the king's servant, and me thy servant, I saw a great tumult, but I knew not what it was."

And the king said unto him, "Turn aside, and stand here." And he turned aside, and stood still.

And, behold, Cushi came; and Cushi said, "Tidings, my lord the king: for the Lord hath avenged thee this day of all them that rose up against thee."

[ 171 ]

*David's lament*   And the king said unto Cushi, "Is the young man Absalom safe?"

And Cushi answered, "The enemies of my lord the king, and all that rise against thee to do thee hurt, be as that young man is."

And the king was much moved, and went up to the chamber over the gate, and wept: and as he went, thus he said, "O my son Absalom, my son, my son Absalom! Would God I had died for thee, O Absalom, my son, my son!"

And it was told Joab, "Behold, the king weepeth and mourneth for Absalom."

And the victory that day was turned into mourning unto all the people: for the people heard say that day how the king was grieved for his son. And the people gat them by stealth that day into the city, as people being ashamed steal away when they flee in battle. But the king covered his face, and the king cried with a loud voice, "O my son Absalom, O Absalom, my son, my son!"

And Joab came into the house to the king, and said, "Thou hast shamed this day the faces of all thy servants, which this day have saved thy life; in that thou lovest thine enemies, and hatest thy friends. For thou hast declared this day, that thou regardest neither princes nor servants: for this day I perceive, that if Absalom had lived, and all we had died this day, then it had pleased thee well. Now therefore arise, go forth, and speak comfortably unto thy servants: for I swear by the LORD, if thou go not forth, there will not tarry one with thee this night: and that will be worse unto thee than all the evil that befell thee from thy youth until now."

Then the king arose, and sat in the gate. And they told unto all the people, saying, "Behold, the king doth sit in the gate."

And all the people came before the king: for Israel had fled every man to his tent. And all the people were at strife throughout all the tribes of Israel, saying, "The king saved us out of the hand of our enemies, and he delivered us out of the hand of the Philistines; and now he is fled out of the land for Absalom."

And he bowed the heart of all the men of Judah, even as the heart of one man; so that they sent this word unto the king, "Return thou, and all thy servants."

So the king returned, and came to Jordan. And Judah came to

Gilgal, to go to meet the king, to conduct the king over Jordan. And there *David's last song* went over a ferry boat to carry over the king's household, and to do what he thought good.

Now Barzillai was a very aged man, even fourscore years old: and he had provided the king of sustenance while he lay at Mahanaim; for he was a very great man. And the king said unto Barzillai, "Come thou over with me, and I will feed thee with me in Jerusalem."

And Barzillai said unto the king, "How long have I to live, that I should go up with the king unto Jerusalem? I am this day fourscore years old: and can I discern between good and evil? can thy servant taste what I eat or what I drink? can I hear any more the voice of singing men and singing women? wherefore then should thy servant be yet a burden unto my lord the king? Thy servant will go a little way over Jordan with the king: and why should the king recompense it me with such a reward? Let thy servant, I pray thee, turn back again, that I may die in mine own city, and be buried by the grave of my father and of my mother. But behold thy servant Chimham; let him go over with my lord the king; and do to him what shall seem good unto thee."

And the king answered, "Chimham shall go over with me, and I will do to him that which shall seem good unto thee: and whatsoever thou shalt require of me, that will I do for thee."

And all the people went over Jordan. And when the king was come over, the king kissed Barzillai, and blessed him; and he returned unto his own place. Then the king went on to Gilgal, and Chimham went on with him: and all the people of Judah conducted the king, and also half the people of Israel. And David came to his house at Jerusalem.

Now these be the last words of David.

> David the son of Jesse said,
> And the man who was raised up on high,
> The anointed of the God of Jacob,
> And the sweet psalmist of Israel, said,
> The Spirit of the LORD spake by me,
> And his word was in my tongue.
> The God of Israel said,
> The Rock of Israel spake to me,

*David's offerings in the temple*

He that ruleth over men must be just, ruling in the fear of God.
And he shall be as the light of the morning, when the sun riseth,
Even a morning without clouds;
As the tender grass springing out of the earth by clear shining after
    rain.
Although my house be not so with God;
Yet he hath made with me an everlasting covenant,
Ordered in all things, and sure:
For this is all my salvation, and all my desire,
Although he make it not to grow.

Furthermore David the king said unto all the congregation, "Solomon my son, whom alone God hath chosen, is yet young and tender, and the work is great: for the palace is not for man, but for the LORD God. Now I have prepared with all my might for the house of my God the gold for things to be made of gold, and the silver for things of silver, and the brass for things of brass, the iron for things of iron, and wood for things of wood; onyx stones, and stones to be set, glistering stones, and of divers colours, and all manner of precious stones, and marble stones in abundance. Moreover, because I have set my affection to the house of my God, I have of mine own proper good, of gold and silver, which I have given to the house of my God, over and above all that I have prepared for the holy house, even three thousand talents of gold, of the gold of Ophir, and seven thousand talents of refined silver, to overlay the walls of the houses withal: the gold for things of gold, and the silver for things of silver, and for all manner of work to be made by the hands of artificers. And who then is willing to consecrate his service this day unto the LORD?"

Then the chief of the fathers and princes of the tribes of Israel, and the captains of thousands and of hundreds, with the rulers of the king's work, offered willingly, and gave for the service of the house of God of gold five thousand talents and ten thousand drams, and of silver ten thousand talents, and of brass eighteen thousand talents, and one hundred thousand talents of iron. And they with whom precious stones were found gave them to the treasure of the house of the LORD, by the hand of Jehiel the Gershonite. Then the people rejoiced, for that they

offered willingly, because with perfect heart they offered willingly to the
LORD: and David the king also rejoiced with great joy.

Wherefore David blessed the LORD before all the congregation: and David said, "Blessed be thou, LORD God of Israel our father, for ever and ever. Thine, O LORD, is the greatness, and the power, and the glory, and the victory, and the majesty: for all that is in the heaven and in the earth is thine; thine is the kingdom, O LORD, and thou art exalted as head above all. Both riches and honour come of thee, and thou reignest over all; and in thine hand is power and might; and in thine hand it is to make great, and to give strength unto all. Now therefore, our God, we thank thee, and praise thy glorious name. But who am I, and what is my people, that we should be able to offer so willingly after this sort? for all things come of thee, and of thine own have we given thee. For we are strangers before thee, and sojourners, as were all our fathers: our days on the earth are as a shadow, and there is none abiding. O LORD our God, all this store that we have prepared to build thee an house for thine holy name cometh of thine hand, and is all thine own. I know also, my God, that thou triest the heart, and hast pleasure in uprightness. As for me, in the uprightness of mine heart I have willingly offered all these things: and now have I seen with joy thy people, which are present here, to offer willingly unto thee. O LORD God of Abraham, Isaac, and of Israel, our fathers, keep this for ever in the imagination of the thoughts of the heart of thy people, and prepare their heart unto thee: and give unto Solomon my son a perfect heart, to keep thy commandments, thy testimonies, and thy statutes, and to do all these things, and to build the palace, for the which I have made provision."

And David said to all the congregation, "Now bless the LORD your God."

And all the congregation blessed the LORD God of their fathers, and bowed down their heads, and worshipped the LORD, and the king. And they sacrificed sacrifices unto the LORD, and offered burnt offerings unto the LORD, on the morrow after that day, even a thousand bullocks, a thousand rams, and a thousand lambs, with their drink offerings, and sacrifices in abundance for all Israel: and did eat and drink before the LORD on that day with great gladness. And they made Solomon the son of

*Solomon made king* David king the second time, and anointed him unto the LORD to be the chief governor, and Zadok to be priest.

And again the anger of the LORD was kindled against Israel, and he moved David against them to say, "Go, number Israel and Judah."

For the king said to Joab the captain of the host, which was with him, "Go now through all the tribes of Israel, from Dan even to Beer-sheba, and number ye the people, that I may know the number of the people."

And Joab said unto the king, "Now the LORD thy God add unto the people, how many soever they be, an hundredfold, and that the eyes of my lord the king may see it: but why doth my lord the king delight in this thing?"

Notwithstanding the king's word prevailed against Joab, and against the captains of the host. And Joab and the captains of the host went out from the presence of the king, to number the people of Israel. And they passed over Jordan, and pitched in Aroer, on the right side of the city that lieth in the midst of the river of Gad, and toward Jazer: then they came to Gilead, and to the land of Tahtim-hodshi; and they came to Dan-jaan, and about to Zidon, and came to the strong hold of Tyre, and to all the cities of the Hivites, and of the Canaanites: and they went out to the south of Judah, even to Beer-sheba.

So when they had gone through all the land, they came to Jerusalem at the end of nine months and twenty days. And Joab gave up the sum of the number of the people unto the king: and there were in Israel eight hundred thousand valiant men that drew the sword; and the men of Judah were five hundred thousand men.

And David's heart smote him after that he had numbered the people. And David said unto the LORD, "I have sinned greatly in that I have done: and now, I beseech thee, O LORD, take away the iniquity of thy servant; for I have done very foolishly."

For when David was up in the morning, the word of the LORD came unto the prophet Gad, David's seer, saying, "Go and say unto David, 'Thus saith the LORD, I offer thee three things; choose thee one of them, that I may do it unto thee.' "

So Gad came to David, and told him, and said unto him, "Shall seven years of famine come unto thee in thy land? or wilt thou flee three months before thine enemies, while they pursue thee? or that there be three

days' pestilence in thy land? now advise, and see what answer I shall re- *The plague*
turn to him that sent me."

And David said unto Gad, "I am in a great strait: let us fall now into
the hand of the LORD; for his mercies are great: and let me not fall into
the hand of man."

So the LORD sent a pestilence upon Israel, and the angel of the LORD
was by the threshingplace of Araunah the Jebusite. And David spake
unto the LORD when he saw the angel that smote the people, and said,
"Lo, I have sinned, and I have done wickedly: but these sheep, what
have they done? let thine hand, I pray thee, be against me, and against
my father's house."

And Gad, David's seer, said unto him, "Go up, rear an altar unto the
LORD in the threshingfloor of Araunah the Jebusite."

And David, according to the saying of Gad, went up as the LORD
commanded. And David built there an altar unto the LORD, and offered
burnt offerings and peace offerings. So the LORD was intreated for the
land, and the plague was stayed from Israel.

Now king David was old and stricken in years. And Bath-sheba went
in unto the king into the chamber. And Bath-sheba bowed, and did
obeisance unto the king. And the king said, "What wouldest thou?"

And she said unto him, "My lord, thou swarest by the LORD thy God
unto thine handmaid, saying, 'Assuredly Solomon thy son shall reign
after me, and he shall sit upon my throne.' And thou, my lord, O king,
the eyes of all Israel are upon thee, that thou shouldest tell them who
shall sit on the throne of my lord the king after him."

And, lo, while she yet talked with the king, Nathan the prophet also
came in. And they told the king, saying, "Behold Nathan the prophet."

And when he was come in before the king, he bowed himself before
the king with his face to the ground.

Then king David said, "Call me Bath-sheba."

And she came into the king's presence, and stood before the king.
And the king sware, and said, "As the LORD liveth, that hath redeemed my
soul out of all distress, even as I sware unto thee by the LORD God of Israel, saying, 'Assuredly Solomon thy son shall reign after me, and he shall
sit upon my throne in my stead;' even so will I certainly do this day."

Then Bath-sheba bowed with her face to the earth, and did reverence to the king, and said, "Let my lord king David live for ever."

And king David said, "Call me Zadok the priest, and Nathan the prophet."

And they came before the king. The king also said unto them, "Take with you the servants of your lord, and cause Solomon my son to ride upon mine own mule, and bring him down to Gihon: and let Zadok the priest and Nathan the prophet anoint him there king over Israel: and blow ye with the trumpet, and say, 'God save king Solomon.' Then ye shall come up after him, that he may come and sit upon my throne; for he shall be king in my stead: and I have appointed him to be ruler over Israel and over Judah."

So Zadok the priest, and Nathan the prophet went down, and caused Solomon to ride upon king David's mule, and brought him to Gihon. And Zadok the priest took an horn of oil out of the tabernacle, and anointed Solomon. And they blew the trumpet; and all the people said, "God save king Solomon." And all the people came up after him, and the people piped with pipes, and rejoiced with great joy, so that the earth rent with the sound of them. And moreover the king's servants came to bless our lord king David, saying, "God make the name of Solomon better than thy name, and make his throne greater than thy throne."

And the king bowed himself upon the bed. And also thus said the king, "Blessed be the LORD God of Israel, which hath given one to sit on my throne this day, mine eyes even seeing it."

Now the days of David drew nigh that he should die; and he charged Solomon his son, saying, "I go the way of all the earth: be thou strong therefore, and shew thyself a man; and keep the charge of the LORD thy God, to walk in his ways, to keep his statutes, and his commandments, and his judgments, and his testimonies, as it is written in the law of Moses, that thou mayest prosper in all that thou doest, and whithersoever thou turnest thyself: and the LORD may continue his word which he spake concerning me, saying, 'If thy children take heed to their way, to walk before me in truth with all their heart and with all their soul, there shall not fail thee' (said he) 'a man on the throne of Israel.' And thou, Solomon my son, know thou the God of thy father, and serve him with a perfect heart and with a willing mind: for the LORD searcheth all hearts, and understandeth all the imaginations of the thoughts: if thou seek him, he will be found of thee; but if thou forsake him, he will cast thee off for ever."

*Solomon chooses understanding*

So David slept with his fathers, and was buried in the city of David. And the days that David reigned over Israel were forty years: seven years reigned he in Hebron, and thirty and three years reigned he in Jerusalem.

Then sat Solomon upon the throne of David his father; and his kingdom was established greatly. And Solomon made affinity with Pharaoh king of Egypt, and took Pharaoh's daughter, and brought her into the city of David, until he had made an end of building his own house, and the house of the LORD, and the wall of Jerusalem round about. Only the people sacrificed in high places, because there was no house built unto the name of the LORD, until those days. And Solomon loved the LORD, walking in the statutes of David his father: only he sacrificed and burnt incense in high places. And the king went to Gibeon to sacrifice there; for that was the great high place: a thousand burnt offerings did Solomon offer upon that altar.

In Gibeon the LORD appeared to Solomon in a dream by night: and God said, "Ask what I shall give thee."

And Solomon said, "Thou hast shewed unto thy servant David my father great mercy, according as he walked before thee in truth, and in righteousness, and in uprightness of heart with thee; and thou hast kept for him this great kindness, that thou hast given him a son to sit on his throne, as it is this day. And now, O LORD my God, thou hast made thy servant king instead of David my father: and I am but a little child: I know not how to go out or come in. And thy servant is in the midst of thy people which thou hast chosen, a great people, that cannot be numbered nor counted for multitude. Give therefore thy servant an understanding heart to judge thy people, that I may discern between good and bad: for who is able to judge this thy so great a people?"

And the speech pleased the LORD, that Solomon had asked this thing. And God said unto him, "Because thou hast asked this thing, and hast not asked for thyself long life; neither hast asked riches for thyself, nor hast asked the life of thine enemies; but hast asked for thyself understanding to discern judgment; behold, I have done according to thy words: lo, I have given thee a wise and an understanding heart; so that there was none like thee before thee, neither after thee shall any arise like unto thee. And I have also given thee that which thou hast not asked, both riches, and honour: so that there shall not be any among the kings like unto thee all thy days. And if thou wilt walk in my ways, to keep my statutes and my commandments, as thy father David did walk, then I will lengthen thy days."

And Solomon awoke; and, behold, it was a dream.

And he came to Jerusalem, and stood before the ark of the covenant of the LORD, and offered up burnt offerings, and offered peace offerings, and made a feast to all his servants.

So king Solomon was king over all Israel. For he was wiser than all men: and his fame was in all nations round about. And he spake three thousand proverbs: and his songs were a thousand and five. And he spake of trees, from the cedar tree that is in Lebanon even unto the hyssop that springeth out of the wall: he spake also of beasts, and of fowl, and of creeping things, and of fishes. And there came of all people to hear the wisdom of Solomon, from all kings of the earth, which had heard of his wisdom.

And Hiram king of Tyre sent his servants unto Solomon; for he had heard that they had anointed him king in the room of his father: for Hiram was ever a lover of David. And Solomon sent to Hiram, saying, "Thou knowest how that David my father could not build an house unto the name of the LORD his God for the wars which were about him on every side, until the LORD put them under the soles of his feet. But now the LORD my God hath given me rest on every side, so that there is neither adversary nor evil occurrent. And, behold, I purpose to build an house unto the name of the LORD my God, as the LORD spake unto David my father, saying, 'Thy son, whom I will set upon thy throne in thy room, he shall build an house unto my name.' Now therefore command thou that they hew me cedar trees out of Lebanon; and my servants shall be with thy servants: and unto thee will I give hire for thy servants according to all that thou shalt appoint: for thou knowest that there is not among us any that can skill to hew timber like unto the Sidonians."

And it came to pass, when Hiram heard the words of Solomon, that he rejoiced greatly, and said, "Blessed be the LORD this day, which hath given unto David a wise son over this great people."

And Hiram sent to Solomon, saying, "I have considered the things *Solomon's temple begun* which thou sentest to me for: and I will do all thy desire concerning timber of cedar, and concerning timber of fir. My servants shall bring them down from Lebanon unto the sea: and I will convey them by sea in floats unto the place that thou shalt appoint me, and will cause them to be discharged there, and thou shalt receive them: and thou shalt accomplish my desire, in giving food for my household."

So Hiram gave Solomon cedar trees and fir trees according to all his desire. And Solomon gave Hiram twenty thousand measures of wheat for food to his household, and twenty measures of pure oil: thus gave Solomon to Hiram year by year. And the LORD gave Solomon wisdom, as he promised him: and there was peace between Hiram and Solomon; and they two made a league together.

And king Solomon raised a levy out of all Israel; and the levy was thirty thousand men. And he sent them to Lebanon, ten thousand a month by courses: a month they were in Lebanon, and two months at home: and Adoniram was over the levy. And Solomon had threescore and ten thousand that bare burdens, and fourscore thousand hewers in the mountains; beside the chief of Solomon's officers which were over the work, three thousand and three hundred, which ruled over the people that wrought in the work. And the king commanded, and they brought great stones, costly stones, and hewed stones, to lay the foundation of the house. And Solomon's builders and Hiram's builders did hew them, and the stonesquarers: so they prepared timber and stones to build the house.

And it came to pass in the four hundred and eightieth year after the children of Israel were come out of the land of Egypt, in the fourth year of Solomon's reign over Israel, in the month Zif, which is the second month, that he began to build the house of the LORD.

And the house which king Solomon built for the LORD, the length thereof was threescore cubits, and the breadth thereof twenty cubits, and the height thereof thirty cubits. And the porch before the temple of the house, twenty cubits was the length thereof, according to the breadth of the house; and ten cubits was the breadth thereof before the house. And for the house he made windows of narrow lights. And against the wall of the house he built chambers round about, against the walls of the

[ 181 ]

*Ornaments of the temple*

house round about. And the house, when it was in building, was built of stone made ready before it was brought thither: so that there was neither hammer nor axe nor any tool of iron heard in the house, while it was in building. The door for the middle chamber was in the right side of the house: and they went up with winding stairs into the middle chamber, and out of the middle into the third. So he built the house, and finished it; and covered the house with beams and boards of cedar. And he built the walls of the house within with boards of cedar, both the floor of the house, and the walls of the ceiling: and he covered them on the inside with wood, and covered the floor of the house with planks of fir. And the cedar of the house within was carved with knops and open flowers: and all was cedar; there was no stone seen. And the oracle he prepared in the house within, to set there the ark of the covenant of the LORD. So Solomon overlaid the house within with pure gold: and he made a partition by the chains of gold before the oracle; and he overlaid it with gold. And the whole house he overlaid with gold, until he had finished all the house: also the whole altar that was by the oracle he overlaid with gold.

And within the oracle he made two cherubims of olive tree, each ten cubits high. And he set the cherubims within the inner house: and they stretched forth the wings of the cherubims, so that the wing of the one touched the one wall, and the wing of the other cherub touched the other wall; and their wings touched one another in the midst of the house. And he overlaid the cherubims with gold. And he carved all the walls of the house round about with carved figures of cherubims and palm trees and open flowers, within and without. And for the entering of the oracle he made doors of olive tree. And he built the inner court with three rows of hewed stone, and a row of cedar beams.

And king Solomon sent and fetched Hiram out of Tyre. He was a worker in brass: and he was filled with wisdom, and understanding, and cunning to work all works in brass. And he came to king Solomon, and wrought all his work. For he cast two pillars of brass, and he set up the pillars in the porch of the temple, and upon the top of the pillars was lily work.

In the fourth year was the foundation of the house of the LORD laid, in the month Zif: and in the eleventh year, in the month Bul, which is the eighth month, was the house finished. So was he seven years in

building it. And the word of the LORD came to Solomon, saying, "Con- *Dedication of the temple*
cerning this house which thou art in building, if thou wilt walk in my
statutes, and execute my judgments, and keep all my commandments to
walk in them; then will I perform my word with thee, which I spake unto
David thy father: and I will dwell among the children of Israel, and will
not forsake my people Israel." So was ended all the work that king
Solomon made for the house of the LORD. And Solomon brought in the
things which David his father had dedicated; even the silver, and the
gold, and the vessels, did he put among the treasures of the house of the
LORD.

Then Solomon assembled the elders of Israel, and all the heads of
the tribes, the chief of the fathers of the children of Israel, unto king
Solomon in Jerusalem, that they might bring up the ark of the covenant
of the LORD out of the city of David, which is Zion. There was nothing in
the ark save the two tables of stone, which Moses put there at Horeb,
when the LORD made a covenant with the children of Israel, when they
came out of the land of Egypt. And it came to pass, when the priests were
come out of the holy place, that the cloud filled the house of the LORD,
so that the priests could not stand to minister because of the cloud: for
the glory of the LORD had filled the house of the LORD.

Then spake Solomon, "The LORD said that he would dwell in the
thick darkness. I have surely built thee an house to dwell in, a settled
place for thee to abide in for ever." And the king turned his face about,
and blessed all the congregation of Israel: (and all the congregation of
Israel stood;) and he said, "Blessed be the LORD God of Israel, which spake
with his mouth unto David my father, and hath with his hand fulfilled it,
saying, 'Since the day that I brought forth my people Israel out of Egypt,
I chose no city out of all the tribes of Israel to build an house, that my
name might be therein; but I chose David to be over my people Israel.'
And it was in the heart of David my father to build an house for the name
of the LORD God of Israel. And the LORD said unto David my father,
'Whereas it was in thine heart to build an house unto my name, thou
didst well that it was in thine heart. Nevertheless thou shalt not build the
house; but thy son that shall come forth, he shall build the house unto
my name.' And the LORD hath performed his word that he spake, and
I am risen up in the room of David my father, and sit on the throne of

*Solomon's blessing and prayer*

Israel, as the LORD promised, and have built an house for the name of the LORD God of Israel. And I have set there a place for the ark, wherein is the covenant of the LORD, which he made with our fathers, when he brought them out of the land of Egypt."

And Solomon stood before the altar of the LORD in the presence of all the congregation of Israel, and spread forth his hands toward heaven: and he said, "LORD God of Israel, there is no God like thee, in heaven above, or on earth beneath, who keepest covenant and mercy with thy servants that walk before thee with all their heart: who hast kept with thy servant David my father that thou promisedst him: therefore now, LORD God of Israel, keep with thy servant David my father that thou promisedst him, saying, 'There shall not fail thee a man in my sight to sit on the throne of Israel; so that thy children take heed to their way, that they walk before me as thou hast walked before me.' And now, O God of Israel, let thy word, I pray thee, be verified, which thou spakest unto thy servant David my father. But will God indeed dwell on the earth? behold, the heaven and heaven of heavens cannot contain thee; how much less this house that I have builded? Yet have thou respect unto the prayer of thy servant, and to his supplication, O LORD my God, to hearken unto the cry and to the prayer, which thy servant prayeth before thee to day: that thine eyes may be open toward this house night and day, even toward the place of which thou hast said, 'My name shall be there': that thou mayest hearken unto the prayer which thy servant shall make toward this place. And hearken thou to the supplication of thy servant, and of thy people Israel, when they shall pray toward this place: and hear thou in heaven thy dwelling place: and when thou hearest, forgive.

"When heaven is shut up, and there is no rain, because they have sinned against thee; if they pray toward this place, and confess thy name, and turn from their sin, when thou afflictest them: then hear thou in heaven, and forgive the sin of thy servants, and of thy people Israel, that thou teach them the good way wherein they should walk, and give rain upon thy land, which thou hast given to thy people for an inheritance.

"If there be in the land famine, if there be pestilence, blasting, mildew, locust, or if there be caterpiller; if their enemy besiege them in the land of their cities; whatsoever plague, whatsoever sickness there be; what prayer and supplication soever be made by any man, or by all thy people

Israel, which shall know every man the plague of his own heart, and spread forth his hands toward this house: then hear thou in heaven thy dwelling place, and forgive, and do, and give to every man according to his ways, whose heart thou knowest; (for thou, even thou, knowest the hearts of all the children of men;) that they may fear thee all the days that they live in the land which thou gavest unto our fathers.

*Solomon's blessing and prayer*

"Moreover concerning a stranger, that is not of thy people Israel, but cometh out of a far country for thy name's sake; (for they shall hear of thy great name, and of thy strong hand, and of thy stretched out arm;) when he shall come and pray toward this house; hear thou in heaven thy dwelling place, and do according to all that the stranger calleth to thee for: that all people of the earth may know thy name, to fear thee, as do thy people Israel; and that they may know that this house, which I have builded, is called by thy name.

"If they sin against thee, (for there is no man that sinneth not,) and thou be angry with them, and deliver them to the enemy, so that they carry them away captives unto the land of the enemy, far or near; yet if they shall bethink themselves in the land whither they were carried captives, and repent, and make supplication unto thee in the land of them that carried them captives, saying, 'We have sinned, and have done perversely'; and so return unto thee with all their heart, and with all their soul: then hear thou their prayer and their supplication in heaven thy dwelling place, and maintain their cause, and forgive thy people that have sinned against thee, and all their transgressions wherein they have transgressed against thee, and give them compassion before them who carried them captive, that they may have compassion on them: for they be thy people, and thine inheritance, which thou broughtest forth out of Egypt, from the midst of the furnace of iron. For thou didst separate them from among all the people of the earth, to be thine inheritance, as thou spakest by the hand of Moses thy servant, when thou broughtest our fathers out of Egypt, O Lord GOD."

And it was so, that when Solomon had made an end of praying all this prayer and supplication unto the LORD, he arose from before the altar of the LORD, from kneeling on his knees with his hands spread up to heaven. And he stood, and blessed all the congregation of Israel with a loud voice, saying, "Blessed be the LORD, that hath given rest unto his people Israel,

[ 185 ]

according to all that he promised: there hath not failed one word of all his good promise, which he promised by the hand of Moses his servant. The LORD our God be with us, as he was with our fathers: let him not leave us, nor forsake us: that he may incline our hearts unto him, to walk in all his ways, and to keep his commandments, and his statutes, and his judgments, which he commanded our fathers: that all the people of the earth may know that the LORD is God, and that there is none else. Let your heart therefore be perfect with the LORD our God, to walk in his statutes, and to keep his commandments, as at this day."

And Solomon built Gezer, and Beth-horon the nether, and Baalath, and Tadmor in the wilderness, in the land, and all the cities of store that Solomon had, and cities for his chariots, and cities for his horsemen, and that which Solomon desired to build in Jerusalem, and in Lebanon, and in all the land of his dominion. And all the people that were left, which were not of the children of Israel, their children that were left after them in the land, whom the children of Israel also were not able utterly to destroy, upon those did Solomon levy a tribute of bondservice unto this day. But of the children of Israel did Solomon make no bondmen: but they were men of war, and his servants, and his princes, and his captains, and rulers of his chariots, and his horsemen. And king Solomon made a navy of ships on the shore of the Red sea. And Hiram sent in the navy his servants, shipmen that had knowledge of the sea, with the servants of Solomon. And they came to Ophir, and fetched from thence gold, four hundred and twenty talents, and brought it to king Solomon.

And when the queen of Sheba heard of the fame of Solomon concerning the name of the LORD, she came to prove him with hard questions. And she came to Jerusalem with a very great train, with camels that bare spices, and very much gold, and precious stones: and when she was come to Solomon, she communed with him of all that was in her heart. And Solomon told her all her questions: there was not any thing hid from the king, which he told her not. And when the queen of Sheba had seen all Solomon's wisdom, and the house that he had built, and the meat of his table, and the sitting of his servants, and the attendance of his ministers, and their apparel, and his cupbearers, and his ascent by which he went up unto the house of the LORD; there was no more spirit in her. And she said to the king, "It was a true report that I heard in mine own land of thy acts and of thy wisdom. Howbeit I believed not the words, until I *Solomon's throne* came, and mine eyes had seen it; and, behold, the half was not told me: thy wisdom and prosperity exceedeth the fame which I heard. Happy are thy men, happy are these thy servants, which stand continually before thee, and that hear thy wisdom. Blessed be the LORD thy God, which delighted in thee, to set thee on the throne of Israel: because the LORD loved Israel for ever, therefore made he thee king, to do judgment and justice."

And she gave the king an hundred and twenty talents of gold, and of spices very great store, and precious stones: there came no more such abundance of spices as these which the queen of Sheba gave to king Solomon. And the navy also of Hiram, that brought gold from Ophir, brought in from Ophir great plenty of almug trees, and precious stones. And the king made of the almug trees pillars for the house of the LORD, and for the king's house, harps also and psalteries for singers: there came no such almug trees, nor were seen unto this day. And king Solomon gave unto the queen of Sheba all her desire, whatsoever she asked, beside that which Solomon gave her of his royal bounty. So she turned and went to her own country, she and her servants.

Moreover the king made a great throne of ivory, and overlaid it with the best gold. The throne had six steps, and the top of the throne was round behind: and there were stays on either side on the place of the seat, and two lions stood beside the stays. And twelve lions stood there on the one side and on the other upon the six steps: there was not the like made in any kingdom. And all king Solomon's drinking vessels were of gold, and all the vessels of the house of the forest of Lebanon were of pure gold; none were of silver: it was nothing accounted of in the days of Solomon. For the king had at sea a navy of Tharshish with the navy of Hiram: once in three years came the navy of Tharshish, bringing gold, and silver, ivory, and apes, and peacocks.

So king Solomon exceeded all the kings of the earth for riches and for wisdom. And all the earth sought to Solomon, to hear his wisdom, which God had put in his heart. And they brought every man his present, vessels of silver, and vessels of gold, and garments, and armour, and spices, horses, and mules, a rate year by year. And Solomon gathered together chariots and horsemen: and he had a thousand and four hundred chariots, and twelve thousand horsemen, whom he bestowed in the cities for chari-

*Solomon's wives* ots, and with the king at Jerusalem. And the king made silver to be in Jerusalem as stones, and cedars made he to be as the sycomore trees that are in the vale, for abundance. And Solomon had horses brought out of Egypt, and linen yarn: the king's merchants received the linen yarn at a price.

But king Solomon loved many strange women. For it came to pass, when Solomon was old, that his wives turned away his heart after other gods: and his heart was not perfect with the LORD his God, as was the heart of David his father. And Solomon did evil in the sight of the LORD, and went not fully after the LORD, as did David his father. And the LORD was angry with Solomon, because his heart was turned from the LORD God of Israel, which had appeared unto him twice, and had commanded him concerning this thing, that he should not go after other gods: but he kept not that which the LORD commanded. Wherefore the LORD said unto Solomon, "Forasmuch as this is done of thee, and thou hast not kept my covenant and my statutes, which I have commanded thee, I will surely rend the kingdom from thee, and will give it to thy servant. Notwithstanding in thy days I will not do it for David thy father's sake: but I will rend it out of the hand of thy son. Howbeit I will not rend away all the kingdom; but will give one tribe to thy son for David my servant's sake, and for Jerusalem's sake which I have chosen."

And the time that Solomon reigned in Jerusalem over all Israel was forty years. And Solomon slept with his fathers, and was buried in the city of David his father: and Rehoboam his son reigned in his stead.

*Rehoboam succeeds Solomon* And Rehoboam went to Shechem: for all Israel were come to Shechem to make him king. And it came to pass, when Jeroboam the son of Nebat, who was yet in Egypt, heard of it, (for he was fled from the presence of king Solomon, and Jeroboam dwelt in Egypt;) that they sent and called him. And Jeroboam and all the congregation of Israel came, and spake unto Rehoboam, saying, "Thy father made our yoke grievous: now therefore make thou the grievous service of thy father, and his heavy yoke which he put upon us, lighter, and we will serve thee."

And he said unto them, "Depart yet for three days, then come again to me." And the people departed.

And king Rehoboam consulted with the old men, that stood before

Solomon his father while he yet lived, and said, "How do ye advise that I *Ten tribes revolt* may answer this people?"

And they spake unto him, saying, "If thou wilt be a servant unto this people this day, and wilt serve them, and answer them, and speak good words to them, then they will be thy servants for ever."

But he forsook the counsel of the old men, which they had given him, and consulted with the young men that were grown up with him, and which stood before him: and he said unto them, "What counsel give ye that we may answer this people, who have spoken to me, saying, 'Make the yoke which thy father did put upon us lighter?' "

And the young men that were grown up with him spake unto him, saying, "Thus shalt thou speak unto this people that spake unto thee, saying, 'Thy father made our yoke heavy, but make thou it lighter unto us'; thus shalt thou say unto them, 'My little finger shall be thicker than my father's loins. And now whereas my father did lade you with a heavy yoke, I will add to your yoke: my father hath chastised you with whips, but I will chastise you with scorpions.' "

So Jeroboam and all the people came to Rehoboam the third day, as the king had appointed, saying, "Come to me again the third day."

And the king answered the people roughly, and forsook the old men's counsel that they gave him; and spake to them after the counsel of the young men, saying, "My father made your yoke heavy, and I will add to your yoke: my father also chastised you with whips, but I will chastise you with scorpions."

Wherefore the king hearkened not unto the people; so when all Israel saw that the king hearkened not unto them, the people answered the king, saying, "What portion have we in David? neither have we inheritance in the son of Jesse: to your tents, O Israel: now see to thine own house, David." So Israel departed unto their tents.

But as for the children of Israel which dwelt in the cities of Judah, Rehoboam reigned over them. Then king Rehoboam sent Adoram, who was over the tribute; and all Israel stoned him with stones, that he died. Therefore king Rehoboam made speed to get him up to his chariot, to flee to Jerusalem.

So Israel rebelled against the house of David unto this day. And it came to pass, when all Israel heard that Jeroboam was come again, that

*Rehoboam's death* they sent and called him unto the congregation, and made him king over all Israel: there was none that followed the house of David, but the tribe of Judah only.

And when Rehoboam was come to Jerusalem, he assembled all the house of Judah, with the tribe of Benjamin, to fight against the house of Israel, to bring the kingdom again to Rehoboam the son of Solomon. But the word of God came unto Shemaiah the man of God, saying, "Speak unto Rehoboam, the son of Solomon, king of Judah, 'Thus saith the LORD, Ye shall not go up, nor fight against your brethren the children of Israel: return every man to his house; for this thing is from me.' " They hearkened therefore to the word of the LORD, and returned to depart, according to the word of the LORD.

And Rehoboam the son of Solomon reigned in Judah. Rehoboam was forty and one years old when he began to reign, and he reigned seventeen years in Jerusalem, the city which the LORD did choose to put his name there. And there was war between Rehoboam and Jeroboam all their days. And Rehoboam slept with his fathers, and was buried with his fathers in the city of David. And Abijam his son reigned in his stead. And the days which Jeroboam reigned were two and twenty years: and he slept with his fathers, and Nadab his son reigned in his stead.

Now in the eighteenth year of king Jeroboam reigned Abijam over Judah. Three years reigned he in Jerusalem. And he walked in all the sins of his father, which he had done before him: and his heart was not perfect with the LORD his God, as the heart of David his father. Nevertheless for David's sake did the LORD his God give him a lamp in Jerusalem, to set up his son after him, and to establish Jerusalem: because David did that which was right in the eyes of the LORD, and turned not aside from any thing that he commanded him all the days of his life, save only in the matter of Uriah the Hittite. And Abijam slept with his fathers; and they buried him in the city of David: and Asa his son reigned in his stead.

And in the twentieth year of Jeroboam king of Israel reigned Asa over Judah. And Asa did that which was right in the eyes of the LORD, as did David his father. And he took away the sodomites out of the land, and removed all the idols that his fathers had made. Asa's heart was perfect with the LORD all his days. And he commanded Judah to seek the LORD God of their fathers, and to do the law and the commandment. And he built fenced cities in Judah: for the land had rest, and he had no war in those years; because the LORD had given him rest.

And the Spirit of God came upon Azariah the son of Oded: and he went out to meet Asa, and said unto him, "Hear ye me, Asa, and all Judah and Benjamin; The LORD is with you, while ye be with him; and if ye seek him, he will be found of you; but if ye forsake him, he will forsake you. Now for a long season Israel hath been without the true God, and without a teaching priest, and without law. But when they in their trouble did turn unto the LORD God of Israel, and sought him, he was found of them. And in those times there was no peace to him that went out, nor to him that came in, but great vexations were upon all the inhabitants of the countries. And nation was destroyed of nation, and city of city: for God did vex them with all adversity. Be ye strong therefore, and let not your hands be weak: for your work shall be rewarded."

And when Asa heard these words, and the prophecy of Oded the prophet, he took courage, and put away the abominable idols out of all the land of Judah and Benjamin, and out of the cities which he had taken from mount Ephraim, and renewed the altar of the LORD, that was before the porch of the LORD. And he gathered all Judah and Benjamin, and the strangers with them out of Ephraim and Manasseh, and out of Simeon: for they fell to him out of Israel in abundance, when they saw that the LORD his God was with him. So they gathered themselves together at Jerusalem in the third month, in the fifteenth year of the reign of Asa. And they entered into a covenant to seek the LORD God of their fathers with all their heart and with all their soul. And they sware unto the LORD with a loud voice, and with shouting, and with trumpets, and with cornets. And all Judah rejoiced at the oath: for they had sworn with all their heart, and sought him with their whole desire; and he was found of them: and the LORD gave them rest round about. And there was no more war unto the five and thirtieth year of the reign of Asa.

And Asa in the thirty and ninth year of his reign was diseased in his feet, until his disease was exceeding great: yet in his disease he sought not to the LORD, but to the physicians. And Asa slept with his fathers, and died in the one and fortieth year of his reign.

And in the thirty and eighth year of Asa king of Judah began Ahab

*Ahab's reign* the son of Omri to reign over Israel: and Ahab the son of Omri reigned over Israel in Samaria twenty and two years. And Ahab the son of Omri did evil in the sight of the LORD above all that were before him. And it came to pass, as if it had been a light thing for him to walk in the sins of Jeroboam the son of Nebat, that he took to wife Jezebel the daughter of Ethbaal king of the Zidonians, and went and served Baal, and worshipped him. And he reared up an altar for Baal in the house of Baal, which he had built in Samaria. And Ahab made a grove; and Ahab did more to provoke the LORD God of Israel to anger than all the kings of Israel that were before him.

# IV

# THE PROPHETS

AND Elijah the Tishbite, who was of the inhabitants of Gilead, said *Elijah fed by ravens* unto Ahab, "As the LORD God of Israel liveth, before whom I stand, there shall not be dew nor rain these years, but according to my word."

And the word of the LORD came unto him, saying, "Get thee hence, and turn thee eastward, and hide thyself by the brook Cherith, that is before Jordan. And it shall be, that thou shalt drink of the brook; and I have commanded the ravens to feed thee there."

So he went and did according unto the word of the LORD: for he went and dwelt by the brook Cherith, that is before Jordan. And the ravens brought him bread and flesh in the morning, and bread and flesh in the evening; and he drank of the brook. And it came to pass after a while, that the brook dried up, because there had been no rain in the land.

And the word of the LORD came unto him, saying, "Arise, get thee to Zarephath, which belongeth to Zidon, and dwell there: behold, I have commanded a widow woman there to sustain thee."

So he arose and went to Zarephath. And when he came to the gate of the city, behold, the widow woman was there gathering of sticks: and he called to her, and said, "Fetch me, I pray thee, a little water in a vessel, that I may drink." And as she was going to fetch it, he called to her, and said, "Bring me, I pray thee a morsel of bread in thine hand."

And she said, "As the LORD thy God liveth, I have not a cake, but an handful of meal in a barrel, and a little oil in a cruse: and, behold, I am gathering two sticks, that I may go in and dress it for me and my son, that we may eat it, and die."

And Elijah said unto her, "Fear not; go and do as thou hast said: but make me thereof a little cake first, and bring it unto me, and after make for thee and for thy son. For thus saith the LORD God of Israel, 'The barrel of meal shall not waste, neither shall the cruse of oil fail, until the day that the LORD sendeth rain upon the earth.'"

And she went and did according to the saying of Elijah: and she, and he, and her house, did eat many days. And the barrel of meal wasted not, neither did the cruse of oil fail, according to the word of the LORD, which he spake by Elijah.

And it came to pass after these things, that the son of the woman, the mistress of the house, fell sick; and his sickness was so sore, that there was no breath left in him. And she said unto Elijah, "What have I to do with thee, O thou man of God? art thou come unto me to call my sin to remembrance, and to slay my son?"

And he said unto her, "Give me thy son."

And he took him out of her bosom, and carried him up into a loft, where he abode, and laid him upon his own bed. And he cried unto the LORD, and said, "O LORD my God, hast thou also brought evil upon the widow with whom I sojourn, by slaying her son?"

And he stretched himself upon the child three times, and cried unto the LORD, and said, "O LORD my God, I pray thee, let this child's soul come into him again."

And the LORD heard the voice of Elijah; and the soul of the child came into him again, and he revived. And Elijah took the child, and brought him down out of the chamber into the house, and delivered him unto his mother: and Elijah said, "See, thy son liveth."

And the woman said to Elijah, "Now by this I know that thou art a man of God, and that the word of the LORD in thy mouth is truth."

And it came to pass after many days, that the word of the LORD came to Elijah in the third year, saying, "Go, shew thyself unto Ahab; and I will send rain upon the earth." And Elijah went to shew himself unto Ahab.

And there was a sore famine in Samaria. And Ahab called Obadiah, which was the governor of his house. And Ahab said unto Obadiah, "Go into the land, unto all fountains of water, and unto all brooks: peradventure we may find grass to save the horses and mules alive, that we lose not all the beasts."

So they divided the land between them to pass throughout it: Ahab went one way by himself, and Obadiah went another way by himself. And as Obadiah was in the way, behold, Elijah met him: and he knew him, and fell on his face, and said, "Art thou that my lord Elijah?"

And he answered him, "I am: go, tell thy lord, 'Behold, Elijah is here.' As the LORD of hosts liveth, before whom I stand, I will surely *Test of Baal's prophets* shew myself unto him to day."

So Obadiah went to meet Ahab, and told him: and Ahab went to meet Elijah. And it came to pass, when Ahab saw Elijah, that Ahab said unto him, "Art thou he that troubleth Israel?"

And he answered, "I have not troubled Israel; but thou, and thy father's house, in that ye have forsaken the commandments of the LORD, and thou hast followed Baalim. Now therefore send, and gather to me all Israel unto mount Carmel, and the prophets of Baal four hundred and fifty, and the prophets of the groves four hundred, which eat at Jezebel's table."

So Ahab sent unto all the children of Israel, and gathered the prophets together unto mount Carmel. And Elijah came unto all the people, and said, "How long halt ye between two opinions? If the LORD be God, follow him: but if Baal, then follow him." And the people answered him not a word.

Then said Elijah unto the people, "I, even I only, remain a prophet of the LORD; but Baal's prophets are four hundred and fifty men. Let them therefore give us two bullocks; and let them choose one bullock for themselves, and cut it in pieces, and lay it on wood, and put no fire under: and I will dress the other bullock, and lay it on wood, and put no fire under: and call ye on the name of your gods, and I will call on the name of the LORD: and the God that answereth by fire, let him be God." And all the people answered and said, "It is well spoken."

And Elijah said unto the prophets of Baal, "Choose you one bullock for yourselves, and dress it first; for ye are many; and call on the name of your gods, but put no fire under."

And they took the bullock which was given them, and they dressed it, and called on the name of Baal from morning even until noon, saying "O Baal, hear us." But there was no voice, nor any that answered. And they leaped upon the altar which was made.

And it came to pass at noon, that Elijah mocked them, and said, "Cry aloud: for he is a god; either he is talking, or he is pursuing, or he is in a journey, or peradventure he sleepeth, and must be awaked."

And they cried aloud, and cut themselves after their manner with

[ 195 ]

*Elijah by prayer obtains rain*

knives and lancets, till the blood gushed out upon them. And it came to pass, when midday was past, and they prophesied until the time of the offering of the evening sacrifice, that there was neither voice, nor any to answer, nor any that regarded.

And Elijah said unto all the people, "Come near unto me."

And all the people came near unto him. And he repaired the altar of the LORD that was broken down. And Elijah took twelve stones, and with the stones he built an altar in the name of the LORD; and he made a trench about the altar, as great as would contain two measures of seed. And he put the wood in order, and cut the bullock in pieces, and laid him on the wood, and said, "Fill four barrels with water, and pour it on the burnt sacrifice, and on the wood." And he said, "Do it the second time." And they did it the second time. And he said, "Do it the third time." And they did it the third time. And the water ran round about the altar; and he filled the trench also with water.

And it came to pass at the time of the offering of the evening sacrifice, that Elijah the prophet came near, and said, "LORD God of Abraham, Isaac, and of Israel, let it be known this day that thou art God in Israel, and that I am thy servant, and that I have done all these things at thy word. Hear me, O LORD, hear me, that this people may know that thou art the LORD God, and that thou hast turned their heart back again."

Then the fire of the LORD fell, and consumed the burnt sacrifice, and the wood, and the stones, and the dust, and licked up the water that was in the trench. And when all the people saw it, they fell on their faces: and they said, "The LORD, he is the God; the LORD, he is the God."

And Elijah said unto Ahab, "Get thee up, eat and drink; for there is a sound of abundance of rain." So Ahab went up to eat and to drink.

And Elijah went up to the top of Carmel; and he cast himself down upon the earth, and put his face between his knees, and said to his servant, "Go up now, look toward the sea."

And he went up, and looked, and said, "There is nothing."

And he said, "Go again seven times."

And it came to pass at the seventh time, that he said, "Behold, there ariseth a little cloud out of the sea, like a man's hand."

And he said, "Go up, say unto Ahab, 'Prepare thy chariot, and get thee down, that the rain stop thee not.' "

And it came to pass in the mean while, that the heaven was black with clouds and wind, and there was a great rain. And Ahab rode, and went to Jezreel. And the hand of the LORD was on Elijah; and he girded up his loins, and ran before Ahab to the entrance of Jezreel.

And Ahab told Jezebel all that Elijah had done, and withal how he had slain all the prophets with the sword. Then Jezebel sent a messenger unto Elijah, saying, "So let the gods do to me, and more also, if I make not thy life as the life of one of them by to morrow about this time."

And Elijah arose, and went for his life, and came to Beer-sheba, which belongeth to Judah, and left his servant there. But he himself went a day's journey into the wilderness, and came and sat down under a juniper tree: and he requested for himself that he might die; and said, "It is enough; now, O LORD, take away my life; for I am not better than my fathers."

And as he lay and slept under a juniper tree, behold, then an angel touched him, and said unto him, "Arise and eat."

And he looked, and, behold, there was a cake baken on the coals, and a cruse of water at his head. And he did eat and drink, and laid him down again. And the angel of the LORD came again the second time, and touched him, and said, "Arise and eat; because the journey is too great for thee."

And he arose, and did eat and drink, and went in the strength of that meat forty days and forty nights unto Horeb the mount of God. And he came thither unto a cave, and lodged there; and, behold, the word of the LORD came to him, and he said unto him, "What doest thou here, Elijah?"

And he said, "I have been very jealous for the LORD God of hosts: for the children of Israel have forsaken thy covenant, thrown down thine altars, and slain thy prophets with the sword; and I, even I only, am left; and they seek my life, to take it away."

And he said, "Go forth, and stand upon the mount before the LORD."

And, behold, the LORD passed by, and a great and strong wind rent the mountains, and brake in pieces the rocks before the LORD; but the LORD was not in the wind: and after the wind an earthquake; but the LORD was not in the earthquake: and after the earthquake a fire; but the

LORD was not in the fire: and after the fire a still small voice. And it was so, when Elijah heard it, that he wrapped his face in his mantle, and went out, and stood in the entering in of the cave. And, behold, there came a voice unto him, and said, "What doest thou here, Elijah?"

And he said, "I have been very jealous for the LORD God of hosts: because the children of Israel have forsaken thy covenant, thrown down thine altars, and slain thy prophets with the sword; and I, even I only, am left; and they seek my life, to take it away."

And the LORD said unto him, "Go, return on thy way to the wilderness of Damascus: and when thou comest, anoint Hazael to be king over Syria: and Jehu the son of Nimshi shalt thou anoint to be king over Israel: and Elisha the son of Shaphat of Abel-meholah shalt thou anoint to be prophet in thy room. Yet I have left me seven thousand in Israel, all the knees which have not bowed unto Baal, and every mouth which hath not kissed him."

So he departed thence, and found Elisha the son of Shaphat, who was ploughing with twelve yoke of oxen before him, and he with the twelfth: and Elijah passed by him, and cast his mantle upon him. And he left the oxen, and ran after Elijah, and said, "Let me, I pray thee, kiss my father and my mother, and then I will follow thee."

And he returned back from him, and took a yoke of oxen, and slew them, and boiled their flesh with the instruments of the oxen, and gave unto the people, and they did eat. Then he arose, and went after Elijah, and ministered unto him.

And it came to pass after these things, that Naboth the Jezreelite had a vineyard, which was in Jezreel, hard by the palace of Ahab king of Samaria. And Ahab spake unto Naboth, saying, "Give me thy vineyard, that I may have it for a garden of herbs, because it is near unto my house: and I will give thee for it a better vineyard than it; or, if it seem good to thee, I will give thee the worth of it in money."

And Naboth said to Ahab, "The LORD forbid it me, that I should give the inheritance of my fathers unto thee."

And Ahab came into his house heavy and displeased because of the word which Naboth the Jezreelite had spoken to him: for he had said, "I will not give thee the inheritance of my fathers." And he laid him down upon his bed, and turned away his face, and would eat no bread.

But Jezebel his wife came to him, and said unto him, "Why is thy spirit so sad, that thou eatest no bread?"

And he said unto her, "Because I spake unto Naboth the Jezreelite, and said unto him, 'Give me thy vineyard for money; or else, if it please thee, I will give thee another vineyard for it': and he answered, 'I will not give thee my vineyard.' "

And Jezebel his wife said unto him, "Dost thou now govern the kingdom of Israel? arise, and eat bread, and let thine heart be merry: I will give thee the vineyard of Naboth the Jezreelite."

So she wrote letters in Ahab's name, and sealed them with his seal, and sent the letters unto the elders and to the nobles that were in the city, dwelling with Naboth. And she wrote in the letters, saying, "Proclaim a fast, and set Naboth on high among the people: and set two men, sons of Belial, before him, to bear witness against him, saying, 'Thou didst blaspheme God and the king.' And then carry him out, and stone him, that he may die."

And the men of the city, even the elders and the nobles who were the inhabitants in his city, did as Jezebel had sent unto them, and as it was written in the letters which she had sent unto them. They proclaimed a fast, and set Naboth on high among the people. And there came in two men, children of Belial, and sat before him: and the men of Belial witnessed against him, even against Naboth, in the presence of the people, saying, "Naboth did blaspheme God and the king."

Then they carried him forth out of the city, and stoned him with stones, that he died.

Then they sent to Jezebel, saying, "Naboth is stoned, and is dead."

And it came to pass, when Jezebel heard that Naboth was stoned, and was dead, that Jezebel said to Ahab, "Arise, take possession of the vineyard of Naboth the Jezreelite, which he refused to give thee for money: for Naboth is not alive, but dead."

And it came to pass, when Ahab heard that Naboth was dead, that Ahab arose up to go down to the vineyard of Naboth the Jezreelite, to take possession of it.

And the word of the LORD came to Elijah the Tishbite, saying, "Arise, go down to meet Ahab king of Israel, which is in Samaria: behold, he is in the vineyard of Naboth, whither he is gone down to possess it. And thou shalt speak unto him, saying, 'Thus saith the LORD, Hast thou killed, and also taken possession?' And thou shalt speak unto him, saying, 'Thus saith the LORD, In the place where dogs licked the blood of Naboth shall dogs lick thy blood, even thine.' "

And Ahab said to Elijah, "Hast thou found me, O mine enemy?"

And he answered, "I have found thee: because thou hast sold thyself to work evil in the sight of the LORD. Behold, I will bring evil upon thee, and will take away thy posterity." But there was none like unto Ahab, which did sell himself to work wickedness in the sight of the LORD, whom Jezebel his wife stirred up. And it came to pass, when Ahab heard those words, that he rent his clothes, and put sackcloth upon his flesh, and fasted, and lay in sackcloth, and went softly.

And Elijah said unto Elisha, "Tarry here, I pray thee; for the LORD hath sent me to Beth-el."

And Elisha said unto him, "As the LORD liveth, and as thy soul liveth, I will not leave thee."

So they went down to Beth-el. And the sons of the prophets that were at Beth-el came forth to Elisha, and said unto him, "Knowest thou that the LORD will take away thy master from thy head to day?"

And he said, "Yea, I know it; hold ye your peace."

And Elijah said unto him, "Elisha, tarry here, I pray thee; for the LORD hath sent me to Jericho."

And he said, "As the LORD liveth, and as thy soul liveth, I will not leave thee."

So they came to Jericho. And the sons of the prophets that were at Jericho came to Elisha, and said unto him, "Knowest thou that the LORD will take away thy master from thy head to day?"

And he answered, "Yea, I know it; hold ye your peace."

And Elijah said unto him, "Tarry, I pray thee, here; for the LORD hath sent me to Jordan."

And he said, "As the LORD liveth, and as thy soul liveth, I will not leave thee."

And they two went on. And fifty men of the sons of the prophets went, and stood to view afar off: and they two stood by Jordan. And Elijah took his mantle, and wrapped it together, and smote the waters, and they were divided hither and thither, so that they two went over on dry ground. And it came to pass, when they were gone over, that Elijah said unto Elisha, "Ask what I shall do for thee, before I be taken away from thee." *Elisha succeeds Elijah*

And Elisha said, "I pray thee, let a double portion of thy spirit be upon me."

And he said, "Thou hast asked a hard thing: nevertheless, if thou see me when I am taken from thee, it shall be so unto thee; but if not, it shall not be so."

And it came to pass, as they still went on, and talked, that, behold, there appeared a chariot of fire, and horses of fire, and parted them both asunder; and Elijah went up by a whirlwind into heaven. And Elisha saw it, and he cried, "My father, my father, the chariot of Israel, and the horsemen thereof!"

And he saw him no more: and he took hold of his own clothes, and rent them in two pieces. He took up also the mantle of Elijah that fell from him, and went back, and stood by the bank of Jordan; and he took the mantle of Elijah that fell from him, and smote the waters, and said, "Where is the LORD God of Elijah?"

And when he also had smitten the waters, they parted hither and thither: and Elisha went over. And when the sons of the prophets which were to view at Jericho saw him, they said, "The spirit of Elijah doth rest on Elisha."

And they came to meet him, and bowed themselves to the ground before him. And they said unto him, "Behold now, there be with thy servants fifty strong men; let them go, we pray thee, and seek thy master: lest peradventure the Spirit of the LORD hath taken him up, and cast him upon some mountain, or into some valley."

And he said, "Ye shall not send."

And when they urged him till he was ashamed, he said, "Send."

They sent therefore fifty men; and they sought three days, but found him not. And when they came again to him, (for he tarried at Jericho,) he said unto them, "Did I not say unto you, 'Go not'? "

And the men of the city said unto Elisha, "Behold, I pray thee, the situation of this city is pleasant, as my lord seeth: but the water is naught, and the ground barren."

And he said, "Bring me a new cruse, and put salt therein."

And they brought it to him. And he went forth unto the spring of the waters, and cast the salt in there, and said, "Thus saith the LORD, 'I have healed these waters; there shall not be from thence any more death or barren land.' "

So the waters were healed unto this day, according to the saying of Elisha which he spake.

Now there cried a certain woman of the wives of the sons of the prophets unto Elisha, saying, "Thy servant my husband is dead; and thou knowest that thy servant did fear the LORD: and the creditor is come to take unto him my two sons to be bondmen."

And Elisha said unto her, "What shall I do for thee? tell me, what hast thou in the house?"

And she said, "Thine handmaid hath not any thing in the house, save a pot of oil."

Then he said, "Go, borrow thee vessels abroad of all thy neighbours, even empty vessels; borrow not a few. And when thou art come in, thou shalt shut the door upon thee and upon thy sons, and shalt pour out into all those vessels, and thou shalt set aside that which is full."

So she went from him, and shut the door upon her and upon her sons, who brought the vessels to her; and she poured out. And it came to pass, when the vessels were full, that she said unto her son, "Bring me yet a vessel."

And he said unto her, "There is not a vessel more." And the oil stayed. Then she came and told the man of God.

And he said, "Go, sell the oil, and pay thy debt, and live thou and thy children of the rest."

And it fell on a day, that Elisha passed to Shunem, where was a great woman; and she constrained him to eat bread. And so it was, that as oft as he passed by, he turned in thither to eat bread. And she said unto her husband, "Behold, now, I perceive that this is an holy man of God, which passeth by us continually. Let us make a little chamber, I pray thee, on the wall; and let us set for him there a bed, and a table, and a stool, and a candlestick: and it shall be, when he cometh to us, that he shall turn in thither."

And it fell on a day, that he came thither, and he turned into the

*ELIJAH IN THE CHARIOT OF FIRE*

chamber, and lay there. And he said to Gehazi his servant, "Call this *Elisha gives a son to the* Shunammite." *good Shunammite*

And when he had called her, she stood before him. And he said unto him, "Say now unto her, 'Behold, thou hast been careful for us with all this care; what is to be done for thee? wouldest thou be spoken for to the king, or to the captain of the host?'"

And she answered, "I dwell among mine own people."

And he said, "What then is to be done for her?"

And Gehazi answered, "Verily she hath no child, and her husband is old."

And he said, "Call her."

And when he had called her, she stood in the door. And he said, "About this season, according to the time of life, thou shalt embrace a son."

And she said, "Nay, my lord, thou man of God, do not lie unto thine handmaid."

And the woman conceived, and bare a son at that season that Elisha had said unto her, according to the time of life. And when the child was grown, it fell on a day, that he went out to his father to the reapers.

And he said unto his father, "My head, my head."

And he said to a lad, "Carry him to his mother."

And when he had taken him, and brought him to his mother, he sat on her knees till noon, and then died. And she went up, and laid him on the bed of the man of God, and shut the door upon him, and went out. And she called unto her husband, and said, "Send me, I pray thee, one of the young men, and one of the asses, that I may run to the man of God, and come again."

And he said, "Wherefore wilt thou go to him to day? it is neither new moon, nor sabbath."

And she said, "It shall be well."

Then she saddled an ass, and said to her servant, "Drive, and go forward; slack not thy riding for me, except I bid thee."

So she went and came unto the man of God to mount Carmel. And it came to pass, when the man of God saw her afar off, that he said to Gehazi his servant, "Behold, yonder is that Shunammite: run now, I pray thee, to meet her, and say unto her, 'Is it well with thee? is it well with thy husband? is it well with the child?' "

And she answered, "It is well."

And when she came to the man of God to the hill, she caught him by the feet: but Gehazi came near to thrust her away. And the man of God said, "Let her alone; for her soul is vexed within her: and the LORD hath hid it from me, and hath not told me."

Then she said, "Did I desire a son of my lord? did I not say, 'Do not deceive me?' "

Then he said to Gehazi, "Gird up thy loins, and take my staff in thine hand, and go thy way: if thou meet any man, salute him not; and if any salute thee, answer him not again: and lay my staff upon the face of the child."

And the mother of the child said, "As the LORD liveth, and as thy soul liveth, I will not leave thee." And he arose, and followed her.

And Gehazi passed on before them, and laid the staff upon the face of the child; but there was neither voice, nor hearing. Wherefore he went again to meet him, and told him, saying, "The child is not awaked."

And when Elisha was come into the house, behold, the child was dead, and laid upon his bed. He went in therefore, and shut the door upon them twain, and prayed unto the LORD. And he went up and lay upon the child, and put his mouth upon his mouth, and his eyes upon his eyes, and his hands upon his hands: and he stretched himself upon the child; and the flesh of the child waxed warm. Then he returned, and walked in the house to and fro; and went up, and stretched himself upon him: and the child sneezed seven times, and the child opened his eyes.

And he called Gehazi, and said, "Call this Shunammite." So he called her.

And when she was come in unto him, he said, "Take up thy son."

Then she went in, and fell at his feet, and bowed herself to the ground, and took up her son, and went out.

And Elisha came again to Gilgal: and there was a dearth in the land; and the sons of the prophets were sitting before him: and he said unto his servant, "Set on the great pot, and seethe pottage for the sons of the prophets."

And one went out into the field to gather herbs, and found a wild

vine, and gathered thereof wild gourds his lap full, and came and shred
them into the pot of pottage: for they knew them not. So they poured out
for the men to eat. And it came to pass, as they were eating of the pottage,
that they cried out, and said, "O thou man of God, there is death in the
pot."

And they could not eat thereof.

But he said, "Then bring meal." And he cast it into the pot; and he
said, "Pour out for the people, that they may eat." And there was no
harm in the pot.

And there came a man from Baal-shalisha, and brought the man of God
bread of the firstfruits, twenty loaves of barley, and full ears of corn in
the husk thereof. And he said, "Give unto the people, that they may eat."
And his servitor said, "What, should I set this before an hundred men?"

He said again, "Give the people, that they may eat: for thus saith
the LORD, 'They shall eat, and shall leave thereof.' "

So he set it before them, and they did eat, and left thereof, according
to the word of the LORD.

Now Naaman, captain of the host of the king of Syria, was a great
man with his master, and honourable, because by him the LORD had
given deliverance unto Syria: he was also a mighty man in valour, but
he was a leper. And the Syrians had gone out by companies, and had
brought away captive out of the land of Israel a little maid; and she
waited on Naaman's wife. And she said unto her mistress, "Would God
my lord were with the prophet that is in Samaria! for he would recover
him of his leprosy."

And one went in, and told his lord, saying, "Thus and thus said the
maid that is of the land of Israel."

And the king of Syria said, "Go to, go, and I will send a letter unto
the king of Israel."

And he departed, and took with him ten talents of silver, and six
thousand pieces of gold, and ten changes of raiment. And he brought
the letter to the king of Israel, saying, "Now when this letter is come
unto thee, behold, I have therewith sent Naaman my servant to thee,
that thou mayest recover him of his leprosy."

And it came to pass, when the king of Israel had read the letter, that

*An hundred fed on
twenty loaves*

he rent his clothes, and said, "Am I God, to kill and to make alive, that this man doth send unto me to recover a man of his leprosy? wherefore consider, I pray you, and see how he seeketh a quarrel against me."

And it was so, when Elisha the man of God had heard that the king of Israel had rent his clothes, that he sent to the king, saying, "Wherefore hast thou rent thy clothes? let him come now to me, and he shall know that there is a prophet in Israel."

So Naaman came with his horses and with his chariot, and stood at the door of the house of Elisha. And Elisha sent a messenger unto him, saying, "Go and wash in Jordan seven times, and thy flesh shall come again to thee, and thou shalt be clean."

But Naaman was wroth, and went away, and said, "Behold, I thought, 'He will surely come out to me, and stand, and call on the name of the LORD his God, and strike his hand over the place, and recover the leper.' Are not Abana and Pharpar, rivers of Damascus, better than all the waters of Israel? may I not wash in them, and be clean?" So he turned and went away in a rage.

And his servants came near, and spake unto him, and said, "My father, if the prophet had bid thee do some great thing, wouldest thou not have done it? how much rather then, when he saith to thee, 'Wash, and be clean'?"

Then went he down, and dipped himself seven times in Jordan, according to the saying of the man of God: and his flesh came again like unto the flesh of a little child, and he was clean. And he returned to the man of God, he and all his company, and came, and stood before him: and he said, "Behold, now I know that there is no God in all the earth, but in Israel: now therefore, I pray thee, take a blessing of thy servant."

But he said, "As the LORD liveth, before whom I stand, I will receive none." And he urged him to take it; but he refused.

And Naaman said, "Shall there not then, I pray thee, be given to thy servant two mules' burden of earth? for thy servant will henceforth offer neither burnt offering nor sacrifice unto other gods, but unto the LORD. In this thing the LORD pardon thy servant, that when my master goeth into the house of Rimmon to worship there, and he leaneth on my hand, and I bow myself in the house of Rimmon: when I bow down myself in the house of Rimmon, the LORD pardon thy servant in this thing."

And he said unto him, "Go in peace." So he departed from him a
little way.

But Gehazi, the servant of Elisha the man of God, said, "Behold, my master hath spared Naaman this Syrian, in not receiving at his hands that which he brought: but as the LORD liveth, I will run after him, and take somewhat of him."

So Gehazi followed after Naaman. And when Naaman saw him running after him, he lighted down from the chariot to meet him, and said, "Is all well?"

And he said, "All is well. My master hath sent me, saying, 'Behold, even now there be come to me from mount Ephraim two young men of the sons of the prophets: give them, I pray thee, a talent of silver, and two changes of garments.'"

And Naaman said, "Be content, take two talents."

And he urged him, and bound two talents of silver in two bags, with two changes of garments, and laid them upon two of his servants; and they bare them before him. And when he came to the tower, he took them from their hand, and bestowed them in the house: and he let the men go, and they departed. But he went in, and stood before his master. And Elisha said unto him, "Whence comest thou, Gehazi?"

And he said, "Thy servant went no whither."

And he said unto him, "Went not mine heart with thee, when the man turned again from his chariot to meet thee? Is it a time to receive money, and to receive garments, and oliveyards, and vineyards, and sheep, and oxen, and menservants, and maidservants? The leprosy therefore of Naaman shall cleave unto thee and unto thy seed for ever." And he went out from his presence a leper as white as snow.

Then the king of Syria warred against Israel, and took counsel with his servants, saying, "In such and such a place shall be my camp."

And the man of God sent unto the king of Israel, saying, "Beware that thou pass not such a place; for thither the Syrians are come down."

And the king of Israel sent to the place which the man of God told him and warned him of, and saved himself there, not once nor twice. Therefore the heart of the king of Syria was sore troubled for this thing; and he called his servants, and said unto them, "Will ye now shew me which of us is for the king of Israel?"

*Elisha and the Syrians*     And one of his servants said, "None, my lord, O king: but Elisha, the prophet that is in Israel, telleth the king of Israel the words that thou speakest in thy bedchamber."

And he said, "Go and spy where he is, that I may send and fetch him."

And it was told him, saying, "Behold, he is in Dothan." Therefore sent he thither horses, and chariots, and a great host: and they came by night, and compassed the city about.

And when the servant of the man of God was risen early, and gone forth, behold, an host compassed the city both with horses and chariots.

And his servant said unto him, "Alas, my master! how shall we do?"

And he answered, "Fear not: for they that be with us are more than they that be with them."

And Elisha prayed, and said, "Lord, I pray thee, open his eyes, that he may see." And the Lord opened the eyes of the young man; and he saw: and, behold, the mountain was full of horses and chariots of fire round about Elisha.

And when they came down to him, Elisha prayed unto the Lord, and said, "Smite this people, I pray thee, with blindness." And he smote them with blindness according to the word of Elisha.

And Elisha said unto them, "This is not the way, neither is this the city: follow me, and I will bring you to the man whom ye seek." But he led them to Samaria.

And it came to pass, when they were come into Samaria, that Elisha said, "Lord, open the eyes of these men, that they may see." And the Lord opened their eyes, and they saw; and, behold, they were in the midst of Samaria.

And the king of Israel said unto Elisha, when he saw them, "My father, shall I smite them? shall I smite them?"

And he answered, "Thou shalt not smite them: wouldest thou smite those whom thou hast taken captive with thy sword and with thy bow? set bread and water before them, that they may eat and drink, and go to their master."

And he prepared great provision for them: and when they had eaten and drunk, he sent them away, and they went to their master. So the bands of Syria came no more into the land of Israel.

Then spake Elisha unto the woman, whose son he had restored to Death of Elisha life, saying, "Arise, and go thou and thine household, and sojourn wheresoever thou canst sojourn: for the LORD hath called for a famine; and it shall also come upon the land seven years."

And the woman arose, and did after the saying of the man of God: and she went with her household, and sojourned in the land of the Philistines seven years. And it came to pass at the seven years' end, that the woman returned out of the land of the Philistines: and she went forth to cry unto the king for her house and for her land.

And the king talked with Gehazi the servant of the man of God, saying, "Tell me, I pray thee, all the great things that Elisha hath done."

And it came to pass, as he was telling the king how he had restored a dead body to life, that, behold, the woman, whose son he had restored to life, cried to the king for her house and for her land. And Gehazi said, "My lord, O king, this is the woman, and this is her son, whom Elisha restored to life."

And when the king asked the woman, she told him. So the king appointed unto her a certain officer, saying, "Restore all that was her's, and all the fruits of the field since the day that she left the land, even until now."

Now Elisha was fallen sick of his sickness whereof he died. And Joash the king of Israel came down unto him, and wept over his face, and said, "O my father, my father, the chariot of Israel, and the horsemen thereof."

And Elisha said unto him, "Take bow and arrows." And he took unto him bow and arrows.

And he said to the king of Israel, "Put thine hand upon the bow." And he put his hand upon it: and Elisha put his hands upon the king's hands.

And he said, "Open the window eastward." And he opened it.

Then Elisha said, "Shoot." And he shot.

And he said, "The arrow of the LORD's deliverance, and the arrow of deliverance from Syria."

And Elisha died, and they buried him.

*The Assyrians capture Samaria*

Then the king of Assyria came up throughout all the land, and went up to Samaria, and besieged it three years. In the ninth year of Hoshea the king of Assyria took Samaria, and carried Israel away into Assyria. For so it was, that the children of Israel had sinned against the LORD their God, which had brought them up out of the land of Egypt, from under the hand of Pharaoh king of Egypt, and had feared other gods, and walked in the statutes of the heathen, whom the LORD cast out from before the children of Israel, and of the kings of Israel, which they had made. And the children of Israel did secretly those things that were not right against the LORD their God, and they built them high places in all their cities, from the tower of the watchmen to the fenced city. And they set them up images and groves in every high hill, and under every green tree: and there they burnt incense in all the high places, as did the heathen whom the LORD carried away before them; and wrought wicked things to provoke the LORD to anger: for they served idols, whereof the LORD had said unto them, "Ye shall not do this thing."

Yet the LORD testified against Israel, and against Judah, by all the prophets, and by all the seers, saying, "Turn ye from your evil ways, and keep my commandments and my statutes, according to all the law which I commanded your fathers, and which I sent to you by my servants the prophets."

Notwithstanding they would not hear, but hardened their necks, like to the neck of their fathers, that did not believe in the LORD their God. And they rejected his statutes, and his covenant that he made with their fathers, and his testimonies which he testified against them; and they followed vanity, and became vain, and went after the heathen that were round about them, concerning whom the LORD had charged them, that they should not do like them. And they left all the commandments of the LORD their God, and made them molten images, even two calves, and made a grove, and worshipped all the host of heaven, and served Baal. And they caused their sons and daughters to pass through the fire, and used divination and enchantments, and sold themselves to do evil in the sight of the LORD, to provoke him to anger. Therefore the LORD was very angry with Israel, and removed them out of his sight. So was Israel carried away out of their own land to Assyria unto this day. And the king of Assyria brought men from Babylon, and placed them in the cities of Samaria instead of the children of Israel: and they possessed Samaria, and dwelt in the cities thereof. There was none left but the tribe of Judah only. Also Judah kept not the commandments of the LORD their God.

Now in the fourteenth year of king Hezekiah did Sennacherib king of Assyria come up against all the fenced cities of Judah, and took them. And the king of Assyria sent Tartan and Rabsaris and Rab-shakeh from Lachish to king Hezekiah with a great host against Jerusalem: and they went up and came to Jerusalem. And when they were come up, they came and stood by the conduit of the upper pool, which is in the highway of the fuller's field. And when they had called to the king, there came out to them Eliakim, which was over the household, and Shebna the scribe, and Joah the son of Asaph the recorder. And Rab-shakeh said unto them, "Speak ye now to Hezekiah, 'Thus saith the great king, the king of Assyria, What confidence is this wherein thou trustest? Thou sayest, (but they are but vain words,) I have counsel and strength for the war. Now on whom dost thou trust, that thou rebellest against me? Now, behold, thou trustest upon the staff of this bruised reed, even upon Egypt, on which if a man lean, it will go into his hand, and pierce it: so is Pharaoh king of Egypt unto all that trust on him. But if ye say unto me, We trust in the LORD our God: is not that he, whose high places and whose altars Hezekiah hath taken away, and hath said to Judah and Jerusalem, Ye shall worship before this altar in Jerusalem? Now therefore, I pray thee, give pledges to my lord the king of Assyria, and I will deliver thee two thousand horses, if thou be able on thy part to set riders upon them. How then wilt thou turn away the face of one captain of the least of my master's servants, and put thy trust on Egypt for chariots and for horsemen? Am I now come up without the LORD against this place to destroy it? The LORD said to me, Go up against this land, and destroy it.' "

Then said Eliakim and Shebna, and Joah, unto Rab-shakeh, "Speak, I pray thee, to thy servants in the Syrian language; for we understand it: and talk not with us in the Jews' language in the ears of the people that are on the wall."

Then Rab-shakeh stood and cried with a loud voice in the Jews' language, and spake, saying, "Hear the word of the great king, the king of Assyria: Thus saith the king, 'Let not Hezekiah deceive you: for he shall not be able to deliver you out of his hand: neither let Hezekiah make you trust in the LORD, saying, "The LORD will surely deliver us, and this city shall not be delivered into the hand of the king of Assyria." ' Hearken not to Hezekiah: for thus saith the king of Assyria, 'Make an agreement with me by a present, and come out to me, and then eat ye every man of his own vine, and every one of his fig tree, and drink ye every one the waters of his cistern: until I come and take you away to a land like your own land, a land of corn and wine, a land of bread and vineyards, a land of oil olive and of honey, that ye may live, and not die: and hearken not unto Hezekiah, when he persuadeth you, saying, "The LORD will deliver us." Hath any of the gods of the nations delivered at all his land out of the hand of the king of Assyria? Who are they among all the gods of the countries, that have delivered their country out of mine hand, that the LORD should deliver Jerusalem out of mine hand?' "

But the people held their peace, and answered him not a word: for the king's commandment was, saying, "Answer him not."

Then came Eliakim which was over the household, and Shebna the scribe, and Joah the son of Asaph the recorder, to Hezekiah with their clothes rent, and told him the words of Rab-shakeh.

And it came to pass, when king Hezekiah heard it, that he rent his clothes, and covered himself with sackcloth, and went into the house of the LORD. And he sent Eliakim, which was over the household, and Shebna the scribe, and the elders of the priests, covered with sackcloth, to Isaiah the prophet the son of Amoz. And they said unto him, "Thus saith Hezekiah, 'This day is a day of trouble, and of rebuke, and blasphemy: for the children are come to the birth, and there is not strength to bring forth. It may be the LORD thy God will hear all the words of Rab-shakeh, whom the king of Assyria his master hath sent to reproach the living God; and will reprove the words which the LORD thy God hath heard: wherefore lift up thy prayer for the remnant that are left.' "

So the servants of king Hezekiah came to Isaiah. And Isaiah said unto them, "Thus shall ye say to your master, 'Thus saith the LORD, Be not afraid of the words which thou hast heard, with which the servants of the king of Assyria have blasphemed me. Behold, I will send a blast upon him, and he shall hear a rumour, and shall return to his own land; and I will Isaiah's prophecy cause him to fall by the sword in his own land. ' "

So Rab-shakeh returned, and he sent messengers again unto Hezekiah, saying, "Thus shall ye speak to Hezekiah king of Judah, saying, 'Let not thy God in whom thou trustest deceive thee, saying, "Jerusalem shall not be delivered into the hand of the king of Assyria." Behold, thou hast heard what the kings of Assyria have done to all lands, by destroying them utterly: and shalt thou be delivered?' "

And Hezekiah received the letter of the hand of the messengers, and read it: and Hezekiah went up into the house of the LORD, and spread it before the LORD. And Hezekiah prayed before the LORD, and said, "O LORD God of Israel, which dwellest between the cherubims, thou art the God, even thou alone, of all the kingdoms of the earth; thou hast made heaven and earth. LORD, bow down thine ear, and hear: open, LORD, thine eyes, and see: and hear the words of Sennacherib, which hath sent him to reproach the living God. Now therefore, O LORD our God, I beseech thee, save thou us out of his hand, that all the kingdoms of the earth may know that thou art the LORD God, even thou only."

Then Isaiah the son of Amoz sent to Hezekiah, saying, "Thus saith the LORD God of Israel, 'That which thou hast prayed to me against Sennacherib king of Assyria I have heard.' This is the word that the LORD hath spoken concerning him; 'The daughter of Zion hath despised thee, and laughed thee to scorn; the daughter of Jerusalem hath shaken her head at thee. Whom hast thou reproached and blasphemed? and against whom hast thou exalted thy voice, and lifted up thine eyes on high? even against the Holy One of Israel. But I know thy abode, and thy going out, and thy coming in, and thy rage against me. Because thy rage against me and thy tumult is come up into mine ears, therefore I will put my hook in thy nose, and my bridle in thy lips, and I will turn thee back by the way by which thou camest.'

"Therefore thus saith the LORD concerning the king of Assyria, 'He shall not come into this city, nor shoot an arrow there, nor come before it with a shield, nor cast a bank against it. By the way that he came, by the same shall he return, and shall not come into this city, for I will defend this city, to save it, for mine own sake, and for my servant David's sake.' "

And it came to pass that night, that the angel of the LORD went out, and smote in the camp of the Assyrians. So Sennacherib king of Assyria departed, and went and returned, and dwelt at Nineveh.

In those days was Hezekiah, son of Ahaz, sick unto death. And the prophet Isaiah the son of Amoz came to him, and said unto him, "Thus saith the LORD, 'Set thine house in order; for thou shalt die, and not live.'" Then he turned his face to the wall and prayed unto the LORD, saying, "I beseech thee, O LORD, remember now how I have walked before thee in truth and with a perfect heart, and have done that which is good in thy sight." And Hezekiah wept sore.

And it came to pass, afore Isaiah was gone out into the middle court, that the word of the LORD came to him, saying, "Turn again, and tell Hezekiah the captain of my people, 'Thus saith the LORD, the God of David thy father, "I have heard thy prayer, I have seen thy tears: behold, I will heal thee: on the third day thou shalt go up unto the house of the LORD. And I will add unto thy days fifteen years; and I will deliver thee and this city out of the hand of the king of Assyria; and I will defend this city for mine own sake, and for my servant David's sake."'"

And Isaiah said, "Take a lump of figs." And they took and laid it on the boil, and he recovered.

At that time Berodach-baladan, the son of Baladan, king of Babylon, sent letters and a present unto Hezekiah: for he had heard that Hezekiah had been sick. And Hezekiah hearkened unto them, and shewed them all the house of his precious things, the silver, and the gold, and the spices, and the precious ointment, and all the house of his armour, and all that was found in his treasures: there was nothing in his house, nor in all his dominion, that Hezekiah shewed them not.

Then came Isaiah the prophet unto king Hezekiah, and said unto him, "What said these men? and from whence came they unto thee?"

And Hezekiah said, "They are come from a far country, even from Babylon."

And he said, "What have they seen in thine house?"

And Hezekiah answered, "All the things that are in mine house have they seen: there is nothing among my treasures that I have not shewed them."

And Isaiah said unto Hezekiah, "Hear the word of the LORD. 'Behold, the days come, that all that is in thine house, and that which thy fathers

have laid up in store unto this day, shall be carried into Babylon: nothing shall be left,' saith the Lord. 'And of thy sons that shall issue from
thee, which thou shalt beget, shall they take away; and they shall be
eunuchs in the palace of the king of Babylon.' ''

Then said Hezekiah unto Isaiah, "Good is the word of the Lord which
thou hast spoken." And he said, "Is it not good, if peace and truth be in
my days?"

And the rest of the acts of Hezekiah, and all his might, and how he
made a pool, and a conduit, and brought water into the city, are they not
written in the book of the chronicles of the kings of Judah? And Hezekiah
slept with his fathers: and Manasseh his son reigned in his stead.

Josiah was eight years old when he began to reign, and he reigned
thirty and one years in Jerusalem. And he did that which was right in the
sight of the Lord, and walked in all the way of David his father, and
turned not aside to the right hand or to the left.

And it came to pass in the eighteenth year of king Josiah, that the king
sent Shaphan the son of Azaliah, the son of Meshullam, the scribe, to the
house of the Lord, saying, "Go up to Hilkiah the high priest, that he may
sum the silver which is brought into the house of the Lord, which the
keepers of the door have gathered of the people: and let them deliver it
into the hand of the doers of the work, that have the oversight of the
house of the Lord: and let them give it to the doers of the work which is
in the house of the Lord, to repair the breaches of the house, unto
carpenters, and builders, and masons, and to buy timber and hewn stone
to repair the house." Howbeit there was no reckoning made with them of
the money that was delivered into their hand, because they dealt faithfully.

And Hilkiah the high priest said unto Shaphan the scribe, "I have
found the book of the law in the house of the Lord." And Hilkiah gave
the book to Shaphan, and he read it.

And Shaphan the scribe came to the king, and brought the king word
again, and said, "Thy servants have gathered the money that was found
in the house, and have delivered it into the hand of them that do the work,
that have the oversight of the house of the Lord."

And Shaphan the scribe shewed the king, saying, "Hilkiah the priest
hath delivered me a book." And Shaphan read it before the king.

So Hilkiah the priest, and Ahikam, and Achbor, and Shaphan, and

Asahiah, went unto Huldah the prophetess, the wife of Shallum, the son of Harhas, keeper of the wardrobe; (now she dwelt in Jerusalem in the college;) and they communed with her. And she said unto them, "Thus saith the LORD God of Israel, Tell the man that sent you to me, Because thine heart was tender, and thou hast humbled thyself before the LORD, when thou heardest what I spake against this place, and against the inhabitants thereof, that they should become a desolation and a curse, and hast rent thy clothes, and wept before me; I also have heard thee, saith the LORD. Behold therefore, I will gather thee unto thy fathers, and thou shalt be gathered into thy grave in peace; and thine eyes shall not see all the evil which I will bring upon this place."

And they brought the king word again. And the king sent, and they gathered unto him all the elders of Judah and of Jerusalem. And the king went up into the house of the LORD, and all the men of Judah and all the inhabitants of Jerusalem with him, and the priests, and the prophets, and all the people, both small and great: and he read in their ears all the words of the book of the covenant which was found in the house of the LORD. And the king stood by a pillar, and made a covenant before the LORD, to walk after the LORD, and to keep his commandments and his testimonies and his statutes with all their heart and all their soul, to perform the words of this covenant that were written in this book. And all the people stood to the covenant.

And the king commanded Hilkiah the high priest, and the priests of the second order, and the keepers of the door, to bring forth out of the temple of the LORD all the vessels that were made for Baal, and for the grove, and for all the host of heaven: and he burned them without Jerusalem in the fields of Kidron, and carried the ashes of them unto Beth-el. And he put down the idolatrous priests, whom the kings of Judah had ordained to burn incense in the high places in the cities of Judah, and in the places round about Jerusalem; them also that burned incense unto Baal, to the sun, and to the moon, and to the planets, and to all the host of heaven. And he brought out the grove from the house of the LORD, without Jerusalem, unto the brook Kidron, and burned it at the brook Kidron, and stamped it small to powder, and cast the powder thereof upon the graves of the children of the people. And he brake down the houses of the sodomites, that were by the house of the LORD, where the women wove

hangings for the grove. And he brought all the priests out of the cities of
Judah, and defiled the high places where the priests had burned incense.

And the king commanded all the people, saying, "Keep the passover
unto the LORD your God, as it is written in the book of this covenant."
Surely there was not holden such a passover from the days of the judges
that judged Israel, nor in all the days of the kings of Israel, nor of the kings
of Judah; but in the eighteenth year of king Josiah, wherein this passover
was holden to the LORD in Jerusalem. And like unto him was there no king
before him, that turned to the LORD with all his heart, and with all his
soul, and with all his might, according to all the law of Moses; neither
after him arose there any like him.

In his days Pharaoh-nechoh king of Egypt went up against the king of
Assyria to the river Euphrates: and king Josiah went against him; and he
slew him at Megiddo, when he had seen him. And his servants carried him
in a chariot dead from Megiddo, and brought him to Jerusalem, and buried
him in his own sepulchre. And the people of the land took Jehoahaz
the son of Josiah, and anointed him, and made him king in his father's
stead.

At that time, the servants of Nebuchadnezzar king of Babylon came
up against Jerusalem, and the city was besieged. And Nebuchadnezzar,
king of Babylon came against the city, and his servants did besiege it. And
Jehoiachin the king of Judah went out to the king of Babylon, he, and his
mother, and his servants, and his princes, and his officers: and the king of
Babylon took him in the eighth year of his reign. And he carried out
thence all the treasures of the house of the LORD, and the treasures of the
king's house, and cut in pieces all the vessels of gold which Solomon king
of Israel had made in the temple of the LORD, as the LORD had said. And
he carried away all Jerusalem, and all the princes, and all the mighty men
of valour, even ten thousand captives, and all the craftsmen and smiths:
none remained, save the poorest sort of the people of the land.

And it came to pass in the ninth year of his reign, in the tenth month,
in the tenth day of the month, that Nebuchadnezzar king of Babylon came,
he, and all his host, against Jerusalem, and pitched against it; and they
built forts against it round about. And the city was besieged unto the
eleventh year of king Zedekiah. And on the ninth day of the fourth month
the famine prevailed in the city, and there was no bread for the people of

the land. And the city was broken up, and all the men of war fled by night by the way of the gate between two walls, which is by the king's garden: (now the Chaldees were against the city round about:) and the king went the way toward the plain. And the army of the Chaldees pursued after the king, and overtook him in the plains of Jericho: and all his army were scattered from him.

Then came Nebuzar-adan, captain of the guard, a servant of the king of Babylon, unto Jerusalem: and he burnt the house of the LORD, and the king's house, and all the houses of Jerusalem, and every great man's house burnt he with fire. And all the army of the Chaldees, that were with the captain of the guard, brake down the walls of Jerusalem round about. Now the rest of the people that were left in the city, and the fugitives that fell away to the king of Babylon, with the remnant of the multitude, did Nebuzar-adan the captain of the guard carry away. But the captain of the guard left of the poor of the land to be vinedressers and husbandmen. And the pillars of brass that were in the house of the LORD, and the bases, and the brasen sea that was in the house of the LORD, did the Chaldees break in pieces, and carried the brass of them to Babylon.

And as for the people that remained in the land of Judah, whom Nebuchadnezzar king of Babylon had left, even over them he made Gedaliah ruler. And Gedaliah sware to them, and to their men, and said unto them, "Fear not to be the servants of the Chaldees: dwell in the land, and serve the king of Babylon; and it shall be well with you."

And it came to pass in the seven and thirtieth year of the captivity of Jehoiachin king of Judah, that Evil-merodach king of Babylon in the year that he began to reign did lift up the head of Jehoiachin king of Judah out of prison; and he spake kindly to him, and set his throne above the throne of the kings that were with him in Babylon; and changed his prison garments: and he did eat bread continually before him all the days of his life. And his allowance was a continual allowance given him of the king, a daily rate for every day, all the days of his life.

THE words of Amos, who was among the herdmen of Tekoa, which he saw concerning Israel in the days of Uzziah king of Judah, and in the days of Jeroboam the son of Joash king of Israel, two years before the earthquake. And he said,

## THE PROPHETS

The LORD will roar from Zion,
And utter his voice from Jerusalem;
And the habitations of the shepherds shall mourn,
And the top of Carmel shall wither.
Can two walk together, except they be agreed?
Will a lion roar in the forest, when he hath no prey?
Will a young lion cry out of his den, if he have taken nothing?
Can a bird fall in a snare upon the earth, where no gin is for him?
Shall one take up a snare from the earth, and have taken nothing at all?
Shall a trumpet be blown in the city, and the people not be afraid?
Shall there be evil in a city, and the LORD hath not done it?
The lion hath roared, who will not fear?
The Lord GOD hath spoken, who can but prophesy?
Thus saith the LORD; "For three transgressions of Moab, and for four,
I will not turn away the punishment thereof;
Because he burned the bones of the king of Edom into lime.
Behold, I am pressed under you,
As a cart is pressed that is full of sheaves."
For thus saith the LORD unto the house of Israel,
"Seek ye me, and ye shall live:
But seek not Beth-el,
Nor enter into Gilgal,
And pass not to Beer-sheba:
For Gilgal shall surely go into captivity,
And Beth-el shall come to nought."
Seek the LORD, and ye shall live;
Lest he break out like fire in the house of Joseph, and devour it,
And there be none to quench it in Beth-el.
Ye who turn judgment to wormwood,
And leave off righteousness in the earth,
Seek him that maketh the seven stars and Orion,
And turneth the shadow of death into the morning,
And maketh the day dark with night:
That calleth for the waters of the sea,
And poureth them out upon the face of the earth:
The LORD is his name.

*A lamentation for Israel*

[ 219 ]

Seek good, and not evil, that ye may live:
And so the LORD, the God of hosts, shall be with you, as ye have spoken.
Hate the evil, and love the good, and establish judgment in the gate:
It may be that the LORD God of hosts will be gracious unto the remnant of Joseph.
Therefore the LORD, the God of hosts, saith thus;
"Though ye offer me burnt offerings and your meat offerings,
I will not accept them:
Neither will I regard the peace offerings of your fat beasts.
Take thou away from me the noise of thy songs;
For I will not hear the melody of thy viols.
But let judgment run down as waters,
And righteousness as a mighty stream."
Publish in the palaces at Ashdod,
And in the palaces in the land of Egypt, and say,
"Assemble yourselves upon the mountains of Samaria,
And behold the great tumults in the midst thereof,
And the oppressed in the midst thereof."
"For they know not to do right," saith the LORD,
"Who store up violence and robbery in their palaces."
Hear this word, ye kine of Bashan, that are in the mountain of Samaria,
Which oppress the poor, which crush the needy,
Which say to their masters, "Bring, and let us drink."
Woe to them that are at ease in Zion,
And trust in the mountain of Samaria,
Which are named chief of the nations, to whom the house of Israel came!
That lie upon beds of ivory,
And stretch themselves upon their couches,
And eat the lambs out of the flock,
And the calves out of the midst of the stall;
That chant to the sound of the viol,
And invent to themselves instruments of musick, like David;
That drink wine in bowls,
And anoint themselves with the chief ointments:
But they are not grieved for the affliction of Joseph.

## THE PROPHETS

Hear this, O ye that swallow up the needy,
Even to make the poor of the land to fail,
Saying, "When will the new moon be gone,
That we may sell corn?
And the sabbath, that we may set forth wheat,
Making the ephah small, and the shekel great,
And falsifying the balances by deceit?
That we may buy the poor for silver,
And the needy for a pair of shoes;
Yea, and sell the refuse of the wheat?"
Forasmuch therefore as your treading is upon the poor,
And ye take from him burdens of wheat:
Ye have built houses of hewn stone, but ye shall not dwell in them;
Ye have planted pleasant vineyards, but ye shall not drink wine of
    them.
For I know your manifold transgressions, and your mighty sins:
They afflict the just, they take a bribe,
And they turn aside the poor in the gate from their right.
Therefore the prudent shall keep silence in that time;
For it is an evil time.
Therefore thus will I do unto thee, O Israel:
And because I will do this unto thee,
Prepare to meet thy God, O Israel.
Shall horses run upon the rock?
Will one plow there with oxen?
For ye have turned judgment into gall,
And the fruit of righteousness into hemlock:
Ye which rejoice in a thing of nought, which say,
"Have we not taken to us horns by our own strength?"
"But, behold, I will raise up against you a nation,
O house of Israel," saith the LORD the God of hosts;
"And they shall afflict you from the entering in of Hemath
Unto the river of the wilderness.
And it shall come to pass in that day," saith the Lord GOD,
"That I will cause the sun to go down at noon,
And I will darken the earth in the clear day:

[ 221 ]

And I will turn your feasts into mourning,
And all your songs into lamentation;
And I will bring up sackcloth upon all loins,
And baldness upon every head;
And I will make it as the mourning of an only son,
And the end thereof as a bitter day."
"Behold, the days come," saith the Lord GOD,
"That I will send a famine in the land,
Not a famine of bread, nor a thirst for water,
But of hearing the words of the LORD:
And they shall wander from sea to sea,
And from the north even to the east,
They shall run to and fro to seek the word of the LORD,
And shall not find it.
Behold, the eyes of the Lord GOD are upon the sinful kingdom,
And I will destroy it from off the face of the earth.
Hear ye this word which I take up against you,
Even a lamentation, O house of Israel.
The virgin of Israel is fallen; she shall no more rise:
She is forsaken upon her land; there is none to raise her up."

Then Amaziah the priest of Beth-el sent to Jeroboam king of Israel, saying, "Amos hath conspired against thee in the midst of the house of Israel: the land is not able to bear all his words. For thus Amos saith, 'Jeroboam shall die by the sword, and Israel shall surely be led away captive out of their own land.'"

Also Amaziah said unto Amos, "O thou seer, go, flee thee away into the land of Judah, and there eat bread, and prophesy there: but prophesy not again any more at Beth-el: for it is the king's chapel, and it is the king's court."

Then answered Amos, and said to Amaziah, "I was no prophet, neither was I a prophet's son; but I was an herdman, and a gatherer of sycomore fruit: and the LORD took me as I followed the flock, and the LORD said unto me, 'Go, prophesy unto my people Israel.'"

I saw the Lord standing upon the altar:
And he said, "Smite the lintel of the door, that the posts may shake:

And cut them in the head, all of them;
And I will slay the last of them with the sword:
He that fleeth of them shall not flee away,
And he that escapeth of them shall not be delivered.
And the Lord GOD of hosts is he that toucheth the land, and it shall
    melt,
And all that dwell therein shall mourn:
And it shall rise up wholly like a flood;
And shall be drowned, as by the flood of Egypt.
Behold, the eyes of the Lord GOD are upon the sinful kingdom,
And I will destroy it from off the face of the earth;
Saving that I will not utterly destroy the house of Jacob," saith the
    LORD.
"For, lo, I will command,
  And I will sift the house of Israel among all nations,
  Like as corn is sifted in a sieve,
  Yet shall not the least grain fall upon the earth.
  All the sinners of my people shall die by the sword, which say,
  'The evil shall not overtake nor prevent us.'
  In that day will I raise up the tabernacle of David that is fallen,
  And close up the breaches thereof;
  And I will raise up his ruins,
  And I will build it as in the days of old:
  That they may possess the remnant of Edom,
  And of all the heathen, which are called by my name,"
  Saith the LORD that doeth this.
"Behold, the days come," saith the LORD,
"That the plowman shall overtake the reaper,
  And the treader of grapes him that soweth seed;
  And the mountains shall drop sweet wine,
  And all the hills shall melt.
  And I will bring again the captivity of my people of Israel,
  And they shall build the waste cities, and inhabit them;
  And they shall plant vineyards, and drink the wine thereof;
  They shall also make gardens, and eat the fruit of them.
  And I will plant them upon their land,

*David's tabernacle to be restored*

And they shall no more be pulled up out of their land which I have
given them,"
Saith the LORD thy God.

THE word of the LORD that came unto Hosea, in the days of Uzziah,
king of Judah, and in the days of Jeroboam, king of Israel.

Hear the word of the LORD, ye children of Israel: for the LORD hath
a controversy with the inhabitants of the land, because there is no truth,
nor mercy, nor knowledge of God in the land. By swearing, and lying,
and killing, and stealing, and committing adultery, they break out, and
blood toucheth blood. Therefore shall the land mourn, and every one
that dwelleth therein shall languish.

My people are destroyed for lack of knowledge: for Israel slideth back
as a backsliding heifer: now the LORD will feed them as a lamb in a large
place. I will go and return to my place, till they acknowledge their
offence, and seek my face: in their affliction they will seek me early.

Come, and let us return unto the LORD:
For he hath torn, and he will heal us;
He hath smitten, and he will bind us up.
After two days will he revive us:
In the third day he will raise us up, and we shall live in his sight.
Then shall we know, if we follow on to know the LORD:
His going forth is prepared as the morning;
And he shall come unto us as the rain,
As the latter and former rain unto the earth.

O Ephraim, what shall I do unto thee? O Judah, what shall I do unto
thee? for your goodness is as a morning cloud, and as the early dew it
goeth away as the chaff that is driven with the whirlwind, and the smoke
out of the chimney. Therefore have I hewed them by the prophets; I have
slain them by the words of my mouth: and thy judgments are as the light
that goeth forth. For I desired mercy, and not sacrifice; and the knowledge of God more than burnt offerings. But they like men have transgressed the covenant: there have they dealt treacherously against me.

Ephraim, he hath mixed himself among the people; Ephraim is a
cake not turned. Strangers have devoured his strength, and he knoweth it

not: yea, gray hairs are here and there upon him, yet he knoweth not.   *Israel's ingratitude to*

Ephraim also is like a silly dove without heart: they call to Egypt,   *God*
they go to Assyria. When they shall go, I will spread my net upon them:
I will bring them down as the fowls of the heaven; I will chastise them,
as their congregation hath heard. For they have sown the wind, and
they shall reap the whirlwind: it hath no stalk: the bud shall yield no
meal: if so be it yield, the strangers shall swallow it up. I have written
to him the great things of my law, but they were counted as a strange
thing.

Ephraim feedeth on wind, and followeth after the east wind: he daily
increaseth lies and desolation; and they do make a covenant with the
Assyrians, and oil is carried into Egypt. The LORD hath also a controversy with Judah, and will punish Jacob according to his ways; according
to his doings will he recompense him. By his strength he had power with
God. Even the LORD God of hosts; the LORD is his memorial. Therefore
turn thou to thy God: keep mercy and judgment and wait on thy God
continually.

And I that am the LORD thy God from the land of Egypt will yet make
thee to dwell in tabernacles, as in the days of the solemn feast. I have also
spoken by the prophets, and I have multiplied visions, and used simili-
tudes, by the ministry of the prophets.

And now they sin more and more.

Yet I am the LORD thy God from the land of Egypt, and thou shalt
know no god but me: for there is no saviour beside me. I did know thee
in the wilderness, in the land of great drought.

According to their pasture, so were they filled; they were filled, and
their heart was exalted; therefore have they forgotten me. And the pride
of Israel testifieth to his face: and they do not return to the LORD their
God, nor seek him for all this.

When Israel was a child, then I loved him, and called my son out of
Egypt. As they called them, so they went from them: they sacrificed unto
Baalim, and burned incense to graven images. I taught Ephraim also to
go, taking them by their arms; but they knew not that I healed them. I
drew them with cords of a man, with bands of love: and I was to them as
they that take off the yoke on their jaws, and I laid meat unto them.

I found Israel like grapes in the wilderness; I saw your fathers as the firstripe in the fig tree at her first time: but they went to Baal-peor, and separated themselves unto that shame; and their abominations were according as they loved.

'O Israel, thou hast destroyed thyself; but in me is thine help. I will be thy king: where is any other that may save thee in all thy cities? and thy judges of whom thou saidst, "Give me a king and princes"?

O Israel, return unto the LORD thy God; for thou hast fallen by thine iniquity. I will heal their backsliding, I will love them freely: for mine anger is turned away from him. I will be as the dew unto Israel: he shall grow as the lily, and cast forth his roots as Lebanon. His branches shall spread, and his beauty shall be as the olive tree, and his smell as Lebanon. They that dwell under his shadow shall return; they shall revive as the corn, and grow as the vine: the scent thereof shall be as the wine of Lebanon.

Ephraim shall say, "What have I to do any more with idols?" I have heard him, and observed him: I am like a green fir tree. From me is thy fruit found.

"How shall I give thee up, Ephraim? how shall I deliver thee, Israel? mine heart is turned within me, my repentings are kindled together. I will not execute the fierceness of mine anger, I will not return to destroy Ephraim: for I am God, and not man; the Holy One in the midst of thee: and I will not enter into the city. They shall walk after the LORD; and I will place them in their houses," saith the LORD.

Sow to yourselves in righteousness, reap in mercy; break up your fallow ground: for it is time to seek the LORD, till he come and rain righteousness upon you.

"Therefore," saith the LORD, "Behold, I will allure her, and bring her into the wilderness, and speak comfortably unto her. And I will give her her vineyards from thence, and the valley of Achor for a door of hope: and she shall sing there, as in the days of her youth, and as in the day when she came up out of the land of Egypt. And it shall be at that day," saith the LORD, "that thou shalt call me Ishi; and shalt call me no more Baali. For I will take away the names of Baalim out of her mouth, and they shall no more be remembered by their name. And in that day will I make a covenant for them with the beasts of the field, and with the fowls of heaven, and with the creeping things of the ground: and I will break the bow and the sword and the battle out of the earth, and will make them to lie down safely. And I will betroth thee unto me for ever; yea, I will betroth thee unto me in righteousness, and in judgment, and in lovingkindness, and in mercies. I will even betroth thee unto me in faithfulness: and thou shalt know the LORD.

"And it shall come to pass in that day, I will hear," saith the LORD, "I will hear the heavens, and they shall hear the earth; and the earth shall hear the corn, and the wine, and the oil; and they shall hear Jezreel. And I will sow her unto me in the earth; and I will have mercy; and I will say to them which were not my people, 'Thou art my people'; and they shall say, 'Thou art my God.' "

Who is wise, and he shall understand these things? prudent, and he shall know them? for the ways of the LORD are right, and the just shall walk in them.

THE vision of Isaiah the son of Amoz, which he saw concerning Judah and Jerusalem in the days of Uzziah, Jotham, Ahaz, and Hezekiah, kings of Judah.

In the year that king Uzziah died I saw also the Lord sitting upon a throne, high and lifted up, and his train filled the temple. Above it stood the seraphims: each one had six wings; with twain he covered his face, and with twain he covered his feet, and with twain he did fly. And one cried unto another, and said, "Holy, holy, holy, is the LORD of hosts: the whole earth is full of his glory." And the posts of the door moved at the voice of him that cried, and the house was filled with smoke.

Then said I, "Woe is me! for I am undone; because I am a man of unclean lips, and I dwell in the midst of a people of unclean lips: for mine eyes have seen the King, the LORD of hosts."

Then flew one of the seraphims unto me, having a live coal in his hand, which he had taken with the tongs from off the altar: and he laid it upon my mouth, and said, "Lo, this hath touched thy lips; and thine iniquity is taken away, and thy sin purged."

Also I heard the voice of the Lord, saying, "Whom shall I send, and who will go for us?"

Then said I, "Here am I; send me."

Now will I sing to my wellbeloved
A song of my beloved touching his vineyard.
My wellbeloved hath a vineyard
In a very fruitful hill:
And he fenced it, and gathered out the stones thereof,
And planted it with the choicest vine,
And built a tower in the midst of it,
And also made a winepress therein:
And he looked that it should bring forth grapes,
And it brought forth wild grapes.
And now, O inhabitants of Jerusalem, and men of Judah,
Judge, I pray you, betwixt me and my vineyard.
What could have been done more to my vineyard,
That I have not done in it?
Wherefore, when I looked that it should bring forth grapes,
Brought it forth wild grapes? And now go to; I will tell you
What I will do to my vineyard:
I will take away the hedge thereof, and it shall be eaten up;
And break down the wall thereof, and it shall be trodden down:
And I will lay it waste; it shall not be pruned, nor digged;
But there shall come up briers and thorns:
I will also command the clouds that they rain no rain upon it.
For the vineyard of the LORD of hosts is the house of Israel,
And the men of Judah his pleasant plant:
And he looked for judgment, but behold oppression;
For righteousness, but behold a cry.
Woe unto them that join house to house,
That lay field to field, till there be no place,
That they may be placed alone in the midst of the earth!
In mine ears said the LORD of hosts,
"Of a truth many houses shall be desolate,
Even great and fair, without inhabitant.
Yea, ten acres of vineyard shall yield one bath,
And the seed of an homer shall yield an ephah.
Woe unto them that rise up early in the morning,
That they may follow strong drink;

That continue until night, till wine inflame them!

And the harp, and the viol, the tabret, and pipe, and wine, are in their
    feasts:

But they regard not the work of the LORD,

Neither consider the operation of his hands.

Therefore my people are gone into captivity,

Because they have no knowledge:

And their honourable men are famished,

And their multitude dried up with thirst.

Therefore hell hath enlarged herself, and opened her mouth without
    measure:

And their glory, and their multitude, and their pomp,

And he that rejoiceth, shall descend into it.

And the mean man shall be brought down,

And the mighty man shall be humbled,

And the eyes of the lofty shall be humbled:

But the LORD of hosts shall be exalted in judgment,

And God that is holy shall be sanctified in righteousness.

Then shall the lambs feed after their manner,

And the waste places of the fat ones shall strangers eat.

Woe unto them that draw iniquity with cords of vanity,

And sin as it were with a cart rope:

That say, "Let him make speed, and hasten his work, that we may
    see it:

And let the counsel of the Holy One of Israel draw nigh and come,
    that we may know it!"

Woe unto them that call evil good, and good evil;

That put darkness for light, and light for darkness;

That put bitter for sweet, and sweet for bitter!

Woe unto them that are wise in their own eyes,

And prudent in their own sight!

Woe unto them that are mighty to drink wine,

And men of strength to mingle strong drink:

Which justify the wicked for reward,

And take away the righteousness of the righteous from him!

Therefore as the fire devoureth the stubble,

*Destruction of the unrighteous*

And the flame consumeth the chaff,
So their root shall be as rottenness,
And their blossom shall go up as dust:
Because they have cast away the law of the LORD of hosts,
And despised the word of the Holy One of Israel.
Woe unto them that decree unrighteous decrees,
And that write grievousness which they have prescribed;
To turn aside the needy from judgment,
And to take away the right from the poor of my people,
That widows may be their prey,
And that they may rob the fatherless!
He will lift up an ensign to the nations from far,
And will hiss unto them from the end of the earth:
And, behold, they shall come with speed swiftly:
None shall be weary nor stumble among them;
None shall slumber nor sleep;
Neither shall the girdle of their loins be loosed,
Nor the latchet of their shoes be broken:
Whose arrows are sharp, and all their bows bent,
Their horses' hoofs shall be counted like flint,
And their wheels like a whirlwind.
Their roaring shall be like a lion, they shall roar like young lions:
Yea, they shall roar, and lay hold of the prey,
And shall carry it away safe, and none shall deliver it.
And in that day they shall roar against them like the roaring of the
        sea:
And if one look unto the land, behold darkness and sorrow,
And the light is darkened in the heavens thereof.

O Assyrian, the rod of mine anger,
And the staff in their hand is mine indignation.
I will send him against an hypocritical nation,
And against the people of my wrath will I give him a charge,
To take the spoil, and to take the prey,
And to tread them down like the mire of the streets. Howbeit he
        meaneth not so,

Neither doth his heart think so;
But it is in his heart to destroy
And cut off nations not a few. For he saith, "Are not my princes alto-
    gether kings?
Is not Calno as Carchemish?
Is not Hamath as Arpad?
Is not Samaria as Damascus?
As my hand hath found the kingdoms of the idols,
And whose graven images did excel them of Jerusalem and of
    Samaria;
Shall I not, as I have done unto Samaria and her idols,
So do to Jerusalem and her idols?"
Wherefore it shall come to pass,
That when the Lord hath performed his whole work upon mount
    Zion and on Jerusalem,
I will punish the fruit of the stout heart of the king of Assyria,
And the glory of his high looks.
For he saith, "By the strength of my hand I have done it,
And by my wisdom; for I am prudent:
And I have removed the bounds of the people,
And have robbed their treasures,
And I have put down the inhabitants like a valiant man:
And my hand hath found as a nest
The riches of the people:
And as one gathereth eggs that are left,
Have I gathered all the earth;
And there was none that moved the wing, or opened the mouth, or
    peeped."
Shall the ax boast itself against him that heweth therewith?
Or shall the saw magnify itself against him that shaketh it?
As if the rod should shake itself against them that lift it up,
Or as if the staff should lift up itself, as if it were no wood.

Wash you, make you clean;
Put away the evil of your doings from before mine eyes;
Cease to do evil;

*Judah's rebellion*     Learn to do well;
Seek judgment, relieve the oppressed,
Judge the fatherless, plead for the widow.
"Come now, and let us reason together,"
Saith the LORD:
"Though your sins be as scarlet,
They shall be as white as snow;
Though they be red like crimson,
They shall be as wool.
If ye be willing and obedient,
Ye shall eat the good of the land:
But if ye refuse and rebel,
Ye shall be devoured with the sword":
For the mouth of the LORD hath spoken it.
Hear, O heavens, and give ear, O earth:
For the LORD hath spoken,
"I have nourished and brought up children,
And they have rebelled against me.
The ox knoweth his owner,
And the ass his master's crib:
But Israel doth not know,
My people doth not consider."
Ah sinful nation, a people laden with iniquity,
A seed of evildoers, children that are corrupters:
They have forsaken the LORD,
They have provoked the Holy One of Israel unto anger,
They are gone away backward. Why should ye be stricken any more?
Ye will revolt more and more:
The whole head is sick, and the whole heart faint.
From the sole of the foot even unto the head there is no soundness
        in it;
But wounds, and bruises, and putrifying sores:
They have not been closed, neither bound up, neither mollified with
        ointment.
Your country is desolate, your cities are burned with fire:
Your land, strangers devour it in your presence,

And it is desolate, as overthrown by strangers.     *A joyful thanksgiving*
And the daughter of Zion is left as a cottage in a vineyard,
As a lodge in a garden of cucumbers, as a besieged city.
The remnant shall return, even the remnant of Jacob,
Unto the mighty God.
For though thy people Israel be as the sand of the sea,
Yet a remnant of them shall return:
The consumption decreed shall overflow with righteousness.
And in that day thou shalt say,
"O LORD, I will praise thee:
Though thou wast angry with me,
Thine anger is turned away,
And thou comfortedst me.
Behold, God is my salvation;
I will trust, and not be afraid:
For the LORD JEHOVAH is my strength and my song;
He also is become my salvation."
Therefore with joy shall ye draw water
Out of the wells of salvation.
And in that day shall ye say,
"Praise the LORD, call upon his name,
Declare his doings among the people,
Make mention that his name is exalted.
Sing unto the LORD;
For he hath done excellent things:
This is known in all the earth.
Cry out and shout, thou inhabitant of Zion:
For great is the Holy One of Israel in the midst of thee."

Thou shalt take up this proverb against the king of Babylon, and say,

"How hath the oppressor ceased!
The golden city ceased!
The LORD hath broken the staff of the wicked,
And the sceptre of the rulers.
He who smote the people in wrath with a continual stroke,
He that ruled the nations in anger,

[ 233 ]

Is persecuted, and none hindereth.
The whole earth is at rest, and is quiet:
They break forth into singing.
Yea, the fir trees rejoice at thee,
And the cedars of Lebanon, saying,
'Since thou art laid down,
No feller is come up against us.'

"How art thou fallen from heaven,
O Lucifer, son of the morning!
How art thou cut down to the ground,
Which didst weaken the nations!
For thou hast said in thine heart,
'I will ascend into heaven,
I will exalt my throne above the stars of God:
I will sit also upon the mount of the congregation,
In the sides of the north:
I will ascend above the heights of the clouds:
I will be like the most High.'
Yet thou shalt be brought down to hell,
To the sides of the pit.
They that see thee shall narrowly look upon thee,
And consider thee, saying,
'Is this the man that made the earth to tremble,
That did shake kingdoms;
That made the world as a wilderness, and destroyed the cities thereof;
That opened not the house of his prisoners?'"
And it shall come to pass in the last days,
That the mountain of the LORD's house
Shall be established in the top of the mountains,
And shall be exalted above the hills;
And all nations shall flow unto it.
And many people shall go and say,
"Come ye, and let us go up to the mountain of the LORD,
To the house of the God of Jacob;
And he will teach us of his ways,

## THE PROPHETS

*Christ's kingdom foretold*

And we will walk in his paths:
For out of Zion shall go forth the law,
And the word of the LORD from Jerusalem." And he shall judge among
    the nations,
And shall rebuke many people:
And they shall beat their swords into plowshares,
And their spears into pruninghooks:
Nation shall not lift up sword against nation,
Neither shall they learn war any more.

O house of Jacob, come ye,
And let us walk in the light of the LORD.
Enter into the rock, and hide thee in the dust,
For fear of the LORD, and for the glory of his majesty.
The lofty looks of man shall be humbled,
And the haughtiness of men shall be bowed down,
And the LORD alone shall be exalted in that day.
For the day of the LORD of hosts
Shall be upon every one that is proud and lofty,
And upon every one that is lifted up;
And he shall be brought low:
And upon all the cedars of Lebanon, that are high and lifted up,
And upon all the oaks of Bashan,
And upon all the high mountains,
And upon all the hills that are lifted up,
And upon every high tower,
And upon every fenced wall,
And upon all the ships of Tarshish,
And upon all pleasant pictures.
And the loftiness of man shall be bowed down, and the haughtiness
    of men shall be made low:
And the LORD alone shall be exalted in that day.
And the idols he shall utterly abolish.
And they shall go into the holes of the rocks,
And into the caves of the earth,
For fear of the LORD, and for the glory of his majesty,

*Israel blessed*

When he ariseth to shake terribly the earth. In that day a man shall
cast his idols of silver, and his idols of gold, which they made each
one for himself to worship, to the moles and to the bats; to go
into the clefts of the rocks, and into the tops of the ragged rocks,
for fear of the LORD, and for the glory of his majesty, when he
ariseth to shake terribly the earth.

Cease ye from man, whose breath is in his nostrils:
For wherein is he to be accounted of?
And the LORD will create upon every dwelling place of mount Zion,
And upon her assemblies,
A cloud and smoke by day, and the shining of a flaming fire by night:
For upon all the glory shall be a defence.
All ye inhabitants of the world, and dwellers on the earth,
See ye, when he lifteth up an ensign on the mountains;
And when he bloweth a trumpet, hear ye.
For so the LORD said unto me, "I will take my rest,
And I will consider in my dwelling place like a clear heat upon herbs,
And like a cloud of dew in the heat of harvest."
In that day shall there be a highway out of Egypt to Assyria,
And the Assyrian shall come into Egypt, and the Egyptian into
Assyria,
And the Egyptians shall serve with the Assyrians.
In that day shall Israel be the third with Egypt and with Assyria,
Even a blessing in the midst of the land:
Whom the LORD of hosts shall bless, saying,
"Blessed be Egypt my people,
And Assyria the work of my hands,
And Israel mine inheritance."
And in this mountain shall the LORD of hosts
Make unto all people a feast of fat things,
A feast of wines on the lees,
Of fat things full of marrow,
Of wines on the lees well refined.
And he will destroy in this mountain
The face of the covering cast over all people,
And the vail that is spread over all nations.

He will swallow up death in victory; *A song of praise to God*
And the Lord GOD will wipe away tears from off all faces;
And the rebuke of his people shall he take away from off all the earth:
For the LORD hath spoken it.
And it shall be said in that day,
"Lo, this is our God; we have waited for him, and he will save us:
This is the LORD; we have waited for him,
We will be glad and rejoice in his salvation."
O LORD, thou art my God; I will exalt thee,
I will praise thy name;
For thou hast done wonderful things;
Thy counsels of old are faithfulness and truth.
Therefore shall the strong people glorify thee,
The city of the terrible nations shall fear thee.
For thou hast been a strength to the poor,
A strength to the needy in his distress,
A refuge from the storm,
A shadow from the heat,
When the blast of the terrible ones
Is as a storm against the wall.

In that day shall this song be sung in the land of Judah;

"We have a strong city;
Salvation will God appoint for walls and bulwarks.
Open ye the gates,
That the righteous nation which keepeth the truth may enter in.
Thou wilt keep him in perfect peace,
Whose mind is stayed on thee:
Because he trusteth in thee.
Trust ye in the LORD for ever:
For in the LORD JEHOVAH is everlasting strength:
For he bringeth down them that dwell on high;
The lofty city, he layeth it low;
He layeth it low, even to the ground;
He bringeth it even to the dust.
The foot shall tread it down,

*Songs of praise and
confidence*

Even the feet of the poor,
And the steps of the needy."
The way of the just is uprightness:
Thou, most upright, dost weigh the path of the just.
Yea, in the way of thy judgments, O LORD,
Have we waited for thee;
The desire of our soul is to thy name,
And to the remembrance of thee.
With my soul have I desired thee in the night;
Yea, with my spirit within me will I seek thee early:
For when thy judgments are in the earth,
The inhabitants of the world will learn righteousness.
LORD, thou wilt ordain peace for us:
For thou also hast wrought all our works in us.
In that day shall the LORD of hosts be for a crown of glory,
And for a diadem of beauty, unto the residue of his people,
And for a spirit of judgment to him that sitteth in judgment,
And for strength to them that turn the battle to the gate.
For precept must be upon precept, precept upon precept;
Line upon line, line upon line;
Here a little, and there a little.
Give ye ear, and hear my voice;
Hearken, and hear my speech.
Doth the plowman plow all day to sow?
Doth he open and break the clods of his ground?
When he hath made plain the face thereof,
Doth he not cast abroad the fitches, and scatter the cummin,
And cast in the principal wheat and the appointed barley and rie in
    their place?
For his God doth instruct him to discretion, and doth teach him.
For the fitches are not threshed with a threshing instrument,
Neither is a cart wheel turned about upon the cummin;
But the fitches are beaten out with a staff,
And the cummin with a rod.
Bread corn is bruised;
Because he will not ever be threshing it,

Nor break it with the wheel of his cart,
Nor bruise it with his horsemen.
This also cometh forth from the LORD of hosts,
Which is wonderful in counsel, and excellent in working.
For thus saith the Lord GOD, the Holy One of Israel;
"In returning and rest shall ye be saved;
In quietness and in confidence shall be your strength":
And ye would not.
And therefore will the LORD wait,
That he may be gracious unto you,
And therefore will he be exalted,
That he may have mercy upon you:
For the LORD is a God of judgment:
Blessed are all they that wait for him.
For the people shall dwell in Zion at Jerusalem:
Thou shalt weep no more:
He will be very gracious unto thee at the voice of thy cry;
When he shall hear it, he will answer thee.
And though the Lord give you the bread of adversity,
And the water of affliction,
Yet shall not thy teachers be removed into a corner any more,
But thine eyes shall see thy teachers:
And thine ears shall hear a word behind thee, saying,
"This is the way, walk ye in it,"
When ye turn to the right hand,
And when ye turn to the left.
Moreover the light of the moon
Shall be as the light of the sun,
And the light of the sun shall be sevenfold,
As the light of seven days, in the day that the LORD bindeth up the
　　breach of his people,
And healeth the stroke of their wound.

Behold, a king shall reign in righteousness,
And princes shall rule in judgment.
And a man shall be as an hiding place from the wind,

*A prophecy of dissolution*

And a covert from the tempest;
As rivers of water in a dry place,
As the shadow of a great rock in a weary land.
And the eyes of them that see shall not be dim,
And the ears of them that hear shall hearken.
The heart also of the rash shall understand knowledge,
And the tongue of the stammerers shall be ready to speak plainly.
Rise up, ye women that are at ease;
Hear my voice, ye careless daughters;
Give ear unto my speech.
Many days and years shall ye be troubled, ye careless women:
For the vintage shall fail, the gathering shall not come.
Tremble, ye women that are at ease;
Be troubled, ye careless ones:
Strip you, and make you bare,
And gird sackcloth upon your loins.
They shall lament for the teats,
For the pleasant fields, for the fruitful vine.
Upon the land of my people shall come up thorns and briers;
Yea, upon all the houses of joy in the joyous city:
Because the palaces shall be forsaken;
The multitude of the city shall be left;
The forts and towers shall be for dens for ever,
A joy of wild asses, a pasture of flocks;
Until the spirit be poured upon us from on high,
And the wilderness be a fruitful field,
And the fruitful field be counted for a forest.
Then judgment shall dwell in the wilderness,
And righteousness remain in the fruitful field.
And the work of righteousness shall be peace;
And the effect of righteousness quietness and assurance for ever.
And my people shall dwell in a peaceable habitation,
And in sure dwellings, and in quiet resting places;
When it shall hail, coming down on the forest;
And the city shall be low in a low place.

## *THE PROPHETS*

Blessed are ye that sow beside all waters,
That send forth thither the feet of the ox and the ass.

Hear, ye that are far off, what I have done;
And, ye that are near, acknowledge my might.
The sinners in Zion are afraid;
Fearfulness hath surprised the hypocrites.
Who among us shall dwell with the devouring fire?
Who among us shall dwell with everlasting burnings?
He that walketh righteously, and speaketh uprightly;
He that despiseth the gain of oppressions,
That shaketh his hands from holding of bribes,
That stoppeth his ears from hearing of blood,
And shutteth his eyes from seeing evil;
He shall dwell on high:
His place of defence shall be the munitions of rocks:
Bread shall be given him;
His waters shall be sure.
Thine eyes shall see the king in his beauty:
They shall behold the land that is very far off.
Look upon Zion, the city of our solemnities:
Thine eyes shall see Jerusalem a quiet habitation,
A tabernacle that shall not be taken down;
Not one of the stakes thereof shall ever be removed,
Neither shall any of the cords thereof be broken.
But there the glorious LORD will be unto us
A place of broad rivers and streams;
Wherein shall go no galley with oars,
Neither shall gallant ship pass thereby.
For the LORD is our judge,
The LORD is our lawgiver,
The LORD is our king;
He will save us.
The wilderness and the solitary place shall be glad for them;
And the desert shall rejoice, and blossom as the rose.

It shall blossom abundantly, and rejoice even with joy and singing:
The glory of Lebanon shall be given unto it, the excellency of Carmel
    and Sharon,
They shall see the glory of the Lord, and the excellency of our God.
Strengthen ye the weak hands,
And confirm the feeble knees.
Say to them that are of a fearful heart, "Be strong, fear not:
Behold, your God will come with vengeance,
Even God with a recompence; he will come and save you."
Then the eyes of the blind shall be opened,
And the ears of the deaf shall be unstopped.
Then shall the lame man leap as an hart
And the tongue of the dumb sing:
For in the wilderness shall waters break out,
And streams in the desert.
And the parched ground shall become a pool,
And the thirsty land springs of water:
In the habitation of dragons, where each lay,
Shall be grass with reeds and rushes.
And an highway shall be there, and a way,
And it shall be called The way of holiness;
The unclean shall not pass over it; but it shall be for those:
The wayfaring men, though fools, shall not err therein.
No lion shall be there, nor any ravenous beast shall go up thereon,
It shall not be found there;
But the redeemed shall walk there:
And the ransomed of the Lord shall return,
And come to Zion with songs and everlasting joy upon their heads:
They shall obtain joy and gladness,
And sorrow and sighing shall flee away.

THE word of the Lord that came to Micah the Morasthite, in the days
of Jotham, Ahaz, and Hezekiah, kings of Judah, which he saw concerning Samaria and Jerusalem.

Hear, all ye people;
Hearken, O earth, and all that therein is:

## THE PROPHETS

And let the Lord GOD be witness against you,
The Lord from his holy temple.
Woe to them that devise iniquity, and work evil.
They covet fields, and take them by violence;
And houses, and take them away:
So they oppress a man and his house,
Even a man and his heritage.
The women of my people have ye cast out from their pleasant houses;
From their children have ye taken away my glory for ever.
Arise ye, and depart;
For this is not your rest.
Hear, I pray you, O heads of Jacob,
And ye princes of the house of Israel;
Is it not for you to know judgment?
Who hate the good, and love the evil;
Then shall they cry unto the LORD,
But he will not hear them:
He will even hide his face from them at that time,
As they have behaved themselves ill in their doings.
But truly I am full of power
By the spirit of the LORD, and of judgment, and of might,
To declare unto Jacob his transgression,
And to Israel his sin.
Hear this, I pray you, ye heads of the house of Jacob,
And princes of the house of Israel,
That abhor judgment,
And pervert all equity.
They build up Zion with blood,
And Jerusalem with iniquity.
The heads thereof judge for reward,
And the priests thereof teach for hire,
And the prophets thereof divine for money:
Yet will they lean upon the LORD, and say,
"Is not the LORD among us?
None evil can come upon us."
Therefore shall Zion for your sake be plowed as a field,

*Judgments against oppression*

[ 243 ]

*God's controversy with*
*his people*

And Jerusalem shall become heaps,
And the mountain of the house as the high places of the forest.
But in the last days it shall come to pass,
That the mountain of the house of the LORD
Shall be established in the top of the mountains,
And it shall be exalted above the hills;
And people shall flow unto it.
And many nations shall come, and say,
"Come, and let us go up to the mountain of the LORD,
And to the house of the God of Jacob;
And he will teach us of his ways,
And we will walk in his paths":
For the law shall go forth of Zion,
And the word of the LORD from Jerusalem.
And he shall judge among many people,
And rebuke strong nations afar off.
But they shall sit every man under his vine
And under his fig tree;
And none shall make them afraid:
For the mouth of the LORD of hosts hath spoken it.
For all the people will walk every one in the name of his god,
And we will walk in the name of the LORD our God for ever and ever.
But they know not the thoughts of the LORD,
Neither understand they his counsel:
For he shall gather them as the sheaves into the floor.
And the remnant of Jacob
Shall be in the midst of many people
As a dew from the LORD,
As the showers upon the grass,
That tarrieth not for man,
Nor waiteth for the sons of men.

Hear ye now what the LORD saith;
"Arise, contend thou before the mountains,
And let the hills hear thy voice."

## THE PROPHETS

*Trust in the Lord*

Wherewith shall I come before the LORD,
And bow myself before the high God?
Shall I come before him with burnt offerings,
With calves of a year old?
Will the LORD be pleased with thousands of rams,
Or with ten thousands of rivers of oil?
Shall I give my firstborn for my transgression,
The fruit of my body for the sin of my soul?
Therefore I will look unto the LORD;
I will wait for the God of my salvation:
My God will hear me.
Rejoice not against me, O mine enemy:
When I fall, I shall arise;
When I sit in darkness, the LORD shall be a light unto me.
I will bear the indignation of the LORD,
Because I have sinned against him,
Until he plead my cause, and execute judgment for me:
He will bring me forth to the light,
And I shall behold his righteousness.
Then she that is mine enemy shall see it,
And shame shall cover her which said unto me,
"Where is the LORD thy God?"
Mine eyes shall behold her:
Now shall she be trodden down as the mire of the streets.
Who is a God like unto thee,
That pardoneth iniquity,
And passeth by the transgression of the remnant of his heritage?
He retaineth not his anger for ever,
Because he delighteth in mercy.
He will turn again,
He will have compassion upon us;
He will subdue our iniquities;
And thou wilt cast all their sins
Into the depths of the sea.
He hath shewed thee, O man, what is good;

And what doth the Lord require of thee,
But to do justly, and to love mercy,
And to walk humbly with thy God?

The burden of Nineveh. The book of the vision of Nahum the El-koshite.

The Lord is slow to anger, and great in power,
And will not at all acquit the wicked:
The Lord hath his way in the whirlwind and in the storm,
And the clouds are the dust of his feet.
He rebuketh the sea, and maketh it dry,
And drieth up all the rivers:
Bashan languisheth, and Carmel,
And the flower of Lebanon languisheth.
The mountains quake at him, and the hills melt,
And the earth is burned at his presence,
Yea, the world, and all that dwell therein.
Who can stand before his indignation?
And who can abide in the fierceness of his anger?
His fury is poured out like fire,
And the rocks are thrown down by him.
The Lord is good, a strong hold in the day of trouble;
And he knoweth them that trust in him.
But Nineveh is of old like a pool of water:
Yet they shall flee away.
"Stand, stand," shall they cry;
But none shall look back.
Take ye the spoil of silver,
Take the spoil of gold:
For there is none end of the store
And glory out of all the pleasant furniture.
She is empty, and void, and waste:
And the heart melteth, and the knees smite together,
And much pain is in all loins,
And the faces of them all gather blackness.
Where is the dwelling of the lions,

## THE PROPHETS

And the feedingplace of the young lions,
Where the lion, even the old lion, walked,
And the lion's whelp, and none made them afraid?
The lion did tear in pieces enough for his whelps,
And strangled for his lionesses,
And filled his holes with prey,
And his dens with ravin.
"Behold, I am against thee," saith the LORD of hosts,
"And I will burn her chariots in the smoke,
And the sword shall devour thy young lions:
And I will cut off thy prey from the earth,
And the voice of thy messengers shall no more be heard.
The horseman lifteth up both the bright sword and the glittering
    spear:
And there is a multitude of slain.
And it shall come to pass,
That all they that look upon thee shall flee from thee,
And say, 'Nineveh is laid waste:
Who will bemoan her?' whence shall I seek comforters for thee?
Art thou better than populous No,
That was situate among the rivers,
That had the waters round about it,
Whose rampart was the sea,
And her wall was from the sea?
Ethiopia and Egypt were her strength,
And it was infinite;
Put and Lubim were thy helpers.
Yet was she carried away,
She went into captivity:
And they cast lots for her honourable men.
All thy strong holds shall be like fig trees with the firstripe figs:
If they be shaken, they shall even fall into the mouth of the eater.
Behold, thy people in the midst of thee are women:
The gates of thy land shall be set wide open unto thine enemies:
The fire shall devour thy bars.
Draw thee waters for the siege, fortify thy strong holds:

*The calling of Jeremiah*

Go into clay, and tread the morter,
Make strong the brickkiln.
Thy crowned are as the locusts,
And thy captains as the great grasshoppers,
Which camp in the hedges in the cold day,
But when the sun ariseth they flee away,
And their place is not known where they are.
Thy shepherds slumber, O king of Assyria:
Thy nobles shall dwell in the dust:
Thy people is scattered upon the mountains,
And no man gathereth them.
There is no healing of thy bruise;
Thy wound is grievous:
All that hear the bruit of thee shall clap the hands over thee:
For upon whom hath not thy wickedness passed continually?"

THE words of Jeremiah the son of Hilkiah, to whom the word of the Lord came in the days of Josiah the king of Judah. It came also in the days of Jehoiakim the son of Josiah king of Judah, unto the end of the eleventh year of Zedekiah the son of Josiah king of Judah, unto the carrying away of Jerusalem captive.

Then the word of the Lord came unto me, saying, "Before I formed thee I knew thee; and I sanctified thee, and I ordained thee a prophet unto the nations."

Then said I, "Ah, Lord God! behold, I cannot speak: for I am a child."

But the Lord said unto me, "Say not, 'I am a child': for thou shalt go to all that I send thee, and whatsoever I command thee thou shalt speak. Be not afraid of their faces: for I am with thee to deliver thee," saith the Lord.

Then the Lord put forth his hand, and touched my mouth. And the Lord said unto me, "Behold, I have put my words in thy mouth. See, I have this day set thee over the nations and over the kingdoms, to root out, and to pull down, and to destroy, and to throw down, to build, and to plant. Thou therefore gird up thy loins, and arise, and speak unto them all that I command thee: be not dismayed. For, behold, I have made thee this day a defenced city, and an iron pillar, and brasen walls against the whole land, against the kings of Judah, against the princes thereof, against the priests thereof, and against the people of the land. And they shall fight against thee; but they shall not prevail against thee; for I am with thee," saith the LORD, "to deliver thee."

Moreover the word of the LORD came to me, saying, "Go and cry in the ears of Jerusalem, saying, 'Thus saith the LORD; I remember thee, the kindness of thy youth, the love of thine espousals, when thou wentest after me in the wilderness, in a land that was not sown.' "

Thus saith the LORD, "What iniquity have your fathers found in me, that they are gone far from me, and have walked after vanity, and are become vain? Neither said they, 'Where is the LORD that brought us up out of the land of Egypt, that led us through the wilderness, through a land of deserts and of pits, through a land of drought, and of the shadow of death, through a land that no man passed through, and where no man dwelt?' Be astonished, O ye heavens, at this, and be horribly afraid, be ye very desolate," saith the LORD. "For my people have committed two evils; they have forsaken me the fountain of living waters, and hewed them out cisterns, broken cisterns, that can hold no water. And now what hast thou to do in the way of Egypt, to drink the waters of Sihor? or what hast thou to do in the way of Assyria, to drink the waters of the river? Know therefore and see that it is an evil thing and bitter, that thou hast forsaken the LORD thy God, and that my fear is not in thee," saith the Lord GOD of hosts. "Yet I had planted thee a noble vine, wholly a right seed: how then art thou turned into the degenerate plant of a strange vine unto me? For though thou wash thee with nitre, and take thee much soap, yet thine iniquity is marked before me," saith the Lord GOD.

O generation, see ye the word of the LORD. "Have I been a wilderness unto Israel? a land of darkness? wherefore say my people, 'We are lords; we will come no more unto thee'? Can a maid forget her ornaments, or a bride her attire? yet my people have forgotten me days without number. Wilt thou not from this time cry unto me, 'My father, thou art the guide of my youth'?"

And the LORD said unto me, "Go and proclaim these words toward the north, and say, 'Return, thou backsliding Israel; and I will not cause mine anger to fall upon you: for I am merciful, and I will not keep anger for ever. And I will give you pastors according to mine heart, which shall feed you with knowledge and understanding. At that time they shall call Jerusalem the throne of the LORD; and all the nations shall be gathered unto it, to the name of the LORD, to Jerusalem. And I said, "Thou shalt call me, 'My father'; and shalt not turn away from me." Return, ye backsliding children, and I will heal your backslidings. If thou wilt return, O Israel, return unto me. And thou shalt swear, "The LORD liveth," in truth, in judgment, and in righteousness; and the nations shall bless themselves in him, and in him shall they glory.' "

Behold, we come unto thee; for thou art the LORD our God. Truly in vain is salvation hoped for from the hills, and from the multitude of mountains: truly in the LORD our God is the salvation of Israel.

Thus saith the LORD to the men of Judah and Jerusalem, "Break up your fallow ground, and sow not among thorns. My bowels, my bowels! I am pained at my very heart; my heart maketh a noise in me; I cannot hold my peace, because thou hast heard, O my soul, the sound of the trumpet, the alarm of war. Destruction upon destruction is cried; for the whole land is spoiled: suddenly are my tents spoiled, and my curtains in a moment. How long shall I see the standard, and hear the sound of the trumpet? For my people is foolish, they have not known me; they are sottish children, and they have none understanding: they are wise to do evil, but to do good they have no knowledge."

I beheld the earth, and, lo, it was without form, and void; and the heavens, and they had no light. I beheld the mountains, and, lo, they trembled, and all the hills moved lightly. I beheld, and, lo, there was no man, and all the birds of the heavens were fled. I beheld, and, lo, the fruitful place was a wilderness, and all the cities thereof were broken down at the presence of the LORD, and by his fierce anger.

For thus hath the LORD said, "The whole land shall be desolate; yet will I not make a full end. For this shall the earth mourn, and the heavens above be black: because I have spoken it, I have purposed it, and will not repent, neither will I turn back from it." The whole city shall flee for the noise of the horsemen and bowmen; they shall go into thickets, and climb up upon the rocks: every city shall be forsaken, and not a man dwell therein. And when thou art spoiled, what wilt thou do? Though thou clothest thyself with crimson, though thou deckest thee with ornaments of gold, though thou rentest thy face with painting, in vain shalt thou make thyself fair; thy lovers will despise thee, they will seek thy life. For I have heard a voice as of a woman in travail, and the anguish as of her that bringeth forth her first child, the voice of the daughter of Zion, that bewaileth herself, that spreadeth her hands, saying, "Woe is me now! for my soul is wearied because of murderers."

"Fear ye not me?" saith the LORD: "will ye not tremble at my presence, which have placed the sand for the bound of the sea by a perpetual decree, that it cannot pass it: and though the waves thereof toss themselves, yet can they not prevail; though they roar, yet can they not pass over it?"

Thus saith the LORD, "Stand ye in the ways, and see, and ask for the old paths, where is the good way, and walk therein, and ye shall find rest for your souls."

But they said, "We will not walk therein."

"From the least of them even unto the greatest of them every one is given to covetousness; and from the prophet even unto the priest every one dealeth falsely. They have healed also the hurt of the daughter of my people slightly, saying, 'Peace, peace'; when there is no peace. Neither say they in their heart, 'Let us now fear the LORD our God, that giveth rain, both the former and the latter, in his season: he reserveth unto us the appointed weeks of the harvest.' To what purpose cometh there to me incense from Sheba, and the sweet cane from a far country? your burnt offerings are not acceptable, nor your sacrifices sweet unto me."

The word that came to Jeremiah from the LORD, saying, "Stand in the gate of the LORD's house, and proclaim there this word, and say, 'Hear the word of the LORD, all ye of Judah, that enter in at these gates to worship the LORD. Thus saith the LORD of hosts, the God of Israel, Amend your ways and your doings, and I will cause you to dwell in this place. Trust ye not in lying words, saying, The temple of the LORD, The temple of the LORD, The temple of the LORD, are these. Behold, ye trust in lying words, that cannot profit. Will ye steal, murder, and commit adultery, and swear falsely, and burn incense unto Baal, and walk after other gods whom ye know not; and come and stand before me in this house, which is called by my name, and say, We are delivered to do all

*Jeremiah threatened* these abominations? Is this house, which is called by my name, become a den of robbers in your eyes? Behold, even I have seen it.' "

Thus saith the LORD of Hosts, the God of Israel, "I spake not unto your fathers, nor commanded them in the day that I brought them out of the land of Egypt, concerning burnt offerings or sacrifices: but this thing commanded I them, saying, 'Obey my voice, and I will be your God, and ye shall be my people: and walk ye in all the ways that I have commanded you, that it may be well unto you.' But they hearkened not, nor inclined their ear, but walked in the counsels and in the imagination of their evil heart, and went backward, and not forward. Since the day that your fathers came forth out of the land of Egypt unto this day I have even sent unto you all my servants the prophets, daily rising up early and sending them: yet they hearkened not unto me, nor inclined their ear, but hardened their neck: they did worse than their fathers. Therefore thou shalt speak all these words unto them; but they will not hearken to thee: thou shalt also call unto them; but they will not answer thee. But thou shalt say unto them, 'This is a nation that obeyeth not the voice of the LORD their God, nor receiveth correction: truth is perished, and is cut off from their mouth.' "

"Do they provoke me to anger?" saith the LORD: "do they not provoke themselves to the confusion of their own faces?"

Now it came to pass, when Jeremiah had made an end of speaking all that the LORD had commanded him to speak unto all the people, that the priests and the prophets and all the people took him, saying, "Thou shalt surely die. Why hast thou prophesied in the name of the LORD, saying, 'This house shall be like Shiloh, and this city shall be desolate without an inhabitant'?" And all the people were gathered against Jeremiah in the house of the LORD.

When the princes of Judah heard these things, then they came up from the king's house unto the house of the LORD, and sat down in the entry of the new gate of the LORD's house. Then spake the priests and the prophets unto the princes and to all the people, saying, "This man is worthy to die; for he hath prophesied against this city, as ye have heard with your ears."

Then spake Jeremiah unto all the princes and to all the people, say-

ing, "The LORD sent me to prophesy against this house and against this
city all the words that ye have heard. Therefore now amend your ways
and your doings, and obey the voice of the LORD your God; and the
LORD will repent him of the evil that he hath pronounced against you.
As for me, behold, I am in your hand: do with me as seemeth good and
meet unto you. But know ye for certain, that if ye put me to death, ye
shall surely bring innocent blood upon yourselves, and upon this city,
and upon the inhabitants thereof: for of a truth the LORD hath sent me
unto you to speak all these words in your ears."

Then said the princes and all the people unto the priests and to
the prophets; "This man is not worthy to die: for he hath spoken to us in
the name of the LORD our God."

Then Jeremiah called Baruch the son of Neriah: and Baruch wrote
from the mouth of Jeremiah all the words of the LORD, which he had
spoken unto him, upon a roll of a book. And Jeremiah commanded
Baruch, saying, "I am shut up; I cannot go into the house of the LORD:
therefore go thou, and read in the roll, which thou hast written from my
mouth, the words of the LORD in the ears of the people in the LORD's
house upon the fasting day: and also thou shalt read them in the ears of all
Judah that come out of their cities. It may be they will present their supplication before the LORD, and will return every one from his evil way."

And Baruch did according to all that Jeremiah the prophet commanded him, reading in the book the words of the LORD in the LORD's
house.

And it came to pass in the fifth year of Jehoiakim the son of Josiah
king of Judah, in the ninth month, that they proclaimed a fast before the
LORD to all the people in Jerusalem, and to all the people that came from
the cities of Judah unto Jerusalem. Then read Baruch in the book the
words of Jeremiah in the house of the LORD, in the chamber of Gemariah,
in the higher court, at the entry of the new gate of the LORD's house, in
the ears of all the people.

When Michaiah the son of Gemariah had heard out of the book all
the words of the LORD, then he went down into the king's house, into the
scribe's chamber: and, lo, all the princes sat there. Then Michaiah declared unto them all the words that he had heard, when Baruch read the
book in the ears of the people. Therefore all the princes sent Jehudi unto

*Jeremiah's prophecy rewritten*

Baruch, saying, "Take in thine hand the roll wherein thou hast read in the ears of the people, and come." So Baruch took the roll in his hand, and came unto them.

And they said unto him, "Sit down now, and read it in our ears." So Baruch read it in their ears.

Now it came to pass, when they had heard all the words, they were afraid both one and other, and said unto Baruch, "We will surely tell the king of all these words."

And they asked Baruch, saying, "Tell us now, How didst thou write all these words at his mouth?"

Then Baruch answered them, "He pronounced all these words unto me with his mouth, and I wrote them with ink in the book."

Then said the princes unto Baruch, "Go, hide thee, thou and Jeremiah; and let no man know where ye be."

And they went in to the king into the court, but they laid up the roll in the chamber of Elishama the scribe, and told all the words in the ears of the king. So the king sent Jehudi to fetch the roll: and he took it out of Elishama the scribe's chamber. And Jehudi read it in the ears of the king, and in the ears of all the princes which stood beside the king.

Now the king sat in the winterhouse in the ninth month: and there was a fire on the hearth burning before him. And it came to pass, that when Jehudi had read three or four leaves, he cut it with the penknife, and cast it into the fire that was on the hearth, until all the roll was consumed in the fire that was on the hearth. Yet they were not afraid, nor rent their garments, neither the king, nor any of his servants that heard all these words. Nevertheless Elnathan and Delaiah and Gemariah had made intercession to the king that he would not burn the roll: but he would not hear them. But the king commanded Jerahmeel and Seraiah and Shelemiah to take Baruch the scribe and Jeremiah the prophet: but the LORD hid them.

Then the word of the LORD came to Jeremiah, after that the king had burned the roll, and the words which Baruch wrote at the mouth of Jeremiah, saying, "Take thee again another roll, and write in it all the former words that were in the first roll, which Jehoiakim the king of Judah hath burned."

Then took Jeremiah another roll, and gave it to Baruch the scribe; *Jeremiah laments the* who wrote therein from the mouth of Jeremiah all the words of the book *sins of the people* which Jehoiakim king of Judah had burned in the fire: and there were added besides unto them many like words.

I hearkened and heard, but they spake not aright: no man repented him of his wickedness, saying, "What have I done?" every one turned to his course, as the horse rusheth into the battle. Yea, the stork in the heaven knoweth her appointed times; and the turtle and the crane and the swallow observe the time of their coming; but my people know not the judgment of the LORD.

We looked for peace, but no good came; and for a time of health, and behold trouble! When I would comfort myself against sorrow, my heart is faint in me.

The harvest is past, the summer is ended, and we are not saved. For the hurt of the daughter of my people am I hurt; I am black; astonishment hath taken hold on me. Is there no balm in Gilead; is there no physician there? why then is not the health of the daughter of my people recovered?

"Oh that my head were waters, and mine eyes a fountain of tears, that I might weep day and night for the slain of the daughter of my people! Oh that I had in the wilderness a lodging place of wayfaring men; that I might leave my people, and go from them! for they be all adulterers, an assembly of treacherous men. And they bend their tongues like their bow for lies: but they are not valiant for the truth upon the earth; for they proceed from evil to evil, and they know not me," saith the LORD.

One speaketh peaceably to his neighbour with his mouth, but in heart he layeth his wait.

Who is the wise man, that may understand this? and who is he to whom the mouth of the LORD hath spoken, that he may declare it?

"Hear ye, and give ear; be not proud: for the LORD hath spoken. Give glory to the LORD your God, before he cause darkness, and before your feet stumble upon the dark mountains, and, while ye look for light, he turn it into the shadow of death, and make it gross darkness. But if ye will not hear it, my soul shall weep in secret places for your pride; and mine eye shall weep sore, and run down with tears, because the LORD's flock is carried away captive. Lift up your eyes, and behold them that come from the north: where is the flock that was given thee, thy beautiful flock? What wilt thou say when he shall punish thee? And if thou say in thine heart, Wherefore come these things upon me? Can the Ethiopian change his skin, or the leopard his spots? then may ye also do good, that are accustomed to do evil. Therefore will I scatter them as the stubble that passeth away by the wind of the wilderness. This is thy lot, the portion of thy measures from me," saith the LORD; "because thou hast forgotten me, and trusted in falsehood. Woe unto thee, O Jerusalem! wilt thou not be made clean? when shall it once be? The cities of the south shall be shut up, and none shall open them: Judah shall be carried away captive all of it, it shall be wholly carried away captive. The land mourneth; the pleasant places of the wilderness are dried up. For I have taken away my peace from this people," saith the LORD, "even lovingkindness and mercies. The sin of Judah is written with a pen of iron, and with the point of a diamond: it is graven upon the table of their heart, and upon the horns of your altars."

O LORD, though our iniquities testify against us, do thou it for thy name's sake: for our backslidings are many; we have sinned against thee. O the hope of Israel, the saviour thereof in time of trouble, why shouldest thou be as a stranger in the land, and as a wayfaring man that turneth aside to tarry for a night? Why shouldest thou be as a man astonied, as a mighty man that cannot save? yet thou, O LORD, art in the midst of us, and we are called by thy name; leave us not.

Hast thou utterly rejected Judah? hath thy soul loathed Zion? why hast thou smitten us, and there is no healing for us? we looked for peace, and there is no good; and for the time of healing, and behold trouble! We acknowledge, O LORD, our wickedness, and the iniquity of our fathers: for we have sinned against thee. Do not abhor us, for thy name's sake, do not disgrace the throne of thy glory: remember, break not thy covenant with us. Are there any among the vanities of the Gentiles that can cause rain? or can the heavens give showers? Art not thou he, O LORD our God? therefore we will wait upon thee: for thou hast made all these things. A glorious high throne from the beginning is the place of our sanctuary. O LORD, the hope of Israel, all that forsake thee shall be ashamed, and they that depart from me shall be written in the earth, because they have forsaken the LORD, the fountain of living waters.

## THE PROPHETS

*Jeremiah prays against his conspirators*

Righteous art thou, O Lord, when I plead with thee: yet let me talk with thee of thy judgments: Wherefore doth the way of the wicked prosper? wherefore are all they happy that deal very treacherously? Thou hast planted them, yea, they have taken root: they grow, yea, they bring forth fruit: thou art near in their mouth, and far from their reins. But thou, O Lord, knowest me. How long shall the land mourn, and the herbs of every field wither, for the wickedness of them that dwell therein? the beasts are consumed, and the birds; because they said, 'He shall not see our last end.' If thou hast run with the footmen, and they have wearied thee, then how canst thou contend with horses? and if in the land of peace, wherein thou trustedst, they wearied thee, then how wilt thou do in the swelling of Jordan? For even thy brethren, and the house of thy father, even they have dealt treacherously with thee; yea, they have called a multitude after thee: believe them not, though they speak fair words unto thee.

O Lord, thou knowest: remember me, and visit me; take me not away in thy longsuffering: know that for thy sake I have suffered rebuke. Thy word was unto me the joy and rejoicing of mine heart: for I am called by thy name, O Lord God of hosts. I sat not in the assembly of the mockers, nor rejoiced; I sat alone because of thy hand: for thou hast filled me with indignation. Why is my pain perpetual, and my wound incurable, which refuseth to be healed? wilt thou be altogether unto me as a liar, and as waters that fail?

Therefore thus saith the Lord, "If thou return, then will I bring thee again, and thou shalt stand before me: and if thou take forth the precious from the vile, thou shalt be as my mouth: let them return unto thee; but return not thou unto them. And I will make thee unto this people a fenced brasen wall: and they shall fight against thee, but they shall not prevail against thee: for I am with thee to save thee and to deliver thee," saith the Lord. "And I will deliver thee out of the hand of the wicked, and I will redeem thee out of the hand of the terrible."

Then said they, "Come, and let us devise devices against Jeremiah; for the law shall not perish from the priest, nor counsel from the wise, nor the word from the prophet. Come, and let us smite him with the tongue, and let us not give heed to any of his words."

Give heed to me, O Lord, and hearken to the voice of them that contend with me. Shall evil be recompensed for good? for they have digged a pit for my soul. Remember that I stood before thee to speak good for them, and to turn away thy wrath from them. Therefore deliver up their children to the famine, and pour out their blood by the force of the sword; and let their wives be bereaved of their children, and be widows; and let their young men be slain by the sword in battle. Let a cry be heard from their houses, when thou shalt bring a troop suddenly upon them: for they have digged a pit to take me, and hid snares for my feet. Yet, LORD, thou knowest all their counsel against me to slay me: forgive not their iniquity, neither blot out their sin from thy sight, but let them be overthrown before thee; deal thus with them in the time of thine anger. Wherefore came I forth out of the womb to see labour and sorrow, that my days should be consumed with shame? Woe is me, my mother, that thou hast borne me a man of strife and a man of contention to the whole earth! I have neither lent on usury, nor men have lent to me on usury; yet every one of them doth curse me.

O LORD, thou hast deceived me, and I was deceived: thou art stronger than I, and hast prevailed: I am in derision daily, every one mocketh me. The word of the LORD was made a reproach unto me, and a derision, daily.

Then I said, "I will not make mention of him, nor speak any more in his name." But his word was in mine heart as a burning fire shut up in my bones, and I was weary with forbearing, and I could not stay. But the LORD is with me as a mighty terrible one: therefore my persecutors shall stumble, and they shall not prevail: they shall be greatly ashamed; for they shall not prosper. But, O LORD of hosts, that triest the righteous, and seest the reins and the heart; unto thee have I opened my cause.

Heal me, O LORD, and I shall be healed; save me, and I shall be saved: for thou art my praise. Behold, they say unto me, "Where is the word of the LORD? let it come now." As for me, I have not hastened from being a pastor to follow thee: neither have I desired the woeful day; thou knowest: that which came out of my lips was right before thee. Be not a terror unto me: thou art my hope in the day of evil. Let not me be confounded: let not me be dismayed. O LORD, I know that the way of man is not in himself: it is not in man that walketh to direct his steps.

O LORD, correct me, but with judgment; not in thine anger, lest thou Trust in God is blessed bring me to nothing.

The word which came to Jeremiah from the LORD, saying, "Arise, and go down to the potter's house, and there I will cause thee to hear my words."

Then I went down to the potter's house, and, behold, he wrought a work on the wheels. And the vessel that he made of clay was marred in the hand of the potter: so he made it again another vessel, as seemed good to the potter to make it.

Then the word of the LORD came to me, saying, "O house of Israel, cannot I do with you as this potter?" saith the LORD. "Behold, as the clay is in the potter's hand, so are ye in mine hand, O house of Israel. Return ye now every one from his evil way, and make your ways and your doings good. Will a man leave the snow of Lebanon which cometh from the rock of the field? or shall the cold flowing waters that come from another place be forsaken?"

Thus saith the LORD, "Let not the wise man glory in his wisdom, neither let the mighty man glory in his might, let not the rich man glory in his riches: but let him that glorieth glory in this, that he understandeth and knoweth me, that I am the LORD which exercise lovingkindness, judgment, and righteousness, in the earth: for in these things I delight," saith the LORD.

"The heart is deceitful above all things, and desperately wicked: who can know it? I the LORD search the heart, I try the reins, even to give every man according to his ways, and according to the fruit of his doings. As the partridge sitteth on eggs, and hatcheth them not; so he that getteth riches, and not by right, shall leave them in the midst of his days, and at his end shall be a fool.

"Blessed is the man that trusteth in the LORD, and whose hope the LORD is. For he shall be as a tree planted by the waters, and that spreadeth out her roots by the river, and shall not see when heat cometh, but her leaf shall be green; and shall not be careful in the year of drought, neither shall cease from yielding fruit.

"And unto this people thou shalt say, 'Thus saith the LORD; Behold, I set before you the way of life, and the way of death.'

[ 259 ]

"Woe unto him that buildeth his house by unrighteousness, and his chambers by wrong; that useth his neighbour's service without wages, and giveth him not for his work; that saith, 'I will build me a wide house and large chambers', and cutteth him out windows; and it is cieled with cedar, and painted with vermilion.

"Shalt thou reign, because thou closest thyself in cedar? did not thy father eat and drink, and do judgment and justice, and then it was well with him? He judged the cause of the poor and needy; then it was well with him: was not this to know me?" saith the LORD. "But thine eyes and thine heart are not but for thy covetousness, and for to shed innocent blood, and for oppression, and for violence, to do it. Moreover I will take from them the voice of mirth, and the voice of gladness, the voice of the bridegroom, and the voice of the bride, the sound of the millstones, and the light of the candle. And this whole land shall be a desolation, and an astonishment; and these nations shall serve the king of Babylon seventy years."

O earth, earth, earth, hear the word of the LORD.

"Woe be unto the pastors that destroy and scatter the sheep of my pasture!" saith the LORD. "I will gather the remnant of my flock out of all countries whither I have driven them, and will bring them again to their folds; and they shall be fruitful and increase. And I will set up shepherds over them which shall feed them: and they shall fear no more, nor be dismayed, neither shall they be lacking," saith the LORD.

"Behold, the days come," saith the LORD, "that I will raise unto David a righteous Branch, and a King shall reign and prosper, and shall execute judgment and justice in the earth. In his days Judah shall be saved, and Israel shall dwell safely: and this is his name whereby he shall be called, THE LORD OUR RIGHTEOUSNESS."

"Am I a God at hand," saith the LORD, "and not a God afar off? Can any hide himself in secret places that I shall not see him?" saith the LORD. "Do not I fill heaven and earth?" saith the LORD. "The prophet that hath a dream, let him tell a dream; and he that hath my word, let him speak my word faithfully. What is the chaff to the wheat?" saith the LORD. "Is not my word like as a fire?" saith the LORD; "and like a hammer that breaketh the rock in pieces?"

The LORD shewed me, and, behold, two baskets of figs were set before the temple of the LORD, after that Nebuchadrezzar king of Babylon
had carried away captive Jeconiah the son of Jehoiakim king of Judah,
and the princes of Judah, with the carpenters and smiths, from Jerusalem,
and had brought them to Babylon. One basket had very good figs, even
like the figs that are first ripe: and the other basket had very naughty
figs, which could not be eaten, they were so bad.

Then said the LORD unto me, "What seest thou, Jeremiah?"

And I said, "Figs; the good figs, very good; and the evil, very evil,
that cannot be eaten, they are so evil."

Again the word of the LORD came unto me, saying, "Thus saith the
LORD, the God of Israel; Like these good figs, so will I acknowledge them
that are carried away captive of Judah, whom I have sent out of this
place into the land of the Chaldeans for their good. For I will set mine
eyes upon them for good, and I will bring them again to this land: and I
will build them, and not pull them down; and I will plant them, and not
pluck them up. And I will give them an heart to know me, that I am the
LORD: and they shall be my people, and I will be their God: for they
shall return unto me with their whole heart."

Thus saith the LORD of hosts, the God of Israel; "Thus shall ye say
unto your masters; I have made the earth, the man and the beast that
are upon the ground, by my great power and by my outstretched arm,
and have given it unto whom it seemed meet unto me. And now have I
given all these lands into the hand of Nebuchadnezzar the king of Babylon, my servant; and the beasts of the field have I given him also to serve
him. But the nations that bring their neck under the yoke of the king of
Babylon, and serve him, those will I let remain still in their own land,"
saith the LORD; "and they shall till it, and dwell therein."

Yea, thus saith the LORD of hosts, the God of Israel, concerning the
vessels that remain in the house of the LORD, and in the house of the
king of Judah and of Jerusalem; "They shall be carried to Babylon, and
there shall they be until the day that I visit them," saith the LORD; "then
will I bring them up, and restore them to this place."

Thus saith the LORD of hosts, the God of Israel, unto all that are
carried away captives, whom I have caused to be carried away from

*Israel comforted* Jerusalem unto Babylon; "Build ye houses, and dwell in them; and plant gardens, and eat the fruit of them; take ye wives, and beget sons and daughters; and take wives for your sons, and give your daughters to husbands, that they may bear sons and daughters; that ye may be increased there, and not diminished. And seek the peace of the city whither I have caused you to be carried away captives, and pray unto the Lord for it: for in the peace thereof shall ye have peace.

"After seventy years be accomplished at Babylon I will visit you, and perform my good word toward you, in causing you to return to this place. For I know the thoughts that I think toward you," saith the Lord, "thoughts of peace, and not of evil, to give you an expected end. Then shall ye call upon me, and ye shall go and pray unto me, and I will hearken unto you. And ye shall seek me, and find me, when ye shall search for me with all your heart. And I will be found of you," saith the Lord: "and I will turn away your captivity, and I will gather you from all the nations, and from all the places whither I have driven you," saith the Lord; "and I will bring you again into the place whence I caused you to be carried away captive. For I am with thee," saith the Lord, "to save thee: I will correct thee in measure, and will not leave thee altogether unpunished. Thy bruise is incurable, and thy wound is grievous. There is none to plead thy cause, that thou mayest be bound up: thou hast no healing medicines. For I will restore health unto thee, and I will heal thee of thy wounds," saith the Lord; "because they called thee an Outcast, saying, 'This is Zion, whom no man seeketh after.' Behold, I will bring again the captivity of Jacob's tents, and have mercy on his dwellingplaces; and the city shall be builded upon her own heap, and the palace shall remain after the manner thereof. And out of them shall proceed thanksgiving and the voice of them that make merry: and I will multiply them, and they shall not be few; I will also glorify them, and they shall not be small. Their children also shall be as aforetime, and their congregation shall be established before me. And their nobles shall be of themselves, and their governor shall proceed from the midst of them; and I will cause him to draw near, and he shall approach unto me: for who is this that engaged his heart to approach unto me?" saith the Lord. "And ye shall be my people, and I will be your God."

The Lord hath appeared of old unto me, saying, "Yea, I have loved

*BY THE WATERS OF BABYLON*

thee with an everlasting love: therefore with lovingkindness have I
drawn thee. Thou shalt yet plant vines upon the mountains of Samaria:
the planters shall plant, and shall eat them as common things. For there
shall be a day, that the watchmen upon the mount Ephraim shall cry,
'Arise ye, and let us go up to Zion unto the LORD our God.' "

*Israel's restoration promised*

For thus saith the LORD; "Sing with gladness for Jacob, and shout
among the chief of the nations: publish ye, praise ye, and say, 'O LORD,
save thy people, the remnant of Israel.' Behold, I will bring them from
the north country, and gather them from the coasts of the earth, and with
them the blind and the lame, the woman with child and her that travaileth
with child together: a great company shall return thither. They shall
come with weeping, and with supplications will I lead them: I will cause
them to walk by the rivers of waters in a straight way, wherein they shall
not stumble: for I am a father to Israel.

"Hear the word of the LORD, O ye nations, and declare it in the isles
afar off, and say, 'He that scattered Israel will gather him, and keep him,
as a shepherd doth his flock.' For the LORD hath redeemed Jacob, and
ransomed him from the hand of him that was stronger than he. Therefore
they shall come and sing in the height of Zion, and shall flow together to
the goodness of the LORD, for wheat, and for wine, and for oil, and for the
young of the flock and of the herd: and their soul shall be as a watered
garden; and they shall not sorrow any more at all.

"Then shall the virgin rejoice in the dance, both young men and old
together: for I will turn their mourning into joy, and will comfort them,
and make them rejoice from their sorrow. My people shall be satisfied
with my goodness," saith the LORD.

Thus saith the LORD; "A voice was heard in Ramah, lamentation, and
bitter weeping; Rahel weeping for her children refused to be comforted
for her children, because they were not." Thus saith the LORD; "Refrain
thy voice from weeping, and thine eyes from tears: for thy work shall be
rewarded," saith the LORD; "and they shall come again from the land of
the enemy. And there is hope in thine end," saith the LORD, "that thy
children shall come again to their own border. Set thee up waymarks,
make thee high heaps: set thine heart toward the highway, even the way
which thou wentest: turn again, O virgin of Israel, turn again to these
thy cities.

"The LORD bless thee, O habitation of justice, and mountain of holiness. And there shall dwell in Judah itself, and in all the cities thereof together, husbandmen, and they that go forth with flocks. For I have satiated the weary soul, and I have replenished every sorrowful soul."

Upon this I awaked, and beheld; and my sleep was sweet unto me.

"Behold, the days come," saith the LORD, "that I will make a new covenant with the house of Israel, and with the house of Judah: not according to the covenant that I made with their fathers in the day that I took them by the hand to bring them out of the land of Egypt; which my covenant they brake, although I was an husband unto them," saith the LORD; "but this shall be the covenant that I will make with the house of Israel; After those days," saith the LORD, "I will put my law in their inward parts, and write it in their hearts; and will be their God, and they shall be my people. And they shall teach no more every man his neighbour, and every man his brother, saying, 'Know the LORD': for they shall all know me, from the least of them unto the greatest of them," saith the LORD: "for I will forgive their iniquity, and I will remember their sin no more."

The word that came to Jeremiah from the LORD in the tenth year of Zedekiah king of Judah, which was the eighteenth year of Nebuchadrezzar. For then the king of Babylon's army besieged Jerusalem: and Jeremiah the prophet was shut up in the court of the prison, which was in the king of Judah's house. For Zedekiah king of Judah had shut him up, saying, "Wherefore dost thou prophesy, and say, 'Thus saith the LORD, Behold, I will give this city into the hand of the king of Babylon, and he shall take it; and Zedekiah king of Judah shall not escape out of the hand of the Chaldeans, but shall surely be delivered into the hand of the king of Babylon, and shall speak with him mouth to mouth, and his eyes shall behold his eyes; and he shall lead Zedekiah to Babylon, and there shall he be until I visit him, saith the LORD: though ye fight with the Chaldeans, ye shall not prosper'."

Ah Lord GOD! behold, thou hast made the heaven and the earth by thy great power and stretched out arm, and there is nothing too hard for thee: thou shewest lovingkindness unto thousands, and recompensest the iniquity of the fathers into the bosom of their children after them: The Great, the Mighty God, the LORD of Hosts, is his name, great in counsel,

and mighty in work: for thine eyes are open upon all the ways of the sons *Jeremiah is arrested*
of men: to give every one according to his ways, and according to the *and imprisoned*
fruit of his doings.

Then came the word of the LORD unto Jeremiah, saying, "Behold, I
am the LORD, the God of all flesh: is there any thing too hard for me? I
will bring them again unto this place, and I will cause them to dwell
safely: and I will give them one heart, and one way, that they may fear
me for ever, for the good of them, and of their children after them: and I
will make an everlasting covenant with them, that I will not turn away
from them, to do them good; but I will put my fear in their hearts, that
they shall not depart from me. Yea, I will rejoice over them to do them
good, and I will plant them in this land assuredly with my whole heart
and with my whole soul."

Thus saith the LORD; "Again there shall be heard in this place the
voice of joy, and the voice of gladness, the voice of the bridegroom, and
the voice of the bride, the voice of them that shall say, 'Praise the LORD
of hosts: for the LORD is good; for his mercy endureth for ever': and of
them that shall bring the sacrifice of praise into the house of the LORD.
For I will cause to return the captivity of the land, as at first," saith the
LORD. "Again in this place, which is desolate without man and without
beast, and in all the cities thereof, shall be an habitation of shepherds
causing their flocks to lie down. In the cities of the mountains, in the
cities of the vale, and in the cities of the south, and in the land of Benjamin, and in the places about Jerusalem, and in the cities of Judah, shall
the flocks pass again under the hands of him that telleth them," saith
the LORD.

Now Jeremiah came in and went out among the people: for they had
not put him into prison. Then Pharaoh's army was come forth out of
Egypt: and when the Chaldeans that besieged Jerusalem heard tidings
of them, they departed from Jerusalem. And it came to pass, that when
the army of the Chaldeans was broken up from Jerusalem for fear of
Pharaoh's army, then Jeremiah went forth out of Jerusalem.

Then Zedekiah the king commanded that they should commit Jeremiah into the court of the prison, and that they should give him daily a
piece of bread out of the bakers' street, until all the bread in the city

*The king spares
Jeremiah's life*

were spent. Thus Jeremiah remained in the court of the prison. Then took they Jeremiah, and cast him into the dungeon of Malchiah the son of Hammelech, that was in the court of the prison: and they let down Jeremiah with cords. And in the dungeon there was no water, but mire: so Jeremiah sunk in the mire.

Now when Ebed-melech the Ethiopian, one of the eunuchs which was in the king's house, heard that they had put Jeremiah in the dungeon; Ebed-melech went forth out of the king's house, and spake to the king, saying, "My lord the king, these men have done evil in all that they have done to Jeremiah the prophet, whom they have cast into the dungeon; and he is like to die for hunger in the place where he is: for there is no more bread in the city."

Then the king commanded Ebed-melech the Ethiopian, saying, "Take from hence thirty men with thee, and take up Jeremiah the prophet out of the dungeon, before he die."

So Ebed-melech took the men with him, and went into the house of the king under the treasury, and took thence old cast clouts and old rotten rags, and let them down by cords into the dungeon to Jeremiah.

And Ebed-melech the Ethiopian said unto Jeremiah, "Put now these old cast clouts and rotten rags under thine armholes under the cords." And Jeremiah did so.

So they drew Jeremiah with cords, and took him out of the dungeon: and Jeremiah remained in the court of the prison.

Then Zedekiah the king sent, and took Jeremiah the prophet unto him into the third entry that is in the house of the LORD: and the king said unto Jeremiah, "I will ask thee a thing; hide nothing from me."

Then Jeremiah said unto Zedekiah, "If I declare it unto thee, wilt thou not surely put me to death? and if I give thee counsel, wilt thou not hearken unto me?" So Zedekiah the king sware secretly unto Jeremiah, saying, "As the LORD liveth, that made us this soul, I will not put thee to death, neither will I give thee into the hand of these men that seek thy life."

But Jeremiah said, "Obey, I beseech thee, the voice of the LORD, which I speak unto thee: so it shall be well unto thee, and thy soul shall live."

So Jeremiah abode in the court of the prison until the day that Jerusalem was taken: and he was there when Jerusalem was taken.

Now Nebuchadrezzar king of Babylon gave charge concerning Jeremiah to Nebuzar-adan the captain of the guard, saying, "Take him, and look well to him, and do him no harm; but do unto him even as he shall say unto thee."

Even they sent, and took Jeremiah out of the court of the prison, and committed him unto Gedaliah the son of Ahikam the son of Shaphan, that he should carry him home: so he dwelt among the people.

And Gedaliah the son of Ahikam sware unto them and to their men, saying, "Fear not to serve the Chaldeans: dwell in the land, and serve the king of Babylon, and it shall be well with you. As for me, behold, I will dwell at Mizpah, to serve the Chaldeans, which will come unto us: but ye, gather ye wine, and summer fruits, and oil, and put them in your vessels, and dwell in your cities that ye have taken."

When all the Jews heard that the king of Babylon had left a remnant of Judah, and that he had set over them Gedaliah; even all the Jews returned out of all places whither they were driven, and came to the land of Judah, to Gedaliah, unto Mizpah, and gathered wine and summer fruits very much.

The word that the LORD spake against Babylon and against the land of the Chaldeans by Jeremiah the prophet.

"Declare ye among the nations, and publish, and set up a standard; publish, and conceal not: say, 'Babylon is taken.' For out of the north there cometh up a nation against her, which shall make her land desolate, and none shall dwell therein: they shall remove, they shall depart, both man and beast. In those days, and in that time," saith the LORD, "the children of Israel shall come, they and the children of Judah together, going and weeping: they shall go, and seek the LORD their God. They shall ask the way to Zion with their faces thitherward, saying, 'Come, and let us join ourselves to the LORD in a perpetual covenant that shall not be forgotten.' My people hath been lost sheep: their shepherds have caused them to go astray, they have turned them away on the mountains: they have gone from mountain to hill, they have forgotten their resting-place. Remove out of the midst of Babylon, and go forth out of the land of the Chaldeans, and be as the he goats before the flocks. Israel is a scattered sheep; the lions have driven him away: first the king of Assyria hath devoured him; and last this Nebuchadrezzar king of Babylon hath broken his bones. And I will bring Israel again to his habitation, and he shall feed on Carmel and Bashan, and his soul shall be satisfied upon mount Ephraim and Gilead."

Thus saith the LORD of hosts; "The children of Israel and the children of Judah were oppressed together: and all that took them captives held them fast; they refused to let them go. Their Redeemer is strong; the LORD of hosts is his name: he shall throughly plead their cause, that he may give rest to the land, and disquiet the inhabitants of Babylon. At the noise of the taking of Babylon the earth is moved, and the cry is heard among the nations.

"Flee out of the midst of Babylon, and deliver every man his soul. Babylon hath been a golden cup in the LORD's hand, that made all the earth drunken: the nations have drunken of her wine; therefore the nations are mad. Babylon is suddenly fallen and destroyed: howl for her; take balm for her pain, if so be she may be healed.

" 'We would have healed Babylon, but she is not healed: forsake her, and let us go every one into his own country: for her judgment reacheth unto heaven, and is lifted up even to the skies.'

"Oh thou that dwellest upon many waters, abundant in treasures, thine end is come, and the measure of thy covetousness."

THE burden which Habakkuk the prophet did see.

O LORD, how long shall I cry,
And thou wilt not hear!
Art thou not from everlasting,
O LORD my God, mine Holy One?
We shall not die.
O LORD, thou hast ordained them for judgment;
And, O mighty God, thou hast established them for correction.
Thou art of purer eyes than to behold evil,
And canst not look on iniquity:
Wherefore lookest thou upon them that deal treacherously,

*Habakkuk's complaint*

And holdest thy tongue when the wicked devoureth
The man that is more righteous than he?
I will stand upon my watch,
And set me upon the tower,
And will watch to see what he will say unto me,
And what I shall answer when I am reproved.
And the LORD answered me, and said,
"Write the vision, and make it plain upon tables,
That he may run that readeth it.
For the vision is yet for an appointed time,
But at the end it shall speak, and not lie:
Though it tarry, wait for it;
Because it will surely come, it will not tarry.
Behold, his soul which is lifted up is not upright in him:
But the just shall live by his faith."
Woe to him that coveteth an evil covetousness to his house,
That he may set his nest on high,
That he may be delivered from the power of evil!
Thou hast consulted shame to thy house by cutting off many people,
And hast sinned against thy soul.
For the stone shall cry out of the wall,
And the beam out of the timber shall answer it.
Woe to him that buildeth a town with blood,
And stablisheth a city by iniquity!
Behold, is it not of the LORD of hosts
That the people shall labour in the very fire,
And the people shall weary themselves for very vanity?
For the earth shall be filled with the knowledge of the glory of the
    LORD,
As the waters cover the sea.
What profiteth the graven image that the maker thereof hath graven
    it;
The molten image, and a teacher of lies,
That the maker of his work trusteth therein,
To make dumb idols?
Woe unto him that saith to the wood, "Awake";

*The confidence of*
*Habakkuk's faith*

To the dumb stone, "Arise, it shall teach!"
Behold, it is laid over with gold and silver,
And there is no breath at all in the midst of it.
But the Lord is in his holy temple:
Let all the earth keep silence before him.

A PRAYER of Habakkuk the prophet upon Shigionoth.

O Lord, I have heard thy speech, and was afraid:
O Lord, revive thy work in the midst of the years,
In the midst of the years make known;
In wrath remember mercy.
Although the fig tree shall not blossom,
Neither shall fruit be in the vines;
The labour of the olive shall fail,
And the fields shall yield no meat;
The flock shall be cut off from the fold,
And there shall be no herd in the stalls:
Yet I will rejoice in the Lord,
I will joy in the God of my salvation.
The Lord God is my strength,
And he will make my feet like hinds' feet,
And he will make me to walk upon mine high places.

*Lamentations*

How doth the city sit solitary, that was full of people!
How is she become as a widow! she that was great among the
    nations,
And princess among the provinces, how is she become tributary!
She weepeth sore in the night, and her tears are on her cheeks:
Among all her lovers she hath none to comfort her:
All her friends have dealt treacherously with her, they are become
    her enemies.
Is it nothing to you, all ye that pass by?
Behold, and see if there be any sorrow like unto my sorrow, which is
    done unto me,
Wherewith the Lord hath afflicted me in the day of his fierce anger.

From above hath he sent fire into my bones, and it prevaileth against  *Lamentations*
   them:
He hath spread a net for my feet, he hath turned me back:
He hath made me desolate and faint all the day.
For these things I weep; mine eye, mine eye runneth down with
   water,
Because the comforter that should relieve my soul is far from me:
My children are desolate, because the enemy prevailed.
The LORD is righteous; for I have rebelled against his commandment:
Hear, I pray you, all people, and behold my sorrow.
It is of the LORD's mercies that we are not consumed, because his
   compassions fail not.
They are new every morning: great is thy faithfulness.
"The LORD is my portion," saith my soul; "therefore will I hope in
   him."
The LORD is good unto them that wait for him, to the soul that seek-
   eth him.
It is good that a man should both hope and quietly wait for the sal-
   vation of the LORD.
For the Lord will not cast off for ever:
But though he cause grief, yet will he have compassion according to
   the multitude of his mercies.
For he doth not afflict willingly, nor grieve the children of men.
Let us search and try our ways, and turn again to the LORD.
Let us lift up our heart with our hands unto God in the heavens.
Thou drewest near in the day that I called upon thee: thou saidst,
   "Fear not."
O LORD, thou hast pleaded the causes of my soul; thou hast redeemed
   my life.
Remember, O LORD, what is come upon us:
Consider, and behold our reproach.
Our inheritance is turned to strangers,
Our houses to aliens.
We are orphans and fatherless,
Our mothers are as widows.
Our necks are under persecution:

*Lamentations*　　We labour, and have no rest.

Our fathers have sinned, and are not; and we have borne their iniqui-
　　ties.

Servants have ruled over us:

There is none that doth deliver us out of their hand.

We gat our bread with the peril of our lives

Because of the sword of the wilderness.

The elders have ceased from the gate,

The young men from their musick.

The joy of our heart is ceased;

Our dance is turned into mourning.

The crown is fallen from our head:

Woe unto us, that we have sinned!

For this our heart is faint;

For these things our eyes are dim.

Because of the mountain of Zion, which is desolate,

The foxes walk upon it.

Thou, O Lord, remainest for ever;

Thy throne from generation to generation.

Wherefore dost thou forget us for ever,

And forsake us so long time?

Turn thou us unto thee, O Lord, and we shall be turned;

Renew our days as of old.

*Ezekiel's vision*　　Now it came to pass, as I was among the captives by the river of Chebar, that the heavens were opened, and I saw visions of God. As the appearance of the bow that is in the cloud in the day of rain, so was the appearance of the brightness round about. This was the appearance of the likeness of the glory of the Lord. And when I saw it, I fell upon my face, and I heard a voice of one that spake. And he said unto me, "Son of man, stand upon thy feet, and I will speak unto thee."

And the spirit entered into me when he spake unto me, and set me upon my feet, and he said unto me, "Son of man, I send thee to the children of Israel, to a rebellious nation that hath rebelled against me: and thou shalt say unto them, 'Thus saith the Lord God.' And they, whether they will hear, or whether they will forbear, (for they are a rebellious house,) yet shall know that there hath been a prophet among them. Be not afraid of their words, nor be dismayed at their looks." Moreover he said unto me, "Son of man, all my words that I shall speak unto thee receive in thine heart, and hear with thine ears."

Then the spirit took me up, and I heard behind me a voice of a great rushing, saying, "Blessed be the glory of the LORD from his place." I heard also the noise of the wings of the living creatures that touched one another, and the noise of the wheels over against them, and a noise of a great rushing. So the spirit lifted me up, and took me away, and I went in bitterness, in the heat of my spirit; but the hand of the LORD was strong upon me. Then I came to them of the captivity at Tel-abib, that dwelt by the river of Chebar, and I sat where they sat, and remained there astonished among them seven days.

And it came to pass at the end of seven days, that the word of the LORD came unto me, saying, "Son of man, I have made thee a watchman unto the house of Israel: therefore hear the word at my mouth, and give them warning from me."

And the hand of the LORD was there upon me; and he said unto me, "Arise, go forth into the plain, and I will there talk with thee."

Then I arose, and went forth into the plain: and, behold, the glory of the LORD stood there, as the glory which I saw by the river of Chebar: and I fell on my face. Then the spirit entered into me, and set me upon my feet, and spake with me, and said unto me, "Go, shut thyself within thine house. But when I speak with thee, I will open thy mouth, and thou shalt say unto them, 'Thus saith the Lord GOD'; He that heareth, let him hear; and he that forbeareth, let him forbear: for they are a rebellious house."

And the Spirit of the LORD fell upon me, and said unto me, "Speak; Thus saith the LORD; Thus have ye said, O house of Israel: for I know the things that come into your mind, every one of them. Therefore say, Thus saith the Lord GOD; Although I have cast them far off among the heathen, and although I have scattered them among the countries, yet will I be to them as a little sanctuary in the countries where they shall come. Therefore say, Thus saith the Lord GOD; I will even gather you from the people, and assemble you out of the countries where ye have been scattered, and I will give you the land of Israel. And I will give them one heart, and I will put a new spirit within you; and I will take the stony heart out of their flesh, and will give them an heart of flesh: that they may walk in my statutes, and keep mine ordinances, and do them: and they shall be my people, and I will be their God. " And the glory of the LORD went up from the midst of the city, and stood upon the mountain which is on the east side of the city.

Afterwards the spirit took me up, and brought me in a vision by the Spirit of God into Chaldea, to them of the captivity. So the vision that I had seen went up from me.

And in the morning came the word of the LORD unto me, saying, "Son of man, put forth a riddle, and speak a parable unto the house of Israel; and say, 'Thus saith the Lord GOD; A great eagle with great wings, longwinged, full of feathers, which had divers colours, came unto Lebanon, and took the highest branch of the cedar: he cropped off the top of his young twigs, and carried it into a land of traffick; he set it in a city of merchants. He took also of the seed of the land, and planted it in a fruitful field; he placed it by great waters, and set it as a willow tree. And it grew, and became a spreading vine of low stature, whose branches turned toward him, and the roots thereof were under him: so it became a vine, and brought forth branches, and shot forth sprigs. There was also another great eagle with great wings and many feathers: and, behold, this vine did bend her roots toward him, and shot forth her branches toward him, that he might water it by the furrows of her plantation. It was planted in a good soil by great waters, that it might bring forth branches, and that it might bear fruit, that it might be a goodly vine.' Say thou, 'Thus saith the Lord GOD; Shall it prosper? shall he not pull up the roots thereof, and cut off the fruit thereof, that it wither? it shall wither in all the leaves of her spring, even without great power or many people to pluck it up by the roots thereof. Yea, behold, being planted, shall it prosper? shall it not utterly wither, when the east wind toucheth it? it shall wither in the furrows where it grew.' "

Moreover the word of the LORD came unto me, saying, "Thus saith the Lord GOD; I will also take of the highest branch of the high cedar, and will set it; I will crop off from the top of his young twigs a tender one, and will plant it upon an high mountain and eminent: in the mountain of the height of Israel will I plant it; and it shall bring forth boughs, and bear fruit, and be a goodly cedar: and under it shall dwell all fowl *Beauty and riches of* of every wing; in the shadow of the branches thereof shall they dwell. And *Tyre* all the trees of the field shall know that I the LORD have brought down the high tree, have exalted the low tree, have dried up the green tree, and have made the dry tree to flourish: I the LORD have spoken and have done it."

The word of the LORD came again unto me, saying, "Now, thou son of man, take up a lamentation for Tyrus; and say unto Tyrus, 'O thou that art situate at the entry of the sea, which art a merchant of the people for many isles, Thus saith the Lord GOD; O Tyrus, thou hast said, "I am of perfect beauty." Thy borders are in the midst of the seas, thy builders have perfected thy beauty. They have made all thy ship boards of fir trees of Senir: they have taken cedars from Lebanon to make masts for thee. Of the oaks of Bashan have they made thine oars; the company of the Ashurites have made thy benches of ivory, brought out of the isles of Chittim. Fine linen with broidered work from Egypt was that which thou spreadest forth to be thy sail; blue and purple from the Isles of Elishah was that which covered thee. The inhabitants of Zidon and Arvad were thy mariners: thy wise men, O Tyrus, that were in thee, were thy pilots. The ancients of Gebal and the wise men thereof were in thee thy calkers: all the ships of the sea with their mariners were in thee to occupy thy merchandise. They of Persia and of Lud and of Phut were in thine army, thy men of war: they hanged the shield and helmet in thee; they set forth thy comeliness. The men of Arvad with thine army were upon thy walls round about, and the Gammadims were in thy towers: they hanged their shields upon thy walls round about; they have made thy beauty perfect. Tarshish was thy merchant by reason of the multitude of all kind of riches; with silver, iron, tin, and lead, they traded in thy fairs. Javan, Tubal, and Meshech, they were thy merchants: they traded the persons of men and vessels of brass in thy market. They of the house of Togarmah traded in thy fairs with horses and horsemen and mules. The men of Dedan were thy merchants; many isles were the merchandise of thine hand: they brought thee for a present horns of ivory and ebony. Syria was thy merchant by reason of the multitude of the wares of thy making: they occupied in thy fairs with emeralds, purple, and broidered work, and fine linen, and coral, and agate. Judah, and the land of Israel, they were thy merchants: they traded in thy market wheat of Minnith, and Pannag, and honey, and oil, and balm. Damascus was thy merchant in the multitude of the wares of thy making, for the multitude of all riches; in the wine of Helbon, and white wool. Dan also and Javan going to and fro occupied in thy fairs: bright iron, cassia, and calamus, were in thy market. Dedan was thy merchant in precious clothes for chariots. Arabia, and all the princes of Kedar, they occupied with thee in lambs, and rams, and goats: in these were they thy merchants. The merchants of Sheba and Raamah, they were thy merchants: they occupied in thy fairs with chief of all spices, and with all precious stones, and gold. Haran, and Canneh, and Eden, the merchants of Sheba, Asshur, and Chilmad, were thy merchants. These were thy merchants in all sorts of things, in blue clothes, and broidered work, and in chests of rich apparel, bound with cords, and made of cedar, among thy merchandise. The ships of Tarshish did sing of thee in thy market: and thou wast replenished, and made very glorious in the midst of the seas. Thy rowers have brought thee into great waters: the east wind hath broken thee in the midst of the seas. And in their wailing they shall take up a lamentation for thee, and lament over thee, saying, "What city is like Tyrus, like the destroyed in the midst of the sea?" When thy wares went forth out of the seas, thou filledst many people; thou didst enrich the kings of the earth with the multitude of thy riches and of thy merchandise.' "

"Son of man, speak unto Pharaoh king of Egypt, and to his multitude; 'Whom art thou like in thy greatness? Behold, the Assyrian was a cedar in Lebanon with fair branches, and with a shadowing shroud, and of an high stature; and his top was among the thick boughs. The waters made him great, the deep set him up on high with her rivers running round about his plants, and sent out her little rivers unto all the trees of the field. Therefore his height was exalted above all the trees of the field, and his boughs were multiplied, and his branches became long because of the multitude of waters, when he shot forth. All the fowls of heaven made their nests in his boughs, and under his branches did all the beasts of the field bring forth their young, and under his shadow dwelt all great nations. Thus was he fair in his greatness, in the length of his branches: for his root was by great waters. The cedars in the garden of God could not hide him: the fir trees were not like his boughs, and the chestnut *The duty of a watchman* trees were not like his branches; nor any tree in the garden of God was like unto him in his beauty. I have made him fair by the multitude of his branches: so that all the trees of Eden, that were in the garden of God, envied him.' Therefore thus saith the Lord GOD; 'Because thou hast lifted up thyself in height, and he hath shot up his top among the thick boughs, and his heart is lifted up in his height; I have therefore delivered him into the hand of the mighty one of the heathen; he shall surely deal with him: I have driven him out for his wickedness. And strangers, the terrible of the nations, have cut him off, and have left him: upon the mountains and in all the valleys his branches are fallen, and his boughs are broken by all the rivers of the land; and all the people of the earth are gone down from his shadow, and have left him. To the end that none of all the trees by the waters exalt themselves for their height, neither shoot up their top among the thick boughs, neither their trees stand up in their height, all that drink water.' "

Again the word of the LORD came unto me, saying, "So thou, O son of man, I have set thee a watchman unto the house of Israel; therefore thou shalt hear the word at my mouth, and warn them from me. Say unto them, ' "As I live," saith the Lord GOD, "I have no pleasure in the death of the wicked; but that the wicked turn from his way, and live: turn ye, turn ye from your evil ways; for why will ye die, O house of Israel?" ' Also, thou son of man, the children of thy people still are talking against thee by the walls and in the doors of the houses, and speak one to another, every one to his brother, saying, 'Come, I pray you, and hear what is the word that cometh forth from the LORD.' And they come unto thee as the people cometh, and they sit before thee as my people, and they hear thy words, but they will not do them: for with their mouth they shew much love, but their heart goeth after their covetousness. And, lo, thou art unto them as a very lovely song of one that hath a pleasant voice, and can play well on an instrument: for they hear thy words, but they do them not. And when this cometh to pass, (lo, it will come,) then shall they know that a prophet hath been among them."

The word of the LORD came unto me again, saying, "What mean ye, that ye use this proverb concerning the land of Israel, saying, 'The fathers have eaten sour grapes, and the children's teeth are set on edge'? As I live," saith the Lord GOD, "ye shall not have occasion any more to use this proverb in Israel. But if a man be just, and do that which is lawful and right, hath given his bread to the hungry, and hath covered the naked with a garment; he that hath not given forth upon usury, neither hath taken any increase, that hath withdrawn his hand from iniquity, hath executed true judgment between man and man, hath walked in my statutes, and hath kept my judgments, to deal truly; he is just, he shall surely live," saith the Lord GOD. "The son shall not bear the iniquity of the father, neither shall the father bear the iniquity of the son: the righteousness of the righteous shall be upon him, and the wickedness of the wicked shall be upon him. Have I any pleasure at all that the wicked should die?" saith the Lord GOD: "and not that he should return from his ways, and live? Yet ye say, 'The way of the Lord is not equal.' Hear now, O house of Israel; Is not my way equal? are not your ways unequal? Therefore I will judge you, O house of Israel, every one according to his ways," saith the Lord GOD. "Repent, and turn yourselves from all your transgressions; so iniquity shall not be your ruin. Cast away from you all your transgressions, whereby ye have transgressed; and make you a new heart and a new spirit: for why will ye die, O house of Israel? For I have no pleasure in the death of him that dieth," saith the Lord GOD: "wherefore turn yourselves, and live ye. I am the LORD your God; walk in my statutes, and keep my judgments, and do them; and hallow my sabbaths; and they shall be a sign between me and you, that ye may know that I am the LORD your God."

Also, the word of the LORD came unto me, saying, "Son of man, behold, I take away from thee the desire of thine eyes with a stroke: yet neither shalt thou mourn nor weep, neither shall thy tears run down. Forbear to cry, make no mourning for the dead, bind the tire of thine head upon thee, and put on thy shoes upon thy feet, and cover not thy lips, and eat not the bread of men."

So I spake unto the people in the morning: and at even my wife died; and I did in the morning as I was commanded.

And the people said unto me, "Wilt thou not tell us what these things are to us, that thou doest so?"

Then I answered them, "The word of the LORD came unto me, saying, 'Speak unto the house of Israel, Thus saith the Lord GOD; Behold,

*THE DEATH OF EZEKIEL'S WIFE*

I will profane my sanctuary, the excellency of your strength, the desire of *Judgment on Tyre* your eyes, and that which your soul pitieth; and your sons and your daughters whom ye have left shall fall by the sword. And ye shall do as I have done: ye shall not cover your lips, nor eat the bread of men. And your tires shall be upon your heads, and your shoes upon your feet: ye shall not mourn nor weep; but ye shall pine away for your iniquities, and mourn one toward another. Thus Ezekiel is unto you a sign: according to all that he hath done shall ye do: and when this cometh, ye shall know that I am the Lord GOD.'

"Also, thou son of man, shall it not be in the day when I take from them their strength, the joy of their glory, the desire of their eyes, and that whereupon they set their minds, their sons and their daughters, that he that escapeth in that day shall come unto thee, to cause thee to hear it with thine ears? In that day shall thy mouth be opened to him which is escaped, and thou shalt speak, and be no more dumb: and thou shalt be a sign unto them; and they shall know that I am the LORD."

The word of the LORD came again unto me, saying, "Son of man, say unto the prince of Tyrus, 'Thus saith the Lord GOD; Because thine heart is lifted up, and thou hast said, "I am a god, I sit in the seat of God, in the midst of the seas"; yet thou art a man, and not God, though thou set thine heart as the heart of God: behold, thou art wiser than Daniel; there is no secret that they can hide from thee: with thy wisdom and with thine understanding thou hast gotten thee riches, and hast gotten gold and silver into thy treasures: by thy great wisdom and by thy traffick hast thou increased thy riches, and thine heart is lifted up because of thy riches: therefore thus saith the Lord GOD; Because thou hast set thine heart as the heart of God; behold, therefore I will bring strangers upon thee, the terrible of the nations: and they shall draw their swords against the beauty of thy wisdom, and they shall defile thy brightness. They shall bring thee down to the pit, and thou shalt die the deaths of them that are slain in the midst of the seas. Wilt thou yet say before him that slayeth thee, "I am God"? but thou shalt be a man, and no God, in the hand of him that slayeth thee: for I have spoken it, saith the Lord GOD.' "

Moreover the word of the LORD came unto me, saying, "Son of man, take up a lamentation upon the king of Tyrus, and say unto him,

'Thus saith the Lord GOD; Thou sealest up the sum, full of wisdom, and perfect in beauty. Thou wast perfect in thy ways from the day that thou wast created, till iniquity was found in thee. Thine heart was lifted up because of thy beauty, thou hast corrupted thy wisdom by reason of thy brightness: I will cast thee to the ground.' "

And the word of the LORD came unto me, saying, "Son of man, prophesy against the shepherds of Israel, prophesy, and say unto them, 'Thus saith the Lord GOD unto the shepherds; "Woe be to the shepherds of Israel that do feed themselves! should not the shepherds feed the flocks? Ye eat the fat, and ye clothe you with the wool, ye kill them that are fed: but ye feed not the flock. The diseased have ye not strengthened, neither have ye healed that which was sick, neither have ye bound up that which was broken, neither have ye brought again that which was driven away, neither have ye sought that which was lost; but with force and with cruelty have ye ruled them. And they were scattered, because there is no shepherd: and they became meat to all the beasts of the field, when they were scattered. My sheep wandered through all the mountains, and upon every high hill: yea, my flock was scattered upon all the face of the earth, and none did search or seek after them." '

" 'For thus saith the Lord GOD; Behold, I, even I, will both search my sheep, and seek them out. As a shepherd seeketh out his flock in the day that he is among his sheep that are scattered; so will I seek out my sheep, and will deliver them out of all places where they have been scattered in the cloudy and dark day. And I will bring them out from the people, and gather them from the countries, and will bring them to their own land, and feed them upon the mountains of Israel by the rivers, and in all the inhabited places of the country. I will feed them in a good pasture, and upon the high mountains of Israel shall their fold be: there shall they lie in a good fold, and in a fat pasture shall they feed upon the mountains of Israel. I will feed my flock, and I will cause them to lie down, saith the Lord GOD. I will seek that which was lost, and bring again that which was driven away, and will bind up that which was broken, and will strengthen that which was sick: but I will destroy the fat and the strong; I will feed them with judgment.

" 'And I will set up one shepherd over them, and he shall feed them, even my servant David; he shall feed them, and he shall be their shepherd. And I the LORD will be their God, and my servant David a prince among them; I the LORD have spoken it. And I will make with them a covenant of peace, and will cause the evil beasts to cease out of the land: and they shall dwell safely in the wilderness, and sleep in the woods. And I will make them and the places round about my hill a blessing; and I will cause the shower to come down in his season; there shall be showers of blessing. And the tree of the field shall yield her fruit, and the earth shall yield her increase, and they shall be safe in their land, and shall know that I am the LORD, when I have broken the bands of their yoke, and delivered them out of the hand of those that served themselves of them. And they shall no more be a prey to the heathen, neither shall the beast of the land devour them; but they shall dwell safely, and none shall make them afraid. And I will raise up for them a plant of renown, and they shall be no more consumed with hunger in the land, neither bear the shame of the heathen any more. Thus shall they know that I the LORD their God am with them, and that they, even the house of Israel, are my people, saith the Lord GOD.

"'And ye my flock, the flock of my pasture, are men, and I am your God,' saith the Lord GOD. 'But ye, O mountains of Israel, ye shall shoot forth your branches, and yield your fruit to my people of Israel; for they are at hand to come. For, behold, I am for you, and I will turn unto you, and ye shall be tilled and sown: and I will multiply men upon you, all the house of Israel, even all of it: and the cities shall be inhabited, and the wastes shall be builded. Then will I sprinkle clean water upon you, and ye shall be clean: from all your filthiness, and from all your idols, will I cleanse you. A new heart also will I give you, and a new spirit will I put within you: and I will take away the stony heart out of your flesh, and I will give you an heart of flesh. And I will put my spirit within you, and cause you to walk in my statutes, and ye shall keep my judgments, and do them. And ye shall dwell in the land that I gave to your fathers; and ye shall be my people, and I will be your God.'"

The hand of the LORD was upon me, and carried me out in the spirit of the LORD, and set me down in the midst of the valley which was full of bones, and caused me to pass by them round about: and, behold, there were very many in the open valley; and, lo, they were very dry. And he said unto me, "Son of man, can these bones live?"

*God's glory comes to the temple*

And I answered, "O Lord GOD, thou knowest."

Again he said unto me, "Prophesy upon these bones, and say unto them, 'O ye dry bones, hear the word of the LORD. Thus saith the Lord GOD unto these bones; Behold, I will cause breath to enter into you, and ye shall live: and I will lay sinews upon you, and will bring up flesh upon you, and cover you with skin, and put breath in you, and ye shall live; and ye shall know that I am the LORD.' "

So I prophesied as I was commanded: and as I prophesied, there was a noise, and behold, a shaking, and the bones came together, bone to his bone. And when I beheld, lo, the sinews and the flesh came up upon them, and the skin covered them above: but there was no breath in them.

Then said he unto me, "Prophesy unto the wind, prophesy, son of man, and say to the wind, 'Thus saith the Lord GOD; Come from the four winds, O breath, and breathe upon these slain, that they may live.' "

So I prophesied as he commanded me, and the breath came into them, and they lived, and stood up upon their feet, an exceeding great army.

Then he said unto me, "Son of man, these bones are the whole house of Israel: behold, they say, 'Our bones are dried, and our hope is lost: we are cut off for our parts.' Therefore prophesy and say unto them, 'Thus saith the Lord GOD; Behold, O my people, I will open your graves, and cause you to come up out of your graves, and bring you into the land of Israel. And ye shall know that I am the LORD, when I have opened your graves, O my people, and brought you up out of your graves, and shall put my spirit in you, and ye shall live, and I shall place you in your own land: then shall ye know that I the LORD have spoken it, and performed it, saith the LORD. Thus will I magnify myself, and sanctify myself; and I will be known in the eyes of many nations, and they shall know that I am the LORD. Neither will I hide my face any more from them: for I have poured out my spirit upon the house of Israel, saith the Lord GOD.' "

Afterward he brought me to the gate, even the gate that looketh toward the east: and, behold, the glory of the God of Israel came from the way of the east: and his voice was like a noise of many waters: and the earth shined with his glory. And it was according to the appearance of the vision which I saw, even according to the vision that I saw when

I came to destroy the city: and the visions were like the vision that I saw by the river Chebar; and I fell upon my face. And the glory of the LORD came into the house by the way of the gate whose prospect is toward the east. So the spirit took me up, and brought me into the inner court; and, behold, the glory of the LORD filled the house. And I heard him speaking unto me out of the house; and the man stood by me.

*Ordinances of the altar*

And he said unto me, "Thou son of man, shew the house to the house of Israel, and if they be ashamed of all that they have done, shew them the form of the house, and the fashion thereof, and the goings out thereof, and the comings in thereof, and all the forms thereof, and all the ordinances thereof, and all the forms thereof, and all the laws thereof: and write it in their sight that they may keep the whole form thereof, and all the ordinances thereof, and do them. This is the law of the house; Upon the top of the mountain the whole limit thereof round about shall be most holy. Behold, this is the law of the house."

Then brought he me the way of the north gate before the house: and I looked, and, behold, the glory of the LORD filled the house of the LORD: and I fell upon my face. And the LORD said unto me, "Son of man, mark well, and behold with thine eyes, and hear with thine ears all that I say unto thee concerning all the ordinances of the house of the LORD, and all the laws thereof; and mark well the entering in of the house, with every going forth of the sanctuary.

"But the priests that kept the charge of my sanctuary when the children of Israel went astray from me, they shall come near to me to minister unto me, and they shall stand before me," saith the Lord GOD: "they shall enter into my sanctuary, and they shall come near to my table, to minister unto me, and they shall keep my charge. And it shall come to pass, that when they enter in at the gates of the inner court, they shall be clothed with linen garments; and no wool shall come upon them, whiles they minister in the gates of the inner court, and within. And when they go forth into the utter court, even into the utter court to the people, they shall put off their garments wherein they ministered, and lay them in the holy chambers, and they shall put on other garments; and they shall not sanctify the people with their garments. And they shall teach my people the difference between the holy and profane, and cause them to discern between the unclean and the clean."

[ 283 ]

Afterward he brought me again unto the door of the house; and, behold, waters issued out from under the threshold of the house eastward: for the forefront of the house stood toward the east, and the waters came down from under from the right side of the house, at the south side of the altar. Then brought he me out of the way of the gate northward, and led me about the way without unto the utter gate by the way that looketh eastward; and, behold, there ran out waters on the right side. And when the man that had the line in his hand went forth eastward, he measured a thousand cubits, and he brought me through the waters; the waters were to the ankles. Again he measured a thousand, and brought me through the waters; the waters were to the knees. Again he measured a thousand, and brought me through; the waters were to the loins. Afterward he measured a thousand, and it was a river that I could not pass over: for the waters were risen, waters to swim in, a river that could not be passed over.

And he said unto me, "Son of man, hast thou seen this?"

Then he brought me, and caused me to return to the brink of the river. Now when I had returned, behold, at the bank of the river were very many trees on the one side and on the other. Then said he unto me, "These waters issue out toward the east country, and go down into the desert, and go into the sea: which being brought forth into the sea, the waters shall be healed. And it shall come to pass, that every thing that liveth, which moveth, whithersoever the rivers shall come, shall live: and there shall be a very great multitude of fish, because these waters shall come thither: for they shall be healed; and every thing shall live whither the river cometh. And it shall come to pass, that the fishers shall stand upon it from En-gedi even unto En-eglaim; they shall be a place to spread forth nets; their fish shall be according to their kinds, as the fish of the great sea, exceeding many. But the miry places thereof and the marishes thereof shall not be healed; they shall be given to salt. And by the river upon the bank thereof, on this side and on that side, shall grow all trees for meat, whose leaf shall not fade, neither shall the fruit thereof be consumed: it shall bring forth new fruit according to his months, because their waters they issued out of the sanctuary: and the fruit thereof shall be for meat, and the leaf thereof for medicine. And the name of the city from that day shall be, 'The LORD is there.' "

## THE PROPHETS

"COMFORT ye, comfort ye my people,"
  Saith your God.
"Speak ye comfortably to Jerusalem,
  And cry unto her,
  That her warfare is accomplished,
  That her iniquity is pardoned:
  For she hath received of the LORD's hand
  Double for all her sins."
  The voice said, "Cry."
  And he said, "What shall I cry?"
"All flesh is grass,
  And all the goodliness thereof is as the flower of the field:
  The grass withereth, the flower fadeth:
  Because the spirit of the LORD bloweth upon it:
  Surely the people is grass.
  The grass withereth, the flower fadeth:
  But the word of our God shall stand for ever."
  O Zion, that bringest good tidings,
  Get thee up into the high mountain;
  O Jerusalem, that bringest good tidings,
  Lift up thy voice with strength;
  Lift it up,
  Be not afraid;
  Say unto the cities of Judah,
"Behold your God!"
  Behold, the Lord GOD will come with strong hand,
  And his arm shall rule for him:
  Behold, his reward is with him,
  And his work before him.
  He shall feed his flock like a shepherd:
  He shall gather the lambs with his arm,
  And carry them in his bosom,
  And shall gently lead those that are with young.
  Who hath measured the waters in the hollow of his hand,
  And meted out heaven with the span,
  And comprehended the dust of the earth in a measure,

*Promulgation of the gospel*

[ 285 ]

*God's incomparableness*
And weighed the mountains in scales,
And the hills in a balance?
Who hath directed the Spirit of the LORD,
Or being his counsellor hath taught him?
With whom took he counsel,
And who instructed him,
And taught him in the path of judgment,
And taught him knowledge,
And shewed to him the way of understanding?
Behold, the nations are as a drop of a bucket,
And are counted as the small dust of the balance:
Behold, he taketh up the isles as a very little thing.
And Lebanon is not sufficient to burn,
Nor the beasts thereof sufficient for a burnt offering.
All nations before him are as nothing;
And they are counted to him less than nothing, and vanity.
To whom then will ye liken God?
Or what likeness will ye compare unto him?
The workman melteth a graven image,
And the goldsmith spreadeth it over with gold,
And casteth silver chains.
He that is so impoverished that he hath no oblation
Chooseth a tree that will not rot;
He seeketh unto him a cunning workman to prepare a graven image,
That shall not be moved.
Have ye not known? have ye not heard?
Hath it not been told you from the beginning?
Have ye not understood from the foundations of the earth?
It is he that sitteth upon the circle of the earth,
And the inhabitants thereof are as grasshoppers;
That stretcheth out the heavens as a curtain,
And spreadeth them out as a tent to dwell in:
That bringeth the princes to nothing;
He maketh the judges of the earth as vanity.
Yea, they shall not be planted;
Yea, they shall not be sown;

## THE PROPHETS

Yea, their stock shall not take root in the earth:
And he shall also blow upon them, and they shall wither,
And the whirlwind shall take them away as stubble.
"To whom then will ye liken me,
Or shall I be equal?" saith the Holy One.
Lift up your eyes on high,
And behold who hath created these things,
That bringeth out their host by number:
He calleth them all by names
By the greatness of his might, for that he is strong in power;
Not one faileth.
Why sayest thou, O Jacob,
And speakest, O Israel,
"My way is hid from the LORD,
And my judgment is passed over from my God?"
Hast thou not known?
Hast thou not heard,
That the everlasting God,
The LORD, the Creator of the ends of the earth,
Fainteth not, neither is weary?
There is no searching of his understanding.
He giveth power to the faint;
And to them that have no might he increaseth strength.
Even the youths shall faint and be weary,
And the young men shall utterly fall:
But they that wait upon the LORD shall renew their strength;
They shall mount up with wings as eagles;
They shall run, and not be weary;
And they shall walk, and not faint.

The LORD shall comfort Zion:
He will comfort all her waste places;
And he will make her wilderness like Eden,
And her desert like the garden of the LORD;
Joy and gladness shall be found therein,
Thanksgiving, and the voice of melody.

[ 287 ]

Awake, awake, stand up, O Jerusalem,
Which hast drunk at the hand of the LORD the cup of his fury;
Thou hast drunken the dregs of the cup of trembling, and wrung
    them out.
There is none to guide her among all the sons whom she hath brought
    forth;
Neither is there any that taketh her by the hand
Of all the sons that she hath brought up.
These two things are come unto thee; who shall be sorry for thee?
Desolation, and destruction, and the famine, and the sword:
By whom shall I comfort thee?
The Lord GOD hath given me the tongue of the learned,
That I should know how to speak a word in season to him that is
    weary:
He wakeneth morning by morning,
He wakeneth mine ear to hear as the learned.
The Lord GOD hath opened mine ear,
And I was not rebellious, neither turned away back. I gave my back
    to the smiters,
And my cheeks to them that plucked off the hair:
I hid not my face from shame and spitting.
For the Lord GOD will help me;
Therefore shall I not be confounded:
Therefore have I set my face like a flint,
And I know that I shall not be ashamed.
He is near that justifieth me; who will contend with me?
Let us stand together: who is mine adversary?
Let him come near to me.
Behold, the Lord GOD will help me;
Who is he that shall condemn me? Lo, they all shall wax old as a gar-
    ment;
The moth shall eat them up.
Who is among you that feareth the LORD,
That obeyeth the voice of his servant,
That walketh in darkness, and hath no light?
Let him trust in the name of the LORD, and stay upon his God.

Behold, all ye that kindle a fire, that compass yourselves about with    *God's care for his church*
    sparks:
Walk in the light of your fire, and in the sparks that ye have kindled.
This shall ye have of mine hand; ye shall lie down in sorrow.


"I have chosen thee," saith the LORD,
"And not cast thee away.
  Fear thou not; for I am with thee:
  Be not dismayed; for I am thy God:
  I will strengthen thee; yea, I will help thee;
  Yea, I will uphold thee with the right hand of my righteousness.
  I will help thee," saith the LORD,
  And thy redeemer, the Holy One of Israel.
"When the poor and needy seek water,
  And there is none, and their tongue faileth for thirst,
  I the LORD will hear them, I the God of Israel will not forsake them.
  I will open rivers in high places, and fountains in the midst of the
    valleys:
  I will make the wilderness a pool of water, and the dry land springs of
    water.
  I will plant in the wilderness the cedar, the shittah tree, and the
    myrtle, and the oil tree;
  I will set in the desert the fir tree, and the pine, and the box tree to-
    gether:
  That they may see, and know, and consider, and understand to-
    gether,
  That the hand of the LORD hath done this,
And the Holy One of Israel hath created it. And I will bring the blind
    by a way that they knew not;
I will lead them in paths that they have not known:
I will make darkness light before them, and crooked things straight.
These things will I do unto them, and not forsake them.
Fear not: for I have redeemed thee,
I have called thee by thy name; thou art mine.
When thou passest through the waters, I will be with thee;
And through the rivers, they shall not overflow thee:

When thou walkest through the fire, thou shalt not be burned;
Neither shall the flame kindle upon thee.
For I am the LORD thy God, the Holy One of Israel, thy Saviour.
Since thou wast precious in my sight, thou hast been honourable,
And I have loved thee.
I, even I, am he that blotteth out thy transgressions for mine own
    sake,
And will not remember thy sins.
I have blotted out, as a thick cloud, thy transgressions,
And, as a cloud, thy sins:
Return unto me; for I have redeemed thee."
Sing, O ye heavens; for the LORD hath done it:
Shout, ye lower parts of the earth:
Break forth into singing, ye mountains, O forest, and every tree
    therein:
For the LORD hath redeemed Jacob, and glorified himself in Israel.
Let all the nations be gathered together, and let the people be as-
    sembled:
Who among them can declare this, and shew us former things? let
    them bring forth their witnesses, that they may be justified:
Or let them hear, and say, "It is truth."

Thus saith the LORD, thy Redeemer, the Holy One of Israel,
"O that thou hadst hearkened to my commandments!
Then had thy peace been as a river,
And thy righteousness as the waves of the sea.
Remember the former things of old:
For I am God, and there is none else;
I am God, and there is none like me,
Declaring the end from the beginning,
And from ancient times the things that are not yet done, saying,
'My counsel shall stand, and I will do all my pleasure.' "

Thus saith the LORD to his anointed,
To Cyrus, whose right hand I have holden,
To subdue nations before him;

## THE PROPHETS

The omnipotence of
God

"I will go before thee,
And make the crooked places straight:
And I will give thee the treasures of darkness,
And hidden riches of secret places,
That thou mayest know that I, the LORD,
Which call thee by thy name, am the God of Israel.
For Jacob my servant's sake,
And Israel mine elect,
I have even called thee by thy name:
I have surnamed thee, though thou hast not known me.
I am the LORD, and there is none else,
There is no God beside me:
I girded thee, though thou hast not known me:
That they may know from the rising of the sun,
And from the west, that there is none beside me.
I am the LORD, and there is none else.
I form the light, and create darkness:
I make peace, and create evil:
I the LORD do all these things.
Drop down, ye heavens, from above,
And let the skies pour down righteousness:
Let the earth open, and let them bring forth salvation,
And let righteousness spring up together;
I the LORD have created it.
Woe unto him that striveth with his Maker!
Let the potsherd strive with the potsherds of the earth.
Shall the clay say to him that fashioneth it, 'What makest thou?'
Or thy work, 'He hath no hands'?
I have made the earth, and created man upon it:
I, even my hands, have stretched out the heavens,
And all their host have I commanded.
I have raised him up in righteousness,
And I will direct all his ways:
He shall build my city, and he shall let go my captives,
Not for price nor reward," saith the LORD of hosts.
"But Israel shall be saved in the LORD with an everlasting salvation:

A light to the Gentiles

Ye shall not be ashamed nor confounded world without end."
For thus saith the LORD that created the heavens;
God himself that formed the earth and made it;
He hath established it, he created it not in vain,
He formed it to be inhabited:
"I am the LORD; and there is none else.
I have not spoken in secret, in a dark place of the earth:
I said not unto the seed of Jacob, 'Seek ye me in vain':
I the LORD speak righteousness,
I declare things that are right.
Assemble yourselves and come;
Draw near together, ye that are escaped of the nations:
Look unto me, and be ye saved, all the ends of the earth:
For I am God, and there is none else.
I have sworn by myself,
The word is gone out of my mouth in righteousness, and shall not re-
    turn,
That unto me every knee shall bow.
There is no God else beside me;
A just God and a Saviour."

Listen, O isles, unto me;
And hearken, ye people, from far;
The LORD hath called me from the womb;
From the bowels of my mother hath he made mention of my name.
And he hath made my mouth like a sharp sword;
In the shadow of his hand hath he hid me,
And made me a polished shaft;
In his quiver hath he hid me;
And said unto me, "Thou art my servant,
O Israel, in whom I will be glorified."
Then I said, "I have laboured in vain,
I have spent my strength for nought, and in vain:
Yet surely my judgment is with the LORD,
And my work with my God."

## THE PROPHETS

And now, saith the LORD that formed me from the womb to be his *God's love is enduring*
    servant,
To bring Jacob again to him,
Though Israel be not gathered,
Yet shall I be glorious in the eyes of the LORD,
And my God shall be my strength.
And he said, "It is a light thing that thou shouldest be my servant
To raise up the tribes of Jacob,
And to restore the preserved of Israel:
I will also give thee for a light to the Gentiles,
That thou mayest be my salvation unto the end of the earth."
Thus saith the LORD, the Redeemer of Israel, and his Holy One,
To him whom man despiseth,
To him whom the nation abhorreth,
To a servant of rulers,
"Kings shall see and arise, princes also shall worship,
Because of the LORD that is faithful,
And the Holy One of Israel,
And he shall choose thee."
Thus saith the LORD,
"In an acceptable time have I heard thee,
And in a day of salvation have I helped thee:
And I will preserve thee,
And give thee for a covenant of the people,
To establish the earth,
To cause to inherit the desolate heritages:
That thou mayest say to the prisoners,
'Go forth';
To them that are in darkness,
'Shew yourselves.'
They shall feed in the ways,
And their pastures shall be in all high places.
They shall not hunger nor thirst;
Neither shall the heat nor sun smite them:
For he that hath mercy on them shall lead them,

[ 293 ]

Even by the springs of water shall he guide them.
And I will make all my mountains a way,
And my highways shall be exalted.
Behold, these shall come from far:
And, lo, these from the north and from the west;
And these from the land of Sinim.
Sing, O heavens; and be joyful, O earth;
And break forth into singing, O mountains:
For the LORD hath comforted his people,
And will have mercy upon his afflicted.
But Zion said, 'The LORD hath forsaken me,
And my Lord hath forgotten me.'
Can a woman forget her sucking child,
That she should not have compassion on the son of her womb?
Yea, they may forget, yet will I not forget thee.
Behold, I have graven thee upon the palms of my hands."

Awake, awake; put on thy strength, O Zion;
Put on thy beautiful garments,
O Jerusalem, the holy city:
How beautiful upon the mountains
Are the feet of him that bringeth good tidings,
That publisheth peace;
That bringeth good tidings of good,
That publisheth salvation;
That saith unto Zion, "Thy God reigneth!"
Thy watchmen shall lift up the voice;
With the voice together shall they sing:
For they shall see eye to eye,
When the LORD shall bring again Zion.
Break forth into joy,
Sing together, ye waste places of Jerusalem:
For the LORD hath comforted his people,
He hath redeemed Jerusalem.
Behold, my servant shall deal prudently,
He shall be exalted and extolled,

And be very high.

"Enlarge the place of thy tent,
And let them stretch forth the curtains of thine habitations:
Spare not, lengthen thy cords,
And strengthen thy stakes;
Fear not; for thou shalt not be ashamed:
Neither be thou confounded; for thou shalt not be put to shame:
For thou shalt forget the shame of thy youth,
And shalt not remember the reproach of thy widowhood any more.
For thy Maker is thine husband;
The LORD of hosts is his name;
And thy Redeemer the Holy One of Israel;
The God of the whole earth shall he be called.
For a small moment have I forsaken thee;
But with great mercies will I gather thee.
In a little wrath I hid my face from thee for a moment;
But with everlasting kindness will I have mercy on thee,"
Saith the LORD thy Redeemer.
"For the mountains shall depart,
And the hills be removed;
But my kindness shall not depart from thee,
Neither shall the covenant of my peace be removed,"
Saith the LORD that hath mercy on thee.
"O thou afflicted,
Tossed with tempest, and not comforted,
Behold, I will lay thy stones with fair colours,
And lay thy foundations with sapphires.

"Ho, every one that thirsteth, come ye to the waters,
And he that hath no money; come ye, buy, and eat;
Yea, come, buy wine and milk
Without money and without price.
Wherefore do ye spend money for that which is not bread?
And your labour for that which satisfieth not?
Hearken diligently unto me, and eat ye that which is good,
And let your soul delight itself in fatness.

[ 295 ]

*Happiness of believers*

Incline your ear, and come unto me;
Hear, and your soul shall live;
And I will make an everlasting covenant with you,
Even the sure mercies of David.
Behold, I have given him for a witness to the people,
A leader and commander to the people.
Behold, thou shalt call a nation that thou knowest not,
And nations that knew not thee shall run unto thee
Because of the Lord thy God,
And for the Holy One of Israel; for he hath glorified thee.
Seek ye the Lord while he may be found,
Call ye upon him while he is near:
Let the wicked forsake his way,
And the unrighteous man his thoughts:
And let him return unto the Lord,
And he will have mercy upon him;
And to our God,
For he will abundantly pardon.
For my thoughts are not your thoughts,
Neither are your ways my ways," saith the Lord.
"For as the heavens
Are higher than the earth,
So are my ways higher than your ways,
And my thoughts than your thoughts.
For as the rain cometh down, and the snow from heaven,
And returneth not thither, but watereth the earth,
And maketh it bring forth and bud,
That it may give seed to the sower, and bread to the eater:
So shall my word be that goeth forth out of my mouth:
It shall not return unto me void,
But it shall accomplish that which I please,
And it shall prosper in the thing whereto I sent it.
For ye shall go out with joy,
And be led forth with peace:
The mountains and the hills shall break forth before you into singing,
And all the trees of the field shall clap their hands.

Instead of the thorn shall come up the fir tree,
And instead of the brier shall come up the myrtle tree:
And it shall be to the LORD for a name,
For an everlasting sign that shall not be cut off."

IN the third year of the reign of Jehoiakim king of Judah came Nebu-chadnezzar king of Babylon unto Jerusalem, and besieged it. And the Lord gave Jehoiakim king of Judah into his hand, with part of the vessels of the house of God: which he carried into the land of Shinar to the house of his god; and he brought the vessels into the treasure house of his god.

And the king spake unto Ashpenaz the master of his eunuchs, that he should bring certain of the children of Israel, and of the king's seed, and of the princes; children in whom was no blemish, but well favoured, and skilful in all wisdom, and cunning in knowledge, and understanding science, and such as had ability in them to stand in the king's palace, and whom they might teach the learning and the tongue of the Chaldeans.

As for these children, God gave them knowledge and skill in all learning and wisdom: and Daniel had understanding in all visions and dreams. And the king communed with them; and among them all was found none like Daniel, Hananiah, Mishael, and Azariah: therefore stood they before the king. And in all matters of wisdom and understanding, that the king enquired of them, he found them ten times better than all the magicians and astrologers that were in all his realm.

Then Daniel answered with counsel and wisdom to Arioch the cap-tain of the king's guard, which was gone forth to slay the wise men of Babylon: "Blessed be the name of God for ever and ever: for wisdom and might are his: and he changeth the times and the seasons: he removeth kings, and setteth up kings: he giveth wisdom unto the wise, and knowl-edge to them that know understanding: he revealeth the deep and secret things: he knoweth what is in the darkness, and the light dwelleth with him. I thank thee, and praise thee, O thou God of my fathers, who hast given me wisdom and might, and hast made known unto me now what we desired of thee: for thou hast now made known unto us the king's matter."

The king answered unto Daniel, and said, "Of a truth it is, that your

God is a God of gods, and a Lord of kings, and a revealer of secrets, seeing thou couldest reveal this secret."

Nebuchadnezzar the king made an image of gold, whose height was threescore cubits, and the breadth thereof six cubits: he set it up in the plain of Dura, in the province of Babylon. Then Nebuchadnezzar the king sent to gather together the princes, the governors, and the captains, the judges, the treasurers, the counsellors, the sheriffs, and all the rulers of the provinces, to come to the dedication of the image which Nebuchadnezzar the king had set up. Then the princes, the governors, and captains, the judges, the treasurers, the counsellors, the sheriffs, and all the rulers of the provinces, were gathered together unto the dedication of the image that Nebuchadnezzar the king had set up; and they stood before the image that Nebuchadnezzar had set up.

Then an herald cried aloud, "To you it is commanded, O people, nations, and languages, that at what time ye hear the sound of the cornet, flute, harp, sackbut, psaltery, dulcimer, and all kinds of musick, ye fall down and worship the golden image that Nebuchadnezzar the king hath set up: and whoso falleth not down and worshippeth shall the same hour be cast into the midst of a burning fiery furnace."

Therefore at that time, when all the people heard the sound of the cornet, flute, harp, sackbut, psaltery, and all kinds of musick, all the people, the nations, and the languages, fell down and worshipped the golden image that Nebuchadnezzar the king had set up.

Wherefore at that time certain Chaldeans came near, and accused the Jews, and said to the king Nebuchadnezzar, "There are certain Jews whom thou hast set over the affairs of the province of Babylon, Shadrach, Meshach, and Abed-nego; these men, O king, have not regarded thee: they serve not thy gods, nor worship the golden image which thou hast set up."

Then Nebuchadnezzar in his rage and fury commanded to bring Shadrach, Meshach, and Abed-nego. Then they brought these men before the king.

Nebuchadnezzar spake and said unto them, "Is it true, O Shadrach, Meshach, and Abed-nego, do not ye serve my gods, nor worship the golden image which I have set up? Now if ye be ready that at what time ye hear the sound of the cornet, flute, harp, sackbut, psaltery, and dulcimer, and all kinds of musick, ye fall down and worship the image which I have made; well: but if ye worship not, ye shall be cast the same hour into the midst of a burning fiery furnace; and who is that God that shall deliver you out of my hands?"

Shadrach, Meshach, and Abed-nego, answered and said to the king, "O Nebuchadnezzar, we are not careful to answer thee in this matter. If it be so, our God whom we serve is able to deliver us from the burning fiery furnace, and he will deliver us out of thine hand, O king. But if not, be it known unto thee, O king, that we will not serve thy gods, nor worship the golden image which thou hast set up."

Then was Nebuchadnezzar full of fury, and the form of his visage was changed against Shadrach, Meshach, and Abed-nego: therefore he spake, and commanded that they should heat the furnace one seven times more than it was wont to be heated. And he commanded the most mighty men that were in his army to bind Shadrach, Meshach, and Abed-nego, and to cast them into the burning fiery furnace. Then these men were bound in their coats, their hosen, and their hats, and their other garments, and were cast into the midst of the burning fiery furnace. Therefore because the king's commandment was urgent, and the furnace exceeding hot, the flame of the fire slew those men that took up Shadrach, Meshach, and Abed-nego. And these three men, Shadrach, Meshach, and Abed-nego, fell down bound into the midst of the burning fiery furnace.

Then Nebuchadnezzar the king was astonied, and rose up in haste, and spake, and said unto his counsellors, "Did not we cast three men bound into the midst of the fire?"

They answered and said unto the king, "True, O king."

He answered, and said, "Lo, I see four men loose, walking in the midst of the fire, and they have no hurt; and the form of the fourth is like the Son of God."

Then Nebuchadnezzar came near to the mouth of the burning fiery furnace, and spake, and said, "Shadrach, Meshach, and Abed-nego, ye servants of the most high God, come forth, and come hither."

Then Shadrach, Meshach, and Abed-nego, came forth of the midst of the fire. And the princes, governors, and captains, and the king's counsellors, being gathered together, saw these men, upon whose bodies the fire had no power, nor was an hair of their head singed, neither were their

*Belshazzar's feast* coats changed, nor the smell of fire had passed on them. Then Nebuchadnezzar spake, and said, "Blessed be the God of Shadrach, Meshach, and Abed-nego, who hath sent his angel, and delivered his servants that trusted in him, and have changed the king's word, and yielded their bodies, that they might not serve nor worship any god, except their own God."

Belshazzar the king made a great feast to a thousand of his lords, and drank wine before the thousand. Belshazzar, whiles he tasted the wine, commanded to bring the golden and silver vessels which his father Nebuchadnezzar had taken out of the temple which was in Jerusalem; that the king, and his princes, his wives, and his concubines, might drink therein. Then they brought the golden vessels that were taken out of the temple of the house of God which was at Jerusalem; and the king and his princes, his wives, and his concubines, drank in them. They drank wine, and praised the gods of gold, and of silver, of brass, of iron, of wood, and of stone.

In the same hour came forth fingers of a man's hand, and wrote over against the candlestick upon the plaister of the wall of the king's palace: and the king saw the part of the hand that wrote. Then the king's countenance was changed, and his thoughts troubled him, so that the joints of his loins were loosed, and his knees smote one against another. The king cried aloud to bring in the astrologers, the Chaldeans, and the soothsayers. And the king spake, and said to the wise men of Babylon, "Whosoever shall read this writing, and shew me the interpretation thereof, shall be clothed with scarlet, and have a chain of gold about his neck, and shall be the third ruler in the kingdom."

Then came in all the king's wise men: but they could not read the writing, nor make known to the king the interpretation thereof. Then was king Belshazzar greatly troubled, and his countenance was changed in him, and his lords were astonied.

Now the queen by reason of the words of the king and his lords came into the banquet house: and the queen spake and said, "O king, live for ever: let not thy thoughts trouble thee, nor let thy countenance be changed: there is a man in thy kingdom, in whom is the spirit of the holy gods; and in the days of thy father light and understanding and wisdom,

like the wisdom of the gods, was found in him; whom the king Nebuchad- *The handwriting on the*
nezzar thy father, the king, I say, thy father, made master of the magicians, *wall*
astrologers, Chaldeans, and soothsayers; forasmuch as an excellent spirit,
and knowledge, and understanding, interpreting of dreams, and shewing
of hard sentences, and dissolving of doubts, were found in the same
Daniel, whom the king named Belteshazzar: now let Daniel be called, and
he will shew the interpretation."

Then was Daniel brought in before the king. And the king spake and
said unto Daniel, "Art thou that Daniel, which art of the children of the
captivity of Judah, whom the king my father brought out of Jewry?
I have even heard of thee, that the spirit of the gods is in thee, and that
light and understanding and excellent wisdom is found in thee. And
now the wise men, the astrologers, have been brought in before me, that
they should read this writing, and make known unto me the interpretation thereof: but they could not shew the interpretation of the thing: and
I have heard of thee, that thou canst make interpretations, and dissolve
doubts: now if thou canst read the writing, and make known to me the
interpretation thereof, thou shalt be clothed with scarlet, and have a
chain of gold about thy neck, and shalt be the third ruler in the kingdom."

Then Daniel answered and said before the king, "Let thy gifts be to
thyself, and give thy rewards to another; yet I will read the writing unto
the king, and make known to him the interpretation. O thou king, the
most high God gave Nebuchadnezzar thy father a kingdom, and majesty,
and glory, and honour: and for the majesty that he gave him, all people,
nations, and languages, trembled and feared before him: whom he would
he slew; and whom he would he kept alive; and whom he would he set
up, and whom he would he put down. But when his heart was lifted up,
and his mind hardened in pride, he was deposed from his kingly throne,
and they took his glory from him: and he was driven from the sons of
men; and his heart was made like the beasts, and his dwelling was with
the wild asses: they fed him with grass like oxen, and his body was wet
with the dew of heaven; till he knew that the most high God ruled in the
kingdom of men, and that he appointeth over it whomsoever he will.

"And thou his son, O Belshazzar, hast not humbled thine heart, though
thou knewest all this; but hast lifted up thyself against the Lord of
heaven; and they have brought the vessels of his house before thee, and

[ 301 ]

*Belshazzar slain* thou, and thy lords, thy wives, and thy concubines, have drunk wine in them; and thou hast praised the gods of silver, and gold, of brass, iron, wood, and stone, which see not, nor hear, nor know: and the God in whose hand thy breath is, and whose are all thy ways, hast thou not glorified: then was the part of the hand sent from him; and this writing was written. And this is the writing that was written, MENE, MENE, TEKEL, UPHARSIN. This is the interpretation of the thing: MENE; God hath numbered thy kingdom, and finished it. TEKEL; Thou art weighed in the balances, and art found wanting. PERES; Thy kingdom is divided, and given to the Medes and Persians."

Then commanded Belshazzar, and they clothed Daniel with scarlet, and put a chain of gold about his neck, and made a proclamation concerning him, that he should be the third ruler in the kingdom.

In that night was Belshazzar the king of the Chaldeans slain. And Darius the Median took the kingdom, being about threescore and two years old.

It pleased Darius to set over the kingdom an hundred and twenty princes, which should be over the whole kingdom; and over these three presidents; of whom Daniel was first: that the princes might give accounts unto them, and the king should have no damage. Then this Daniel was preferred above the presidents and princes, because an excellent spirit was in him; and the king thought to set him over the whole realm.

Then the presidents and princes sought to find occasion against Daniel concerning the kingdom; but they could find none occasion nor fault; forasmuch as he was faithful, neither was there any error or fault found in him. Then said these men, "We shall not find any occasion against this Daniel, except we find it against him concerning the law of his God."

Then these presidents and princes assembled together to the king, and said thus unto him, "King Darius, live for ever. All the presidents of the kingdom, the governors, and the princes, the counsellors, and the captains, have consulted together to establish a royal statute, and to make a firm decree, that whosoever shall ask a petition of any God or man for thirty days, save of thee, O king, he shall be cast into the den of lions. Now, O king, establish the decree, and sign the writing, that it be not

# ANCIENT PALESTINE

# KEY TO MAP

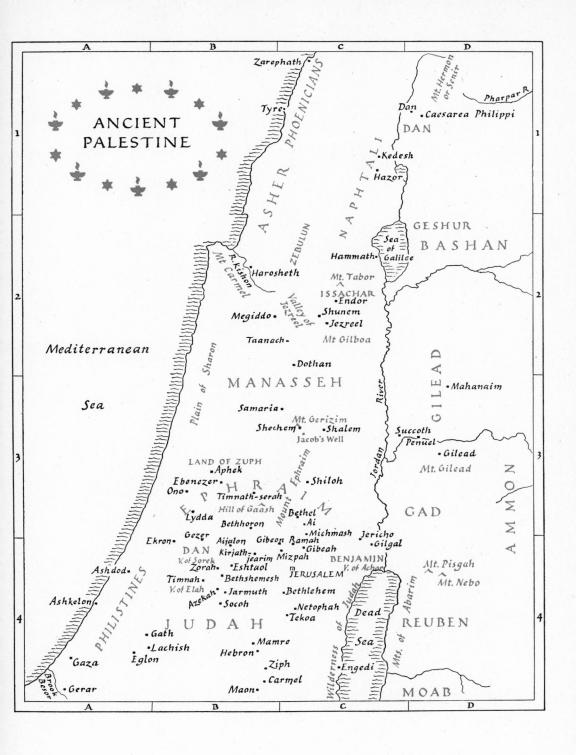

# ANCIENT PALESTINE

Zarephath

Tyre

PHOENICIANS

ASHER

ZEBULUN

NAPHTALI

Dan

Caesarea Philippi

Mt. Hermon or Senir

Pharpar R.

DAN

Kedesh

Hazor

GESHUR

BASHAN

Sea of Galilee

Hammath

R. Kishon

Mt. Carmel

Harosheth

Mt. Tabor

ISSACHAR

Endor

Shunem

Jezreel

Mt Gilboa

Valley of Jezreel

Megiddo

Taanach

Mediterranean

Sea

Plain of Sharon

Dothan

MANASSEH

Samaria

Shechem

Mt. Gerizim

Shalem

Jacob's Well

Mahanaim

GILEAD

River

Succoth

Penuel

Gilead

Mt. Gilead

AMMON

GAD

LAND OF ZUPH

Aphek

Ebenezer

Ono

Timnath-serah

Hill of Gaash

Lydda

Bethhoron

Ekron

Gezer

DAN

V. of Sorek

Zorah

Timnah

V. of Elah

Azekah

Ashdod

Ashkelon

PHILISTINES

Mount Ephraim

Shiloh

Bethel

Ai

Michmash

Gibeah

Gibeon

Ramah

Mizpah

Kirjath-jearim

Eshtaol

Bethshemesh

Jarmuth

Socoh

JERUSALEM

BENJAMIN

V. of Achor

Bethlehem

Netophah

Tekoa

JUDAH

Gath

Lachish

Eglon

Mamre

Hebron

Ziph

Carmel

Maon

Gaza

Gerar

Brook Besor

Wilderness of Judah

Dead Sea

Engedi

Mts. of Abarim

Mt. Pisgah

Mt. Nebo

REUBEN

MOAB

EPHRAIM

changed, according to the law of the Medes and Persians, which altereth not."

Wherefore king Darius signed the writing and the decree.

Now when Daniel knew that the writing was signed, he went into his house; and his windows being open in his chamber toward Jerusalem, he kneeled upon his knees three times a day, and prayed, and gave thanks before his God, as he did aforetime. Then these men assembled, and found Daniel praying and making supplication before his God.

Then they came near, and spake before the king concerning the king's decree; "Hast thou not signed a decree, that every man that shall ask a petition of any God or man within thirty days, save of thee, O king, shall be cast into the den of lions?"

The king answered and said, "The thing is true, according to the law of the Medes and Persians, which altereth not."

Then answered they and said before the king, "That Daniel, which is of the children of the captivity of Judah, regardeth not thee, O king, nor the decree that thou hast signed, but maketh his petition three times a day."

Then the king, when he heard these words, was sore displeased with himself, and set his heart on Daniel to deliver him: and he laboured till the going down of the sun to deliver him. Then these men assembled unto the king, and said unto the king, "Know, O king, that the law of the Medes and Persians is, That no decree nor statute which the king establisheth may be changed."

Then the king commanded, and they brought Daniel, and cast him into the den of lions.

Now the king spake and said unto Daniel, "Thy God whom thou servest continually, he will deliver thee." And a stone was brought, and laid upon the mouth of the den; and the king sealed it with his own signet, and with the signet of his lords; that the purpose might not be changed concerning Daniel.

Then the king went to his palace, and passed the night fasting: neither were instruments of musick brought before him: and his sleep went from him. Then the king arose very early in the morning, and went in haste unto the den of lions. And when he came to the den, he cried with a lamentable voice unto Daniel: and the king spake and said to

*Haggai reproves the people*

Daniel, "O Daniel, servant of the living God, is thy God, whom thou servest continually, able to deliver thee from the lions?"

Then said Daniel unto the king, "O king, live for ever. My God hath sent his angel, and hath shut the lions' mouths, that they have not hurt me: forasmuch as before him innocency was found in me; and also before thee, O king, have I done no hurt."

Then was the king exceeding glad for him, and commanded that they should take Daniel up out of the den. So Daniel was taken up out of the den, and no manner of hurt was found upon him, because he believed in his God.

Then king Darius wrote unto all people, nations, and languages, that dwell in all the earth; "Peace be multiplied unto you. I make a decree, That in every dominion of my kingdom men tremble and fear before the God of Daniel: for he is the living God, and stedfast for ever, and his kingdom that which shall not be destroyed, and his dominion shall be even unto the end. He delivereth and rescueth, and he worketh signs and wonders in heaven and in earth, who hath delivered Daniel from the power of the lions."

In the second year of Darius the king, in the sixth month, in the first day of the month, came the word of the LORD by Haggai the prophet unto Zerubbabel, governor of Judah, and to Joshua, the high priest, saying, "Thus speaketh the LORD of hosts, saying, This people say, 'The time is not come, the time that the LORD's house should be built.'"

Then came the word of the LORD by Haggai the prophet, saying, "Is it time for you, O ye, to dwell in your cieled houses, and this house lie waste? Now therefore, thus saith the LORD of hosts; Consider your ways. Ye have sown much, and bring in little; ye eat, but ye have not enough; ye drink, but ye are not filled with drink; ye clothe you, but there is none warm; and he that earneth wages earneth wages to put it into a bag with holes.

"Thus saith the LORD of hosts; Consider your ways. Go up to the mountain, and bring wood, and build the house; and I will take pleasure in it, and I will be glorified, saith the LORD. Ye looked for much, and, lo, it came to little; and when ye brought it home, I did blow upon it. Why? saith the LORD of hosts. Because of mine house that is waste, and ye run every man unto his own house. Therefore the heaven over you is stayed from dew, and the earth is stayed from her fruit. And I called for a drought upon the land, and upon the mountains, and upon the corn, and upon the new wine, and upon the oil, and upon that which the ground bringeth forth, and upon men, and upon cattle, and upon all the labour of the hands."

Then Zerubbabel, and Joshua, the high priest, with all the remnant of the people, obeyed the voice of the LORD their God, and the words of Haggai the prophet, as the LORD their God had sent him, and the people did fear before the LORD. Then spake Haggai the LORD's messenger in the LORD's message unto the people, saying, "I am with you, saith the LORD."

And the LORD stirred up the spirit of Zerubbabel, governor of Judah, and the spirit of Joshua, the high priest, and the spirit of all the remnant of the people; and they came and did work in the house of the LORD of hosts, their God, in the four and twentieth day of the sixth month, in the second year of Darius the king.

In the seventh month, in the one and twentieth day of the month, came the word of the LORD by the prophet Haggai, saying, "Speak now to Zerubbabel, governor of Judah, and to Joshua, the high priest, and to the residue of the people, saying, 'Who is left among you that saw this house in her first glory? and how do ye see it now? is it not in your eyes in comparison of it as nothing? Yet now be strong, O Zerubbabel, saith the LORD; and be strong, O Joshua; and be strong, all ye people of the land, saith the LORD, and work: for I am with you, saith the LORD of hosts: according to the word that I covenanted with you when ye came out of Egypt, so my spirit remaineth among you: fear ye not. For thus saith the LORD of hosts; Yet once, it is a little while, and I will shake the heavens, and the earth, and the sea, and the dry land; and I will shake all nations, and the desire of all nations shall come: and I will fill this house with glory, saith the LORD of hosts. The silver is mine, and the gold is mine, saith the LORD of hosts. The glory of this latter house shall be greater than of the former, saith the LORD of hosts: and in this place will I give peace, saith the LORD of hosts.

" 'Consider now from this day and upward, from the four and twentieth day of the ninth month, even from the day that the foundation of the

LORD's temple was laid, consider it. Is the seed yet in the barn? yea, as yet the vine, and the fig tree, and the pomegranate, and the olive tree, hath not brought forth: from this day will I bless you. In that day, saith the LORD of hosts, will I take thee, O Zerubbabel, my servant, the son of Shealtiel, saith the LORD, and will make thee as a signet: for I have chosen thee, saith the LORD of hosts.' "

IN the eighth month, in the second year of Darius, came the word of the LORD unto Zechariah, the son of Berechiah, the son of Iddo the prophet, saying, "The LORD hath been sore displeased with your fathers. Therefore say thou unto them, 'Thus saith the LORD of hosts; Turn ye unto me, saith the LORD of hosts, and I will turn unto you, saith the LORD of hosts.' "

I lifted up mine eyes again, and looked, and behold a man with a measuring line in his hand.

Then said I, "Whither goest thou?"

And he said unto me, "To measure Jerusalem, to see what is the breadth thereof, and what is the length thereof."

And, behold, the angel that talked with me went forth, and another angel went out to meet him, and said unto him, "Run, speak to this young man, saying, 'Jerusalem shall be inhabited as towns without walls for the multitude of men and cattle therein: for I, saith the LORD, will be unto her a wall of fire round about, and will be the glory in the midst of her. Ho, ho, come forth, and flee from the land of the north, saith the LORD: for I have spread you abroad as the four winds of the heaven, saith the LORD. Deliver thyself, O Zion, that dwellest with the daughter of Babylon. Sing and rejoice, O daughter of Zion: for, lo, I come, and I will dwell in the midst of thee, saith the LORD. And many nations shall be joined to the LORD in that day, and shall be my people: and I will dwell in the midst of thee, and thou shalt know that the LORD of hosts hath sent me unto thee.

" 'Thus saith the LORD of hosts; If thou wilt walk in my ways, and if thou wilt keep my charge, then thou shalt also judge my house, and shalt also keep my courts, and I will give thee places to walk among these that stand by. Hear now, O Joshua the high priest, thou, and thy fellows that sit before thee: for they are men wondered at: for, behold, I will bring

forth my servant the BRANCH. In that day, saith the LORD of hosts, *Christ the Branch*
shall ye call every man his neighbour under the vine and under the fig *typified*
tree.

" 'This is the word of the LORD unto Zerubbabel, saying, Not by might, nor by power, but by my spirit, saith the LORD of hosts. Who art thou, O great mountain? before Zerubbabel thou shalt become a plain: and he shall bring forth the headstone thereof with shoutings, crying, "Grace, grace" unto it. Moreover the word of the LORD came unto me, saying, "The hands of Zerubbabel have laid the foundation of this house; his hands shall also finish it"; and thou shalt know that the LORD of hosts hath sent me unto you. For who hath despised the day of small things? for they shall rejoice, and shall see the plummet in the hand of Zerubbabel with those seven; they are the eyes of the LORD, which run to and fro through the whole earth.' "

And the word of the LORD came unto me, saying, "Take of them of the captivity, which are come from Babylon, and come thou the same day, and go into the house of Josiah the son of Zephaniah; then take silver and gold, and make crowns, and set them upon the head of Joshua the son of Josedech, the high priest; and speak unto him, saying, 'Thus speaketh the LORD of hosts, saying, Behold the man whose name is The BRANCH; and he shall grow up out of his place, and he shall build the temple of the LORD: even he shall build the temple of the LORD; and he shall bear the glory, and shall sit and rule upon his throne; and he shall be a priest upon his throne: and the counsel of peace shall be between them both. And they that are far off shall come and build in the temple of the LORD, and ye shall know that the LORD of hosts hath sent me unto you. And this shall come to pass, if ye will diligently obey the voice of the LORD your God.' "

Then came the word of the LORD of hosts unto Zechariah, saying, "Thus speaketh the LORD of hosts, saying, Execute true judgment, and shew mercy and compassions every man to his brother: and oppress not the widow, nor the fatherless, the stranger, nor the poor; and let none of you imagine evil against his brother in your heart.

"Thus saith the LORD; I am returned unto Zion, and will dwell in the midst of Jerusalem: and Jerusalem shall be called a city of truth; and the mountain of the LORD of hosts the holy mountain. Thus saith the LORD of hosts; There shall yet old men and old women dwell in the streets of Jerusalem, and every man with his staff in his hand for very age. And the streets of the city shall be full of boys and girls playing in the streets thereof.

"These are the things that ye shall do; Speak ye every man the truth to his neighbour; execute the judgment of truth and peace in your gates: and let none of you imagine evil in your hearts against his neighbour; and love no false oath: for all these are things that I hate, saith the LORD.

"Thus saith the LORD of hosts; It shall yet come to pass, that there shall come people and the inhabitants of many cities: and the inhabitants of one city shall go to another, saying, 'Let us go speedily to pray before the LORD, and to seek the LORD of hosts: I will go also. Yea, many people and strong nations shall come to seek the LORD of hosts in Jerusalem, and to pray before the LORD.' Thus saith the LORD of hosts; In those days it shall come to pass, that ten men shall take hold out of all languages of the nations, even shall take hold of the skirt of him that is a Jew, saying, 'We will go with you: for we have heard that God is with you.'"

THE burden of the word of the LORD to Israel by Malachi. "A son honoureth his father, and a servant his master: if then I be a father, where is mine honour? and if I be a master, where is my fear?" saith the LORD of hosts unto you, "O priests, that despise my name. And ye say, 'Wherein have we despised thy name?' Ye offer polluted bread upon mine altar; and ye say, 'Wherein have we polluted thee?' In that ye say, 'The table of the LORD is contemptible.' And if ye offer the blind for sacrifice, is it not evil? and if ye offer the lame and sick, is it not evil? offer it now unto thy governor; will he be pleased with thee, or accept thy person?" saith the LORD of hosts.

"Who is there even among you that would shut the doors for nought? neither do ye kindle fire on mine altar for nought. I have no pleasure in you," saith the LORD of hosts, "neither will I accept an offering at your hand. For, from the rising of the sun even unto the going down of the same, my name shall be great among the Gentiles; and in every place incense shall be offered unto my name, and a pure offering: for my name shall be great among the heathen," saith the LORD of hosts.

"And now, O ye priests, this commandment is for you. And ye shall *The priests and people* know that I have sent this commandment unto you, that my covenant *reproved* might be with Levi," saith the LORD of hosts. "My covenant was with him of life and peace. The law of truth was in his mouth, and iniquity was not found in his lips: he walked with me in peace and equity, and did turn many away from iniquity."

Have we not all one father? hath not one God created us? why do we deal treacherously every man against his brother, by profaning the covenant of our fathers? And this have ye done again, covering the altar of the LORD with tears, with weeping, and with crying out, insomuch that he regardeth not the offering any more, or receiveth it with good will at your hand. Yet ye say, "Wherefore?" Because the LORD hath been witness between thee and the wife of thy youth, against whom thou hast dealt treacherously: yet is she thy companion, and the wife of thy covenant. And did not he make one? Yet had he the residue of the spirit. And wherefore one? That he might seek a godly seed. Therefore take heed to your spirit, and let none deal treacherously against the wife of his youth. For the LORD, the God of Israel, saith that he hateth putting away: "for one covereth violence with his garment," saith the LORD of hosts: therefore take heed to your spirit, that ye deal not treacherously.

Ye have wearied the LORD with your words. Yet ye say, "Wherein have we wearied him?" When ye say, "Every one that doeth evil is good in the sight of the LORD, and he delighteth in them"; or, "Where is the God of judgment?" Ye have said, "It is vain to serve God: and what profit is it that we have kept his ordinance, and that we have walked mournfully before the Lord of hosts?"

"Behold, I will send my messenger, and he shall prepare the way before me: and the Lord, whom ye seek, shall suddenly come to his temple, even the messenger of the covenant, whom ye delight in: behold, he shall come," saith the LORD of hosts. But who may abide the day of his coming? and who shall stand when he appeareth? for he is like a refiner's fire and like fullers' soap: and he shall sit as a refiner and a purifier of silver: and he shall purify the sons of Levi, and purge them as gold and silver, that they may offer unto the LORD an offering in righteousness. Then shall the offering of Judah and Jerusalem be pleasant unto the LORD, as in the days of old, and as in former years.

"And I will come near to you to judgment; and I will be a swift witness against the sorcerers, and against the adulterers, and against false swearers, and against those that oppress the hireling in his wages, the widow, and the fatherless, and that turn aside the stranger from his right, and fear not me," saith the LORD of hosts. "Unto you that fear my name shall the Sun of righteousness arise with healing in his wings. And all nations shall call you blessed: for ye shall be a delightsome land," saith the LORD of hosts.

Now in the first year of Cyrus king of Persia, that the word of the LORD by the mouth of Jeremiah might be fulfilled, the LORD stirred up the spirit of Cyrus king of Persia, that he made a proclamation throughout all his kingdom, and put it also in writing, saying, "Thus saith Cyrus king of Persia, 'The LORD God of heaven hath given me all the kingdoms of the earth; and he hath charged me to build him an house at Jerusalem, which is in Judah. Who is there among you of all his people? his God be with him, and let him go up to Jerusalem, which is in Judah, and build the house of the LORD God of Israel, (he is the God,) which is in Jerusalem. And whosoever remaineth in any place where he sojourneth, let the men of his place help him with silver, and with gold, and with goods, and with beasts, beside the freewill offering for the house of God that is in Jerusalem.' "

Then rose up the chief of the fathers of Judah and Benjamin, and the priests, and the Levites, with all them whose spirit God had raised, to go up to build the house of the LORD which is in Jerusalem. And all they that were about them strengthened their hands with vessels of silver, with gold, with goods, and with beasts, and with precious things, beside all that was willingly offered.

Also Cyrus the king brought forth the vessels of the house of the LORD, which Nebuchadnezzar had brought forth out of Jerusalem, and had put them in the house of his gods; even those did Cyrus king of Persia bring forth by the hand of Mithredath the treasurer, and numbered them unto Sheshbazzar, the prince of Judah. And this is the number of them: thirty chargers of gold, a thousand chargers of silver, nine and twenty knives, thirty basons of gold, silver basons of a second sort four hundred and ten, and other vessels a thousand. All the vessels of

gold and of silver were five thousand and four hundred. All these did
Sheshbazzar bring up with them of the captivity that were brought up
from Babylon unto Jerusalem. The whole congregation together was
forty and two thousand three hundred and threescore. And when the
builders laid the foundation of the temple of the LORD, they set the priests
in their apparel with trumpets, and the Levites the sons of Asaph with
cymbals, to praise the LORD, after the ordinance of David king of Israel.
And they sang together by course in praising and giving thanks unto the
LORD; because he is good, for his mercy endureth for ever toward
Israel. And all the people shouted with a great shout, when they praised
the LORD, because the foundation of the house of the LORD was laid.

But many of the priests and Levites and chief of the fathers, who
were ancient men, that had seen the first house, when the foundation of
this house was laid before their eyes, wept with a loud voice; and many
shouted aloud for joy: so that the people could not discern the noise of
the shout of joy from the noise of the weeping of the people: for the
people shouted with a loud shout, and the noise was heard afar off.

Now when the adversaries of Judah and Benjamin heard that the
children of the captivity builded the temple unto the LORD God of Israel;
then they came to Zerubbabel, and to the chief of the fathers, and said
unto them, "Let us build with you: for we seek your God, as ye do; and
we do sacrifice unto him since the days of Esar-haddon king of Assur,
which brought us up hither."

But Zerubbabel, and Jeshua, and the rest of the chief of the fathers of
Israel, said unto them, "Ye have nothing to do with us to build an house
unto our God; but we ourselves together will build unto the LORD God of
Israel, as king Cyrus the king of Persia hath commanded us." Then the
people of the land weakened the hands of the people of Judah, and
troubled them in building, and hired counsellors against them, to frus-
trate their purpose, all the days of Cyrus king of Persia, even until the
reign of Darius king of Persia. And in the reign of Ahasuerus, in the
beginning of his reign, wrote they unto him an accusation against the inhabitants of Judah and Jerusalem.

And in the days of Artaxerxes wrote Bishlam, Mithredath, Tabeel,
and the rest of their companions, unto Artaxerxes king of Persia; and the

writing of the letter was written in the Syrian tongue, and interpreted in the Syrian tongue. Rehum the chancellor and Shimshai the scribe wrote a letter against Jerusalem to Artaxerxes the king in this sort: then wrote Rehum the chancellor, and Shimshai the scribe, and the rest of their companions, and the rest of the nations whom the great and noble Asnapper brought over, and set in the cities of Samaria, and the rest that are on this side the river, and at such a time.

This is the copy of the letter that they sent unto him, even unto Artaxerxes the king;

THY SERVANTS THE MEN ON THIS SIDE THE RIVER, AND AT SUCH A TIME.

BE it known unto the king, that the Jews which came up from thee to us are come unto Jerusalem, building the rebellious and the bad city, and have set up the walls thereof, and joined the foundations. Be it known now unto the king, that, if this city be builded, and the walls set up again, then will they not pay toll, tribute, and custom, and so thou shalt endamage the revenue of the kings. Now because we have maintenance from the king's palace, and it was not meet for us to see the king's dishonour, therefore have we sent and certified the king; that search may be made in the book of the records of thy fathers: so shalt thou find in the book of the records, and know that this city is a rebellious city, and hurtful unto kings and provinces, and that they have moved sedition within the same of old time: for which cause was this city destroyed. We certify the king that, if this city be builded again, and the walls thereof set up, by this means thou shalt have no portion on this side the river.

*Artaxerxes' decree* Then sent the king an answer unto Rehum the chancellor, and to Shimshai the scribe, and to the rest of their companions that dwell in Samaria, and unto the rest beyond the river,

PEACE, AND AT SUCH A TIME.

THE letter which ye sent unto us hath been plainly read before me. And I commanded, and search hath been made, and it is found that this city of old time hath made insurrection against kings, and that rebellion and sedition have been made therein. There have been mighty kings also over Jerusalem, which have ruled over all countries beyond the river; and toll, tribute, and custom, was paid unto them. Give ye now commandment to cause these men to cease, and that this city be not builded, until another commandment shall be given from me. Take heed now that ye fail not to do this: why should damage grow to the hurt of the kings?

Now when the copy of king Artaxerxes' letter was read before Rehum, and Shimshai the scribe, and their companions, they went up in haste to Jerusalem unto the Jews, and made them to cease by force and power. Then the prophets, Haggai the prophet, and Zechariah the son of Iddo, prophesied unto the Jews that were in Judah and Jerusalem in the name of the God of Israel, even unto them. Then rose up Zerubbabel the son of Shealtiel, and Jeshua the son of Jozadak, and began to build the house of God which is at Jerusalem: and with them were the prophets of God helping them.

*Hanani informs Nehemiah*

THE words of Nehemiah the son of Hachaliah.

And it came to pass in the month Chisleu, in the twentieth year, as I was in Shushan the palace, that Hanani, one of my brethren, came, he and certain men of Judah; and I asked them concerning the Jews that had escaped, which were left of the captivity, and concerning Jerusalem. And they said unto me, "The remnant that are left of the captivity there in the province are in great affliction and reproach: the wall of Jerusalem also is broken down, and the gates thereof are burned with fire."

And it came to pass, when I heard these words, that I sat down and wept, and mourned certain days, and fasted, and prayed before the God of heaven, and said, "I beseech thee, O LORD God of heaven, the great and terrible God, that keepeth covenant and mercy for them that love him and observe his commandments: Let thine ear now be attentive, and thine eyes open, that thou mayest hear the prayer of thy servant, which I pray before thee now, day and night, for the children of Israel thy servants, and confess the sins of the children of Israel, which we have sinned against thee: both I and my father's house have sinned. We have dealt very corruptly against thee, and have not kept the commandments, nor the statutes, nor the judgments, which thou commandedst thy servant Moses. Remember, I beseech thee, the word that thou commandedst thy servant Moses, saying, 'If ye transgress, I will scatter you abroad among the nations: but if ye turn unto me, and keep my commandments, and do them; though there were of you cast out unto the uttermost part of the heaven, yet will I gather them from thence, and will bring them unto the place that I have chosen to set my name there.' Now these are thy servants and thy people, whom thou hast redeemed by thy great power, and by thy strong hand.

[ 313 ]

*Nehemiah returns to*
*Jerusalem*

"O Lord, I beseech thee, let now thine ear be attentive to the prayer of thy servant, and to the prayer of thy servants, who desire to fear thy name: and prosper, I pray thee, thy servant this day, and grant him mercy in the sight of this man."

I was the king's cupbearer. And it came to pass in the month Nisan, in the twentieth year of Artaxerxes the king, that wine was before him: and I took up the wine, and gave it unto the king. Now I had not been beforetime sad in his presence. Wherefore the king said unto me, "Why is thy countenance sad, seeing thou art not sick? this is nothing else but sorrow of heart."

Then I was very sore afraid, and said unto the king, "Let the king live for ever: why should not my countenance be sad, when the city, the place of my fathers' sepulchres, lieth waste, and the gates thereof are consumed with fire?"

Then the king said unto me, "For what dost thou make request?"

So I prayed to the God of heaven. And I said unto the king, "If it please the king, and if thy servant have found favour in thy sight, that thou wouldest send me unto Judah, unto the city of my fathers' sepulchres, that I may build it."

And the king said unto me, (the queen also sitting by him,) "For how long shall thy journey be? and when wilt thou return?"

So it pleased the king to send me; and I set him a time. Moreover I said unto the king, "If it please the king, let letters be given me to the governors beyond the river, that they may convey me over till I come into Judah; and a letter unto Asaph the keeper of the king's forest, that he may give me timber to make beams for the gates of the palace which appertained to the house, and for the wall of the city, and for the house that I shall enter into." And the king granted me, according to the good hand of my God upon me. Then I came to the governors beyond the river, and gave them the king's letters. Now the king had sent captains of the army and horsemen with me. When Sanballat the Horonite, and Tobiah the servant, the Ammonite, heard of it, it grieved them exceedingly that there was come a man to seek the welfare of the children of Israel.

So I came to Jerusalem, and was there three days. And I arose in the night, I and some few men with me; neither told I any man what my

God had put in my heart to do at Jerusalem: neither was there any beast with me, save the beast that I rode upon. And I went out by night by the gate of the valley, even before the dragon well, and to the dung port, and viewed the walls of Jerusalem, which were broken down, and the gates thereof were consumed with fire. Then I went on to the gate of the fountain, and to the king's pool: but there was no place for the beast that was under me to pass. Then went I up in the night by the brook, and viewed the wall, and turned back, and entered by the gate of the valley, and so returned. And the rulers knew not whither I went, or what I did; neither had I as yet told it to the Jews, nor to the priests, nor to the nobles, nor to the rulers, nor to the rest that did the work. Then said I unto them, "Ye see the distress that we are in, how Jerusalem lieth waste, and the gates thereof are burned with fire: come, and let us build up the wall of Jerusalem, that we be no more a reproach."

*The wall of Jerusalem rebuilt*

Then I told them of the hand of my God which was good upon me; as also the king's words that he had spoken unto me. And they said, "Let us rise up and build."

So they strengthened their hands for this good work. But when Sanballat the Horonite, and Tobiah the servant, the Ammonite, and Geshem the Arabian, heard it, they laughed us to scorn, and despised us, and said, "What is this thing that ye do? will ye rebel against the king?"

Then answered I them, and said unto them, "The God of heaven, he will prosper us; therefore we his servants will arise and build: but ye have no portion, nor right, nor memorial, in Jerusalem."

But it came to pass, that when Sanballat heard that we builded the wall, he was wroth, and took great indignation, and mocked the Jews. And he spake before his brethren and the army of Samaria, and said, "What do these feeble Jews? will they fortify themselves? will they sacrifice? will they make an end in a day? will they revive the stones out of the heaps of the rubbish which are burned?"

Now Tobiah the Ammonite was by him, and he said, "Even that which they build, if a fox go up, he shall even break down their stone wall." Hear, O our God; for we are despised: and turn their reproach upon their own head, and give them for a prey in the land of captivity.

So built we the wall; and all the wall was joined together unto the half thereof: for the people had a mind to work. But it came to pass, that

*Nehemiah arms the labourers*

when Sanballat, and Tobiah, and the Arabians, and the Ammonites, and the Ashdodites, heard that the walls of Jerusalem were made up, and that the breaches began to be stopped, then they were very wroth, and conspired all of them together to come and to fight against Jerusalem, and to hinder it. Nevertheless we made our prayer unto our God, and set a watch against them day and night, because of them.

And Judah said, "The strength of the bearers of burdens is decayed, and there is much rubbish; so that we are not able to build the wall."

And our adversaries said, "They shall not know, neither see, till we come in the midst among them, and slay them, and cause the work to cease."

And it came to pass, that when the Jews which dwelt by them came, they said unto us ten times, "From all places whence ye shall return unto us they will be upon you."

Therefore set I in the lower places behind the wall, and on the higher places, I even set the people after their families with their swords, their spears, and their bows. And I looked, and rose up, and said unto the nobles, and to the rulers, and to the rest of the people, "Be not ye afraid of them: remember the Lord, which is great and terrible, and fight for your brethren, your sons, and your daughters, your wives, and your houses."

And it came to pass, when our enemies heard that it was known unto us, and God had brought their counsel to nought, that we returned all of us to the wall, every one unto his work. And it came to pass from that time forth, that the half of my servants wrought in the work, and the other half of them held both the spears, the shields, and the bows, and the habergeons; and the rulers were behind all the house of Judah. They which builded on the wall, and they that bare burdens, with those that laded, every one with one of his hands wrought in the work, and with the other hand held a weapon. For the builders, every one had his sword girded by his side, and so builded. And he that sounded the trumpet was by me. And I said unto the nobles, and to the rulers, and to the rest of the people, "The work is great and large, and we are separated upon the wall, one far from another. In what place therefore ye hear the sound of the trumpet, resort ye thither unto us: our God shall fight for us."

So we laboured in the work: and half of them held the spears from the rising of the morning till the stars appeared. Likewise at the same time said I unto the people, "Let every one with his servant lodge within Jerusalem, that in the night they may be a guard to us, and labour on the day."

So neither I, nor my brethren, nor my servants, nor the men of the guard which followed me, none of us put off our clothes, saving that every one put them off for washing.

And there was a great cry of the people and of their wives against their brethren the Jews.

For there were that said, "We, our sons, and our daughters, are many: therefore we take up corn for them, that we may eat, and live."

Some also there were that said, "We have mortgaged our lands, vine-yards, and houses, that we might buy corn, because of the dearth."

There were also that said, "We have borrowed money for the king's tribute, and that upon our lands and vineyards. Yet now our flesh is as the flesh of our brethren, our children as their children: and, lo, we bring into bondage our sons and our daughters to be servants, and some of our daughters are brought into bondage already: neither is it in our power to redeem them; for other men have our lands and vineyards."

And I was very angry when I heard their cry and these words. Then I consulted with myself, and I rebuked the nobles, and the rulers, and said unto them, "Ye exact usury, every one of his brother."

And I set a great assembly against them. And I said unto them, "We after our ability have redeemed our brethren the Jews, which were sold unto the heathen; and will ye even sell your brethren? or shall they be sold unto us?" Then held they their peace, and found nothing to answer. Also I said, "It is not good that ye do: ought ye not to walk in the fear of our God because of the reproach of the heathen our enemies? Restore, I pray you, to them, even this day, their lands, their vineyards, their olive-yards, and their houses, also the hundredth part of the money, and of the corn, the wine, and the oil, that ye exact of them."

Then said they, "We will restore them, and will require nothing of them; so will we do as thou sayest."

Then I called the priests, and took an oath of them, that they should do according to this promise. Also I shook my lap, and said, "So God shake out every man from his house, and from his labour, that performeth not this promise, even thus be he shaken out, and emptied."

And all the congregation said, "Amen," and praised the Lord. And the people did according to this promise.

Moreover from the time that I was appointed to be their governor in the land of Judah, from the twentieth year even unto the two and thirtieth year of Artaxerxes the king, that is, twelve years, I and my brethren have not eaten the bread of the governor. But the former governors that had been before me were chargeable unto the people, and had taken of them bread and wine, besides forty shekels of silver; yea, even their servants bare rule over the people: but so did not I, because of the fear of God. Yea, also I continued in the work of this wall, neither bought we any land: and all my servants were gathered thither unto the work. Moreover there were at my table an hundred and fifty of the Jews and rulers, besides those that came unto us from among the heathen that are about us. Now that which was prepared for me daily was one ox and six choice sheep; also fowls were prepared for me, and once in ten days store of all sorts of wine: yet for all this required not I the bread of the governor, because the bondage was heavy upon this people. Think upon me, my God, for good, according to all that I have done for this people.

Now it came to pass when Sanballat, and Tobiah, and Geshem the Arabian, and the rest of our enemies, heard that I had builded the wall, and that there was no breach left therein; (though at that time I had not set up the doors upon the gates;) that Sanballat and Geshem sent unto me, saying, "Come, let us meet together in some one of the villages of the plain of Ono."

But they thought to do me mischief. And I sent messengers unto them, saying, "I am doing a great work, so that I cannot come down: why should the work cease, whilst I leave it, and come down to you?"

Yet they sent unto me four times after this sort; and I answered them after the same manner. Then sent Sanballat his servant unto me in like manner the fifth time with an open letter in his hand; wherein was written,

IT is reported among the heathen, and Gashmu saith it, that thou and the Jews think to rebel: for which cause thou buildest the wall, that thou mayest be their king, according to these words. And thou hast also appointed prophets to preach of thee at Jerusalem, saying, "There is a king in Judah": and now shall it be reported to the king according to these words. Come now therefore, and let us take counsel together.

Then I sent unto him, saying, "There are no such things done as thou sayest, but thou feignest them out of thine own heart." For they all made us afraid, saying, "Their hands shall be weakened from the work," that it be not done. Now therefore, O God, strengthen my hands. Afterward I came unto the house of Shemaiah, who was shut up; and he said, "Let us meet together in the house of God, within the temple, and let us shut the doors of the temple: for they will come to slay thee; yea, in the night will they come to slay thee."

· And I said, "Should such a man as I flee? and who is there, that, being as I am, would go into the temple to save his life? I will not go in."

And, lo, I perceived that God had not sent him; but that he pronounced this prophecy against me: for Tobiah and Sanballat had hired him. Therefore was he hired, that I should be afraid, and do so, and sin, and that they might have matter for an evil report, that they might reproach me. My God, think thou upon Tobiah and Sanballat according to these their works, and on the prophetess Noadiah, and the rest of the prophets, that would have put me in fear.

So the wall was finished in the twenty and fifth day of the month Elul, in fifty and two days. And it came to pass, that when all our enemies heard thereof, and all the heathen that were about us saw these things, they were much cast down in their own eyes: for they perceived that this work was wrought of our God.

Now it came to pass, when the wall was built, and I Nehemiah had set up the doors, and the porters and the singers and the Levites were appointed, that I gave my brother Hanani, and Hananiah the ruler of the palace, charge over Jerusalem: for he was a faithful man, and feared God above many.

And I said unto them, "Let not the gates of Jerusalem be opened until the sun be hot; and while they stand by, let them shut the doors, and bar them: and appoint watches of the inhabitants of Jerusalem, every one in his watch, and every one to be over against his house."

Now the city was large and great: but the people were few therein,

*The feast of tabernacles* and the houses were not builded. And all the people gathered themselves together as one man into the street that was before the water gate; and they spake unto Ezra the scribe to bring the book of the law of Moses, which the LORD had commanded to Israel. And Ezra the priest brought the law before the congregation both of men and women, and all that could hear with understanding, upon the first day of the seventh month. And he read therein before the street that was before the water gate from the morning until midday, before the men and the women, and those that could understand; and the ears of all the people were attentive unto the book of the law. And Ezra the scribe stood upon a pulpit of wood, which they had made for the purpose. And Ezra opened the book in the sight of all the people; (for he was above all the people;) and when he opened it, all the people stood up: and Ezra blessed the LORD, the great God, and all the people answered, "Amen, Amen," with lifting up their hands: and they bowed their heads, and worshipped the LORD with their faces to the ground. So they read in the book in the law of God distinctly, and gave the sense, and caused them to understand the reading.

And Nehemiah, which is the Tirshatha, and Ezra the priest the scribe, and the Levites that taught the people, said unto all the people, "This day is holy unto the LORD your God; mourn not, nor weep." For all the people wept, when they heard the words of the law.

Then he said unto them, "Go your way, eat the fat, and drink the sweet, and send portions unto them for whom nothing is prepared: for this day is holy unto our Lord: neither be ye sorry; for the joy of the LORD is your strength."

So the Levites stilled all the people, saying, "Hold your peace, for the day is holy; neither be ye grieved."

And all the people went their way to eat, and to drink, and to send portions, and to make great mirth, because they had understood the words that were declared unto them.

And on the second day were gathered together the chief of the fathers of all the people, the priests, and the Levites, unto Ezra the scribe, even to understand the words of the law. And they found written in the law which the LORD had commanded by Moses, that the children of Israel should dwell in booths in the feast of the seventh month: and that they should publish and proclaim in all their cities, and in Jerusalem, saying,

"Go forth unto the mount, and fetch olive branches, and pine branches, *Dedication of the wall* and myrtle branches, and palm branches, and branches of thick trees, to make booths, as it is written."

So the people went forth, and brought them, and made themselves booths, every one upon the roof of his house, and in their courts, and in the courts of the house of God, and in the street of the water gate, and in the street of the gate of Ephraim. And all the congregation of them that were come again out of the captivity made booths, and sat under the booths: for since the days of Jeshua the son of Nun unto that day had not the children of Israel done so. And there was very great gladness. Also day by day, from the first day unto the last day, he read in the book of the law of God. And they kept the feast seven days; and on the eighth day was a solemn assembly, according unto the manner.

And at the dedication of the wall of Jerusalem they sought the Levites out of all their places, to bring them to Jerusalem, to keep the dedication with gladness, both with thanksgivings, and with singing, with cymbals, psalteries, and with harps. And the sons of the singers gathered themselves together, both out of the plain country round about Jerusalem, and from the villages of Netophathi; also from the house of Gilgal, and out of the fields of Geba and Azmaveth: for the singers had builded them villages round about Jerusalem.

Then I brought up the princes of Judah upon the wall, and appointed two great companies of them that gave thanks, whereof one went on the right hand upon the wall toward the dung gate: and the priests and the Levites purified themselves, and purified the people, and the gates, and the wall. And at the fountain gate, which was over against them, they went up by the stairs of the city of David, at the going up of the wall, above the house of David, even unto the water gate eastward. And the other company of them that gave thanks went over against them, and I after them, and the half of the people upon the wall, from beyond the tower of the furnaces even unto the broad wall; and from above the gate of Ephraim, and above the old gate, and above the fish gate, and the tower of Hananeel and the tower of Meah, even unto the sheep gate: and they stood still in the prison gate. So stood the two companies of them that gave thanks in the house of God, and I, and the half of the rulers with me. And the singers sang loud, with Jezrahiah their overseer. Also that day they offered great sacrifices, and rejoiced: for God had made them rejoice with great joy: the wives also and the children rejoiced: so that the joy of Jerusalem was heard even afar off.

There dwelt men of Tyre also therein, which brought fish, and all manner of ware, and sold on the sabbath unto the children of Judah, and in Jerusalem. Then I contended with the nobles of Judah, and said unto them, "What evil thing is that that ye do, and profane the sabbath day? Did not your fathers thus, and did not our God bring all this evil upon us, and upon this city? yet ye bring more wrath upon Israel by profaning the sabbath."

And it came to pass, that when the gates of Jerusalem began to be dark before the sabbath, I commanded that the gates should be shut, and charged that they should not be opened till after the sabbath: and some of my servants set I at the gates, that there should no burden be brought in on the sabbath day. So the merchants and sellers of all kinds of ware lodged without Jerusalem once or twice. Then I testified against them, and said unto them, "Why lodge ye about the wall? if ye do so again, I will lay hands on you."

From that time forth came they no more on the sabbath. And I commanded the Levites that they should cleanse themselves, and that they should come and keep the gates, to sanctify the sabbath day. Remember me, O my God, concerning this also, and spare me according to the greatness of thy mercy.

THE word of the LORD that came to Joel the son of Pethuel.

Fear not, O land; be glad and rejoice:
For the LORD will do great things.
Be not afraid, ye beasts of the field:
For the pastures of the wilderness do spring,
For the tree beareth her fruit,
The fig tree and the vine do yield their strength. Be glad then, ye
    children of Zion,
And rejoice in the LORD your God:
For he hath given you the former rain moderately,
And he will cause to come down for you the rain,

## THE PROPHETS

The former rain, and the latter rain in the first month.
And the floors shall be full of wheat,
And the fats shall overflow with wine and oil.
And I will restore to you the years that the locust hath eaten,
The cankerworm, and the caterpiller, and the palmerworm,
My great army which I sent among you. And ye shall eat in plenty,
    and be satisfied,
And praise the name of the LORD your God,
That hath dealt wondrously with you:
And my people shall never be ashamed.
And ye shall know that I am in the midst of Israel,
And that I am the LORD your God, and none else:
And my people shall never be ashamed.
And it shall come to pass afterward,
That I will pour out my spirit upon all flesh;
And your sons and your daughters shall prophesy,
Your old men shall dream dreams,
Your young men shall see visions.

REJOICE greatly, O daughter of Zion:
    Shout, O daughter of Jerusalem:
Behold, thy King cometh unto thee:
He is just, and having salvation;
Lowly, and riding upon an ass,
And upon a colt the foal of an ass.
And I will cut off the chariot from Ephraim,
And the horse from Jerusalem,
And the battle bow shall be cut off:
And he shall speak peace unto the heathen:
And his dominion shall be from sea even to sea,
And from the river even to the ends of the earth.
And the LORD shall be seen over them,
And his arrow shall go forth as the lightning:
And the Lord GOD shall blow the trumpet,
And shall go with whirlwinds of the south.
For how great is his goodness,

*Zechariah exhorts Zion*
*to rejoice*

And how great is his beauty!
Corn shall make the young men cheerful,
And new wine the maids.
Ask ye of the LORD rain in the time of the latter rain;
So the LORD shall make bright clouds,
And give them showers of rain,
To every one grass in the field.
"The burden of the word of the LORD for Israel,"
Saith the LORD, which stretcheth forth the heavens,
And layeth the foundation of the earth,
And formeth the spirit of man within him.
"And I will refine them as silver is refined,
And will try them as gold is tried:
They shall call on my name, and I will hear them:
I will say, 'It is my people':
And they shall say, 'The LORD is my God.'"

MINE house shall be called an house of prayer for all people.
For thus saith the high and lofty One
That inhabiteth eternity, whose name is Holy;
"I dwell in the high and holy place,
With him also that is of a contrite and humble spirit,
To revive the spirit of the humble,
And to revive the heart of the contrite ones.
I create the fruit of the lips;
Peace, peace to him that is far off,
And to him that is near," saith the LORD;
"And I will heal him."
"But the wicked are like the troubled sea, when it cannot rest,
Whose waters cast up mire and dirt.
There is no peace," saith my God, "to the wicked."

Cry aloud, spare not,
Lift up thy voice like a trumpet,
And shew my people their transgression,
And the house of Jacob their sins.

Yet they seek me daily, and delight to know my ways,  *The acceptable fast*
As a nation that did righteousness,
And forsook not the ordinance of their God:
They ask of me the ordinances of justice;
They take delight in approaching to God.
"Wherefore have we fasted," say they, "and thou seest not?
Wherefore have we afflicted our soul, and thou takest no knowledge?"
Behold, in the day of your fast ye find pleasure,
And exact all your labours.
Behold, ye fast for strife and debate,
And to smite with the fist of wickedness:
Ye shall not fast as ye do this day,
To make your voice to be heard on high.
Is it such a fast that I have chosen?
A day for a man to afflict his soul?
Is it to bow down his head as a bulrush,
And to spread sackcloth and ashes under him?
Wilt thou call this a fast,
And an acceptable day to the LORD?
Is not this the fast that I have chosen?
To loose the bands of wickedness,
To undo the heavy burdens,
And to let the oppressed go free,
And that ye break every yoke?
Is it not to deal thy bread to the hungry,
And that thou bring the poor that are cast out to thy house?
When thou seest the naked, that thou cover him;
And that thou hide not thyself from thine own flesh?
Then shall thy light break forth as the morning,
And thine health shall spring forth speedily:
And thy righteousness shall go before thee;
The glory of the LORD shall be thy rereward.
Then shalt thou call, and the LORD shall answer;
Thou shalt cry, and he shall say, "Here I am."
If thou take away from the midst of thee the yoke,
The putting forth of the finger, and speaking vanity;

And if thou draw out thy soul to the hungry,
And satisfy the afflicted soul;
Then shall thy light rise in obscurity,
And thy darkness be as the noon day:
And the LORD shall guide thee continually,
And satisfy thy soul in drought,
And make fat thy bones:
And thou shalt be like a watered garden,
And like a spring of water, whose waters fail not.
And they that shall be of thee shall build the old waste places:
Thou shalt raise up the foundations of many generations;
And thou shalt be called, "The repairer of the breach,
The restorer of paths to dwell in."
Then shalt thou delight thyself in the LORD.
Behold, the LORD's hand is not shortened, that it cannot save;
Neither his ear heavy, that it cannot hear:
Therefore is judgment far from us,
Neither doth justice overtake us:
We wait for light, but behold obscurity;
For brightness, but we walk in darkness.
We grope for the wall like the blind,
And we grope as if we had no eyes:
We stumble at noon day as in the night;
We are in desolate places as dead men.

Arise, shine! for thy light is come,
And the glory of the LORD is risen upon thee.
For, behold, the darkness shall cover the earth,
And gross darkness the people:
But the LORD shall arise upon thee,
And his glory shall be seen upon thee.
And the Gentiles shall come to thy light,
And kings to the brightness of thy rising.
Lift up thine eyes round about, and see:
All they gather themselves together, they come to thee:
Thy sons shall come from far,

# THE PROPHETS

And thy daughters shall be nursed at thy side.
And the sons of strangers shall build up thy walls,
And their kings shall minister unto thee:
For in my wrath I smote thee,
But in my favour have I had mercy on thee.
Therefore thy gates shall be open continually;
They shall not be shut day nor night;
That men may bring unto thee the forces of the Gentiles,
And that their kings may be brought.
Violence shall no more be heard in thy land,
Wasting nor destruction within thy borders;
But thou shalt call thy walls Salvation,
And thy gates Praise.
The sun shall be no more thy light by day;
Neither for brightness shall the moon give light unto thee:
But the Lord shall be unto thee an everlasting light,
And thy God thy glory.
Thy sun shall no more go down;
Neither shall thy moon withdraw itself:
For the Lord shall be thine everlasting light,
And the days of thy mourning shall be ended.
Thy people also shall be all righteous:
They shall inherit the land for ever,
The branch of my planting, the work of my hands,
That I may be glorified.
A little one shall become a thousand,
And a small one a strong nation:
I the Lord will hasten it in his time.

The Spirit of the Lord God is upon me;
Because the Lord hath anointed me
To preach good tidings unto the meek;
He hath sent me to bind up the brokenhearted,
To proclaim liberty to the captives,
And the opening of the prison to them that are bound;
To proclaim the acceptable year of the Lord,

*God's mercy to the church*

And the day of vengeance of our God;
To comfort all that mourn;
To appoint unto them that mourn in Zion,
To give unto them beauty for ashes,
The oil of joy for mourning,
The garment of praise for the spirit of heaviness;
That they might be called trees of righteousness,
The planting of the LORD, that he might be glorified.
And they shall build the old wastes,
They shall raise up the former desolations,
And they shall repair the waste cities,
The desolations of many generations.
For as the earth bringeth forth her bud,
And as the garden causeth the things that are sown in it to spring
    forth;
So the Lord GOD will cause righteousness and praise
To spring forth before all the nations.
I will greatly rejoice in the LORD,
My soul shall be joyful in my God;
For he hath clothed me with the garments of salvation,
He hath covered me with the robe of righteousness,
As a bridegroom decketh himself with ornaments,
And as a bride adorneth herself with her jewels.

Go through, go through the gates;
Prepare ye the way of the people;
Cast up, cast up the highway;
Gather out the stones;
Lift up a standard for the people.
Behold, the LORD hath proclaimed unto the end of the world,
"Say ye to the daughter of Zion,
'Behold, thy salvation cometh;
Behold, his reward is with him,
And his work before him.'
And they shall call them, 'The holy people,
The redeemed of the LORD':

## THE PROPHETS

*Blessed state of the
New Jerusalem*

And thou shalt be called, 'Sought out,
A city not forsaken.' "
I will mention the lovingkindnesses of the LORD,
And the praises of the LORD,
According to all that the LORD hath bestowed on us,
And the great goodness toward the house of Israel,
Which he hath bestowed on them according to his mercies,
And according to the multitude of his lovingkindnesses.
For he said, "Surely they are my people,
Children that will not lie":
So he was their Saviour.
In all their affliction he was afflicted,
And the angel of his presence saved them:
In his love and in his pity he redeemed them;
And he bare them, and carried them all the days of old.
"Where is he that brought them up out of the sea with the shepherd of
        his flock?
Where is he that put his holy Spirit within him?
That led them by the right hand of Moses
With his glorious arm,
Dividing the water before them,
To make himself an everlasting name?
That led them through the deep,
As an horse in the wilderness,
That they should not stumble?"
So didst thou lead thy people,
To make thyself a glorious name.
Where is thy strength and thy mercies toward me?
Thou art our father,
Thou, O LORD, art our father, our redeemer;
Thy name is from everlasting.
For since the beginning of the world
Men have not heard,
Nor perceived by the ear,
Neither hath the eye seen, O God, beside thee,
What he hath prepared for him that waiteth for him.

[ 329 ]

*Calling of the Gentiles*

But now, O Lord, thou art our father;
We are the clay,
And thou our potter; and we all are the work of thy hand.

"For, behold, I create new heavens and a new earth:
And the former shall not be remembered, nor come into mind.
But be ye glad and rejoice for ever in that which I create:
For, behold, I create Jerusalem a rejoicing,
And her people a joy.
And I will rejoice in Jerusalem, and joy in my people:
And the voice of weeping shall be no more heard in her,
Nor the voice of crying.
There shall be no more thence an infant of days,
Nor an old man that hath not filled his days:
For the child shall die an hundred years old;
But the sinner being an hundred years old shall be accursed.
And they shall build houses, and inhabit them;
And they shall plant vineyards, and eat the fruit of them.
They shall not build, and another inhabit;
They shall not plant, and another eat:
For as the days of a tree are the days of my people,
And mine elect shall long enjoy the work of their hands.
They shall not labour in vain,
Nor bring forth for trouble;
For they are the seed of the blessed of the Lord,
And their offspring with them.
And it shall come to pass,
That before they call, I will answer;
And while they are yet speaking, I will hear.
The wolf and the lamb shall feed together,
And the lion shall eat straw like the bullock:
And dust shall be the serpent's meat.
They shall not hurt nor destroy
In all my holy mountain," saith the Lord.
Thus saith the Lord,
"The heaven is my throne,

## THE PROPHETS

And the earth is my footstool:
Where is the house that ye build unto me?
And where is the place of my rest?
For all those things hath mine hand made,
And all those things have been," saith the LORD:
"But to this man will I look,
Even to him that is poor and of a contrite spirit,
And trembleth at my word.
As one whom his mother comforteth, so will I comfort you:
And ye shall be comforted in Jerusalem.
For I know their works and their thoughts:
It shall come, that I will gather all nations and tongues;
And they shall come, and see my glory.
And I will set a sign among them,
And I will send those that escape of them unto the nations,
To Tarshish, Pul, and Lud, that draw the bow,
To Tubal, and Javan, to the isles afar off,
That have not heard my fame, neither have seen my glory;
And they shall declare my glory among the Gentiles.
And they shall bring all your brethren
For an offering unto the LORD out of all nations
Upon horses, and in chariots, and in litters,
And upon mules, and upon swift beasts,
To my holy mountain Jerusalem," saith the LORD,
"As the children of Israel bring an offering in a clean vessel
Into the house of the LORD.
And I will also take of them
For priests and for Levites," saith the LORD.
"For as the new heavens and the new earth, which I will make,
Shall remain before me," saith the LORD,
"So shall your seed and your name remain.
And it shall come to pass,
That from one new moon to another,
And from one sabbath to another,
Shall all flesh come to worship before me," saith the LORD.

*The Gentiles shall have
a holy church*

# V

# PROPHECIES OF THE MESSIAH

IN the first year of Belshazzar king of Babylon Daniel had a dream and visions of his head upon his bed: then he wrote the dream, and told the sum of the matters.

"I beheld till the thrones were cast down, and the Ancient of days did sit, whose garment was white as snow, and the hair of his head like the pure wool: his throne was like the fiery flame, and his wheels as burning fire. I saw in the night visions, and, behold, one like the Son of man came with the clouds of heaven, and came to the Ancient of days, and they brought him near before him. And there was given him dominion, and glory, and a kingdom, that all people, nations, and languages, should serve him: his dominion is an everlasting dominion, which shall not pass away, and his kingdom that which shall not be destroyed.

"And I set my face unto the Lord God, to seek by prayer and supplications, with fasting, and sackcloth, and ashes: and I prayed unto the LORD my God, and made my confession, and said, 'O Lord, the great and dreadful God, keeping the covenant and mercy to them that love him, and to them that keep his commandments; we have sinned, and have committed iniquity, and have done wickedly, and have rebelled, even by departing from thy precepts and from thy judgments: neither have we hearkened unto thy servants the prophets, which spake in thy name to our kings, our princes, and our fathers, and to all the people of the land. O Lord, righteousness belongeth unto thee, but unto us confusion of faces, as at this day; to the men of Judah, and to the inhabitants of Jerusalem, and unto all Israel, that are near, and that are far off, through all the countries whither thou hast driven them, because of their trespass that they have trespassed against thee. To the Lord our God belong mercies and forgivenesses, though we have rebelled against him; neither have we obeyed the voice of the LORD our God, to walk in his laws, which he set before us by his servants the prophets. Now therefore, O our God, hear the prayer of thy servant, and his supplications, and cause thy face to shine upon thy sanctuary that is desolate, for the Lord's sake. O Lord, hear; O Lord, forgive; O Lord, hearken and do; defer not, for

thine own sake, O my God: for thy city and thy people are called by thy *Daniel's vision*
name.'

"And whiles I was speaking, and praying, and confessing my sin and the sin of my people Israel, and presenting my supplication before the LORD my God for the holy mountain of my God; yea, whiles I was speaking in prayer, even the man Gabriel, whom I had seen in the vision at the beginning, being caused to fly swiftly, touched me about the time of the evening oblation. And he informed me, and talked with me, and said, 'O Daniel, I am now come forth to give thee skill and understanding. At the beginning of thy supplications the commandment came forth, and I am come to shew thee; for thou art greatly beloved: therefore understand the matter, and consider the vision. Know therefore and understand, that from the going forth of the commandment to restore and to build Jerusalem unto the Messiah the Prince shall be seven weeks, and threescore and two weeks: the street shall be built again, and the wall, even in troublous times.' "

In the third year of Cyrus king of Persia a thing was revealed unto Daniel.

"And I Daniel alone saw the vision: for the men that were with me saw not the vision; but a great quaking fell upon them, so that they fled to hide themselves. Therefore I was left alone, and saw this great vision, and there remained no strength in me. Yet heard I the voice of his words: and when I heard the voice of his words, then was I in a deep sleep on my face, and my face toward the ground.

"And, behold, an hand touched me, which set me upon my knees and upon the palms of my hands. And he said unto me, 'O Daniel, a man greatly beloved, understand the words that I speak unto thee, and stand upright: for unto thee am I now sent.' And when he had spoken this word unto me, I stood trembling.

"Then said he unto me, 'Fear not, Daniel: for from the first day that thou didst set thine heart to understand, and to chasten thyself before thy God, thy words were heard, and I am come for thy words.'

"Then there came and touched me one like the appearance of a man and said, 'O man greatly beloved, fear not: peace be unto thee; be strong, yea, be strong.' And when he had spoken unto me, I was strengthened, and said, 'Let my lord speak; for thou hast strengthened me.'

" 'Many of them that sleep in the dust of the earth shall awake, some to everlasting life, and some to shame and everlasting contempt. And they that be wise shall shine as the brightness of the firmament; and they that turn many to righteousness, as the stars for ever and ever.'

"And I heard, but I understood not: then said I, 'O my Lord, what shall be the end of these things?' And he said, 'Go thy way, Daniel. Many shall be purified, and made white, and tried; but the wise shall understand. Blessed is he that waiteth. But go thou thy way till the end be: for thou shalt rest, and stand in thy lot at the end of the days.' "

The voice of him that crieth in the wilderness,
"Prepare ye the way of the LORD,
Make straight in the desert a highway for our God.
Every valley shall be exalted,
And every mountain and hill shall be made low:
And the crooked shall be made straight,
And the rough places plain:
And the glory of the LORD shall be revealed,
And all flesh shall see it together: for the mouth of the
    LORD hath spoken it."
The Lord himself shall give you a sign;
Behold, a virgin shall conceive, and bear a son,
And shall call his name Immanuel.
Butter and honey shall he eat,
That he may know to refuse the evil,
And choose the good.
There shall come forth a rod out of the stem of Jesse,
And a Branch shall grow out of his roots:
And the spirit of the LORD shall rest upon him,
The spirit of wisdom and understanding,
The spirit of counsel and might,
The spirit of knowledge and of the fear of the LORD;
And shall make him of quick understanding in the fear of the LORD:
And he shall not judge after the sight of his eyes,
Neither reprove after the hearing of his ears:
But with righteousness shall he judge the poor,

## PROPHECIES OF THE MESSIAH

And reprove with equity for the meek of the earth:
And he shall smite the earth with the rod of his mouth,
And with the breath of his lips shall he slay the wicked.
And righteousness shall be the girdle of his loins,
And faithfulness the girdle of his reins.
The wolf also shall dwell with the lamb,
And the leopard shall lie down with the kid;
And the calf and the young lion and the fatling together;
And a little child shall lead them.
And the cow and the bear shall feed;
Their young ones shall lie down together:
And the lion shall eat straw like the ox.
And the sucking child shall play on the hole of the asp,
And the weaned child shall put his hand on the cockatrice' den.
They shall not hurt nor destroy
In all my holy mountain:
For the earth shall be full of the knowledge of the LORD,
As the waters cover the sea.

Thou, Beth-lehem Ephratah,
Though thou be little among the thousands of Judah,
Yet out of thee shall he come forth unto me that is to be ruler in
    Israel;
Whose goings forth have been from of old, from everlasting.
And he shall stand and feed in the strength of the LORD,
In the majesty of the name of the LORD his God;
And they shall abide:
For now shall he be great unto the ends of the earth.
And this man shall be the peace.

The people that walked in darkness
Have seen a great light:
They that dwell in the land of the shadow of death,
Upon them hath the light shined.
Thou hast multiplied the nation, and not increased the joy:
They joy before thee according to the joy in harvest,

*The office of Christ*  And as men rejoice when they divide the spoil.
For unto us a child is born, unto us a son is given:
And the government shall be upon his shoulder:
And his name shall be called Wonderful, Counsellor, The mighty
    God,
The everlasting Father, The Prince of Peace.
Of the increase of his government and peace
There shall be no end,
Upon the throne of David, and upon his kingdom,
To order it, and to establish it
With judgment and with justice
From henceforth even for ever.
The zeal of the LORD of hosts will perform this.

Behold my servant, whom I uphold;
Mine elect, in whom my soul delighteth;
I have put my spirit upon him:
He shall bring forth judgment to the Gentiles.
He shall not cry, nor lift up,
Nor cause his voice to be heard in the street.
A bruised reed shall he not break,
And the smoking flax shall he not quench:
He shall bring forth judgment unto truth.
He shall not fail nor be discouraged,
Till he have set judgment in the earth:
And the isles shall wait for his law.

Who hath believed our report?
And to whom is the arm of the LORD revealed?
For he shall grow up before him as a tender plant,
And as a root out of a dry ground:
He hath no form nor comeliness;
And when we shall see him,
There is no beauty that we should desire him.
He is despised and rejected of men;
A man of sorrows, and acquainted with grief:

## PROPHECIES OF THE MESSIAH

And we hid as it were our faces from him;
He was despised, and we esteemed him not.
Surely he hath borne our griefs, and carried our sorrows:
Yet we did esteem him stricken, smitten of God, and afflicted.
But he was wounded for our transgressions,
He was bruised for our iniquities:
The chastisement of our peace was upon him;
And with his stripes we are healed.
All we like sheep have gone astray;
We have turned every one to his own way;
And the LORD hath laid on him the iniquity of us all.
He was oppressed, and he was afflicted,
Yet he opened not his mouth:
He is brought as a lamb to the slaughter,
And as a sheep before her shearers is dumb,
So he openeth not his mouth.
He was taken from prison and from judgment:
And who shall declare his generation?
For he was cut off out of the land of the living:
For the transgression of my people was he stricken.
And he made his grave with the wicked,
And with the rich in his death;
Because he had done no violence,
Neither was any deceit in his mouth.
Yet it pleased the LORD to bruise him;
He hath put him to grief:
When thou shalt make his soul an offering for sin,
He shall see his seed,
He shall prolong his days,
And the pleasure of the LORD shall prosper in his hand.
He shall see of the travail of his soul,
And shall be satisfied:
By his knowledge shall my righteous servant justify many;
For he shall bear their iniquities.
Therefore will I divide him a portion with the great,
And he shall divide the spoil with the strong;

*The humiliation and
suffering of Christ*

Because he hath poured out his soul unto death:
And he was numbered with the transgressors;
And he bare the sin of many,
And made intercession for the transgressors.

Behold, my servant shall deal prudently,
He shall be exalted and extolled,
And be very high.
As many were astonied at thee;
His visage was so marred more than any man,
And his form more than the sons of men:
So shall he sprinkle many nations;
The kings shall shut their mouths at him:
For that which had not been told them shall they see;
And that which they had not heard shall they consider.

Give the king thy judgments, O God,
And thy righteousness unto the king's son.
He shall judge thy people with righteousness,
And thy poor with judgment.
The mountains shall bring peace to the people,
And the little hills, by righteousness.
He shall judge the poor of the people,
He shall save the children of the needy,
And shall break in pieces the oppressor.
They shall fear thee as long as the sun and moon endure,
Throughout all generations.
He shall come down like rain upon the mown grass:
As showers that water the earth.
In his days shall the righteous flourish;
And abundance of peace so long as the moon endureth.
He shall have dominion also from sea to sea,
And from the river unto the ends of the earth.
They that dwell in the wilderness shall bow before him;
And his enemies shall lick the dust.
The kings of Tarshish and of the isles shall bring presents:

## PROPHECIES OF THE MESSIAH

The kings of Sheba and Seba shall offer gifts.
Yea, all kings shall fall down before him:
All nations shall serve him.
For he shall deliver the needy when he crieth;
The poor also, and him that hath no helper.
He shall spare the poor and needy,
And shall save the souls of the needy.
He shall redeem their soul from deceit and violence:
And precious shall their blood be in his sight.
And he shall live, and to him shall be given of the gold of Sheba:
Prayer also shall be made for him continually;
And daily shall he be praised.
There shall be an handful of corn in the earth upon the top of the
    mountains;
The fruit thereof shall shake like Lebanon:
And they of the city shall flourish like grass of the earth.
His name shall endure for ever:
His name shall be continued as long as the sun:
And men shall be blessed in him:
All nations shall call him blessed.
Blessed be the Lord God, the God of Israel,
Who only doeth wondrous things.
And blessed be his glorious name for ever:
And let the whole earth be filled with his glory;
Amen, and Amen.

"The Book of my Remembrance"

THE LORD bless thee, and keep thee: the LORD make his face shine upon thee, and be gracious unto thee: the LORD lift up his countenance upon thee, and give thee peace.

# PART II

# I

# THE LIFE OF JESUS

THE beginning of the gospel of Jesus Christ, the Son of God. *Christ the Word*
In the beginning was the Word, and the Word was with God, and the Word was God. The same was in the beginning with God. All things were made by him; and without him was not any thing made that was made. In him was life; and the life was the light of men. And the light shineth in darkness; and the darkness comprehended it not.

That was the true Light, which lighteth every man that cometh into the world. He was in the world, and the world was made by him, and the world knew him not. He came unto his own, and his own received him not. But as many as received him, to them gave he power to become the sons of God, even to them that believe on his name: which were born, not of blood, nor of the will of the flesh, nor of the will of man, but of God.

And the Word was made flesh, and dwelt among us, (and we beheld his glory, the glory as of the only begotten of the Father,) full of grace and truth.

There was in the days of Herod, the king of Judæa, a certain priest *Birth of John foretold*
named Zacharias, of the course of Abia: and his wife was of the daughters of Aaron, and her name was Elisabeth. And they were both righteous before God, walking in all the commandments and ordinances of the Lord blameless. And they had no child, and both were now well stricken in years. And it came to pass, that while he executed the priest's office before God in the order of his course, there appeared unto him an angel of the Lord standing on the right side of the altar of incense. And when Zacharias saw him, he was troubled, and fear fell upon him. But the angel said unto him, "Fear not, Zacharias: for thy prayer is heard; and thy wife Elisabeth shall bear thee a son and thou shalt call his name John. And thou shalt have joy and gladness; and many shall rejoice at his birth. For he shall be great in the sight of the Lord, and shall drink neither wine nor strong drink; and he shall be filled with the Holy Ghost, even

*Birth of Jesus foretold* from his mother's womb. And many of the children of Israel shall he turn to the Lord their God. And he shall go before him in the spirit and power of Elias, to turn the hearts of the fathers to the children, and the disobedient to the wisdom of the just; to make ready a people prepared for the Lord."

And in the sixth month the angel Gabriel was sent from God unto a city of Galilee, named Nazareth, to a virgin espoused to a man whose name was Joseph, of the house of David; and the virgin's name was Mary. And the angel came in unto her, and said, "Hail, thou that art highly favoured, the Lord is with thee: blessed art thou among women."

And when she saw him, she was troubled at his saying, and cast in her mind what manner of salutation this should be.

And the angel said unto her, "Fear not, Mary: for thou hast found favour with God. And, behold, thou shalt conceive in thy womb, and bring forth a son, and shalt call his name JESUS. He shall be great, and shall be called the Son of the Highest: and the Lord God shall give unto him the throne of his father David: and he shall reign over the house of Jacob for ever; and of his kingdom there shall be no end."

Then said Mary unto the angel, "How shall this be?"

And the angel answered and said unto her, "The Holy Ghost shall come upon thee, and the power of the Highest shall overshadow thee: therefore also that holy thing which shall be born of thee shall be called the Son of God. And, behold, thy cousin Elisabeth, she hath also conceived a son in her old age: and this is the sixth month with her, who was called barren. For with God nothing shall be impossible."

And Mary said, "Behold the handmaid of the Lord; be it unto me according to thy word." And the angel departed from her.

And Mary arose in those days, and went into the hill country with haste, into a city of Juda; and entered into the house of Zacharias, and saluted Elisabeth.

And it came to pass, that, when Elisabeth heard the salutation of Mary, the babe leaped in her womb; and Elisabeth was filled with the Holy Ghost: and she spake out with a loud voice, and said, "Blessed art thou among women, and blessed is the fruit of thy womb. And whence is this to me, that the mother of my Lord should come to me? For, lo, as soon as the voice of thy salutation sounded in mine ears, the babe leaped

*THE DESCENT OF PEACE*

in my womb for joy." And blessed is she that believed: for there shall be     *Mary's song of thanks-*
a performance of those things which were told her from the Lord.     *giving*

And Mary said,

My soul doth magnify the Lord,
And my spirit hath rejoiced in God my Saviour.
For he hath regarded the low estate of his handmaiden:
For, behold, from henceforth all generations shall call me blessed.
For he that is mighty hath done to me great things;
And holy is his name.
And his mercy is on them that fear him from generation to generation.
He hath shewed strength with his arm;
He hath scattered the proud in the imagination of their hearts.
He hath put down the mighty from their seats,
And exalted them of low degree.
He hath filled the hungry with good things;
And the rich he hath sent empty away.
He hath holpen his servant Israel,
In remembrance of his mercy;
As he spake to our fathers,
To Abraham, and to his seed for ever.

And Mary abode with her about three months, and returned to her own house.

Now Elisabeth's full time came that she should be delivered; and she     *Prophecy of Zacharias*
brought forth a son. And her neighbours and her cousins heard how the
Lord had shewed great mercy upon her; and they rejoiced with her.
And his mother said, "He shall be called John." And his father Zacharias
was filled with the Holy Ghost, and prophesied, saying,

Blessed be the Lord God of Israel;
For he hath visited and redeemed his people.
And thou, child, shalt be called the prophet of the Highest:
For thou shalt go before the face of the Lord to prepare his ways;
To give knowledge of salvation unto his people

By the remission of their sins,
Through the tender mercy of our God;
Whereby the dayspring from on high hath visited us,
To give light to them that sit in darkness and in the shadow of death,
To guide our feet into the way of peace.

And the child grew, and waxed strong in spirit, and was in the deserts till the day of his shewing unto Israel.

And it came to pass in those days, that there went out a decree from Cæsar Augustus, that all the world should be taxed. (And this taxing was first made when Cyrenius was governor of Syria.) And all went to be taxed, every one into his own city. And Joseph also went up from Galilee, out of the city of Nazareth, unto Judæa, unto the city of David, which is called Bethlehem; (because he was of the house and lineage of David:) to be taxed with Mary his espoused wife, being great with child. And so it was, that, while they were there, the days were accomplished that she should be delivered. And she brought forth her firstborn son, and wrapped him in swaddling clothes, and laid him in a manger; because there was no room for them in the inn.

And there were in the same country shepherds abiding in the field, keeping watch over their flock by night. And, lo, the angel of the Lord came upon them, and the glory of the Lord shone round about them: and they were sore afraid. And the angel said unto them, "Fear not: for, behold, I bring you good tidings of great joy, which shall be to all people. For unto you is born this day in the city of David a Saviour, which is Christ the Lord. And this shall be a sign unto you; Ye shall find the babe wrapped in swaddling clothes, lying in a manger."

And suddenly there was with the angel a multitude of the heavenly host praising God, and saying, "Glory to God in the highest, and on earth peace, good will toward men."

And it came to pass, as the angels were gone away from them into heaven, the shepherds said one to another, "Let us now go even unto Bethlehem, and see this thing which is come to pass, which the Lord hath made known unto us. And they came with haste, and found Mary, and Joseph, and the babe lying in a manger. And when they had seen it, they made known abroad the saying which was told them concerning this child. And all they that heard it wondered at those things which were told them by the shepherds. But Mary kept all these things, and pon- dered them in her heart. And the shepherds returned, glorifying and praising God for all the things that they had heard and seen, as it was told unto them.

And when eight days were accomplished for the circumcising of the child, his name was called JESUS, which was so named of the angel before he was conceived in the womb.

And when the days of her purification according to the law of Moses were accomplished, they brought him to Jerusalem, to present him to the Lord; and to offer a sacrifice according to that which is said in the law of the Lord, A pair of turtledoves, or two young pigeons.

And, behold, there was a man in Jerusalem, whose name was Simeon; and the same man was just and devout, and the Holy Ghost was upon him. And it was revealed unto him by the Holy Ghost, that he should not see death, before he had seen the Lord's Christ. And he came by the Spirit into the temple: and when the parents brought in the child Jesus, to do for him after the custom of the law, then took he him up in his arms, and blessed God, and said,

> Lord, now lettest thou thy servant depart in peace,
> According to thy word:
> For mine eyes have seen thy salvation,
> Which thou hast prepared before the face of all people;
> A light to lighten the Gentiles,
> And the glory of thy people Israel.

And Joseph and his mother marvelled at those things which were spoken of him. And Simeon blessed them, and said unto Mary his mother, "Behold, this child is set for the fall and rising again of many in Israel."

And there was one Anna, a prophetess; and she was a widow of about fourscore and four years, which departed not from the temple, but served God with fastings and prayers night and day. And she coming in that instant gave thanks likewise unto the Lord, and spake of him to all them that looked for redemption in Jerusalem. And when they had performed all things according to the law of the Lord, they returned into Galilee, to their own city Nazareth.

Now when Jesus was born in Bethlehem of Judæa in the days of Herod the king, behold, there came wise men from the east to Jerusalem, saying, "Where is he that is born King of the Jews? for we have seen his star in the east, and are come to worship him."

When Herod the king had heard these things, he was troubled, and all Jerusalem with him. And when he had gathered all the chief priests and scribes of the people together, he demanded of them where Christ should be born. And they said unto him, "In Bethlehem of Judæa: for thus it is written by the prophet,

> And thou Bethlehem, in the land of Juda,
> Art not the least among the princes of Juda:
> For out of thee shall come a Governor,
> That shall rule my people Israel."

Then Herod, when he had privily called the wise men, enquired of them diligently what time the star appeared. And he sent them to Bethlehem, and said, "Go and search diligently for the young child; and when ye have found him, bring me word again, that I may come and worship him also."

When they had heard the king, they departed; and, lo, the star, which they saw in the east, went before them, till it came and stood over where the young child was. When they saw the star, they rejoiced with exceeding great joy. And when they were come into the house, they saw the young child with Mary his mother, and fell down, and worshipped him: and when they had opened their treasures, they presented unto him gifts; gold, and frankincense, and myrrh. And being warned of God in a dream that they should not return to Herod, they departed into their own country another way.

And when they were departed, behold, the angel of the Lord appeareth to Joseph in a dream, saying, "Arise, and take the young child and his mother, and flee into Egypt, and be thou there until I bring thee word: for Herod will seek the young child to destroy him."

When he arose, he took the young child and his mother by night, and departed into Egypt: and was there until the death of Herod: that it might be fulfilled which was spoken of the Lord by the prophet, saying, "Out of Egypt have I called my son."

*SIMEON PROPHESYING OVER THE INFANT CHRIST*

But when Herod was dead, behold, an angel of the Lord appeareth in *Death of Herod* a dream to Joseph in Egypt, saying, "Arise, and take the young child and his mother, and go into the land of Israel: for they are dead which sought the young child's life."

And he arose, and took the young child and his mother, and came into the land of Israel. But when he heard that Archelaus did reign in Judæa in the room of his father Herod, he was afraid to go thither: notwithstanding, being warned of God in a dream, he turned aside into the parts of Galilee: And he came and dwelt in a city called Nazareth: that it might be fulfilled which was spoken by the prophets, "He shall be called a Nazarene."

And the child grew, and waxed strong in spirit, filled with wisdom: and the grace of God was upon him.

Now his parents went to Jerusalem every year at the feast of the passover. And when he was twelve years old, they went up to Jerusalem after the custom of the feast. And when they had fulfilled the days, as they returned, the child Jesus tarried behind in Jerusalem; and Joseph and his mother knew not of it. But they, supposing him to have been in the company, went a day's journey; and they sought him among their kinsfolk and acquaintance. And when they found him not, they turned back again to Jerusalem, seeking him.

And it came to pass, that after three days they found him in the temple, sitting in the midst of the doctors, both hearing them, and asking them questions. And all that heard him were astonished at his understanding and answers. And when they saw him, they were amazed: and his mother said unto him, "Son, why hast thou thus dealt with us? behold, thy father and I have sought thee sorrowing."

And he said unto them, "How is it that ye sought me? wist ye not that I must be about my Father's business?" And they understood not the saying which he spake unto them.

And he went down with them, and came to Nazareth, and was subject unto them: but his mother kept all these sayings in her heart. And Jesus increased in wisdom and stature, and in favour with God and man.

There was a man sent from God, whose name was John. In the fifteenth year of the reign of Tiberius Cæsar, Pontius Pilate being

*Christt the Light*

governor of Judæa, and Herod being tetrarch of Galilee, Annas and Caiaphas being the high priests, the word of God came unto John the son of Zacharias in the wilderness. And John was clothed with camel's hair, and with a girdle of a skin about his loins; and he did eat locusts and wild honey.

The same came for a witness, to bear witness of the Light, that all men through him might believe. He was not that Light, but was sent to bear witness of that Light. John bare witness of him, and cried, saying, "This was he of whom I spake, 'He that cometh after me is preferred before me: for he was before me.'" And of his fulness have all we received, and grace for grace. For the law was given by Moses, but grace and truth came by Jesus Christ. No man hath seen God at any time; the only begotten Son, which is in the bosom of the Father, he hath declared him.

And he came into all the country about Jordan, preaching the baptism of repentance for the remission of sins; saying, "Repent ye: for the kingdom of heaven is at hand. As it is written in the book of the words of Esaias the prophet, The voice of one crying in the wilderness, 'Prepare ye the way of the Lord, make his paths straight. Every valley shall be filled, and every mountain and hill shall be brought low; and the crooked shall be made straight, and the rough ways shall be made smooth; and all flesh shall see the salvation of God.'"

And there went out unto him all the land of Judæa, and they of Jerusalem, and were all baptized of him in the river of Jordan, confessing their sins.

But when he saw many of the Pharisees and Sadducees come to his baptism, he said unto them, "O generation of vipers, who hath warned you to flee from the wrath to come? Bring forth fruits worthy of repentance."

Then said he to the multitude that came forth to be baptized of him, "Now also the axe is laid unto the root of the trees: every tree therefore which bringeth not forth good fruit is hewn down, and cast into the fire."

And the people asked him, saying, "What shall we do then?"

He answereth and saith unto them, "He that hath two coats, let him impart to him that hath none; and he that hath meat, let him do likewise."

*THE FLIGHT INTO EGYPT*

Then came also publicans to be baptized, and said unto him, "Master, *Jesus baptized*
what shall we do?"

And he said unto them, "Exact no more than that which is appointed
you."

And the soldiers likewise demanded of him, saying, "And what shall
we do?"

And he said unto them, "Do violence to no man, neither accuse any
falsely; and be content with your wages."

And as the people were in expectation, and all men mused in their
hearts of John, whether he were the Christ, or not; John answered, saying unto them all, "I am not the Christ. I indeed baptize you with water;
but one mightier than I cometh, the latchet of whose shoes I am not
worthy to unloose: he shall baptize you with the Holy Ghost and with
fire: whose fan is in his hand, and he will throughly purge his floor, and
will gather the wheat into his garner; but the chaff he will burn with fire
unquenchable." And many other things in his exhortation preached he
unto the people.

These things were done in Bethabara beyond Jordan, where John
was baptizing.

Then cometh Jesus from Galilee to Jordan unto John, to be baptized
of him. But John forbad him, saying, "I have need to be baptized of thee,
and comest thou to me?"

And Jesus answering said unto him, "Suffer it to be so now: for thus
it becometh us to fulfil all righteousness." Then he suffered him.

And Jesus, when he was baptized, went up straightway out of the
water: and, lo, the heavens were opened unto him, and he saw the
Spirit of God descending like a dove, and lighting upon him: and lo a
voice from heaven, saying, "This is my beloved Son, in whom I am well
pleased."

And Jesus himself began to be about thirty years of age.

Then was Jesus led up of the spirit into the wilderness to be tempted *The temptation*
of the devil. And when he had fasted forty days and forty nights, he was
afterward an hungred. And when the tempter came to him, he said, "If
thou be the Son of God, command that these stones be made bread."

But he answered and said, "It is written,

[ 9 ]

Man shall not live by bread alone,
But by every word that proceedeth out of the mouth of God."

Then the devil taketh him up into the holy city, and setteth him on a pinnacle of the temple, and saith unto him, "If thou be the Son of God, cast thyself down: for it is written,

He shall give his angels charge concerning thee:
And in their hands they shall bear thee up,
Lest at any time thou dash thy foot against a stone."

Jesus said unto him, "It is written again, Thou shalt not tempt the Lord thy God."

Again, the devil taketh him up into an exceeding high mountain, and sheweth him all the kingdoms of the world, and the glory of them; and saith unto him, "All these things will I give thee, if thou wilt fall down and worship me."

Then saith Jesus unto him, "Get thee hence, Satan: for it is written, Thou shalt worship the Lord thy God, and him only shalt thou serve."

Then the devil leaveth him, and, behold, angels came and ministered unto him.

The next day John seeth Jesus coming unto him, and saith, "Behold the Lamb of God, which taketh away the sin of the world. This is he of whom I said, 'After me cometh a man which is preferred before me: for he was before me.' And I knew him not: but that he should be made manifest to Israel, therefore am I come baptizing with water."

And John bare record, saying, "I saw the Spirit descending from heaven like a dove, and it abode upon him. And I knew him not: but he that sent me to baptize with water, the same said unto me, 'Upon whom thou shalt see the Spirit descending, and remaining on him, the same is he which baptizeth with the Holy Ghost.' And I saw, and bare record that this is the Son of God."

Again the next day after John stood, and two of his disciples; and looking upon Jesus as he walked, he saith, "Behold the Lamb of God!"

And the two disciples heard him speak, and they followed Jesus. Then Jesus turned, and saw them following, and saith unto them, "What seek ye?"

*THE BAPTISM OF CHRIST*

They said unto him, "Rabbi," (which is to say, being interpreted, *The disciples called*
"Master,") "where dwellest thou?"

He saith unto them, "Come and see." They came and saw where he
dwelt, and abode with him that day: for it was about the tenth hour.

One of the two which heard John speak, and followed him, was
Andrew, Simon Peter's brother. He first findeth his own brother Simon,
and saith unto him, "We have found the Messias," which is, being interpreted, the Christ.

And he brought him to Jesus. And when Jesus beheld him, he said,
"Thou art Simon the son of Jona: thou shalt be called Cephas," which is
by interpretation, "A stone."

The day following Jesus would go forth into Galilee, and findeth
Philip, and saith unto him, "Follow me." Now Philip was of Bethsaida,
the city of Andrew and Peter.

Philip findeth Nathanael, and saith unto him, "We have found him,
of whom Moses in the law, and the prophets, did write, Jesus of Nazareth,
the son of Joseph."

And Nathanael said unto him, "Can there any good thing come out
of Nazareth?"

Philip saith unto him, "Come and see."

Jesus saw Nathanael coming to him, and saith of him, "Behold an
Israelite indeed, in whom is no guile!"

Nathanael saith unto him, "Whence knowest thou me?"

Jesus answered and said unto him, "Before that Philip called thee,
when thou wast under the fig tree, I saw thee."

Nathanael answered and saith unto him, "Rabbi, thou art the Son of
God; thou art the King of Israel."

Jesus answered and said unto him, "Because I said unto thee 'I saw
thee under the fig tree,' believest thou? thou shalt see greater things than
these." And he saith unto him, "Verily, verily, I say unto you, Hereafter
ye shall see heaven open, and the angels of God ascending and descending upon the Son of man."

And the third day there was a marriage in Cana of Galilee; and the
mother of Jesus was there: and both Jesus was called, and his disciples,
to the marriage. And when they wanted wine, the mother of Jesus saith
unto him, "They have no wine."

[ 11 ]

*The wedding feast at Cana*

Jesus saith unto her, "Woman, what have I to do with thee? mine hour is not yet come."

His mother saith unto the servants, "Whatsoever he saith unto you, do it."

And there were set there six waterpots of stone, after the manner of the purifying of the Jews, containing two or three firkins apiece.

Jesus saith unto them, "Fill the waterpots with water." And they filled them up to the brim. And he saith unto them, "Draw out now, and bear unto the governor of the feast." And they bare it.

When the ruler of the feast had tasted the water that was made wine, and knew not whence it was: (but the servants which drew the water knew;) the governor of the feast called the bridegroom, and saith unto him, "Every man at the beginning doth set forth good wine; and when men have well drunk, then that which is worse: but thou hast kept the good wine until now."

This beginning of miracles did Jesus in Cana of Galilee, and manifested forth his glory; and his disciples believed on him. After this he went down to Capernaum, he, and his mother, and his brethren, and his disciples: and he taught them on the sabbath days. And they were astonished at his doctrine: for his word was with power.

And the Jews' passover was at hand, and Jesus went up to Jerusalem.

Now when he was in Jerusalem at the passover, in the feast day, many believed in his name, when they saw the miracles which he did. But Jesus did not commit himself unto them, because he knew all men, and needed not that any should testify of man: for he knew what was in man.

There was a man of the Pharisees, named Nicodemus, a ruler of the Jews: the same came to Jesus by night, and said unto him, "Rabbi, we know that thou art a teacher come from God: for no man can do these miracles that thou doest, except God be with him."

Jesus answered and said unto him, "Verily, verily, I say unto thee, Except a man be born again, he cannot see the kingdom of God."

Nicodemus saith unto him, "How can a man be born when he is old? can he enter the second time into his mother's womb, and be born?"

Jesus answered, "Verily, verily, I say unto thee, Except a man be born of water and of the Spirit, he cannot enter into the kingdom of God.

CHRIST TEMPTED TO TURN STONES INTO BREAD

That which is born of the flesh is flesh; and that which is born of the Spirit is spirit. Marvel not that I said unto thee, 'Ye must be born again.' The wind bloweth where it listeth, and thou hearest the sound thereof, but canst not tell whence it cometh, and whither it goeth: so is every one that is born of the Spirit." *Nicodemus taught the necessity of regeneration*

Nicodemus answered and said unto him, "How can these things be?"

Jesus answered and said unto him, "Art thou a master of Israel, and knowest not these things? Verily, verily, I say unto thee, We speak that we do know, and testify that we have seen; and ye receive not our witness. If I have told you earthly things, and ye believe not, how shall ye believe, if I tell you of heavenly things? And no man hath ascended up to heaven, but he that came down from heaven, even the Son of man which is in heaven. And as Moses lifted up the serpent in the wilderness, even so must the Son of man be lifted up: that whosoever believeth in him should not perish, but have eternal life. For God so loved the world, that he gave his only begotten Son, that whosoever believeth in him should not perish, but have everlasting life. For God sent not his Son into the world to condemn the world; but that the world through him might be saved. He that believeth on him is not condemned: but he that believeth not is condemned already, because he hath not believed in the name of the only begotten Son of God. And this is the condemnation, that light is come into the world, and men loved darkness rather than light, because their deeds were evil. For every one that doeth evil hateth the light, neither cometh to the light, lest his deeds should be reproved. But he that doeth truth cometh to the light, that his deeds may be made manifest, that they are wrought in God."

After these things came Jesus and his disciples into the land of Judæa; and there he tarried with them, and baptized. And John also was baptizing in Ænon near to Salim, because there was much water there: and they came, and were baptized. For John was not yet cast into prison.

Then there arose a question between some of John's disciples and the Jews about purifying. And they came unto John, and said unto him, "Rabbi, he that was with thee beyond Jordan, to whom thou barest witness, behold, the same baptizeth, and all men come to him."

John answered and said, "A man can receive nothing, except it be given him from heaven. Ye yourselves bear me witness, that I said, I am

*The Samaritan woman* not the Christ, but that I am sent before him. He that hath the bride is the bridegroom: but the friend of the bridegroom, which standeth and heareth him, rejoiceth greatly because of the bridegroom's voice: this my joy therefore is fulfilled. He must increase, but I must decrease. He that cometh from above is above all: he that is of the earth is earthly, and speaketh of the earth: he that cometh from heaven is above all. And what he hath seen and heard, that he testifieth; and no man receiveth his testimony. He that hath received his testimony hath set to his seal that God is true. For he whom God hath sent speaketh the words of God: for God giveth not the Spirit by measure unto him. The Father loveth the Son, and hath given all things into his hand. He that believeth on the Son hath everlasting life."

Jesus left Judæa, and departed again into Galilee. And he must needs go through Samaria. Then cometh he to a city of Samaria, which is called Sychar, near to the parcel of ground that Jacob gave to his son Joseph. Now Jacob's well was there. Jesus therefore, being wearied with his journey, sat thus on the well: and it was about the sixth hour.

There cometh a woman of Samaria to draw water: Jesus saith unto her, "Give me to drink." (For his disciples were gone away unto the city to buy meat.)

Then saith the woman of Samaria unto him, "How is it that thou, being a Jew, askest drink of me, which am a woman of Samaria?" for the Jews have no dealings with the Samaritans.

Jesus answered and said unto her, "If thou knewest the gift of God, and who it is that saith to thee, 'Give me to drink'; thou wouldest have asked of him, and he would have given thee living water."

The woman saith unto him, "Sir, thou hast nothing to draw with, and the well is deep: from whence then hast thou that living water? Art thou greater than our father Jacob, which gave us the well, and drank thereof himself, and his children, and his cattle?"

Jesus answered and said unto her, "Whosoever drinketh of this water shall thirst again: but whosoever drinketh of the water that I shall give him shall never thirst; but the water that I shall give him shall be in him a well of water springing up into everlasting life."

The woman saith unto him, "Sir, give me this water, that I thirst not, neither come hither to draw. I perceive that thou art a prophet. Our

fathers worshipped in this mountain; and ye say, that in Jerusalem is the
place where men ought to worship."

Jesus saith unto her, "Woman, believe me, the hour cometh when ye shall neither in this mountain, nor yet at Jerusalem, worship the Father. Ye worship ye know not what: we know what we worship: but the hour cometh, and now is, when the true worshippers shall worship the Father in spirit and in truth: for the Father seeketh such to worship him. God is a Spirit: and they that worship him must worship him in spirit and in truth."

The woman saith unto him, "I know that Messias cometh, which is called Christ: when he is come, he will tell us all things."

Jesus saith unto her, "I that speak unto thee am he."

And upon this came his disciples, and marvelled that he talked with the woman: yet no man said, "What seekest thou?" or, "Why talkest thou with her?"

The woman then left her waterpot, and went her way into the city, and saith to the men, "Come, see a man, which told me all things that ever I did: is not this the Christ?"

Then they went out of the city, and came unto him.

In the mean while his disciples prayed him, saying, "Master, eat."

But he said unto them, "I have meat to eat that ye know not of."

Therefore said the disciples one to another, "Hath any man brought him ought to eat?"

Jesus saith unto them, "My meat is to do the will of him that sent me, and to finish his work. Say not ye, 'There are yet four months, and then cometh harvest'? behold, I say unto you, 'Lift up your eyes, and look on the fields; for they are white already to harvest.' And he that reapeth receiveth wages, and gathereth fruit unto life eternal: that both he that soweth and he that reapeth may rejoice together. And herein is that saying true, 'One soweth, and another reapeth.' I sent you to reap that whereon ye bestowed no labour: other men laboured, and ye are entered into their labours."

And many of the Samaritans of that city believed on him for the saying of the woman, which testified, "He told me all that ever I did." So when the Samaritans were come unto him, they besought him that he would tarry with them: and he abode there two days. And many more believed because of his own word; and said unto the woman, "Now we believe, not because of thy saying: for we have heard him ourselves, and know that this is indeed the Christ, the Saviour of the world."

Now after two days Jesus departed thence and returned in the power of the Spirit into Galilee: and there went out a fame of him through all the region round about. The Galilæans received him, having seen all the things that he did at Jerusalem at the feast: for they also went unto the feast. And he taught in their synagogues, being glorified of all.

So Jesus came again into Cana of Galilee, where he made the water wine. And there was a certain nobleman, whose son was sick at Capernaum. When he heard that Jesus was come out of Judæa into Galilee, he went unto him, and besought him that he would come down, and heal his son: for he was at the point of death.

Then said Jesus unto him, "Except ye see signs and wonders, ye will not believe."

The nobleman saith unto him, "Sir, come down ere my child die."

Jesus saith unto him, "Go thy way; thy son liveth." And the man believed the word that Jesus had spoken unto him, and he went his way. And as he was now going down, his servants met him, and told him, saying, "Thy son liveth." Then enquired he of them the hour when he began to amend. And they said unto him, "Yesterday at the seventh hour the fever left him." So the father knew that it was at the same hour, in the which Jesus said unto him, "Thy son liveth": and himself believed, and his whole house.

This is again the second miracle that Jesus did, when he was come out of Judæa into Galilee.

And he came to Nazareth, where he had been brought up: and, as his custom was, he went into the synagogue on the sabbath day, and stood up for to read. And there was delivered unto him the book of the prophet Esaias. And when he had opened the book, he found the place where it was written,

The Spirit of the Lord is upon me,
Because he hath anointed me to preach the gospel to the poor;
He hath sent me to heal the brokenhearted,
To preach deliverance to the captives,

[ 16 ]

And recovering of sight to the blind,
To set at liberty them that are bruised,
To preach the acceptable year of the Lord.

And he closed the book, and he gave it again to the minister, and sat down. And the eyes of all them that were in the synagogue were fastened on him. And he began to say unto them, "This day is this scripture fulfilled in your ears."

And all bare him witness, and wondered at the gracious words which proceeded out of his mouth. And they said, "Is not this Joseph's son?"

And he said unto them, "Ye will surely say unto me this proverb, 'Physician, heal thyself: whatsoever we have heard done in Capernaum, do also here in thy country.'" And he said, "Verily I say unto you, No prophet is accepted in his own country. But I tell you of a truth, many widows were in Israel in the days of Elias, when the heaven was shut up three years and six months, when great famine was throughout all the land; but unto none of them was Elias sent, save unto Sarepta, a city of Sidon, unto a woman that was a widow. And many lepers were in Israel in the time of Eliseus the prophet; and none of them was cleansed, saving Naaman the Syrian."

And all they in the synagogue, when they heard these things, were filled with wrath, and rose up, and thrust him out of the city, and led him unto the brow of the hill whereon their city was built, that they might cast him down headlong. But he passing through the midst of them went his way.

And leaving Nazareth, he came and dwelt in Capernaum, which is upon the sea coast, in the borders of Zabulon and Nephthalim: that it might be fulfilled which was spoken by Esaias the prophet, saying,

The land of Zabulon, and the land of Nephthalim,
By the way of the sea, beyond Jordan,
Galilee of the Gentiles;
The people which sat in darkness
Saw great light;
And to them which sat in the region and shadow of death
Light is sprung up.

[ 17 ]

*The miraculous draught of fishes*

And it came to pass, that, as the people pressed upon him to hear the word of God, he stood by the lake of Gennesaret, and saw two ships standing by the lake: but the fishermen were gone out of them, and were washing their nets. And he entered into one of the ships, which was Simon's, and prayed him that he would thrust out a little from the land. And he sat down, and taught the people out of the ship.

Now when he had left speaking, he said unto Simon, "Launch out into the deep, and let down your nets for a draught." And Simon answering said unto him, "Master, we have toiled all the night, and have taken nothing: nevertheless at thy word I will let down the net."

And when they had this done, they inclosed a great multitude of fishes: and their net brake. And they beckoned unto their partners, which were in the other ship, that they should come and help them. And they came, and filled both the ships, so that they began to sink.

When Simon Peter saw it, he fell down at Jesus' knees, saying, "Depart from me; for I am a sinful man, O Lord." For he was astonished, and all that were with him, at the draught of the fishes which they had taken: and so was also James, and John, the sons of Zebedee, which were partners with Simon. And Jesus said unto Simon, "Fear not; from henceforth thou shalt catch men."

And when they had brought their ships to land, they forsook all, and followed him. And they went into Capernaum; and straightway on the sabbath day he entered into the synagogue, and taught. And they were astonished at his doctrine: for he taught them as one that had authority, and not as the scribes.

And there was in their synagogue a man with an unclean spirit; and he cried out, saying, "Let us alone; what have we to do with thee, thou Jesus of Nazareth? art thou come to destroy us? I know thee who thou art, the Holy One of God."

And Jesus rebuked him, saying, "Hold thy peace, and come out of him."

And when the unclean spirit had torn him, and cried with a loud voice, he came out of him. And they were all amazed, insomuch that they questioned among themselves, saying, "What thing is this? what new doctrine is this? for with authority commandeth he even the unclean

spirits, and they do obey him." And immediately his fame spread
abroad throughout all the region round about Galilee.

And forthwith, when they were come out of the synagogue, they
entered into the house of Simon and Andrew, with James and John.
But Simon's wife's mother lay sick of a fever, and anon they tell him of
her. And he came and took her by the hand, and lifted her up; and immediately the fever left her, and she ministered unto them. And all the
city was gathered together at the door.

Now when the sun was setting, all they that had any sick with divers
diseases brought them unto him; and he laid his hands on every one of
them, and healed them.

And in the morning, rising up a great while before day, he went out,
and departed into a solitary place, and there prayed. And when it was
day, the people sought him, and came unto him, and stayed him, that he
should not depart from them.

And he said unto them, "I must preach the kingdom of God to other
cities also: for therefore am I sent."

And Jesus went about all Galilee, teaching in their synagogues, and
preaching the gospel of the kingdom, and healing all manner of sickness
and all manner of disease among the people. And his fame went throughout all Syria: and they brought unto him all sick people that were taken
with divers diseases and torments, and those which were possessed with
devils, and those which were lunatick, and those that had the palsy; and
he healed them.

And there came a leper to him, beseeching him, and kneeling down
to him, and saying unto him, "If thou wilt, thou canst make me clean."
And Jesus, moved with compassion, put forth his hand, and touched
him, and saith unto him, "I will; be thou clean." And as soon as he had
spoken, immediately the leprosy departed from him, and he was cleansed.

And he straitly charged him, and forthwith sent him away; and saith
unto him, "See thou say nothing to any man: but go thy way, shew thyself to the priest, and offer for thy cleansing those things which Moses
commanded, for a testimony unto them."

But he went out, and began to publish it much, and to blaze abroad
the matter, insomuch that Jesus could no more openly enter into the
city, and he withdrew himself into the wilderness, and prayed.

*Works of healing*

And again he entered into Capernaum after some days; and it was noised that he was in the house. And it came to pass, as he was teaching, that there were Pharisees and doctors of the law sitting by, which were come out of every town of Galilee, and Judæa, and Jerusalem: and the power of the Lord was present to heal them. And straightway many were gathered together, insomuch that there was no room to receive them, no, not so much as about the door: and he preached the word unto them.

And, behold, men brought in a bed a man which was taken with a palsy: and they sought means to bring him in, and to lay him before him. And when they could not find by what way they might bring him in because of the multitude, they went upon the housetop, and let him down through the tiling with his couch into the midst before Jesus.

And when he saw their faith, he said unto him, "Man, thy sins are forgiven thee."

And the scribes and the Pharisees began to reason, saying, "Who is this which speaketh blasphemies? Who can forgive sins, but God alone?"

But when Jesus perceived their thoughts, he answering said unto them, "What reason ye in your hearts? Whether is easier, to say, 'Thy sins be forgiven thee'; or to say, 'Rise up and walk'? But that ye may know that the Son of man hath power upon earth to forgive sins, (he said unto the sick of the palsy,) I say unto thee, 'Arise, and take up thy couch, and go into thine house.' "

And immediately he rose up before them, and took up that whereon he lay, and departed to his own house, glorifying God. And they were all amazed, and they glorified God, and were filled with fear, saying, "We have seen strange things to day."

And he went forth again by the sea side; and all the multitude resorted unto him, and he taught them.

*Matthew the publican*

And as Jesus passed forth from thence, he saw a man, named Matthew, sitting at the receipt of custom: and he saith unto him, "Follow me." And he arose, and followed him.

And it came to pass, as Jesus sat at meat in the house, behold, many publicans and sinners came and sat down with him and his disciples. And when the Pharisees saw it, they said unto his disciples, "Why eateth your Master with publicans and sinners?"

But when Jesus heard that, he said unto them,

*"They that be whole need not a physician, but they that are sick. But go ye*   *Jesus talks about fasting*
*and learn what that meaneth, 'I will have mercy, and not sacrifice': for I am*
*not come to call the righteous, but sinners to repentance."*

And the disciples of John and of the Pharisees used to fast: and they
come and say unto him, "Why do the disciples of John and of the
Pharisees fast, but thy disciples fast not?"
And Jesus said unto them,

*"Can the children of the bridechamber fast, while the bridegroom is with*
*them? as long as they have the bridegroom with them, they cannot fast. But*
*the days will come, when the bridegroom shall be taken away from them, and*
*then shall they fast in those days.*
*"No man also seweth a piece of new cloth on an old garment: else the new*
*piece that filled it up taketh away from the old, and the rent is made worse.*
*"And no man putteth new wine into old bottles; else the new wine doth*
*burst the bottles, and the wine is spilled, and the bottles will be marred: but*
*new wine must be put into new bottles."*

After this there was a feast of the Jews; and Jesus went up to Jeru-   *Healing on the sabbath*
salem. Now there is at Jerusalem by the sheep market a pool, which is
called in the Hebrew tongue Bethesda, having five porches. In these lay
a great multitude of impotent folk, of blind, halt, withered, waiting for
the moving of the water. And a certain man was there, which had an
infirmity thirty and eight years. When Jesus saw him lie, and knew that
he had been now a long time in that case, he saith unto him, "Wilt thou
be made whole?"
The impotent man answered him, "Sir, I have no man, when the
water is troubled, to put me into the pool: but while I am coming, another steppeth down before me."
Jesus saith unto him, "Rise, take up thy bed, and walk."
And immediately the man was made whole, and took up his bed, and
walked: and on the same day was the sabbath.
The Jews therefore said unto him that was cured, "It is the sabbath
day: it is not lawful for thee to carry thy bed."
He answered them, "He that made me whole, the same said unto me,
'Take up thy bed, and walk.' "

*Jesus tells who he is*      And he that was healed wist not who it was: for Jesus had conveyed himself away, a multitude being in that place.

Afterward Jesus findeth him in the temple, and said unto him, "Behold, thou art made whole: sin no more, lest a worse thing come unto thee." The man departed, and told the Jews that it was Jesus, which had made him whole.

And therefore did the Jews persecute Jesus, and sought to slay him, because he had done these things on the sabbath day.

But Jesus answered them, "My Father worketh hitherto, and I work." Therefore the Jews sought the more to kill him, because he not only had broken the sabbath, but said also that God was his Father, making himself equal with God.

Then answered Jesus and said unto them, "Verily, verily, I say unto you, He that heareth my word, and believeth on him that sent me, hath everlasting life, and shall not come into condemnation; but is passed from death unto life. I can of mine own self do nothing: as I hear, I judge: and my judgment is just; because I seek not mine own will, but the will of the Father which hath sent me. If I bear witness of myself, my witness is not true. There is another that beareth witness of me; and I know that the witness which he witnesseth of me is true. Ye sent unto John, and he bare witness unto the truth. He was a burning and a shining light: and ye were willing for a season to rejoice in his light. But I have greater witness than that of John: for the works which the Father hath given me to finish, the same works that I do, bear witness of me, that the Father hath sent me. And the Father himself, which hath sent me, hath borne witness of me. Ye have neither heard his voice at any time, nor seen his shape. And ye have not his word abiding in you: for whom he hath sent, him ye believe not.

"Search the scriptures; for in them ye think ye have eternal life: and they are they which testify of me. And ye will not come to me, that ye might have life. I receive not honour from men. But I know you, that ye have not the love of God in you. I am come in my Father's name, and ye receive me not: if another shall come in his own name, him ye will receive. How can ye believe, which receive honour one of another, and seek not the honour that cometh from God only? Do not think that I will accuse you to the Father: there is one that accuseth you, even Moses, in

whom ye trust. For had ye believed Moses, ye would have believed me:
for he wrote of me. But if ye believe not his writings, how shall ye believe
my words?"

At that time Jesus went on the sabbath day through the corn; and
his disciples were an hungred, and began to pluck the ears of corn, and
did eat, rubbing them in their hands. But when the Pharisees saw it,
they said unto him, "Behold, thy disciples do that which is not lawful to
do upon the sabbath day."

And he said unto them, "The sabbath was made for man, and not
man for the sabbath."

And it came to pass also on another sabbath, that he entered into the
synagogue and taught: and there was a man whose right hand was
withered. And the scribes and Pharisees watched him, whether he would
heal on the sabbath day; that they might find an accusation against him.
But he knew their thoughts, and said to the man which had the withered
hand, "Rise up, and stand forth in the midst." And he arose and stood
forth.

Then said Jesus unto them, "I will ask you one thing; Is it lawful on
the sabbath days to do good, or to do evil? to save life, or to destroy it?"
And he said unto them,

*"What man shall there be among you, that shall have one sheep, and if it
fall into a pit on the sabbath day, will he not lay hold on it, and lift it out?
How much then is a man better than a sheep? Wherefore it is lawful to do
well on the sabbath days."*

And looking round about upon them all, he said unto the man,
"Stretch forth thy hand." And he did so: and his hand was restored
whole as the other.

And they were filled with madness; and communed one with another
what they might do to Jesus.

But Jesus withdrew himself with his disciples to the sea: and a great
multitude from Galilee followed him, and from Judæa, and from Jerusalem, and from Idumæa, and from beyond Jordan; and they about Tyre
and Sidon, a great multitude, when they had heard what great things he
did, came unto him.

And he spake to his disciples, that a small ship should wait on him

*The twelve apostles* because of the multitude, lest they should throng him. For he had healed many; insomuch that they pressed upon him for to touch him, for there went virtue out of him, and healed them all.

He charged them that they should not make him known: that it might be fulfilled which was spoken by Esaias the prophet, saying,

Behold my servant, whom I have chosen;
My beloved, in whom my soul is well pleased:
I will put my spirit upon him,
And he shall shew judgment to the Gentiles.
He shall not strive, nor cry;
Neither shall any man hear his voice in the streets.
A bruised reed shall he not break,
And smoking flax shall he not quench,
Till he send forth judgment unto victory.
And in his name shall the Gentiles trust.

*The sermon on the mount*

And it came to pass in those days, that he went out into a mountain to pray, and continued all night in prayer to God. And when it was day, he called unto him his disciples: and of them he chose twelve, whom also he named apostles; that they should be with him, and that he might send them forth to preach, and to have power to heal sicknesses. Now the names of the twelve apostles are these; The first, Simon, who is called Peter, and Andrew his brother; James the son of Zebedee, and John his brother; Philip, and Bartholomew; Thomas, and Matthew the publican; James the son of Alphæus, and Lebbæus, whose surname was Thaddæus; Simon the Canaanite, and Judas Iscariot, who also betrayed him.

And he came down with them, and stood in the plain, and the company of his disciples, and a great multitude of people which came to hear him, and to be healed of their diseases.

And seeing the multitudes, he went up into a mountain: and when he was set, his disciples came unto him: and he opened his mouth, and taught them, saying,

"Blessed are the poor in spirit:
For their's is the kingdom of heaven.
Blessed are they that mourn:

For they shall be comforted.
Blessed are the meek:
For they shall inherit the earth.
Blessed are they which do hunger and thirst after righteousness:
For they shall be filled.
Blessed are the merciful:
For they shall obtain mercy.
Blessed are the pure in heart:
For they shall see God.
Blessed are the peacemakers:
For they shall be called the children of God.
Blessed are they which are persecuted for righteousness' sake:
For their's is the kingdom of heaven.
Blessed are ye, when men shall revile you, and persecute you,
And shall say all manner of evil against you falsely, for my sake.
Rejoice, and be exceeding glad: for great is your reward in heaven:
For so persecuted they the prophets which were before you.

But woe unto you that are rich!
For ye have received your consolation.
Woe unto you that are full!
For ye shall hunger.
Woe unto you that laugh now!
For ye shall mourn and weep.
Woe unto you, when all men shall speak well of you!
For so did their fathers to the false prophets.

"Ye are the salt of the earth: but if the salt have lost his savour, wherewith shall it be salted? it is thenceforth good for nothing, but to be cast out, and to be trodden under foot of men.

"Ye are the light of the world. A city that is set on an hill cannot be hid. Neither do men light a candle, and put it under a bushel, but on a candlestick; and it giveth light unto all that are in the house. Let your light so shine before men, that they may see your good works, and glorify your Father which is in heaven.

"Think not that I am come to destroy the law, or the prophets: I am not come to destroy, but to fulfil. For verily I say unto you, Till heaven and earth pass, one jot or one tittle shall in no wise pass from the law, till all be fulfilled. Whosoever therefore shall break one of these least commandments, and shall teach men so, he shall be called the least in the kingdom of heaven: but whosoever shall do and teach them, the same shall be called great in the kingdom of heaven. For I say unto you, Except your righteousness shall exceed the righteousness of the scribes and Pharisees, ye shall in no case enter into the kingdom of heaven.

"Ye have heard that it was said by them of old time, 'Thou shalt not kill'; and 'whosoever shall kill shall be in danger of the judgment': but I say unto you, Whosoever is angry with his brother without a cause shall be in danger of the judgment. Therefore if thou bring thy gift to the altar, and there rememberest that thy brother hath ought against thee; leave there thy gift before the altar, and go thy way; first be reconciled to thy brother, and then come and offer thy gift.

"Ye have heard that it was said by them of old time, 'Thou shalt not commit adultery': but I say unto you, Whosoever looketh on a woman to lust after her hath committed adultery with her already in his heart.

"Again, ye have heard that it hath been said by them of old time, 'Thou shalt not forswear thyself, but shalt perform unto the Lord thine oaths': but I say unto you, Swear not at all; neither by heaven; for it is God's throne: nor by the earth; for it is his footstool: neither by Jerusalem; for it is the city of the great King. Neither shalt thou swear by thy head, because thou canst not make one hair white or black.

"Ye have heard that it hath been said, 'An eye for an eye, and a tooth for a tooth': but I say unto you, Resist not evil: but whosoever shall smite thee on thy right cheek, turn to him the other also. And if any man will sue thee at the law, and take away thy coat, let him have thy cloke also. And whosoever shall compel thee to go a mile, go with him twain. Give to him that asketh thee, and from him that would borrow of thee turn not thou away.

"Ye have heard that it hath been said, 'Thou shalt love thy neighbour, and hate thine enemy.' But I say unto you, Love your enemies, bless them that curse you, do good to them that hate you, and pray for them which despitefully use you, and persecute you; that ye may be the children of your Father which is in heaven: for he maketh his sun to rise on the evil and on the good, and sendeth rain on the just and on the unjust. For if ye love them which love you, what reward have ye? do not even the publicans the same? And if ye salute your brethren only, what do ye more than others? do not even the publicans so?

"And if ye lend to them of whom ye hope to receive, what thank have ye? for sinners also lend to sinners, to receive as much again. But love ye your enemies, and do good, and lend, hoping for nothing again; and your reward shall be great, and ye shall be the children of the Highest: for he is kind unto the unthankful and to the evil. Be ye therefore merciful, as your Father also is merciful.

"Take heed that ye do not your alms before men, to be seen of them: otherwise ye have no reward of your Father which is in heaven. Therefore when thou doest thine alms, do not sound a trumpet before thee, as the hypocrites do in the synagogues and in the streets, that they may have glory of men. Verily I say unto you, They have their reward. But when thou doest alms, let not thy left hand know what thy right hand doeth: that thine alms may be in secret: and thy Father which seeth in secret himself shall reward thee openly.

"And when thou prayest, thou shalt not be as the hypocrites are: for they love to pray standing in the synagogues and in the corners of the streets, that they may be seen of men. Verily I say unto you, They have their reward. But thou, when thou prayest, enter into thy closet, and when thou hast shut thy door, pray to thy Father which is in secret; and thy Father which seeth in secret shall reward thee openly. But when ye pray, use not vain repetitions, as the heathen do: for they think that they shall be heard for their much speaking. Be not ye therefore like unto them: for your Father knoweth what things ye have need of, before ye ask him.

"Moreover when ye fast, be not, as the hypocrites, of a sad countenance: for they disfigure their faces, that they may appear unto men to fast. Verily I say unto you, They have their reward. But thou, when thou fastest, anoint thine head, and wash thy face; that thou appear not unto men to fast, but unto thy Father which is in secret: and thy Father, which seeth in secret, shall reward thee openly.

"Lay not up for yourselves treasures upon earth, where moth and rust doth corrupt, and where thieves break through and steal: but lay up for yourselves treasures in heaven, where neither moth nor rust doth corrupt, and where thieves do not break through nor steal: for where your treasure is, there will your heart be also.

"The light of the body is the eye: if therefore thine eye be single, thy whole body shall be full of light. But if thine eye be evil, thy whole body shall be full of darkness. If therefore the light that is in thee be darkness, how great is that darkness! No man can serve two masters: for either he will hate the one, and love the other; or else he will hold to the one, and despise the other. Ye cannot serve God and mammon.

"Therefore I say unto you, Take no thought for your life, what ye shall eat, or what ye shall drink; nor yet for your body, what ye shall put on. Is not the life more than meat, and the body than raiment? Behold the fowls of the air: for they sow not, neither do they reap, nor gather into barns; yet your heavenly Father feedeth them. Are ye not much better than they? Which of you by taking thought can add one cubit unto his stature? And why take ye thought for raiment? Consider the lilies of the field, how they grow; they toil not, neither do they spin: and yet I say unto you, that even Solomon in all his glory was not arrayed like one of these. Wherefore, if God so clothe the grass of the field, which to day is and to morrow is cast into the oven, shall he not much more clothe you, O ye of little faith? Therefore take no thought, saying, 'What shall we eat?' or, 'What shall we drink?' or, 'Wherewithal shall we be clothed?' for your heavenly Father knoweth that ye have need of all these things. Neither be ye of doubtful mind, but seek ye first the kingdom of God, and his righteousness; and all these things shall be added unto you. Take therefore no thought for the morrow: for the morrow shall take thought for the things of itself. Sufficient unto the day is the evil thereof.

"Judge not, and ye shall not be judged: condemn not, and ye shall not be condemned: forgive, and ye shall be forgiven: give, and it shall be given unto you; good measure, pressed down, and shaken together, and running over, shall men give into your bosom. For with the same measure that ye mete withal it shall be measured to you again."

And he spake a parable unto them,

*"Can the blind lead the blind? shall they not both fall into the ditch? The disciple is not above his master: but every one that is perfect shall be as his*

[ 28 ]

*master. And why beholdest thou the mote that is in thy brother's eye, but considerest not the beam that is in thine own eye? Or how wilt thou say to thy brother, 'Let me pull out the mote out of thine eye'; and, behold, a beam is in thine own eye? Thou hypocrite, first cast out the beam out of thine own eye; and then shalt thou see clearly to cast out the mote out of thy brother's eye.*

*"Beware of false prophets, which come to you in sheep's clothing, but inwardly they are ravening wolves. Ye shall know them by their fruits. Do men gather grapes of thorns, or figs of thistles? Even so every good tree bringeth forth good fruit; but a corrupt tree bringeth forth evil fruit. A good tree cannot bring forth evil fruit, neither can a corrupt tree bring forth good fruit. Every tree that bringeth not forth good fruit is hewn down, and cast into the fire. Wherefore by their fruits ye shall know them. A good man out of the good treasure of his heart bringeth forth that which is good; and an evil man out of the evil treasure of his heart bringeth forth that which is evil: for of the abundance of the heart his mouth speaketh. But I say unto you, That every idle word that men shall speak, they shall give account thereof. For by thy words thou shalt be justified, and by thy words thou shalt be condemned.*

"Be ye therefore perfect, even as your Father which is in heaven is perfect. And as ye would that men should do to you, do ye also to them likewise.

"Enter ye in at the strait gate: for wide is the gate, and broad is the way, that leadeth to destruction, and many there be which go in thereat: because strait is the gate, and narrow is the way, which leadeth unto life, and few there be that find it.

"Not every one that saith unto me, 'Lord, Lord,' shall enter into the kingdom of heaven; but he that doeth the will of my Father which is in heaven. Many will say to me in that day, 'Lord, Lord, have we not prophesied in thy name? and in thy name have cast out devils? and in thy name done many wonderful works?' And then will I profess unto them, 'I never knew you: depart from me, ye that work iniquity.'

*"Therefore whosoever heareth these sayings of mine, and doeth them, I will liken him unto a wise man, which built his house upon a rock: and the rain descended, and the floods came, and the winds blew, and beat upon that house; and it fell not: for it was founded upon a rock. And every one that*

*The sermon on the mount*

*heareth these sayings of mine, and doeth them not, shall be likened unto a foolish man, which built his house upon the sand: and the rain descended, and the floods came, and the winds blew, and beat upon that house; and it fell: and great was the fall of it."*

And it came to pass, when Jesus had ended these sayings, the people were astonished at his doctrine: for he taught them as one having authority.

When he was come down from the mountain, great multitudes followed him. And he went round about the villages, teaching. "Come unto me, all ye that labour and are heavy laden, and I will give you rest. Take my yoke upon you, and learn of me; for I am meek and lowly in heart: and ye shall find rest unto your souls. For my yoke is easy, and my burden is light."

*The centurion's servant healed*

And when Jesus was entered into Capernaum, a certain centurion's servant, who was dear unto him, was sick, and ready to die. And when he heard of Jesus, he sent unto him the elders of the Jews, beseeching him that he would come and heal his servant. And when they came to Jesus, they besought him instantly, saying, that he was worthy for whom he should do this: "For he loveth our nation, and he hath built us a synagogue."

And Jesus saith, "I will come and heal him."

Then Jesus went with them. And when he was now not far from the house, the centurion sent friends to him, saying unto him, "Lord, trouble not thyself: for I am not worthy that thou shouldest enter under my roof: wherefore neither thought I myself worthy to come unto thee: but say in a word, and my servant shall be healed. For I also am a man set under authority, having under me soldiers, and I say unto one, 'Go,' and he goeth; and to another, 'Come,' and he cometh; and to my servant, 'Do this,' and he doeth it."

When Jesus heard these things, he marvelled at him, and turned him about, and said unto the people that followed him, "I say unto you, I have not found so great faith, no, not in Israel."

And Jesus said unto the centurion, "Go thy way; and as thou hast believed, so be it done unto thee." And his servant was healed in the selfsame hour.

And it came to pass the day after, that he went into a city called Nain; *The widow's son raised* and many of his disciples went with him, and much people. Now when *from the dead* he came nigh to the gate of the city, behold, there was a dead man carried out, the only son of his mother, and she was a widow: and much people of the city was with her. And when the Lord saw her, he had compassion on her, and said unto her, "Weep not."

And he came and touched the bier: and they that bare him stood still. And he said, "Young man, I say unto thee, Arise."

And he that was dead sat up, and began to speak. And he delivered him to his mother.

And there came a fear on all: and they glorified God, saying, "A great prophet is risen up among us"; and, "God hath visited his people." And this rumour of him went forth throughout all Judæa, and throughout all the region round about.

Now when John had heard the works of Christ, he sent two of his *John's disciples sent to* disciples, and said unto him, "Art thou he that should come, or do we *Jesus* look for another?"

When the men were come unto him, they said, "John Baptist hath sent us unto thee, saying, 'Art thou he that should come? or look we for another?'" And in that same hour he cured many of their infirmities and plagues, and of evil spirits; and unto many that were blind he gave sight.

Then Jesus answering said unto them, "Go your way, and tell John what things ye have seen and heard; how that the blind see, the lame walk, the lepers are cleansed, the deaf hear, the dead are raised, to the poor the gospel is preached. And blessed is he, whosoever shall not be offended in me."

And when the messengers of John were departed, he began to speak unto the people concerning John, "What went ye out into the wilderness for to see? A reed shaken with the wind? But what went ye out for to see? A man clothed in soft raiment? Behold, they which are gorgeously apparelled, and live delicately, are in kings' courts. But what went ye out for to see? A prophet? Yea, I say unto you, and much more than a prophet. This is he, of whom it is written, 'Behold, I send my messenger before thy face, which shall prepare thy way before thee.' For I say unto you, Among those that are born of women there is not a greater prophet

than John the Baptist: but he that is least in the kingdom of God is greater than he."

And all the people that heard him, and the publicans, justified God, being baptized with the baptism of John. But the Pharisees and lawyers rejected the counsel of God against themselves, being not baptized of him.

And one of the Pharisees desired him that he would eat with him. And he went into the Pharisee's house, and sat down to meat.

And, behold, a woman in the city, which was a sinner, when she knew that Jesus sat at meat in the Pharisee's house, brought an alabaster box of ointment, and stood at his feet behind him weeping, and began to wash his feet with tears, and did wipe them with the hairs of her head, and kissed his feet, and anointed them with the ointment.

Now when the Pharisee which had bidden him saw it, he spake within himself, saying, "This man, if he were a prophet, would have known who and what manner of woman this is that toucheth him: for she is a sinner."

And Jesus answering said unto him, "Simon, I have somewhat to say unto thee."

And he saith, "Master, say on."

*"There was a certain creditor which had two debtors: the one owed five hundred pence, and the other fifty. And when they had nothing to pay, he frankly forgave them both. Tell me therefore, which of them will love him most?"*

*Simon answered and said, "I suppose that he, to whom he forgave most."*

*And he said unto him, "Thou hast rightly judged."*

And he turned to the woman, and said unto Simon, "Seest thou this woman? I entered into thine house, thou gavest me no water for my feet: but she hath washed my feet with tears, and wiped them with the hairs of her head. Thou gavest me no kiss: but this woman since the time I came in hath not ceased to kiss my feet. My head with oil thou didst not anoint: but this woman hath anointed my feet with ointment. Wherefore I say unto thee, Her sins, which are many, are forgiven; for she loved much: but to whom little is forgiven, the same loveth little."

And he said unto her, "Thy sins are forgiven."

And they that sat at meat with him began to say within themselves, "Who is this that forgiveth sins also?"

*Jesus reproves the Pharisees*

And he said to the woman, "Thy faith hath saved thee; go in peace."

And it came to pass afterward, that he went throughout every city and village, preaching and shewing the glad tidings of the kingdom of God: and the twelve were with him, and certain women, which had been healed of evil spirits and infirmities, Mary called Magdalene, and Joanna, and Susanna, and many others, which ministered unto him of their substance.

And they went into an house. And the multitude cometh together again, so that they could not so much as eat bread. And when his friends heard of it, they went out to lay hold on him: for they said, "He is beside himself."

Then was brought unto him one possessed with a devil, blind, and dumb: and he healed him, insomuch that the blind and dumb both spake and saw.

And all the people were amazed, and said, "Is not this the son of David?"

But when the Pharisees heard it, they said, "This fellow doth not cast out devils, but by Beelzebub the prince of the devils."

And Jesus knew their thoughts, and said unto them, "Every kingdom divided against itself is brought to desolation; and every city or house divided against itself shall not stand: and if Satan cast out Satan, he is divided against himself; how shall then his kingdom stand? And if I by Beelzebub cast out devils, by whom do your children cast them out? therefore they shall be your judges. But if I cast out devils by the Spirit of God, then the kingdom of God is come unto you. He that is not with me is against me; and he that gathereth not with me scattereth abroad. Either make the tree good, and his fruit good; or else make the tree corrupt, and his fruit corrupt: for the tree is known by his fruit.

"O generation of vipers, how can ye, being evil, speak good things? for out of the abundance of the heart the mouth speaketh. A good man out of the good treasure of the heart bringeth forth good things: and an evil man out of the evil treasure bringeth forth evil things. But I say unto you, Every idle word that men shall speak, they shall give account thereof in the day of judgment. For by thy words thou shalt be justified, and by thy words thou shalt be condemned."

Then certain of the scribes and of the Pharisees answered, saying, "Master, we would see a sign from thee."

But he answered and said unto them, "An evil and adulterous generation seeketh after a sign; and there shall no sign be given to it, but the sign of the prophet Jonas: for as Jonas was three days and three nights in the whale's belly; so shall the Son of man be three days and three nights in the heart of the earth. The men of Nineveh shall rise in judgment with this generation, and shall condemn it: because they repented at the preaching of Jonas; and, behold, a greater than Jonas is here."

While he yet talked to the people, behold, his mother and his brethren stood without, and could not come at him for the press. And it was told him by certain which said, "Thy mother and thy brethren stand without, desiring to see thee."

And he answered and said unto them, "My mother and my brethren are these which hear the word of God, and do it."

The same day went Jesus out of the house, and sat by the sea side. And great multitudes were gathered together unto him, so that he went into a ship, and sat; and the whole multitude was by the sea on the land. And he taught them many things by parables, and said unto them in his doctrine, "Hearken;

"*Behold, a sower went forth to sow; and when he sowed, some seeds fell by the way side, and the fowls came and devoured them up: some fell upon stony places, where they had not much earth: and forthwith they sprung up, because they had no deepness of earth: and when the sun was up, they were scorched; and because they had no root, they withered away. And some fell among thorns; and the thorns sprung up, and choked them: but other fell into good ground, and brought forth fruit, some an hundredfold, some sixtyfold, some thirtyfold.*

"*Who hath ears to hear, let him hear.*

"*Hear ye therefore the parable of the sower. When any one heareth the word of the kingdom, and understandeth it not, then cometh the wicked one, and catcheth away that which was sown in his heart. This is he which*

[ 34 ]

*received seed by the way side. But he that received the seed into stony places, the same is he that heareth the word, and anon with joy receiveth it; yet hath he not root in himself, but dureth for a while: for when tribulation or persecution ariseth because of the word, by and by he is offended. He also that received seed among the thorns is he that heareth the word; and the care of this world, and the deceitfulness of riches, choke the word, and he becometh unfruitful. But he that received seed into the good ground is he that heareth the word, and understandeth it; which also beareth fruit, and bringeth forth, some an hundredfold, some sixty, some thirty."*

And he said unto them,

*"Is a candle brought to be put under a bushel, or under a bed? and not to be set on a candlestick? For there is nothing hid, which shall not be manifested; neither was any thing kept secret, but that it should come abroad. If any man have ears to hear, let him hear."*

Another parable put he forth unto them, saying,

*"The kingdom of heaven is likened unto a man which sowed good seed in his field: but while men slept, his enemy came and sowed tares among the wheat, and went his way. But when the blade was sprung up, and brought forth fruit, then appeared the tares also. So the servants of the householder came and said unto him, 'Sir, didst not thou sow good seed in thy field? from whence then hath it tares?'*

*"He said unto them, 'An enemy hath done this.'*

*"The servants said unto him, 'Wilt thou then that we go and gather them up?'*

*"But he said, 'Nay; lest while ye gather up the tares, ye root up also the wheat with them. Let both grow together until the harvest: and in the time of harvest I will say to the reapers, Gather ye together first the tares, and bind them in bundles to burn them: but gather the wheat into my barn.'"*

Then Jesus sent the multitude away, and went into the house: and his disciples came unto him, saying, "Declare unto us the parable of the tares of the field."

He answered and said unto them,

"*He that soweth the good seed is the Son of man; the field is the world; the good seed are the children of the kingdom; but the tares are the children of the wicked one; the enemy that sowed them is the devil; the harvest is the end of the world; and the reapers are the angels. As therefore the tares are gathered and burned in the fire; so shall it be in the end of this world. The Son of man shall send forth his angels, and they shall gather out of his kingdom all things that offend, and them which do iniquity; and shall cast them into a furnace of fire: there shall be wailing and gnashing of teeth. Then shall the righteous shine forth as the sun in the kingdom of their Father. Who hath ears to hear, let him hear.*"

Jesus saith unto them, "Have ye understood all these things?"

They say unto him, "Yea, Lord."

Then said he unto them, "Therefore every scribe which is instructed unto the kingdom of heaven is like unto a man that is an householder, which bringeth forth out of his treasure things new and old."

And he began again to teach by the sea side. And he said,

"*So is the kingdom of God, as if a man should cast seed into the ground; and should sleep, and rise night and day, and the seed should spring and grow up, he knoweth not how. For the earth bringeth forth fruit of herself; first the blade, then the ear, after that the full corn in the ear. But when the fruit is brought forth, immediately he putteth in the sickle, because the harvest is come.*"

Another parable spake he unto them:

"*The kingdom of heaven is like unto leaven, which a woman took, and hid in three measures of meal, till the whole was leavened.*"

And he said,

"*Whereunto shall we liken the kingdom of God? or with what comparison shall we compare it? It is like a grain of mustard seed, which, when it is sown in the earth, is less than all the seeds that be in the earth: but when it is sown, it groweth up, and becometh greater than all herbs, and shooteth out great branches; so that the fowls of the air may lodge under the shadow of it.*"

Again,

*"The kingdom of heaven is like unto treasure hid in a field; the which when a man hath found, he hideth, and for joy thereof goeth and selleth all that he hath, and buyeth that field."*

Again,

*"The kingdom of heaven is like unto a merchant man, seeking goodly pearls: who, when he had found one pearl of great price, went and sold all that he had, and bought it."*

Again,

*"The kingdom of heaven is like unto a net, that was cast into the sea, and gathered of every kind: which, when it was full, they drew to shore, and sat down, and gathered the good into vessels, but cast the bad away."*

With many such parables spake he the word unto them, as they were able to hear it. But without a parable spake he not unto them: and when they were alone, he expounded all things to his disciples. And he said unto them, "Unto you it is given to know the mystery of the kingdom of God: but unto them that are without, all these things are done in parables."

And it came to pass, that when Jesus had finished these parables, he departed thence. And the same day, when the even was come, he saith unto them, "Let us pass over unto the other side."

And when they had sent away the multitude, they took him even as he was in the ship. And there were also with him other little ships. And there arose a great storm of wind, and the waves beat into the ship, so that it was now full. And he was in the hinder part of the ship, asleep on a pillow: and they awake him, and say unto him, "Master, carest thou not that we perish?"

And he arose, and rebuked the wind, and said unto the sea, "Peace, be still." And the wind ceased, and there was a great calm.

And he said unto them, "Why are ye so fearful? how is it that ye have no faith?"

And they feared exceedingly, and said one to another, "What manner of man is this, that even the wind and the sea obey him?"

And when Jesus was passed over again by ship unto the other side, much people gathered unto him: and he was nigh unto the sea. And, behold, there cometh one of the rulers of the synagogue, Jairus by name; and when he saw him, he fell at his feet, and besought him greatly, saying, "My little daughter lieth at the point of death: I pray thee, come and lay thy hands on her, that she may be healed; and she shall live."

And Jesus went with him; and much people followed him, and thronged him.

There came from the ruler of the synagogue's house certain which said, "Thy daughter is dead: why troublest thou the Master any further?"

As soon as Jesus heard the word that was spoken, he saith unto the ruler of the synagogue, "Be not afraid, only believe."

And he suffered no man to follow him, save Peter, and James, and John the brother of James. And he cometh to the house of the ruler of the synagogue, and seeth the tumult, and them that wept and wailed greatly.

And when he was come in, he saith unto them, "Why make ye this ado, and weep? the damsel is not dead, but sleepeth."

And they laughed him to scorn. But when he had put them all out, he taketh the father and the mother of the damsel, and them that were with him, and entereth in where the damsel was lying. And he took the damsel by the hand, and said unto her, *Talitha cumi;* which is, being interpreted, "Damsel, I say unto thee, arise."

And straightway the damsel arose, and walked; for she was of the age of twelve years. And they were astonished with a great astonishment. And he charged them straitly that no man should know it; and commanded that something should be given her to eat.

And a woman having an issue of blood twelve years, which had spent all her living upon physicians, neither could be healed of any, came behind him, and touched the border of his garment: and immediately her issue of blood stanched.

And Jesus said, "Who touched me?"

When all denied, Peter and they that were with him said, "Master, the multitude throng thee and press thee, and sayest thou, 'Who touched me?'"

And Jesus said, "Somebody hath touched me: for I perceive that virtue is gone out of me."

And when the woman saw that she was not hid, she came trembling, *The apostles instructed* and falling down before him, she declared unto him before all the people for what cause she had touched him, and how she was healed immediately.

And he said unto her, "Daughter, be of good comfort: thy faith hath made thee whole; go in peace."

And he went out from thence, and came into his own country; and his disciples follow him. And when the sabbath day was come, he began to teach in the synagogue: and many hearing him were astonished, saying, "From whence hath this man these things? and what wisdom is this which is given unto him, that even such mighty works are wrought by his hands? Is not this the carpenter, the son of Mary, the brother of James, and Joses, and of Juda, and Simon? and are not his sisters here with us?" And they were offended at him.

But Jesus said unto them, "A prophet is not without honour, but in his own country, and among his own kin, and in his own house."

And he could there do no mighty work, save that he laid his hands upon a few sick folk, and healed them. And he marvelled because of their unbelief.

And Jesus went about all the cities and villages, teaching in their synagogues, and preaching the gospel of the kingdom, and healing every sickness and every disease among the people. But when he saw the multitudes, he was moved with compassion on them, because they fainted, and were scattered abroad, as sheep having no shepherd.

Then saith he unto his disciples, "The harvest truly is plenteous, but the labourers are few; pray ye therefore the Lord of the harvest, that he will send forth labourers into his harvest."

Then he called his twelve disciples together, and gave them power and authority over all devils, and to cure diseases, and began to send them forth by two and two, and he sent them to preach the kingdom of God, and to heal the sick; and commanded them that they should take nothing for their journey, save a staff only; no scrip, no bread, no money in their purse. And he commanded them, saying, "Into whatsoever city or town ye shall enter, enquire who in it is worthy; and there abide till ye go thence. And when ye come into an house, salute it. And if the house be worthy, let your peace come upon it: but if it be not worthy, let your peace return to you.

"Behold, I send you forth as sheep in the midst of wolves: be ye there-fore wise as serpents, and harmless as doves. But beware of men: for they will deliver you up to the councils, and they will scourge you in their synagogues; and ye shall be brought before governors and kings for my sake, for a testimony against them and the Gentiles. But when they deliver you up, take no thought how or what ye shall speak: for it shall be given you in that same hour what ye shall speak. For it is not ye that speak, but the Spirit of your Father which speaketh in you. The disciple is not above his master, nor the servant above his lord. It is enough for the disciple that he be as his master, and the servant as his lord. If they have called the master of the house Beelzebub, how much more shall they call them of his household? There is nothing covered, that shall not be revealed; and hid, that shall not be known. What I tell you in darkness, that speak ye in light: and what ye hear in the ear, that preach ye upon the housetops. And fear not them which kill the body, but are not able to kill the soul: but rather fear him which is able to destroy both soul and body. Are not two sparrows sold for a farthing? and one of them shall not fall on the ground without your Father. But the very hairs of your head are all numbered. Fear ye not therefore, ye are of more value than many sparrows. Whosoever therefore shall confess me before men, him will I confess also before my Father which is in heaven."

And they departed, and went through the towns, preaching the gospel, and healing every where.

And it came to pass, when Jesus had made an end of commanding his twelve disciples, he departed thence to teach and to preach in their cities.

And the apostles gathered themselves together unto Jesus, and told him all things, both what they had done, and what they had taught.

And he said unto them, "Come ye yourselves apart into a desert place, and rest a while": for there were many coming and going, and they had no leisure so much as to eat. And they departed into a desert place by ship privately. And the people saw them departing, and many knew him, and ran afoot thither out of all cities, and outwent them, and came together unto him. And Jesus, when he came out, saw much people, and was moved with compassion toward them: and began to teach them many things.

And when the day was now far spent, his disciples came unto him, and said, "This is a desert place, and now the time is far passed: send *Miracle of the five* them away, that they may go into the country round about, and into the *loaves and two fishes* villages, and buy themselves bread: for they have nothing to eat."

He answered and said unto them, "They need not depart; give ye them to eat."

And they say unto him, "Shall we go and buy two hundred penny-worth of bread, and give them to eat?"

He saith unto them, "How many loaves have ye? go and see."

And when they knew, they say, "Five, and two fishes."

And he commanded them to make all sit down by companies upon the green grass. And they sat down in ranks, by hundreds, and by fifties.

And when he had taken the five loaves and the two fishes, he looked up to heaven, and blessed, and brake the loaves, and gave them to his disciples to set before them; and the two fishes divided he among them all. And they did all eat, and were filled. And they took up twelve baskets full of the fragments, and of the fishes. And they that did eat of the loaves were about five thousand men.

Then those men, when they had seen the miracle that Jesus did, said, "This is of a truth that prophet that should come into the world."

Jesus therefore perceived that they would come and take him by force, to make him a king, and straightway Jesus constrained his disciples to get into a ship, and to go before him unto the other side, while he sent the multitudes away.

And when he had sent the multitudes away, he went up into a mountain apart to pray: and when the evening was come, he was there alone.

But the ship was now in the midst of the sea, tossed with waves: *Jesus walks on the sea* for the wind was contrary. And he saw them toiling in rowing. And in the fourth watch of the night Jesus went unto them, walking on the sea. And when the disciples saw him walking on the sea, they were troubled, saying, "It is a spirit"; and they cried out for fear.

But straightway Jesus spake unto them, saying, "Be of good cheer; it is I; be not afraid."

And Peter answered him and said, "Lord, if it be thou, bid me come unto thee on the water."

And he said, "Come."

And when Peter was come down out of the ship, he walked on the

Many are healed water, to go to Jesus. But when he saw the wind boisterous, he was afraid; and beginning to sink, he cried, saying, "Lord, save me."

And immediately Jesus stretched forth his hand, and caught him, and said unto him, "O thou of little faith, wherefore didst thou doubt?"

And when they were come into the ship, the wind ceased, and they were sore amazed in themselves beyond measure, and wondered. Then they that were in the ship came and worshipped him, saying, "Of a truth thou art the Son of God."

And when they had passed over, they came into the land of Gennesaret, and drew to the shore.

And when they were come out of the ship, straightway they knew him, and ran through that whole region round about, and began to carry about in beds those that were sick, where they heard he was. And whithersoever he entered, into villages, or cities, or country, they laid the sick in the streets, and besought him that they might touch if it were but the border of his garment: and as many as touched him were made whole.

The day following, when the people which stood on the other side of the sea saw that there was none other boat there, save that one whereinto his disciples were entered, and that Jesus went not with his disciples into the boat, but that his disciples were gone away alone; (Howbeit there came other boats from Tiberias nigh unto the place where they did eat bread, after that the Lord had given thanks:) When the people therefore saw that Jesus was not there, neither his disciples, they also took shipping, and came to Capernaum, seeking for Jesus. And when they had found him on the other side of the sea, they said unto him, "Rabbi, when camest thou hither?"

Jesus answered them and said, "Verily, verily, I say unto you, Ye seek me, not because ye saw the miracles, but because ye did eat of the loaves, and were filled.

*"Labour not for the meat which perisheth, but for that meat which endureth unto everlasting life, which the Son of man shall give unto you: for him hath God the Father sealed."*

*Then said they unto him, "What shall we do, that we might work the works of God?"*

[ 42 ]

Jesus answered and said unto them, "This is the work of God, that ye believe on him whom he hath sent." *The bread of life*

They said therefore unto him, "What sign shewest thou then, that we may see, and believe thee? what dost thou work? Our fathers did eat manna in the desert; as it is written, 'He gave them bread from heaven to eat.'"

Then Jesus said unto them, "Verily, verily, I say unto you, Moses gave you not that bread from heaven; but my Father giveth you the true bread from heaven. For the bread of God is he which cometh down from heaven, and giveth life unto the world."

Then said they unto him, "Lord, evermore give us this bread."

And Jesus said unto them, "I am the bread of life: he that cometh to me shall never hunger; and he that believeth on me shall never thirst. But I said unto you, that ye also have seen me, and believe not. All that the Father giveth me shall come to me; and him that cometh to me I will in no wise cast out. For I came down from heaven, not to do mine own will, but the will of him that sent me. And this is the Father's will which hath sent me, that of all which he hath given me I should lose nothing, but should raise it up again at the last day. And this is the will of him that sent me, that every one which seeth the Son, and believeth on him, may have everlasting life: and I will raise him up at the last day."

The Jews then murmured at him, because he said, "I am the bread which came down from heaven." And they said, "Is not this Jesus, the son of Joseph, whose father and mother we know? how is it then that he saith, 'I came down from heaven'?"

Jesus therefore answered and said unto them, "Murmur not among yourselves. No man can come to me, except the Father which hath sent me draw him: and I will raise him up at the last day. It is written in the prophets, 'And they shall be all taught of God.' Every man therefore that hath heard, and hath learned of the Father, cometh unto me. Not that any man hath seen the Father, save he which is of God, he hath seen the Father. Verily, verily, I say unto you, He that believeth on me hath everlasting life. I am that bread of life. Your fathers did eat manna in the wilderness, and are dead. This is the bread which cometh down from heaven, that a man may eat thereof, and not die. I am the living bread which came down from heaven: if any man eat of this bread, he shall live for ever: and the bread that I will give is my flesh, which I will give for the life of the world."

*The Lord's Supper
foreshadowed*

*The Jews therefore strove among themselves, saying, "How can this man give us his flesh to eat?"*

*Then Jesus said unto them, "Verily, verily, I say unto you, Except ye eat the flesh of the Son of man, and drink his blood, ye have no life in you. Whoso eateth my flesh, and drinketh my blood, hath eternal life; and I will raise him up at the last day. For my flesh is meat indeed, and my blood is drink indeed. He that eateth my flesh, and drinketh my blood, dwelleth in me, and I in him. As the living Father hath sent me, and I live by the Father: so he that eateth me, even he shall live by me. This is that bread which came down from heaven: not as your fathers did eat manna, and are dead: he that eateth of this bread shall live for ever."*

Many therefore of his disciples, when they had heard this, said, "This is an hard saying; who can hear it?"

When Jesus knew in himself that his disciples murmured at it, he said unto them, "Doth this offend you? What and if ye shall see the Son of man ascend up where he was before? It is the spirit that quickeneth; the flesh profiteth nothing: the words that I speak unto you, they are spirit, and they are life. But there are some of you that believe not."

For Jesus knew from the beginning who they were that believed not, and who should betray him. And he said, "Therefore said I unto you, that no man can come unto me, except it were given unto him of my Father."

*Many disciples depart
from Christ*

From that time many of his disciples went back, and walked no more with him.

Then said Jesus unto the twelve, "Will ye also go away?"

Then Simon Peter answered him, "Lord, to whom shall we go? thou hast the words of eternal life. And we believe, and are sure that thou art that Christ, the Son of the living God."

Then came together unto him the Pharisees, and certain of the scribes, which came from Jerusalem. And when they saw some of his disciples eat bread with defiled, that is to say, with unwashen, hands, they found fault. For the Pharisees, and all the Jews, except they wash their hands oft, eat not, holding the tradition of the elders. And when they come from the market, except they wash, they eat not. And many other things there be, which they have received to hold, as the washing of cups, and pots, brasen vessels, and of tables.

Then the Pharisees and scribes asked him, "Why walk not thy disciples according to the tradition of the elders, but eat bread with unwashen hands?"

He answered and said unto them, "Well hath Esaias prophesied of you hypocrites, as it is written,

> This people honoureth me with their lips,
> But their heart is far from me.
> Howbeit in vain do they worship me,
> Teaching for doctrines the commandments of men.

"For laying aside the commandment of God, ye hold the tradition of men, as the washing of pots and cups: and many other such like things ye do." And he said unto them, "Full well ye reject the commandment of God, that ye may keep your own tradition."

And when he had called all the people unto him, he said unto them,

*"Hearken unto me every one of you, and understand: There is nothing from without a man, that entering into him can defile him: but the things which come out of him, those are they that defile the man. If any man have ears to hear, let him hear."*

And when he was entered into the house from the people, his disciples asked him concerning the parable.

And he saith unto them, "Are ye so without understanding also? Do ye not perceive, that whatsoever thing from without entereth into the man, it cannot defile him; because it entereth not into his heart, but into the belly, and goeth out into the draught, purging all meats?"

And he said, "That which cometh out of the man, that defileth the man. But those things which proceed out of the mouth come forth from the heart; and they defile the man. For from within, out of the heart of men, proceed evil thoughts, adulteries, fornications, murders, thefts, covetousness, wickedness, deceit, lasciviousness, an evil eye, blasphemy, pride, foolishness: all these evil things come from within, and defile the man."

And from thence he arose, and went into the borders of Tyre and

Sidon, and entered into an house, and would have no man know it: but he could not be hid.

And again, departing from the coasts of Tyre and Sidon, he came unto the sea of Galilee, through the midst of the coasts of Decapolis, and went up into a mountain, and sat down there. And great multitudes came unto him, having with them those that were lame, blind, dumb, maimed, and many others, and cast them down at Jesus' feet; and he healed them: insomuch that the multitude wondered, when they saw the dumb to speak, the maimed to be whole, the lame to walk, and the blind to see: and they glorified the God of Israel.

And they bring unto him one that was deaf, and had an impediment in his speech; and they beseech him to put his hand upon him. And he took him aside from the multitude, and put his fingers into his ears, and he spit, and touched his tongue; and looking up to heaven, he sighed, and saith unto him, *Ephphatha,* that is, "Be opened." And straightway his ears were opened, and the string of his tongue was loosed, and he spake plain. And he charged them that they should tell no man: but the more he charged them, so much the more a great deal they published it; and were beyond measure astonished, saying, "He hath done all things well: he maketh both the deaf to hear, and the dumb to speak." And he sent away the multitude, and took ship, and came into the coasts of Magdala.

And the Pharisees came forth, and began to question with him, seeking of him a sign from heaven, tempting him. And he sighed deeply in his spirit, and saith, "Why doth this generation seek after a sign? verily I say unto you, There shall no sign be given unto this generation. When it is evening, ye say, 'It will be fair weather: for the sky is red.' And in the morning, 'It will be foul weather to day: for the sky is red and lowring.' "

And he said also to the people, "When ye see a cloud rise out of the west, straightway ye say, 'There cometh a shower'; and so it is. And when ye see the south wind blow, ye say, 'There will be heat'; and it cometh to pass. Ye hypocrites, ye can discern the face of the sky and of the earth; but how is it that ye do not discern this time?"

And he left them, and entering into the ship again departed to the other side.

Now the disciples had forgotten to take bread, neither had they in the ship with them more than one loaf.

And he charged them, saying, "Take heed, beware of the leaven of *The blind man restored to sight* the Pharisees, and of the leaven of Herod."

And they reasoned among themselves, saying, "It is because we have no bread."

And when Jesus knew it, he saith unto them, "Why reason ye, because ye have no bread? perceive ye not yet, neither understand? have ye your heart yet hardened? Having eyes, see ye not? and having ears, hear ye not? and do ye not remember? When I brake the five loaves among five thousand, how many baskets full of fragments took ye up?"

They say unto him, "Twelve."

"How is it that ye do not understand that I spake it not to you concerning bread, that ye should beware of the leaven of the Pharisees and of the Sadducees?" Then understood they how that he bade them beware of the doctrine of the Pharisees and the Sadducees.

And he cometh to Bethsaida; and they bring a blind man unto him, and besought him to touch him. And he took the blind man by the hand, and led him out of the town; and when he had spit on his eyes, and put his hands upon him, he asked him if he saw ought.

And he looked up, and said, "I see men as trees, walking."

After that he put his hands again upon his eyes, and made him look up: and he was restored, and saw every man clearly. And he sent him away to his house, saying, "Neither go into the town, nor tell it to any in the town."

And Jesus went out, and his disciples, into the towns of Cæsarea *Jesus' promise to Peter* Philippi: and by the way he asked his disciples, saying unto them, "Whom do men say that I am?"

And they answered, "John the Baptist: but some say, 'Elias'; and others, 'One of the prophets.'"

And he saith unto them, "But whom say ye that I am?"

Simon Peter answereth and saith, "Thou art the Christ, the Son of the living God."

And Jesus answered and said unto him, "Blessed art thou, Simon Barjona: for flesh and blood hath not revealed it unto thee, but my Father which is in heaven. And I say also unto thee, That thou art Peter, and upon this rock I will build my church; and the gates of hell shall not prevail against it. And I will give unto thee the keys of the kingdom

[ 47 ]

*Jesus warns of suffering to come*

of heaven: and whatsoever thou shalt bind on earth shall be bound in heaven: and whatsoever thou shalt loose on earth shall be loosed in heaven."

And he charged them that they should tell no man that he was Jesus the Christ.

And he began to teach them, that the Son of man must suffer many things, and be rejected of the elders, and of the chief priests, and scribes, and be killed, and after three days rise again. And he spake that saying openly. And Peter took him, and began to rebuke him. But when he had turned about and looked on his disciples, he rebuked Peter, saying, "Get thee behind me, Satan: for thou savourest not the things that be of God, but the things that be of men."

And when he had called the people unto him with his disciples also, he said unto them, "Whosoever will come after me, let him deny himself, and take up his cross daily, and follow me. And he that taketh not his cross, and followeth after me is not worthy of me. For whosoever will save his life shall lose it; but whosoever shall lose his life for my sake and the gospel's, the same shall save it. For what shall it profit a man, if he shall gain the whole world, and lose his own soul? Or what shall a man give in exchange for his soul?"

*The transfiguration*

And after six days Jesus taketh with him Peter, and James, and John, and leadeth them up into an high mountain apart by themselves: and he was transfigured before them. And his face did shine as the sun. And his raiment became shining, exceeding white as snow; so as no fuller on earth can white them.

And there appeared unto them Elias with Moses: and they were talking with Jesus. But Peter and they that were with him were heavy with sleep: and when they were awake, they saw his glory, and the two men that stood with him.

And Peter answered and said to Jesus, "Master, it is good for us to be here: and let us make three tabernacles; one for thee, and one for Moses, and one for Elias." For he wist not what to say; for they were sore afraid.

And there was a cloud that overshadowed them: and a voice came out of the cloud, saying, "This is my beloved Son in whom I am well pleased; hear ye him."

And Jesus came and touched them, and said, "Arise, and be not afraid."

*Jesus instructs his disciples in humility*

And when they had lifted up their eyes, they saw no man, save Jesus only.

And as they came down from the mountain, he charged them that they should tell no man what things they had seen, till the Son of man were risen from the dead. And they kept that saying with themselves, questioning one with another what the rising from the dead should mean.

And they departed thence, and passed through Galilee; and he would not that any man should know it. For he taught his disciples, and said unto them, "The Son of man is delivered into the hands of men, and they shall kill him; and after that he is killed, he shall rise the third day." But they understood not that saying, and were afraid to ask him.

And he came to Capernaum: and being in the house he asked them, "What was it that ye disputed among yourselves by the way?" But they held their peace: for by the way they had disputed among themselves, who should be the greatest.

And he sat down, and called the twelve, and saith unto them, "If any man desire to be first, the same shall be last of all, and servant of all."

And he took a child, and set him in the midst of them: and when he had taken him in his arms, he said unto them,

*"Verily, I say unto you, Except ye be converted, and become as little children, ye shall not enter into the kingdom of heaven. Whosoever therefore shall humble himself as this little child, the same is greatest in the kingdom of heaven. Whosoever shall receive one of such children in my name, receiveth me: and whosoever shall receive me, receiveth not me, but him that sent me. But whoso shall offend one of these little ones which believe in me, it were better for him that a millstone were hanged about his neck, and that he were drowned in the depth of the sea. Woe unto the world because of offences! for it must needs be that offences come; but woe to that man by whom the offence cometh! And whosoever shall give to drink unto one of these little ones a cup of cold water only in the name of a disciple, verily I say unto you, he shall in no wise lose his reward.*

"Moreover if thy brother shall trespass against thee, go and tell him his fault between thee and him alone: if he shall hear thee, thou hast gained thy brother. Verily I say unto you, Whatsoever ye shall bind on earth shall be bound in heaven: and whatsoever ye shall loose on earth shall be loosed in heaven.

"Again I say unto you, If two of you shall agree on earth as touching any thing that they shall ask, it shall be done for them of my Father which is in heaven. For where two or three are gathered together in my name, there am I in the midst of them."

Then came Peter to him, and said, "Lord, how oft shall my brother sin against me, and I forgive him? till seven times?"

Jesus saith unto him, "I say not unto thee, Until seven times: but, Until seventy times seven.

"*Therefore is the kingdom of heaven likened unto a certain king, which would take account of his servants. And when he had begun to reckon, one was brought unto him, which owed him ten thousand talents. But forasmuch as he had not to pay, his lord commanded him to be sold, and his wife, and children, and all that he had, and payment to be made. The servant therefore fell down, and worshipped him, saying, 'Lord, have patience with me, and I will pay thee all.' Then the lord of that servant was moved with compassion, and loosed him, and forgave him the debt.*

"*But the same servant went out, and found one of his fellowservants, which owed him an hundred pence: and he laid hands on him, and took him by the throat, saying, 'Pay me that thou owest.' And his fellowservant fell down at his feet, and besought him, saying, 'Have patience with me, and I will pay thee all.' And he would not: but went and cast him into prison, till he should pay the debt.*

"*So when his fellowservants saw what was done, they were very sorry, and came and told unto their lord all that was done. Then his lord, after that he had called him, said unto him, 'O thou wicked servant, I forgave thee all that debt, because thou desiredst me: shouldest not thou also have had compassion on thy fellowservant, even as I had pity on thee?' And his lord was wroth, and delivered him to the tormentors, till he should pay all that was due unto him.*

"*So likewise shall my heavenly Father do also unto you, if ye from your hearts forgive not every one his brother their trespasses.*"

# PALESTINE AT THE TIME OF CHRIST

## WITH A PLAN OF JERUSALEM

# KEY TO MAP

| | | | |
|---|---|---|---|
| Antonia, Tower of | *Jerusalem* | Hippicus | *Jerusalem* |
| Ascalon | A–2 | Jerusalem | B–2 |
| Azotus | A–2 | Jezreel | B–1 |
| Bethany | B–2 | Joppa | A–2 |
| Bethel | B–2 | Judaea | A–2 |
| Bethesda, Pool of | *Jerusalem* | Lower City | *Jerusalem* |
| Bethlehem | B–2 | Lydda | A–2 |
| Bethsaida | B–1 | Magdala | B–1 |
| Caesarea | A–1 | Mariamme (Mariamne) | *Jerusalem* |
| Cana | B–1 | Mediterranean Sea | A–2 |
| Capernaum | B–1 | Nain | B–1 |
| Carmel, Mount | A–1 | Nazareth | B–1 |
| Cedron, Valley of | *Jerusalem* | Olives, Mount of | *Jerusalem* |
| Dead Sea | B–2 | Peraea | B–2 |
| Decapolis | B–1 | Phasael | *Jerusalem* |
| Emmaus | A–2 | Phoenicia | B–1 |
| Galilee | B–1 | Salim | B–1, B–2 |
| Galilee, Sea of | B–1 | Samaria | B–2 |
| Gennesaret, Plain of | B–1 | Samaria (town) | B–2 |
| Gennesaret, Sea of, *see* Gali- | | Sharon, Plain of | A–2 |
| lee, Sea of | | Siloam, Pool of | *Jerusalem* |
| Gerizim, Mount | B–2 | Suburb | *Jerusalem* |
| Gethsemane | *Jerusalem* | Sychar | B–2 |
| Gihon | *Jerusalem* | Tabor, Mount | B–1 |
| Ginaea | B–1 | Temple | *Jerusalem* |
| Herod's Palace | *Jerusalem* | Tiberias | B–1 |
| Hinnom, Valley of | *Jerusalem* | Upper City | *Jerusalem* |

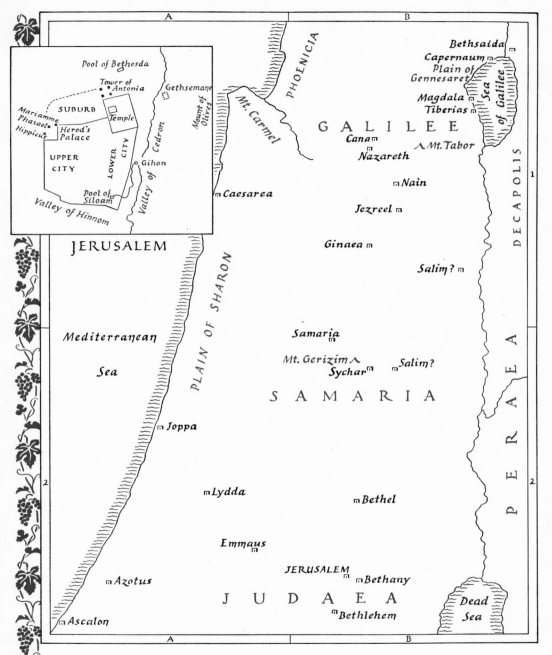

**Inset: JERUSALEM**

Pool of Bethesda

Tower of Antonia

Gethsemane

Mariamme
Phasael
Hippicus

SUBURB

Temple

Mount of Olives

Herod's Palace

UPPER CITY

LOWER CITY

Valley of Cedron

Gihon

Pool of Siloam

Valley of Hinnom

JERUSALEM

**Main map**

A

B

PHOENICIA

Bethsaida
Capernaum
Plain of Gennesaret

Mt. Carmel

Magdala
Tiberias

Sea of Galilee

GALILEE

DECAPOLIS

Cana

∧ Mt. Tabor

Nazareth

Caesarea

Nain

Jezreel

Ginaea

Salim?

1

PLAIN OF SHARON

Mediterranean

Sea

Samaria

Mt. Gerizim ∧
Sychar

Salim?

S A M A R I A

P E R A E A

Joppa

Lydda

Bethel

2

Emmaus

JERUSALEM

Bethany

Azotus

J U D A E A

Dead Sea

Ascalon

Bethlehem

A

B

PALESTINE AT THE TIME OF CHRIST

After these things Jesus walked in Galilee: for he would not walk in Jewry, because the Jews sought to kill him.

*Jesus teaches in the temple*

Now the Jews' feast of tabernacles was at hand. His brethren therefore said unto him, "Depart hence, and go into Judæa, that thy disciples also may see the works that thou doest. For there is no man that doeth any thing in secret, and he himself seeketh to be known openly. If thou do these things, shew thyself to the world." For neither did his brethren believe in him.

Then Jesus said unto them, "My time is not yet come, but your time is alway ready. The world cannot hate you; but me it hateth, because I testify of it, that the works thereof are evil. Go ye up unto this feast: I go not up yet unto this feast; for my time is not yet full come."

When he had said these words unto them, he abode still in Galilee.

But when his brethren were gone up, then went he also up unto the feast, not openly, but as it were in secret. Then the Jews sought him at the feast, and said, "Where is he?" And there was much murmuring among the people concerning him: for some said, "He is a good man": others said, "Nay; but he deceiveth the people." Howbeit no man spake openly of him for fear of the Jews.

Now about the midst of the feast Jesus went up into the temple, and taught.

And the Jews marvelled, saying, "How knoweth this man letters, having never learned?"

Jesus answered them, and said, "My doctrine is not mine, but his that sent me. If any man will do his will, he shall know of the doctrine, whether it be of God, or whether I speak of myself. He that speaketh of himself seeketh his own glory: but he that seeketh his glory that sent him, the same is true, and no unrighteousness is in him. Judge not according to the appearance, but judge righteous judgment."

Then said some of them of Jerusalem, "Is not this he, whom they seek to kill? But, lo, he speaketh boldly, and they say nothing unto him. Do the rulers know indeed that this is the very Christ? Howbeit we know this man whence he is: but when Christ cometh, no man knoweth whence he is."

Then cried Jesus in the temple as he taught, saying, "Ye both know me, and ye know whence I am: and I am not come of myself, but he that sent me is true, whom ye know not. But I know him: for I am from him, and he hath sent me."

Then they sought to take him: but no man laid hands on him, because his hour was not yet come. And many of the people believed on him, and said, "When Christ cometh, will he do more miracles than these which this man hath done?"

The Pharisees heard that the people murmured such things concerning him; and the Pharisees and the chief priests sent officers to take him.

Then said Jesus unto them, "Yet a little while am I with you, and then I go unto him that sent me. Ye shall seek me, and shall not find me: and where I am, thither ye cannot come."

Then said the Jews among themselves, "Whither will he go, that we shall not find him? will he go unto the dispersed among the Gentiles, and teach the Gentiles? What manner of saying is this that he said, 'Ye shall seek me, and shall not find me: and where I am, thither ye cannot come'?"

In the last day, that great day of the feast, Jesus stood and cried, saying, "If any man thirst, let him come unto me, and drink. He that believeth on me, as the scripture hath said, out of his belly shall flow rivers of living water." (But this spake he of the Spirit, which they that believe on him should receive: for the Holy Ghost was not yet given; because that Jesus was not yet glorified.)

Many of the people therefore, when they heard this saying, said, "Of a truth this is the Prophet." Others said, "This is the Christ." But some said, "Shall Christ come out of Galilee? Hath not the scripture said, That Christ cometh of the seed of David, and out of the town of Bethlehem, where David was?"

So there was a division among the people because of him. And some of them would have taken him; but no man laid hands on him.

Then came the officers to the chief priests and Pharisees; and they said unto them, "Why have ye not brought him?"

The officers answered, "Never man spake like this man."

Then answered them the Pharisees, "Are ye also deceived? Have any of the rulers or of the Pharisees believed on him? But this people who knoweth not the law are cursed."

Nicodemus saith unto them, (he that came to Jesus by night, being one of them,) "Doth our law judge any man, before it hear him, and *Jesus and the adulteress* know what he doeth?"

They answered and said unto him, "Art thou also of Galilee? Search, and look: for out of Galilee ariseth no prophet."

And every man went unto his own house.

Jesus went unto the mount of Olives. And early in the morning he came again into the temple, and all the people came unto him; and he sat down, and taught them.

And the scribes and Pharisees brought unto him a woman taken in adultery; and when they had set her in the midst, they say unto him, "Master, this woman was taken in adultery. Now Moses in the law commanded us, that such should be stoned: but what sayest thou?" This they said, tempting him, that they might have to accuse him.

But Jesus stooped down, and with his finger wrote on the ground, as though he heard them not. So when they continued asking him, he lifted up himself, and said unto them, "He that is without sin among you, let him first cast a stone at her." And again he stooped down, and wrote on the ground.

And they which heard it, being convicted by their own conscience, went out one by one, beginning at the eldest, even unto the last: and Jesus was left alone, and the woman standing in the midst.

When Jesus had lifted up himself, and saw none but the woman, he said unto her, "Woman, where are those thine accusers? hath no man condemned thee?"

She said, "No man, Lord."

And Jesus said unto her, "Neither do I condemn thee: go, and sin no more."

Then spake Jesus again unto them, saying, "I am the light of the world: he that followeth me shall not walk in darkness, but shall have the light of life."

The Pharisees therefore said unto him, "Thou bearest record of thyself; thy record is not true."

Jesus answered and said unto them, "Though I bear record of myself, yet my record is true: for I know whence I came, and whither I go; but ye cannot tell whence I come, and whither I go. Ye judge after the flesh; I judge no man. And yet if I judge, my judgment is true: for I

[ 53 ]

*Jesus answers the Jews* am not alone, but I and the Father that sent me. It is also written in your law, that the testimony of two men is true. I am one that bear witness of myself, and the Father that sent me beareth witness of me."

Then said they unto him, "Where is thy Father?"

Jesus answered, "Ye neither know me, nor my Father: if ye had known me, ye should have known my Father also."

These words spake Jesus in the treasury, as he taught in the temple: and no man laid hands on him; for his hour was not yet come.

Then said Jesus again unto them, "I go my way, and ye shall seek me, and shall die in your sins: whither I go, ye cannot come."

Then said the Jews, "Will he kill himself? because he saith, 'Whither I go, ye cannot come.'"

And he said unto them, "Ye are from beneath; I am from above: ye are of this world; I am not of this world. I said therefore unto you, that ye shall die in your sins, if ye believe not that I am he."

Then said they unto him, "Who art thou?"

And Jesus saith unto them, "Even the same that I said unto you from the beginning. I have many things to say and to judge of you: but he that sent me is true; and I speak to the world those things which I have heard of him." They understood not that he spake to them of the Father.

Then said Jesus unto them, "When ye have lifted up the Son of man, then shall ye know that I am he, and that I do nothing of myself; but as my Father hath taught me, I speak these things. And he that sent me is with me: the Father hath not left me alone; for I do always those things that please him." As he spake these words, many believed on him.

Then said Jesus to those Jews which believed on him, "If ye continue in my word, then are ye my disciples indeed; and ye shall know the truth, and the truth shall make you free."

They answered him, "We be Abraham's seed, and were never in bondage to any man: how sayest thou, 'Ye shall be made free'?"

Jesus answered them, "Verily, verily, I say unto you, Whosoever committeth sin is the servant of sin. And the servant abideth not in the house for ever: but the Son abideth ever. If the Son therefore shall make you free, ye shall be free indeed. And because I tell you the truth, ye believe me not. Which of you convinceth me of sin? And if I say the truth, why do ye not believe me? He that is of God heareth God's words: *The Jews call Jesus a bedeviled Samaritan* ye therefore hear them not, because ye are not of God."

Then answered the Jews, and said unto him, "Say we not well that thou art a Samaritan, and hast a devil?"

Jesus answered, "I have not a devil; but I honour my Father, and ye do dishonour me. And I seek not mine own glory: there is one that seeketh and judgeth. Verily, verily, I say unto you, If a man keep my saying, he shall never see death. If I honour myself, my honour is nothing: it is my Father that honoureth me; of whom ye say, that he is your God: yet ye have not known him; but I know him: and if I should say, 'I know him not,' I shall be a liar like unto you: but I know him, and keep his saying. Verily, verily, I say unto you, Before Abraham was, I am."

Then took they up stones to cast at him: but Jesus hid himself, and went out of the temple, going through the midst of them, and so passed by.

And he arose from thence, and cometh into the coasts of Judæa by the farther side of Jordan: and the people resort unto him again; and, as he was wont, he taught them again.

And it came to pass, when the time was come that he should be received up, he stedfastly set his face to go to Jerusalem, and sent messengers before his face: and they went, and entered into a village of the Samaritans, to make ready for him. And they did not receive him, because his face was as though he would go to Jerusalem. And when his disciples James and John saw this, they said, "Lord, wilt thou that we command fire to come down from heaven, and consume them, even as Elias did?"

But he turned, and said, "The son of man is not come to destroy men's lives, but to save them." And they went to another village.

And it came to pass, that, as they went in the way, a certain man said unto him, "Lord, I will follow thee whithersoever thou goest."

And Jesus said unto him, "Foxes have holes, and birds of the air have nests; but the Son of man hath not where to lay his head."

And he said unto another, "Follow me."

But he said, "Lord, suffer me first to go and bury my father."

Jesus said unto him, "Let the dead bury their dead: but go thou and preach the kingdom of God."

*The great
commandment* And another also said, "Lord, I will follow thee; but let me first go bid them farewell, which are at home at my house."

And Jesus said unto him, "No man, having put his hand to the plough, and looking back, is fit for the kingdom of God."

And, behold, a certain lawyer stood up, and tempted him, saying, "Master, what shall I do to inherit eternal life?"

He said unto him, "What is written in the law? how readest thou?"

And he answering said, "Thou shalt love the Lord thy God with all thy heart, and with all thy soul, and with all thy strength, and with all thy mind; and thy neighbour as thyself."

And he said unto him, "Thou hast answered right: this do, and thou shalt live."

But he, willing to justify himself, said unto Jesus, "And who is my neighbour?"

And Jesus answering said,

*The good
Samaritan* *"A certain man went down from Jerusalem to Jericho, and fell among thieves, which stripped him of his raiment, and wounded him, and departed, leaving him half dead. And by chance there came down a certain priest that way: and when he saw him, he passed by on the other side. And likewise a Levite, when he was at the place, came and looked on him, and passed by on the other side. But a certain Samaritan, as he journeyed, came where he was: and when he saw him, he had compassion on him, and went to him, and bound up his wounds, pouring in oil and wine, and set him on his own beast, and brought him to an inn, and took care of him. And on the morrow when he departed, he took out two pence, and gave them to the host, and said unto him, 'Take care of him; and whatsoever thou spendest more, when I come again, I will repay thee.' Which now of these three, thinkest thou, was neighbour unto him that fell among the thieves?"*

*And he said, "He that shewed mercy on him."*

*Then said Jesus unto him, "Go, and do thou likewise."*

After these things the Lord appointed other seventy also, and sent them two and two before his face into every city and place, whither he himself would come. Therefore said he unto them, "Go your ways: Carry neither purse, nor scrip, nor shoes: and salute no man by the way. And into whatsoever house ye enter, first say, 'Peace be to this house.' And if the son of peace be there, your peace shall rest upon it: if not, it shall turn *The mission of the* to you again. And in the same house remain, eating and drinking such *seventy* things as they give: for the labourer is worthy of his hire. Go not from house to house. And into whatsoever city ye enter, and they receive you, eat such things as are set before you: and heal the sick that are therein, and say unto them, 'The kingdom of God is come nigh unto you.' He that heareth you heareth me; and he that despiseth you despiseth me; and he that despiseth me despiseth him that sent me."

And the seventy returned again with joy. In that hour Jesus rejoiced in spirit, and said, "I thank thee, O Father, Lord of heaven and earth, that thou hast hid these things from the wise and prudent, and hast revealed them unto babes: even so, Father; for so it seemed good in thy sight. All things are delivered to me of my Father: and no man knoweth who the Son is, but the Father; and who the Father is, but the Son, and he to whom the Son will reveal him."

And he turned him unto his disciples, and said privately, "Blessed are the eyes which see the things that ye see: for I tell you, that many prophets and kings have desired to see those things which ye see, and have not seen them; and to hear those things which ye hear, and have not heard them."

Now it came to pass, as they went, that he entered into a certain village: and a certain woman named Martha received him into her house. And she had a sister called Mary, which also sat at Jesus' feet, and heard his word. But Martha was cumbered about much serving, and came to him, and said, "Lord, dost thou not care that my sister hath left me to serve alone? bid her therefore that she help me."

And Jesus answered and said unto her, "Martha, Martha, thou art careful and troubled about many things: but one thing is needful: and Mary hath chosen that good part, which shall not be taken away from her."

And as Jesus passed by, he saw a man which was blind from his birth, and he said, "I must work the works of him that sent me, while it is day: the night cometh, when no man can work. As long as I am in the world, I am the light of the world."

When he had thus spoken, he spat on the ground, and made clay of the spittle, and he anointed the eyes of the blind man with the clay. And

*Sight restored to a blind man* said unto him, "Go, wash in the pool of Siloam." He went his way therefore, and washed, and came seeing.

The neighbours therefore, and they which before had seen him that he was blind, said, "Is not this he that sat and begged?"

Some said, "This is he"; others said, "He is like him": but he said, "I am he."

Therefore said they unto him, "How were thine eyes opened?"

He answered and said, "A man that is called Jesus made clay, and anointed mine eyes, and said unto me, 'Go to the pool of Siloam, and wash': and I went and washed, and I received sight."

Then said they unto him, "Where is he?"

He said, "I know not."

They brought to the Pharisees him that aforetime was blind. And it was the sabbath day when Jesus made the clay, and opened his eyes. Then again the Pharisees also asked him how he had received his sight.

He said unto them, "He put clay upon mine eyes, and I washed, and do see."

Therefore said some of the Pharisees, "This man is not of God, because he keepeth not the sabbath day."

Others said, "How can a man that is a sinner do such miracles?"

And there was a division among them. They say unto the blind man again, "What sayest thou of him, that he hath opened thine eyes?"

He said, "He is a prophet."

But the Jews did not believe concerning him, that he had been blind, and received his sight, until they called the parents of him that had received his sight. And they asked them, saying, "Is this your son, who ye say was born blind? how then doth he now see?"

His parents answered them and said, "We know that this is our son, and that he was born blind: but by what means he now seeth, we know not: he is of age; ask him: he shall speak for himself."

These words spake his parents, because they feared the Jews: for the Jews had agreed already, that if any man did confess that he was Christ, he should be put out of the synagogue. Therefore said his parents, "He is of age; ask him."

Then again called they the man that was blind, and said unto him, "Give God the praise: we know that this man is a sinner."

[ 58 ]

He answered and said, "Whether he be a sinner or no, I know not: *Pharisees reproved for* one thing I know, that, whereas I was blind, now I see." *unbelief*

Then said they to him again, "What did he to thee? how opened he thine eyes?"

He answered them, "I have told you already, and ye did not hear: wherefore would ye hear it again? will ye also be his disciples?"

Then they reviled him, and said, "Thou art his disciple; but we are Moses' disciples. We know that God spake unto Moses: as for this fellow, we know not from whence he is."

The man answered and said unto them, "Why herein is a marvellous thing, that ye know not from whence he is, and yet he hath opened mine eyes. Now we know that God heareth not sinners: but if any man be a worshipper of God, and doeth his will, him he heareth. Since the world began was it not heard that any man opened the eyes of one that was born blind. If this man were not of God, he could do nothing."

They answered and said unto him, "Thou wast altogether born in sins, and dost thou teach us?" And they cast him out.

Jesus heard that they had cast him out; and when he had found him, he said unto him, "Dost thou believe on the Son of God?"

He answered and said, "Who is he, Lord, that I might beleive on him?"

And Jesus said unto him, "Thou hast both seen him, and it is he that talketh with thee."

And he said, "Lord, I believe." And he worshipped him.

And Jesus said, "For judgment I am come into this world, that they which see not might see; and that they which see might be made blind."

And some of the Pharisees which were with him heard these words, and said unto him, "Are we blind also?"

Jesus said unto them, "If ye were blind, ye should have no sin: but now ye say, 'We see'; therefore your sin remaineth."

*"Verily, verily, I say unto you, he that entereth not by the door into the sheepfold, but climbeth up some other way, the same is a thief and a robber. But he that entereth in by the door is the shepherd of the sheep. To him the porter openeth; and the sheep hear his voice; and he calleth his own sheep by name, and leadeth them out. And when he putteth forth his own sheep, he*

[ 59 ]

*goeth before them, and the sheep follow him: for they know his voice. And a stranger will they not follow, but will flee from him: for they know not the voice of strangers."*

*This parable spake Jesus unto them: but they understood not what things they were which he spake unto them.*

*Then said Jesus unto them again, "Verily, verily, I say unto you, I am the door of the sheep. All that ever came before me are thieves and robbers: but the sheep did not hear them.*

*"I am the door: by me if any man enter in, he shall be saved, and shall go in and out, and find pasture. The thief cometh not, but for to steal, and to kill, and to destroy: I am come that they might have life, and that they might have it more abundantly.*

*"I am the good shepherd: the good shepherd giveth his life for the sheep. But he that is an hireling, and not the shepherd, whose own the sheep are not, seeth the wolf coming, and leaveth the sheep, and fleeth: and the wolf catcheth them, and scattereth the sheep. The hireling fleeth, because he is an hireling, and careth not for the sheep. I am the good shepherd, and know my sheep, and am known of mine. As the Father knoweth me, even so know I the Father: and I lay down my life for the sheep. And other sheep I have which are not of this fold: them also I must bring, and they shall hear my voice; and there shall be one fold, and one shepherd. Therefore doth my Father love me, because I lay down my life, that I might take it again. No man taketh it from me, but I lay it down of myself. I have power to lay it down, and I have power to take it again. This commandment have I received of my Father."*

There was a division therefore again among the Jews. And many of them said, "He hath a devil, and is mad; why hear ye him?" Others said, "These are not the words of him that hath a devil. Can a devil open the eyes of the blind?"

And it was at Jerusalem the feast of the dedication, and it was winter. And Jesus walked in the temple in Solomon's porch. Then came the Jews round about him, and said unto him, "How long dost thou make us to doubt? If thou be the Christ, tell us plainly."

Jesus answered them, "I told you, and ye believed not: the works that I do in my Father's name, they bear witness of me. But ye believe not, because ye are not of my sheep, as I said unto you. My sheep hear my *Jesus escapes from the* voice, and I know them, and they follow me: and I give unto them *Jews* eternal life; and they shall never perish, neither shall any man pluck them out of my hand. My Father, which gave them me, is greater than all; and no man is able to pluck them out of my Father's hand. I and my Father are one."

Then the Jews took up stones again to stone him.

Jesus answered them, "Many good works have I shewed you from my Father; for which of those works do ye stone me? If I do not the works of my Father, believe me not. But if I do, though ye believe not me, believe the works: that ye may know, and believe, that the Father is in me, and I in him."

Therefore they sought again to take him: but he escaped out of their hand, and went away again beyond Jordan into the place where John at first baptized; and there he abode. And many resorted unto him, and said, "John did no miracle: but all things that John spake of this man were true." And many believed on him there.

And it came to pass, that, as he was praying in a certain place, when he ceased, one of his disciples said unto him, "Lord, teach us to pray, as John also taught his disciples."

And he said unto them, "After this manner therefore pray ye: *The Lord's Prayer*

> Our Father which art in heaven,
> Hallowed be thy name.
> Thy kingdom come.
> Thy will be done
> In earth, as it is in heaven.
> Give us this day our daily bread.
> And forgive us our debts,
> As we forgive our debtors.
> And lead us not into temptation,
> But deliver us from evil:
> For thine is the kingdom,
> And the power,
> And the glory,
> Forever. Amen.

[ 61 ]

"For if ye forgive men their trespasses, your heavenly Father will also forgive you: but if ye forgive not men their trespasses, neither will your Father forgive your trespasses. And all things, whatsoever ye shall ask in prayer, believing, ye shall receive."

And he said unto them,

*"Which of you shall have a friend, and shall go unto him at midnight, and say unto him, 'Friend, lend me three loaves; for a friend of mine in his journey is come to me, and I have nothing to set before him'? And he from within shall answer and say, 'Trouble me not: the door is now shut, and my children are with me in bed; I cannot rise and give thee.' I say unto you, Though he will not rise and give him, because he is his friend, yet because of his importunity he will rise and give him as many as he needeth.*

"And I say unto you, Ask, and it shall be given you; seek, and ye shall find; knock, and it shall be opened unto you. For every one that asketh receiveth; and he that seeketh findeth; and to him that knocketh it shall be opened. If a son shall ask bread of any of you that is a father, will he give him a stone? or if he ask a fish, will he for a fish give him a serpent? If ye then, being evil, know how to give good gifts unto your children: how much more shall your heavenly Father give the Holy Spirit to them that ask him? Therefore all things whatsoever ye would that men should do to you, do ye even so to them: for this is the law and the prophets.

"No man, when he hath lighted a candle, putteth it in a secret place, neither under a bushel, but on a candlestick, that they which come in may see the light. The light of the body is the eye: therefore when thine eye is single, thy whole body also is full of light; but when thine eye is evil, thy body also is full of darkness. Take heed therefore that the light which is in thee be not darkness. If thy whole body therefore be full of light, having no part dark, the whole shall be full of light, as when the bright shining of a candle doth give thee light."

In the mean time, when there were gathered together an innumerable multitude of people, insomuch that they trode one upon another, he began to say unto his disciples first of all, "Beware ye of the leaven of the Pharisees, which is hypocrisy. For there is nothing covered, that shall not be revealed; neither hid, that shall not be known. Therefore whatsoever ye have spoken in darkness shall be heard in the light; and that which ye have spoken in the ear in closets shall be proclaimed upon the housetops."

And one of the company said unto him, "Master, speak to my brother, that he divide the inheritance with me."

And he said unto him, "Man, who made me a judge or a divider over you?" And he said unto them, "Take heed, and beware of covetousness: for a man's life consisteth not in the abundance of the things which he possesseth."

And he spake a parable unto them, saying,

*"The ground of a certain rich man brought forth plentifully: and he thought within himself, saying, 'What shall I do, because I have no room where to bestow my fruits?' And he said, 'This will I do: I will pull down my barns, and build greater; and there will I bestow all my fruits and my goods. And I will say to my soul, "Soul, thou hast much goods laid up for many years; take thine ease, eat, drink, and be merry."' But God said unto him, 'Thou fool, this night thy soul shall be required of thee: then whose shall those things be, which thou hast provided?' So is he that layeth up treasure for himself, and is not rich toward God.*

"Fear not, little flock; for it is your Father's good pleasure to give you the kingdom. Sell that ye have, and give alms; provide yourselves bags which wax not old, a treasure in the heavens that faileth not, where no thief approacheth, neither moth corrupteth. For where your treasure is, there will your heart be also.

"Let your loins be girded about, and your lights burning; And ye yourselves like unto men that wait for their lord, when he will return from the wedding; that when he cometh and knocketh, they may open unto him immediately. Blessed are those servants, whom the lord when he cometh shall find watching: verily I say unto you, that he shall gird himself, and make them to sit down to meat, and will come forth and serve them. And if he shall come in the second watch, or come in the third watch, and find them so, blessed are those servants. And this know, that if the goodman of the house had known what hour the thief would come, he would have watched, and not have suffered his house to be broken through. Be ye therefore ready also: for the Son of man cometh at an hour when ye think not."

Then Peter said unto him, "Lord, speakest thou this parable unto us, or even to all?"

And the Lord said,

*"Who then is that faithful and wise steward, whom his lord shall make ruler over his household, to give them their portion of meat in due season? Blessed is that servant, whom his lord when he cometh shall find so doing. Of a truth I say unto you, that he will make him ruler over all that he hath. But and if that servant say in his heart, 'My lord delayeth his coming'; and shall begin to beat the menservants and maidens, and to eat and drink, and to be drunken; the lord of that servant will come in a day when he looketh not for him, and at an hour when he is not aware, and will cut him in sunder, and will appoint him his portion with the unbelievers. And that servant, which knew his lord's will, and prepared not himself, neither did according to his will, shall be beaten with many stripes. But he that knew not, and did commit things worthy of stripes, shall be beaten with few stripes. For unto whomsoever much is given, of him shall be much required: and to whom men have committed much, of him they will ask the more."*

He spake also this parable;

*"A certain man had a fig tree planted in his vineyard; and he came and sought fruit thereon, and found none. Then said he unto the dresser of his vineyard, 'Behold, these three years I come seeking fruit on this fig tree, and find none: cut it down; why cumbereth it the ground?' And he answering said unto him, 'Lord, let it alone this year also, till I shall dig about it, and dung it; and if it bear fruit, well: and if not, then after that thou shalt cut it down.' "*

He was teaching in one of the synagogues on the sabbath. And, behold, there was a woman which had a spirit of infirmity eighteen years, and was bowed together, and could in no wise lift up herself. And when Jesus saw her, he called her to him, and said unto her, "Woman, thou art loosed from thine infirmity." And he laid his hands on her: and immediately she was made straight, and glorified God.

And the ruler of the synagogue answered with indignation, because that Jesus had healed on the sabbath day, and said unto the people,

"There are six days in which men ought to work: in them therefore come   *A lament for Jerusalem* and be healed, and not on the sabbath day."

The Lord then answered him, and said, "Thou hypocrite, doth not each one of you on the sabbath loose his ox or his ass from the stall, and lead him away to watering? And ought not this woman, being a daughter of Abraham, whom Satan hath bound, lo, these eighteen years, be loosed from this bond on the sabbath day?"

And when he had said these things, all his adversaries were ashamed: and all the people rejoiced for all the glorious things that were done by him.

And he went through the cities and villages, teaching, and journeying toward Jerusalem.

And he said unto them, "Strive to enter in at the strait gate: for many, I say unto you, will seek to enter in, and shall not be able. And, behold, there are last which shall be first, and there are first which shall be last."

The same day there came certain of the Pharisees, saying unto him, "Get thee out, and depart hence: for Herod will kill thee."

And he said unto them, "Go ye, and tell that fox, 'Behold, I cast out devils, and I do cures to day and to morrow, and the third day I shall be perfected: Nevertheless I must walk to day and to morrow and the day following: for it cannot be said that a prophet perish out of Jerusalem.'

"O Jerusalem, Jerusalem, which killest the prophets, and stonest them that are sent unto thee; how often would I have gathered thy children together, as a hen doth gather her brood under her wings, and ye would not! Behold, your house is left unto you desolate: and verily I say unto you, Ye shall not see me, until the time comes when ye shall say, 'Blessed is he that cometh in the name of the Lord.' "

And it came to pass, as he went into the house of one of the chief Pharisees to eat bread on the sabbath day, that they watched him. And, behold, there was a certain man before him which had the dropsy. And Jesus answering spake unto the lawyers and Pharisees, saying, "Is it lawful to heal on the sabbath day?"

And they held their peace. And he took him, and healed him, and let him go; and answered them, saying, "Which of you shall have an ass or

[ 65 ]

an ox fallen into a pit, and will not straightway pull him out on the sabbath day?"

And they could not answer him again to these things.

And he put forth a parable to those which were bidden, when he marked how they chose out the chief rooms; saying unto them,

*"When thou art bidden of any man to a wedding, sit not down in the highest room; lest a more honourable man than thou be bidden of him; and he that bade thee and him come and say to thee, 'Give this man place'; and thou begin with shame to take the lowest room. But when thou art bidden, go and sit down in the lowest room; that when he that bade thee cometh, he may say unto thee, 'Friend, go up higher': then shalt thou have worship in the presence of them that sit at meat with thee. For whosoever exalteth himself shall be abased; and he that humbleth himself shall be exalted."*

Then said he also to him that bade him, "When thou makest a dinner or a supper, call not thy friends, nor thy brethren, neither thy kinsmen, nor thy rich neighbours; lest they also bid thee again, and a recompence be made thee. But when thou makest a feast, call the poor, the maimed, the lame, and the blind: and thou shalt be blessed; for they cannot recompense thee: for thou shalt be recompensed at the resurrection of the just."

And when one of them that sat at meat with him heard these things, he said unto him, "Blessed is he that shall eat bread in the kingdom of God."

Then said he unto him,

*"A certain man made a great supper, and bade many: and sent his servant at supper time to say to them that were bidden, 'Come; for all things are now ready.' And they all with one consent began to make excuse. The first said unto him, 'I have bought a piece of ground, and I must needs go and see it: I pray thee have me excused.' And another said, 'I have bought five yoke of oxen, and I go to prove them: I pray thee have me excused.' And another said, 'I have married a wife, and therefore I cannot come.'*

*"So that servant came, and shewed his lord these things. Then the master of the house being angry said to his servant, 'Go out quickly into the streets and lanes of the city, and bring in hither the poor, and the maimed, and the halt,*

*and the blind.' And the servant said, 'Lord, it is done as thou hast com-*
*manded, and yet there is room.' And the lord said unto the servant, 'Go out
into the highways and hedges, and compel them to come in, that my house
may be filled. For I say unto you, None of those men which were bidden shall
taste of my supper.' "*

And there went great multitudes with him: and he turned, and said
unto them,

*"Which of you, intending to build a tower, sitteth not down first, and
counteth the cost, whether he have sufficient to finish it? Lest haply, after he
hath laid the foundation, and is not able to finish it, all that behold it begin
to mock him, saying, 'This man began to build, and was not able to finish.'
"Or what king, going to make war against another king, sitteth not down
first, and consulteth whether he be able with ten thousand to meet him that
cometh against him with twenty thousand? Or else, while the other is yet
a great way off, he sendeth an ambassage, and desireth conditions of peace.
So likewise, whosoever he be of you that forsaketh not all that he hath, he
cannot be my disciple. He that hath ears to hear, let him hear."*

Then drew near unto him all publicans and sinners for to hear him.
And the Pharisees and scribes murmured, saying, "This man receiveth
sinners, and eateth with them."
And he spake this parable unto them, saying,

*"What man of you, having an hundred sheep, if he lose one of them, doth
not leave the ninety and nine in the wilderness, and go after that which is lost,
until he find it? And when he hath found it, he layeth it on his shoulders, rejoicing. And when he cometh home, he calleth together his friends and neighbours, saying unto them, 'Rejoice with me; for I have found my sheep which
was lost.' I say unto you, that likewise joy shall be in heaven over one sinner
that repenteth, more than over ninety and nine just persons, which need no
repentance.
"Even so it is not the will of your Father which is in heaven, that one of
these little ones should perish.
"Either what woman having ten pieces of silver, if she lose one piece,
doth not light a candle, and sweep the house, and seek diligently till she find
it? And when she hath found it, she calleth her friends and her neighbours*

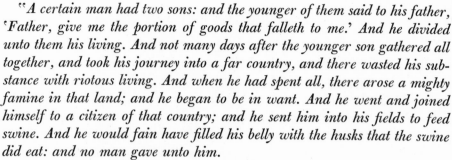
together, saying, 'Rejoice with me; for I have found the piece which I had lost.' Likewise, I say unto you, there is joy in the presence of the angels of God over one sinner that repenteth."

And he said,

"A certain man had two sons: and the younger of them said to his father, 'Father, give me the portion of goods that falleth to me.' And he divided unto them his living. And not many days after the younger son gathered all together, and took his journey into a far country, and there wasted his substance with riotous living. And when he had spent all, there arose a mighty famine in that land; and he began to be in want. And he went and joined himself to a citizen of that country; and he sent him into his fields to feed swine. And he would fain have filled his belly with the husks that the swine did eat: and no man gave unto him.

"And when he came to himself, he said, 'How many hired servants of my father's have bread enough and to spare, and I perish with hunger! I will arise and go to my father, and will say unto him, "Father, I have sinned against heaven, and before thee, and am no more worthy to be called thy son: make me as one of thy hired servants." '

"And he arose, and came to his father. But when he was yet a great way off, his father saw him, and had compassion, and ran, and fell on his neck, and kissed him. And the son said unto him, 'Father, I have sinned against heaven, and in thy sight, and am no more worthy to be called thy son.' But the father said to his servants, 'Bring forth the best robe, and put it on him; and put a ring on his hand, and shoes on his feet: and bring hither the fatted calf, and kill it; and let us eat, and be merry: For this my son was dead, and is alive again; he was lost, and is found.' And they began to be merry.

"Now his elder son was in the field: and as he came and drew nigh to the house, he heard musick and dancing. And he called one of the servants, and asked what these things meant. And he said unto him, 'Thy brother is come; and thy father hath killed the fatted calf, because he hath received him safe and sound.' And he was angry, and would not go in: therefore came his father out, and intreated him. And he answering said to his father, 'Lo, these many years do I serve thee, neither transgressed I at any time thy commandment: and yet thou never gavest me a kid, that I might make merry with my friends: but as soon as this thy son was come, which hath devoured thy living with harlots, thou hast killed for him the fatted calf.' And he said unto him, 'Son, thou art ever with me, and all that I have is thine. It was meet that we should make merry, and be glad: for this thy brother was dead, and is alive again; and was lost, and is found.' "

And he said also unto his disciples,

"*There was a certain rich man, which had a steward; and the same was accused unto him that he had wasted his goods. And he called him, and said unto him, 'How is it that I hear this of thee? give an account of thy steward-ship; for thou mayest be no longer steward.' Then the steward said within himself, 'What shall I do? for my lord taketh away from me the stewardship: I cannot dig; to beg I am ashamed. I am resolved what to do, that, when I am put out of the stewardship, they may receive me into their houses.' So he called every one of his lord's debtors unto him, and said unto the first, 'How much owest thou unto my lord?' And he said, 'An hundred measures of oil.' And he said unto him, 'Take thy bill, and sit down quickly, and write fifty.' Then said he to another, 'And how much owest thou?' And he said, 'An hundred measures of wheat.' And he said unto him, 'Take thy bill, and write fourscore.'*

"*And the lord commended the unjust steward, because he had done wisely: for the children of this world are in their generation wiser than the children of light. And I say unto you, 'Make to yourselves friends of the mammon of unrighteousness'; that, when ye fail, they may receive you into everlasting habitations. He that is faithful in that which is least is faithful also in much: and he that is unjust in the least is unjust also in much. If therefore ye have not been faithful in the unrighteous mammon, who will commit to your trust the true riches? And if ye have not been faithful in that which is another man's, who shall give you that which is your own?*

"*No servant can serve two masters: for either he will hate the one, and love the other; or else he will hold to the one, and despise the other. Ye can-not serve God and mammon.*"

And the Pharisees also, who were covetous, heard all these things: and they derided him. And he said unto them, "Ye are they which justify yourselves before men; but God knoweth your hearts: for that which is highly esteemed among men is abomination in the sight of God. The law

*The rich man and Lazarus* and the prophets were until John: since that time the kingdom of God is preached, and every man presseth into it."

"*There was a certain rich man, which was clothed in purple and fine linen, and fared sumptuously every day: and there was a certain beggar named Lazarus, which was laid at his gate, full of sores, and desiring to be fed with the crumbs which fell from the rich man's table: moreover the dogs came and licked his sores. And it came to pass, that the beggar died, and was carried by the angels into Abraham's bosom: the rich man also died, and was buried; and in hell he lift up his eyes, being in torments, and seeth Abraham afar off, and Lazarus in his bosom. And he cried and said, 'Father Abraham, have mercy on me, and send Lazarus, that he may dip the tip of his finger in water, and cool my tongue; for I am tormented in this flame.' But Abraham said, 'Son, remember that thou in thy lifetime receivedst thy good things, and likewise Lazarus evil things: but now he is comforted and thou art tormented. And beside all this, between us and you there is a great gulf fixed: so that they which would pass from hence to you cannot; neither can they pass to us, that would come from thence.'*

"*Then he said, 'I pray thee therefore, father, that thou wouldest send him to my father's house: for I have five brethren; that he may testify unto them, lest they also come into this place of torment.' Abraham saith unto him, 'They have Moses and the prophets; let them hear them.' And he said, 'Nay, father Abraham: but if one went unto them from the dead, they will repent.' And he said unto him, 'If they hear not Moses and the prophets, neither will they be persuaded, though one rose from the dead.' *"

"*But which of you, having a servant plowing or feeding cattle, will say unto him by and by, when he is come from the field, 'Go and sit down to meat'? And will not rather say unto him, 'Make ready wherewith I may sup, and gird thyself, and serve me, till I have eaten and drunken; and afterward thou shalt eat and drink'? Doth he thank that servant because he did the things that were commanded him? I trow not.*

"*So likewise ye, when ye shall have done all those things which are commanded you, say, 'We are unprofitable servants: we have done that which was our duty to do.' *"

Now a certain man was sick, named Lazarus, of Bethany, the town of Mary and her sister Martha. (It was that Mary which anointed the *Sickness and death of* Lord with ointment, and wiped his feet with her hair, whose brother *Lazarus* Lazarus was sick). Therefore his sisters sent unto him, saying, "Lord, behold, he whom thou lovest is sick."

When Jesus heard that, he said, "This sickness is not unto death, but for the glory of God, that the Son of God might be glorified thereby."

Now Jesus loved Martha, and her sister, and Lazarus. When he had heard therefore that he was sick, he abode two days still in the same place where he was.

Then after that saith he to his disciples, "Let us go into Judæa again."

His disciples say unto him, "Master, the Jews of late sought to stone thee; and goest thou thither again?"

Jesus answered, "Are there not twelve hours in the day? If any man walk in the day, he stumbleth not, because he seeth the light of this world. But if a man walk in the night, he stumbleth, because there is no light in him." These things said he: and after that he saith unto them, "Our friend Lazarus sleepeth; but I go, that I may awake him out of sleep."

Then said his disciples, "Lord, if he sleep, he shall do well." Howbeit Jesus spake of his death: but they thought that he had spoken of taking of rest in sleep.

Then said Jesus unto them plainly, "Lazarus is dead. And I am glad for your sakes that I was not there, to the intent ye may believe; nevertheless let us go unto him."

Then said Thomas, which is called Didymus, unto his fellowdisciples, "Let us also go, that we may die with him."

Then when Jesus came, he found that he had lain in the grave four days already.

Now Bethany was nigh unto Jerusalem, about fifteen furlongs off: and many of the Jews came to Martha and Mary, to comfort them concerning their brother.

Then Martha, as soon as she heard that Jesus was coming, went and met him: but Mary sat still in the house.

Then said Martha unto Jesus, "Lord, if thou hadst been here, my brother had not died. But I know, that even now, whatsoever thou wilt ask of God, God will give it thee."

Jesus saith unto her, "Thy brother shall rise again."

Martha saith unto him, "I know that he shall rise again in the resurrection at the last day."

Jesus said unto her, "I am the resurrection, and the life: he that believeth in me, though he were dead, yet shall he live: and whosoever liveth and believeth in me shall never die. Believest thou this?"

She saith unto him, "Yea, Lord: I believe that thou art the Christ, the Son of God, which should come into the world."

And when she had so said, she went her way, and called Mary her sister secretly, saying, "The Master is come, and calleth for thee." As soon as she heard that, she arose quickly, and came unto him.

Now Jesus was not yet come into the town, but was in that place where Martha met him. The Jews then which were with her in the house, and comforted her, when they saw Mary, that she rose up hastily and went out, followed her, saying, "She goeth unto the grave to weep there."

Then when Mary was come where Jesus was, and saw him, she fell down at his feet, saying unto him, "Lord, if thou hadst been here, my brother had not died."

When Jesus therefore saw her weeping, and the Jews also weeping which came with her, he groaned in the spirit, and was troubled, and said, "Where have ye laid him?"

They said unto him, "Lord, come and see."

Jesus wept.

Then said the Jews, "Behold how he loved him!"

And some of them said, "Could not this man, which opened the eyes of the blind, have caused that even this man should not have died?"

Jesus therefore again groaning in himself cometh to the grave. It was a cave, and a stone lay upon it.

Jesus said, "Take ye away the stone." Martha, the sister of him that was dead, saith unto him, "Lord, he hath been dead four days."

Jesus saith unto her, "Said I not unto thee, that, if thou wouldest believe, thou shouldest see the glory of God?"

Then they took away the stone from the place where the dead was laid. And Jesus lifted up his eyes, and said, "Father, I thank thee that thou hast heard me. And I knew that thou hearest me always: but because of the people which stand by I said it, that they may believe that *The resurrection of* thou hast sent me." And when he thus had spoken, he cried out with a *Lazarus* loud voice, "Lazarus, come forth."

And he that was dead came forth, bound hand and foot with grave-clothes: and his face was bound about with a napkin.

Jesus saith unto them, "Loose him, and let him go."

Then many of the Jews which came to Mary, and had seen the things which Jesus did, believed on him. But some of them went their ways to the Pharisees, and told them what things Jesus had done. Then from that day forth they took counsel together for to put him to death.

Jesus therefore walked no more openly among the Jews; but went *Ten lepers cleansed* thence unto a country near to the wilderness, into a city called Ephraim, and there continued with his disciples.

And it came to pass, as he went to Jerusalem, that he passed through the midst of Samaria and Galilee. And as he entered into a certain village, there met him ten men that were lepers, which stood afar off: and they lifted up their voices, and said, "Jesus, Master, have mercy on us."

And when he saw them, he said unto them, "Go shew yourselves unto the priests."

And it came to pass, that, as they went, they were cleansed. And one of them, when he saw that he was healed, turned back, and with a loud voice glorified God, and fell down on his face at his feet, giving him thanks: and he was a Samaritan.

And Jesus answering said, "Were there not ten cleansed? but where are the nine? There are not found that returned to give glory to God, save this stranger." And he said unto him, "Arise, go thy way: thy faith hath made thee whole."

And when he was demanded of the Pharisees, when the kingdom of God should come, he answered them and said, "The kingdom of God cometh not with observation: neither shall they say, 'Lo here!' or, 'lo there!' for, behold, the kingdom of God is within you."

And he said unto the disciples, "For as the lightning, that lighteneth out of the one part under heaven, shineth unto the other part under heaven; so shall also the Son of man be in his day. But first must he suffer many things, and be rejected of this generation. Whosoever shall seek

to save his life shall lose it; and whosoever shall lose his life shall preserve it."

And he spake this parable unto certain which trusted in themselves
that they were righteous, and despised others:

*"Two men went up into the temple to pray; the one a Pharisee, and the
other a publican. The Pharisee stood and prayed thus with himself, 'God, I
thank thee, that I am not as other men are, extortioners, unjust, adulterers,
or even as this publican. I fast twice in the week. I give tithes of all that I
possess.' And the publican, standing afar off, would not lift up so much as
his eyes unto heaven, but smote upon his breast, saying, 'God be merciful to
me a sinner.' I tell you, this man went down to his house justified rather than
the other: for every one that exalteth himself shall be abased; and he that
humbleth himself shall be exalted."*

The Pharisees also came unto him, tempting him, and saying unto
him, "Is it lawful for a man to put away his wife for every cause?"

And he answered and said unto them, "Have ye not read, that he
which made them at the beginning made them male and female, and said,
'For this cause shall a man leave father and mother, and shall cleave to
his wife: and they twain shall be one flesh'? Wherefore they are no more
twain, but one flesh. What therefore God hath joined together, let not
man put asunder."

Then were there brought unto him little children, that he should put
his hands on them, and pray: and the disciples rebuked them. But Jesus
called them unto him, and said, "Suffer little children to come unto me,
and forbid them not: for of such is the kingdom of God. Verily I say unto
you, Whosoever shall not receive the kingdom of God as a little child, he
shall not enter therein." And he took them up in his arms, put his hands
upon them, and blessed them.

And when he was gone forth into the way, there came one running,
and kneeled to him, and asked him, "Good Master, what shall I do that
I may inherit eternal life?"

And Jesus said unto him, "Why callest thou me good? there is none
good but one, that is, God. Thou knowest the commandments, 'Do not
commit adultery, Do not kill, Do not steal, Do not bear false witness,
Defraud not, Honour thy father and thy mother.' "

And he answered and said unto him, "Master, all these have I observed from my youth."

Then Jesus beholding him loved him, and said unto him, "One thing thou lackest: go thy way, sell whatsoever thou hast, and give to the poor, and thou shalt have treasure in heaven: and come, take up the cross, and follow me."

And he was sad at that saying, and went away grieved: for he had great possessions.

And Jesus looked round about, and saith unto his disciples, "How hardly shall they that have riches enter into the kingdom of God!" And the disciples were astonished at his words. But Jesus answereth again, and saith unto them, "Children, how hard is it for them that trust in riches to enter into the kingdom of God! It is easier for a camel to go through the eye of a needle, than for a rich man to enter into the kingdom of God."

And they were astonished out of measure, saying among themselves, "Who then can be saved?"

*"Many that are first shall be last; and the last shall be first. For the kingdom of heaven is like unto a man that is an householder, which went out early in the morning to hire labourers into his vineyard. And when he had agreed with the labourers for a penny a day, he sent them into his vineyard. And he went out about the third hour, and saw others standing idle in the marketplace, and said unto them; 'Go ye also into the vineyard, and whatsoever is right I will give you.' And they went their way. Again he went out about the sixth and ninth hour, and did likewise. And about the eleventh hour he went out, and found others standing idle, and saith unto them, 'Why stand ye here all the day idle?' They say unto him, 'Because no man hath hired us.' He saith unto them, 'Go ye also into the vineyard; and whatsoever is right, that shall ye receive.'*

*"So when even was come, the lord of the vineyard saith unto his steward, 'Call the labourers, and give them their hire, beginning from the last unto the first.' And when they came that were hired about the eleventh hour, they received every man a penny. But when the first came, they supposed that they should have received more; and they likewise received every man a penny. And when they had received it, they murmured against the goodman*

*Jesus again foretells his death and resurrection*

of the house, saying, 'These last have wrought but one hour, and thou hast made them equal unto us, which have borne the burden and heat of the day.' But he answered one of them, and said, 'Friend, I do thee no wrong: didst not thou agree with me for a penny? Take that thine is, and go thy way: I will give unto this last, even as unto thee. Is it not lawful for me to do what I will with mine own? Is thine eye evil, because I am good?'

"So the last shall be first, and the first last: for many be called, but few chosen."

And they were in the way going up to Jerusalem; and Jesus went before them: and they were amazed; and as they followed, they were afraid. And he took again the twelve, and began to tell them what things should happen unto him, saying, "Behold, we go up to Jerusalem; and the Son of man shall be delivered unto the chief priests, and unto the scribes; and they shall condemn him to death, and shall deliver him to the Gentiles: and they shall mock him, and shall scourge him, and shall spit upon him, and shall kill him: and the third day he shall rise again."

Then came to him the mother of Zebedee's children, with her sons, worshipping him, and desiring a certain thing of him.

And he said unto her, "What wilt thou?"

She saith unto him, "Grant that these my two sons may sit, the one on thy right hand, and the other on the left, in thy kingdom."

But Jesus answered and said, "Ye know not what ye ask. Are ye able to drink of the cup that I shall drink of, and to be baptized with the baptism that I am baptized with?"

They say unto him, "We are able."

And he saith unto them, "Ye shall drink indeed of my cup, and be baptized with the baptism that I am baptized with: but to sit on my right hand, and on my left, is not mine to give, but it shall be given to them for whom it is prepared of my Father."

And when the ten heard it, they were moved with indignation against the two brethren.

But Jesus called them unto him, and said, "Ye know that the princes of the Gentiles exercise dominion over them, and they that are great exercise authority upon them. But it shall not be so among you: but whosoever will be great among you, let him be your minister; and whosoever will be chief among you, let him be your servant: even as the Son of man came not to be ministered unto, but to minister, and to give his life a ransom for many."

*The blind man's sight restored*

A great multitude followed him. And it came to pass, that as he was come nigh unto Jericho, a certain blind man sat by the way side begging: and hearing the multitude pass by, he asked what it meant. And they told him, that Jesus of Nazareth passeth by. And he cried, saying, "Jesus, thou son of David, have mercy on me." And they which went before rebuked him, that he should hold his peace: but he cried so much the more, "Thou son of David, have mercy on me."

And Jesus stood still, and commanded him to be called. And they call the blind man, saying unto him, "Be of good comfort, rise; he calleth thee."

And he, casting away his garment, rose, and came to Jesus. And Jesus answered and said unto him, "What wilt thou that I should do unto thee?"

The blind man said unto him, "Lord, that I might receive my sight."

And Jesus said unto him, "Go thy way; thy faith hath made thee whole."

And immediately he received his sight, and followed Jesus in the way, glorifying God: and all the people, when they saw it, gave praise unto God.

And Jesus entered and passed through Jericho. And, behold, there was a man named Zacchæus, which was the chief among the publicans, and he was rich. And he sought to see Jesus who he was; and could not for the press, because he was of little stature. And he ran before, and climbed up into a sycomore tree to see him: for he was to pass that way.

And when Jesus came to the place, he looked up, and saw him, and said unto him, "Zacchæus, make haste, and come down; for to day I must abide at thy house." And he made haste, and came down, and received him joyfully.

And when they saw it, they all murmured, saying, That he was gone to be guest with a man that is a sinner.

And Zacchæus stood, and said unto the Lord; "Behold, Lord, the half of my goods I give to the poor; and if I have taken any thing from any man by false accusation, I restore him fourfold."

And Jesus said unto him, "This day is salvation come to this house, for the Son of man is come to seek and to save that which was lost."

And as they heard these things, he added and spake a parable, because he was nigh to Jerusalem, and because they thought that the kingdom of God should immediately appear. He said therefore,

*"A certain nobleman went into a far country to receive for himself a kingdom, and to return. And he called his ten servants, and delivered them ten pounds, and said unto them, 'Occupy till I come.' But his citizens hated him, and sent a message after him, saying, 'We will not have this man to reign over us.'*

*"And it came to pass, that when he was returned, having received the kingdom, then he commanded these servants to be called unto him, to whom he had given the money, that he might know how much every man had gained by trading.*

*"Then came the first, saying, 'Lord, thy pound hath gained ten pounds.' And he said unto him, 'Well, thou good servant: because thou hast been faithful in a very little, have thou authority over ten cities.'*

*"And the second came, saying, 'Lord, thy pound hath gained five pounds.' And he said likewise to him, 'Be thou also over five cities.'*

*"And another came, saying, 'Lord, behold, here is thy pound, which I have kept laid up in a napkin: for I feared thee, because thou art an austere man: thou takest up that thou layedst not down, and reapest that thou didst not sow.'*

*"And he saith unto him, 'Out of thine own mouth will I judge thee, thou wicked servant. Thou knewest that I was an austere man, taking up that I laid not down, and reaping that I did not sow: wherefore then gavest not thou my money into the bank, that at my coming I might have required mine own with usury?' And he said unto them that stood by, 'Take from him the pound, and give it to him that hath ten pounds.' (And they said unto him, 'Lord, he hath ten pounds.') 'For I say unto you, Unto every one which hath shall be given; and from him that hath not, even that he hath shall be taken away from him.' "*

And when he had thus spoken, he went before, ascending up to Jerusalem.

And the Jews' passover was nigh at hand: and many went out of the country up to Jerusalem before the passover, to purify themselves.

Then sought they for Jesus, and spake among themselves, as they stood in the temple, "What think ye, that he will not come to the feast?"

Now both the chief priests and the Pharisees had given a commandment, that, if any man knew where he were, he should shew it, that they might take him.

Then Jesus six days before the passover came to Bethany, where Lazarus was which had been dead, whom he raised from the dead. There they made him a supper; and Martha served: but Lazarus was one of them that sat at the table with him.

Then took Mary a pound of ointment of spikenard, very costly, and anointed the feet of Jesus, and wiped his feet with her hair: and the house was filled with the odour of the ointment. Then saith one of his disciples, Judas Iscariot, Simon's son, which should betray him, "Why was not this ointment sold for three hundred pence, and given to the poor?"

This he said, not that he cared for the poor; but because he was a thief, and had the bag, and bare what was put therein.

Then said Jesus, "Let her alone: against the day of my burying hath she kept this. For the poor always ye have with you; but me ye have not always. Verily I say unto you, Wheresoever this gospel shall be preached throughout the whole world, this also that she hath done shall be spoken of for a memorial of her."

Much people of the Jews therefore knew that he was there: and they came not for Jesus' sake only, but that they might see Lazarus also, whom he had raised from the dead. But the chief priests consulted that they might put Lazarus also to death; because that by reason of him many of the Jews went away, and believed on Jesus.

And when they came nigh to Jerusalem, unto Bethphage and Bethany, at the mount of Olives, he sendeth forth two of his disciples, and saith unto them, "Go your way into the village over against you: and as soon as ye be entered into it, ye shall find a colt tied, whereon never man sat; loose him, and bring him. And if any man say unto you, 'Why do ye this?' say ye that the Lord hath need of him; and straightway he will send him hither."

*Jesus enters Jerusalem*  All this was done, that it might be fulfilled which was spoken by the prophet, saying, "Tell ye the daughter of Sion, 'Behold, thy King cometh unto thee, meek, and sitting upon an ass, and a colt the foal of an ass.'"

And they went their way, and found the colt tied by the door without in a place where two ways met; and they loose him. And certain of them that stood there said unto them, "What do ye, loosing the colt?" And they said unto them even as Jesus had commanded: and they let them go. And they brought the colt to Jesus, and cast their garments on him; and he sat upon him.

And when he was come nigh, even now at the descent of the mount of Olives, the whole multitude of the disciples began to rejoice and praise God with a loud voice for all the mighty works that they had seen; saying, "Blessed be the King that cometh in the name of the Lord: peace in heaven, and glory in the highest."

And some of the Pharisees from among the multitude said unto him, "Master, rebuke thy disciples."

And he answered and said unto them, "I tell you that, if these should hold their peace, the stones would immediately cry out."

And when he was come near, he beheld the city, and wept over it, saying, "If thou hadst known, even thou, at least in this thy day, the things which belong unto thy peace! but now they are hid from thine eyes. For the days shall come upon thee, that thine enemies shall cast a trench about thee, and compass thee round, and keep thee in on every side, and shall lay thee even with the ground, and thy children within thee; and they shall not leave in thee one stone upon another; because thou knewest not the time of thy visitation."

And many spread their garments in the way: and others cut down branches off the trees, and strawed them in the way. And they that went before, and they that followed, cried, saying, "Hosanna; Blessed is he that cometh in the name of the Lord: blessed be the kingdom of our father David, that cometh in the name of the Lord: Hosanna in the highest."

And when he was come into Jerusalem, all the city was moved, saying, "Who is this?"

And the multitude said, "This is Jesus the prophet of Nazareth of Galilee."

The Pharisees therefore said among themselves, "Perceive ye how ye prevail nothing? behold, the world is gone after him."

*Jesus drives the money-changers from the temple*

And Jesus entered into Jerusalem, and into the temple: and when he had looked round about upon all things, and now the eventide was come, he went out unto Bethany with the twelve.

And they come to Jerusalem: and Jesus went into the temple, and began to cast out them that sold and bought in the temple, and overthrew the tables of the moneychangers, and the seats of them that sold doves; and would not suffer that any man should carry any vessel through the temple. And he taught, saying unto them, "Is it not written, 'My house shall be called of all nations the house of prayer'? but ye have made it a den of thieves."

And the blind and the lame came to him in the temple; and he healed them. And when the chief priests and scribes saw the wonderful things that he did, and the children crying in the temple, and saying, "Hosanna to the son of David"; they were sore displeased, and said unto him, "Hearest thou what these say?"

And Jesus saith unto them, "Yea; have ye never read, 'Out of the mouth of babes and sucklings thou hast perfected praise' ? "

And he taught daily in the temple. But the chief priests and the scribes and the chief of the people sought to destroy him, and could not find what they might do: for all the people were very attentive to hear him.

And when even was come, he went out of the city.

And in the morning, as they passed by, Jesus saith unto them, "Have faith in God. For verily I say unto you, That whosoever shall say unto this mountain, 'Be thou removed, and be thou cast into the sea'; and shall not doubt in his heart, but shall believe that those things which he saith shall come to pass; he shall have whatsoever he saith. Therefore I say unto you, What things soever ye desire, when ye pray, believe that ye receive them, and ye shall have them. And when ye stand praying, forgive, if ye have ought against any: that your Father also which is in heaven may forgive you your trespasses. But if ye do not forgive, neither will your Father which is in heaven forgive your trespasses."

And it came to pass, that on one of those days, as he taught the people in the temple, and preached the gospel, the chief priests and the scribes

*Parable of the vineyard* came upon him with the elders, and spake unto him, saying, "Tell us, by what authority doest thou these things? or who is he that gave thee this authority?"

And he answered and said unto them, "I will also ask you one thing; and answer me: The baptism of John, was it from heaven, or of men?"

And they reasoned with themselves, saying, "If we shall say, 'From heaven'; he will say, 'Why then believed ye him not?' But and if we say, 'Of men'; all the people will stone us: for they be persuaded that John was a prophet." And they answered, that they could not tell whence it was.

And Jesus said unto them, "Neither tell I you by what authority I do these things."

And he began to speak unto them by parables:

*"A certain man had two sons; and he came to the first, and said, 'Son, go work to day in my vineyard.' He answered and said, 'I will not': but afterward he repented, and went. And he came to the second, and said likewise. And he answered and said, 'I go, sir': and went not. Whether of them twain did the will of his father?"*

*They say unto him, "The first."*

Hear another parable:

*"A certain man planted a vineyard, and set an hedge about it, and digged a place for the winefat, and built a tower, and let it out to husbandmen, and went into a far country. And at the season he sent to the husbandmen a servant, that he might receive from the husbandmen of the fruit of the vineyard. And they caught him, and beat him, and sent him away empty. And again he sent unto them another servant; and at him they cast stones, and wounded him in the head, and sent him away shamefully handled. And again he sent another; and him they killed, and many others; beating some, and killing some. Having yet therefore one son, his wellbeloved, he sent him also last unto them, saying, 'They will reverence my son.' But those husbandmen said among themselves, 'This is the heir; come, let us kill him, and the inheritance shall be our's.' And they took him, and killed him, and cast him out of the vineyard. What shall therefore the lord of the vineyard do? he will come and destroy the husbandmen, and will give the vineyard unto others. And have ye not read this scripture;*

*The stone which the builders rejected*
*Is become the head of the corner:*
*This was the Lord's doing,*
*And it is marvellous in our eyes?"*

And Jesus answered and spake unto them again by parables, and said,

*"The kingdom of heaven is like unto a certain king, which made a mar-*
*riage for his son, and sent forth his servants to call them that were bidden to*
*the wedding: and they would not come. Again, he sent forth other servants,*
*saying, 'Tell them which are bidden, Behold, I have prepared my dinner:*
*my oxen and my fatlings are killed, and all things are ready: come unto the*
*marriage.' But they made light of it, and went their ways, one to his farm,*
*another to his merchandise: and the remnant took his servants, and en-*
*treated them spitefully, and slew them.*

*"But when the king heard thereof, he was wroth: and he sent forth his*
*armies, and destroyed those murderers, and burned up their city. Then saith*
*he to his servants, 'The wedding is ready, but they which were bidden were*
*not worthy. Go ye therefore into the highways, and as many as ye shall find,*
*bid to the marriage.' So those servants went out into the highways, and*
*gathered together all as many as they found, both bad and good: and the*
*wedding was furnished with guests."*

And the chief priests and the scribes sought to lay hold on him, but
feared the people: for they knew that he had spoken the parable against
them: and they left him, and went their way.

And they send unto him certain of the Pharisees and of the Herodians,
to catch him in his words. And when they were come, they say unto him,
"Master, we know that thou art true, and carest for no man: for thou regardest not the person of men, but teachest the way of God in truth: Is it
lawful to give tribute to Cæsar, or not? Shall we give, or shall we not
give?"

But he, knowing their hypocrisy, said unto them, "Why tempt ye me?
bring me a penny, that I may see it." And they brought it.

And he saith unto them, "Whose is this image and superscription?"
And they said unto him, "Cæsar's."

And Jesus answering said unto them, "Render to Cæsar the things that are Cæsar's, and to God the things that are God's." And they marvelled at him and left him, and went their way.

Then come unto him the Sadducees, which say there is no resurrection.

Jesus said unto them, "Ye know not the scriptures, neither the power of God. And as touching the dead, that they rise. God is not the God of the dead, but the God of the living: ye therefore do greatly err."

And one of the scribes came, and having heard them reasoning together, and perceiving that he had answered them well, asked him, "Which is the first commandment of all?"

And Jesus answered him, "The first of all the commandments is, 'Hear, O Israel; The Lord our God is one Lord: and thou shalt love the Lord thy God with all thy heart, and with all thy soul, and with all thy mind, and with all thy strength': this is the first and great commandment. And the second is like, namely this, 'Thou shalt love thy neighbour as thyself.' There is none other commandment greater than these. On these two commandments hang all the law and the prophets."

And the scribe said unto him, "Well, Master, thou hast said the truth: for there is one God; and there is none other but he: and to love him with all the heart, and with all the understanding, and with all the soul, and with all the strength, and to love his neighbour as himself, is more than all whole burnt offerings and sacrifices."

And when Jesus saw that he answered discreetly, he said unto him, "Thou art not far from the kingdom of God." And no man after that durst ask him any question.

Then spake Jesus to the multitude, and to his disciples, saying, "The scribes and the Pharisees sit in Moses' seat; all therefore whatsoever they bid you observe, that observe and do; but do not ye after their works: for they say, and do not. For they bind heavy burdens and grievous to be borne, and lay them on men's shoulders; but they themselves will not move them with one of their fingers. But all their works they do for to be seen of men: they make broad their phylacteries, and enlarge the borders of their garments, and love the uppermost rooms at feasts, and the chief seats in the synagogues, and greetings in the markets, and to be called of men, 'Rabbi, Rabbi.' But be not ye called 'Rabbi': for one is your Master, even Christ; and all ye are brethren. And call no man your father upon the earth: for one is your Father, which is in heaven. Neither be ye called masters: for one is your Master, even Christ. But he that is greatest among you shall be your servant. And whosoever shall exalt himself shall be abased; and he that shall humble himself shall be exalted.

"But woe unto you, scribes and Pharisees, hypocrites! for ye shut up the kingdom of heaven against men: for ye neither go in yourselves, neither suffer ye them that are entering to go in. Woe unto you, scribes and Pharisees, hypocrites! for ye pay tithe of mint and anise and cummin, and have omitted the weightier matters of the law, judgment, mercy, and faith: these ought ye to have done, and not to leave the other undone. Ye blind guides, which strain at a gnat, and swallow a camel. Woe unto you, scribes and Pharisees, hypocrites! for ye make clean the outside of the cup and of the platter, but within they are full of extortion and excess. Thou blind Pharisee, cleanse first that which is within the cup and platter, that the outside of them may be clean also. Woe unto you, scribes and Pharisees, hypocrites! for ye are like unto whited sepulchres, which indeed appear beautiful outward, but are within full of dead men's bones, and of all uncleanness. Even so ye also outwardly appear righteous unto men, but within ye are full of hypocrisy and iniquity."

And Jesus sat over against the treasury, and beheld how the people cast money into the treasury: and many that were rich cast in much. And there came a certain poor widow, and she threw in two mites, which make a farthing. And he called unto him his disciples, and saith unto them, "Verily I say unto you, This poor widow hath cast more in, than all they which have cast into the treasury: for all they did cast in of their abundance; but she of her want did cast in all that she had, even all her living."

And there were certain Greeks among them that came up to worship at the feast: the same came therefore to Philip, which was of Bethsaida of Galilee, and desired him, saying, "Sir, we would see Jesus." Philip cometh and telleth Andrew: and again Andrew and Philip tell Jesus.

And Jesus answered them, saying, "The hour is come, that the Son of man should be glorified. Verily, verily, I say unto you, Except a corn of wheat fall into the ground and die, it abideth alone: but if it die, it bringeth forth much fruit. He that loveth his life shall lose it; and he that

*Jesus calls earnestly for confession of faith*

hateth his life in this world shall keep it unto life eternal. If any man serve me, let him follow me; and where I am, there shall also my servant be: if any man serve me, him will my Father honour. Now is my soul troubled; and what shall I say? 'Father, save me from this hour': but for this cause came I unto this hour. 'Father, glorify thy name.' "

Then came there a voice from heaven, saying, "I have both glorified it, and will glorify it again."

The people therefore, that stood by, and heard it, said that it thundered: others said, "An angel spake to him."

Jesus answered and said, "This voice came not because of me, but for your sakes. Now is the judgment of this world: now shall the prince of this world be cast out. And I, if I be lifted up from the earth, will draw all men unto me." This he said, signifying what death he should die.

The people answered him, "We have heard out of the law that Christ abideth for ever: and how sayest thou, 'The Son of man must be lifted up? who is this Son of man?' "

Then Jesus said unto them, "Yet a little while is the light with you. Walk while ye have the light, lest darkness come upon you: for he that walketh in darkness knoweth not whither he goeth. While ye have light, believe in the light, that ye may be the children of light." These things spake Jesus, and departed, and did hide himself from them.

But though he had done so many miracles before them, yet they believed not on him. Nevertheless among the chief rulers also many believed on him; but because of the Pharisees they did not confess him, lest they should be put out of the synagogue: for they loved the praise of men more than the praise of God.

Jesus cried and said, "He that believeth on me, believeth not on me, but on him that sent me. And he that seeth me seeth him that sent me. I am come a light into the world, that whosoever believeth on me should not abide in darkness. And if any man hear my words, and believe not, I judge him not: for I came not to judge the world, but to save the world. He that rejecteth me, and receiveth not my words, hath one that judgeth him: the word that I have spoken, the same shall judge him in the last day. For I have not spoken of myself; but the Father which sent me, he gave me a commandment, what I should say, and what I should speak."

And as he sat upon the mount of Olives, the disciples came unto him privately, saying, "Tell us, when shall these things be? and what shall be the sign of thy coming, and of the end of the world?"

*Jesus describes the last days*

And he said, "Take heed that ye be not deceived: for many shall come in my name, saying, 'I am Christ'; and 'the time draweth near': go ye not therefore after them. But when ye shall hear of wars and commotions, be not terrified: for these things must first come to pass; but the end is not by and by."

Then said he unto them, "Nation shall rise against nation, and kingdom against kingdom: and great earthquakes shall be in divers places, and famines, and pestilences; and fearful sights and great signs shall there be from heaven. But before all these, they shall lay their hands on you, and persecute you, delivering you up to the synagogues, and into prisons, being brought before kings and rulers for my name's sake. And it shall turn to you for a testimony. Settle it therefore in your hearts, not to meditate before what ye shall answer: for I will give you a mouth and wisdom, which all your adversaries shall not be able to gainsay nor resist. And ye shall be betrayed both by parents, and brethren, and kinsfolks, and friends; and some of you shall they cause to be put to death. And ye shall be hated of all men for my name's sake. But there shall not an hair of your head perish. And this gospel of the kingdom shall be preached in all the world for a witness unto all nations.

"In your patience possess ye your souls. For as the lightning cometh out of the east, and shineth even unto the west; so shall also the coming of the Son of man be. And then shall appear the sign of the Son of man in heaven: and then shall all the tribes of the earth mourn, and they shall see the Son of man coming in the clouds of heaven with power and great glory. And he shall send his angels with a great sound of a trumpet, and they shall gather together his elect from the four winds, from one end of heaven to the other. And when these things begin to come to pass, then look up, and lift up your heads; for your redemption draweth nigh."

And he spake to them a parable;

*"Behold the fig tree, and all the trees; when they now shoot forth, ye see and know of your own selves that summer is now nigh at hand. So likewise ye, when ye see these things come to pass, know ye that the kingdom of God is nigh at hand.*

[ 87 ]

*Parable of the ten virgins*

"*Verily I say unto you, This generation shall not pass away, till all be ful-filled. Heaven and earth shall pass away: but my words shall not pass away.*

"*Take ye heed, watch and pray: for ye know not when the time is. For the Son of man is as a man taking a far journey, who left his house, and gave authority to his servants, and to every man his work, and commanded the porter to watch. Blessed is that servant, whom his lord when he cometh shall find so doing. Verily I say unto you, That he shall make him ruler over all his goods. Watch ye therefore: for ye know not when the master of the house cometh, at even, or at midnight, or at the cock-crowing, or in the morning: lest coming suddenly he find you sleeping. And what I say unto you, I say unto all, 'Watch.'*

"*Then shall the kingdom of heaven be likened unto ten virgins, which took their lamps, and went forth to meet the bridegroom. And five of them were wise, and five were foolish. They that were foolish took their lamps, and took no oil with them: but the wise took oil in their vessels with their lamps. While the bridegroom tarried, they all slumbered and slept. And at midnight there was a cry made, 'Behold, the bridegroom cometh; go ye out to meet him.' Then all those virgins arose, and trimmed their lamps. And the foolish said unto the wise, 'Give us of your oil; for our lamps are gone out.' But the wise answered, saying, 'Not so; lest there be not enough for us and you: but go ye rather to them that sell, and buy for yourselves.'*

"*And while they went to buy, the bridegroom came; and they that were ready went in with him to the marriage: and the door was shut. Afterward came also the other virgins, saying, 'Lord, Lord, open to us.' But he an-swered and said, 'Verily I say unto you, I know you not.'*

"*Watch therefore, for ye know neither the day nor the hour wherein the Son of man cometh.*"

*Parable of the talents*

"*For the kingdom of heaven is as a man travelling into a far country, who called his own servants, and delivered unto them his goods. And unto one he gave five talents, to another two, and to another one; to every man according to his several ability; and straightway took his journey. Then he that had received the five talents went and traded with the same, and made them other five talents. And likewise he that had received two, he also gained other two. But he that had received one went and digged in the earth, and hid his lord's money.*

[ 88 ]

*THE WISE AND FOOLISH VIRGINS*

"*After a long time the lord of those servants cometh, and reckoneth with* *them. And so he that had received five talents came and brought other five talents, saying, 'Lord, thou deliveredst unto me five talents: behold, I have gained beside them five talents more.' His lord said unto him, 'Well done, thou good and faithful servant: thou hast been faithful over a few things, I will make thee ruler over many things: enter thou into the joy of thy lord.' He also that had received two talents came and said, 'Lord, thou deliveredst unto me two talents: behold, I have gained two other talents beside them.' His lord said unto him, 'Well done, good and faithful servant; thou hast been faithful over a few things, I will make thee ruler over many things: enter thou into the joy of thy lord.' Then he which had received the one talent came and said, 'Lord, I knew thee that thou art an hard man, reaping where thou hast not sown, and gathering where thou hast not strawed: and I was afraid, and went and hid thy talent in the earth: lo, there thou hast that is thine.' His lord answered and said unto him, 'Thou wicked and slothful servant, thou knewest that I reap where I sowed not, and gather where I have not strawed: thou oughtest therefore to have put my money to the exchangers, and then at my coming I should have received mine own with usury. Take therefore the talent from him, and give it unto him which hath ten talents. For unto every one that hath shall be given, and he shall have abundance: but from him that hath not shall be taken away even that which he hath.'*

"*When the Son of man shall come in his glory, and all the holy angels with him, then shall he sit upon the throne of his glory: and before him shall be gathered all nations: and he shall separate them one from another, as a shepherd divideth his sheep from the goats: and he shall set the sheep on his right hand, but the goats on the left.*

"*Then shall the King say unto them on his right hand, 'Come, ye blessed of my Father, inherit the kingdom prepared for you from the foundation of the world: for I was an hungred, and ye gave me meat: I was thirsty, and ye gave me drink: I was a stranger, and ye took me in: naked, and ye clothed me: I was sick, and ye visited me: I was in prison, and ye came unto me.' Then shall the righteous answer him, saying, 'Lord, when saw we thee an hungred, and fed thee? or thirsty, and gave thee drink? When saw we thee a stranger, and took thee in? or naked, and clothed thee? Or when saw we thee sick, or in prison, and came unto thee?' And the King shall answer and say unto them, 'Verily I say unto you, Inasmuch as ye have done it unto one of the least of these my brethren, ye have done it unto me.'*

*"Then shall he say also unto them on the left hand, 'Depart from me, for I was an hungred, and ye gave me no meat: I was thirsty, and ye gave me no drink: I was a stranger, and ye took me not in: naked, and ye clothed me not: sick, and in prison, and ye visited me not.' Then shall they also answer him, saying, 'Lord, when saw we thee an hungred, or athirst, or a stranger, or naked, or sick, or in prison, and did not minister unto thee?' Then shall he answer them, saying, 'Verily I say unto you, Inasmuch as ye did it not to one of the least of these, ye did it not to me.' "*

And it came to pass, when Jesus had finished all these sayings, he said unto his disciples, "Ye know that after two days is the feast of the passover, and the Son of man is betrayed to be crucified."

And in the day time he was teaching in the temple; and at night he went out, and abode in the mount that is called the mount of Olives. And all the people came early in the morning to him in the temple, for to hear him.

Now the feast of unleavened bread drew nigh, which is called the Passover. And the chief priests and scribes sought how they might kill him; for they feared the people. But they said, "Not on the feast day, lest there be an uproar among the people."

Then entered Satan into Judas surnamed Iscariot, being of the number of the twelve. And he went his way, and communed with the chief priests and captains, how he might betray him unto them. And they were glad, and covenanted to give him money. And he promised, and sought opportunity to betray him unto them in the absence of the multitude.

Then came the day of unleavened bread, when the passover must be killed. And he sent Peter and John, saying, "Go and prepare us the passover, that we may eat."

And they said unto him, "Where wilt thou that we prepare?"

And he said unto them, "Behold, when ye are entered into the city, there shall a man meet you, bearing a pitcher of water; follow him into the house where he entereth in. And ye shall say unto the goodman of the house, 'The Master saith unto thee, "Where is the guestchamber, where

I shall eat the passover with my disciples?" ' And he shall shew you a
large upper room furnished: there make ready."

And they went, and found as he had said unto them: and they made ready the passover.

Now before the feast of the passover, when Jesus knew that his hour was come that he should depart out of this world unto the Father, having loved his own which were in the world, he loved them unto the end. And when the hour was come, he sat down, and the twelve apostles with him. And he said unto them, "With desire I have desired to eat this passover with you before I suffer: for I say unto you, I will not any more eat thereof, until it be fulfilled in the kingdom of God."

Jesus knowing that the Father had given all things into his hands, and that he was come from God, and went to God; he riseth from supper, and laid aside his garments; and took a towel, and girded himself. After that he poureth water into a bason, and began to wash the disciples' feet, and to wipe them with the towel wherewith he was girded.

Then cometh he to Simon Peter: and Peter saith unto him, "Lord, dost thou wash my feet?"

Jesus answered and said unto him, "What I do thou knowest not now; but thou shalt know hereafter."

Peter saith unto him, "Thou shalt never wash my feet."

Jesus answered him, "If I wash thee not, thou hast no part with me."

Simon Peter saith unto him, "Lord, not my feet only, but also my hands and my head."

Jesus saith unto him, "He that is washed needeth not save to wash his feet, but is clean every whit: and ye are clean, but not all." For he knew who should betray him; therefore said he, "Ye are not all clean."

So after he had washed their feet, and had taken his garments, and was set down again, he said unto them, "Know ye what I have done to you? Ye call me Master and Lord: and ye say well; for so I am. If I then, your Lord and Master, have washed your feet; ye also ought to wash one another's feet. For I have given you an example, that ye should do as I have done to you. Verily, verily, I say unto you, The servant is not greater than his lord; neither he that is sent greater than he that sent him. If ye know these things, happy are ye if ye do them. I speak not of

*Judas indicated as the betrayer*

you all: I know whom I have chosen: but that the scripture may be fulfilled, 'He that eateth bread with me hath lifted up his heel against me.' Now I tell you before it come, that, when it is come to pass, ye may believe that I am he. Verily, verily, I say unto you, He that receiveth whomsoever I send receiveth me; and he that receiveth me receiveth him that sent me."

When Jesus had thus said, he was troubled in spirit, and testified, and said, "Verily, verily, I say unto you, that one of you shall betray me."

Then the disciples looked one on another, doubting of whom he spake. And they were exceeding sorrowful, and began every one of them to say unto him, "Lord, is it I?"

Now there was leaning on Jesus' bosom one of his disciples, whom Jesus loved. Simon Peter therefore beckoned to him, that he should ask who it should be of whom he spake. He then lying on Jesus' breast saith unto him, "Lord, who is it?"

Jesus answered, "He it is, to whom I shall give a sop, when I have dipped it." And when he had dipped the sop, he gave it to Judas Iscariot, the son of Simon.

Then Judas, which betrayed him, answered and said, "Master, is it I?"

He said unto him, "Thou hast said." And after the sop Satan entered into him.

Then said Jesus unto him, "That thou doest, do quickly."

Now no man at the table knew for what intent he spake this unto him. For some of them thought, because Judas had the bag, that Jesus had said unto him, "Buy those things that we have need of against the feast"; or, that he should give something to the poor. He then having received the sop went immediately out: and it was night.

And there was also a strife among them, which of them should be accounted the greatest. And Jesus said unto them, "The Kings of the Gentiles exercise lordship over them; and they that exercise authority upon them are called benefactors. But ye shall not be so: but he that is greatest among you, let him be as the younger; and he that is chief, as he that doth serve. For whether is greater, he that sitteth at meat, or he that serveth? is not he that sitteth at meat? but I am among you as he that serveth. Ye are they which have continued with me in my temptations.

And I appoint unto you a kingdom, as my Father hath appointed unto me; that ye may eat and drink at my table in my kingdom."

And as they were eating, Jesus took bread, and blessed it, and brake it, and gave it to the disciples, and said, "Take, eat; this is my body." Likewise also the cup after supper, saying, "This cup is the new testament in my blood, which is shed for you." And when he had given thanks, he gave it to them, saying, "Drink ye all of it; for this is my blood of the new testament, which is shed for many for the remission of sins. But I say unto you, I will not drink henceforth of this fruit of the vine, until that day when I drink it new with you in my Father's kingdom."

Therefore, when Judas was gone out, Jesus said, "Now is the Son of man glorified, and God is glorified in him. Little children, yet a little while I am with you. Ye shall seek me: and as I said unto the Jews, 'Whither I go, ye cannot come'; so now I say to you. A new commandment I give unto you, that ye love one another; as I have loved you, that ye also love one another. By this shall all men know that ye are my disciples, if ye have love one to another."

And Jesus saith unto them, "All ye shall be offended because of me this night: for it is written, 'I will smite the shepherd, and the sheep shall be scattered.' But after that I am risen, I will go before you into Galilee."

Simon Peter said unto him, "Lord, whither goest thou?"

Jesus answered him, "Whither I go, thou canst not follow me now; but thou shalt follow me afterwards."

Peter said unto him, "Lord, why cannot I follow thee now? I will lay down my life for thy sake."

Jesus answered him, "Wilt thou lay down thy life for my sake? Simon, Simon, behold, Satan hath desired to have you, that he may sift you as wheat: but I have prayed for thee, that thy faith fail not: and when thou art converted, strengthen thy brethren."

And he said unto him, "Lord, I am ready to go with thee, both into prison, and to death. Although all shall be offended, yet will not I." Jesus said, "Verily, verily, I say unto thee, Peter, the cock shall not crow this day till thou shalt thrice deny that thou knowest me." But Peter spake the more vehemently, "If I should die with thee, I will not deny thee in any wise." Likewise also said they all.

*The disciples comforted*

And Jesus said, "Let not your heart be troubled: ye believe in God, believe also in me. In my Father's house are many mansions: if it were not so, I would have told you. I go to prepare a place for you. And if I go and prepare a place for you, I will come again, and receive you unto myself; that where I am, there ye may be also. And whither I go ye know, and the way ye know."

Thomas saith unto him, "Lord, we know not whither thou goest; and how can we know the way?"

Jesus saith unto him, "I am the way, the truth, and the life: no man cometh unto the Father, but by me. If ye had known me, ye should have known my Father also: and from henceforth ye know him, and have seen him."

Philip saith unto him, "Lord, shew us the Father, and it sufficeth us."

Jesus saith unto him, "Have I been so long time with you, and yet hast thou not known me, Philip? he that hath seen me hath seen the Father; and how sayest thou then, 'Shew us the Father'? Believest thou not that I am in the Father, and the Father in me? the words that I speak unto you I speak not of myself: but the Father that dwelleth in me, he doeth the works. Believe me that I am in the Father, and the Father in me: or else believe me for the very works' sake. Verily, verily, I say unto you, He that believeth on me, the works that I do shall he do also; and greater works than these shall he do; because I go unto my Father. And whatsoever ye shall ask in my name, that will I do, that the Father may be glorified in the Son. If ye shall ask any thing in my name, I will do it.

"If ye love me, keep my commandments. And I will pray the Father, and he shall give you another Comforter, that he may abide with you for ever; even the Spirit of truth; whom the world cannot receive, because it seeth him not, neither knoweth him: but ye know him; for he dwelleth with you, and shall be in you. I will not leave you comfortless: I will come to you. Yet a little while, and the world seeth me no more; but ye see me: because I live, ye shall live also. At that day ye shall know that I am in my Father, and ye in me, and I in you. He that hath my commandments, and keepeth them, he it is that loveth me: and he that loveth me shall be loved of my Father, and I will love him, and will manifest myself to him."

Judas saith unto him, not Iscariot, "Lord, how is it that thou wilt manifest thyself unto us, and not unto the world?"

*Jesus answered and said unto him, "If a man love me, he will keep my words: and my Father will love him, and we will come unto him, and make our abode with him. He that loveth me not keepeth not my sayings: and the word which ye hear is not mine, but the Father's which sent me. These things have I spoken unto you, being yet present with you. But the Comforter, which is the Holy Ghost, whom the Father will send in my name, he shall teach you all things, and bring all things to your remembrance, whatsoever I have said unto you.*

*The true vine and the branches*

*"Peace I leave with you, my peace I give unto you: not as the world giveth, give I unto you. Let not your heart be troubled, neither let it be afraid. Ye have heard how I said unto you, 'I go away, and come again unto you.' If ye loved me, ye would rejoice, because I said, 'I go unto the Father': for my Father is greater than I.*

*"And now I have told you before it come to pass, that, when it is come to pass, ye might believe. Hereafter I will not talk much with you: for the prince of this world cometh, and hath nothing in me. But that the world may know that I love the Father; and as the Father gave me commandment, even so I do. Arise, let us go hence.*

*"I am the true vine, and my Father is the husbandman. Every branch in me that beareth not fruit he taketh away; and every branch that beareth fruit, he purgeth it, that it may bring forth more fruit. Now ye are clean through the word which I have spoken unto you. Abide in me, and I in you. As the branch cannot bear fruit of itself, except it abide in the vine; no more can ye, except ye abide in me. I am the vine, ye are the branches: He that abideth in me, and I in him, the same bringeth forth much fruit: for without me ye can do nothing. If a man abide not in me, he is cast forth as a branch, and is withered; and men gather them, and cast them into the fire, and they are burned. If ye abide in me, and my words abide in you, ye shall ask what ye will, and it shall be done unto you. Herein is my Father glorified, that ye bear much fruit; so shall ye be my disciples.*

*"As the Father hath loved me, so have I loved you: continue ye in my love. If ye keep my commandments, ye shall abide in my love; even as I have kept my Father's commandments, and abide in his love. These things have I spoken unto you, that my joy might remain in you, and that your joy might be full. This is my commandment, That ye love one another, as I have loved you. Greater love hath no man than this, that a man lay down his life for his*

*friends. Ye are my friends, if ye do whatsoever I command you. Henceforth I call you not servants; for the servant knoweth not what his lord doeth: but I have called you friends; for all things that I have heard of my Father I have made known unto you. Ye have not chosen me, but I have chosen you, and ordained you, that ye should go and bring forth fruit, and that your fruit should remain: that whatsoever ye shall ask of the Father in my name, he may give it you.*

*"These things I command you, that ye love one another. If the world hate you, ye know that it hated me before it hated you. If ye were of the world, the world would love his own, but because ye are not of the world, but I have chosen you out of the world, therefore the world hateth you. Remember the word that I said unto you, 'The servant is not greater than his lord.' If they have persecuted me, they will also persecute you; if they have kept my saying, they will keep your's also. But all these things will they do unto you for my name's sake, because they know not him that sent me. If I had not come and spoken unto them, they had not had sin: but now they have no cloke for their sin. He that hateth me hateth my Father also. If I had not done among them the works which none other man did, they had not had sin: but now have they both seen and hated both me and my Father. But this cometh to pass, that the word might be fulfilled that is written in their law, 'They hated me without a cause.' But when the Comforter is come, whom I will send unto you from the Father, even the Spirit of truth, which proceedeth from the Father, he shall testify of me: and ye also shall bear witness, because ye have been with me from the beginning.*

*"I have yet many things to say unto you, but ye cannot bear them now. Howbeit when he, the Spirit of truth, is come, he will guide you into all truth: for he shall not speak of himself; but whatsoever he shall hear, that shall he speak: and he will shew you things to come. He shall glorify me: for he shall receive of mine, and shall shew it unto you. All things that the Father hath are mine: therefore said I, that he shall take of mine, and shall shew it unto you. A little while, and ye shall not see me: and again, a little while, and ye shall see me, because I go to the Father."*

*Then said some of his disciples among themselves,"What is this that he saith unto us, 'A little while, and ye shall not see me': and again, 'a little while, and ye shall see me': and, 'Because I go to the Father'?" They said therefore,"What is this that he saith, 'A little while'? we cannot tell what he saith."*

*Now Jesus knew that they were desirous to ask him, and said unto them,* *Jesus speaks plainly*
*"Do ye enquire among yourselves of that I said, 'A little while, and ye shall* *to the disciples*
*not see me': and again, 'a little while, and ye shall see me'? Verily, verily,
I say unto you, That ye shall weep and lament, but the world shall rejoice:
and ye shall be sorrowful, but your sorrow shall be turned into joy. A
woman when she is in travail hath sorrow, because her hour is come: but as
soon as she is delivered of the child, she remembereth no more the anguish,
for joy that a man is born into the world. And ye now therefore have
sorrow: but I will see you again, and your heart shall rejoice, and your joy
no man taketh from you. And in that day ye shall ask me nothing. Verily,
verily, I say unto you, Whatsoever ye shall ask the Father in my name, he
will give it you. Hitherto have ye asked nothing in my name: ask, and ye
shall receive, that your joy may be full. These things have I spoken unto you
in proverbs: but the time cometh, when I shall no more speak unto you in
proverbs, but I shall shew you plainly of the Father. At that day ye shall ask
in my name: and I say not unto you, that I will pray the Father for you: for
the Father himself loveth you, because ye have loved me, and have believed
that I came out from God. I came forth from the Father, and am come into
the world: again, I leave the world, and go to the Father."*

*His disciples said unto him, "Lo, now speakest thou plainly, and
speakest no proverb. Now are we sure that thou knowest all things, and
needest not that any man should ask thee: by this we believe that thou camest
forth from God."*

*Jesus answered them, "Do ye now believe? Behold, the hour cometh,
yea, is now come, that ye shall be scattered, every man to his own, and shall
leave me alone: and yet I am not alone, because the Father is with me. These
things I have spoken unto you, that in me ye might have peace. In the world
ye shall have tribulation: but be of good cheer; I have overcome the world."*

*These words spake Jesus, and lifted up his eyes to heaven and said,
"Father, the hour is come; glorify thy Son, that thy Son also may glorify thee:
as thou hast given him power over all flesh, that he should give eternal life
to as many as thou hast given him. And this is life eternal, that they might
know thee the only true God, and Jesus Christ, whom thou hast sent. I have
glorified thee on the earth: I have finished the work which thou gavest me
to do.*

*"And now, O Father, glorify thou me with thine own self with the glory*

*He prays for all believers*

*which I had with thee before the world was. I have manifested thy name unto the men which thou gavest me out of the world: thine they were, and thou gavest them me; and they have kept thy word. Now they have known that all things whatsoever thou hast given me are of thee. For I have given unto them the words which thou gavest me; and they have received them, and have known surely that I came out from thee, and they have believed that thou didst send me. I pray for them: I pray not for the world, but for them which thou hast given me; for they are thine. And all mine are thine, and thine are mine; and I am glorified in them.*

*"And now I am no more in the world, but these are in the world, and I come to thee. Holy Father, keep through thine own name those whom thou hast given me, that they may be one, as we are. While I was with them in the world, I kept them in thy name: those that thou gavest me I have kept, and none of them is lost, but the son of perdition; that the scripture might be fulfilled. And now come I to thee; and these things I speak in the world, that they might have my joy fulfilled in themselves. I have given them thy word; and the world hath hated them, because they are not of the world, even as I am not of the world. I pray not that thou shouldest take them out of the world, but that thou shouldest keep them from the evil. They are not of the world, even as I am not of the world. Sanctify them through thy truth: thy word is truth. As thou hast sent me into the world, even so have I also sent them into the world. And for their sakes I sanctify myself, that they also might be sanctified through the truth.*

*"Neither pray I for these alone, but for them also which shall believe on me through their word; that they all may be one; as thou, Father, art in me, and I in thee, that they also may be one in us: that the world may believe that thou hast sent me. And the glory which thou gavest me I have given them; that they may be one, even as we are one: I in them, and thou in me, that they may be made perfect in one; and that the world may know that thou hast sent me, and hast loved them, as thou hast loved me. Father, I will that they also, whom thou hast given me, be with me where I am; that they may behold my glory, which thou hast given me: for thou lovedst me before the foundation of the world. O righteous Father, the world hath not known thee: but I have known thee, and these have known that thou hast sent me. And I have declared unto them thy name, and will declare it: that the love wherewith thou hast loved me may be in them, and I in them."*

And when they had sung an hymn, they went out into the mount of *The agony in the*
Olives. *garden of Gethsemane*

When Jesus had spoken these words, he went forth with his disciples over the brook Cedron, unto a place called Gethsemane, where was a garden, into the which he entered, and his disciples. And he saith unto the disciples, "Sit ye here, while I go and pray yonder."

And he took with him Peter and the two sons of Zebedee, and began to be sorrowful and very heavy. Then saith he unto them, "My soul is exceeding sorrowful, even unto death: tarry ye here, and watch with me."

And he went forward a little, and fell on the ground, and prayed that, if it were possible, the hour might pass from him. And he said, "Abba, Father, all things are possible unto thee; take away this cup from me: nevertheless not what I will, but what thou wilt."

And being in an agony he prayed more earnestly: and his sweat was as it were great drops of blood falling down to the ground.

And he cometh, and findeth them sleeping, and saith unto Peter, "Simon, sleepest thou? couldest not thou watch one hour? Watch ye and pray, lest ye enter into temptation. The spirit truly is ready, but the flesh is weak."

He went away again the second time, and prayed, saying, "O my Father, if this cup may not pass away from me, except I drink it, thy will be done."

And when he returned, he found them asleep again, (for their eyes were heavy,) neither wist they what to answer him. And he left them, and went away again, and prayed the third time, saying the same words. And he cometh the third time, and saith unto them, "Sleep on now, and take your rest: it is enough, the hour is come; behold, the Son of man is betrayed into the hands of sinners. Rise up, let us go; lo, he that betrayeth me is at hand."

Judas also, which betrayed him, knew the place: for Jesus ofttimes *The betrayal* resorted thither with his disciples. Judas then, having received a band of men and officers from the chief priests and Pharisees, cometh thither with lanterns and torches and weapons. And he that betrayed him had given them a token, saying, "Whomsoever I shall kiss, that same is he; take him, and lead him away safely."

And Judas went before them, and drew near unto Jesus to kiss him.

[ 99 ]

*The arrest* But Jesus said unto him, "Judas, betrayest thou the Son of man with a kiss?"

Jesus therefore, knowing all things that should come upon him, went forth, and said unto them, "Whom seek ye?"

They answered him, "Jesus of Nazareth."

Jesus saith unto them, "I am he."

And Judas also, which betrayed him, stood with them. As soon then as he had said unto them, "I am he," they went backward, and fell to the ground. Then asked he them again, "Whom seek ye?"

And they said, "Jesus of Nazareth."

Jesus answered, "I have told you that I am he: if therefore ye seek me, let these go their way."

When they which were about him saw what would follow, they said unto him, "Lord, shall we smite with the sword?"

Then Simon Peter having a sword drew it, and smote the high priest's servant, and cut off his right ear. The servant's name was Malchus. Then said Jesus unto Peter, "Put up thy sword into the sheath: for all they that take the sword shall perish with the sword." And Jesus said, "Suffer ye thus far." And he touched his ear, and healed him.

"Thinkest thou that I cannot now pray to my Father, and he shall presently give me more than twelve legions of angels? The cup which the Father hath given me, shall I not drink it?"

Then Jesus said unto the chief priests, and captains of the temple, and the elders, which were come to him, "Be ye come out, as against a thief, with swords and staves? When I was daily with you in the temple, ye stretched forth no hands against me: but this is your hour, and the power of darkness."

Then all the disciples forsook him, and fled. And there followed him a certain young man, having a linen cloth cast about his naked body; and the young men laid hold on him: and he left the linen cloth, and fled from them naked.

Then the band and the captain and officers of the Jews took Jesus, and bound him, and led him away to Annas first; for he was father in law to Caiaphas, which was the high priest that same year.

The high priest then asked Jesus of his disciples, and of his doctrine. Jesus answered him, "I spake openly to the world; I ever taught in the synagogue, and in the temple, whither the Jews always resort; and in secret have I said nothing. Why askest thou me? ask them which heard me, what I have said unto them: behold, they know what I said."

And when he had thus spoken, one of the officers which stood by struck Jesus with the palm of his hand, saying, "Answerest thou the high priest so?"

Jesus answered him, "If I have spoken evil, bear witness of the evil: but if well, why smitest thou me?"

And Simon Peter followed Jesus, and so did another disciple: that disciple was known unto the high priest, and went in with Jesus into the palace of the high priest. But Peter stood at the door without. Then went out that other disciple, which was known unto the high priest, and spake unto her that kept the door, and brought in Peter. And the servants and officers stood there, who had made a fire of coals; for it was cold: and they warmed themselves: and Peter stood with them, and warmed himself. But a certain maid beheld him as he sat by the fire, and earnestly looked upon him, and said, "This man was also with him."

And he denied him, saying, "Woman, I know him not."

And after a little while another saw him, and said, "Thou art also of them."

And Peter said, "Man, I am not."

And about the space of one hour after another confidently affirmed, saying, "Of a truth this fellow also was with him: for he is a Galilæan."

And Peter said, "Man, I know not what thou sayest." And immediately, while he yet spake, the cock crew. And the Lord turned, and looked upon Peter. And Peter remembered the word of the Lord, how he had said unto him, "Before the cock crow, thou shalt deny me thrice." And Peter went out, and wept bitterly.

Now Annas had sent him bound unto Caiaphas the high priest. Caiaphas was he, which gave counsel to the Jews, that it was expedient that one man should die for the people.

And as soon as it was day, the elders of the people and the chief priests and the scribes came together, and led him into their council. And the chief priests and all the council sought for witness against Jesus to put him to death; and found none. For many bare false witness against him, but their witness agreed not together. And there arose certain and bare

*Jesus is accused* false witness against him, saying, "We heard him say, 'I will destroy this temple that is made with hands, and within three days I will build another made without hands.'" But neither so did their witness agree together.

And the high priest stood up in the midst, and asked Jesus, saying, "Answerest thou nothing? what is it which these witness against thee?"

But he held his peace, and answered nothing. Again the high priest asked him and said unto him, "Art thou the Christ? Tell us."

And he said unto them, "If I tell you, ye will not believe: and if I also ask you, ye will not answer me, nor let me go. Hereafter shall the Son of man sit on the right hand of the power of God."

Then said they all, "Art thou then the Son of God?"

And he said unto them, "Ye say that I am."

Then the high priest rent his clothes, and saith, "What need we any further witnesses? Ye have heard the blasphemy: what think ye?"

And they all condemned him to be guilty of death.

And the men that held Jesus mocked him, and smote him. And when they had blindfolded him, they struck him on the face, and asked him, saying, "Prophesy, who is it that smote thee?"

And many other things blasphemously spake they against him.

Then led they Jesus from Caiaphas unto the hall of judgment unto Pilate: and it was early. And they began to accuse him, saying, "We found this fellow perverting the nation, and forbidding to give tribute to Cæsar, saying that he himself is Christ a King."

Then said Pilate unto him, "Hearest thou not how many things they witness against thee?"

And he answered him to never a word; insomuch that the governor marvelled greatly.

And they themselves went not into the judgment hall, lest they should be defiled; but that they might eat the passover. Pilate then went out unto them, and said, "What accusation bring ye against this man?"

They answered and said unto him, "If he were not a malefactor, we would not have delivered him up unto thee."

Then said Pilate unto them, "Take ye him, and judge him according to your law."

The Jews therefore said unto him, "It is not lawful for us to put any

man to death": that the saying of Jesus might be fulfilled, which he *Pilate passes judgment*
spake, signifying what death he should die.

Then Pilate entered into the judgment hall again, and called Jesus, and said unto him, "Art thou the King of the Jews?"

Jesus answered him, "Sayest thou this thing of thyself, or did others tell it thee of me?"

Pilate answered, "Am I a Jew? Thine own nation and the chief priests have delivered thee unto me: what hast thou done?"

Jesus answered, "My kingdom is not of this world: if my kingdom were of this world, then would my servants fight, that I should not be delivered to the Jews: but now is my kingdom not from hence."

Pilate therefore said unto him, "Art thou a king then?"

Jesus answered, "Thou sayest that I am a king. To this end was I born, and for this cause came I into the world, that I should bear witness unto the truth. Everyone that is of the truth heareth my voice."

Pilate saith unto him, "What is truth?" And when he had said this, he went out again unto the Jews.

Then said Pilate to the chief priests and to the people, "I find no fault in this man."

And they were the more fierce, saying, "He stirreth up the people, teaching throughout all Jewry, beginning from Galilee to this place."

When Pilate heard of Galilee, he asked whether the man were a Galilæan. And as soon as he knew that he belonged unto Herod's jurisdiction, he sent him to Herod, who himself also was at Jerusalem at that time. And when Herod saw Jesus, he was exceeding glad: for he was desirous to see him of a long season, because he had heard many things of him; and he hoped to have seen some miracle done by him. Then he questioned with him in many words; but he answered him nothing. And the chief priests and scribes stood and vehemently accused him. And Herod with his men of war set him at nought, and mocked him, and arrayed him in a gorgeous robe, and sent him again to Pilate. And the same day Pilate and Herod were made friends together: for before they were at enmity between themselves.

When Pilate was set down on the judgment seat, his wife sent unto him, saying, "Have thou nothing to do with that just man: for I have suffered many things this day in a dream because of him."

And Pilate, when he had called together the chief priests and the rulers and the people, said unto them, "Ye have brought this man unto me, as one that perverteth the people: and, behold, I, having examined him before you, have found no fault in this man touching those things whereof ye accuse him: no, nor yet Herod: for I sent you to him; and, lo, nothing worthy of death is done unto him. Ye have a custom, that I should release unto you one at the passover: will ye therefore that I release unto you the King of the Jews?"

But the chief priests and elders persuaded the multitude that they should ask Barabbas, and destroy Jesus. And they cried out all at once, saying, "Away with this man, and release unto us Barabbas": (who for a certain sedition made in the city, and for murder, was cast into prison.) Pilate therefore, willing to release Jesus, spake again to them. But they cried, saying, "Crucify him, crucify him."

And he said unto them the third time, "Why, what evil hath he done? I have found no cause of death in him: I will therefore chastise him, and let him go."

And they were instant with loud voices, requiring that he might be crucified. And when Pilate saw that he could prevail nothing, but that rather a tumult was made, he took water, and washed his hands before the multitude, saying, "I am innocent of the blood of this just person: see ye to it."

And the voices of them and of the chief priests prevailed. And so Pilate, willing to content the people, gave sentence that it should be as they required. And he released unto them him that for sedition and murder was cast into prison, whom they had desired; but he delivered Jesus to their will.

Then Pilate therefore took Jesus, and scourged him. And the soldiers platted a crown of thorns, and put it on his head, and they put on him a purple robe, and said, "Hail, King of the Jews!" and they smote him with their hands, and did spit upon him and bowing their knees worshipped him.

Pilate therefore went forth again, and saith unto them, "Behold, I bring him forth to you, that ye may know that I find no fault in him."

Then came Jesus forth, wearing the crown of thorns, and the purple robe.

And Pilate saith unto them, "Behold the man!"

*Jesus is given to be crucified*

When the chief priests therefore and officers saw him, they cried out, saying, "Crucify him, crucify him."

Pilate saith unto them, "Take ye him, and crucify him: for I find no fault in him." The Jews answered him, "We have a law, and by our law he ought to die, because he made himself the Son of God."

When Pilate therefore heard that saying, he was the more afraid; and went again into the judgment hall, and saith unto Jesus, "Whence art thou?"

But Jesus gave him no answer.

Then saith Pilate unto him, "Speakest thou not unto me? knowest thou not that I have power to crucify thee, and have power to release thee?"

Jesus answered, "Thou couldest have no power at all against me, except it were given thee from above: therefore he that delivered me unto thee hath the greater sin."

And from thenceforth Pilate sought to release him: but the Jews cried out, saying, "If thou let this man go, thou art not Cæsar's friend: whosoever maketh himself a king speaketh against Cæsar."

When Pilate therefore heard that saying, he brought Jesus forth, and sat down in the judgment seat in a place that is called the Pavement, but in the Hebrew, Gabbatha. And it was the preparation of the passover, and about the sixth hour: and he saith unto the Jews, "Behold your King!"

But they cried out, "Away with him, crucify him."

Pilate saith unto them, "Shall I crucify your King?"

The chief priests answered, "We have no king but Cæsar."

Then delivered he him therefore unto them to be crucified.

And when they had mocked him, they took off the purple from him, and put his own clothes on him, and led him out to crucify him. And he bearing his cross went forth unto the place Golgotha, which is, being interpreted, "The place of a skull." And they gave him to drink wine mingled with myrrh: but he received it not.

And as they led him away, they laid hold upon one Simon, a Cyrenian, coming out of the country, and on him they laid the cross, that he might bear it after Jesus.

*The crucifixion on Calvary*

And there followed him a great company of people, and of women, which also bewailed and lamented him. But Jesus turning unto them said, "Daughters of Jerusalem, weep not for me, but weep for yourselves, and for your children."

And when they were come to the place, which is called Calvary, there they crucified him, and two other with him, on either side one, and Jesus in the midst. And it was the third hour.

Then said Jesus, "Father, forgive them; for they know not what they do."

And Pilate wrote a title, and put it on the cross. And the writing was JESUS OF NAZARETH THE KING OF THE JEWS. This title then read many of the Jews: for the place where Jesus was crucified was nigh to the city: and it was written in Hebrew, and Greek, and Latin.

Then said the chief priests of the Jews to Pilate, "Write not, 'The King of the Jews'; but that he said, 'I am King of the Jews.' "

Pilate answered, "What I have written I have written."

*The soldiers cast lots*

Then the soldiers, when they had crucified Jesus, took his garments, and made four parts, to every soldier a part; and also his coat: now the coat was without seam, woven from the top throughout. They said therefore among themselves, "Let us not rend it, but cast lots for it, whose it shall be": that the scripture might be fulfilled, which saith,

> They parted my raiment among them,
> And for my vesture they did cast lots.

These things therefore the soldiers did.

And the people stood beholding. And the rulers also with them derided him, saying, "He saved others; let him save himself, if he be Christ, the chosen of God."

Likewise also the chief priests mocking said among themselves with the scribes, "He saved others; himself he cannot save. Let Christ the King of Israel descend now from the cross, that we may see and believe."

And the soldiers also mocked him, coming to him, and offering him vinegar, and saying, "If thou be the king of the Jews, save thyself."

And they that were crucified with him reviled him. And one of the malefactors which were hanged railed on him, saying, "If thou be Christ, save thyself and us."

*SOLDIERS CASTING LOTS FOR CHRIST'S GARMENT*

But the other answering rebuked him, saying, "Dost not thou fear *Jesus and the* God, seeing thou art in the same condemnation? And we indeed justly; *malefactors crucified* for we receive the due reward of our deeds: but this man hath done *with him* nothing amiss."

And he said unto Jesus, "Lord, remember me when thou comest into thy kingdom."

And Jesus said unto him, "Verily I say unto thee, To day shalt thou be with me in paradise."

Now there stood by the cross of Jesus his mother, and his mother's sister, Mary the wife of Cleophas, and Mary Magdalene. When Jesus therefore saw his mother, and the disciple standing by, whom he loved, he saith unto his mother, "Woman, behold thy son!"

Then saith he to the disciple, "Behold thy mother!"

And from that hour that disciple took her unto his own home.

And when the sixth hour was come, there was darkness over the whole land until the ninth hour. And at the ninth hour Jesus cried with a loud voice, saying, *Eloi, Eloi, lama sabachthani?* which is, being interpreted, "My God, my God, why hast thou forsaken me?"

After this, Jesus knowing that all things were now accomplished, that the scripture might be fulfilled, saith, "I thirst." Now there was set a vessel full of vinegar: and they filled a spunge with vinegar, and put it upon hyssop, and put it to his mouth. When Jesus therefore had received the vinegar, he said, "It is finished: Father, into thy hands I commend my spirit": and he bowed his head, and gave up the ghost.

And the veil of the temple was rent in twain from the top to the bottom. And the earth did quake, and the rocks rent. And when the centurion, which stood over against him, saw that he so cried out, and gave up the ghost, he said, "Truly this man was the Son of God."

And now when the even was come, because it was the preparation, that is, the day before the sabbath, Joseph of Arimathæa, an honourable counsellor, which also waited for the kingdom of God, came, and went in boldly unto Pilate, and craved the body of Jesus. Then Pilate commanded the body to be delivered. And there came also Nicodemus, which at the first came to Jesus by night, and brought a mixture of myrrh and aloes, about an hundred pound weight. Then took they the body of Jesus, and wound it in linen clothes with the spices, as the manner of the Jews

*Burial by Joseph* is to bury. Now in the place where he was crucified there was a garden. And Joseph laid it in his own new tomb, which he had hewn out in the rock: and he rolled a great stone to the door of the sepulchre, and departed.

And Mary Magdalene and Mary the mother of Joses beheld where he was laid. And they returned, and prepared spices and ointments; and rested the sabbath day according to the commandment.

Now the next day, that followed the day of the preparation, the chief priests and Pharisees came together unto Pilate, saying, "Sir, we remember that that deceiver said, while he was yet alive, 'After three days I will rise again.' Command therefore that the sepulchre be made sure until the third day, lest his disciples come by night, and steal him away, and say unto the people, 'He is risen from the dead': so the last error shall be worse than the first."

Pilate said unto them, "Ye have a watch: go your way, make it as sure as ye can." So they went, and made the sepulchre sure, sealing the stone, and setting a watch.

Now upon the first day of the week, very early in the morning, came Mary Magdalene and the other Mary unto the sepulchre, bringing the spices which they had prepared, and certain others with them. And they said among themselves, "Who shall roll us away the stone from the door of the sepulchre?"

*The resurrection* And, behold, there was a great earthquake: for the angel of the Lord descended from heaven, and came and rolled back the stone from the door, and sat upon it. His countenance was like lightning, and his raiment white as snow. And when they looked, they saw that the stone was rolled away: for it was very great. And they entered in, and found not the body of the Lord Jesus. And it came to pass, as they were much perplexed thereabout, behold, two men stood by them in shining garments: and as they were afraid, and bowed down their faces to the earth, they said unto them, "Fear not ye. Ye seek Jesus of Nazareth, which was crucified. Why seek ye the living among the dead? He is not here, but is risen. Come, see the place where the Lord lay. Remember how he spake unto you when he was yet in Galilee, saying 'The Son of man must be delivered into the hands of sinful men, and be crucified, and the third day rise

ANGELS HOVERING OVER THE BODY OF JESUS
IN THE SEPULCHRE

again.' Go quickly and tell his disciples that he is risen from the dead;  *The sepulchre found empty*
and, behold, he goeth before you into Galilee; there shall ye see him: lo,
I have told you."

And they remembered his words, and returned from the sepulchre.

Mary Magdalene runneth, and cometh to Simon Peter, and to the
other disciple, whom Jesus loved, and saith unto them, "They have taken
away the Lord out of the sepulchre, and we know not where they have
laid him."

Peter therefore went forth, and that other disciple, and came to the
sepulchre. So they ran both together: and the other disciple did outrun
Peter, and came first to the sepulchre. And he stooping down, and looking
in, saw the linen clothes lying; yet went he not in. Then cometh Simon
Peter following him, and went into the sepulchre, and seeth the linen
clothes lie, and the napkin, that was about his head, not lying with the
linen clothes, but wrapped together in a place by itself. Then went in
also that other disciple, which came first to the sepulchre, and he saw,
and believed. For as yet they knew not the scripture, that he must rise
again from the dead. Then the disciples went away again unto their own
home, wondering at that which was come to pass.

And as they went to tell his disciples, behold, Jesus met them, saying, *Jesus reappears*
"All hail." And they came and held him by the feet, and worshipped him.

Then said Jesus unto them, "Be not afraid: go tell my brethren that
they go into Galilee, and there shall they see me."

But Mary stood without at the sepulchre weeping: and as she wept,
she stooped down, and looked into the sepulchre, and seeth two angels
in white sitting, the one at the head, and the other at the feet, where
the body of Jesus had lain. And they say unto her, "Woman, why weepest thou?"

She saith unto them, "Because they have taken away my Lord, and
I know not where they have laid him."

And when she had thus said, she turned herself back, and saw Jesus
standing, and knew not that it was Jesus.

Jesus saith unto her, "Woman, why weepest thou? whom seekest
thou?"

She, supposing him to be the gardener, saith unto him, "Sir, if thou have borne him hence, tell me where thou hast laid him, and I will take him away."

Jesus saith unto her, "Mary."

She turned herself, and saith unto him, *Rabboni;* which is to say, "Master."

Jesus saith unto her, "Touch me not; for I am not yet ascended to my Father: but go to my brethren, and say unto them, I ascend unto my Father, and your Father; and to my God, and your God."

And she went and told them that had been with him, as they mourned and wept. And they, when they had heard that he was alive, and had been seen of her, believed not.

After that he appeared in another form unto two of them, as they walked, and went into the country.

And, behold, two of them went that same day to a village called Emmaus, which was from Jerusalem about threescore furlongs. And they talked together of all these things which had happened. And it came to pass, that, while they communed together and reasoned, Jesus himself drew near, and went with them. But their eyes were holden that they should not know him.

And he said unto them, "What manner of communications are these that ye have one to another, as ye walk, and are sad?"

And the one of them, whose name was Cleopas, answering said unto him, "Art thou only a stranger in Jerusalem, and hast not known the things which are come to pass there in these days?"

And he said unto them, "What things?"

And they said unto him, "Concerning Jesus of Nazareth, which was a prophet mighty in deed and word before God and all the people: and how the chief priests and our rulers delivered him to be condemned to death, and have crucified him. But we trusted that it had been he which should have redeemed Israel: and beside all this, to day is the third day since these things were done. Yea, and certain women also of our company made us astonished, which were early at the sepulchre; and when they found not his body, they came, saying, that they had also seen a vision of angels, which said that he was alive. And certain of them which were with us went to the sepulchre, and found it even so as the women had said: but him they saw not."

Then he said unto them, "O fools, and slow of heart to believe all *Jesus in the midst of* that the prophets have spoken: Ought not Christ to have suffered these *the disciples* things and to enter into his glory?"

And beginning at Moses and all the prophets, he expounded unto them in all the scriptures the things concerning himself. And they drew nigh unto the village, whither they went: and he made as though he would have gone further.

But they constrained him, saying, "Abide with us: for it is toward evening, and the day is far spent." And he went in to tarry with them.

And it came to pass, as he sat at meat with them, he took bread, and blessed it, and brake, and gave to them. And their eyes were opened, and they knew him; and he vanished out of their sight.

And they said one to another, "Did not our heart burn within us, while he talked with us by the way, and while he opened to us the scriptures?"

And they rose up the same hour, and returned to Jerusalem, and found the eleven gathered together, and them that were with them, saying, "The Lord is risen indeed, and hath appeared to Simon."

And they told what things were done in the way, and how he was known of them in breaking of bread.

Then the same day at evening, being the first day of the week, when the doors were shut where the disciples were assembled for fear of the Jews, and while they yet believed not for joy, and wondered, came Jesus and stood in the midst, and saith unto them, "Peace be unto you." But they were terrified and affrighted, and supposed that they had seen a spirit. He shewed unto them his hands and his side. Then were the disciples glad, when they saw the Lord.

Then said Jesus to them again, "Peace be unto you: as my Father hath sent me, even so send I you."

And when he had said this, he breathed on them, and saith unto them, "Receive ye the Holy Ghost: whose soever sins ye remit, they are remitted unto them; and whose soever sins ye retain, they are retained."

But Thomas, one of the twelve, called Didymus, was not with them when Jesus came. The other disciples therefore said unto him, "We have seen the Lord."

But he said unto them, "Except I shall see in his hands the print of

*Jesus and doubting Thomas* the nails, and put my finger into the print of the nails, and thrust my hand into his side, I will not believe."

And after eight days again his disciples were within, and Thomas with them: then came Jesus, the doors being shut, and stood in the midst, and said, "Peace be unto you."

Then saith he to Thomas, "Reach hither thy finger and behold my hands; and reach hither thy hand, and thrust it into my side: and be not faithless, but believing."

And Thomas answered and said unto him, "My Lord and my God."

Jesus saith unto him, "Thomas, because thou hast seen me, thou hast believed: blessed are they that have not seen, and yet have believed."

After these things Jesus shewed himself again to the disciples at the sea of Tiberias; and on this wise shewed he himself. There were together Simon Peter, and Thomas called Didymus, and Nathanael of Cana in Galilee, and the sons of Zebedee, and two other of his disciples.

Simon Peter saith unto them, "I go a fishing."

They say unto him, "We also go with thee."

They went forth, and entered into a ship immediately; and that night they caught nothing.

But when the morning was now come, Jesus stood on the shore: but the disciples knew not that it was Jesus.

Then Jesus saith unto them, "Children, have ye any meat?"

They answered him, "No."

And he said unto them, "Cast the net on the right side of the ship, and ye shall find."

They cast therefore, and now they were not able to draw it for the multitude of fishes. Therefore that disciple whom Jesus loved saith unto Peter, "It is the Lord."

Now when Simon Peter heard that it was the Lord, he girt his fisher's coat unto him, (for he was naked,) and did cast himself into the sea. And the other disciples came in a little ship; (for they were not far from land, but as it were two hundred cubits,) dragging the net with fishes. As soon then as they were come to land, they saw a fire of coals there, and fish laid thereon, and bread.

Jesus saith unto them, "Bring of the fish which ye have now caught."

Simon Peter went up, and drew the net to land full of great fishes, an

**CHRIST APPEARING TO HIS APOSTLES**
*AFTER THE RESURRECTION*

hundred and fifty and three: and for all there were so many, yet was not the net broken.

Jesus saith unto them, "Come and dine."

And none of the disciples durst ask him, "Who art thou?" knowing that it was the Lord.

Jesus then cometh, and taketh bread, and giveth them, and fish likewise.

So when they had dined, Jesus saith to Simon Peter, "Simon, son of Jonas, lovest thou me more than these?" He saith unto him, "Yea, Lord; thou knowest that I love thee." He saith unto him, "Feed my lambs."

He saith to him again the second time, "Simon, son of Jonas, lovest thou me?" He saith unto him, "Yea, Lord; thou knowest that I love thee." He saith unto him, "Feed my sheep."

He saith unto him the third time, "Simon, son of Jonas, lovest thou me?" Peter was grieved because he said unto him the third time, "Lovest thou me?" And he said unto him, "Lord, thou knowest all things; thou knowest that I love thee." Jesus saith unto him, "Feed my sheep. Verily, verily, I say unto thee, When thou wast young, thou girdedst thyself, and walkedst whither thou wouldest: but when thou shalt be old, thou shalt stretch forth thy hands, and another shall gird thee, and carry thee whither thou wouldest not." This spake he, signifying by what death he should glorify God. And when he had spoken this, he saith unto him, "Follow me."

Then Peter, turning about, seeth the disciple whom Jesus loved following; which also leaned on his breast at supper, and said, "Lord, which is he that betrayeth thee?"

Peter seeing him saith to Jesus, "Lord, and what shall this man do?"

Jesus saith unto him, "If I will that he tarry till I come, what is that to thee? follow thou me." Then went this saying abroad among the brethren, that that disciple should not die: yet Jesus said not unto him, "He shall not die"; but, "If I will that he tarry till I come, what is that to thee?"

Judas, which had betrayed him, when he saw that he was condemned, repented himself, and brought again the thirty pieces of silver to the chief priests and elders, saying, "I have sinned in that I have betrayed the innocent blood." And they said, "What is that to us? see thou to that." And he cast down the pieces of silver in the temple, and departed, and went and hanged himself.

Then the eleven disciples went away into Galilee, into a mountain where Jesus had appointed them. And when they saw him, they worshipped him: but some doubted.

And Jesus came and spake unto them, saying, "All power is given unto me in heaven and in earth. Go ye therefore, and teach all nations, baptizing them in the name of the Father, and of the Son, and of the Holy Ghost: teaching them to observe all things whatsoever I have commanded you: and, lo, I am with you alway, even unto the end of the world."

Then opened he their understanding, that they might understand the scriptures, and said unto them, "Thus it is written, and thus it behoved Christ to suffer, and to rise from the dead the third day: and that repentance and remission of sins should be preached in his name among all nations, beginning at Jerusalem. And ye are witnesses of these things. And, behold, I send the promise of my Father upon you: but tarry ye in the city of Jerusalem, until ye be endued with power from on high."

And he led them out as far as to Bethany, and he lifted up his hands, and blessed them.

And it came to pass, while he blessed them, he was parted from them, and carried up into heaven. And they worshipped him, and returned to Jerusalem with great joy: and were continually in the temple, praising and blessing God.

And they went forth, and preached every where, the Lord working with them, and confirming the word with signs following.

And many other signs truly did Jesus in the presence of his disciples, which are not written in this book: but these are written, that ye might believe that Jesus is the Christ, the Son of God; and that believing ye might have life through his name. And there are also many other things which Jesus did, the which, if they should be written every one, I suppose that even the world itself could not contain the books that should be written. Amen.

*THE ASCENSION*

# II

# PAUL THE APOSTLE

## *His Life*

THE former treatise have I made, O Theophilus, of all that Jesus *Christ prepares his*
began both to do and teach, until the day in which he was taken *apostles for the*
up, after that he through the Holy Ghost had given command- *ascension*
ments unto the apostles whom he had chosen: to whom also he
shewed himself alive after his passion by many infallible proofs,
being seen of them forty days, and speaking of the things pertaining to
the kingdom of God: and, being assembled together with them, commanded them that they should not depart from Jerusalem, but wait for
the promise of the Father, "which," saith he, "ye have heard of me. For
John truly baptized with water; but ye shall be baptized with the Holy
Ghost not many days hence."

When they therefore were come together, he said unto them, "Ye
shall receive power, after that the Holy Ghost is come upon you: and ye
shall be witnesses unto me both in Jerusalem, and in all Judæa, and in
Samaria, and unto the uttermost part of the earth."

And when he had spoken these things, while they beheld, he was
taken up; and a cloud received him out of their sight. And while they
looked stedfastly toward heaven as he went up, behold, two men stood
by them in white apparel; which also said, "Ye men of Galilee, why stand
ye gazing up into heaven? this same Jesus, which is taken up from you
into heaven, shall so come in like manner as ye have seen him go into
heaven."

Then returned they unto Jerusalem from the mount called Olivet,
which is from Jerusalem a sabbath day's journey. And when they were
come in, they went up into an upper room, where abode both Peter, and
James, and John, and Andrew, Philip, and Thomas, Bartholomew, and
Matthew, James the son of Alphæus, and Simon Zelotes, and Judas the
brother of James. These all continued with one accord in prayer and
supplication, with the women, and Mary the mother of Jesus, and with
his brethren.

And in those days Peter stood up in the midst of the disciples, and said,

*Matthias chosen by lot* (the number of names together were about an hundred and twenty,) "Men and brethren, this scripture must needs have been fulfilled. Wherefore of these men which have companied with us all the time that the Lord Jesus went in and out among us, beginning from the baptism of John, unto that same day that he was taken up from us, must one be ordained to be a witness with us of his resurrection."

And they appointed two, Joseph called Barsabas, who was surnamed Justus, and Matthias. And they prayed, and said, "Thou, Lord, which knowest the hearts of all men, shew whether of these two thou hast chosen, that he may take part of this ministry and apostleship, from which Judas by transgression fell, that he might go to his own place."

And they gave forth their lots; and the lot fell upon Matthias; and he was numbered with the eleven apostles.

*The descent of the Holy Ghost* And when the day of Pentecost was fully come, they were all with one accord in one place. And suddenly there came a sound from heaven as of a rushing mighty wind, and it filled all the house where they were sitting. And there appeared unto them cloven tongues like as of fire, and it sat upon each of them. And they were all filled with the Holy Ghost, and began to speak with other tongues, as the Spirit gave them utterance.

And there were dwelling at Jerusalem Jews, devout men, out of every nation under heaven. Now when this was noised abroad, the multitude came together, and were confounded, because that every man heard them speak in his own language. And they were all amazed and marvelled, saying one to another, "Behold, are not all these which speak Galilæans? And how hear we every man in our own tongue, wherein we were born? Parthians, and Medes, and Elamites, and the dwellers in Mesopotamia, and in Judæa, and Cappadocia, in Pontus, and Asia, Phrygia, and Pamphylia, in Egypt, and in the parts of Libya about Cyrene, and strangers of Rome, Jews and proselytes, Cretes and Arabians, we do hear them speak in our tongues the wonderful works of God."

And they were all amazed, and were in doubt, saying one to another, "What meaneth this?" Others mocking said, "These men are full of new wine."

But Peter, standing up with the eleven, lifted up his voice, and said unto them, "Ye men of Judæa, and all ye that dwell at Jerusalem, be this known unto you, and hearken to my words: for these are not drunken, as ye suppose, seeing it is but the third hour of the day.

"Ye men of Israel, hear these words; Jesus of Nazareth, a man approved of God among you by miracles and wonders and signs, which God did by him in the midst of you, as ye yourselves also know: him, being delivered by the determinate counsel and foreknowledge of God, ye have taken, and by wicked hands have crucified and slain: whom God hath raised up. For David speaketh concerning him,

> I foresaw the Lord always before my face,
> For he is on my right hand,
> That I should not be moved:
> Therefore did my heart rejoice,
> And my tongue was glad;
> Moreover also my flesh shall rest in hope;
> Because thou wilt not leave my soul in hell,
> Neither wilt thou suffer thine Holy One to see corruption.
> Thou hast made known to me the ways of life;
> Thou shalt make me full of joy with thy countenance.

"This Jesus hath God raised up, whereof we all are witnesses. Therefore being by the right hand of God exalted, and having received of the Father the promise of the Holy Ghost, he hath shed forth this, which ye now see and hear. Therefore let all the house of Israel know assuredly, that God hath made that same Jesus, whom ye have crucified, both Lord and Christ."

Now when they heard this, they were pricked in their heart, and said unto Peter and to the rest of the apostles, "Men and brethren, what shall we do?"

Then Peter said unto them, "Repent, and be baptized every one of you in the name of Jesus Christ for the remission of sins, and ye shall receive the gift of the Holy Ghost. For the promise is unto you, and to your children, and to all that are afar off, even as many as the Lord our God shall call." And with many other words did he testify and exhort, saying, "Save yourselves from this untoward generation."

Then they that gladly received his word were baptized: and the same day there were added unto them about three thousand souls. And they continued stedfastly in the apostles' doctrine and fellowship, and in breaking of bread, and in prayers. And fear came upon every soul: and many wonders and signs were done by the apostles.

And all that believed were together, and had all things common; and sold their possessions and goods, and parted them to all men, as every man had need.

And they, continuing daily with one accord in the temple, and breaking bread from house to house, did eat their meat with gladness and singleness of heart, praising God, and having favour with all the people. And the Lord added to the church daily such as should be saved.

Now Peter and John went up together into the temple at the hour of prayer, being the ninth hour. And a certain man lame from his mother's womb was carried, whom they laid daily at the gate of the temple which is called "Beautiful," to ask alms of them that entered into the temple; who seeing Peter and John about to go into the temple asked an alms.

And Peter, fastening his eyes upon him with John, said, "Look on us." And he gave heed unto them, expecting to receive something of them.

Then Peter said, "Silver and gold have I none; but such as I have give I thee: In the name of Jesus Christ of Nazareth rise up and walk." And he took him by the right hand, and lifted him up: and immediately his feet and ankle bones received strength. And he leaping up stood, and walked, and entered with them into the temple, walking, and leaping, and praising God. And all the people saw him walking and praising God: and they knew that it was he which sat for alms at the "Beautiful" gate of the temple: and they were filled with wonder and amazement at that which had happened unto him. And as the lame man which was healed held Peter and John, all the people ran together unto them in the porch that is called Solomon's, greatly wondering.

And when Peter saw it, he answered unto the people, "Ye men of Israel, why marvel ye at this? Or why look ye so earnestly on us, as though by our own power or holiness we had made this man to walk? The God of Abraham, and of Isaac, and of Jacob, the God of our fathers, hath glorified his Son Jesus; whom ye delivered up, and denied him in the presence of Pilate, when he was determined to let him go. But ye denied the Holy One and the Just, and desired a murderer to be granted unto you; and killed the Prince of life, whom God hath raised from the dead; whereof we are witnesses. And his name through faith in his name hath made this man strong, whom ye see and know: yea, the faith which is by him hath given him this perfect soundness in the presence of you all. And now, brethren, I wot that through ignorance ye did it, as did also your rulers. But those things, which God before had shewed by the mouth of all his prophets, that Christ should suffer, he hath so fulfilled."

*Peter and John imprisoned*

And as they spake unto the people, the priests, and the captain of the temple, and the Sadducees, came upon them, being grieved that they taught the people, and preached through Jesus the resurrection from the dead. And they laid hands on them, and put them in hold unto the next day: for it was now eventide. Howbeit many of them which heard the word believed; and the number of the men was about five thousand.

And it came to pass on the morrow, that their rulers, and elders, and scribes, and Annas the high priest, and Caiaphas, and John, and Alexander, and as many as were of the kindred of the high priest, were gathered together at Jerusalem. And when they had set them in the midst, they asked, "By what power, or by what name, have ye done this?"

Then Peter, filled with the Holy Ghost, said unto them, "Ye rulers of the people, and elders of Israel, if we this day be examined of the good deed done to the impotent man, by what means he is made whole; be it known unto you all, and to all the people of Israel, that by the name of Jesus Christ of Nazareth, whom ye crucified, whom God raised from the dead, even by him doth this man stand here before you whole. This is the stone which was set at nought of you builders, which is become the head of the corner. Neither is there salvation in any other: for there is none other name under heaven given among men, whereby we must be saved."

Now when they saw the boldness of Peter and John, and perceived that they were unlearned and ignorant men, they marvelled; and they took knowledge of them, that they had been with Jesus. And beholding the man which was healed standing with them, they could say nothing against it. But when they had commanded them to go aside out of the council, they conferred among themselves, saying, "What shall we do to these men? for that indeed a notable miracle hath been done by them is manifest to all them that dwell in Jerusalem; and we cannot deny it. But that it spread no further among the people, let us straitly threaten them, that they speak henceforth to no man in this name."

And they called them, and commanded them not to speak at all nor teach in the name of Jesus. But Peter and John answered and said unto them, "Whether it be right in the sight of God to hearken unto you more than unto God, judge ye. For we cannot but speak the things which we have seen and heard."

So when they had further threatened them, they let them go, finding nothing how they might punish them, because of the people: for all men glorified God for that which was done. For the man was above forty years old, on whom this miracle of healing was shewed.

And being let go, they went to their own company, and reported all that the chief priests and elders had said unto them. And when they heard that, they lifted up their voice to God with one accord, and said, "Lord, thou art God, which hast made heaven, and earth, and the sea, and all that in them is: who by the mouth of thy servant David hast said,

> Why did the heathen rage,
> And the people imagine vain things?
> The kings of the earth stood up,
> And the rulers were gathered together
> Against the Lord, and against his Christ.

"For of a truth against thy holy child Jesus, whom thou hast anointed, both Herod, and Pontius Pilate, with the Gentiles, and the people of Israel, were gathered together, for to do whatsoever thy hand and thy counsel determined before to be done. And now, Lord, behold their threatenings: and grant unto thy servants, that with all boldness they may speak thy word, by stretching forth thine hand to heal; and that signs and wonders may be done by the name of thy holy child Jesus."

And when they had prayed, the place was shaken where they were assembled together; and they were all filled with the Holy Ghost, and they spake the word of God with boldness.

And the multitude of them that believed were of one heart and of one soul: neither said any of them that ought of the things which he possessed was his own; but they had all things common. And with great power gave the apostles witness of the resurrection of the Lord Jesus:

and great grace was upon them all. Neither was there any among them that lacked: for as many as were possessors of lands or houses sold them, and brought the prices of the things that were sold, and laid them down at the apostles' feet: and distribution was made unto every man according as he had need.

And Joses, who by the apostles was surnamed Barnabas, (which is, being interpreted, "The son of consolation,") a Levite, and of the country of Cyprus, having land, sold it, and brought the money, and laid it at the apostles' feet.

But a certain man named Ananias, with Sapphira his wife, sold a possession, and kept back part of the price, his wife also being privy to it, and brought a certain part, and laid it at the apostles' feet.

But Peter said, "Ananias, why hath Satan filled thine heart to lie to the Holy Ghost, and to keep back part of the price of the land? Whiles it remained, was it not thine own? and after it was sold, was it not in thine own power? why hast thou conceived this thing in thine heart? thou hast not lied unto men, but unto God."

And Ananias hearing these words fell down, and gave up the ghost: and great fear came on all them that heard these things. And the young men arose, wound him up, and carried him out, and buried him.

And it was about the space of three hours after, when his wife, not knowing what was done, came in.

And Peter answered unto her, "Tell me whether ye sold the land for so much?"

And she said, "Yea, for so much."

Then Peter said unto her, "How is it that ye have agreed together to tempt the Spirit of the Lord? behold, the feet of them which have buried thy husband are at the door, and shall carry thee out."

Then fell she down straightway at his feet, and yielded up the ghost: and the young men came in, and found her dead, and, carrying her forth, buried her by her husband. And great fear came upon all the church, and upon as many as heard these things.

And by the hands of the apostles were many signs and wonders wrought among the people; (and they were all with one accord in Solomon's porch. And of the rest durst no man join himself to them: but the people magnified them. And believers were the more added to the

Lord, multitudes both of men, and women.) Insomuch that they brought forth the sick into the streets, and laid them on beds and couches, that at the least the shadow of Peter passing by might overshadow some of them. There came also a multitude out of the cities round about unto Jerusalem, bringing sick folks, and them which were vexed with unclean spirits: and they were healed every one.

Then the high priest rose up, and all they that were with him, (which is the sect of the Sadducees,) and were filled with indignation, and laid their hands on the apostles, and put them in the common prison.

But the angel of the Lord by night opened the prison doors, and brought them forth, and said, "Go, stand and speak in the temple to the people all the words of this life."

And when they heard that, they entered into the temple early in the morning, and taught. But the high priest came, and they that were with him, and called the council together, and all the senate of the children of Israel, and sent to the prison to have them brought. But when the officers came, and found them not in the prison, they returned, and told, saying, "The prison truly found we shut with all safety, and the keepers standing without before the doors: but when we had opened, we found no man within."

Now when the high priest and the captain of the temple and the chief priests heard these things, they doubted of them whereunto this would grow. Then came one and told them, saying, "Behold, the men whom ye put in prison are standing in the temple, and teaching the people."

Then went the captain with the officers, and brought them without violence: for they feared the people, lest they should have been stoned. And when they had brought them, they set them before the council: and the high priest asked them, saying, "Did not we straitly command you that ye should not teach in this name? and, behold, ye have filled Jerusalem with your doctrine, and intend to bring this man's blood upon us."

Then Peter and the other apostles answered and said, "We ought to obey God rather than men. The God of our fathers raised up Jesus, whom ye slew and hanged on a tree. Him hath God exalted with his right hand to be a Prince and a Saviour, for to give repentance to Israel, and forgiveness of sins. And we are his witnesses of these things; and so is also the Holy Ghost, whom God hath given to them that obey him." *Gamaliel's advice*

When they heard that, they were cut to the heart, and took counsel to slay them. Then stood there up one in the council, a Pharisee, named Gamaliel, a doctor of the law, had in reputation among all the people, and commanded to put the apostles forth a little space; and said, "Refrain from these men, and let them alone: for if this counsel or this work be of men, it will come to nought: but if it be of God, ye cannot overthrow it; lest haply ye be found even to fight against God."

And to him they agreed: and when they had called the apostles, and beaten them, they commanded that they should not speak in the name of Jesus, and let them go. And they departed from the presence of the council, rejoicing that they were counted worthy to suffer shame for his name.

Then the twelve called the multitude of the disciples unto them, *Stephen chosen* and they chose Stephen, a man full of faith and of the Holy Ghost. And Stephen, full of faith and power, did great wonders and miracles among the people. Then there arose certain of the synagogue, disputing with Stephen. And they were not able to resist the wisdom and the spirit by which he spake. Then they suborned men, which said, "We have heard him speak blasphemous words against Moses, and against God."

And they stirred up the people, and the elders, and the scribes, and came upon him, and caught him, and brought him to the council, and set up false witnesses, which said, "This man ceaseth not to speak blasphemous words against this holy place, and the law: for we have heard him say, that this Jesus of Nazareth shall destroy this place, and shall change the customs which Moses delivered us."

And all that sat in the council, looking stedfastly on him, saw his face as it had been the face of an angel. Then said the high priest, "Are these things so?" And he said, "Men, brethren, and fathers, hearken: the most High dwelleth not in temples made with hands; as saith the prophet,

> Heaven is my throne,
> And earth is my footstool:
> What house will ye build me? saith the Lord:
> Or what is the place of my rest?
> Hath not my hand made all these things?

*Stephen stoned to death*    "Ye stiffnecked and uncircumcised in heart and ears, ye do always resist the Holy Ghost: as your fathers did, so do ye. Which of the prophets have not your fathers persecuted? and they have slain them which shewed before of the coming of the Just One; of whom ye have been now the betrayers and murderers: Who have received the law by the disposition of angels, and have not kept it."

When they heard these things, they were cut to the heart, and they gnashed on him with their teeth. But he, being full of the Holy Ghost, looked up stedfastly into heaven, and saw the glory of God, and Jesus standing on the right hand of God, and said, "Behold, I see the heavens opened, and the Son of man standing on the right hand of God."

Then they cried out with a loud voice, and stopped their ears, and ran upon him with one accord, and cast him out of the city, and stoned him: and the witnesses laid down their clothes at a young man's feet, whose name was Saul.

And they stoned Stephen, calling upon God, and saying, "Lord Jesus receive my spirit." And he kneeled down, and cried with a loud voice, "Lord, lay not this sin to their charge."

And when he had said this, he fell asleep. And devout men carried Stephen to his burial, and made great lamentation over him.

And Saul was consenting unto his death. And at that time there was a great persecution against the church which was at Jerusalem; and they were all scattered abroad throughout the regions of Judæa and Samaria, except the apostles.

As for Saul, he made havock of the church, entering into every house, and haling men and women committed them to prison.

Therefore they that were scattered abroad went every where preaching the word.

*Philip preaches in Samaria*    Then Philip went down to the city of Samaria, and preached Christ unto them. And the people with one accord gave heed unto those things which Philip spake, hearing and seeing the miracles which he did. And there was great joy in that city.

But there was a certain man, called Simon, which beforetime in the same city used sorcery, and bewitched the people of Samaria, giving out that himself was some great one: to whom they all gave heed, from the least to the greatest, saying, "This man is the great power of God." And to him they had regard, because that of long time he had bewitched them with sorceries. But when they believed Philip preaching the things concerning the kingdom of God, and the name of Jesus Christ, they were baptized, both men and women. Then Simon himself believed also: and when he was baptized, he continued with Philip, and wondered, beholding the miracles and signs which were done.

*Simon Magus seeks to purchase the power of the Holy Ghost*

Now when the apostles which were at Jerusalem heard that Samaria had received the word of God, they sent unto them Peter and John: who, when they were come down, prayed for them, that they might receive the Holy Ghost: then laid they their hands on them, and they received the Holy Ghost.

And when Simon saw that through laying on of the apostles' hands the Holy Ghost was given, he offered them money, saying, "Give me also this power, that on whomsoever I lay hands, he may receive the Holy Ghost."

But Peter said unto him, "Thy money perish with thee, because thou hast thought that the gift of God may be purchased with money. Thou hast neither part nor lot in this matter: for thy heart is not right in the sight of God."

And they, when they had testified and preached the word of the Lord, returned to Jerusalem, and preached the gospel in many villages of the Samaritans.

And the angel of the Lord spake unto Philip, saying, "Arise, and go toward the south unto the way that goeth down from Jerusalem unto Gaza," which is desert. And he arose and went: and, behold, a man of Ethiopia, an eunuch of great authority under Candace queen of the Ethiopians, who had the charge of all her treasure, and had come to Jerusalem for to worship, was returning, and sitting in his chariot read Esaias the prophet.

*Philip and the Ethiopian*

Then the Spirit said unto Philip, "Go near, and join thyself to this chariot."

And Philip ran thither to him, and heard him read the prophet Esaias, and said, "Understandest thou what thou readest?"

And he said, "How can I, except some man should guide me?" And he desired Philip that he would come up and sit with him.

The place of the scripture which he read was this,

*The Ethiopian baptized*

He was led as a sheep to the slaughter;
And like a lamb dumb before his shearer,
So opened he not his mouth:
In his humiliation his judgment was taken away:
And who shall declare his generation?
For his life is taken from the earth.

And the eunuch answered Philip, and said, "I pray thee, of whom speaketh the prophet this? of himself, or of some other man?"

Then Philip opened his mouth, and began at the same scripture, and preached unto him Jesus. And as they went on their way, they came unto a certain water: and the eunuch said, "See, here is water; what doth hinder me to be baptized?"

And Philip said, "If thou believest with all thine heart, thou mayest."

And he answered and said, "I believe that Jesus Christ is the Son of God."

And he commanded the chariot to stand still: and they went down both into the water, both Philip and the eunuch; and he baptized him. And when they were come up out of the water, the Spirit of the Lord caught away Philip, that the eunuch saw him no more: and he went on his way rejoicing. But Philip was found at Azotus: and passing through he preached in all the cities, till he came to Cæsarea.

*The conversion of Saul*

And Saul, yet breathing out threatenings and slaughter against the disciples of the Lord, went unto the high priest, and desired of him letters to Damascus to the synagogues, that if he found any of this way, whether they were men or women, he might bring them bound unto Jerusalem.

And as he journeyed, he came near Damascus: and suddenly there shined round about him a light from heaven: and he fell to the earth, and heard a voice saying unto him, "Saul, Saul, why persecutest thou me?"

And he said, "Who art thou, Lord?"

And the Lord said, "I am Jesus whom thou persecutest: it is hard for thee to kick against the pricks."

And he trembling and astonished said, "Lord, what wilt thou have me to do?"

*THE CONVERSION OF SAUL*

And the Lord said unto him, "Arise, and go into the city, and it shall be told thee what thou must do."

*Saul preaches in Damascus*

And the men which journeyed with him stood speechless, hearing a voice, but seeing no man. And Saul arose from the earth; and when his eyes were opened, he saw no man: but they led him by the hand, and brought him into Damascus. And he was three days without sight, and neither did eat nor drink.

And there was a certain disciple at Damascus, named Ananias; and to him said the Lord in a vision, "Ananias."

And he said, "Behold, I am here, Lord."

And the Lord said unto him, "Arise, and go into the street which is called 'Straight,' and enquire in the house of Judas for one called Saul, of Tarsus: for, behold, he prayeth, and hath seen in a vision a man named Ananias coming in, and putting his hand on him, that he might receive his sight."

Then Ananias answered, "Lord, I have heard by many of this man, how much evil he hath done to thy saints at Jerusalem: and here he hath authority from the chief priests to bind all that call on thy name."

But the Lord said unto him, "Go thy way: for he is a chosen vessel unto me, to bear my name before the Gentiles, and kings, and the children of Israel: for I will shew him how great things he must suffer for my name's sake."

And Ananias went his way, and entered into the house; and putting his hands on him said, "Brother Saul, the Lord, even Jesus, that appeared unto thee in the way as thou camest, hath sent me, that thou mightest receive thy sight, and be filled with the Holy Ghost."

And immediately there fell from his eyes as it had been scales: and he received sight forthwith, and arose, and was baptized. And when he had received meat, he was strengthened.

Then was Saul certain days with the disciples which were at Damascus. And straightway he preached Christ in the synagogues, that he is the Son of God. But all that heard him were amazed, and said; "Is not this he that destroyed them which called on this name in Jerusalem, and came hither for that intent, that he might bring them bound unto the chief priests?" But Saul increased the more in strength, and confounded the Jews which dwelt at Damascus, proving that this is very Christ.

*Conspiracy to kill Saul*

And after that many days were fulfilled, the Jews took counsel to kill him: but their laying await was known of Saul. And they watched the gates day and night to kill him. Then the disciples took him by night, and let him down by the wall in a basket.

And when Saul was come to Jerusalem, he assayed to join himself to the disciples: but they were all afraid of him, and believed not that he was a disciple. But Barnabas took him, and brought him to the apostles, and declared unto them how he had seen the Lord in the way, and that he had spoken to him, and how he had preached boldly at Damascus in the name of Jesus. And he was with them coming in and going out at Jerusalem. And he spake boldly in the name of the Lord Jesus, and disputed against the Grecians: but they went about to slay him, which when the brethren knew, they brought him down to Cæsarea, and sent him forth to Tarsus.

Then had the churches rest throughout all Judæa and Galilee and Samaria, and were edified; and walking in the fear of the Lord, and in the comfort of the Holy Ghost, were multiplied.

*Peter's miracles*

And it came to pass, as Peter passed throughout all quarters, he came down also to the saints which dwelt at Lydda. And there he found a certain man named Æneas, which had kept his bed eight years, and was sick of the palsy.

And Peter said unto him, "Æneas, Jesus Christ maketh thee whole: arise, and make thy bed." And he arose immediately. And all that dwelt at Lydda and Saron saw him, and turned to the Lord. And forasmuch as Lydda was nigh to Joppa, and the disciples had heard that Peter was there, they sent unto him two men, desiring him that he would not delay to come to them. And it came to pass, that he tarried many days in Joppa with one Simon a tanner.

There was a certain man in Cæsarea called Cornelius, a centurion of the band called the Italian band, a devout man, and one that feared God with all his house, which gave much alms to the people, and prayed to God alway. He saw in a vision evidently about the ninth hour of the day an angel of God coming in to him, and saying unto him, "Cornelius."

And when he looked on him, he was afraid, and said, "What is it, Lord?"

And he said unto him, "Thy prayers and thine alms are come up for *Peter goes to Cornelius* a memorial before God. And now send men to Joppa, and call for one Simon, whose surname is Peter: he lodgeth with one Simon a tanner, whose house is by the sea side: he shall tell thee what thou oughtest to do."

And when the angel which spake unto Cornelius was departed, he called two of his household servants, and a devout soldier of them that waited on him continually; and when he had declared all these things unto them, he sent them to Joppa.

The men which were sent from Cornelius had made enquiry for Simon's house, and stood before the gate, and called, and asked whether Simon, which was surnamed Peter, were lodged there.

Then Peter went down to the men which were sent unto him from Cornelius; and said, "Behold, I am he whom ye seek: what is the cause wherefore ye are come?"

And they said, "Cornelius the centurion, a just man, and one that feareth God, and of good report among all the nation of the Jews, was warned from God by an holy angel to send for thee into his house, and to hear words of thee."

Then called he them in, and lodged them. And on the morrow Peter went away with them, and certain brethren from Joppa accompanied him.

And the morrow after they entered into Cæsarea. And Cornelius waited for them, and had called together his kinsmen and near friends. And as Peter was coming in, Cornelius met him, and fell down at his feet, and worshipped him. But Peter took him up, saying, "Stand up; I myself also am a man."

And as he talked with him, he went in, and found many that were come together. And he said unto them, "Ye know how that it is an unlawful thing for a man that is a Jew to keep company, or come unto one of another nation; but God hath shewed me that I should not call any man common or unclean. Therefore came I unto you without gainsaying, as soon as I was sent for: I ask therefore for what intent ye have sent for me?"

And Cornelius said, "Four days ago I was fasting until this hour; and at the ninth hour I prayed in my house, and, behold, a man stood before me in bright clothing, and said, 'Cornelius, thy prayer is heard, and thine alms are had in remembrance in the sight of God. Send therefore to Joppa, and call hither Simon, whose surname is Peter; he is lodged in the house of one Simon a tanner by the sea side: who, when he cometh, shall speak unto thee.' Immediately therefore I sent to thee; and thou hast well done that thou art come. Now therefore are we all here present before God, to hear all things that are commanded thee of God."

Then Peter opened his mouth, and said, "Of a truth I perceive that God is no respecter of persons: but in every nation he that feareth him, and worketh righteousness, is accepted with him. The word which God sent unto the children of Israel, preaching peace by Jesus Christ: (he is Lord of all:) That word, I say, ye know, which was published throughout all Judæa, and began from Galilee, after the baptism which John preached; how God anointed Jesus of Nazareth with the Holy Ghost and with power: who went about doing good, and healing all that were oppressed of the devil; for God was with him. And we are witnesses of all things which he did both in the land of the Jews, and in Jerusalem; whom they slew and hanged on a tree: him God raised up the third day, and shewed him openly; not to all the people, but unto witnesses chosen before of God, even to us, who did eat and drink with him after he rose from the dead. And he commanded us to preach unto the people, and to testify that it is he which was ordained of God to be the Judge of quick and dead. To him give all the prophets witness, that through his name whosoever believeth in him shall receive remission of sins."

While Peter yet spake these words, the Holy Ghost fell on all them which heard the word. And they of the circumcision which believed were astonished, as many as came with Peter, because that on the Gentiles also was poured out the gift of the Holy Ghost. For they heard them speak with tongues, and magnify God.

Then answered Peter, "Can any man forbid water, that these should not be baptized, which have received the Holy Ghost as well as we?" And he commanded them to be baptized in the name of the Lord. Then prayed they him to tarry certain days.

And the apostles and brethren that were in Judæa heard that the Gentiles had also received the word of God. And when Peter was come up to Jerusalem, they that were of the circumcision contended with him, saying, "Thou wentest in to men uncircumcised, and didst eat with them."

But Peter rehearsed the matter from the beginning, and expounded it *Peter defends himself* by order unto them, saying, "I was in the city of Joppa praying: and in a trance I saw a vision, A certain vessel descend, as it had been a great sheet, let down from heaven by four corners; and it came even to me: upon the which when I had fastened mine eyes, I considered, and saw fourfooted beasts of the earth, and wild beasts, and creeping things, and fowls of the air. And I heard a voice saying unto me, 'Arise, Peter; slay and eat.' But I said, 'Not so, Lord: for nothing common or unclean hath at any time entered into my mouth.' But the voice answered me again from heaven, 'What God hath cleansed that call not thou common.' And this was done three times: and all were drawn up again into heaven. And, behold, immediately there were three men already come unto the house where I was, sent from Cæsarea unto me. And the Spirit bade me go with them, nothing doubting. Moreover these six brethren accompanied me, and we entered into the man's house: and he shewed us how he had seen an angel in his house, which stood and said unto him, 'Send men to Joppa, and call for Simon, whose surname is Peter; who shall tell thee words, whereby thou and all thy house shall be saved.' And as I began to speak, the Holy Ghost fell on them, as on us at the beginning. Then remembered I the word of the Lord, how that he said, 'John indeed baptized with water; but ye shall be baptized with the Holy Ghost.' Forasmuch then as God gave them the like gift as he did unto us, who believed on the Lord Jesus Christ, what was I, that I could withstand God?"

When they heard these things, they held their peace, and glorified God, saying, "Then hath God also to the Gentiles granted repentance unto life."

Now they which were scattered abroad upon the persecution that arose about Stephen travelled as far as Phenice, and Cyprus, and Antioch, preaching the word to none but unto the Jews only. And some of them were men of Cyprus and Cyrene, which, when they were come to Antioch, spake unto the Grecians, preaching the Lord Jesus. And the hand of the Lord was with them: and a great number believed, and turned unto the Lord.

Then tidings of these things came unto the ears of the church which

*The gospel preached in Antioch*

was in Jerusalem: and they sent forth Barnabas, that he should go as far as Antioch. Who, when he came, and had seen the grace of God, was glad, and exhorted them all, that with purpose of heart they would cleave unto the Lord. For he was a good man, and full of the Holy Ghost and of faith: and much people was added unto the Lord.

Then departed Barnabas to Tarsus, for to seek Saul: and when he had found him, he brought him unto Antioch. And it came to pass, that a whole year they assembled themselves with the church, and taught much people. And the disciples were called Christians first in Antioch.

And in these days came prophets from Jerusalem unto Antioch. And there stood up one of them named Agabus, and signified by the Spirit that there should be great dearth throughout all the world: which came to pass in the days of Claudius Cæsar. Then the disciples, every man according to his ability, determined to send relief unto the brethren which dwelt in Judæa: which also they did, and sent it to the elders by the hands of Barnabas and Saul.

The word of God grew and multiplied. And Barnabas and Saul returned from Jerusalem, when they had fulfilled their ministry, and took with them John, whose surname was Mark.

Now there were in the church that was at Antioch certain prophets and teachers. As they ministered to the Lord, and fasted, the Holy Ghost said, "Separate me Barnabas and Saul for the work whereunto I have called them." And when they had fasted and prayed, and laid their hands on them, they sent them away.

So they, being sent forth by the Holy Ghost, departed unto Seleucia; and from thence they sailed to Cyprus. And when they were at Salamis, they preached the word of God in the synagogues of the Jews: and they had also John to their minister. And when they had gone through the isle unto Paphos, they found a certain sorcerer, a false prophet, a Jew, whose name was Bar-jesus: which was with the deputy of the country, Sergius Paulus, a prudent man; who called for Barnabas and Saul, and desired to hear the word of God. But Elymas the sorcerer (for so is his name by interpretation) withstood them, seeking to turn away the deputy from the faith.

Then Saul, (who also is called Paul,) filled with the Holy Ghost, set his eyes on him, and said, "O full of all subtilty and all mischief, thou

*Paul's sermon at Antioch*

child of the devil, thou enemy of all righteousness, wilt thou not cease to pervert the right ways of the Lord? And now, behold, the hand of the Lord is upon thee, and thou shalt be blind, not seeing the sun for a season."

And immediately there fell on him a mist and a darkness; and he went about seeking some to lead him by the hand. Then the deputy, when he saw what was done, believed, being astonished at the doctrine of the Lord.

Now when Paul and his company loosed from Paphos, they came to Perga in Pamphylia: and John departing from them returned to Jerusalem.

But when they departed from Perga, they came to Antioch in Pisidia, and went into the synagogue on the sabbath day, and sat down. And after the reading of the law and the prophets the rulers of the synagogue sent unto them, saying, "Ye men and brethren, if ye have any word of exhortation for the people, say on."

Then Paul stood up, and beckoning with his hand said, "Men of Israel, and ye that fear God, give audience. God according to his promise, raised unto Israel a Saviour, Jesus. And though they found no cause of death in him, yet desired they Pilate that he should be slain. And when they had fulfilled all that was written of him, they took him down from the tree, and laid him in a sepulchre. But God raised him from the dead: and he was seen many days of them which came up with him from Galilee to Jerusalem, who are his witnesses unto the people. And we declare unto you glad tidings, how that the promise which was made unto the fathers, God hath fulfilled the same unto us their children, in that he hath raised up Jesus again; as it is also written in the second psalm,

> Thou art my Son,
> This day have I begotten thee.

"Be it known unto you therefore, men and brethren, that through this man is preached unto you the forgiveness of sins."

And when the Jews were gone out of the synagogue, the Gentiles besought that these words might be preached to them the next sabbath.

Now when the congregation was broken up, many of the Jews and

*Persecution of Paul and Barnabas*

religious proselytes followed Paul and Barnabas: who, speaking to them, persuaded them to continue in the grace of God. And the next sabbath day came almost the whole city together to hear the word of God.

But when the Jews saw the multitudes, they were filled with envy, and spake against those things which were spoken by Paul, contradicting and blaspheming. Then Paul and Barnabas waxed bold, and said, "It was necessary that the word of God should first have been spoken to you: but seeing ye put it from you, and judge yourselves unworthy of everlasting life, lo, we turn to the Gentiles. For so hath the Lord commanded us, saying, 'I have set thee to be a light of the Gentiles, that thou shouldest be for salvation unto the ends of the earth.'"

And when the Gentiles heard this, they were glad, and glorified the word of the Lord. And the word of the Lord was published throughout all the region. But the Jews stirred up the devout and honourable women, and the chief men of the city, and raised persecution against Paul and Barnabas, and expelled them out of their coasts.

But they shook off the dust of their feet against them, and came unto Iconium. And the disciples were filled with joy, and with the Holy Ghost.

And it came to pass in Iconium, that they went both together into the synagogue of the Jews, and so spake, that a great multitude both of the Jews and also of the Greeks believed. But the unbelieving Jews stirred up the Gentiles, and made their minds evil affected against the brethren.

Long time therefore abode they speaking boldly in the Lord, which gave testimony unto the word of his grace, and granted signs and wonders to be done by their hands. But the multitude of the city was divided: and part held with the Jews, and part with the apostles. And when there was an assault made both of the Gentiles, and also of the Jews with their rulers, to use them despitefully, and to stone them, they were ware of it, and fled unto Lystra and Derbe, cities of Lycaonia, and unto the region that lieth round about: and there they preached the gospel.

And there came thither certain Jews from Antioch and Iconium, who persuaded the people, and, having stoned Paul, drew him out of the city, supposing he had been dead. Howbeit, as the disciples stood round about him, he rose up, and came into the city: and the next day he departed with Barnabas to Derbe.

And when they had preached the gospel to that city, and had taught

many, they returned again to Lystra, and to Iconium, and Antioch, con- *Return to Antioch*
firming the souls of the disciples, and exhorting them to continue in the
faith, and that we must through much tribulation enter into the kingdom
of God. And when they had ordained them elders in every church, and
had prayed with fasting, they commended them to the Lord, on whom
they believed.

And after they had passed throughout Pisidia, they came to Pamphylia. And when they had preached the word in Perga, they went down
to Attalia: and thence sailed to Antioch, from whence they had been
recommended to the grace of God for the work which they fulfilled.

And when they were come, and had gathered the church together,
they rehearsed all that God had done with them, and how he had opened
the door of faith unto the Gentiles. And there they abode long time with
the disciples.

They determined that Paul and Barnabas, and certain other of them, *Paul and Barnabas*
should go up to Jerusalem unto the apostles and elders. And being *report to the church*
brought on their way by the church, they passed through Phenice and *in Jerusalem*
Samaria, declaring the conversion of the Gentiles: and they caused great
joy unto all the brethren.

And when they were come to Jerusalem, they were received of the
church, and of the apostles and elders, and they declared all things that
God had done with them. And the apostles and elders came together.

Peter rose up, and said unto them, "Men and brethren, ye know how
that a good while ago God made choice among us, that the Gentiles by my
mouth should hear the word of the gospel, and believe. And God, which
knoweth the hearts, bare them witness, giving them the Holy Ghost,
even as he did unto us; and put no difference between us and them, purifying their hearts by faith."

Then all the multitude kept silence, and gave audience to Barnabas
and Paul, declaring what miracles and wonders God had wrought among
the Gentiles by them.

Then pleased it the apostles and elders, with the whole church, to
send chosen men of their own company to Antioch with Paul and Barnabas; namely, Judas surnamed Barsabas, and Silas, chief men among the
brethren: and they wrote letters by them after this manner;

# PAUL THE APOSTLE

*Letter to the Gentiles* THE APOSTLES AND ELDERS AND BRETHREN SEND GREETING UNTO THE BRETHREN WHICH ARE OF THE GENTILES IN ANTIOCH AND SYRIA AND CILICIA:

IT seemed good unto us, being assembled with one accord, to send chosen men unto you with our beloved Barnabas and Paul, men that have hazarded their lives for the name of our Lord Jesus Christ. We have sent therefore Judas and Silas, who shall also tell you the same things by mouth.

Fare ye well.

So when they were dismissed, they came to Antioch: and when they had gathered the multitude together, they delivered the epistle: which when they had read, they rejoiced for the consolation. And Judas and Silas, being prophets also themselves, exhorted the brethren with many words, and confirmed them. And after they had tarried there a space, they were let go in peace from the brethren unto the apostles. Notwithstanding it pleased Silas to abide there still.

Paul also and Barnabas continued in Antioch, teaching and preaching the word of the Lord, with many others also. And some days after Paul said unto Barnabas, "Let us go again and visit our brethren in every city where we have preached the word of the Lord, and see how they do."

And Barnabas determined to take with them John, whose surname was Mark. But Paul thought not good to take him with them, who departed from them from Pamphylia, and went not with them to the work. And the contention was so sharp between them, that they departed asunder one from the other: and so Barnabas took Mark, and sailed unto Cyprus; and Paul chose Silas, and departed, being recommended by the brethren unto the grace of God. And he went through Syria and Cilicia, confirming the churches.

Then came he to Derbe and Lystra: and, behold, a certain disciple was there, named Timotheus, the son of a certain woman, which was a Jewess, and believed; but his father was a Greek: which was well reported of by the brethren that were at Lystra and Iconium. Him would Paul have to go forth with him; and took and circumcised him because of the Jews which were in those quarters: for they knew all that his father was a Greek.

And as they went through the cities, they delivered them the decrees for to keep, that were ordained of the apostles and elders which were at

Jerusalem. And so were the churches established in the faith, and in-  *Lydia is converted*
creased in number daily.

Now when they had gone throughout Phrygia and the region of
Galatia, and were forbidden of the Holy Ghost to preach the word in
Asia, after they were come to Mysia, they assayed to go into Bithynia:
but the Spirit suffered them not. And they passing by Mysia came down
to Troas.

And a vision appeared to Paul in the night; There stood a man of
Macedonia, and prayed him, saying, "Come over into Macedonia, and
help us." After he had seen the vision, immediately we endeavoured to
go into Macedonia, assuredly gathering that the Lord had called us for
to preach the gospel unto them. Therefore, loosing from Troas, we came
with a straight course to Samothracia, and the next day to Neapolis; and
from thence to Philippi, which is the chief city of that part of Macedonia,
and a colony: and we were in that city abiding certain days.

And on the sabbath we went out of the city by a river side, where
prayer was wont to be made; and we sat down, and spake unto the women
which resorted thither. And a certain woman named Lydia, a seller of
purple, of the city of Thyatira, which worshipped God, heard us: whose
heart the Lord opened, that she attended unto the things which were
spoken of Paul. And when she was baptized, and her household, she besought us, saying, "If ye have judged me to be faithful to the Lord, come
into my house, and abide there." And she constrained us.

They caught Paul and Silas, and drew them into the marketplace unto  *Paul and Silas*
the rulers, and brought them to the magistrates, saying, "These men,  *apprehended*
being Jews, do exceedingly trouble our city, and teach customs, which
are not lawful for us to receive, neither to observe, being Romans."

And the multitude rose up together against them: and the magistrates rent off their clothes, and commanded to beat them. And when
they had laid many stripes upon them, they cast them into prison, charg-
ing the jailor to keep them safely: who, having received such a charge,
thrust them into the inner prison, and made their feet fast in the stocks.

And at midnight Paul and Silas prayed, and sang praises unto God:
and the prisoners heard them. And suddenly there was a great earthquake, so that the foundations of the prison were shaken: and immediately all the doors were opened, and every one's bands were loosed. And

*Paul and Silas released from prison*

the keeper of the prison awaking out of his sleep, and seeing the prison doors open, he drew out his sword, and would have killed himself, supposing that the prisoners had been fled. But Paul cried with a loud voice, saying, "Do thyself no harm: for we are all here."

Then he called for a light, and sprang in, and came trembling, and fell down before Paul and Silas, and brought them out, and said, "Sirs, what must I do to be saved?"

And they said, "Believe on the Lord Jesus Christ, and thou shalt be saved, and thy house." And they spake unto him the word of the Lord, and to all that were in his house. And he took them the same hour of the night, and washed their stripes; and was baptized, he and all his, straightway. And when he had brought them into his house, he set meat before them, and rejoiced, believing in God with all his house.

And when it was day, the magistrates sent the serjeants, saying, "Let those men go."

And the keeper of the prison told this saying to Paul, "The magistrates have sent to let you go: now therefore depart, and go in peace."

But Paul said unto them, "They have beaten us openly uncondemned, being Romans, and have cast us into prison; and now do they thrust us out privily? nay verily; but let them come themselves and fetch us out."

And the serjeants told these words unto the magistrates: and they feared, when they heard that they were Romans. And they came and besought them, and brought them out, and desired them to depart out of the city. And they went out of the prison, and entered into the house of Lydia: and when they had seen the brethren, they comforted them, and departed.

Now when they had passed through Amphipolis and Apollonia, they came to Thessalonica, where was a synagogue of the Jews: and Paul, as his manner was, went in unto them, and three sabbath days reasoned with them out of the scriptures, opening and alleging, that Christ must needs have suffered, and risen again from the dead; and that "this Jesus, whom I preach unto you, is Christ."

And some of them believed, and consorted with Paul and Silas; and of the devout Greeks a great multitude, and of the chief women not a few. But the Jews, which believed not, moved with envy, drew certain brethren unto the rulers of the city, crying, "These that have turned the world upside down are come hither also; these all do contrary to the *Paul preaches at Athens* decrees of Cæsar, saying that there is another king, one Jesus."

And they troubled the people and the rulers of the city, when they heard these things.

And the brethren immediately sent away Paul and Silas by night unto Berea: who coming thither went into the synagogue of the Jews. These were more noble than those in Thessalonica, in that they received the word with all readiness of mind, and searched the scriptures daily, whether those things were so. Therefore many of them believed; also of honourable women which were Greeks, and of men, not a few.

But when the Jews of Thessalonica had knowledge that the word of God was preached of Paul at Berea, they came thither also, and stirred up the people. And then immediately the brethren sent away Paul to go as it were to the sea: but Silas and Timotheus abode there still.

And they that conducted Paul brought him unto Athens: and receiving a commandment unto Silas and Timotheus for to come to him with all speed, they departed.

Now while Paul waited for them at Athens, his spirit was stirred in him, when he saw the city wholly given to idolatry. Therefore disputed he in the synagogue with the Jews, and with the devout persons, and in the market daily with them that met with him.

Then certain philosophers of the Epicureans, and of the Stoicks, encountered him. And some said, "What will this babbler say?" other some, "He seemeth to be a setter forth of strange gods": because he preached unto them Jesus, and the resurrection.

And they took him, and brought him unto Areopagus, saying, "May we know what this new doctrine, whereof thou speakest, is? For thou bringest certain strange things to our ears: we would know therefore what these things mean." (For all the Athenians and strangers which were there spent their time in nothing else, but either to tell, or to hear some new thing.)

Then Paul stood in the midst of Mars' hill, and said, "Ye men of Athens, I perceive that in all things ye are too superstitious. For as I passed by, and beheld your devotions, I found an altar with this inscription, TO THE UNKNOWN GOD. Whom therefore ye ignorantly worship, him declare I unto you. God that made the world and all things

*Paul at Corinth* therein, seeing that he is Lord of heaven and earth, dwelleth not in temples made with hands; neither is worshipped with men's hands, as though he needed any thing, seeing he giveth to all life, and breath, and all things; and hath made of one blood all nations of men for to dwell on all the face of the earth, and hath determined the times before appointed, and the bounds of their habitation; that they should seek the Lord, if haply they might feel after him, and find him, though he be not far from every one of us: for in him we live, and move, and have our being; as certain also of your own poets have said, 'For we are also his offspring.' Forasmuch then as we are the offspring of God, we ought not to think that the Godhead is like unto gold, or silver, or stone, graven by art and man's device. Because he hath appointed a day, in the which he will judge the world in righteousness by that man whom he hath ordained; whereof he hath given assurance unto all men, in that he hath raised him from the dead."

And when they heard of the resurrection of the dead, some mocked: and others said, "We will hear thee again of this matter." So Paul departed from among them. Howbeit certain men clave unto him, and believed: among the which was Dionysius the Areopagite, and a woman named Damaris, and others with them.

After these things Paul departed from Athens, and came to Corinth; and found a certain Jew named Aquila, born in Pontus, lately come from Italy, with his wife Priscilla; (because that Claudius had commanded all Jews to depart from Rome:) and came unto them. And because he was of the same craft, he abode with them, and wrought: for by their occupation they were tentmakers. And he reasoned in the synagogue every sabbath, and persuaded the Jews and the Greeks.

And when Silas and Timotheus were come from Macedonia, Paul was pressed in the spirit, and testified to the Jews that Jesus was Christ. And when they opposed themselves, and blasphemed, he shook his raiment, and said unto them, "Your blood be upon your own heads; I am clean: from henceforth I will go unto the Gentiles."

And he departed thence, and entered into a certain man's house, named Justus, one that worshipped God, whose house joined hard to the synagogue. And Crispus, the chief ruler of the synagogue, believed on

*SAINT PAUL PREACHING AT ATHENS*

the Lord with all his house; and many of the Corinthians hearing believed, and were baptized.

Then spake the Lord to Paul in the night by a vision, "Be not afraid, but speak, and hold not thy peace: for I am with thee, and no man shall set on thee to hurt thee: for I have much people in this city." And he continued there a year and six months, teaching the word of God among them.

And Paul after this tarried there yet a good while, and then took his leave of the brethren, and sailed thence into Syria, and with him Priscilla and Aquila. And he came to Ephesus, and left them there: but he himself entered into the synagogue, and reasoned with the Jews. When they desired him to tarry longer time with them, he consented not; but bade them farewell, saying, "I must by all means keep this feast that cometh in Jerusalem: but I will return again unto you, if God will."

And he sailed from Ephesus. And when he had landed at Cæsarea and gone up, and saluted the church, he went down to Antioch. And after he had spent some time there, he departed, and went over all the country of Galatia and Phrygia in order, strengthening all the disciples.

And a certain Jew named Apollos, born at Alexandria, an eloquent man, and mighty in the scriptures, came to Ephesus. This man was instructed in the way of the Lord; and being fervent in the spirit, he spake and taught diligently the things of the Lord, knowing only the baptism of John. And he began to speak boldly in the synagogue: whom when Aquila and Priscilla had heard, they took him unto them, and expounded unto him the way of God more perfectly. And when he was disposed to pass into Achaia, the brethren wrote, exhorting the disciples to receive him: who, when he was come, helped them much which had believed through grace: for he mightily convinced the Jews, and that publickly, shewing by the scriptures that Jesus was Christ.

And it came to pass, that, while Apollos was at Corinth, Paul having passed through the upper coasts came to Ephesus: and finding certain disciples, he said unto them, "Have ye received the Holy Ghost since ye believed?"

And they said unto him, "We have not so much as heard whether there be any Holy Ghost."

*Paul at Ephesus*

*Apollos teaches according to the baptism of John*

And he said unto them, "Unto what then were ye baptized?"

And they said, "Unto John's baptism."

Then said Paul, "John verily baptized with the baptism of repentance, saying unto the people, that they should believe on him which should come after him, that is, on Christ Jesus."

When they heard this, they were baptized in the name of the Lord Jesus. And when Paul had laid his hands upon them, the Holy Ghost came on them; and they spake with tongues, and prophesied. And all the men were about twelve.

And he went into the synagogue, and spake boldly for the space of three months, disputing and persuading the things concerning the kingdom of God. But when divers were hardened, and believed not, but spake evil of that way before the multitude, he departed from them, and separated the disciples, disputing daily in the school of one Tyrannus. And this continued by the space of two years; so that all they which dwelt in Asia heard the word of the Lord Jesus, both Jews and Greeks. And God wrought special miracles by the hands of Paul. So mightily grew the word of God and prevailed.

After these things were ended, Paul purposed in the spirit, when he had passed through Macedonia and Achaia, to go to Jerusalem, saying, "After I have been there, I must also see Rome."

So he sent into Macedonia two of them that ministered unto him, Timotheus and Erastus; but he himself stayed in Asia for a season.

And the same time there arose no small stir about that way. For a certain man named Demetrius, a silversmith, which made silver shrines for Diana, brought no small gain unto the craftsmen; whom he called together with the workmen of like occupation, and said, "Sirs, ye know that by this craft we have our wealth. Moreover ye see and hear, that not alone at Ephesus, but almost throughout all Asia, this Paul hath persuaded and turned away much people, saying that they be no gods, which are made with hands: so that not only this our craft is in danger to be set at nought; but also that the temple of the great goddess Diana should be despised, and her magnificence should be destroyed, whom all Asia and the world worshippeth."

And when they heard these sayings, they were full of wrath, and cried out, saying, "Great is Diana of the Ephesians."

And the whole city was filled with confusion: and having caught *Uproar about Diana at* Gaius and Aristarchus, men of Macedonia, Paul's companions in travel, *Ephesus* they rushed with one accord into the theatre. And when Paul would have entered in unto the people, the disciples suffered him not.

And certain of the chief of Asia, which were his friends, sent unto him, desiring him that he would not adventure himself into the theatre. Some therefore cried one thing, and some another: for the assembly was confused; and the more part knew not wherefore they were come together. And they drew Alexander out of the multitude, the Jews putting him forward. And Alexander beckoned with the hand, and would have made his defence unto the people. But when they knew that he was a Jew, all with one voice about the space of two hours cried out, "Great is Diana of the Ephesians."

And when the townclerk had appeased the people, he said, "Ye men of Ephesus, what man is there that knoweth not how that the city of the Ephesians is a worshipper of the great goddess Diana, and of the image which fell down from Jupiter? Seeing then that these things cannot be spoken against, ye ought to be quiet, and to do nothing rashly. For ye have brought hither these men, which are neither robbers of churches, nor yet blasphemers of your goddess. Wherefore if Demetrius, and the craftsmen which are with him, have a matter against any man, the law is open, and there are deputies: let them implead one another. But if ye enquire any thing concerning other matters, it shall be determined in a lawful assembly. For we are in danger to be called in question for this day's uproar, there being no cause whereby we may give an account of this concourse."

And when he had thus spoken, he dismissed the assembly. And after the uproar was ceased, Paul called unto him the disciples, and embraced them, and departed for to go to Macedonia.

And when he had gone over those parts, and had given them much exhortation, he came unto Greece, and there abode three months. And when the Jews laid wait for him, as he was about to sail into Syria, he purposed to return through Macedonia. And there accompanied him into Asia Sopater of Berea; and of the Thessalonians, Aristarchus and Secundus; and Gaius of Derbe, and Timotheus; and of Asia, Tychicus and

Paul's charge to the
elders of Ephesus

Trophimus. These going before tarried for us at Troas. And we sailed away from Philippi after the days of unleavened bread, and came unto them to Troas in five days; where we abode seven days.

And upon the first day of the week, when the disciples came together to break bread, Paul preached unto them, ready to depart on the morrow; and continued his speech until midnight. And there were many lights in the upper chamber, where they were gathered together. And there sat in a window a certain young man named Eutychus, being fallen into a deep sleep: and as Paul was long preaching, he sunk down with sleep, and fell down from the third loft, and was taken up dead. And Paul went down, and fell on him, and embracing him said, "Trouble not yourselves; for his life is in him." When he therefore was come up again, and had broken bread, and eaten, and talked a long while, even till break of day, so he departed. And they brought the young man alive, and were not a little comforted.

And we went before to ship, and sailed unto Assos, there intending to take in Paul: for so had he appointed, minding himself to go afoot. And when he met with us at Assos, we took him in, and came to Mitylene. And we sailed thence, and came the next day over against Chios; and the next day we arrived at Samos, and tarried at Trogyllium; and the next day we came to Miletus. For Paul had determined to sail by Ephesus, because he would not spend the time in Asia: for he hasted, if it were possible for him, to be at Jerusalem the day of Pentecost.

And from Miletus he sent to Ephesus, and called the elders of the church. And when they were come to him, he said unto them, "Ye know, from the first day that I came into Asia, after what manner I have been with you at all seasons, serving the Lord with all humility of mind, and with many tears, and temptations, which befell me by the lying in wait of the Jews: and how I kept back nothing that was profitable unto you, but have shewed you, and have taught you publickly, and from house to house, testifying both to the Jews, and also to the Greeks, repentance toward God, and faith toward our Lord Jesus Christ. And now, behold, I go bound in the spirit unto Jerusalem, not knowing the things that shall befall me there: save that the Holy Ghost witnesseth in every city, saying that bonds and afflictions abide me. But none of these things move me, neither count I my life dear unto myself, so that I might finish my course with joy, and the ministry, which I have received of the Lord Jesus, to testify the gospel of the grace of God. And now, behold, I know that ye all, among whom I have gone preaching the kingdom of God, shall see my face no more. Wherefore I take you to record this day, that I am pure from the blood of all men. For I have not shunned to declare unto you all the counsel of God. Take heed therefore unto yourselves, and to all the flock, over the which the Holy Ghost hath made you overseers, to feed the church of God, which he hath purchased with his own blood. For I know this, that after my departing shall grievous wolves enter in among you, not sparing the flock. Also of your own selves shall men arise, speaking perverse things, to draw away disciples after them. Therefore watch, and remember, that by the space of three years I ceased not to warn every one night and day with tears.

"And now, brethren, I commend you to God, and to the word of his grace, which is able to build you up, and to give you an inheritance among all them which are sanctified. I have coveted no man's silver, or gold, or apparel. Yea, ye yourselves know, that these hands have ministered unto my necessities, and to them that were with me. I have shewed you all things, how that so labouring ye ought to support the weak, and to remember the words of the Lord Jesus, how he said, 'It is more blessed to give than to receive.' "

And when he had thus spoken, he kneeled down, and prayed with them all. And they all wept sore, and fell on Paul's neck, and kissed him, sorrowing most of all for the words which he spake, that they should see his face no more. And they accompanied him unto the ship.

And it came to pass, that after we were gotten from them, and had launched, we came with a straight course unto Coos, and the day following unto Rhodes, and from thence unto Patara: and finding a ship sailing over unto Phenicia, we went aboard, and set forth.

Now when we had discovered Cyprus, we left it on the left hand, and sailed into Syria, and landed at Tyre: for there the ship was to unlade her burden. And finding disciples, we tarried there seven days: who said to Paul through the Spirit, that he should not go up to Jerusalem. And when we had accomplished those days, we departed and went our way; and they all brought us on our way, with wives and children, till we were out of the city: and we kneeled down on the shore, and prayed. And when we had taken our leave one of another, we took ship; and they returned home again.

And when we had finished our course from Tyre, we came to Ptolemais, and saluted the brethren, and abode with them one day.

And the next day we that were of Paul's company departed, and came unto Cæsarea: and we entered into the house of Philip the evangelist, which was one of the seven; and abode with him. And as we tarried there many days, there came down from Judæa a certain prophet, named Agabus. And when he was come unto us, he took Paul's girdle, and bound his own hands and feet, and said, "Thus saith the Holy Ghost, 'So shall the Jews at Jerusalem bind the man that owneth this girdle, and shall deliver him into the hands of the Gentiles.'"

And when we heard these things, both we, and they of that place, besought him not to go up to Jerusalem.

Then Paul answered, "What mean ye to weep and to break mine heart? for I am ready not to be bound only, but also to die at Jerusalem for the name of the Lord Jesus."

And when he would not be persuaded, we ceased, saying, "The will of the Lord be done."

And after those days we took up our carriages, and went up to Jerusalem. There went with us also certain of the disciples of Cæsarea, and brought with them one Mnason of Cyprus, an old disciple, with whom we should lodge. And when we were come to Jerusalem, the brethren received us gladly. And the day following Paul went in with us unto James; and all the elders were present. And when he had saluted them, he declared particularly what things God had wrought among the Gentiles by his ministry.

And when they heard it, they glorified the Lord, and said unto him, "Thou seest, brother, how many thousands of Jews there are which believe; and they are all zealous of the law: and they are informed of thee, that thou teachest all the Jews which are among the Gentiles to forsake Moses, saying that they ought not to circumcise their children, neither to walk after the customs."

Paul entered into the temple. The Jews which were of Asia, when they saw him in the temple, stirred up all the people, and laid hands on him, crying out, "Men of Israel, help: This is the man, that teacheth all men every where against the people, and the law, and this place: and further brought Greeks also into the temple, and hath polluted this holy place."

And all the city was moved, and the people ran together: and they took Paul, and drew him out of the temple: and forthwith the doors were shut. And as they went about to kill him, tidings came unto the chief captain of the band, that all Jerusalem was in an uproar. Who immediately took soldiers and centurions, and ran down unto them: and when they saw the chief captain and the soldiers, they left beating of Paul.

Then the chief captain came near, and took him, and commanded him to be bound with two chains; and demanded who he was, and what he had done. And some cried one thing, some another, among the multitude: and when he could not know the certainty for the tumult, he commanded him to be carried into the castle. And when he came upon the stairs, so it was, that he was borne of the soldiers for the violence of the people. For the multitude of the people followed after, crying, "Away with him."

And as Paul was to be led into the castle, he said unto the chief captain, "May I speak unto thee?"

Who said, "Canst thou speak Greek?"

But Paul said, "I am a man which am a Jew of Tarsus, a city in Cilicia, a citizen of no mean city: and, I beseech thee, suffer me to speak unto the people."

And when he had given him licence, Paul stood on the stairs, and beckoned with the hand unto the people. And when there was made a great silence, he spake unto them in the Hebrew tongue, saying, "Men, brethren, and fathers, hear ye my defence which I make now unto you." (And when they heard that he spake in the Hebrew tongue to them, they kept the more silence: and he saith,) "I am verily a man which am a Jew, born in Tarsus, a city in Cilicia, yet brought up in this city at the feet of Gamaliel, and taught according to the perfect manner of the law of the fathers, and was zealous toward God, as ye all are this day. And I persecuted this way unto the death, binding and delivering into prisons both men and women, and went to Damascus, to bring them which were there bound unto Jerusalem, for to be punished.

"And it came to pass, that, as I made my journey, and was come nigh unto Damascus about noon, suddenly there shone from heaven a great light round about me. And I fell unto the ground, and heard a voice saying unto me, 'Saul, Saul, why persecutest thou me?' And I answered, 'Who art thou, Lord?' And he said unto me, 'I am Jesus of Nazareth, whom thou persecutest.' And they that were with me saw indeed the light, and were afraid; but they heard not the voice of him that spake to me. And I said, 'What shall I do, Lord?' And the Lord said unto me, 'Arise, and go into Damascus; and there it shall be told thee of all things which are appointed for thee to do.' And when I could not see for the glory of that light, being led by the hand of them that were with me, I came into Damascus.

"And one Ananias, a devout man according to the law, having a good report of all the Jews which dwelt there, came unto me, and stood, and said unto me, 'Brother Saul, receive thy sight.' And the same hour I looked up upon him. And he said, 'The God of our fathers hath chosen thee, that thou shouldest know his will, and see that Just One, and shouldest hear the voice of his mouth. For thou shalt be his witness unto all men of what thou hast seen and heard. And now why tarriest thou? arise, and be baptized, and wash away thy sins, calling on the name of the Lord.'

"And it came to pass, that, when I was come again to Jerusalem, even while I prayed in the temple, I was in a trance; and saw him saying unto me, 'Make haste, and get thee quickly out of Jerusalem: for they will not receive thy testimony concerning me.' And I said, 'Lord, they know that I imprisoned and beat in every synagogue them that believed on thee: and when the blood of thy martyr Stephen was shed, I also was standing by, and consenting unto his death, and kept the raiment of them that slew him.' And he said unto me, 'Depart: for I will send thee far hence unto the Gentiles.' "

And they gave him audience unto this word, and then lifted up their voices, and said, "Away with such a fellow from the earth: for it is not fit that he should live."

And as they cried out, and cast off their clothes, and threw dust into the air, the chief captain commanded him to be brought into the castle, and bade that he should be examined by scourging; that he might know wherefore they cried so against him. And as they bound him with thongs,

Paul said unto the centurion that stood by, "Is it lawful for you to scourge a man that is a Roman, and uncondemned?"

*Paul before the council*

When the centurion heard that, he went and told the chief captain, saying, "Take heed what thou doest: for this man is a Roman."

Then the chief captain came, and said unto him, "Tell me, art thou a Roman?"

He said, "Yea."

And the chief captain answered, "With a great sum obtained I this freedom."

And Paul said, "But I was free born."

Then straightway they departed from him which should have examined him: and the chief captain also was afraid, after he knew that he was a Roman, and because he had bound him.

On the morrow, because he would have known the certainty wherefore he was accused of the Jews, he loosed him from his bands, and commanded the chief priests and all their council to appear, and brought Paul down, and set him before them.

And Paul, earnestly beholding the council, said, "Men and brethren, I have lived in all good conscience before God until this day."

And the high priest Ananias commanded them that stood by him to smite him on the mouth.

Then said Paul unto him, "God shall smite thee, thou whited wall: for sittest thou to judge me after the law, and commandest me to be smitten contrary to the law?"

And they that stood by said, "Revilest thou God's high priest?"

Then said Paul, "I wist not, brethren, that he was the high priest": for it is written, "Thou shalt not speak evil of the ruler of thy people."

But when Paul perceived that the one part were Sadducees, and the other Pharisees, he cried out in the council, "Men and brethren, I am a Pharisee, the son of a Pharisee: of the hope and resurrection of the dead I am called in question."

And when he had so said, there arose a dissension between the Pharisees and the Sadducees: and the multitude was divided. For the Sadducees say that there is no resurrection, neither angel, nor spirit: but the Pharisees confess both. And there arose a great cry: and the scribes that were of the Pharisees' part arose, and strove, saying, "We find no evil in this man: but if a spirit or an angel hath spoken to him, let us not fight against God."

And when there arose a great dissension, the chief captain, fearing lest Paul should have been pulled in pieces of them, commanded the soldiers to go down, and to take him by force from among them, and to bring him into the castle.

And the night following the Lord stood by him, and said, "Be of good cheer, Paul: for as thou hast testified of me in Jerusalem, so must thou bear witness also at Rome."

And when it was day, certain of the Jews banded together, and bound themselves under a curse, saying that they would neither eat nor drink till they had killed Paul. And they were more than forty which had made this conspiracy. And they came to the chief priests and elders, and said, "We have bound ourselves under a great curse, that we will eat nothing until we have slain Paul. Now therefore ye with the council signify to the chief captain that he bring him down unto you to morrow, as though ye would enquire something more perfectly concerning him: and we, or ever he come near, are ready to kill him."

And when Paul's sister's son heard of their lying in wait, he went and entered into the castle, and told Paul. Then Paul called one of the centurions unto him, and said, "Bring this young man unto the chief captain: for he hath a certain thing to tell him."

So he took him, and brought him to the chief captain, and said, "Paul the prisoner called me unto him, and prayed me to bring this young man unto thee, who hath something to say unto thee."

Then the chief captain took him by the hand, and went with him aside privately, and asked him, "What is that thou hast to tell me?"

And he said, "The Jews have agreed to desire thee that thou wouldest bring down Paul to morrow into the council, as though they would enquire somewhat of him more perfectly. But do not thou yield unto them: for there lie in wait for him of them more than forty men, which have bound themselves with an oath, that they will neither eat nor drink till they have killed him: and now are they ready, looking for a promise from thee."

So the chief captain then let the young man depart, and charged him, "See thou tell no man that thou hast shewed these things to me." And he called unto him two centurions, saying, "Make ready two hundred soldiers to go to Cæsarea, and horsemen threescore and ten, and spearmen two hundred, at the third hour of the night; and provide them beasts, that they may set Paul on, and bring him safe unto Felix the governor." *Paul is sent to Felix the governor*

And he wrote a letter after this manner:

CLAUDIUS LYSIAS UNTO THE MOST EXCELLENT GOVERNOR FELIX SENDETH GREETING.

THIS man was taken of the Jews, and should have been killed of them: then came I with an army, and rescued him, having understood that he was a Roman. And when I would have known the cause wherefore they accused him, I brought him forth into their council: whom I perceived to be accused of questions of their law, but to have nothing laid to his charge worthy of death or of bonds. And when it was told me how that the Jews laid wait for the man, I sent straightway to thee, and gave commandment to his accusers also to say before thee what they had against him.

Farewell.

Then the soldiers, as it was commanded them, took Paul, and brought him by night to Antipatris.

On the morrow they left the horsemen to go with him, and returned to the castle: who, when they came to Cæsarea, and delivered the epistle to the governor, presented Paul also before him. And when the governor had read the letter, he asked of what province he was. And when he understood that he was of Cilicia; "I will hear thee," said he, "when thine accusers are also come." And he commanded him to be kept in Herod's judgment hall.

And after five days Ananias the high priest descended with the elders, and with a certain orator named Tertullus, who informed the governor against Paul. And when he was called forth, Tertullus began to accuse him, saying, "Seeing that by thee we enjoy great quietness, and that very worthy deeds are done unto this nation by thy providence, we accept it always, and in all places, most noble Felix, with all thankfulness. Notwithstanding, that I be not further tedious unto thee, I pray thee that thou wouldest hear us of thy clemency a few words. For we have found this man a pestilent fellow, and a mover of sedition among all the Jews throughout the world, and a ringleader of the sect of the Nazarenes: who also hath gone about to profane the temple: whom we took, and would have judged according to our law. But the chief captain Lysias came upon us, and with great violence took him away out of our hands, commanding his accusers to come unto thee: by examining of whom thyself mayest take knowledge of all these things, whereof we accuse him."

And the Jews also assented, saying that these things were so.

Then Paul, after that the governor had beckoned unto him to speak, answered, "Forasmuch as I know that thou hast been of many years a judge unto this nation, I do the more cheerfully answer for myself: because that thou mayest understand, that there are yet but twelve days since I went up to Jerusalem for to worship. And they neither found me in the temple disputing with any man, neither raising up the people, neither in the synagogues, nor in the city: neither can they prove the things whereof they now accuse me. But this I confess unto thee, that after the way which they call heresy, so worship I the God of my fathers, believing all things which are written in the law and in the prophets: and have hope toward God, which they themselves also allow, that there shall be a resurrection of the dead, both of the just and unjust. And herein do I exercise myself, to have always a conscience void of offence toward God, and toward men. Now after many years I came to bring alms to my nation, and offerings. Whereupon certain Jews from Asia found me purified in the temple, neither with multitude, nor with tumult, who ought to have been here before thee, and object, if they had ought against me. Or else let these same here say, if they have found any evil doing in me, while I stood before the council, except it be for this one voice, that I cried standing among them, 'Touching the resurrection of the dead I am called in question by you this day.'"

And when Felix heard these things, having more perfect knowledge of that way, he deferred them, and said, "When Lysias the chief captain shall come down, I will know the uttermost of your matter."

And he commanded a centurion to keep Paul, and to let him have liberty, and that he should forbid none of his acquaintance to minister or come unto him.

And after certain days, when Felix came with his wife Drusilla, which was a Jewess, he sent for Paul, and heard him concerning the faith in Christ. And as he reasoned of righteousness, temperance, and judgment

to come, Felix trembled, and answered, "Go thy way for this time;   *Paul before Festus*
when I have a convenient season, I will call for thee."

He hoped also that money should have been given him of Paul, that
he might loose him: wherefore he sent for him the oftener, and communed
with him. But after two years Porcius Festus came into Felix' room: and
Felix, willing to shew the Jews a pleasure, left Paul bound.

Now when Festus was come into the province, after three days he ascended from Cæsarea to Jerusalem. Then the high priest and the chief
of the Jews informed him against Paul, and besought him, and desired
favour against him, that he would send for him to Jerusalem, laying wait
in the way to kill him. But Festus answered, that Paul should be kept at
Cæsarea, and that he himself would depart shortly thither.

"Let them therefore," said he, "which among you are able, go down
with me, and accuse this man, if there be any wickedness in him."

And when he had tarried among them more than ten days, he went
down unto Cæsarea; and the next day sitting on the judgment seat commanded Paul to be brought. And when he was come, the Jews which
came down from Jerusalem stood round about, and laid many and
grievous complaints against Paul, which they could not prove. While he
answered for himself, "Neither against the law of the Jews, neither against
the temple, nor yet against Cæsar, have I offended any thing at all."

But Festus, willing to do the Jews a pleasure, answered Paul, and
said, "Wilt thou go up to Jerusalem, and there be judged of these things
before me?"

Then said Paul, "I stand at Cæsar's judgment seat, where I ought to
be judged: to the Jews have I done no wrong, as thou very well knowest.
For if I be an offender, or have committed any thing worthy of death,
I refuse not to die: but if there be none of these things whereof these
accuse me, no man may deliver me unto them. I appeal unto Cæsar."

Then Festus, when he had conferred with the council, answered,
"Hast thou appealed unto Cæsar? unto Cæsar shalt thou go."

And after certain days king Agrippa and Bernice came unto Cæsarea
to salute Festus. And when they had been there many days, Festus declared Paul's cause unto the king, saying, "There is a certain man left in
bonds by Felix: about whom, when I was at Jerusalem, the chief priests
and the elders of the Jews informed me, desiring to have judgment against

him. To whom I answered, 'It is not the manner of the Romans to deliver any man to die, before that he which is accused have the accusers face to face, and have licence to answer for himself concerning the crime laid against him.' Therefore, when they were come hither, without any delay on the morrow I sat on the judgment seat, and commanded the man to be brought forth. Against whom when the accusers stood up, they brought none accusation of such things as I supposed: but had certain questions against him of their own superstition, and of one Jesus, which was dead, whom Paul affirmed to be alive. And because I doubted of such manner of questions, I asked him whether he would go to Jerusalem, and there be judged of these matters. But when Paul had appealed to be reserved unto the hearing of Augustus, I commanded him to be kept till I might send him to Cæsar."

Then Agrippa said unto Festus, "I would also hear the man myself."

"To morrow," said he, "thou shalt hear him."

And on the morrow, when Agrippa was come, and Bernice, with great pomp, and was entered into the place of hearing, with the chief captains, and principal men of the city, at Festus' commandment Paul was brought forth. And Festus said, "King Agrippa, and all men which are here present with us, ye see this man, about whom all the multitude of the Jews have dealt with me, both at Jerusalem, and also here, crying that he ought not to live any longer. But when I found that he had committed nothing worthy of death, and that he himself hath appealed to Augustus, I have determined to send him. Of whom I have no certain thing to write unto my lord. Wherefore I have brought him forth before you, and specially before thee, O king Agrippa, that, after examination had, I might have somewhat to write. For it seemeth to me unreasonable to send a prisoner, and not withal to signify the crimes laid against him."

Then Agrippa said unto Paul, "Thou art permitted to speak for thyself."

Then Paul stretched forth the hand, and answered for himself:

"I think myself happy, king Agrippa, because I shall answer for myself this day before thee touching all the things whereof I am accused of the Jews: especially because I know thee to be expert in all customs and questions which are among the Jews: wherefore I beseech thee to hear me patiently. My manner of life from my youth, which was at the first

among mine own nation at Jerusalem, know all the Jews; which knew me
from the beginning, if they would testify, that after the most straitest sect
of our religion I lived a Pharisee. And now I stand and am judged for the
hope of the promise made of God unto our fathers: unto which promise
our twelve tribes, instantly serving God day and night, hope to come. For
which hope's sake, king Agrippa, I am accused of the Jews. Why should
it be thought a thing incredible with you, that God should raise the dead?
I verily thought with myself, that I ought to do many things contrary to
the name of Jesus of Nazareth. Which thing I also did in Jerusalem: and
many of the saints did I shut up in prison, having received authority
from the chief priests; and when they were put to death, I gave my voice
against them. And I punished them oft in every synagogue, and compelled them to blaspheme; and being exceedingly mad against them, I
persecuted them even unto strange cities. Whereupon as I went to
Damascus with authority and commission from the chief priests, at midday, O king, I saw in the way a light from heaven, above the brightness
of the sun, shining round about me and them which journeyed with me.
And when we were all fallen to the earth, I heard a voice speaking unto me,
and saying in the Hebrew tongue, 'Saul, Saul, why persecutest thou me?
it is hard for thee to kick against the pricks.' And I said, 'Who art thou,
Lord?' And he said, 'I am Jesus whom thou persecutest. But rise, and
stand upon thy feet: for I have appeared unto thee for this purpose, to
make thee a minister and a witness both of these things which thou hast
seen, and of those things in the which I will appear unto thee; delivering
thee from the people, and from the Gentiles, unto whom now I send thee,
to open their eyes, and to turn them from darkness to light, and from the
power of Satan unto God, that they may receive forgiveness of sins, and
inheritance among them which are sanctified by faith that is in me.'

"Whereupon, O king Agrippa, I was not disobedient unto the heavenly
vision: but shewed first unto them of Damascus, and at Jerusalem, and
throughout all the coasts of Judæa, and then to the Gentiles, that they
should repent and turn to God, and do works meet for repentance. For
these causes the Jews caught me in the temple, and went about to kill me.
Having therefore obtained help of God, I continue unto this day, wit-
nessing both to small and great, saying none other things than those
which the prophets and Moses did say should come: That Christ should

suffer, and that he should be the first that should rise from the dead, and should shew light unto the people, and to the Gentiles."

And as he thus spake for himself, Festus said with a loud voice, "Paul, thou art beside thyself; much learning doth make thee mad."

But he said, "I am not mad, most noble Festus; but speak forth the words of truth and soberness. For the king knoweth of these things, before whom also I speak freely: for I am persuaded that none of these things are hidden from him; for this thing was not done in a corner. King Agrippa, believest thou the prophets? I know that thou believest."

Then Agrippa said unto Paul, "Almost thou persuadest me to be a Christian."

And Paul said, "I would to God, that not only thou, but also all that hear me this day, were both almost, and altogether such as I am, except these bonds."

And when he had thus spoken, the king rose up, and the governor, and Bernice, and they that sat with them: and when they were gone aside, they talked between themselves, saying, "This man doeth nothing worthy of death or of bonds."

Then said Agrippa unto Festus, "This man might have been set at liberty, if he had not appealed unto Cæsar."

And when it was determined that we should sail into Italy, they delivered Paul and certain other prisoners unto one named Julius, a centurion of Augustus' band. And entering into a ship of Adramyttium, we launched, meaning to sail by the coasts of Asia; one Aristarchus, a Macedonian of Thessalonica, being with us.

And the next day we touched at Sidon. And Julius courteously entreated Paul, and gave him liberty to go unto his friends to refresh himself. And when we had launched from thence, we sailed under Cyprus, because the winds were contrary.

And when we had sailed over the sea of Cilicia and Pamphylia, we came to Myra, a city of Lycia. And there the centurion found a ship of Alexandria sailing into Italy; and he put us therein.

And when we had sailed slowly many days, and scarce were come over against Cnidus, the wind not suffering us, we sailed under Crete, over against Salmone; and, hardly passing it, came unto a place which is called The fair havens; nigh whereunto was the city of Lasea.

# PAUL THE APOSTLE

Now when much time was spent, and when sailing was now dangerous, because the fast was now already past, Paul admonished them, and said unto them, "Sirs, I perceive that this voyage will be with hurt and much damage, not only of the lading and ship, but also of our lives."

Nevertheless the centurion believed the master and the owner of the ship, more than those things which were spoken by Paul. And because the haven was not commodious to winter in, the more part advised to depart thence also, if by any means they might attain to Phenice, and there to winter; which is an haven of Crete, and lieth toward the south west and north west.

And when the south wind blew softly, supposing that they had obtained their purpose, loosing thence, they sailed close by Crete. But not long after there arose against it a tempestuous wind, called Euroclydon. And when the ship was caught, and could not bear up into the wind, we let her drive. And running under a certain island which is called Clauda, we had much work to come by the boat: which when they had taken up, they used helps, undergirding the ship; and, fearing lest they should fall into the quicksands, strake sail, and so were driven.

And we being exceedingly tossed with a tempest, the next day they lightened the ship; and the third day we cast out with our own hands the tackling of the ship. And when neither sun nor stars in many days appeared, and no small tempest lay on us, all hope that we should be saved was then taken away.

But after long abstinence Paul stood forth in the midst of them, and said, "Sirs, ye should have hearkened unto me, and not have loosed from Crete, and to have gained this harm and loss. And now I exhort you to be of good cheer: for there shall be no loss of any man's life among you, but of the ship. For there stood by me this night the angel of God, whose I am, and whom I serve, saying, 'Fear not, Paul; thou must be brought before Cæsar: and, lo, God hath given thee all them that sail with thee.' Wherefore, sirs, be of good cheer: for I believe as it was told me. Howbeit we must be cast upon a certain island."

But when the fourteenth night was come, as we were driven up and down in Adria, about midnight the shipmen deemed that they drew near to some country; and sounded, and found it twenty fathoms: and when they had gone a little further, they sounded again, and found it fifteen

*The shipwreck and escape to Melita* fathoms. Then fearing lest we should have fallen upon rocks, they cast four anchors out of the stern, and wished for the day.

And as the shipmen were about to flee out of the ship, when they had let down the boat into the sea, under colour as though they would have cast anchors out of the foreship, Paul said to the centurion and to the soldiers, "Except these abide in the ship, ye cannot be saved."

Then the soldiers cut off the ropes of the boat, and let her fall off.

And while the day was coming on, Paul besought them all to take meat, saying, "This day is the fourteenth day that ye have tarried and continued fasting, having taken nothing. Wherefore I pray you to take some meat: for this is for your health: for there shall not an hair fall from the head of any of you."

And when he had thus spoken, he took bread, and gave thanks to God in presence of them all: and when he had broken it, he began to eat. Then were they all of good cheer, and they also took some meat. And we were in all in the ship two hundred threescore and sixteen souls. And when they had eaten enough, they lightened the ship, and cast out the wheat into the sea.

And when it was day, they knew not the land: but they discovered a certain creek with a shore, into the which they were minded, if it were possible, to thrust in the ship. And when they had taken up the anchors, they committed themselves unto the sea, and loosed the rudder bands, and hoised up the mainsail to the wind, and made toward shore. And falling into a place where two seas met, they ran the ship aground; and the forepart stuck fast, and remained unmoveable, but the hinder part was broken with the violence of the waves.

And the soldiers' counsel was to kill the prisoners, lest any of them should swim out, and escape. But the centurion, willing to save Paul, kept them from their purpose; and commanded that they which could swim should cast themselves first into the sea, and get to land: and the rest, some on boards, and some on broken pieces of the ship. And so it came to pass, that they escaped all safe to land.

Now when they were escaped, then they knew that the island was called Melita. And the barbarous people shewed us no little kindness: for they kindled a fire, and received us every one, because of the present rain, and because of the cold.

[ 158 ]

# PAUL THE APOSTLE

And when Paul had gathered a bundle of sticks, and laid them on the fire, there came a viper out of the heat, and fastened on his hand. And when the barbarians saw the venomous beast hang on his hand, they said among themselves, "No doubt this man is a murderer, whom, though he hath escaped the sea, yet vengeance suffereth not to live."

*Paul and the viper*

And he shook off the beast into the fire, and felt no harm. Howbeit they looked when he should have swollen, or fallen down dead suddenly: but after they had looked a great while, and saw no harm come to him, they changed their minds, and said that he was a god.

In the same quarters were possessions of the chief man of the island, whose name was Publius; who received us, and lodged us three days courteously. And it came to pass, that the father of Publius lay sick of a fever and of a bloody flux: to whom Paul entered in, and prayed, and laid his hands on him, and healed him. So when this was done, others also, which had diseases in the island, came, and were healed: who also honoured us with many honours; and when we departed, they laded us with such things as were necessary.

And after three months we departed in a ship of Alexandria, which had wintered in the isle, whose sign was Castor and Pollux. And landing at Syracuse, we tarried there three days. And from thence we fetched a compass, and came to Rhegium: and after one day the south wind blew, and we came the next day to Puteoli: where we found brethren, and were desired to tarry with them seven days: and so we went toward Rome.

*The arrival at Rome*

And from thence, when the brethren heard of us, they came to meet us as far as Appii forum, and The three taverns: whom when Paul saw, he thanked God, and took courage. And when we came to Rome, the centurion delivered the prisoners to the captain of the guard: but Paul was suffered to dwell by himself with a soldier that kept him.

And it came to pass, that after three days Paul called the chief of the Jews together: and when they were come together, he said unto them, "Men and brethren, though I have committed nothing against the people, or customs of our fathers, yet was I delivered prisoner from Jerusalem into the hands of the Romans. Who, when they had examined me, would have let me go, because there was no cause of death in me. But when the Jews spake against it, I was constrained to appeal unto Cæsar; not that I had ought to accuse my nation of. For this cause therefore have I called

for you, to see you, and to speak with you: because that for the hope of
Israel I am bound with this chain."

And they said unto him, "We neither received letters out of Judæa
concerning thee, neither any of the brethren that came shewed or spake
any harm of thee. But we desire to hear of thee what thou thinkest: for
as concerning this sect, we know that every where it is spoken against."

And when they had appointed him a day, there came many to him into
his lodging; to whom he expounded and testified the kingdom of God,
persuading them concerning Jesus, both out of the law of Moses, and out
of the prophets, from morning till evening. And some believed the things
which were spoken, and some believed not. And when they agreed not
among themselves, they departed, after that Paul had spoken one word,
"Well spake the Holy Ghost by Esaias the prophet unto our fathers,
saying,

> Go unto this people, and say,
> Hearing ye shall hear, and shall not understand;
> And seeing ye shall see, and not perceive:
> For the heart of this people is waxed gross,
> And their ears are dull of hearing,
> And their eyes have they closed;
> Lest they should see with their eyes,
> And hear with their ears,
> And understand with their heart,
> And should be converted,
> And I should heal them.

"Be it known therefore unto you, that the salvation of God is sent
unto the Gentiles, and that they will hear it."

And when he had said these words, the Jews departed, and had great
reasoning among themselves.

And Paul dwelt two whole years in his own hired house, and received
all that came in unto him, preaching the kingdom of God, and teaching
those things which concern the Lord Jesus Christ, with all confidence,
no man forbidding him.

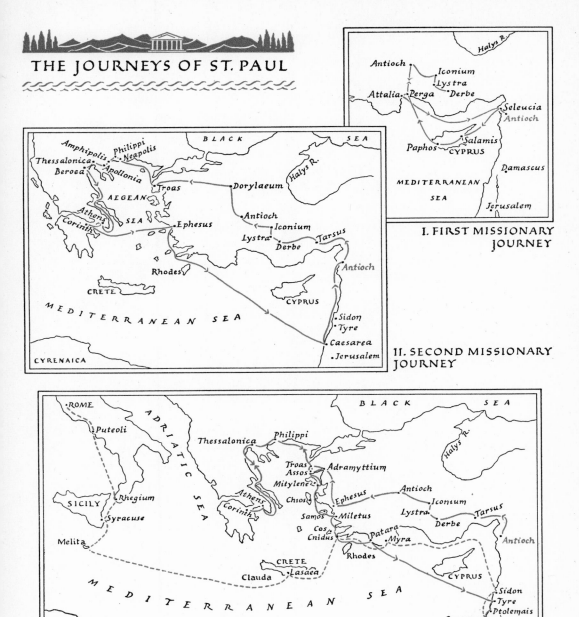

# THE JOURNEYS OF ST. PAUL

**I. FIRST MISSIONARY JOURNEY**

**II. SECOND MISSIONARY JOURNEY**

**III. THIRD MISSIONARY JOURNEY & VOYAGE TO ROME**

*Antioch in Syria from which St. Paul started on his missionary journeys, is shown in color.*

# Paul's Message

*Paul, a servant of Jesus Christ, called to be an apostle.*

As much as in me is, I am ready to preach the gospel to you. Am I not an apostle? am I not free? have I not seen Jesus Christ our Lord? are not ye my work in the Lord? *Christ the only foundation*

For though I preach the gospel, I have nothing to glory of: for necessity is laid upon me; yea, woe is unto me, if I preach not the gospel! But God forbid that I should glory, save in the cross of our Lord Jesus Christ, by whom the world is crucified unto me, and I unto the world. For the preaching of the cross is unto us the power of God.

For the Jews require a sign, and the Greeks seek after wisdom: but we preach Christ crucified, unto the Jews a stumblingblock, and unto the Greeks foolishness; but unto them which are called, both Jews and Greeks, Christ the power of God, and the wisdom of God. There is no respect of persons with God, for the same Lord over all is rich unto all that call upon him. For ye are all the children of God by faith in Christ Jesus. For as many of you as have been baptized into Christ have put on Christ. There is neither Jew nor Greek, there is neither bond nor free, there is neither male nor female: for ye are all one in Christ Jesus.

One saith, "I am of Paul"; and another, "I am of Apollos." Who then is Paul, and who is Apollos, but ministers by whom ye believed, even as the Lord gave to every man? I have planted, Apollos watered; but God gave the increase. So then neither is he that planteth any thing, neither he that watereth; but God that giveth the increase. Now he that planteth and he that watereth are one: and every man shall receive his own reward according to his own labour. For we are labourers together with God.

Ye are God's husbandry, ye are God's building. According to the grace of God which is given unto me, as a wise masterbuilder, I have laid the foundation, and another buildeth thereon. But let every man take heed how he buildeth thereupon. For other foundation can no man lay than that is laid, which is Jesus Christ.

All things are your's; whether Paul, or Apollos, or the world, or life, or death, or things present, or things to come; all are your's.

And ye are Christ's; and Christ is God's.

Let a man so account of us, as of the ministers of Christ, and stewards of the mysteries of God, who hath made us able ministers of the new testament. Moreover it is required in stewards, that a man be found faithful. Do ye not know that they which minister about holy things live of the things of the temple? and they which wait at the altar are partakers with the altar? Even so hath the Lord ordained that they which preach the gospel should live of the gospel. Our sufficiency is of God. Therefore judge nothing before the time, until the Lord come, who both will bring to light the hidden things of darkness, and will make manifest the counsels of the hearts: and then shall every man have praise of God. And these things, brethren, I have in a figure transferred to myself and to Apollos for your sakes; that ye might learn in us not to think of men above that which is written, that no one of you be puffed up for one against another.

Even unto this present hour we both hunger, and thirst, and are naked, and are buffeted, and have no certain dwellingplace; and labour, working with our own hands: being reviled, we bless; being persecuted, we suffer it: but in all things approving ourselves as the ministers of God, in much patience, in afflictions, in necessities, in distresses, in stripes, in imprisonments, in tumults, in labours, in watchings, in fastings; by pureness, by knowledge, by longsuffering, by kindness, by the Holy Ghost, by love unfeigned, by the word of truth, by the power of God, by the armour of righteousness on the right hand and on the left, by honour and dishonour, by evil report and good report: as deceivers, and yet true; as unknown, and yet well known; as dying, and, behold, we live; as chastened, and not killed; as sorrowful, yet alway rejoicing; as poor, yet making many rich; as having nothing, and yet possessing all things.

And not only so, but we glory in tribulations also: knowing that tribulation worketh patience; and patience, experience; and experience, hope: and hope maketh not ashamed; because the love of God is shed abroad in our hearts by the Holy Ghost which is given unto us.

Wherefore, my beloved, as ye have always obeyed, not as in my presence only, but now much more in my absence, work out your own salvation with fear and trembling. For it is God which worketh in you both to will and to do of his good pleasure. Do all things without murmurings and disputings: that ye may be blameless and harmless, the sons of God, without rebuke, in the midst of a crooked and perverse nation, among whom ye shine as lights in the world; holding forth the word of life; that I may rejoice in the day of Christ, that I have not run in vain, neither laboured in vain.

But I trust in the Lord Jesus to send Timotheus shortly unto you, that I also may be of good comfort, when I know your state. For I have no man likeminded, who will naturally care for your state. For all seek their own, not the things which are Jesus Christ's. But ye know the proof of him, that, as a son with the father, he hath served with me in the gospel. He shall bring you into remembrance of my ways which be in Christ, as I teach every where in every church.

Therefore, my brethren dearly beloved and longed for, my joy and crown, so stand fast in the Lord, my dearly beloved. Rejoice in the Lord alway: and again I say, Rejoice. Let your moderation be known unto all men. The Lord is at hand. Be careful for nothing; but in every thing by prayer and supplication with thanksgiving let your requests be made known unto God.

Though I be absent in the flesh, yet am I with you in the spirit, joying and beholding your order, and the stedfastness of your faith in Christ.

As ye have therefore received Christ Jesus the Lord, so walk ye in him: rooted and built up in him, and stablished in the faith, as ye have been taught, abounding therein with thanksgiving. Beware lest any man spoil you through philosophy and vain deceit, after the tradition of men, after the rudiments of the world, and not after Christ. For in him dwelleth all the fulness of the Godhead bodily.

Finally, brethren, whatsoever things are true, whatsoever things are honest, whatsoever things are just, whatsoever things are pure, whatsoever things are lovely, whatsoever things are of good report; if there be any virtue, and if there be any praise, think on these things.

And the peace of God, which passeth all understanding, shall keep your hearts and minds through Christ Jesus. Amen.

# PAUL THE APOSTLE

*Paul, an apostle of Jesus Christ by the will of God, according to the promise of life which is in Christ Jesus, To Timothy, my dearly beloved son: Grace, mercy, and peace, from God the Father and Christ Jesus our Lord.*

*Paul's love of Timothy*

I THANK GOD, whom I serve from my forefathers with pure conscience, that without ceasing I have remembrance of thee in my prayers night and day; greatly desiring to see thee, that I may be filled with joy; when I call to remembrance the unfeigned faith that is in thee, which dwelt first in thy grandmother Lois, and thy mother Eunice; and I am persuaded that in thee also. Wherefore I put thee in remembrance that thou stir up and neglect not the gift of God, which is in thee by the putting on of my hands. For God hath not given us the spirit of fear; but of power, and of love, and of a sound mind. Be not thou therefore ashamed of the testimony of our Lord, nor of me his prisoner: but be thou partaker of the afflictions of the gospel according to the power of God; who hath called us with an holy calling, not according to our works, but according to his own purpose and grace, which was given us in Christ Jesus before the world began, but is now made manifest by the appearing of our Saviour Jesus Christ, who hath abolished death, and hath brought life and immortality to light through the gospel: whereunto I am appointed a preacher, and an apostle, and a teacher of the Gentiles.

Thou therefore, my son, be strong in the grace that is in Christ Jesus. And the things that thou hast heard of me among many witnesses, the same commit thou to faithful men, who shall be able to teach others also. Thou hast fully known my doctrine, manner of life, purpose, faith, longsuffering, charity, patience. Continue thou in the things which thou hast learned and hast been assured of, knowing of whom thou hast learned them; and that from a child thou hast known the holy scriptures, which are able to make thee wise unto salvation through faith which is in Christ Jesus. If we believe not, yet he abideth faithful: he cannot deny himself. Consider what I say; and the Lord give thee understanding in all things.

Thou therefore endure hardness, as a good soldier of Jesus Christ. Study to shew thyself approved unto God, a workman that needeth not to be ashamed, rightly dividing the word of truth. The foundation of God standeth sure, having this seal, "The Lord knoweth them that are his," and, "Let every one that nameth the name of Christ depart from ini- *Godliness is great gain* quity." Flee also youthful lusts: but follow righteousness, faith, charity, peace, with them that call on the Lord out of a pure heart.

And the servant of the Lord must not strive; but be gentle unto all men, apt to teach, patient. All scripture is given by inspiration of God, and is profitable for doctrine, for reproof, for correction, for instruction in righteousness: that the man of God may be perfect, throughly furnished unto all good works. Let no man despise thy youth; but be thou an example of the believers, in word, in conversation, in charity, in spirit, in faith. Keep thyself pure. But watch thou in all things, endure afflictions, do the work of an evangelist, make full proof of thy ministry.

I exhort therefore, that, first of all, supplications, prayers, intercessions, and giving of thanks, be made for all men; I will therefore that men pray every where, lifting up holy hands, without wrath and doubting.

Without controversy great is the mystery of godliness: God was manifest in the flesh, justified in the Spirit, seen of angels, preached unto the Gentiles, believed on in the world, received up into glory. Therefore we both labour and suffer reproach, because we trust in the living God, who is the Saviour of all men.

Godliness with contentment is great gain. For we brought nothing into this world, and it is certain we can carry nothing out. And having food and raiment let us be therewith content. But they that will be rich fall into temptation and a snare, and into many foolish and hurtful lusts, which drown men in destruction and perdition. For the love of money is the root of all evil: which while some coveted after, they have erred from the faith, and pierced themselves through with many sorrows. Charge them that are rich in this world, that they be not highminded, nor trust in uncertain riches, but in the living God, who giveth us richly all things to enjoy; that they do good, that they be rich in good works, ready to distribute, willing to communicate.

But thou, O man of God, flee these things; and follow after righteousness, godliness, faith, love, patience, meekness. Fight the good fight of faith, lay hold on eternal life, whereunto thou art also called, and hast professed a good profession before many witnesses.

I give thee charge in the sight of God, who quickeneth all things, and before Christ Jesus, who before Pontius Pilate witnessed a good con-

*Advice to Timothy* fession; that thou keep this commandment without spot, unrebukeable, until the appearing of our Lord Jesus Christ: who is the blessed and only Potentate, the King of kings, and Lord of lords; who only hath immortality, dwelling in the light which no man can approach unto; whom no man hath seen, nor can see: to whom be honour and power everlasting.

O Timothy, keep that which is committed to thy trust. This charge I commit unto thee, son Timothy, according to the prophecies which went before on thee, that thou by them mightest war a good warfare; holding faith, and a good conscience; which some having put away concerning faith have made shipwreck.

Grace be with thee.

Now unto the King eternal, immortal, invisible, the only wise God, be honour and glory for ever and ever. Amen.

*Paul, a prisoner of Jesus Christ, and Timothy our brother, unto Philemon our dearly beloved, and fellowlabourer, and to our beloved Apphia, and Archippus our fellowsoldier, and to the church in thy house: grace to you, and peace, from God our Father and the Lord Jesus Christ.*

*Paul's joy in Philemon's love* I THANK MY GOD, making mention of thee always in my prayers, hearing of thy love and faith, which thou hast toward the Lord Jesus, and toward all saints; that the communication of thy faith may become effectual by the acknowledging of every good thing which is in you in Christ Jesus.

For we have great joy and consolation in thy love, because the bowels of the saints are refreshed by thee, brother.

Wherefore, though I might be much bold in Christ to enjoin thee that which is convenient, yet for love's sake I rather beseech thee, being such an one as Paul the aged, and now also a prisoner of Jesus Christ.

I beseech thee for my son Onesimus, whom I have begotten in my bonds: which in time past was to thee unprofitable, but now profitable to thee and to me: whom I have sent again: thou therefore receive him, that is, mine own bowels: whom I would have retained with me, that in thy stead he might have ministered unto me in the bonds of the gospel: but without thy mind would I do nothing; that thy benefit should not be as it were of necessity, but willingly.

For perhaps he therefore departed for a season, that thou shouldest receive him for ever; not now as a servant, but above a servant, a brother beloved, specially to me, but how much more unto thee, both in the flesh, and in the Lord?

*Forgiveness asked for Onesimus*

If thou count me therefore a partner, receive him as myself.

If he hath wronged thee, or oweth thee ought, put that on mine account; I Paul have written it with mine own hand, I will repay it: albeit I do not say to thee how thou owest unto me even thine own self besides.

Yea, brother, let me have joy of thee in the Lord: refresh my bowels in the Lord.

Having confidence in thy obedience I wrote unto thee, knowing that thou wilt also do more than I say.

But withal prepare me also a lodging: for I trust that through your prayers I shall be given unto you.

There salute thee Epaphras, my fellowprisoner in Christ Jesus; Marcus, Aristarchus, Demas, Lucas, my fellowlabourers.

The grace of our Lord Jesus Christ be with your spirit. Amen.

*Paul, an apostle, (not of men, neither by man, but by Jesus Christ, and God the Father, who raised him from the dead;) Grace be to you and peace from God the Father, and from our Lord Jesus Christ.*

*Paul's gospel is of God*

I CERTIFY YOU, brethren, that the gospel which was preached of me is not after man. For I neither received it of man, neither was I taught it, but by the revelation of Jesus Christ. For ye have heard of my conversation in time past in the Jews' religion, how that beyond measure I persecuted the church of God, and wasted it: and profited in the Jews' religion above many my equals in mine own nation, being more exceedingly zealous of the traditions of my fathers. But when it pleased God to reveal his Son in me, that I might preach him among the heathen; immediately I conferred not with flesh and blood: neither went I up to Jerusalem to them which were apostles before me; but I went into Arabia, and returned again unto Damascus.

Then after three years I went up to Jerusalem to see Peter, and abode with him fifteen days. But other of the apostles saw I none, save James the Lord's brother. Now the things which I write unto you, behold, before God, I lie not.

Afterwards I came into the regions of Syria and Cilicia; and was unknown by face unto the churches of Judæa which were in Christ: but

*The kingdom of God is in power*

they had heard only, That he which persecuted us in times past now preacheth the faith which once he destroyed. And they glorified God in me.

I am not ashamed of the gospel of Christ: for it is the power of God unto salvation to every one that believeth. Christ sent me not to baptize, but to preach the gospel: not with wisdom of words, lest the cross of Christ should be made of none effect. And I, brethren, when I came to you, came not with excellency of speech or of wisdom, declaring unto you the testimony of God. For I determined not to know any thing among you, save Jesus Christ, and him crucified.

For the kingdom of God is not in word, but in power.

We speak the wisdom of God in a mystery, even the hidden wisdom, which God ordained before the world unto our glory: as it is written,

> Eye hath not seen, nor ear heard,
> Neither have entered into the heart of man,
> The things which God hath prepared for them that love him.

But God hath revealed them unto us by his Spirit: for the Spirit searcheth all things, yea, the deep things of God.

For what man knoweth the things of a man, save the spirit of man which is in him? even so the things of God knoweth no man, but the Spirit of God. Now we have received, not the spirit of the world, but the spirit which is of God; that we might know the things that are freely given to us of God. Which things also we speak, not in the words which man's wisdom teacheth, but which the Holy Ghost teacheth; comparing spiritual things with spiritual. But he that is spiritual judgeth all things, yet he himself is judged of no man. For who hath known the mind of the Lord, that he may instruct him? But we have the mind of Christ.

I fear, lest by any means, your minds should be corrupted from the simplicity that is in Christ. This I say then, Walk in the Spirit, and ye shall not fulfil the lust of the flesh. For the flesh lusteth against the Spirit, and the Spirit against the flesh: and these are contrary the one to the other: so that ye cannot do the things that ye would. Now the works of the flesh are manifest.

The fruit of the Spirit is love, joy, peace, longsuffering, gentleness,

goodness, faith, meekness, temperance: against such there is no law. If
we live in the Spirit, let us also walk in the Spirit. *The spirit of the Lord brings freedom*

Stand fast therefore in the liberty wherewith Christ hath made us
free, for, brethren, ye have been called unto liberty, the glorious liberty
of the children of God; only use not liberty for an occasion to the flesh,
but by love serve one another. For all the law is fulfilled in one word, even
in this; "Thou shalt love thy neighbour as thyself."

The letter killeth, but the spirit giveth life. Now the Lord is that
Spirit: and where the Spirit of the Lord is, there is liberty.

But we all, with open face beholding as in a glass the glory of the
Lord, are changed into the same image from glory to glory even as by the
Spirit of the Lord. For God, who commanded the light to shine out of
darkness, hath shined in our hearts, to give the light of the knowledge of
the glory of God in the face of Jesus Christ.

We are troubled on every side, yet not distressed; we are perplexed,
but not in despair; persecuted, but not forsaken; cast down, but not
destroyed; always bearing about in the body the dying of the Lord Jesus,
that the life also of Jesus might be made manifest in our body. For which
cause we faint not; but though our outward man perish, yet the inward
man is renewed day by day. For our light affliction, which is but for a
moment, worketh for us a far more exceeding and eternal weight of glory;
while we look not at the things which are seen, but at the things which
are not seen: for the things which are seen are temporal; but the things
which are not seen are eternal. We know that if our earthly house of this
tabernacle were dissolved, we have a building of God, an house not made
with hands, eternal in the heavens.

Now he that hath wrought us for the selfsame thing is God, who also
hath given unto us the earnest of the Spirit. For we walk by faith, not by
sight. Therefore if any man be in Christ, he is a new creature: old things
are passed away; behold, all things are become new.

To be spiritually minded is life and peace. For as many as are led by
the Spirit of God, they are the sons of God. Ye have not received the spirit
of bondage again to fear; but ye have received the Spirit of adoption,
whereby we cry, "Abba, Father." The Spirit itself beareth witness with
our spirit, that we are the children of God: and if children, then heirs;
heirs of God, and joint-heirs with Christ; if so be that we suffer with him,

*The Christian hope* that we may be also glorified together. For I reckon that the sufferings of this present time are not worthy to be compared with the glory which shall be revealed in us. For the earnest expectation of the creature waiteth for the manifestation of the sons of God. For we are saved by hope: but hope that is seen is not hope: for what a man seeth, why doth he yet hope for? But if we hope for that we see not, then do we with patience wait for it. And we know that all things work together for good to them that love God, to them who are the called according to his purpose.

What shall we then say to these things? If God be for us, who can be against us? He that spared not his own Son, but delivered him up for us all, how shall he not with him also freely give us all things? Who shall lay any thing to the charge of God's elect? It is God that justifieth. Who is he that condemneth? It is Christ that died, yea rather, that is risen again, who is even at the right hand of God, who also maketh intercession for us.

Who shall separate us from the love of Christ? shall tribulation, or distress, or persecution, or famine, or nakedness, or peril, or sword? Nay, in all these things we are more than conquerors through him that loved us. For I am persuaded, that neither death, nor life, nor angels, nor principalities, nor powers, nor things present, nor things to come, nor height, nor depth, nor any other creature, shall be able to separate us from the love of God, which is in Christ Jesus our Lord.

If thou shalt confess with thy mouth the Lord Jesus, and shalt believe in thine heart that God hath raised him from the dead, thou shalt be saved. For with the heart man believeth unto righteousness; and with the mouth confession is made unto salvation.

Behold therefore the goodness and severity of God. O the depth of the riches both of the wisdom and knowledge of God! how unsearchable are his judgments, and his ways past finding out! For who hath known the mind of the Lord? or who hath been his counsellor? Or who hath first given to him, and it shall be recompensed unto him again? For of him, and through him, and to him, are all things: to whom be glory for ever. Amen.

## PAUL THE APOSTLE

*Paul, called to be an apostle of Jesus Christ through the will of God, grace be unto you, and peace, from God our Father, and from the Lord Jesus Christ.*

I THANK MY GOD always on your behalf, for the grace of God which is given you by Jesus Christ; who is the image of the invisible God, that in every thing ye are enriched by him, in all utterance, and in all knowledge; for it pleased the Father that in him should all fulness dwell.

Every one of us shall give account of himself to God. Let us not therefore judge one another any more: but judge this rather, that no man put a stumblingblock or an occasion to fall in his brother's way.

For the kingdom of God is not meat and drink; but righteousness, and peace, and joy in the Holy Ghost. Let us therefore follow after the things which make for peace, and things wherewith one may edify another.

We then that are strong ought to bear the infirmities of the weak, and not to please ourselves. Brethren, if a man be overtaken in a fault, ye which are spiritual, restore such an one in the spirit of meekness; considering thyself, lest thou also be tempted. Bear ye one another's burdens, and so fulfil the law of Christ. For if a man think himself to be something, when he is nothing, he deceiveth himself.

But let every man prove his own work, and then shall he have rejoicing in himself alone, and not in another. For every man shall bear his own burden. Every man's work shall be made manifest: for the day shall declare it, because it shall be revealed by fire; and the fire shall try every man's work of what sort it is. If any man's work abide which he hath built thereupon, he shall receive a reward.

Be not deceived; God is not mocked: for whatsoever a man soweth, that shall he also reap. But this I say, He which soweth sparingly shall reap also sparingly; and he which soweth bountifully shall reap also bountifully. For he that soweth to his flesh shall of the flesh reap corruption; but he that soweth to the Spirit shall of the Spirit reap life everlasting.

Know ye not that ye are the temple of God, and that the Spirit of God dwelleth in you? What? know ye not that your body is the temple of the Holy Ghost which is in you, which ye have of God, and ye are not your own? For ye are bought with a price: therefore glorify God in your body, and in your spirit, which are God's. He that is joined unto the Lord is one spirit.

[ 171 ]

*Death the wages of sin*

Know ye not, that so many of us as were baptized into Jesus Christ were baptized into his death? that like as Christ was raised up from the dead by the glory of the Father, even so we also should walk in newness of life. For if we have been planted together in the likeness of his death, we shall be also in the likeness of his resurrection. For in that he died, he died unto sin once: but in that he liveth, he liveth unto God. Let not sin therefore reign in your mortal body. For sin shall not have dominion over you: for ye are not under the law, but under grace.

Know ye not, that to whom ye yield yourselves servants to obey, his servants ye are to whom ye obey; whether of sin unto death, or of obedience unto righteousness? For the wages of sin is death; but the gift of God is eternal life through Jesus Christ our Lord.

And let us not be weary in well doing: for in due season we shall reap, if we faint not. As we have therefore opportunity, let us do good unto all men. Every man according as he purposeth in his heart, so let him give; not grudgingly, or of necessity: for God loveth a cheerful giver. Remember the words of the Lord Jesus, how he said, "It is more blessed to give than to receive."

Let him that is taught in the word communicate unto him that teacheth in all good things. Let us not be desirous of vain glory, provoking one another, envying one another.

I beseech you therefore, brethren, by the mercies of God, that ye present your bodies a living sacrifice, holy, acceptable unto God, which is your reasonable service.

Be not conformed to this world: but be ye transformed by the renewing of your mind, that ye may prove what is that good, and acceptable, and perfect, will of God.

Know ye not that they which run in a race run all, but one receiveth the prize? So run, that ye may obtain. And every man that striveth for the mastery is temperate in all things.

Know ye not that a little leaven leaveneth the whole lump? Purge out therefore the old leaven, that ye may be a new lump, as ye are unleavened. For even Christ our passover is sacrificed for us: therefore let us keep the feast, not with old leaven, neither with the leaven of malice and wickedness; but with the unleavened bread of sincerity and truth.

Casting down imaginations, and every high thing that exalteth itself against the knowledge of God, and bringing into captivity every thought to the obedience of Christ; he that glorieth, let him glory in the Lord. For not he that commendeth himself is approved, but whom the Lord commendeth.

*Duties of the Christian believer*

Wherefore let him that thinketh he standeth take heed lest he fall.

There hath no temptation taken you but such as is common to man: but God is faithful, who will not suffer you to be tempted above that ye are able; but will with the temptation also make a way to escape, that ye may be able to bear it.

Let love be without dissimulation. Abhor that which is evil; cleave to that which is good. Be kindly affectioned one to another with brotherly love; in honour preferring one another; not slothful in business; fervent in spirit; serving the Lord; rejoicing in hope; patient in tribulation; continuing instant in prayer; distributing to the necessity of saints; given to hospitality.

Bless them which persecute you: bless, and curse not. Rejoice with them that do rejoice, and weep with them that weep. Be of the same mind one toward another. Mind not high things, but condescend to men of low estate. Be not wise in your own conceits.

Recompense to no man evil for evil. Provide things honest in the sight of all men. If it be possible, as much as lieth in you, live peaceably with all men.

Dearly beloved, avenge not yourselves, but rather give place unto wrath: for it is written, " 'Vengeance is mine; I will repay,' saith the Lord." Therefore if thine enemy hunger, feed him; if he thirst, give him drink: for in so doing thou shalt heap coals of fire on his head.

Be not overcome of evil, but overcome evil with good.

Be ye therefore followers of God, as dear children; for ye were sometimes darkness, but now are ye light in the Lord: walk as children of light; but all things that are reproved are made manifest by the light: for whatsoever doth make manifest is light. See then that ye walk circumspectly, not as fools, but as wise. Wherefore be ye not unwise, but understanding what the will of the Lord is.

Ye are all the children of light, and the children of the day: we are not of the night, nor of darkness.

But let us, who are of the day, be sober, putting on the breastplate of faith and love; and for an helmet, the hope of salvation. For God hath not appointed us to wrath, but to obtain salvation by our Lord Jesus Christ, who died for us, that, whether we wake or sleep, we should live together with him.

Wherefore comfort yourselves together. And be at peace among yourselves. Support the weak, be patient toward all men. See that none render evil for evil unto any man; but ever follow that which is good, both among yourselves, and to all men.

Rejoice evermore. Pray without ceasing. In every thing give thanks: for this is the will of God in Christ Jesus concerning you. Quench not the Spirit. Despise not prophesyings. Prove all things; hold fast that which is good. Abstain from all appearance of evil. And the very God of peace sanctify you wholly; and I pray God your whole spirit and soul and body be preserved blameless unto the coming of our Lord Jesus Christ. Therefore, brethren, stand fast, and hold the traditions which ye have been taught, whether by word or our epistle.

Now the God of patience and consolation grant you to be likeminded one toward another according to Christ Jesus: that ye may with one mind and one mouth glorify God, even the Father of our Lord Jesus Christ. To God only wise, be glory through Jesus Christ for ever. Amen.

*Grace be to you, and peace, from God our Father, and from the Lord Jesus Christ.*

I CEASE NOT to give thanks for you, making mention of you in my prayers; that the God of our Lord Jesus Christ, the Father of glory, may give unto you the spirit of wisdom and revelation in the knowledge of him: the eyes of your understanding being enlightened; that ye may know what is the hope of his calling, and what the riches of the glory of his inheritance in the saints, and what is the exceeding greatness of his power to us-ward who believe, according to the working of his mighty power, which he wrought in Christ, when he raised him from the dead, and set him at his own right hand in the heavenly places, far above all principality, and power, and might, and dominion, and every name that is named, not only in this world, but also in that which is to come: and hath put all things under his feet, and gave him to be the head over all

things to the church, which is his body, the fulness of him that filleth *We are members one of*
all in all. *another*

But God is rich in mercy, for his great love wherewith he loved us hath quickened us together with Christ. By grace are ye saved through faith; and that not of yourselves: it is the gift of God. But now in Christ Jesus ye who sometimes were far off are made nigh.

He is our peace. For through him we both have access by one Spirit unto the Father.

Now therefore ye are no more strangers and foreigners, but fellow-citizens with the saints, and of the household of God; and are built upon the foundation of the apostles and prophets, Jesus Christ himself being the chief corner stone; in whom all the building fitly framed together groweth unto an holy temple in the Lord: in whom ye also are builded together for an habitation of God through the Spirit.

For this cause I bow my knees unto the Father of our Lord Jesus Christ, of whom the whole family in heaven and earth is named, that he would grant you, according to the riches of his glory, to be strengthened with might by his Spirit in the inner man; that Christ may dwell in your hearts by faith; that ye, being rooted and grounded in love, may be able to comprehend with all saints what is the breadth, and length, and depth, and height; and to know the love of Christ, which passeth knowledge, that ye might be filled with all the fulness of God.

And this I pray, that your love may abound yet more and more in knowledge and in all judgment; that ye may approve things that are excellent; that ye may be sincere and without offence till the day of Christ; being filled with the fruits of righteousness, which are by Jesus Christ, unto the glory and praise of God.

If so be that ye have heard Christ, and have been taught by him, as the truth is in Jesus: that ye put off the old man, and be renewed in the spirit of your mind; and that ye put on the new man, which after God is created in righteousness and true holiness. Wherefore putting away lying, speak every man truth with his neighbour: for we are members one of another. Be ye angry, and sin not: let not the sun go down upon your wrath. Let him that stole steal no more: but rather let him labour, working with his hands the thing which is good, that he may have to give to him that needeth. Let no corrupt communication proceed out

[ 175 ]

*Paul exhorts them to unity*

of your mouth, but that which is good to the use of edifying, that it may minister grace unto the hearers. And grieve not the holy Spirit of God, whereby ye are sealed unto the day of redemption. Let all bitterness, and wrath, and anger, and clamour, and evil speaking, be put away from you, with all malice: and be ye kind one to another, tenderhearted, forgiving one another, even as God for Christ's sake hath forgiven you.

If there be therefore any consolation in Christ, if any comfort of love, if any fellowship of the Spirit, if any bowels and mercies, fulfil ye my joy, that ye be likeminded, having the same love, being of one accord, of one mind.

Let nothing be done through strife or vainglory; but in lowliness of mind let each esteem other better than themselves. Look not every man on his own things, but every man also on the things of others.

Let this mind be in you, which was also in Christ Jesus: who, being in the form of God, thought it not robbery to be equal with God: but made himself of no reputation, and took upon him the form of a servant, and was made in the likeness of men: and being found in fashion as a man, he humbled himself, and became obedient unto death, even the death of the cross. Wherefore God also hath highly exalted him, and given him a name which is above every name: that at the name of Jesus every knee should bow, of things in heaven, and things in earth, and things under the earth; and that every tongue should confess that Jesus Christ is Lord, to the glory of God the Father.

*The Christian soldier*

Finally, my brethren, be strong in the Lord, and in the power of his might. Put on the whole armour of God, that ye may be able to stand against the wiles of the devil. For we wrestle not against flesh and blood, but against principalities, against powers, against the rulers of the darkness of this world, against spiritual wickedness in high places. Wherefore take unto you the whole armour of God, that ye may be able to withstand in the evil day, and having done all, to stand. Stand therefore, having your loins girt about with truth, and having on the breastplate of righteousness; and your feet shod with the preparation of the gospel of peace; above all, taking the shield of faith, wherewith ye shall be able to quench all the fiery darts of the wicked. And take the helmet of salvation, and the sword of the Spirit, which is the word of God: praying always with all prayer and supplication in the Spirit, and watching thereunto *Exhortation to prayer* with all perseverance and supplication for all saints.

And for me, that utterance may be given unto me, that I may open my mouth boldly, to make known the mystery of the gospel, for which I am an ambassador in bonds: that therein I may speak boldly, as I ought to speak.

Peace be to the brethren, and love with faith, from God the Father and the Lord Jesus Christ.

Grace be with all them that love our Lord Jesus Christ in sincerity. Amen.

*Paul, a servant of God, and an apostle of Jesus Christ, according to the faith of God's elect, and the acknowledging of the truth which is after godliness; in hope of eternal life, which God, that cannot lie, promised before the world began; but hath in due times manifested his word through preaching, which is committed unto me according to the commandment of God our Saviour.*

BRETHREN, I declare unto you the gospel which I preached unto you, *The gospel of Paul* which also ye have received, and wherein ye stand.

For I delivered unto you first of all that which I also received, how that Christ died for our sins according to the scriptures; and that he was buried, and that he rose again the third day according to the scriptures: and that he was seen of Cephas, then of the twelve: after that, he was seen of above five hundred brethren at once; of whom the greater part remain unto this present, but some are fallen asleep. After that, he was seen of James; then of all the apostles. And last of all he was seen of me also, as of one born out of due time.

For I am the least of the apostles, that am not meet to be called an apostle, because I persecuted the church of God. But by the grace of God I am what I am: and his grace which was bestowed upon me was not in vain; but I laboured more abundantly than they all: yet not I, but the grace of God which was with me. Therefore whether it were I or they, so we preach, and so ye believed.

Now if Christ be preached that he rose from the dead, how say some among you that there is no resurrection of the dead? But if there be no

resurrection of the dead, then is Christ not risen: and if Christ be not risen, then is our preaching vain, and your faith is also vain.

But some man will say, "How are the dead raised up? and with what body do they come?" Thou fool, that which thou sowest is not quickened, except it die: and that which thou sowest, thou sowest not that body that shall be, but bare grain, it may chance of wheat, or of some other grain: but God giveth it a body as it hath pleased him, and to every seed his own body.

All flesh is not the same flesh: but there is one kind of flesh of men, another flesh of beasts, another of fishes, and another of birds. There are also celestial bodies, and bodies terrestrial: but the glory of the celestial is one, and the glory of the terrestrial is another. There is one glory of the sun, and another glory of the moon, and another glory of the stars; for one star differeth from another star in glory.

So also is the resurrection of the dead. It is sown in corruption; it is raised in incorruption: it is sown in dishonour; it is raised in glory: it is sown in weakness; it is raised in power: it is sown a natural body; it is raised a spiritual body. There is a natural body, and there is a spiritual body. And as we have borne the image of the earthy, we shall also bear the image of the heavenly.

Behold, I shew you a mystery; We shall not all sleep, but we shall all be changed, so when this corruptible shall have put on incorruption, and this mortal shall have put on immortality, then shall be brought to pass the saying that is written, "Death is swallowed up in victory. O death, where is thy sting? O grave, where is thy victory?" But thanks be to God, which giveth us the victory through our Lord Jesus Christ.

Therefore, my beloved brethren, be ye stedfast, unmoveable, always abounding in the work of the Lord, forasmuch as ye know that your labour is not in vain in the Lord. Watch ye, stand fast in the faith, quit you like men, be strong.

If ye then be risen with Christ, seek those things which are above, where Christ sitteth on the right hand of God. Set your affection on things above, not on things on the earth. Your life is hid with Christ in God.

Put on therefore, as the elect of God, holy and beloved, bowels of mercies, kindness, humbleness of mind, meekness, longsuffering; forbear-

ing one another, and forgiving one another, if any man have a quarrel   *Put on charity*
against any: even as Christ forgave you, so also do ye. And above all
these things put on charity, which is the bond of perfectness.

And let the peace of God rule in your hearts, to the which also ye are
called in one body; and be ye thankful.

Let the word of Christ dwell in you richly in all wisdom; teaching and
admonishing one another in psalms and hymns and spiritual songs, singing with grace in your hearts to the Lord. And whatsoever ye do in word
or deed, do it heartily, as to the Lord, and not unto men, giving thanks to
God and the Father.

But I would not have you to be ignorant, brethren, concerning them
which are asleep, that ye sorrow not, even as others which have no hope.
For if we believe that Jesus died and rose again, even so them also which
sleep in Jesus will God bring with him. Wherefore comfort one another
with these words.

Brethren, the grace of our Lord Jesus Christ be with your spirit. Amen.


*Paul, an apostle of Jesus Christ whom we preach, warning every man, and
teaching every man in all wisdom; that we may present every man perfect
in Christ Jesus.*

As GOD hath distributed to every man, as the Lord hath called every one,   *Of spiritual gifts*
so let him walk. And so ordain I in all churches. Let every man abide
in the same calling wherein he was called. Every man hath his proper gift
of God, one after this manner, and another after that.

Now there are diversities of gifts, but the same Spirit. And there are
differences of administrations, but the same Lord. And there are diversities of operations, but it is the same God which worketh all in all.

But the manifestation of the Spirit is given to every man to profit
withal. For to one is given by the Spirit the word of wisdom; to another
the word of knowledge by the same Spirit; to another faith by the same
Spirit; to another the gifts of healing by the same Spirit; to another the
working of miracles; to another prophecy; to another discerning of
spirits; to another divers kinds of tongues; to another the interpretation
of tongues. But all these worketh that one and the selfsame Spirit, dividing to every man severally as he will. For as the body is one, and hath

*We are the members of the body of Christ* many members, and all the members of that one body, being many, are one body: so also is Christ. For by one Spirit are we all baptized into one body, whether we be Jews or Gentiles, whether we be bond or free; and have been all made to drink into one Spirit.

For the body is not one member, but many. If the foot shall say, "Because I am not the hand, I am not of the body"; is it therefore not of the body? And if the ear shall say, "Because I am not the eye, I am not of the body"; is it therefore not of the body? If the whole body were an eye, where were the hearing? If the whole were hearing, where were the smelling? But now hath God set the members every one of them in the body, as it hath pleased him. And if they were all one member, where were the body? But now are they many members, yet but one body. And the eye cannot say unto the hand, "I have no need of thee": nor again the head to the feet, "I have no need of you." Nay, much more those members of the body, which seem to be more feeble, are necessary: and those members of the body, which we think to be less honourable, upon these we bestow more abundant honour; and our uncomely parts have more abundant comeliness. For our comely parts have no need: but God hath tempered the body together, having given more abundant honour to that part which lacked: that there should be no schism in the body; but that the members should have the same care one for another. And whether one member suffer, all the members suffer with it; or one member be honoured, all the members rejoice with it.

Now ye are the body of Christ, and members in particular. And God hath set some in the church, first apostles, secondarily prophets, thirdly teachers, after that miracles, then gifts of healings, helps, governments, diversities of tongues. Are all apostles? are all prophets? are all teachers? are all workers of miracles? have all the gifts of healing? do all speak with tongues? do all interpret?

For I say, through the grace given unto me, to every man that is among you, not to think of himself more highly than he ought to think; but to think soberly, according as God hath dealt to every man the measure of faith. Having then gifts differing according to the grace that is given to us, whether prophecy, let us prophesy according to the proportion of faith; or ministry, let us wait on our ministering: or he that teacheth, on teaching; or he that exhorteth, on exhortation: he that giveth, let him do it with simplicity; he that ruleth, with diligence; he *Gifts nothing without* that sheweth mercy, with cheerfulness. *charity*

I therefore, the prisoner of the Lord, beseech you that ye walk worthy of the vocation wherewith ye are called, with all lowliness and meekness, with longsuffering, forbearing one another in love; endeavouring to keep the unity of the Spirit in the bond of peace. There is one body, and one Spirit, even as ye are called in one hope of your calling; one Lord, one faith, one baptism, one God and Father of all, who is above all, and through all, and in you all. But unto every one of us is given grace according to the measure of the gift of Christ.

And he gave some, apostles; and some, prophets; and some, evangelists; and some, pastors and teachers; for the perfecting of the saints, for the work of the ministry, for the edifying of the body of Christ: till we all come in the unity of the faith, and of the knowledge of the Son of God, unto a perfect man, unto the measure of the stature of the fulness of Christ: that we henceforth be no more children, tossed to and fro, and carried about with every wind of doctrine, by the sleight of men, and cunning craftiness, whereby they lie in wait to deceive; but speaking the truth in love, may grow up into him in all things, which is the head, even Christ: from whom the whole body fitly joined together and compacted by that which every joint supplieth, according to the effectual working in the measure of every part, maketh increase of the body unto the edifying of itself in love.

Brethren, be not children in understanding: howbeit in malice be ye children, but in understanding be men. Yet I would have you wise unto that which is good, and simple concerning evil. And that ye study to be quiet, and to do your own business, and to work with your own hands, as we commanded you. But covet earnestly the best gifts: and yet shew I unto you a more excellent way.

Though I speak with the tongues of men and of angels, and have not *Hymn to love* charity, I am become as sounding brass, or a tinkling cymbal. And though I have the gift of prophecy, and understand all mysteries, and all knowledge; and though I have all faith, so that I could remove mountains, and have not charity, I am nothing. And though I bestow all my goods to feed the poor, and though I give my body to be burned, and have not charity, it profiteth me nothing.

[ 181 ]

*In praise of charity*

Charity suffereth long, and is kind; charity envieth not; charity vaunteth not itself, is not puffed up, doth not behave itself unseemly, seeketh not her own, is not easily provoked, thinketh no evil; rejoiceth not in iniquity, but rejoiceth in the truth; beareth all things, believeth all things, hopeth all things, endureth all things. Charity never faileth: but whether there be prophecies, they shall fail; whether there be tongues, they shall cease; whether there be knowledge, it shall vanish away.

For we know in part, and we prophesy in part. But when that which is perfect is come, then that which is in part shall be done away. When I was a child, I spake as a child, I understood as a child, I thought as a child: but when I became a man, I put away childish things. For now we see through a glass, darkly; but then face to face: now I know in part; but then shall I know even as also I am known.

And now abideth faith, hope, charity, these three; but the greatest of these is charity.

Follow after charity, and desire spiritual gifts.

Now unto him that is able to do exceeding abundantly above all that we ask or think, according to the power that worketh in us, unto him be glory in the church by Christ Jesus throughout all ages, world without end. Amen.

## Paul's Affirmation

*The ministry*

I PAUL am made a minister, according to the dispensation of God which is given to me for you, to fulfil the word of God; even the mystery which hath been hid from ages and from generations, but now is made manifest to his saints: to whom God would make known what is the riches of the glory of this mystery among the Gentiles; which is Christ in you, the hope of glory.

Therefore seeing we have this ministry, as we have received mercy, we faint not, commending ourselves to every man's conscience in the sight of God, by manifestation of the truth. For we preach not ourselves, but Christ Jesus the Lord; and ourselves your servants for Jesus' sake. For God, who commanded the light to shine out of darkness, hath shined in our hearts, to give the light of the knowledge of the glory of God in the

face of Jesus Christ. But we have this treasure in earthen vessels, that the *Paul's suffering for*
excellency of the power may be of God, and not of us. Are they Hebrews? *the gospel*
so am I. Are they Israelites? so am I. Are they the seed of Abraham? so
am I.

Are they ministers of Christ? I am more; in labours more abundant,
in stripes above measure, in prisons more frequent, in deaths, oft. Of the
Jews five times received I forty stripes save one. Thrice was I beaten with
rods, once was I stoned, thrice I suffered shipwreck, a night and a day I
have been in the deep; in journeyings often, in perils of waters, in perils
of robbers, in perils by mine own countrymen, in perils by the heathen,
in perils in the city, in perils in the wilderness, in perils in the sea, in
perils among false brethren; in weariness and painfulness, in watchings
often, in hunger and thirst, in fastings often, in cold and nakedness.

Beside those things that are without, that which cometh upon me
daily, the care of all the churches. Who is weak, and I am not weak? who
is offended, and I burn not? For the good that I would I do not: but the
evil which I would not, that I do. If I must needs glory, I will glory of
the things which concern mine infirmities.

I knew a man in Christ above fourteen years ago, (whether in the
body, I cannot tell; or whether out of the body, I cannot tell: God knoweth;) such an one caught up to the third heaven. And I knew such a man,
(whether in the body, or out of the body, I cannot tell: God knoweth;)
how that he was caught up into paradise, and heard unspeakable words,
which it is not lawful for a man to utter. Of such an one will I glory: yet
of myself I will not glory, but in mine infirmities. For though I would desire to glory, I shall not be a fool; for I will say the truth: but now I forbear, lest any man should think of me above that which he seeth me to be,
or that he heareth of me. And lest I should be exalted above measure
through the abundance of the revelations, there was given to me a thorn
in the flesh. For this thing I besought the Lord thrice, that it might depart from me. And he said unto me, "My grace is sufficient for thee: for
my strength is made perfect in weakness." Therefore I take pleasure in
infirmities, in reproaches, in necessities, in persecutions, in distresses for
Christ's sake: for when I am weak, then am I strong.

Not that I speak in respect of want: for I have learned, in whatsoever
state I am, therewith to be content. I know both how to be abased, and I

*Paul acknowledges his own imperfection*

know how to abound: every where and in all things I am instructed both to be full and to be hungry, both to abound and to suffer need.

Yea doubtless, and I count all things but loss for the excellency of the knowledge of Christ Jesus my Lord: for whom I have suffered the loss of all things, and do count them but dung, that I may win Christ, and be found in him, not having mine own righteousness, which is of the law, but that which is through the faith of Christ, the righteousness which is of God by faith: that I may know him, and the power of his resurrection, and the fellowship of his sufferings, being made conformable unto his death; if by any means I might attain unto the resurrection of the dead.

Not as though I had already attained, either were already perfect: but I follow after, if that I may apprehend that for which also I am apprehended of Christ Jesus. Brethren, I count not myself to have apprehended: but this one thing I do, forgetting those things which are behind, and reaching forth unto those things which are before, I press toward the mark for the prize of the high calling of God in Christ Jesus. According to my earnest expectation and my hope, that in nothing I shall be ashamed, but that with all boldness, as always, so now also Christ shall be magnified in my body, whether it be by life, or by death. For to me to live is Christ, and to die is gain.

I am crucified with Christ: nevertheless I live; yet not I, but Christ liveth in me: and the life which I now live in the flesh I live by the faith of the Son of God, who loved me, and gave himself for me.

I therefore so run, not as uncertainly; so fight I, not as one that beateth the air: but I keep under my body, and bring it into subjection: lest that by any means, when I have preached to others, I myself should be a castaway.

I can do all things through Christ which strengtheneth me.

I have fought a good fight, I have finished my course, I have kept the faith: from henceforth, let no man trouble me: for I bear in my body the marks of the Lord Jesus.

But my God shall supply all your need according to his riches in glory by Christ Jesus.

Finally, brethren, farewell. Be perfect, be of good comfort, be of one mind, live in peace; and the God of love and peace shall be with you. Amen.

*CHRIST CRUCIFIED*

# III

# THE EPISTLES OF
# JAMES, PETER AND JOHN

*James, a servant of God and of the Lord Jesus Christ, to the twelve tribes which are scattered abroad, greeting.*

MY BRETHREN, count it all joy when ye fall into divers temptations; knowing this, that the trying of your faith worketh patience. But let patience have her perfect work, that ye may be perfect and entire, wanting nothing. *Pray in faith*

If any of you lack wisdom, let him ask of God, that giveth to all men liberally, and upbraideth not; and it shall be given him. But let him ask in faith, nothing wavering. For he that wavereth is like a wave of the sea driven with the wind and tossed. For let not that man think that he shall receive any thing of the Lord. A double minded man is unstable in all his ways.

Let the brother of low degree rejoice in that he is exalted: but the rich, in that he is made low: because as the flower of the grass he shall pass away. For the sun is no sooner risen with a burning heat, but it withereth the grass, and the flower thereof falleth, and the grace of the fashion of it perisheth: so also shall the rich man fade away in his ways.

Blessed is the man that endureth temptation: for when he is tried, he shall receive the crown of life, which the Lord hath promised to them that love him. Let no man say when he is tempted, "I am tempted of God": for God cannot be tempted with evil, neither tempteth he any man: but every man is tempted, when he is drawn away of his own lust, and enticed. Then when lust hath conceived, it bringeth forth sin: and sin, when it is finished, bringeth forth death.

Do not err, my beloved brethren. Every good gift and every perfect gift is from above, and cometh down from the Father of lights, with whom is no variableness, neither shadow of turning. Of his own will begat he us with the word of truth, that we should be a kind of firstfruits of his creatures.

Wherefore, my beloved brethren, let every man be swift to hear,

*Be doers of the word* slow to speak, slow to wrath: for the wrath of man worketh not the righteousness of God. Wherefore lay apart all filthiness and superfluity of naughtiness, and receive with meekness the engrafted word, which is able to save your souls.

But be ye doers of the word, and not hearers only, deceiving your own selves. For if any be a hearer of the word, and not a doer, he is like unto a man beholding his natural face in a glass: for he beholdeth himself, and goeth his way, and straightway forgetteth what manner of man he was. But whoso looketh into the perfect law of liberty, and continueth therein, he being not a forgetful hearer, but a doer of the work, this man shall be blessed in his deed.

If a man among you seem to be religious, and bridleth not his tongue, but deceiveth his own heart, this man's religion is vain. Pure religion and undefiled before God and the Father is this, to visit the fatherless and widows in their affliction, and to keep himself unspotted from the world.

Hearken, my beloved brethren, Hath not God chosen the poor of this world rich in faith, and heirs of the kingdom which he hath promised to them that love him?

So speak ye, and so do, as they that shall be judged by the law of liberty. What doth it profit, my brethren, though a man say he hath faith, and have not works? can faith save him? Even so faith, if it hath not works, is dead, being alone.

*Faith and works* Yea, a man may say, "Thou hast faith, and I have works": shew me thy faith without thy works, and I will shew thee my faith by my works. And the scripture was fulfilled which saith, "Abraham believed God, and it was imputed unto him for righteousness: and he was called the Friend of God." Ye see then how that by works a man is justified, and not by faith only. For as the body without the spirit is dead, so faith without works is dead also. If any man offend not in word, the same is a perfect man, and able also to bridle the whole body. Behold, we put bits in the horses' mouths, that they may obey us; and we turn about their whole body. Behold also the ships, which though they be so great, and are driven of fierce winds, yet are they turned about with a very small helm, whithersoever the governor listeth. Even so the tongue is a little member, and boasteth great things. Behold, how great a matter a little fire kindleth! And the tongue is a fire, a world of iniquity: so is the tongue among our members, that it defileth the whole body, and setteth on fire the course of *The tongue to be bridled* nature; and it is set on fire of hell. For every kind of beasts, and of birds, and of serpents, and of things in the sea, is tamed, and hath been tamed of mankind: but the tongue can no man tame; it is an unruly evil, full of deadly poison. Therewith bless we God, even the Father; and therewith curse we men, which are made after the similitude of God. Out of the same mouth proceedeth blessing and cursing. My brethren, these things ought not so to be. Doth a fountain send forth at the same place sweet water and bitter? Can the fig tree, my brethren, bear olive berries? either a vine, figs? so can no fountain both yield salt water and fresh.

Who is a wise man and endued with knowledge among you? let him shew out of a good conversation his works with meekness of wisdom. But if ye have bitter envying and strife in your hearts, glory not, and lie not against the truth. This wisdom descendeth not from above, but is earthly, sensual, devilish. For where envying and strife is, there is confusion and every evil work. But the wisdom that is from above is first pure, then peaceable, gentle, and easy to be intreated, full of mercy and good fruits, without partiality, and without hypocrisy. And the fruit of righteousness is sown in peace of them that make peace.

He giveth more grace. Wherefore he saith, "God resisteth the proud, but giveth grace unto the humble." Submit yourselves therefore to God. Resist the devil, and he will flee from you. Draw nigh to God, and he will draw nigh to you. Cleanse your hands, ye sinners; and purify your hearts, ye double minded. Be afflicted, and mourn, and weep: let your laughter be turned to mourning, and your joy to heaviness. Humble yourselves in the sight of the Lord, and he shall lift you up.

Speak not evil one of another, brethren. He that speaketh evil of his brother, and judgeth his brother, speaketh evil of the law, and judgeth the law: but if thou judge the law, thou art not a doer of the law, but a judge. There is one lawgiver, who is able to save and to destroy: who art thou that judgest another?

Go to now, ye that say, "To day or to morrow we will go into such a city, and continue there a year, and buy and sell, and get gain": whereas ye know not what shall be on the morrow. For what is your life? It is even a vapour, that appeareth for a little time, and then vanisheth away. For that ye ought to say, "If the Lord will, we shall live, and do this, or that."

*Patience under
afflictions*

Be patient therefore, brethren, unto the coming of the Lord. Behold, the husbandman waiteth for the precious fruit of the earth, and hath long patience for it, until he receive the early and latter rain. Be ye also patient; stablish your hearts: for the coming of the Lord draweth nigh. Grudge not one against another, brethren, lest ye be condemned: behold, the judge standeth before the door.

Take, my brethren, the prophets, who have spoken in the name of the Lord, for an example of suffering affliction, and of patience. Behold, we count them happy which endure. Ye have heard of the patience of Job, and have seen the end of the Lord; that the Lord is very pitiful, and of tender mercy. But above all things, my brethren, swear not, neither by heaven, neither by the earth, neither by any other oath: but let your yea be yea; and your nay, nay. Confess your faults one to another, and pray one for another, that ye may be healed. The effectual fervent prayer of a righteous man availeth much.

*Peter, an apostle of Jesus Christ, to the strangers scattered throughout Pontus, Galatia, Cappadocia, Asia, and Bithynia, grace unto you, and peace, be multiplied.*

*Blessing for
spiritual graces*

BLESSED be the God and Father of our Lord Jesus Christ, which according to his abundant mercy hath begotten us again unto a lively hope by the resurrection of Jesus Christ from the dead, to an inheritance incorruptible, and undefiled, and that fadeth not away, reserved in heaven for you, that the trial of your faith, being much more precious than of gold that perisheth, though it be tried with fire, might be found unto praise and honour and glory at the appearing of Jesus Christ: whom having not seen, ye love; in whom, though now ye see him not, yet believing, ye rejoice with joy unspeakable and full of glory: receiving the end of your faith, even the salvation of your souls.

Wherefore gird up the loins of your mind, be sober, and hope to the end for the grace that is to be brought unto you at the revelation of Jesus Christ; as obedient children, not fashioning yourselves according to the former lusts in your ignorance: but as he which hath called you is holy, so be ye holy in all manner of conversation; because it is written, "Be ye holy; for I am holy."

Wherefore laying aside all malice, and all guile, and hypocrisies, and envies, and all evil speakings, see that ye love one another with a pure heart fervently.

Dearly beloved, I beseech you as strangers and pilgrims, abstain from fleshly lusts, which war against the soul. For ye were as sheep going astray; but are now returned unto the Shepherd and Bishop of your souls. Ye are a chosen generation, a royal priesthood, an holy nation, a peculiar people; that ye should shew forth the praises of him who hath called you out of darkness into his marvellous light.

Finally, be ye all of one mind, having compassion one of another, love as brethren, be pitiful, be courteous: not rendering evil for evil, or railing for railing: but contrariwise blessing; knowing that ye are thereunto called, that ye should inherit a blessing.

For he that will love life, and see good days, let him refrain his tongue from evil, and his lips that they speak no guile: let him eschew evil, and do good; let him seek peace, and ensue it. For the eyes of the Lord are over the righteous, and his ears are open unto their prayers: but the face of the Lord is against them that do evil. And who is he that will harm you, if ye be followers of that which is good?

Be ye therefore sober, and watch unto prayer. And above all things have fervent charity among yourselves: for charity shall cover the multitude of sins. Use hospitality one to another without grudging. As every man hath received the gift, even so minister the same one to another, as good stewards of the manifold grace of God. If any man speak, let him speak as the oracles of God; if any man minister, let him do it as of the ability which God giveth: that God in all things may be glorified through Jesus Christ, to whom be praise and dominion for ever and ever.

Yet, if any man suffer as a Christian, let him not be ashamed; but let him glorify God on this behalf. Wherefore let them that suffer according to the will of God commit the keeping of their souls to him in well doing, as unto a faithful Creator.

The elders which are among you I exhort, who am also an elder, and a witness of the sufferings of Christ, and also a partaker of the glory that shall be revealed: feed the flock of God which is among you, taking the oversight thereof, not by constraint, but willingly; not for filthy lucre, but of a ready mind; neither as being lords over God's heritage, but being

*Obedience and humility* ensamples to the flock. And when the chief Shepherd shall appear, ye shall receive a crown of glory that fadeth not away.

Likewise, ye younger, submit yourselves unto the elder. Yea, all of you be subject one to another, and be clothed with humility: for God resisteth the proud, and giveth grace to the humble. Humble yourselves therefore under the mighty hand of God, that he may exalt you in due time: casting all your care upon him; for he careth for you.

Be sober, be vigilant; greet ye one another with a kiss of charity. Peace be with you all that are in Christ Jesus.

The God of all grace, who hath called us unto his eternal glory by Christ Jesus, after that ye have suffered a while, make you perfect, stablish, strengthen, settle you. To him be glory and dominion for ever and ever. Amen.

*Simon Peter, a servant and an apostle of Jesus Christ, to them that have obtained like precious faith with us through the righteousness of God and our Saviour Jesus Christ:*

*Divers exhortations* GRACE and peace be multiplied unto you through the knowledge of God, and of Jesus our Lord, according as his divine power hath given unto us all things that pertain unto life and godliness, through the knowledge of him that hath called us to glory and virtue: whereby are given unto us exceeding great and precious promises: that by these ye might be partakers of the divine nature.

And beside this, giving all diligence, add to your faith virtue; and to virtue knowledge; and to knowledge temperance; and to temperance patience; and to patience godliness; and to godliness brotherly kindness; and to brotherly kindness charity. For if these things be in you, and abound, they make you that ye shall neither be barren nor unfruitful in the knowledge of our Lord Jesus Christ. But he that lacketh these things is blind, and cannot see afar off, and hath forgotten that he was purged from his old sins.

Wherefore the rather, brethren, give diligence to make your calling and election sure: for if ye do these things, ye shall never fall: for so an entrance shall be ministered unto you abundantly into the everlasting kingdom of our Lord and Saviour Jesus Christ. Wherefore I will not be negligent to put you always in remembrance of these things, though ye *Exhortation to* know them, and be established in the present truth. Yea, I think it meet, *stedfastness* as long as I am in this tabernacle, to stir you up by putting you in remembrance; knowing that shortly I must put off this my tabernacle, even as our Lord Jesus Christ hath shewed me.

Moreover I will endeavour that ye may be able after my decease to have these things always in remembrance. For we have not followed cunningly devised fables, when we made known unto you the power and coming of our Lord Jesus Christ, but were eyewitnesses of his majesty. For he received from God the Father honour and glory, when there came such a voice to him from the excellent glory, "This is my beloved Son, in whom I am well pleased." And this voice which came from heaven we heard, when we were with him in the holy mount.

We have also a more sure word of prophecy; whereunto ye do well that ye take heed, as unto a light that shineth in a dark place, until the day dawn, and the day star arise in your hearts: knowing this first, that no prophecy of the scripture is of any private interpretation. For the prophecy came not in old time by the will of man: but holy men of God spake as they were moved by the Holy Ghost.

But, beloved, be not ignorant of this one thing, that one day is with the Lord as a thousand years, and a thousand years as one day.

Ye therefore, beloved, beware lest ye also, being led away with the error of the wicked, fall from your own stedfastness. But grow in grace, and in the knowledge of our Lord and Saviour Jesus Christ. To him be glory both now and for ever. Amen.

*The elder [John] unto the wellbeloved Gaius, whom I love in the truth.*

BELOVED, I wish above all things that thou mayest prosper and be in *Gaius commended for* health, even as thy soul prospereth. For I rejoiced greatly, when the *piety and charity* brethren came and testified of the truth that is in thee, even as thou walkest in the truth. I have no greater joy than to hear that my children walk in truth.

Beloved, thou doest faithfully whatsoever thou doest to the brethren, and to strangers; which have borne witness of thy charity before the church: whom if thou bring forward on their journey after a godly sort, thou shalt do well: because that for his name's sake, they went forth. We therefore ought to receive such, that we might be fellowhelpers to the truth.

Beloved, follow not that which is evil, but that which is good. He that doeth good is of God: but he that doeth evil hath not seen God. But I trust I shall shortly see thee, and we shall speak face to face.

Peace be to thee. Our friends salute thee. Greet the friends by name.

THAT which was from the beginning, which we have heard, which we have seen with our eyes, which we have looked upon, and our hands have handled, of the Word of life; (for the life was manifested, and we have seen it, and bear witness, and shew unto you that eternal life, which was with the Father, and was manifested unto us;) that which we have seen and heard declare we unto you, that ye also may have fellowship with us: and truly our fellowship is with the Father, and with his Son Jesus Christ.

And these things write we unto you, that your joy may be full.

This then is the message which we have heard of him, and declare unto you, that God is light, and in him is no darkness at all. If we say that we have fellowship with him, and walk in darkness, we lie, and do not the truth: but if we walk in the light, as he is in the light, we have fellowship one with another, and the blood of Jesus Christ his Son cleanseth us from all sin.

If we say that we have no sin, we deceive ourselves, and the truth is not in us. If we confess our sins, he is faithful and just to forgive us our sins, and to cleanse us from all unrighteousness. If we say that we have not sinned, we make him a liar, and his word is not in us.

My little children, these things write I unto you, that ye sin not. And if any man sin, we have an advocate with the Father, Jesus Christ the righteous: and he is the propitiation for our sins: and not for our's only, but also for the sins of the whole world. And hereby we do know that we know him, if we keep his commandments. He that saith, "I know him," and keepeth not his commandments, is a liar, and the truth is not in him. But whoso keepeth his word, in him verily is the love of God perfected: hereby know we that we are in him.

He that saith he abideth in him ought himself also so to walk, even as he walked. Brethren, I write no new commandment unto you, but an old commandment which ye had from the beginning. The old commandment is the word which ye have heard from the beginning. Again, a new commandment I write unto you, which thing is true in him and in you: because the darkness is past, and the true light now shineth. He that saith he is in the light, and hateth his brother, is in darkness even until now. He that loveth his brother abideth in the light, and there is none occasion of stumbling in him. But he that hateth his brother is in darkness, and walketh in darkness, and knoweth not whither he goeth, because that darkness hath blinded his eyes.

I write unto you, little children, because your sins are forgiven you for his name's sake. I write unto you, fathers, because ye have known him that is from the beginning. I write unto you, young men, because ye have overcome the wicked one. I write unto you, little children, because ye have known the Father.

I have written unto you, fathers, because ye have known him that is from the beginning. I have written unto you, young men, because ye are strong, and the word of God abideth in you, and ye have overcome the wicked one.

Love not the world, neither the things that are in the world. If any man love the world, the love of the Father is not in him. For all that is in the world, the lust of the flesh, and the lust of the eyes, and the pride of life, is not of the Father, but is of the world. And the world passeth away, and the lust thereof: but he that doeth the will of God abideth for ever.

Let that therefore abide in you, which ye have heard from the beginning. If that which ye have heard from the beginning shall remain in you, ye also shall continue in the Son, and in the Father. And this is the promise that he hath promised us, even eternal life.

If ye know that he is righteous, ye know that every one that doeth righteousness is born of him. Behold, what manner of love the Father hath bestowed upon us, that we should be called the sons of God: therefore the world knoweth us not, because it knew him not.

Beloved, now are we the sons of God, and it doth not yet appear what we shall be: but we know that, when he shall appear, we shall be like him; for we shall see him as he is. And every man that hath this hope

*The love of God* in him purifieth himself, even as he is pure. Whosoever committeth sin transgresseth also the law: for sin is the transgression of the law. And ye know that he was manifested to take away our sins; and in him is no sin. Whosoever abideth in him sinneth not: whosoever sinneth hath not seen him, neither known him.

Little children, let no man deceive you: he that doeth righteousness is righteous, even as he is righteous. Whosoever is born of God doth not commit sin; for his seed remaineth in him: and he cannot sin, because he is born of God. In this the children of God are manifest: whosoever doeth not righteousness is not of God, neither he that loveth not his brother. For this is the message that ye heard from the beginning, that we should love one another.

Hereby perceive we the love of God, because he laid down his life for us: and we ought to lay down our lives for the brethren. But whoso hath this world's good, and seeth his brother have need, and shutteth up his bowels of compassion from him, how dwelleth the love of God in him?

My little children, let us not love in word, neither in tongue; but in deed and in truth. And hereby we know that we are of the truth, and shall assure our hearts before him. For if our heart condemn us, God is greater than our heart, and knoweth all things.

Beloved, if our heart condemn us not, then have we confidence toward God. And whatsoever we ask, we receive of him, because we keep his commandments, and do those things that are pleasing in his sight. And this is his commandment, That we should believe on the name of his Son Jesus Christ, and love one another, as he gave us commandment. And he that keepeth his commandments dwelleth in him, and he in him. And hereby we know that he abideth in us, by the Spirit which he hath given us.

Beloved, believe not every spirit, but try the spirits whether they are of God: because many false prophets are gone out into the world. Hereby know ye the Spirit of God: Every spirit that confesseth that Jesus Christ is come in the flesh is of God.

Beloved, let us love one another: for love is of God; and every one that loveth is born of God, and knoweth God. He that loveth not knoweth not God; for God is love. In this was manifested the love of God toward us, because that God sent his only begotten Son into the world, that we might live through him. Herein is love, not that we loved God, but that *The effects of the* he loved us, and sent his Son to be the propitiation of our sins. *love of God*

Beloved, if God so loved us, we ought also to love one another. No man hath seen God at any time. If we love one another, God dwelleth in us, and his love is perfected in us.

Hereby know we that we dwell in him, and he in us, because he hath given us of his Spirit. And we have seen and do testify that the Father sent the Son to be the Saviour of the world. Whosoever shall confess that Jesus is the Son of God, God dwelleth in him, and he in God. And we have known and believed the love that God hath to us. God is love; and he that dwelleth in love dwelleth in God, and God in him. Herein is our love made perfect, that we may have boldness in the day of judgment: because as he is, so are we in this world.

There is no fear in love; but perfect love casteth out fear: because fear hath torment. He that feareth is not made perfect in love. We love him, because he first loved us. If a man say, "I love God," and hateth his brother, he is a liar: for he that loveth not his brother whom he hath seen, how can he love God whom he hath not seen? And this commandment have we from him, That he who loveth God love his brother also.

For this is the love of God, that we keep his commandments: and his commandments are not grievous. For whatsoever is born of God overcometh the world: and this is the victory that overcometh the world, even our faith. Who is he that overcometh the world, but he that believeth that Jesus is the Son of God?

This is he that came by water and blood, even Jesus Christ; not by water only, but by water and blood. And it is the Spirit that beareth witness, because the Spirit is truth. For there are three that bear record in heaven, the Father, the Word, and the Holy Ghost: and these three are one. And there are three that bear witness in earth, the Spirit, and the water, and the blood: and these three agree in one.

And this is the record, that God hath given to us eternal life, and this life is in his Son. He that hath the Son hath life; and he that hath not the Son of God hath not life.

These things have I written unto you that believe on the name of the Son of God; that ye may know that ye have eternal life, and that ye may believe on the name of the Son of God. And this is the confidence that

*God will hear prayer*  we have in him, that, if we ask any thing according to his will, he heareth us: and if we know that he hear us, whatsoever we ask, we know that we have the petitions that we desired of him.

We know that whosoever is born of God sinneth not; but he that is begotten of God keepeth himself, and that wicked one toucheth him not. And we know that the Son of God is come, and hath given us an understanding, that we may know him that is true, and we are in him that is true, even in his Son Jesus Christ. This is the true God, and eternal life.

Grace be with you, mercy, and peace, from God the Father, and from the Lord Jesus Christ, the Son of the Father, in truth and love. Amen.

# IV

# AN ANCIENT HOMILY

*Why Christic assumed human nature*

GOD, who at sundry times and in divers manners spake in time past unto the fathers by the prophets, hath in these last days spoken unto us by his Son, whom he hath appointed heir of all things, who being the brightness of his glory, and the express image of his person, and upholding all things by the word of his power, when he had by himself purged our sins, sat down on the right hand of the Majesty on high; being made so much better than the angels, as he hath by inheritance obtained a more excellent name than they.

For unto which of the angels said he at any time, "Thou art my Son, this day have I begotten thee"? And again, "I will be to him a Father, and he shall be to me a Son"? And again, when he bringeth in the first-begotten into the world, he saith, "And let all the angels of God worship him." And of the angels he saith, "Who maketh his angels spirits, and his ministers a flame of fire."

But unto the Son he saith, "Thy throne, O God, is for ever and ever: a sceptre of righteousness is the sceptre of thy kingdom. Thou hast loved righteousness, and hated iniquity; therefore God, even thy God, hath anointed thee with the oil of gladness above thy fellows." And, "Thou, Lord, in the beginning hast laid the foundation of the earth; and the heavens are the works of thine hands: they shall perish; but thou remainest; and they all shall wax old as doth a garment; and as a vesture shalt thou fold them up, and they shall be changed: but thou art the same, and thy years shall not fail."

We see Jesus, who was made a little lower than the angels for the suffering of death, crowned with glory and honour; that he by the grace of God should taste death for every man. For it became him, for whom are all things, and by whom are all things, in bringing many sons unto glory, to make the captain of their salvation perfect through sufferings. Wherefore in all things it behoved him to be made like unto his brethren, that he might be a merciful and faithful high priest in things pertaining to God, to make reconciliation for the sins of the people. For in that

*Power of God's word*  he himself hath suffered being tempted, he is able to succour them that are tempted.

Though he were a Son, yet learned he obedience by the things which he suffered; and being made perfect, he became the author of eternal salvation unto all them that obey him; called of God an high priest after the order of Melchisedec.

The word of God is quick, and powerful, and sharper than any two-edged sword, piercing even to the dividing asunder of soul and spirit, and of the joints and marrow, and is a discerner of the thoughts and intents of the heart. Neither is there any creature that is not manifest in his sight: but all things are naked and opened into the eyes of him with whom we have to do.

Seeing then that we have a great high priest, that is passed into the heavens, Jesus the Son of God, let us hold fast our profession. For we have not an high priest which cannot be touched with the feeling of our infirmities; but was in all points tempted like as we are, yet without sin. Let us therefore come boldly unto the throne of grace, that we may obtain mercy, and find grace to help in time of need.

But this man, because he continueth ever, hath an unchangeable priesthood. Wherefore he is able also to save them to the uttermost that come unto God by him, seeing he ever liveth to make intercession for them. For such an high priest became us, who is holy, harmless, undefiled, separate from sinners, and made higher than the heavens; who needeth not daily, as those high priests, to offer up sacrifice, first for his own sins, and then for the people's: for this he did once, when he offered up himself.

*Faith defined*  The just shall live by faith: Now faith is the substance of things hoped for, the evidence of things not seen. Through faith we understand that the worlds were framed by the word of God, so that things which are seen were not made of things which do appear.

By faith Abel offered unto God a more excellent sacrifice than Cain, by which he obtained witness that he was righteous, God testifying of his gifts: and by it he being dead yet speaketh.

By faith Enoch was translated that he should not see death; and was not found, because God had translated him: for before his translation he had this testimony, that he pleased God. But without faith it is impossible to please him: for he that cometh to God must believe that he is, and that he is a rewarder of them that diligently seek him.

By faith Noah, being warned of God of things not seen as yet, moved with fear, prepared an ark to the saving of his house; by the which he condemned the world, and became heir of the righteousness which is by faith.

By faith Abraham, when he was called to go out into a place which he should after receive for an inheritance, obeyed; and he went out, not knowing whither he went. By faith he sojourned in the land of promise, as in a strange country, dwelling in tabernacles with Isaac and Jacob, the heirs with him of the same promise: for he looked for a city which hath foundations, whose builder and maker is God.

Through faith also Sara herself received strength to conceive, and was delivered of a child when she was past age, because she judged him faithful who had promised. Therefore sprang there even of one, and him as good as dead, so many as the stars of the sky in multitude, and as the sand which is by the sea shore innumerable.

These all died in faith, not having received the promises, but having seen them afar off, and were persuaded of them, and embraced them, and confessed that they were strangers and pilgrims on the earth. For they that say such things declare plainly that they seek a country. And truly, if they had been mindful of that country from whence they came out, they might have had opportunity to have returned. But now they desire a better country, that is, an heavenly: wherefore God is not ashamed to be called their God: for he hath prepared for them a city.

By faith Moses, when he was born, was hid three months of his parents, because they saw he was a proper child; and they were not afraid of the king's commandment. By faith Moses, when he was come to years, refused to be called the son of Pharaoh's daughter; choosing rather to suffer affliction with the people of God, esteeming the reproach of Christ greater riches than the treasures in Egypt. By faith he forsook Egypt, not fearing the wrath of the king: for he endured, as seeing him who is invisible. Through faith he kept the passover. By faith they passed through the Red sea as by dry land: which the Egyptians assaying to do were drowned.

And what shall I more say? for the time would fail me to tell of Gedeon,

*The Lord's chastenings*

and of Barak, and of Samson, and of Jephthæ; of David also, and Samuel, and of the prophets: who through faith subdued kingdoms, wrought righteousness, obtained promises, stopped the mouths of lions, quenched the violence of fire, escaped the edge of the sword, out of weakness were made strong, waxed valiant in fight, turned to flight the armies of the aliens. Women received their dead raised to life again: and others were tortured, not accepting deliverance; that they might obtain a better resurrection: and others had trial of cruel mockings and scourgings, yea, moreover of bonds and imprisonment: they were stoned, they were sawn asunder, were tempted, were slain with the sword: they wandered about in sheepskins and goatskins; being destitute, afflicted, tormented; (of whom the world was not worthy:) they wandered in deserts, and in mountains, and in dens and caves of the earth. And these all, having obtained a good report through faith, received not the promise: God having provided some better thing for us, that they without us should not be made perfect.

Wherefore seeing we also are compassed about with so great a cloud of witnesses, let us lay aside every weight, and the sin which doth so easily beset us, and let us run with patience the race that is set before us, looking unto Jesus the author and finisher of our faith; who for the joy that was set before him endured the cross, despising the shame, and is set down at the right hand of the throne of God.

For consider him that endured such contradiction of sinners against himself, lest ye be wearied and faint in your minds. Ye have not yet resisted unto blood, striving against sin. And ye have forgotten the exhortation which speaketh unto you as unto children, "My son, despise not thou the chastening of the Lord, nor faint when thou art rebuked of him: for whom the Lord loveth he chasteneth, and scourgeth every son whom he receiveth." If ye endure chastening, God dealeth with you as with sons; for what son is he whom the father chasteneth not?

Furthermore we have had fathers of our flesh which corrected us, and we gave them reverence: shall we not much rather be in subjection unto the Father of spirits, and live? For they verily for a few days chastened us after their own pleasure; but he for our profit, that we might be partakers of his holiness. Now no chastening for the present seemeth to be joyous, but grievous: nevertheless afterward it yieldeth the peaceable fruit of righteousness unto them which are exercised *Serve God with* thereby. *reverence*

Wherefore lift up the hands which hang down, and the feeble knees; and make straight paths for your feet, lest that which is lame be turned out of the way; but let it rather be healed. Follow peace with all men, and holiness, without which no man shall see the Lord: looking diligently lest any man fail of the grace of God; lest any root of bitterness springing up trouble you, and thereby many be defiled.

For ye are not come unto the mount that might be touched, and that burned with fire, nor unto blackness, and darkness, and tempest, but ye are come unto mount Sion, and unto the city of the living God, the heavenly Jerusalem, and to an innumerable company of angels, to the general assembly and church of the firstborn, which are written in heaven, and to God the Judge of all, and to the spirits of just men made perfect, and to Jesus the mediator of the new covenant.

Wherefore we receiving a kingdom which cannot be moved, let us have grace, whereby we may serve God acceptably with reverence and godly fear: for our God is a consuming fire.

Let brotherly love continue. Be not forgetful to entertain strangers: for thereby some have entertained angels unawares. Remember them that are in bonds, as bound with them; and them which suffer adversity, as being yourselves also in the body. Let your conversation be without covetousness; and be content with such things as ye have: for he hath said, "I will never leave thee, nor forsake thee." So that we may boldly say, "The Lord is my helper, and I will not fear what man shall do unto me." Remember them which have the rule over you, who have spoken unto you the word of God: whose faith follow, considering the end of their conversation.

Jesus Christ the same yesterday, and to day, and for ever.

Let us go forth therefore unto him without the camp, bearing his reproach. For here have we no continuing city, but we seek one to come. By him therefore let us offer the sacrifice of praise to God continually, that is, the fruit of our lips giving thanks to his name. But to do good and to communicate forget not: for with such sacrifices God is well pleased.

Obey them that have the rule over you, and submit yourselves: for

[ 201 ]

*Benediction* they watch for your souls, as they that must give account, that they may do it with joy, and not with grief: for that is unprofitable for you.

Now the God of peace, that brought again from the dead our Lord Jesus, that great shepherd of the sheep, through the blood of the everlasting covenant, make you perfect in every good work to do his will, working in you that which is wellpleasing in his sight, through Jesus Christ; to whom be glory for ever and ever. Grace be with you all. Amen.

# PSALMS AND TWO SONGS

## I. Psalms of Praise and Worship

PRAISE ye the Lord. Praise, O ye servants of the Lord,
  Praise the name of the Lord.
  Blessed be the name of the Lord from this time forth and
  for evermore.
  From the rising of the sun unto the going down of the
  same the Lord's name is to be praised.
The Lord is high above all nations, and his glory above the heavens.
Who is like unto the Lord our God, who dwelleth on high,
Who humbleth himself to behold the things that are in heaven, and
  in the earth!

Keep not thou silence, O God:
Hold not thy peace, and be not still, O God.
That men may know that thou, whose name alone is JEHOVAH,
  art the most high over all the earth.

God standeth in the congregation of the mighty.
Arise, O God, judge the earth:
For thou shalt inherit all nations.

Praise ye the Lord.
Sing unto the Lord a new song,
And his praise in the congregation of saints.
Let Israel rejoice in him that made him:

Let the children of Zion be joyful in their King.
Let them praise his name in the dance:
Let them sing praises unto him with the timbrel and harp.
For the LORD taketh pleasure in his people:
He will beautify the meek with salvation.

O LORD our Lord,
How excellent is thy name in all the earth!
Who hast set thy glory above the heavens.
When I consider thy heavens, the work of thy fingers,
The moon and the stars, which thou hast ordained;
What is man, that thou art mindful of him?
And the son of man, that thou visitest him?
For thou hast made him a little lower than the angels,
And hast crowned him with glory and honour.
Thou madest him to have dominion over the works of thy hands;
Thou hast put all things under his feet:
All sheep and oxen,
Yea, and the beasts of the field;
The fowl of the air, and the fish of the sea,
And whatsoever passeth through the paths of the seas.
O LORD our Lord,
How excellent is thy name in all the earth!

The heavens declare the glory of God;
And the firmament sheweth his handywork.
Day unto day uttereth speech,
And night unto night sheweth knowledge.
There is no speech nor language,
Where their voice is not heard.
Their line is gone out through all the earth,
And their words to the end of the world.
In them hath he set a tabernacle for the sun,
Which is as a bridegroom coming out of his chamber,
And rejoiceth as a strong man to run a race.
His going forth is from the end of the heaven,

And his circuit unto the ends of it:
And there is nothing hid from the heat thereof.

Thy mercy, O Lord, is in the heavens;
And thy faithfulness reacheth unto the clouds.
Thy righteousness is like the great mountains;
Thy judgments are a great deep:
O Lord, thou preservest man and beast.
How excellent is thy lovingkindness, O God!
Therefore the children of men put their trust
Under the shadow of thy wings.
They shall be abundantly satisfied with the fatness of thy house;
And thou shalt make them drink of the river of thy pleasures.
For with thee is the fountain of life:
In thy light shall we see light.

Give unto the Lord, O ye mighty,
Give unto the Lord glory and strength.
Give unto the Lord the glory due unto his name;
Worship the Lord in the beauty of holiness.
The voice of the Lord is upon the waters:
The God of glory thundereth,
The Lord is upon many waters.
The voice of the Lord is powerful;
The voice of the Lord is full of majesty.
The voice of the Lord breaketh the cedars;
Yea, the Lord breaketh the cedars of Lebanon.
He maketh them also to skip like a calf;
Lebanon and Sirion like a young unicorn.
The voice of the Lord divideth the flames of fire.
The voice of the Lord shaketh the wilderness;
The Lord shaketh the wilderness of Kadesh.
The voice of the Lord maketh the hinds to calve,
And discovereth the forests:
And in his temple doth every one speak of his glory.
The Lord sitteth upon the flood;

Yea, the LORD sitteth King for ever.
The LORD will give strength unto his people;
The LORD will bless his people with peace.

Rejoice in the LORD, O ye righteous:
For praise is comely for the upright.
Praise the LORD with harp:
Sing unto him with the psaltery and an instrument of ten strings.
Sing unto him a new song;
Play skilfully with a loud noise.
For the word of the LORD is right;
And all his works are done in truth.
He loveth righteousness and judgment:
The earth is full of the goodness of the LORD.
By the word of the LORD were the heavens made;
And all the host of them by the breath of his mouth.
He gathereth the waters of the sea together as an heap:
He layeth up the depth in storehouses.
Let all the earth fear the LORD:
Let all the inhabitants of the world stand in awe of him.
For he spake, and it was done;
He commanded, and it stood fast.
The counsel of the LORD standeth for ever,
The thoughts of his heart to all generations.
Blessed is the nation whose God is the LORD;
And the people whom he hath chosen for his own inheritance.

Praise waiteth for thee, O God, in Sion:
And unto thee shall the vow be performed.
O thou that hearest prayer,
Unto thee shall all flesh come.
Iniquities prevail against me:
As for our transgressions, thou shalt purge them away.
Blessed is the man whom thou choosest, and causest to approach unto
     thee,
That he may dwell in thy courts:

We shall be satisfied with the goodness of thy house,
Even of thy holy temple.
By terrible things in righteousness wilt thou answer us,
O God of our salvation;
Who art the confidence of all the ends of the earth,
And of them that are afar off upon the sea:
Which by his strength setteth fast the mountains;
Being girded with power:
Which stilleth the noise of the seas, the noise of their waves,
And the tumult of the people.
They also that dwell in the uttermost parts are afraid at thy tokens:
Thou makest the outgoings of the morning and evening to rejoice.
Thou visitest the earth, and waterest it:
Thou greatly enrichest it
With the river of God, which is full of water:
Thou preparest them corn, when thou hast so provided for it.
Thou waterest the ridges thereof abundantly:
Thou settlest the furrows thereof:
Thou makest it soft with showers:
Thou blessest the springing thereof.
Thou crownest the year with thy goodness;
And thy paths drop fatness.
They drop upon the pastures of the wilderness:
And the little hills rejoice on every side.
The pastures are clothed with flocks;
The valleys also are covered over with corn;
They shout for joy, they also sing.

The Lord reigneth, he is clothed with majesty;
The Lord is clothed with strength, wherewith he hath girded himself:
The world also is stablished, that it cannot be moved.

*Of Praise and Worship*

Thy throne is established of old:
Thou art from everlasting.
The floods have lifted up, O LORD,
The floods have lifted up their voice;
The floods lift up their waves.
The LORD on high is mightier than the noise of many waters,
Yea, than the mighty waves of the sea.
Thy testimonies are very sure:
Holiness becometh thine house, O LORD, for ever.

Praise ye the LORD:
For it is good to sing praises unto our God;
For it is pleasant; and praise is comely.
The LORD doth build up Jerusalem:
He gathereth together the outcasts of Israel.
He healeth the broken in heart,
And bindeth up their wounds.
He telleth the number of the stars;
He calleth them all by their names.
Great is our Lord, and of great power:
His understanding is infinite.
Sing unto the LORD with thanksgiving;
Sing praise upon the harp unto our God:
Who covereth the heaven with clouds,
Who prepareth rain for the earth,
Who maketh grass to grow upon the mountains.
He giveth to the beast his food,
And to the young ravens which cry.
He delighteth not in the strength of the horse:
He taketh not pleasure in the legs of a man.
The LORD taketh pleasure in them that fear him,
In those that hope in his mercy.
Praise the LORD, O Jerusalem;
Praise thy God, O Zion.
For he hath strengthened the bars of thy gates;
He hath blessed thy children within thee.

He maketh peace in thy borders,
And filleth thee with the finest of the wheat.
He sendeth forth his commandment upon earth:
His word runneth very swiftly.
He giveth snow like wool:
He scattereth the hoarfrost like ashes.
He casteth forth his ice like morsels:
Who can stand before his cold?
He sendeth out his word, and melteth them:
He causeth his wind to blow, and the waters flow.
He sheweth his word unto Jacob,
His statutes and his judgments unto Israel.

The mountains shall bring peace to the people,
And the little hills, by righteousness.
They shall fear thee as long as the sun and moon endure,
Throughout all generations.
He shall come down like rain upon the mown grass:
As showers that water the earth.
In his days shall the righteous flourish;
And abundance of peace so long as the moon endureth.
He shall have dominion also from sea to sea,
And from the river unto the ends of the earth.
They that dwell in the wilderness shall bow before him;
And his enemies shall lick the dust.
His name shall endure for ever:
His name shall be continued as long as the sun:
And men shall be blessed in him:
All nations shall call him blessed.
Blessed be the LORD God, the God of Israel,
Who only doeth wondrous things.

And blessed be his glorious name for ever:
And let the whole earth be filled with his glory;
Amen, and Amen.

Praise ye the LORD.
Praise ye the LORD from the heavens:
Praise him in the heights.
Praise ye him, all his angels:
Praise ye him, all his hosts.
Praise ye him, sun and moon:
Praise him, all ye stars of light.
Praise him, ye heavens of heavens,
And ye waters that be above the heavens.
Let them praise the name of the LORD:
For he commanded, and they were created.
He hath also stablished them for ever and ever:
He hath made a decree which shall not pass.
Praise the LORD from the earth,
Ye dragons, and all deeps:
Fire, and hail; snow, and vapours;
Stormy wind fulfilling his word:
Mountains, and all hills;
Fruitful trees, and all cedars:
Beasts, and all cattle;
Creeping things, and flying fowl:
Kings of the earth, and all people;
Princes, and all judges of the earth:
Both young men, and maidens;
Old men, and children:
Let them praise the name of the LORD:
For his name alone is excellent;
His glory is above the earth and heaven.

If it had not been the LORD who was on our side,
Now may Israel say;
If it had not been the LORD who was on our side,

When men rose up against us:
Then they had swallowed us up quick,
When their wrath was kindled against us:
Then the waters had overwhelmed us,
The stream had gone over our soul:
Then the proud waters had gone over our soul.
Blessed be the LORD,
Who hath not given us as a prey to their teeth.
Our soul is escaped as a bird out of the snare of the fowlers:
The snare is broken, and we are escaped.
Our help is in the name of the LORD,
Who made heaven and earth.

When the LORD turned again the captivity of Zion,
We were like them that dream.
Then was our mouth filled with laughter,
And our tongue with singing:
Then said they among the heathen,
The LORD hath done great things for them.
The LORD hath done great things for us;
Whereof we are glad.
Turn again our captivity, O LORD,
As the streams in the south.
They that sow in tears shall reap in joy.
He that goeth forth and weepeth, bearing precious seed,
Shall doubtless come again with rejoicing, bringing his sheaves with
    him.

LORD, who shall abide in thy tabernacle?
Who shall dwell in thy holy hill?
He that walketh uprightly, and worketh righteousness,
And speaketh the truth in his heart.
He that backbiteth not with his tongue,
Nor doeth evil to his neighbour,
Nor taketh up a reproach against his neighbour.
In whose eyes a vile person is contemned;

[ 211 ]

But he honoureth them that fear the LORD.
He that sweareth to his own hurt, and changeth not.
He that putteth not out his money to usury,
Nor taketh reward against the innocent.
He that doeth these things shall never be moved.

The earth is the LORD's, and the fulness thereof;
The world, and they that dwell therein.
For he hath founded it upon the seas,
And established it upon the floods.
Who shall ascend into the hill of the LORD?
Or who shall stand in his holy place?
He that hath clean hands, and a pure heart;
Who hath not lifted up his soul unto vanity, nor sworn deceitfully.
He shall receive the blessing from the LORD,
And righteousness from the God of his salvation.
This is the generation of them that seek him,
That seek thy face, O Jacob.

How amiable are thy tabernacles,
O LORD of hosts!
My soul longeth, yea, even fainteth for the courts of the LORD:
My heart and my flesh crieth out for the living God.
Yea, the sparrow hath found an house,
And the swallow a nest for herself, where she may lay her young,
Even thine altars, O LORD of hosts,
My King, and my God.
Blessed are they that dwell in thy house:
They will be still praising thee.
Blessed is the man whose strength is in thee;
In whose heart are the ways of them.
Who passing through the valley of Baca make it a well;
The rain also filleth the pools.
They go from strength to strength,
Every one of them in Zion appeareth before God.
O LORD God of hosts, hear my prayer:

Give ear, O God of Jacob.
Behold, O God our shield,
And look upon the face of thine anointed.
For a day in thy courts is better than a thousand.
I had rather be a doorkeeper in the house of my God,
Than to dwell in the tents of wickedness.
For the LORD God is a sun and shield:
The LORD will give grace and glory:
No good thing will he withhold from them that walk uprightly.
O LORD of hosts,
Blessed is the man that trusteth in thee.

Lift up your heads, O ye gates;
And be ye lift up, ye everlasting doors;
And the King of glory shall come in.
Who is this King of glory?
The LORD strong and mighty,
The LORD mighty in battle.
Lift up your heads, O ye gates;
Even lift them up, ye everlasting doors;
And the King of glory shall come in.
Who is this King of glory?
The LORD of hosts,
He is the King of glory.

It is a good thing to give thanks unto the LORD,
And to sing praises unto thy name, O most High:
To shew forth thy lovingkindness in the morning,
And thy faithfulness every night,
Upon an instrument of ten strings, and upon the psaltery;
Upon the harp with a solemn sound.

For thou, Lord, hast made me glad through thy work:
I will triumph in the works of thy hands.
O Lord, how great are thy works!
And thy thoughts are very deep.
But thou, Lord, art most high for evermore.
The righteous shall flourish like the palm tree:
He shall grow like a cedar in Lebanon.
Those that be planted in the house of the Lord
Shall flourish in the courts of our God.
They shall still bring forth fruit in old age;
To shew that the Lord is upright:
He is my rock, and there is no unrighteousness in him.

O come, let us sing unto the Lord:
Let us make a joyful noise to the rock of our salvation.
Let us come before his presence with thanksgiving,
And make a joyful noise unto him with psalms.
For the Lord is a great God,
And a great King above all gods.
In his hand are the deep places of the earth:
The strength of the hills is his also.
The sea is his, and he made it:
And his hands formed the dry land.
O come, let us worship and bow down:
Let us kneel before the Lord our maker.
For he is our God;
And we are the people of his pasture, and the sheep of his hand.

I will lift up mine eyes unto the hills,
From whence cometh my help.
My help cometh from the Lord,

Which made heaven and earth.
He will not suffer thy foot to be moved:
He that keepeth thee will not slumber.
Behold, he that keepeth Israel
Shall neither slumber nor sleep.
The LORD is thy keeper:
The LORD is thy shade upon thy right hand.
The sun shall not smite thee by day,
Nor the moon by night.
The LORD shall preserve thee from all evil:
He shall preserve thy soul.
The LORD shall preserve thy going out and thy coming in
From this time forth, and even for evermore.

I was glad when they said unto me,
Let us go into the house of the LORD.
Our feet shall stand
Within thy gates, O Jerusalem.
Jerusalem is builded
As a city that is compact together:
Whither the tribes go up, the tribes of the LORD,
Unto the testimony of Israel,
To give thanks unto the name of the LORD.
For there are set thrones of judgment,
The thrones of the house of David.
Pray for the peace of Jerusalem:
They shall prosper that love thee.
Peace be within thy walls,
And prosperity within thy palaces.
For my brethren and companions' sakes,
I will now say, Peace be within thee.
Because of the house of the LORD our God
I will seek thy good.

Unto thee lift I up mine eyes,
O thou that dwellest in the heavens.

*Of Praise and Worship*

Behold, as the eyes of servants look unto the hand of their masters,
And as the eyes of a maiden unto the hand of her mistress;
So our eyes wait upon the LORD our God,
Until that he have mercy upon us.
Have mercy upon us, O LORD, have mercy upon us:
For we are exceedingly filled with contempt.

They that trust in the LORD
Shall be as mount Zion, which cannot be removed, but abideth for
    ever.
As the mountains are round about Jerusalem,
So the LORD is round about his people
From henceforth even for ever.
Do good, O LORD, unto those that be good,
And to them that are upright in their hearts.

O sing unto the LORD a new song:
Sing unto the LORD, all the earth.
Sing unto the LORD, bless his name;
Shew forth his salvation from day to day.
Declare his glory among the heathen, his wonders among all people.
For the LORD is great, and greatly to be praised:
He is to be feared above all gods.
For all the gods of the nations are idols:
But the LORD made the heavens.
Honour and majesty are before him:
Strength and beauty are in his sanctuary.
Give unto the LORD, O ye kindreds of the people,
Give unto the LORD glory and strength.
Give unto the LORD the glory due unto his name:
Bring an offering, and come into his courts.
O worship the LORD in the beauty of holiness:
Fear before him, all the earth.
Say among the heathen that the LORD reigneth:
The world also shall be established that it shall not be moved:

He shall judge the people righteously.
Let the heavens rejoice, and let the earth be glad;
Let the sea roar, and the fulness thereof.
Let the field be joyful, and all that is therein:
Then shall all the trees of the wood rejoice
Before the LORD:
For he cometh, for he cometh to judge the earth:
He shall judge the world with righteousness,
And the people with his truth.

The LORD reigneth; let the earth rejoice;
Let the multitude of isles be glad thereof.
Clouds and darkness are round about him:
Righteousness and judgment are the habitation of his throne.
The heavens declare his righteousness,
And all the people see his glory.
For thou, LORD, art high above all the earth:
Thou art exalted far above all gods.
Ye that love the LORD, hate evil:
He preserveth the souls of his saints;
He delivereth them out of the hand of the wicked.
Light is sown for the righteous,
And gladness for the upright in heart.
Rejoice in the LORD, ye righteous;
And give thanks at the remembrance of his holiness.

O sing unto the LORD a new song;
For he hath done marvellous things:
His right hand, and his holy arm, hath gotten him the victory.
The LORD hath made known his salvation:

*Of Praise and Worship*

His righteousness hath he openly shewed in the sight of the heathen.
He hath remembered his mercy and his truth toward the house of
    Israel:
All the ends of the earth have seen the salvation of our God.
Make a joyful noise unto the Lord, all the earth:
Make a loud noise, and rejoice, and sing praise.
Sing unto the Lord with the harp;
With the harp, and the voice of a psalm.
With trumpets and sound of cornet
Make a joyful noise before the Lord, the King.
Let the sea roar, and the fulness thereof;
The world, and they that dwell therein.
Let the floods clap their hands:
Let the hills be joyful together
Before the Lord; for he cometh to judge the earth:
With righteousness shall he judge the world,
And the people with equity.

Make a joyful noise unto the Lord, all ye lands.
Serve the Lord with gladness:
Come before his presence with singing.
Know ye that the Lord he is God:
It is he that hath made us, and not we ourselves;
We are his people, and the sheep of his pasture.
Enter into his gates with thanksgiving,
And into his courts with praise:
Be thankful unto him, and bless his name.
For the Lord is good; his mercy is everlasting;
And his truth endureth to all generations.

Praise ye the Lord.
Praise God in his sanctuary:
Praise him in the firmament of his power.
Praise him for his mighty acts:
Praise him according to his excellent greatness.
Praise him with the sound of the trumpet:

## PSALMS

Praise him with the psaltery and harp.
Praise him with the timbrel and dance:
Praise him with stringed instruments and organs.
Praise him upon the loud cymbals:
Praise him upon the high sounding cymbals.
Let every thing that hath breath praise the LORD.
Praise ye the LORD.

God be merciful unto us, and bless us;
And cause his face to shine upon us;
That thy way may be known upon earth,
Thy saving health among all nations.
Let the people praise thee, O God;
Let all the people praise thee.
O let the nations be glad and sing for joy:
For thou shalt judge the people righteously,
And govern the nations upon earth.
Let the people praise thee, O God;
Let all the people praise thee.
Then shall the earth yield her increase;
And God, even our own God, shall bless us.
God shall bless us;
And all the ends of the earth shall fear him.

O give thanks unto the LORD; call upon his name:
Make known his deeds among the people.
Sing unto him, sing psalms unto him:
Talk ye of all his wondrous works.
Glory ye in his holy name:
Let the heart of them rejoice that seek the LORD.
Seek the LORD, and his strength:
Seek his face evermore.
Remember his marvellous works that he hath done;
His wonders, and the judgments of his mouth;
He is the LORD our God:
His judgments are in all the earth.

He hath remembered his covenant for ever,
The word which he commanded to a thousand generations.

Praise ye the LORD. O give thanks unto the LORD;
For he is good:
For his mercy endureth for ever.
Who can utter the mighty acts of the LORD?
Who can shew forth all his praise?
Blessed are they that keep judgment,
And he that doeth righteousness at all times.
Remember me, O LORD, with the favour that thou bearest unto thy
 people:
O visit me with thy salvation;
That I may see the good of thy chosen,
That I may rejoice in the gladness of thy nation,
That I may glory with thine inheritance.

Make a joyful noise unto God, all ye lands:
Sing forth the honour of his name:
Make his praise glorious.
Say unto God, How terrible art thou in thy works!
Through the greatness of thy power shall thine enemies submit them-
 selves unto thee.
All the earth shall worship thee, and shall sing unto thee;
They shall sing to thy name.
Come and see the works of God:
He is terrible in his doing toward the children of men.
He turned the sea into dry land:
They went through the flood on foot:
There did we rejoice in him.
He ruleth by his power for ever; his eyes behold the nations:
Let not the rebellious exalt themselves.
O bless our God, ye people,
And make the voice of his praise to be heard:
Which holdeth our soul in life,
And suffereth not our feet to be moved.

For thou, O God, hast proved us:
Thou hast tried us, as silver is tried.
Come and hear, all ye that fear God,
And I will declare what he hath done for my soul.
I cried unto him with my mouth,
And he was extolled with my tongue.
If I regard iniquity in my heart,
The Lord will not hear me:
But verily God hath heard me;
He hath attended to the voice of my prayer.
Blessed be God, which hath not turned away my prayer, nor his
     mercy from me.

O give thanks unto the Lord; for he is good:
For his mercy endureth for ever.
O give thanks unto the God of gods:
For his mercy endureth for ever.
O give thanks to the Lord of lords:
For his mercy endureth for ever.
To him who alone doeth great wonders:
For his mercy endureth for ever.
To him that by wisdom made the heavens:
For his mercy endureth for ever.
To him that stretched out the earth above the waters:
For his mercy endureth for ever.
To him that made great lights:
For his mercy endureth for ever:
The sun to rule by day:
For his mercy endureth for ever:
The moon and the stars to rule by night:
For his mercy endureth for ever.
O give thanks unto the God of heaven:
For his mercy endureth for ever.

Great is the Lord, and greatly to be praised
In the city of our God, in the mountain of his holiness.

## PSALMS

Beautiful for situation, the joy of the whole earth,
Is Mount Zion, on the sides of the north,
The city of the great King.
God is known in her palaces for a refuge.
For, lo, the kings were assembled,
They passed by together.
They saw it, and so they marvelled;
They were troubled, and hasted away.
Fear took hold upon them there,
And pain, as of a woman in travail.
Thou breakest the ships of Tarshish with an east wind.
As we have heard, so have we seen
In the city of the LORD of hosts, in the city of our God:
God will establish it for ever.
We have thought of thy lovingkindness, O God,
In the midst of thy temple.
According to thy name, O God,
So is thy praise unto the ends of the earth:
Thy right hand is full of righteousness.
Let Mount Zion rejoice,
Let the daughters of Judah be glad,
Because of thy judgments.
Walk about Zion, and go round about her:
Tell the towers thereof.
Mark ye well her bulwarks,
Consider her palaces;
That ye may tell it to the generation following.
For this God is our God for ever and ever:
He will be our guide even unto death.

I will extol thee, my God, O king;
And I will bless thy name for ever and ever.
Every day will I bless thee;
And I will praise thy name for ever and ever.
Great is the LORD, and greatly to be praised;
And his greatness is unsearchable.

One generation shall praise thy works to another,
And shall declare thy mighty acts.
I will speak of the glorious honour of thy majesty,
And of thy wondrous works.
And men shall speak of the might of thy terrible acts:
And I will declare thy greatness.
They shall abundantly utter the memory of thy great goodness,
And shall sing of thy righteousness.
The LORD is gracious, and full of compassion;
Slow to anger, and of great mercy.
The LORD is good to all:
And his tender mercies are over all his works.
All thy works shall praise thee, O LORD;
And thy saints shall bless thee.
They shall speak of the glory of thy kingdom,
And talk of thy power;
To make known to the sons of men his mighty acts,
And the glorious majesty of his kingdom.
Thy kingdom is an everlasting kingdom,
And thy dominion endureth throughout all generations.
The LORD upholdeth all that fall,
And raiseth up all those that be bowed down.
The eyes of all wait upon thee;
And thou givest them their meat in due season.
Thou openest thine hand,
And satisfiest the desire of every living thing.
The LORD is righteous in all his ways,
And holy in all his works.
The LORD is nigh unto all them that call upon him,
To all that call upon him in truth.
He will fulfil the desire of them that fear him:
He also will hear their cry, and will save them.
The LORD preserveth all them that love him:
But all the wicked will he destroy.
My mouth shall speak the praise of the LORD:
And let all flesh bless his holy name for ever and ever.

[ 223 ]

Bless the LORD, O my soul:
And all that is within me, bless his holy name.
Bless the LORD, O my soul,
And forget not all his benefits:
Who forgiveth all thine iniquities;
Who healeth all thy diseases;
Who redeemeth thy life from destruction;
Who crowneth thee with lovingkindness and tender mercies;
Who satisfieth thy mouth with good things;
So that thy youth is renewed like the eagle's.
The LORD executeth righteousness
And judgment for all that are oppressed.
He made known his ways unto Moses,
His acts unto the children of Israel.
The LORD is merciful and gracious,
Slow to anger, and plenteous in mercy.
He will not always chide:
Neither will he keep his anger for ever.
He hath not dealt with us after our sins;
Nor rewarded us according to our iniquities.
For as the heaven is high above the earth,
So great is his mercy toward them that fear him.
As far as the east is from the west,
So far hath he removed our transgressions from us.
Like as a father pitieth his children,
So the LORD pitieth them that fear him.
For he knoweth our frame;
He remembereth that we are dust.
As for man, his days are as grass:
As a flower of the field, so he flourisheth.
For the wind passeth over it, and it is gone;

And the place thereof shall know it no more.

But the mercy of the LORD is from everlasting to everlasting upon
    them that fear him,

And his righteousness unto children's children;

To such as keep his covenant,

And to those that remember his commandments to do them.

The LORD hath prepared his throne in the heavens;

And his kingdom ruleth over all.

Bless the LORD, ye his angels,

That excel in strength, that do his commandments,

Hearkening unto the voice of his word.

Bless ye the LORD, all ye his hosts;

Ye ministers of his, that do his pleasure.

Bless the LORD, all his works

In all places of his dominion:

Bless the LORD, O my soul.


Give ear, O my people, to my law:

Incline your ears to the words of my mouth.

I will open my mouth in a parable:

I will utter dark sayings of old:

Which we have heard and known,

And our fathers have told us.

We will not hide them from their children,

Shewing to the generation to come the praises of the LORD,

And his strength, and his wonderful works that he hath done.

For he established a testimony in Jacob, and appointed a law in Israel,

Which he commanded our fathers,

That they should make them known to their children:

That the generation to come might know them,

Even the children which should be born;

Who should arise and declare them to their children:

That they might set their hope in God,

And not forget the works of God,

But keep his commandments.

God is our refuge and strength,
A very present help in trouble.
Therefore will not we fear, though the earth be removed,
And though the mountains be carried into the midst of the sea;
Though the waters thereof roar and be troubled,
Though the mountains shake with the swelling thereof.
The LORD of hosts is with us;
The God of Jacob is our refuge.
There is a river, the streams whereof shall make glad the city of God,
The holy place of the tabernacles of the most High.
God is in the midst of her; she shall not be moved:
God shall help her, and that right early.
The heathen raged, the kingdoms were moved:
He uttered his voice, the earth melted.
The LORD of hosts is with us;
The God of Jacob is our refuge.
Come, behold the works of the LORD,
What desolations he hath made in the earth.
He maketh wars to cease unto the end of the earth;
He breaketh the bow, and cutteth the spear in sunder;
He burneth the chariot in the fire.
Be still, and know that I am God:
I will be exalted among the heathen,
I will be exalted in the earth.
The LORD of hosts is with us;
The God of Jacob is our refuge.

Be thou exalted, O God, above the heavens;
Let thy glory be above all the earth.
They have prepared a net for my steps;
My soul is bowed down:
They have digged a pit before me, into the midst whereof they are
    fallen themselves.
My heart is fixed, O God, my heart is fixed:
I will sing and give praise.
Awake up, my glory; awake, psaltery and harp:

I myself will awake early.
I will praise thee, O Lord, among the people:
I will sing unto thee among the nations.
For thy mercy is great unto the heavens,
And thy truth unto the clouds.
Be thou exalted, O God, above the heavens:
Let thy glory be above all the earth.

Blessed is every one that feareth the LORD;
That walketh in his ways.
For thou shalt eat the labour of thine hands:
Happy shalt thou be, and it shall be well with thee.
Thy wife shall be as a fruitful vine by the sides of thine house:
Thy children like olive plants round about thy table.
Behold, that thus shall the man be blessed
That feareth the LORD.
The LORD shall bless thee out of Zion:
And thou shalt see the good of Jerusalem all the days of thy life.
Yea, thou shalt see thy children's children,
And peace upon Israel.

O give thanks unto the LORD, for he is good:
For his mercy endureth for ever.
Let the redeemed of the LORD say so,
Whom he hath redeemed from the hand of the enemy;
And gathered them out of the lands,
From the east, and from the west,
From the north, and from the south.
They wandered in the wilderness in a solitary way;
They found no city to dwell in.
Hungry and thirsty, their soul fainted in them.
Then they cried unto the LORD in their trouble,
And he delivered them out of their distresses.
And he led them forth by the right way,
That they might go to a city of habitation.
Oh that men would praise the LORD for his goodness,

And for his wonderful works to the children of men!
For he satisfieth the longing soul,
And filleth the hungry soul with goodness.
Such as sit in darkness and in the shadow of death,
Being bound in affliction and iron;
Because they rebelled against the words of God,
And contemned the counsel of the most High:
Therefore he brought down their heart with labour;
They fell down, and there was none to help.
Then they cried unto the LORD in their trouble,
And he saved them out of their distresses.
He brought them out of darkness and the shadow of death,
And brake their bands in sunder.
Oh that men would praise the LORD for his goodness,
And for his wonderful works to the children of men!
For he hath broken the gates of brass,
And cut the bars of iron in sunder.
Fools because of their transgression,
And because of their iniquities, are afflicted.
Their soul abhorreth all manner of meat;
And they draw near unto the gates of death.
Then they cry unto the LORD in their trouble,
And he saveth them out of their distresses.
He sent his word, and healed them,
And delivered them from their destructions.
Oh that men would praise the LORD for his goodness,
And for his wonderful works to the children of men!
And let them sacrifice the sacrifices of thanksgiving,
And declare his works with rejoicing.
They that go down to the sea in ships, that do business in great waters;
These see the works of the LORD, and his wonders in the deep.

For he commandeth, and raiseth the stormy wind, which lifteth up *Of Praise and Worship*
 the waves thereof.
They mount up to the heaven, they go down again to the depths:
Their soul is melted because of trouble.
They reel to and fro, and stagger like a drunken man,
And are at their wit's end.
Then they cry unto the LORD in their trouble,
And he bringeth them out of their distresses.
He maketh the storm a calm,
So that the waves thereof are still.
Then are they glad because they be quiet;
So he bringeth them unto their desired haven.
Oh that men would praise the LORD for his goodness,
And for his wonderful works to the children of men!
Let them exalt him also in the congregation of the people,
And praise him in the assembly of the elders.
He turneth rivers into a wilderness,
And the watersprings into dry ground;
A fruitful land into barrenness, for the wickedness of them that dwell
 therein.
He turneth the wilderness into a standing water,
And dry ground into watersprings.
And there he maketh the hungry to dwell,
That they may prepare a city for habitation;
And sow the fields, and plant vineyards, which may yield fruits of in-
 crease.
He blesseth them also, so that they are multiplied greatly;
And suffereth not their cattle to decrease.
Again, they are minished and brought low through oppression, afflic-
 tion, and sorrow.
He poureth contempt upon princes,
And causeth them to wander in the wilderness,
Where there is no way.
Yet setteth he the poor on high from affliction,
And maketh him families like a flock.
The righteous shall see it, and rejoice:

And all iniquity shall stop her mouth.
Whoso is wise, and will observe these things,
Even they shall understand the lovingkindness of the LORD.

O give thanks unto the LORD; for he is good:
Because his mercy endureth for ever.
Let them now that fear the LORD say,
That his mercy endureth for ever.
I called upon the LORD in distress:
The LORD answered me, and set me in a large place.
The LORD is on my side; I will not fear:
What can man do unto me?
It is better to trust in the LORD
Than to put confidence in man.
The LORD is my strength and song,
And is become my salvation.
The voice of rejoicing and salvation is in the tabernacles of the right-
eous:
The right hand of the LORD doeth valiantly.
I shall not die, but live, and declare the works of the LORD.
The LORD hath chastened me sore:
But he hath not given me over unto death.
Open to me the gates of righteousness:
I will go into them, and I will praise the LORD;
This gate of the LORD, into which the righteous shall enter.
I will praise thee:
For thou hast heard me, and art become my salvation.
The stone which the builders refused is become the head stone of the
corner.
This is the LORD's doing;
It is marvellous in our eyes.
This is the day which the LORD hath made;
We will rejoice and be glad in it.
Save now, I beseech thee, O LORD:
O LORD, I beseech thee, send now prosperity.
God is the LORD, which hath shewed us light.

# PSALMS

Thou art my God, and I will praise thee:
Thou art my God, I will exalt thee.
O give thanks unto the LORD; for he is good:
For his mercy endureth for ever.

O LORD God of hosts,
Who is a strong LORD like unto thee?
Or to thy faithfulness round about thee?
Thou rulest the raging of the sea:
When the waves thereof arise, thou stillest them.
The heavens are thine, the earth also is thine:
As for the world and the fulness thereof,
Thou hast founded them.
The north and the south thou hast created them:
Tabor and Hermon shall rejoice in thy name.
Thou hast a mighty arm:
Strong is thy hand, and high is thy right hand.
Justice and judgment are the habitation of thy throne:
Mercy and truth shall go before thy face.
Blessed is the people that know the joyful sound:
They shall walk, O LORD, in the light of thy countenance.
In thy name shall they rejoice all the day:
And in thy righteousness shall they be exalted.
For thou art the glory of their strength:
And in thy favour our horn shall be exalted.
For the LORD is our defence;
And the Holy One of Israel is our king.

Behold, bless ye the LORD, all ye servants of the LORD,
Which by night stand in the house of the LORD.
Lift up your hands in the sanctuary,
And bless the LORD.
The LORD that made heaven and earth
Bless thee out of Zion.

The LORD reigneth; let the people tremble:

[ 231 ]

He sitteth between the cherubims; let the earth be moved.
Exalt ye the Lord our God, and worship at his footstool;
For he is holy.
Exalt the Lord our God, and worship at his holy hill;
For the Lord our God is holy.

They shall fear thee as long as the sun and moon endure,
Throughout all generations.
He shall come down like rain upon the mown grass:
As showers that water the earth.
In his days shall the righteous flourish;
And abundance of peace so long as the moon endureth.
He shall have dominion also from sea to sea,
And from the river unto the ends of the earth.
They that dwell in the wilderness shall bow before him.

O praise the Lord, all ye nations:
Praise him, all ye people.
For his merciful kindness is great toward us:
And the truth of the Lord endureth for ever.
Praise ye the Lord.

Praise ye the Lord.
Praise, O ye servants of the Lord,
Praise the name of the Lord.
Blessed be the name of the Lord
From this time forth and for evermore.
From the rising of the sun
Unto the going down of the same
The Lord's name is to be praised.
The Lord is high above all nations,
And his glory above the heavens.
Who is like unto the Lord our God,
Who dwelleth on high,
Who humbleth himself to behold
The things that are in heaven, and in the earth!

## II. *Psalms of Petition and Confession of Faith*

THE LORD is my strength and my shield;
My heart trusted in him, and I am helped:
Therefore my heart greatly rejoiceth;
And with my song will I praise him.
Save thy people, and bless thine inheritance:
Feed them also, and lift them up for ever.

Let all those that seek thee rejoice and be glad in thee:
And let such as love thy salvation say continually,
Let God be magnified.

In God have I put my trust:
I will not be afraid what man can do unto me.
What time I am afraid,
I will trust in thee.

I will walk within my house with a perfect heart.

I cried unto the LORD with my voice,
And he heard me out of his holy hill.
I laid me down and slept; I awaked;
For the LORD sustained me.

Teach me to do thy will; for thou art my God:
Thy spirit is good; lead me into the land of uprightness.

Blessed be the LORD:
For he hath shewed me his marvellous kindness in a strong city.
O love the LORD, all ye his saints:
For the LORD preserveth the faithful,
And plentifully rewardeth the proud doer.
Be of good courage,
And he shall strengthen your heart,
All ye that hope in the LORD.

*Of Petition and
Confession of Faith*

Behold, how good and how pleasant it is for brethren
To dwell together in unity!
As the dew of Hermon, and as the dew
That descended upon the mountains of Zion:
For there the Lord commanded the blessing,
Even life for evermore.

Set a watch, O Lord, before my mouth;
Keep the door of my lips.

Teach me thy way, O Lord;
I will walk in thy truth:
Unite my heart to fear thy name.
I will praise thee, O Lord my God, with all my heart:
And I will glorify thy name for evermore.

Be merciful unto me, O God,
Be merciful unto me:
For my soul trusteth in thee:
Yea, in the shadow of thy wings will I make my refuge,
Until these calamities be overpast.

Shew us thy mercy, O Lord,
And grant us thy salvation.
I will hear what God the Lord will speak:
For he will speak peace unto his people, and to his saints:
Surely his salvation is nigh them that fear him;
That glory may dwell in our land.
Mercy and truth are met together;
Righteousness and peace have kissed each other.
Truth shall spring out of the earth;
And righteousness shall look down from heaven.
Yea, the Lord shall give that which is good;
And our land shall yield her increase.
Righteousness shall go before him;
And shall set us in the way of his steps.

# PSALMS

Blessed is he whose transgression is forgiven, whose sin is covered. *Of Petition and*
Blessed is the man unto whom the LORD imputeth not iniquity,     *Confession of Faith*
And in whose spirit there is no guile.
For day and night thy hand was heavy upon me:
My moisture is turned into the drought of summer.
I acknowledge my sin unto thee, and mine iniquity have I not hid.
I said, I will confess my transgressions unto the LORD;
And thou forgavest the iniquity of my sin.
For this shall every one that is godly pray unto thee
In a time when thou mayest be found:
Surely in the floods of great waters they shall not come nigh unto him.
Thou art my hiding place;
Thou shalt preserve me from trouble;
Thou shalt compass me about with songs of deliverance.
I will instruct thee and teach thee in the way which thou shalt go:
I will guide thee with mine eye.
Be ye not as the horse, or as the mule,
Which have no understanding:
Whose mouth must be held in with bit and bridle,
Lest they come near unto thee.
Many sorrows shall be to the wicked:
But he that trusteth in the LORD,
Mercy shall compass him about.
Be glad in the LORD, and rejoice, ye righteous:
And shout for joy, all ye that are upright in heart.

In the day of my trouble I sought the Lord.
I remembered God, and was troubled:
I complained, and my spirit was overwhelmed.
I am so troubled that I cannot speak.
I have considered the days of old,
The years of ancient times.
I call to remembrance my song in the night:
I commune with mine own heart:
And my spirit made diligent search.
Will the Lord cast off for ever?

[ 235 ]

And will he be favourable no more?
Is his mercy clean gone for ever?
Doth his promise fail for evermore?
Hath God forgotten to be gracious?
Hath he in anger shut up his tender mercies?
And I said, This is my infirmity:
But I will remember the years of the right hand of the most High.
I will remember the works of the LORD:
Surely I will remember thy wonders of old.
I will meditate also of all thy work, and talk of thy doings.
Thy way, O God, is in the sanctuary:
Who is so great a God as our God?
Thou art the God that doest wonders:
Thou hast declared thy strength among the people.
Thou hast with thine arm redeemed thy people,
The sons of Jacob and Joseph.
The waters saw thee, O God, the waters saw thee;
They were afraid:
The depths also were troubled.
The clouds poured out water:
The skies sent out a sound:
Thine arrows also went abroad.
The voice of thy thunder was in the heaven:
The lightnings lightened the world:
The earth trembled and shook.
Thy way is in the sea,
And thy path in the great waters,
And thy footsteps are not known.
Thou leddest thy people like a flock by the hand of Moses and Aaron.

Out of the depths have I cried unto thee, O LORD.

[ 236 ]

# *PSALMS*

Lord, hear my voice:
Let thine ears be attentive to the voice of my supplications.
If thou, LORD, shouldest mark iniquities,
O Lord, who shall stand?
But there is forgiveness with thee,
That thou mayest be feared.
I wait for the LORD, my soul doth wait,
And in his word do I hope.
My soul waiteth for the Lord
More than they that watch for the morning:
I say, more than they that watch for the morning.
Let Israel hope in the LORD:
For with the LORD there is mercy,
And with him is plenteous redemption.
And he shall redeem Israel
From all his iniquities.

Judge me, O LORD; for I have walked in mine integrity:
I have trusted also in the LORD;
Therefore I shall not slide.
Examine me, O LORD, and prove me;
Try my reins and my heart.
For thy lovingkindness is before mine eyes:
And I have walked in thy truth.
That I may publish with the voice of thanksgiving,
And tell of all thy wondrous works.
LORD, I have loved the habitation of thy house,
And the place where thine honour dwelleth.
But as for me, I will walk in mine integrity:
Redeem me, and be merciful unto me.
My foot standeth in an even place:
In the congregations will I bless the LORD.

Hear my prayer, O LORD, give ear to my supplications:
In thy faithfulness answer me, and in thy righteousness.
And enter not into judgment with thy servant:

*Of Petition and*
*Confession of Faith*

For in thy sight shall no man living be justified.
I remember the days of old;
I meditate on all thy works;
I muse on the work of thy hands.
I stretch forth my hands unto thee:
My soul thirsteth after thee, as a thirsty land.
Hear me speedily, O LORD:
My spirit faileth:
Hide not thy face from me,
Lest I be like unto them that go down into the pit.
Cause me to hear thy lovingkindness in the morning;
For in thee do I trust:
Cause me to know the way wherein I should walk;
For I lift up my soul unto thee.
Teach me to do thy will; for thou art my God:
Thy spirit is good; lead me into the land of uprightness.
Quicken me, O LORD, for thy name's sake:
For thy righteousness' sake bring my soul out of trouble.

Hear the right, O LORD, attend unto my cry,
Give ear unto my prayer, that goeth not out of feigned lips.
Let my sentence come forth from thy presence;
Let thine eyes behold the things that are equal.
Thou hast proved mine heart;
Thou hast visited me in the night;
Thou hast tried me, and shalt find nothing;
I am purposed that my mouth shall not transgress.
Concerning the works of men, by the word of thy lips
I have kept me from the paths of the destroyer.
Hold up my goings in thy paths,
That my footsteps slip not.
I have called upon thee, for thou wilt hear me, O God:
Incline thine ear unto me, and hear my speech.
Shew thy marvellous lovingkindness,
O thou that savest by thy right hand them
Which put their trust in thee from those that rise up against them.

# PSALMS

Keep me as the apple of the eye,
Hide me under the shadow of thy wings.
As for me, I will behold thy face in righteousness:
I shall be satisfied, when I awake, with thy likeness.


Bow down thine ear, O LORD, hear me:
For I am poor and needy.
Preserve my soul; for I am holy:
O thou my God, save thy servant that trusteth in thee.
Be merciful unto me, O Lord:
For I cry unto thee daily.
Rejoice the soul of thy servant:
For unto thee, O Lord, do I lift up my soul.
For thou, Lord, art good, and ready to forgive;
And plenteous in mercy unto all them that call upon thee.
Give ear, O LORD, unto my prayer;
And attend to the voice of my supplications.
In the day of my trouble I will call upon thee:
For thou wilt answer me.
Among the gods there is none like unto thee, O Lord;
Neither are there any works like unto thy works.
All nations whom thou hast made shall come
And worship before thee, O Lord;
And shall glorify thy name.
For thou art great, and doest wondrous things:
Thou art God alone.
Teach me thy way, O LORD;
I will walk in thy truth:
Unite my heart to fear thy name.
I will praise thee, O Lord my God, with all my heart:
And I will glorify thy name for evermore.
Thou, O Lord, art a God full of compassion, and gracious, long-
    suffering, and plenteous in mercy and truth.
O turn unto me, and have mercy upon me;
Give thy strength unto thy servant, and save the son of thine hand-
    maid.

Shew me a token for good;
Because thou, LORD, hast holpen me, and comforted me.

Have mercy upon me, O God, according to thy lovingkindness:
According unto the multitude of thy tender mercies blot out my
    transgressions.
Wash me throughly from mine iniquity,
And cleanse me from my sin.
For I acknowledge my transgressions:
And my sin is ever before me.
Against thee, thee only, have I sinned, and done this evil in thy sight.
Behold, thou desirest truth in the inward parts:
And in the hidden part thou shalt make me to know wisdom.
Purge me with hyssop, and I shall be clean:
Wash me, and I shall be whiter than snow.
Make me to hear joy and gladness;
That the bones which thou hast broken may rejoice.
Hide thy face from my sins,
And blot out all mine iniquities.
Create in me a clean heart, O God;
And renew a right spirit within me.
Cast me not away from thy presence;
And take not thy holy spirit from me.
Restore unto me the joy of thy salvation;
And uphold me with thy free spirit.
Then will I teach transgressors thy ways;
And sinners shall be converted unto thee.
O Lord, open thou my lips;
And my mouth shall shew forth thy praise.
For thou desirest not sacrifice; else would I give it:
Thou delightest not in burnt offering.
The sacrifices of God are a broken spirit:
A broken and a contrite heart, O God, thou wilt not despise.

I waited patiently for the LORD;
And he inclined unto me, and heard my cry.

He brought me up also out of an horrible pit, out of the miry clay,
And set my feet upon a rock, and established my goings.
And he hath put a new song in my mouth, even praise unto our God:
Many shall see it, and fear, and shall trust in the Lord.
Blessed is that man that maketh the Lord his trust,
And respecteth not the proud,
Nor such as turn aside to lies.
Many, O Lord my God, are thy wonderful works which thou hast
    done,
And thy thoughts which are to us-ward:
They cannot be reckoned up in order unto thee:
If I would declare and speak of them,
They are more than can be numbered.
Sacrifice and offering thou didst not desire;
Mine ears hast thou opened:
Burnt offering and sin offering hast thou not required.
Then said I, Lo, I come:
In the volume of the book it is written of me,
I delight to do thy will, O my God:
Yea, thy law is within my heart.
I have preached righteousness in the great congregation:
Lo, I have not refrained my lips, O Lord, thou knowest.
I have not hid thy righteousness within my heart;
I have declared thy faithfulness and thy salvation:
I have not concealed thy lovingkindness and thy truth from the great
    congregation.
Withhold not thou thy tender mercies from me, O Lord:
Let thy lovingkindness and thy truth continually preserve me.
Let all those that seek thee rejoice and be glad in thee:
Let such as love thy salvation say continually,
The Lord be magnified.
But I am poor and needy;
Yet the Lord thinketh upon me:
Thou art my help and my deliverer;
Make no tarrying, O my God.

*Of Petition and
Confession of Faith*

[ 241 ]

O God, thou art my God; early will I seek thee:
My soul thirsteth for thee, my flesh longeth for thee
In a dry and thirsty land, where no water is;
To see thy power and thy glory,
So as I have seen thee in the sanctuary.
Because thy lovingkindness is better than life,
My lips shall praise thee.
Thus will I bless thee while I live:
I will lift up my hands in thy name.
My soul shall be satisfied as with marrow and fatness;
And my mouth shall praise thee with joyful lips:
When I remember thee upon my bed,
And meditate on thee in the night watches.
Because thou hast been my help,
Therefore in the shadow of thy wings will I rejoice.
My soul followeth hard after thee:
Thy right hand upholdeth me.

Truly God is good to Israel, even to such as are of a clean heart.
But as for me, my feet were almost gone;
My steps had well nigh slipped.
For I was envious at the foolish,
When I saw the prosperity of the wicked.
They are not in trouble as other men;
Neither are they plagued like other men.
Therefore pride compasseth them about as a chain;
Violence covereth them as a garment.
Their eyes stand out with fatness:
They have more than heart could wish.
They speak loftily.
And they say, How doth God know?
And is there knowledge in the most High?
Behold, these are the ungodly, who prosper in the world;
They increase in riches.
Verily I have cleansed my heart in vain,

And washed my hands in innocency.
For all the day long have I been plagued,
And chastened every morning.
If I say, I will speak thus;
Behold, I should offend against the generation of thy children.
When I thought to know this, it was too painful for me;
Until I went into the sanctuary of God;
Then understood I their end.
Surely thou didst set them in slippery places.
How are they brought into desolation, as in a moment!
They are utterly consumed with terrors.
Nevertheless I am continually with thee:
Thou hast holden me by my right hand.
Thou shalt guide me with thy counsel,
And afterward receive me to glory.
But it is good for me to draw near to God:
I have put my trust in the Lord God,
That I may declare all thy works.

I will praise thee with my whole heart:
Before the gods will I sing praise unto thee.
I will worship toward thy holy temple,
And praise thy name for thy lovingkindness and for thy truth:
For thou hast magnified thy word above all thy name.
In the day when I cried thou answeredst me,
And strengthenedst me with strength in my soul.
All the kings of the earth shall praise thee, O Lord,
When they hear the words of thy mouth.
Yea, they shall sing in the ways of the Lord:
For great is the glory of the Lord.
Though the Lord be high, yet hath he respect unto the lowly:
But the proud he knoweth afar off.
Though I walk in the midst of trouble, thou wilt revive me:
Thou shalt stretch forth thine hand against the wrath of mine enemies,
    and thy right hand shall save me.

*Of Petition and
Confession of Faith*

[ 243 ]

The LORD will perfect that which concerneth me:
Thy mercy, O LORD, endureth for ever:
Forsake not the works of thine own hands.

Preserve me, O God:
For in thee do I put my trust.
O my soul, thou hast said unto the LORD,
The LORD is the portion of mine inheritance and of my cup:
Thou maintainest my lot.
The lines are fallen unto me in pleasant places;
Yea, I have a goodly heritage.
I will bless the LORD, who hath given me counsel:
My reins also instruct me in the night seasons.
I have set the LORD always before me:
Because he is at my right hand, I shall not be moved.
Therefore my heart is glad, and my glory rejoiceth:
My flesh also shall rest in hope.
For thou wilt not leave my soul in hell;
Neither wilt thou suffer thine Holy One to see corruption.
Thou wilt shew me the path of life:
In thy presence is fulness of joy;
At thy right hand there are pleasures for evermore.

I will love thee, O LORD, my strength.
The LORD is my rock, and my fortress, and my deliverer;
My God, my strength, in whom I will trust;
My buckler, and the horn of my salvation, and my high tower.
In my distress I called upon the LORD, and cried unto my God:
He heard my voice out of his temple,
And my cry came before him, even into his ears.
He made darkness his secret place;
His pavilion round about him were dark waters and thick clouds of
    the skies.
He sent from above, he took me, he drew me out of many waters.
But the LORD was my stay.
He brought me forth also into a large place;

He delivered me, because he delighted in me.

For I have kept the ways of the LORD, and have not wickedly departed from my God.

For all his judgments were before me,

And I did not put away his statutes from me.

I was also upright before him,

And I kept myself from mine iniquity.

Therefore hath the LORD recompensed me according to my righteousness,

According to the cleanness of my hands in his eyesight.

For thou wilt light my candle:

The LORD my God will enlighten my darkness.

For by thee I have run through a troop;

And by my God have I leaped over a wall.

As for God, his way is perfect:

The word of the LORD is tried:

He is a buckler to all those that trust in him.

For who is God save the LORD?

Or who is a rock save our God?

It is God that girdeth me with strength, and maketh my way perfect.

He maketh my feet like hinds' feet, and setteth me upon my high places.

Thou hast also given me the shield of thy salvation:

And thy right hand hath holden me up,

And thy gentleness hath made me great.

Thou hast enlarged my steps under me, that my feet did not slip.

The LORD liveth;

And blessed be my rock;

And let the God of my salvation be exalted.

Therefore will I give thanks unto thee, O LORD,

And sing praises unto thy name.

The LORD is my shepherd; I shall not want.

He maketh me to lie down in green pastures:

He leadeth me beside the still waters.

He restoreth my soul:

He leadeth me in the paths of righteousness for his name's sake.
Yea, though I walk through the valley of the shadow of death,
I will fear no evil: for thou art with me;
Thy rod and thy staff they comfort me.
Thou preparest a table before me in the presence of mine enemies:
Thou anointest my head with oil; my cup runneth over.
Surely goodness and mercy shall follow me all the days of my life:
And I will dwell in the house of the Lord for ever.

Unto thee, O Lord, do I lift up my soul.
O my God, I trust in thee:
Let me not be ashamed.
Shew me thy ways, O Lord;
Teach me thy paths.
Lead me in thy truth, and teach me:
For thou art the God of my salvation;
On thee do I wait all the day.
Remember, O Lord, thy tender mercies and thy lovingkindnesses;
For they have been ever of old.
Remember not the sins of my youth, nor my transgressions:
According to thy mercy remember thou me for thy goodness' sake, O
    Lord.
All the paths of the Lord are mercy and truth unto such as keep his
    covenant and his testimonies.
For thy name's sake, O Lord, pardon mine iniquity; for it is great.
Turn thee unto me, and have mercy upon me;
For I am desolate and afflicted.
The troubles of my heart are enlarged:
O bring thou me out of my distresses.
Look upon mine affliction and my pain;
And forgive all my sins.
What man is he that feareth the Lord?
Him shall he teach in the way that he shall choose.
His soul shall dwell at ease.

O keep my soul, and deliver me:

## PSALMS

Let me not be ashamed;
For I put my trust in thee.
Let integrity and uprightness preserve me;
For I wait on thee.

I will bless the LORD at all times:
His praise shall continually be in my mouth.
My soul shall make her boast in the LORD:
The humble shall hear thereof, and be glad.
O magnify the LORD with me, and let us exalt his name together.
I sought the LORD, and he heard me,
And delivered me from all my fears.
They looked unto him, and were lightened:
And their faces were not ashamed.
The angel of the LORD encampeth round about them that fear him,
    and delivereth them.
O taste and see that the LORD is good:
Blessed is the man that trusteth in him.
Come, ye children, hearken unto me:
I will teach you the fear of the LORD.
What man is he that desireth life, and loveth many days, that he may
    see good?
Keep thy tongue from evil, and thy lips from speaking guile.
Depart from evil, and do good;
Seek peace, and pursue it.
The eyes of the LORD are upon the righteous,
And his ears are open unto their cry.
The face of the LORD is against them that do evil.
The righteous cry, and the LORD heareth, and delivereth them out of
    all their troubles.
The LORD is nigh unto them that are of a broken heart;
And saveth such as be of a contrite spirit.
Many are the afflictions of the righteous:
But the LORD delivereth him out of them all.
The LORD redeemeth the soul of his servants:
And none of them that trust in him shall be desolate.

*Of Petition and
Confession of Faith*

As the hart panteth after the water brooks,
So panteth my soul after thee, O God.
My soul thirsteth for God, for the living God:
When shall I come and appear before God?
My tears have been my meat day and night,
While they continually say unto me, Where is thy God?
When I remember these things, I pour out my soul in me:
For I had gone with the multitude, I went with them to the house of
    God,
With the voice of joy and praise, with a multitude that kept holyday.
Why art thou cast down, O my soul?
And why art thou disquieted in me?
Hope thou in God: for I shall yet praise him
For the help of his countenance.
O my God, my soul is cast down within me:
Therefore will I remember thee from the land of Jordan,
And of the Hermonites, from the hill Mizar.
Deep calleth unto deep at the noise of thy waterspouts:
All thy waves and thy billows are gone over me.
Yet the LORD will command his lovingkindness in the daytime,
And in the night his song shall be with me,
And my prayer unto the God of my life.
I will say unto God my rock, Why hast thou forgotten me?
Why go I mourning because of the oppression of the enemy?
As with a sword in my bones, mine enemies reproach me;
While they say daily unto me, Where is thy God?
Why art thou cast down, O my Soul?
And why art thou disquieted within me?
Hope thou in God: for I shall yet praise him,
Who is the health of my countenance, and my God.
Judge me, O God, and plead my cause against an ungodly nation:

# PSALMS

O deliver me from the deceitful and unjust man.
For thou art the God of my strength:
Why dost thou cast me off?
Why go I mourning because of the oppression of the enemy?
O send out thy light and thy truth:
Let them lead me;
Let them bring me unto thy holy hill, and to thy tabernacles.
Then will I go unto the altar of God, unto God my exceeding joy:
Yea, upon the harp will I praise thee, O God my God.
Why art thou cast down, O my soul?
And why art thou disquieted within me?
Hope in God: for I shall yet praise him,
Who is the health of my countenance, and my God.

The LORD is my light and my salvation; whom shall I fear?
The LORD is the strength of my life; of whom shall I be afraid?
Though an host should encamp against me,
My heart shall not fear:
Though war should rise against me,
In this will I be confident.
One thing have I desired of the LORD, that will I seek after;
That I may dwell in the house of the LORD all the days of my life,
To behold the beauty of the LORD, and to enquire in his temple.
For in the time of trouble he shall hide me in his pavilion:
In the secret of his tabernacle shall he hide me;
He shall set me up upon a rock.
And now shall mine head be lifted up:
Therefore will I offer in his tabernacle sacrifices of joy;
I will sing, yea, I will sing praises unto the LORD.
Hear, O LORD, when I cry with my voice:
Have mercy also upon me, and answer me.

*Of Petition and*
*Confession of Faith*

When thou saidst, Seek ye my face; my heart said unto thee,
Thy face, LORD, will I seek.
Hide not thy face far from me;
Put not thy servant away in anger:
Thou hast been my help;
Leave me not, neither forsake me, O God of my salvation.
Teach me thy way, O LORD,
And lead me in a plain path.
I had fainted, unless I had believed to see the goodness of the LORD
In the land of the living.
Wait on the LORD:
Be of good courage, and he shall strengthen thine heart:
Wait, I say, on the LORD.

The law of the LORD is perfect, converting the soul:
The testimony of the LORD is sure, making wise the simple.
The statutes of the LORD are right, rejoicing the heart:
The commandment of the LORD is pure, enlightening the eyes.
The fear of the LORD is clean, enduring for ever:
The judgments of the LORD are true and righteous altogether.
More to be desired are they than gold, yea, than much fine gold:
Sweeter also than honey and the honeycomb.
Moreover by them is thy servant warned:
And in keeping of them there is great reward.
Who can understand his errors?
Cleanse thou me from secret faults.
Keep back thy servant also from presumptuous sins;
Let them not have dominion over me: then shall I be upright,
And I shall be innocent from the great transgression.
Let the words of my mouth, and the meditation of my heart, be ac-
    ceptable in thy sight,
O LORD, my strength, and my redeemer.

Praise ye the LORD.  Praise the LORD, O my soul.
While I live will I praise the LORD:
I will sing praises unto my God while I have any being.

Happy is he that hath the God of Jacob for his help,
Whose hope is in the LORD his God:
Which made heaven, and earth, the sea, and all that therein is:
Which keepeth truth for ever:
Which executeth judgment for the oppressed:
Which giveth food to the hungry.
The LORD looseth the prisoners:
The LORD openeth the eyes of the blind:
The LORD raiseth them that are bowed down:
The LORD loveth the righteous:
The LORD preserveth the strangers;
He relieveth the fatherless and widow:
But the way of the wicked he turneth upside down.
The LORD shall reign for ever, even thy God, O Zion, unto all gen-
　　erations.
Praise ye the LORD.


He that dwelleth in the secret place of the most High
Shall abide under the shadow of the Almighty.
I will say of the LORD, He is my refuge and my fortress:
My God; in him will I trust.
Surely he shall deliver thee from the snare of the fowler,
And from the noisome pestilence.
He shall cover thee with his feathers,
And under his wings shalt thou trust:
His truth shall be thy shield and buckler.
Thou shalt not be afraid for the terror by night;
Nor for the arrow that flieth by day;
Nor for the pestilence that walketh in darkness;
Nor for the destruction that wasteth at noonday.
Because thou hast made the LORD, which is my refuge,

Even the most High, thy habitation;
There shall no evil befall thee,
Neither shall any plague come nigh thy dwelling.
For he shall give his angels charge over thee,
To keep thee in all thy ways.
They shall bear thee up in their hands,
Lest thou dash thy foot against a stone.
Thou shalt tread upon the lion and adder:
The young lion and the dragon shalt thou trample under feet.
Because he hath set his love upon me, therefore will I deliver him:
I will set him on high, because he hath known my name.
He shall call upon me, and I will answer him:
I will be with him in trouble;
I will deliver him, and honour him.
With long life will I satisfy him,
And show him my salvation.

Praise ye the LORD.
I will praise the LORD with my whole heart,
In the assembly of the upright, and in the congregation.
The works of the LORD are great,
Sought out of all them that have pleasure therein.
His work is honourable and glorious:
And his righteousness endureth for ever.
He hath made his wonderful works to be remembered:
The LORD is gracious and full of compassion.
He hath given meat unto them that fear him:
He will ever be mindful of his covenant.
He hath shewed his people the power of his works,
That he may give them the heritage of the heathen.
The works of his hands are verity and judgment;
All his commandments are sure.
They stand fast for ever and ever,
And are done in truth and uprightness.
He sent redemption unto his people:

## PSALMS

He hath commanded his covenant for ever:
Holy and reverend is his name.
The fear of the LORD is the beginning of wisdom:
A good understanding have all they that do his commandments:
His praise endureth for ever.

Truly my soul waiteth upon God:
From him cometh my salvation.
He only is my rock and my salvation;
He is my defence; I shall not be greatly moved.
My soul, wait thou only upon God;
For my expectation is from him.
He only is my rock and my salvation:
He is my defence; I shall not be moved.
In God is my salvation and my glory:
The rock of my strength, and my refuge, is in God.
Trust in him at all times; ye people,
Pour out your heart before him:
God is a refuge for us.
God hath spoken once;
Twice have I heard this;
That power belongeth unto God.
Also unto thee, O Lord, belongeth mercy:
For thou renderest to every man according to his work.

Hear my cry, O God; attend unto my prayer.
From the end of the earth will I cry unto thee, when my heart is over-
  whelmed:
Lead me to the rock that is higher than I.
For thou hast been a shelter for me, and a strong tower from the
  enemy.
I will abide in thy tabernacle for ever:
I will trust in the covert of thy wings.
For thou, O God, hast heard my vows:
Thou hast given me the heritage of those that fear thy name.

*Of Petition and*
*Confession of Faith*

Thou wilt prolong the king's life: and his years as many generations.
He shall abide before God for ever:
O prepare mercy and truth, which may preserve him.
So will I sing praise unto thy name for ever,
That I may daily perform my vows.

In thee, O LORD, do I put my trust:
Let me never be put to confusion.
Be thou my strong habitation, whereunto I may continually resort:
Thou hast given commandment to save me;
For thou art my rock and my fortress.
For thou art my hope, O Lord GOD:
Thou art my trust from my youth.
Let my mouth be filled with thy praise and with thy honour all the
    day.
But I will hope continually,
And will yet praise thee more and more.
My mouth shall shew forth thy righteousness and thy salvation all the
    day;
For I know not the numbers thereof.
I will go in the strength of the Lord GOD:
I will make mention of thy righteousness, even of thine only.
O God, thou hast taught me from my youth:
And hitherto have I declared thy wondrous works.
Now also when I am old and greyheaded, O God, forsake me not;
Until I have shewed thy strength unto this generation,
And thy power to every one that is to come.
Thy righteousness also, O God, is very high, who hast done great
    things:
O God, who is like unto thee!

Give ear to my words, O LORD,
Consider my meditation.
Hearken unto the voice of my cry, my King, and my God:
For unto thee will I pray.
My voice shalt thou hear in the morning, O LORD;

In the morning will I direct my prayer unto thee, and will look up.
Lead me, O Lord, in thy righteousness;
Make thy way straight before my face.
But let all those that put their trust in thee rejoice:
Let them ever shout for joy, because thou defendest them:
Let them also that love thy name be joyful in thee.

Whom have I in heaven but thee?
And there is none upon earth that I desire beside thee.
My flesh and my heart faileth:
But God is the strength of my heart,
And my portion for ever.
But it is good for me to draw near to God:
I have put my trust in the Lord God,
That I may declare all thy works.

## III. Psalms of Reflection

Happy is that people, that is in such a case:
Yea, happy is that people, whose God is the Lord.

In the multitude of my thoughts within me
Thy comforts delight my soul.

Our help is in the name of the Lord,
Who made heaven and earth.

Surely the righteous shall give thanks unto thy name:
The upright shall dwell in thy presence.
For the righteous Lord loveth righteousness;
His countenance doth behold the upright.

Blessed is the man that walketh not in the counsel of the ungodly,
Nor standeth in the way of sinners,

*Of Reflection*  Nor sitteth in the seat of the scornful.
But his delight is in the law of the Lord;
And in his law doth he meditate day and night.
And he shall be like a tree planted by the rivers of water,
That bringeth forth his fruit in his season;
His leaf also shall not wither;
And whatsoever he doeth shall prosper.
The ungodly are not so:
But are like the chaff which the wind driveth away.
Therefore the ungodly shall not stand in the judgment,
Nor sinners in the congregation of the righteous.
For the Lord knoweth the way of the righteous:
But the way of the ungodly shall perish.

But know that the Lord hath set apart him that is godly for himself:
Stand in awe, and sin not:
Commune with your own heart upon your bed, and be still.
Offer the sacrifices of righteousness,
And put your trust in the Lord.
There be many that say, Who will shew us any good?
Lord, lift thou up the light of thy countenance upon us.
Thou hast put gladness in my heart,
More than in the time that their corn and their wine increased.
I will both lay me down in peace, and sleep:
For thou, Lord, only makest me dwell in safety.

Why standest thou afar off, O Lord?
Why hidest thou thyself in times of trouble?
The wicked in his pride doth persecute the poor.
God is not in all his thoughts.
He hath said in his heart, I shall not be moved:
For I shall never be in adversity.
He hath said in his heart, God hath forgotten:
He hideth his face; he will never see it.
Thou hast seen it; for thou beholdest mischief and spite,
To requite it with thy hand.

## PSALMS

Arise, O LORD; O God, lift up thine hand:
Forget not the humble.
The poor committeth himself unto thee;
Thou art the helper of the fatherless.
The LORD is King for ever and ever.
LORD, thou hast heard the desire of the humble:
Thou wilt prepare their heart,
Thou wilt cause thine ear to hear:
To judge the fatherless and the oppressed,
That the man of the earth may no more oppress.

Thy mercy, O LORD, is in the heavens;
And thy faithfulness reacheth unto the clouds.
Thy righteousness is like the great mountains;
Thy judgments are a great deep:
O LORD, thou preservest man and beast.
How excellent is thy lovingkindness, O God!
Therefore the children of men put their trust under the shadow of thy
    wings.
They shall be abundantly satisfied with the fatness of thy house;
And thou shalt make them drink of the river of thy pleasures.
For with thee is the fountain of life:
In thy light shall we see light.
O continue thy lovingkindness unto them that know thee;
And thy righteousness to the upright in heart.

Fret not thyself because of evildoers,
Neither be thou envious against the workers of iniquity.
For they shall soon be cut down like the grass,
And wither as the green herb.
Trust in the LORD, and do good;
So shalt thou dwell in the land, and verily thou shalt be fed.
Delight thyself also in the LORD;
And he shall give thee the desires of thine heart.
Commit thy way unto the LORD;
Trust also in him; and he shall bring it to pass.

*Of Reflection*

And he shall bring forth thy righteousness as the light,
And thy judgment as the noonday.
Rest in the LORD, and wait patiently for him:
Fret not thyself because of him who prospereth in his way,
Because of the man who bringeth wicked devices to pass.
Cease from anger, and forsake wrath:
Fret not thyself in any wise to do evil.
A little that a righteous man hath
Is better than the riches of many wicked.
The steps of a good man are ordered by the LORD:
And he delighteth in his way.
Though he fall, he shall not be utterly cast down:
For the LORD upholdeth him with his hand.
I have been young, and now am old;
Yet have I not seen the righteous forsaken,
Nor his seed begging bread.
Depart from evil, and do good;
And dwell for evermore.
For the LORD loveth judgment,
And forsaketh not his saints.
The mouth of the righteous speaketh wisdom,
And his tongue talketh of judgment.
The law of his God is in his heart;
None of his steps shall slide.
Wait on the LORD, and keep his way.
I have seen the wicked in great power,
And spreading himself like a green bay tree.
Yet he passed away, and lo, he was not:
Yea, I sought him, but he could not be found.
Mark the perfect man, and behold the upright:
For the end of that man is peace.

LORD, thou hast been our dwelling place
In all generations.
Before the mountains were brought forth,
Or ever thou hadst formed the earth and the world,

## PSALMS

Even from everlasting to everlasting, thou art God.
Thou turnest man to destruction;
And sayest, Return, ye children of men.
For a thousand years in thy sight
Are but as yesterday when it is past,
And as a watch in the night.
Thou carriest them away as with a flood; they are as a sleep:
In the morning they are like grass which groweth up.
In the morning it flourisheth, and groweth up;
In the evening it is cut down, and withereth.
For we are consumed by thine anger,
And by thy wrath are we troubled.
Thou hast set our iniquities before thee,
Our secret sins in the light of thy countenance.
For all our days are passed away in thy wrath:
We spend our years as a tale that is told.
The days of our years are threescore years and ten;
And if by reason of strength they be fourscore years,
Yet is their strength labour and sorrow;
For it is soon cut off, and we fly away.
Who knoweth the power of thine anger?
Even according to thy fear, so is thy wrath.
So teach us to number our days,
That we may apply our hearts unto wisdom.
Return, O Lord, how long?
And let it repent thee concerning thy servants.
O satisfy us early with thy mercy;
That we may rejoice and be glad all our days.
Make us glad according to the days wherein thou hast afflicted us,
And the years wherein we have seen evil.
Let thy work appear unto thy servants,
And thy glory unto their children.
And let the beauty of the Lord our God be upon us:
And establish thou the work of our hands upon us;
Yea, the work of our hands establish thou it.

I love the LORD, because he hath heard
My voice and my supplications.
Because he hath inclined his ear unto me,
Therefore will I call upon him as long as I live.
Gracious is the LORD, and righteous;
Yea, our God is merciful.
The LORD preserveth the simple:
I was brought low, and he helped me.
Return unto thy rest, O my soul;
For the LORD hath dealt bountifully with thee.
For thou hast delivered my soul from death,
Mine eyes from tears,
And my feet from falling.
What shall I render unto the LORD
For all his benefits toward me?
I will take the cup of salvation,
And call upon the name of the LORD.
I will pay my vows unto the LORD
Now in the presence of all his people.
Precious in the sight of the LORD
Is the death of his saints.
O LORD, truly I am thy servant;
I am thy servant, and the son of thine handmaid:
Thou hast loosed my bonds.
I will offer to thee the sacrifice of thanksgiving,
And will call upon the name of the LORD.
I will pay my vows unto the LORD
Now in the presence of all his people,
In the courts of the LORD's house,
In the midst of thee, O Jerusalem.
Praise ye the LORD.

But thou, O LORD, shalt endure for ever;
And thy remembrance unto all generations.
Thy years are throughout all generations.
Of old hast thou laid the foundation of the earth:

And the heavens are the work of thy hands.
They shall perish, but thou shalt endure:
Yea, all of them shall wax old like a garment;
As a vesture shalt thou change them, and they shall be changed:
But thou art the same,
And thy years shall have no end.

O Lord, thou hast searched me, and known me.
Thou knowest my downsitting and mine uprising,
Thou understandest my thought afar off.
Thou compassest my path and my lying down,
And art acquainted with all my ways.
For there is not a word in my tongue,
But lo, O Lord, thou knowest it altogether.
Thou hast beset me behind and before,
And laid thine hand upon me.
Such knowledge is too wonderful for me;
It is high, I cannot attain unto it.
Whither shall I go from thy spirit?
Or whither shall I flee from thy presence?
If I ascend up into heaven, thou art there:
If I make my bed in hell, behold, thou art there.
If I take the wings of the morning,
And dwell in the uttermost parts of the sea;
Even there shall thy hand lead me,
And thy right hand shall hold me.
If I say, Surely the darkness shall cover me;
Even the night shall be light about me.
Yea, the darkness hideth not from thee;
But the night shineth as the day:
The darkness and the light are both alike to thee.
I will praise thee; for I am fearfully and wonderfully made:
Marvellous are thy works;
And that my soul knoweth right well.
My substance was not hid from thee,
When I was made in secret,

And curiously wrought in the lowest parts of the earth.
Thine eyes did see my substance, yet being unperfect;
And in thy book all my members were written,
Which in continuance were fashioned,
When as yet there was none of them.
How precious also are thy thoughts unto me, O God!
How great is the sum of them!
If I should count them, they are more in number than the sand:
When I awake, I am still with thee.
Search me, O God, and know my heart:
Try me, and know my thoughts:
And see if there be any wicked way in me,
And lead me in the way everlasting.

Blessed are the undefiled in the way,
Who walk in the law of the LORD.
Blessed are they that keep his testimonies,
And that seek him with the whole heart.
Wherewithal shall a young man cleanse his way?
By taking heed thereto according to thy word.
With my whole heart have I sought thee:
O let me not wander from thy commandments.
Thy word have I hid in mine heart,
That I might not sin against thee.
Open thou mine eyes,
That I may behold wondrous things out of thy law.
My soul cleaveth unto the dust:
Quicken thou me according to thy word.
Remove from me the way of lying.
I will run the way of thy commandments,
When thou shalt enlarge my heart.
Incline my heart unto thy testimonies,
And not to covetousness.
Turn away mine eyes from beholding vanity;
And quicken thou me in thy way.
And take not the word of truth utterly out of my mouth;

For I have hoped in thy judgments.
So shall I keep thy law continually for ever and ever.
And I will walk at liberty:
For I seek thy precepts.
The proud have had me greatly in derision:
Yet have I not declined from thy law.
Thy statutes have been my songs in the house of my pilgrimage.
It is good for me that I have been afflicted;
That I might learn thy statutes.
The law of thy mouth is better unto me than thousands of gold and
silver.
Thy hands have made me and fashioned me:
Give me understanding, that I may learn thy commandments.
For thy law is my delight.
For ever, O LORD, thy word is settled in heaven.
Thy faithfulness is unto all generations:
Thou hast established the earth, and it abideth.
O how love I thy law!
It is my meditation all the day.
Thy word is a lamp unto my feet, and a light unto my path.
Thy testimonies have I taken as an heritage for ever:
For they are the rejoicing of my heart.
Thou art my hiding place and my shield:
I hope in thy word.
Uphold me according unto thy word, that I may live:
And let me not be ashamed of my hope.
Hold thou me up, and I shall be safe:
And I will have respect unto thy statutes continually.
Therefore I love thy commandments above gold;
Yea, above fine gold.
Make thy face to shine upon thy servant;
And teach me thy statutes.
Righteous art thou, O LORD, and upright are thy judgments.
Thy testimonies that thou hast commanded are righteous and very
faithful.
Thy word is very pure:

Therefore thy servant loveth it.
Let thine hand help me; for I have chosen thy precepts.
I have longed for thy salvation, O LORD;
And thy law is my delight.
Great peace have they which love thy law.

When Israel went out of Egypt,
The house of Jacob from a people of strange language;
Judah was his sanctuary, and Israel his dominion.
The sea saw it, and fled:
Jordan was driven back.
The mountains skipped like rams,
And the little hills like lambs.
What ailed thee, O thou sea, that thou fleddest?
Thou Jordan, that thou wast driven back?
Ye mountains, that ye skipped like rams;
And ye little hills, like lambs?
Tremble, thou earth, at the presence of the Lord,
At the presence of the God of Jacob;
Which turned the rock into a standing water,
The flint into a fountain of waters.

By the rivers of Babylon,
There we sat down, yea, we wept,
When we remembered Zion.
We hanged our harps
Upon the willows in the midst thereof.
For there they that carried us away captive required of us a song;
And they that wasted us required of us mirth, saying,
Sing us one of the songs of Zion.
How shall we sing the LORD's song

In a strange land?
If I forget thee, O Jerusalem,
Let my right hand forget her cunning.
If I do not remember thee,
Let my tongue cleave to the roof of my mouth;
If I prefer not Jerusalem above my chief joy.

The LORD looketh from heaven;
He beholdeth all the sons of men.
From the place of his habitation he looketh upon all the inhabitants
    of the earth.
He fashioneth their hearts alike;
He considereth all their works.
There is no king saved by the multitude of an host:
A mighty man is not delivered by much strength.
An horse is a vain thing for safety:
Neither shall he deliver any by his great strength.
Behold, the eye of the LORD is upon them that fear him,
Upon them that hope in his mercy;
To deliver their soul from death,
And to keep them alive in famine.
Our soul waiteth for the LORD:
He is our help and our shield.
For our heart shall rejoice in him,
Because we have trusted in his holy name.
Let thy mercy, O LORD, be upon us,
According as we hope in thee.

Except the LORD build the house,
They labour in vain that build it:
Except the LORD keep the city,
The watchman waketh but in vain.
It is vain for you to rise up early, to sit up late,
To eat the bread of sorrows:
For so he giveth his beloved sleep.
Lo, children are an heritage of the LORD:

And the fruit of the womb is his reward.
As arrows are in the hand of a mighty man;
So are children of the youth.
Happy is the man that hath his quiver full of them:
They shall not be ashamed.

Hear me, O LORD; for thy lovingkindness is good:
Turn unto me according to the multitude of thy tender mercies.
Let the heaven and earth praise him, the seas, and every thing that
    moveth therein.
For God will save Zion, and will build the cities of Judah.

O praise the LORD, all ye nations:
Praise him, all ye people.
For his merciful kindness is great toward us:
And the truth of the LORD endureth for ever.
Praise ye the LORD.

For God is my King of old, working salvation in the midst of the
    earth.
Thou didst divide the sea by thy strength:
Thou brakest the heads of the dragons in the waters.
Thou didst cleave the fountain and the flood:
Thou driedst up mighty rivers.
The day is thine, the night also is thine:
Thou hast prepared the light and the sun.
Thou hast set all the borders of the earth:
Thou hast made summer and winter.

Not unto us, O LORD, not unto us,
But unto thy name give glory,

For thy mercy, and for thy truth's sake.
The heaven, even the heavens, are the LORD's:
But the earth hath he given to the children of men.

Thou hast a mighty arm:
Strong is thy hand, and high is thy right hand.
Justice and judgment are the habitation of thy throne:
Mercy and truth shall go before thy face.
Blessed is the people that know the joyful sound:
They shall walk, O LORD, in the light of thy countenance.
In thy name shall they rejoice all the day:
And in thy righteousness shall they be exalted.
For thou art the glory of their strength:
And in thy favour our horn shall be exalted.

I will hear what God the LORD will speak:
For he will speak peace unto his people, and to his saints:
But let them not turn again to folly.
Surely his salvation is nigh them that fear him;
That glory may dwell in our land.
Mercy and truth are met together;
Righteousness and peace have kissed each other.
Truth shall spring out of the earth;
And righteousness shall look down from heaven.
Yea, the LORD shall give that which is good;
And our land shall yield her increase.
Righteousness shall go before him;
And shall set us in the way of his steps.

My heart is inditing a good matter:
I speak of the things which I have made
Touching the king:
My tongue is the pen of a ready writer.
Thou art fairer than the children of men:
Grace is poured into thy lips:
Therefore God hath blessed thee for ever.

[ 267 ]

*Of Reflection*    Gird thy sword upon thy thigh, O most mighty,
With thy glory and thy majesty.
And in thy majesty ride prosperously
Because of truth and meekness and righteousness;
And thy right hand shall teach thee terrible things.
Thine arrows are sharp in the heart of the king's enemies;
Whereby the people fall under thee.
Thy throne, O God, is for ever and ever:
The sceptre of thy kingdom is a right sceptre.
Thou lovest righteousness, and hatest wickedness:
Therefore God, thy God, hath anointed thee
With the oil of gladness above thy fellows.
All thy garments smell of myrrh, and aloes, and cassia,
Out of the ivory palaces, whereby they have made thee glad.
Kings' daughters were among thy honourable women:
Upon thy right hand did stand the queen in gold of Ophir.
Hearken, O daughter, and consider, and incline thine ear;
Forget also thine own people, and thy father's house;
So shall the king greatly desire thy beauty:
For he is thy Lord; and worship thou him.
And the daughter of Tyre shall be there with a gift;
Even the rich among the people shall intreat thy favour.
The king's daughter is all glorious within:
Her clothing is of wrought gold.
She shall be brought unto the king in raiment of needlework:
The virgins her companions that follow her shall be brought unto
    thee.
With gladness and rejoicing shall they be brought:
They shall enter into the king's palace.
Instead of thy fathers shall be thy children,
Whom thou mayest make princes in all the earth.
I will make thy name to be remembered in all generations:
Therefore shall the people praise thee for ever and ever.

## *Two Songs*

MY BELOVED spake, and said unto me,
Rise up, my love, my fair one, and come away.
For, lo, the winter is past,
The rain is over and gone;
The flowers appear on the earth;
The time of the singing of birds is come,
And the voice of the turtle is heard in our land;
The fig tree putteth forth her green figs,
And the vines with the tender grape give a good smell.
Arise, my love, my fair one, and come away.
O my dove, that art in the clefts of the rock,
In the secret places of the stairs,
Let me see thy countenance,
Let me hear thy voice;
For sweet is thy voice, and thy countenance is comely.
Take us the foxes, the little foxes,
That spoil the vines:
For our vines have tender grapes.
My beloved is mine, and I am his:
He feedeth among the lilies.
Until the day break, and the shadows flee away,
Turn, my beloved, and be thou like a roe or a young hart
Upon the mountains of Bether.

Set me as a seal upon thine heart,
As a seal upon thine arm:
For love is strong as death;
Jealousy is cruel as the grave:
The coals thereof are coals of fire,
Which hath a most vehement flame.
Many waters cannot quench love,
Neither can the floods drown it:

If a man would give all the substance of his house for love,
It would utterly be contemned.

And all the men of Shechem gathered together, and all the house of
Millo, and went, and made Abimelech king, by the plain of the pillar that
was in Shechem. And when they told it to Jotham, he went and stood in
the top of mount Gerizim, and lifted up his voice, and cried, and said
unto them, "Hearken unto me, ye men of Shechem, that God may
hearken unto you:

> The trees went forth on a time
> To anoint a king over them;
> And they said unto the olive tree,
> 'Reign thou over us.'
> But the olive tree said unto them,
> 'Should I leave my fatness,
> Wherewith by me they honour God and man,
> And go to be promoted over the trees?'
> And the trees said to the fig tree,
> 'Come thou, and reign over us.'
> But the fig tree said unto them,
> 'Should I forsake my sweetness,
> And my good fruit,
> And go to be promoted over the trees?'
> Then said the trees unto the vine,
> 'Come thou, and reign over us.'
> And the vine said unto them,
> 'Should I leave my wine,
> Which cheereth God and man,
> And go to be promoted over the trees?'
> Then said all the trees unto the bramble,
> 'Come thou, and reign over us.'
> And the bramble said unto the trees,
> 'If in truth ye anoint me king over you,
> Then come and put your trust in my shadow:
> And if not, let fire come out of the bramble,
> And devour the cedars of Lebanon.' "

# VI

# JOB AND WISDOM LITERATURE

THERE was a man in the land of Uz, whose name was Job; and *Job and his situation* that man was perfect and upright, and one that feared God, and eschewed evil. And there were born unto him seven sons and three daughters. His substance also was seven thousand sheep, and three thousand camels, and five hundred yoke of oxen, and five hundred she asses, and a very great household; so that this man was the greatest of all the men of the east. And his sons went and feasted in their houses, every one his day; and sent and called for their three sisters to eat and to drink with them. And it was so, when the days of their feasting were gone about, that Job sent and sanctified them, and rose up early in the morning, and offered burnt offerings according to the number of them all: for Job said, "It may be that my sons have sinned, and cursed God in their hearts." Thus did Job continually.

Now there was a day when the sons of God came to present themselves before the LORD, and Satan came also among them.

And the LORD said unto Satan, "Whence comest thou?"

Then Satan answered the LORD, and said, "From going to and fro in the earth, and from walking up and down in it."

And the LORD said unto Satan, "Hast thou considered my servant Job, that there is none like him in the earth, a perfect and an upright man, one that feareth God, and escheweth evil?"

Then Satan answered the LORD, and said, "Doth Job fear God for nought? Hast not thou made an hedge about him, and about his house, and about all that he hath on every side? thou hast blessed the work of his hands, and his substance is increased in the land. But put forth thine hand now, and touch all that he hath, and he will curse thee to thy face."

And the LORD said unto Satan, "Behold, all that he hath is in thy power; only upon himself put not forth thine hand." So Satan went forth from the presence of the LORD.

And there was a day when his sons and his daughters were eating and drinking wine in their eldest brother's house: And there came a messenger unto Job, and said, "The oxen were plowing, and the asses feeding beside

them: and the Sabeans fell upon them, and took them away; yea, they have slain the servants with the edge of the sword; and I only am escaped alone to tell thee."

While he was yet speaking, there came also another, and said, "The fire of God is fallen from heaven, and hath burned up the sheep, and the servants, and consumed them; and I only am escaped alone to tell thee."

While he was yet speaking, there came also another, and said, "The Chaldeans made out three bands, and fell upon the camels, and have carried them away, yea, and slain the servants with the edge of the sword; and I only am escaped alone to tell thee."

While he was yet speaking, there came also another, and said, "Thy sons and thy daughters were eating and drinking wine in their eldest brother's house: and, behold, there came a great wind from the wilderness, and smote the four corners of the house, and it fell upon the young men, and they are dead; and I only am escaped alone to tell thee."

Then Job arose, and rent his mantle, and shaved his head, and fell down upon the ground, and worshipped, and said, "Naked came I out of my mother's womb, and naked shall I return thither: the LORD gave, and the LORD hath taken away; blessed be the name of the LORD." In all this Job sinned not, nor charged God foolishly.

Again there was a day when the sons of God came to present themselves before the LORD, and Satan came also among them to present himself before the LORD.

And the LORD said unto Satan, "From whence comest thou?"

And Satan answered the LORD, and said, "From going to and fro in the earth, and from walking up and down in it."

And the LORD said unto Satan, "Hast thou considered my servant Job, that there is none like him in the earth, a perfect and an upright man, one that feareth God, and escheweth evil? and still he holdeth fast his integrity, although thou movedst me against him, to destroy him without cause."

And Satan answered the LORD, and said, "Skin for skin, yea, all that a man hath will he give for his life. But put forth thine hand now, and touch his bone and his flesh, and he will curse thee to thy face."

And the LORD said unto Satan, "Behold, he is in thine hand; but save his life."

So went Satan forth from the presence of the LORD, and smote Job *Job's trials increased* with sore boils from the sole of his foot unto his crown. And he took him a potsherd to scrape himself withal; and he sat down among the ashes.

Then said his wife unto him, "Dost thou still retain thine integrity? curse God, and die."

But he said unto her, "Thou speakest as one of the foolish women speaketh. What? shall we receive good at the hand of God, and shall we not receive evil?" In all this did not Job sin with his lips.

Now when Job's three friends heard of all this evil that was come upon him, they came every one from his own place; Eliphaz the Temanite, and Bildad the Shuhite, and Zophar the Naamathite: for they had made an appointment together to come to mourn with him and to comfort him. And when they lifted up their eyes afar off, and knew him not, they lifted up their voice, and wept; and they rent every one his mantle, and sprinkled dust upon their heads toward heaven. So they sat down with him upon the ground seven days and seven nights, and none spake a word unto him: for they saw that his grief was very great.

After this opened Job his mouth, and cursed his day. And Job spake, *Job curses the day of* and said, *his birth*

"Let the day perish wherein I was born.
Let that day be darkness;
Let not God regard it from above,
Neither let the light shine upon it.
Let darkness and the shadow of death stain it;
Let a cloud dwell upon it;
Let the blackness of the day terrify it.
Let the stars of the twilight thereof be dark;
Let it look for light, but have none;
Neither let it see the dawning of the day.
For now should I have lain still and been quiet,
I should have slept: then had I been at rest.
There the wicked cease from troubling;
And there the weary be at rest.
There the prisoners rest together;
They hear not the voice of the oppressor.
The small and great are there;

*Job's complaint*

And the servant is free from his master.
Wherefore is light given to him that is in misery,
And life unto the bitter in soul;
Which long for death, but it cometh not;
And dig for it more than for hid treasures;
Which rejoice exceedingly,
And are glad, when they can find the grave?
Why is light given to a man whose way is hid,
And whom God hath hedged in?
For my sighing cometh before I eat,
And my roarings are poured out like the waters.
For the thing which I greatly feared is come upon me,
And that which I was afraid of is come unto me.
I was not in safety, neither had I rest, neither was I quiet;
Yet trouble came."

*Eliphaz reproves Job*    Then Eliphaz the Temanite answered and said,

"If we assay to commune with thee, wilt thou be grieved?
But who can withhold himself from speaking?
Behold, thou hast instructed many,
And thou hast strengthened the weak hands.
Thy words have upholden him that was falling,
And thou hast strengthened the feeble knees.
But now it is come upon thee, and thou faintest;
It toucheth thee, and thou art troubled.
Is not this thy fear, thy confidence,
Thy hope, and the uprightness of thy ways?
Remember, I pray thee, who ever perished, being innocent?
Or where were the righteous cut off?
Even as I have seen, they that plow iniquity,
And sow wickedness, reap the same.
By the blast of God they perish,
And by the breath of his nostrils are they consumed.
Now a thing was secretly brought to me,
And mine ear received a little thereof.
In thoughts from the visions of the night,

## JOB

When deep sleep falleth on men,
Fear came upon me, and trembling,
Which made all my bones to shake.
Then a spirit passed before my face;
The hair of my flesh stood up;
It stood still, but I could not discern the form thereof:
An image was before mine eyes,
There was silence, and I heard a voice, saying,
'Shall mortal man be more just than God?
Shall a man be more pure than his maker?'
Yet man is born unto trouble,
As the sparks fly upward.
I would seek unto God,
And unto God would I commit my cause:
Which doeth great things and unsearchable;
Marvellous things without number:
Who giveth rain upon the earth,
And sendeth waters upon the fields:
To set up on high those that be low;
That those which mourn may be exalted to safety.
He disappointeth the devices of the crafty,
So that their hands cannot perform their enterprise.
They meet with darkness in the daytime,
And grope in the noonday as in the night.
But he saveth the poor from the hand of the mighty.
So the poor hath hope,
And iniquity stoppeth her mouth.
Behold, happy is the man whom God correcteth:
Therefore despise not thou the chastening of the Almighty:
For he maketh sore, and bindeth up:
He woundeth, and his hands make whole.
In famine he shall redeem thee from death;
And in war from the power of the sword.
Thou shalt be hid from the scourge of the tongue:
Neither shalt thou be afraid of destruction when it cometh.
At destruction and famine thou shalt laugh:

[ 275 ]

*God's chastening brings confidence*

Neither shalt thou be afraid of the beasts of the earth.
For thou shalt be in league with the stones of the field:
And the beasts of the field shall be at peace with thee.
And thou shalt know that thy tabernacle shall be in peace;
And thou shalt visit thy habitation, and shalt not sin.
Thou shalt know also that thy seed shall be great,
And thine offspring as the grass of the earth.
Thou shalt come to thy grave in a full age,
Like as a shock of corn cometh in in his season.
Lo this, we have searched it, so it is;
Hear it, and know thou it for thy good."

*Job wishes for death*

But Job answered and said,

"Oh that my grief were throughly weighed,
And my calamity laid in the balances together!
For now it would be heavier than the sand of the sea:
Therefore my words are swallowed up.
For the arrows of the Almighty are within me,
The poison whereof drinketh up my spirit.
Oh that I might have my request;
And that God would grant me the thing that I long for!
Then should I yet have comfort;
Yea, I would harden myself in sorrow: let him not spare;
For I have not concealed the words of the Holy One.
What is my strength, that I should hope?
And what is mine end, that I should prolong my life?
Is my strength the strength of stones?
Or is my flesh of brass?
Is not my help in me?
And is wisdom driven quite from me?
To him that is afflicted pity should be shewed from his friend;
But he forsaketh the fear of the Almighty.
My brethren have dealt deceitfully as a brook,
And as the stream of brooks they pass away.
Teach me, and I will hold my tongue:
And cause me to understand wherein I have erred.

9

Shall mortal Man be more Just than God? Shall a Man be more Pure than his Maker? Behold he putteth no trust in his Saints & his Angels he chargeth with folly

WBlake inven. sculp

Then a Spirit pafsed before my Face
the hair of my flesh stood up

London, Published as the Act directs March 8: 1825 by William Blake N 3 Fountain Court Strand

Proof

## JOB

How forcible are right words!
But what doth your arguing reprove?
Do ye imagine to reprove words,
And the speeches of one that is desperate, which are as wind?
Now therefore be content, look upon me;
For it is evident unto you if I lie.
Return, I pray you, let it not be iniquity;
Yea, return again, my righteousness is in it.
Is there iniquity in my tongue?
Cannot my taste discern perverse things?
When I lie down, I say, 'When shall I arise,
And the night be gone?'
And I am full of tossings to and fro unto the dawning of the day.
My days are swifter than a weaver's shuttle,
And are spent without hope.
O remember that my life is wind."

*Job detests the hopelessness of his life*

Then answered Bildad the Shuhite, and said,

*Bildad's reproof*

"How long wilt thou speak these things?
And how long shall the words of thy mouth be like a strong wind?
Doth God pervert judgment?
Or doth the Almighty pervert justice?
If thy children have sinned against him,
And he have cast them away for their transgression;
If thou wouldest seek unto God betimes,
And make thy supplication to the Almighty;
If thou wert pure and upright;
Surely now he would awake for thee,
And make the habitation of thy righteousness prosperous.
Can the rush grow up without mire?
Can the flag grow without water?
Whilst it is yet in his greenness, and not cut down,
It withereth before any other herb.
So are the paths of all that forget God;
And the hypocrite's hope shall perish:
Whose hope shall be cut off,

[ 277 ]

*Bildad's reassurance* And whose trust shall be a spider's web.
He shall lean upon his house, but it shall not stand:
He shall hold it fast, but it shall not endure.
He is green before the sun,
And his branch shooteth forth in his garden.
His roots are wrapped about the heap,
And seeth the place of stones.
If he destroy him from his place,
Then it shall deny him, saying, 'I have not seen thee.'
Behold, this is the joy of his way,
And out of the earth shall others grow.
Behold, God will not cast away a perfect man,
Neither will he help the evil doers:
Till he fill thy mouth with laughing,
And thy lips with rejoicing.
They that hate thee shall be clothed with shame;
And the dwelling place of the wicked shall come to nought."

*Job's resignation* Then Job answered and said,

"I know it is so of a truth:
But how should man be just with God?
If he will contend with him,
He cannot answer him one of a thousand.
He is wise in heart, and mighty in strength:
Who hath hardened himself against him, and hath prospered?
Which removeth the mountains, and they know not:
Which overturneth them in his anger.
Which shaketh the earth out of her place,
And the pillars thereof tremble.
Which commandeth the sun, and it riseth not;
And sealeth up the stars.
Which alone spreadeth out the heavens,
And treadeth upon the waves of the sea.
Which maketh Arcturus, Orion, and Pleiades,
And the chambers of the south.
Which doeth great things past finding out;

## JOB

Yea, and wonders without number.
Lo, he goeth by me, and I see him not:
He passeth on also, but I perceive him not.
Behold, he taketh away, who can hinder him?
Who will say unto him, What doest thou?
If God will not withdraw his anger,
The proud helpers do stoop under him.
How much less shall I answer him,
And choose out my words to reason with him?
For he breaketh me with a tempest,
And multiplieth my wounds without cause.
He will not suffer me to take my breath,
But filleth me with bitterness.
He destroyeth the perfect and the wicked.
If I be wicked,
Why then labour I in vain?
If I wash myself with snow water,
And make my hands never so clean;
Yet shalt thou plunge me in the ditch,
And mine own clothes shall abhor me.
For he is not a man, as I am, that I should answer him,
And we should come together in judgment.
Let him take his rod away from me,
And let not his fear terrify me:
Then would I speak, and not fear him;
But it is not so with me.
I will say unto God, 'Do not condemn me;
Shew me wherefore thou contendest with me.
Is it good unto thee that thou shouldest oppress,
That thou shouldest despise the work of thine hands,
And shine upon the counsel of the wicked?
Thou knowest that I am not wicked;
And there is none that can deliver out of thine hand.
Thou hast granted me life and favour,
And thy visitation hath preserved my spirit.
Are not my days few? cease then,

[ 279 ]

*Job prays for respite*

And let me alone, that I may take comfort a little,
Before I go whence I shall not return,
Even to the land of darkness and the shadow of death;
A land of darkness, as darkness itself;
And of the shadow of death, without any order,
And where the light is as darkness.' "

*Zophar answers in reproof*

Then answered Zophar the Naamathite, and said,

"Should not the multitude of words be answered?
And should a man full of talk be justified?
For thou hast said, 'My doctrine is pure,
And I am clean in thine eyes.'
But oh that God would speak,
And open his lips against thee;
And that he would shew thee the secrets of wisdom,
That they are double to that which is!
Know therefore that God exacteth of thee less than thine iniquity deserveth.
Canst thou by searching find out God?
Canst thou find out the Almighty unto perfection?
It is as high as heaven; what canst thou do?
Deeper than hell; what canst thou know?
The measure thereof is longer than the earth,
And broader than the sea.
If he cut off, and shut up,
Or gather together, then who can hinder him?
For he knoweth vain men:
He seeth wickedness also; will he not then consider it?
If thou prepare thine heart,
And stretch out thine hands toward him;
If iniquity be in thine hand, put it far away,
And let not wickedness dwell in thy tabernacles.
For then shalt thou lift up thy face without spot;
Yea, thou shalt be stedfast, and shalt not fear:
Because thou shalt forget thy misery,
And remember it as waters that pass away:

# JOB

And thine age shall be clearer than the noonday;
Thou shalt shine forth, thou shalt be as the morning.
And thou shalt be secure, because there is hope;
Yea, thou shalt dig about thee,
And thou shalt take thy rest in safety.
Also thou shalt lie down, and none shall make thee afraid;
Yea, many shall make suit unto thee."

And Job answered and said,

"No doubt but ye are the people,
And wisdom shall die with you.
But I have understanding as well as you.
What ye know, the same do I know also:
I am not inferior unto you.
Surely I would speak to the Almighty,
And I desire to reason with God.
But ye are forgers of lies,
Ye are all physicians of no value.
Oh that ye would altogether hold your peace!
And it should be your wisdom.
Shall not his excellency make you afraid?
And his dread fall upon you?
Your remembrances are like unto ashes,
Your bodies to bodies of clay.
Hold your peace, let me alone, that I may speak,
And let come on me what will.
Though he slay me, yet will I trust in him:
But I will maintain mine own ways before him.
He also shall be my salvation:
For an hypocrite shall not come before him.
Hear diligently my speech,
And my declaration with your ears.
Behold now, I have ordered my cause;
I know that I shall be justified.
Withdraw thine hand far from me:
And let not thy dread make me afraid.

Then call thou, and I will answer:
Or let me speak, and answer thou me.
How many are mine iniquities and sins?
Make me to know my transgression and my sin.
Wherefore hidest thou thy face,
And holdest me for thine enemy?
Wilt thou break a leaf driven to and fro?
And wilt thou pursue the dry stubble?
For thou writest bitter things against me,
And makest me to possess the iniquities of my youth.
Thou puttest my feet also in the stocks,
And lookest narrowly unto all my paths;
Thou settest a print upon the heels of my feet.
Man that is born of a woman
Is of few days, and full of trouble.
He cometh forth like a flower, and is cut down:
He fleeth also as a shadow, and continueth not.
And dost thou open thine eyes upon such an one,
And bringest me into judgment with thee?
Who can bring a clean thing out of an unclean? Not one.
Turn from him, that he may rest,
Till he shall accomplish, as an hireling, his day.
For there is hope of a tree,
If it be cut down, that it will sprout again,
And that the tender branch thereof will not cease.
Though the root thereof wax old in the earth,
And the stock thereof die in the ground;
Yet through the scent of water it will bud,
And bring forth boughs like a plant.
If a man die, shall he live again?
All the days of my appointed time will I wait,
Till my change come.
Thou shalt call, and I will answer thee:
Thou wilt have a desire to the work of thine hands.
And surely the mountain falling cometh to nought,
And the rock is removed out of his place.

The waters wear the stones:

Thou washest away the things which grow out of the dust of the earth;

And thou destroyest the hope of man.

Thou prevailest for ever against him, and he passeth:

Thou changest his countenance, and sendest him away."

Then answered Eliphaz the Temanite, and said,

"Thine own mouth condemneth thee, and not I:

Yea, thine own lips testify against thee.

Art thou the first man that was born?

Or wast thou made before the hills?

Hast thou heard the secret of God?

And dost thou restrain wisdom to thyself?

What knowest thou, that we know not?

What understandest thou, which is not in us?

With us are both the grayheaded and very aged men,

Much elder than thy father.

Are the consolations of God small with thee?

Is there any secret thing with thee?

Why doth thine heart carry thee away?

And what do thy eyes wink at,

That thou turnest thy spirit against God,

And lettest such words go out of thy mouth?

I will shew thee, hear me;

And that which I have seen I will declare;

Which wise men have told

From their fathers, and have not hid it:

The wicked man travaileth with pain all his days.

For he stretcheth out his hand against God,

And strengtheneth himself against the Almighty."

Then Job answered and said,

"Shall vain words have an end?

I also could speak as ye do:

If your soul were in my soul's stead,

I could heap up words against you, and shake mine head at you.

But I would strengthen you with my mouth,
And the moving of my lips should asswage your grief.
God hath delivered me to the ungodly,
And turned me over into the hands of the wicked.
I was at ease, but he hath broken me asunder:
He hath also taken me by my neck,
And shaken me to pieces, and set me up for his mark.
His archers compass me round about.
My face is foul with weeping,
And on my eyelids is the shadow of death;
Not for any injustice in mine hands:
Also my prayer is pure.
O earth, cover not thou my blood,
And let my cry have no place.
Also now, behold, my witness is in heaven,
And my record is on high.
My friends scorn me:
But mine eye poureth out tears unto God.
Oh that one might plead for a man with God,
As a man pleadeth for his neighbour!
When a few years are come,
Then I shall go the way whence I shall not return.
My days are past, my purposes are broken off,
Even the thoughts of my heart.
And where is now my hope?"

Then answered Bildad the Shuhite, and said,

"How long will it be ere ye make an end of words?
Mark, and afterwards we will speak.
Wherefore are we counted as beasts,
And reputed vile in your sight?
He teareth himself in his anger:
Shall the earth be forsaken for thee?
And shall the rock be removed out of his place?
Yea, the light of the wicked shall be put out,
And the spark of his fire shall not shine.

The light shall be dark in his tabernacle,
And his candle shall be put out with him.
The steps of his strength shall be straitened,
And his own counsel shall cast him down.
For he is cast into a net by his own feet,
And he walketh upon a snare.
Terrors shall make him afraid on every side,
And destruction shall be ready at his side.
His remembrance shall perish from the earth,
And he shall have no name in the street.
Surely such are the dwellings of the wicked,
And this is the place of him that knoweth not God."

*Bildad pictures the lot
of the wicked*

Then Job answered and said,

*Job's attempt at
self justification*

"How long will ye vex my soul,
And break me in pieces with words?
And be it indeed that I have erred,
Mine error remaineth with myself.
If indeed ye will magnify yourselves against me,
And plead against me my reproach:
Know now that God hath overthrown me,
And hath compassed me with his net.
Behold, I cry out of wrong, but I am not heard:
I cry aloud, but there is no judgment.
He hath fenced up my way that I cannot pass,
And he hath set darkness in my paths.
He hath stripped me of my glory,
And taken the crown from my head.
He hath destroyed me on every side, and I am gone:
And mine hope hath he removed like a tree.
He hath also kindled his wrath against me,
And he counteth me unto him as one of his enemies.
His troops come together,
And raise up their way against me,
And encamp round about my tabernacle.
He hath put my brethren far from me,

*Job asks the pity of his friends*

And mine acquaintance are verily estranged from me.
My kinsfolk have failed,
And my familiar friends have forgotten me.
They that dwell in mine house, and my maids, count me for a stranger:
I am an alien in their sight.
I called my servant, and he gave me no answer.
My breath is strange to my wife.
Yea, young children despised me.
All my inward friends abhorred me;
And they whom I loved are turned against me.
My bone cleaveth to my skin and to my flesh,
And I am escaped with the skin of my teeth.
Have pity upon me, have pity upon me, O ye my friends;
For the hand of God hath touched me.
Why do ye persecute me as God,
And are not satisfied with my flesh?
Oh that my words were now written!
Oh that they were printed in a book!
That they were graven with an iron pen
And lead in the rock for ever!
For I know that my redeemer liveth,
And that he shall stand at the latter day upon the earth:
Yet in my flesh shall I see God:
Whom I shall see for myself,
And mine eyes shall behold, and not another."

*Zophar argues that the triumph of the wicked is short*

Then answered Zophar the Naamathite, and said,

"Knowest thou not this of old,
Since man was placed upon earth,
That the triumphing of the wicked is short,
And the joy of the hypocrite but for a moment?
Though his excellency mount up to the heavens,
And his head reach unto the clouds;
Yet he shall perish for ever:
They which have seen him shall say, 'Where is he?'
He shall fly away as a dream, and shall not be found:

Yea, he shall be chased away as a vision of the night.

Because he hath oppressed and hath forsaken the poor;
Because he hath violently taken away an house which he builded not;
He shall not save of that which he desired.
The heaven shall reveal his iniquity;
And the earth shall rise up against him.
The increase of his house shall depart,
And his goods shall flow away in the day of his wrath.
This is the portion of a wicked man from God,
And the heritage appointed unto him by God."

But Job answered and said,

"Hear diligently my speech,
And let this be your consolations.
Suffer me that I may speak;
And after that I have spoken, mock on.
As for me, is my complaint to man?
And if it were so, why should not my spirit be troubled?
Mark me, and be astonished,
And lay your hand upon your mouth.
Even when I remember I am afraid,
And trembling taketh hold on my flesh.
Wherefore do the wicked live,
Become old, yea, are mighty in power?
Their seed is established in their sight with them,
And their offspring before their eyes.
Their houses are safe from fear,
Neither is the rod of God upon them.
They send forth their little ones like a flock,
And their children dance.
They take the timbrel and harp,
And rejoice at the sound of the organ.
They spend their days in wealth,
And in a moment go down to the grave.
Therefore they say unto God, 'Depart from us;
For we desire not the knowledge of thy ways.

What is the Almighty, that we should serve him?
And what profit should we have, if we pray unto him?"
How oft is the candle of the wicked put out!
And how oft cometh their destruction upon them!
God distributeth sorrows in his anger.
They are as stubble before the wind,
And as chaff that the storm carrieth away.
God layeth up his iniquity for his children:
He rewardeth him, and he shall know it.
His eyes shall see his destruction,
And he shall drink of the wrath of the Almighty.
For what pleasure hath he in his house after him,
When the number of his months is cut off in the midst?
One dieth in his full strength,
Being wholly at ease and quiet.
His breasts are full of milk,
And his bones are moistened with marrow.
And another dieth in the bitterness of his soul,
And never eateth with pleasure.
They shall lie down alike in the dust.
How then comfort ye me in vain,
Seeing in your answers there remaineth falsehood?"

Then Eliphaz the Temanite answered and said,

"Can a man be profitable unto God,
As he that is wise may be profitable unto himself?
Is it any pleasure to the Almighty, that thou art righteous?
Or is it gain to him, that thou makest thy ways perfect?
Will he reprove thee for fear of thee?
Will he enter with thee into judgment?
Is not thy wickedness great?
And thine iniquities infinite?
For thou hast taken a pledge from thy brother for nought,
And stripped the naked of their clothing.
Thou hast not given water to the weary to drink,
And thou hast withholden bread from the hungry.

Thou hast sent widows away empty,
And the arms of the fatherless have been broken.
Therefore snares are round about thee,
And sudden fear troubleth thee;
Or darkness, that thou canst not see;
And abundance of waters cover thee.
Is not God in the height of heaven?
And behold the height of the stars, how high they are!
And thou sayest, 'How doth God know?
Can he judge through the dark cloud?
Thick clouds are a covering to him, that he seeth not;
And he walketh in the circuit of heaven.'
Hast thou marked the old way
Which wicked men have trodden?
Acquaint now thyself with him, and be at peace:
Thereby good shall come unto thee.
Receive, I pray thee, the law from his mouth,
And lay up his words in thine heart.
If thou return to the Almighty, thou shalt be built up,
Thou shalt put away iniquity far from thy tabernacles.
Then shalt thou lay up gold as dust,
And the gold of Ophir as the stones of the brooks.
Yea, the Almighty shall be thy defence,
And thou shalt have plenty of silver.
For then shalt thou have thy delight in the Almighty,
And shalt lift up thy face unto God.
Thou shalt make thy prayer unto him, and he shall hear thee.
And the light shall shine upon thy ways.
When men are cast down, then thou shalt say, 'There is lifting up';
And he shall save the humble person.
He shall deliver the island of the innocent:
And it is delivered by the pureness of thine hands."

Then Job answered and said,

"Oh that I knew where I might find him!
That I might come even to his seat!

*Eliphaz accuses Job of sin*

I would order my cause before him.
I would know the words which he would answer me,
And understand what he would say unto me.
Will he plead against me with his great power?
No; but he would put strength in me.
Behold, I go forward, but he is not there;
And backward, but I cannot perceive him:
On the left hand, where he doth work, but I cannot behold him:
He hideth himself on the right hand, that I cannot see him:
But he knoweth the way that I take:
When he hath tried me, I shall come forth as gold.
My foot hath held his steps,
His way have I kept, and not declined.
Neither have I gone back from the commandment of his lips;
I have esteemed the words of his mouth more than my necessary food.
But he is in one mind, and who can turn him?
And what his soul desireth, even that he doeth.
Therefore am I troubled at his presence:
When I consider, I am afraid of him.
For God maketh my heart soft,
And the Almighty troubleth me."

Then answered Bildad the Shuhite, and said,

"Dominion and fear are with him,
He maketh peace in his high places.
Is there any number of his armies?
And upon whom doth not his light arise?"

But Job answered and said,

"How hast thou helped him that is without power?
How savest thou the arm that hath no strength?
How hast thou counselled him that hath no wisdom?
And how hast thou plentifully declared the thing as it is?
He stretcheth out the north over the empty place,
And hangeth the earth upon nothing.
He bindeth up the waters in his thick clouds;

And the cloud is not rent under them.

He holdeth back the face of his throne,

And spreadeth his cloud upon it.

He hath compassed the waters with bounds,

Until the day and night come to an end.

The pillars of heaven tremble,

And are astonished at his reproof.

He divideth the sea with his power.

By his spirit he hath garnished the heavens.

Lo, these are parts of his ways;

But how little a portion is heard of him?

But the thunder of his power who can understand?

As God liveth, who hath taken away my judgment;

And the Almighty, who hath vexed my soul;

All the while my breath is in me,

And the spirit of God is in my nostrils;

My lips shall not speak wickedness,

Nor my tongue utter deceit.

God forbid that I should justify you:

Till I die I will not remove mine integrity from me.

My righteousness I hold fast,

And will not let it go:

My heart shall not reproach me so long as I live.

"Oh that I were as in months past,

As in the days when God preserved me;

When his candle shined upon my head,

And when by his light I walked through darkness;

As I was in the days of my youth,

When the secret of God was upon my tabernacle;

When the Almighty was yet with me,

When my children were about me;

When I washed my steps with butter,

And the rock poured me out rivers of oil;

When I went out to the gate through the city,

When I prepared my seat in the street!

*The parts of God's ways*

*Job recalls his God-guided past*

The young men saw me, and hid themselves:
And the aged arose, and stood up.
The princes refrained talking.
The nobles held their peace.

"Unto me men gave ear, and waited,
And kept silence at my counsel.
After my words they spake not again;
And my speech dropped upon them.
And they waited for me as for the rain;
And they opened their mouth wide as for the latter rain.
When the ear heard me, then it blessed me;
And when the eye saw me, it gave witness to me:
Because I delivered the poor that cried,
And the fatherless, and him that had none to help him.
The blessing of him that was ready to perish came upon me:
And I caused the widow's heart to sing for joy.
I put on righteousness, and it clothed me:
My judgment was as a robe and a diadem.
I was eyes to the blind,
And feet was I to the lame.
I was a father to the poor:
And the cause which I knew not I searched out.
Then I said, 'I shall die in my nest,
And I shall multiply my days as the sand.'
My root was spread out by the waters,
And the dew lay all night upon my branch.
My glory was fresh in me, and my bow was renewed in my hand.
And the light of my countenance they cast not down.

"But now they that are younger than I have me in derision.
And now am I their song,
Yea, I am their byword.
They abhor me, they flee far from me,
And spare not to spit in my face.
They mar my path,

[ 292 ]

# JOB

*Job's honour is turned to contempt*

They set forward my calamity.
They came upon me as a wide breaking in of waters:
In the desolation they rolled themselves upon me.
Terrors are turned upon me:
They pursue my soul as the wind:
And my welfare passeth away as a cloud.
And now my soul is poured out upon me;
The days of affliction have taken hold upon me.
I am become like dust and ashes.
I cry unto thee, and thou dost not hear me:
I stand up, and thou regardest me not.
Thou art become cruel to me:
With thy strong hand thou opposest thyself against me.
Thou liftest me up to the wind;
Thou causest me to ride upon it.
When I looked for good, then evil came unto me:
And when I waited for light, there came darkness.
My harp also is turned to mourning,
And my organ into the voice of them that weep.

"I made a covenant with mine eyes;
Why then should I think upon a maid?
Doth not he see my ways,
And count all my steps?
Let me be weighed in an even balance,
That God may know mine integrity.
If my step hath turned out of the way,
And mine heart walked after mine eyes,
And if any blot hath cleaved to mine hands;
Then let me sow, and let another eat.
If mine heart have been deceived by a woman,
Or if I have laid wait at my neighbour's door;
Then let my wife grind unto another.
For this is an heinous crime;
Yea, it is an iniquity to be punished by the judges.
For it is a fire that consumeth to destruction.

*He makes solemn protestation of his integrity*

If I did despise the cause of my manservant or of my maidservant,
When they contended with me;
What then shall I do when God riseth up?
And when he visiteth, what shall I answer him?
Did not he that made me in the womb make him?
If I have withheld the poor from their desire,
Or have caused the eyes of the widow to fail;
Or have eaten my morsel myself alone,
And the fatherless hath not eaten thereof;
If I have seen any perish for want of clothing,
Or any poor without covering;
If he were not warmed with the fleece of my sheep;
If I have lifted up my hand against the fatherless,
When I saw my help in the gate:
Then let mine arm fall from my shoulder blade,
And mine arm be broken from the bone.
If I have made gold my hope,
Or have said to the fine gold, 'Thou art my confidence';
If I rejoiced because my wealth was great,
And because mine hand had gotten much;
If I rejoiced at the destruction of him that hated me,
Or lifted up myself when evil found him:
This also were an iniquity to be punished by the judge:
For I should have denied the God that is above.
If my land cry against me,
Or that the furrows likewise thereof complain;
If I have eaten the fruits thereof without money,
Or have caused the owners thereof to lose their life:
Let thistles grow instead of wheat,
And cockle instead of barley.

"Oh that one would hear me!
Behold, my desire is, that the Almighty would answer me,
And that mine adversary had written a book.
Surely I would take it upon my shoulder,
And bind it as a crown to me.

[ 294 ]

Canst thou bind the sweet influences of Pleiades or loose the bands of Orion

14

Let there Be

Light

And God made Two Great Lights

Sun

Moon

Let there be A

Firmament

Let the Waters bring forth abundantly

Let the Waters be gathered together into one place

Let the Earth bring forth

& let the Dry Land appear

Cattle & Creeping thing & Beast

When the morning Stars sang together, & all the
Sons of God shouted for joy

W Blake Inven.it & Sc

London, Published as the Act directs March 8. 1825 by Will. Blake N 3 Fountain Court Strand

I would declare unto him the number of my steps;
As a prince would I go near unto him."

Then the LORD answered out of the whirlwind, and said,

"Who is this that darkeneth counsel
By words without knowledge?
Gird up now thy loins like a man;
For I will demand of thee, and answer thou me.
Where wast thou when I laid the foundations of the earth?
Declare, if thou hast understanding.
Who hath laid the measures thereof, if thou knowest?
Or who hath stretched the line upon it?
Whereupon are the foundations thereof fastened?
Or who laid the corner stone thereof;
When the morning stars sang together,
And all the sons of God shouted for joy?
Or who shut up the sea with doors,
When it brake forth, as if it had issued out of the womb?
When I made the cloud the garment thereof,
And thick darkness a swaddlingband for it,
And brake up for it my decreed place,
And set bars and doors,
And said, 'Hitherto shalt thou come, but no further:
And here shall thy proud waves be stayed'?
Hast thou commanded the morning since thy days;
And caused the dayspring to know his place;
Hast thou entered into the springs of the sea?
Or hast thou walked in the search of the depth?
Have the gates of death been opened unto thee?
Or hast thou seen the doors of the shadow of death?
Hast thou perceived the breadth of the earth?
Declare if thou knowest it all.
Where is the way where light dwelleth?
And as for darkness, where is the place thereof,
That thou shouldest take it to the bound thereof,
And that thou shouldest know the paths to the house thereof?

*God impresses his
knowledge and
omnipotence upon Job*

Knowest thou it, because thou wast then born?
Or because the number of thy days is great?
Hast thou entered into the treasures of the snow?
Or hast thou seen the treasures of the hail,
Which I have reserved against the time of trouble,
Against the day of battle and war?
By what way is the light parted,
Which scattereth the east wind upon the earth?
Who hath divided a watercourse for the overflowing of waters,
Or a way for the lightning of thunder;
To cause it to rain on the earth, where no man is;
On the wilderness, wherein there is no man;
To satisfy the desolate and waste ground;
And to cause the bud of the tender herb to spring forth?
Hath the rain a father?
Or who hath begotten the drops of dew?
Out of whose womb came the ice?
And the hoary frost of heaven, who hath gendered it?
The waters are hid as with a stone,
And the face of the deep is frozen.
Canst thou bind the sweet influences of Pleiades,
Or loose the bands of Orion?
Canst thou bring forth Mazzaroth in his season?
Or canst thou guide Arcturus with his sons?
Knowest thou the ordinances of heaven?
Canst thou set the dominion thereof in the earth?
Canst thou lift up thy voice to the clouds,
That abundance of waters may cover thee?
Canst thou send lightnings, that they may go,
And say unto thee, 'Here we are'?
Who hath put wisdom in the inward parts?
Or who hath given understanding to the heart?
Who can number the clouds in wisdom?
Or who can stay the bottles of heaven,
When the dust groweth into hardness,
And the clods cleave fast together?

## JOB

"Wilt thou hunt the prey for the lion?
  Or fill the appetite of the young lions,
  When they couch in their dens,
  And abide in the covert to lie in wait?
  Who provideth for the raven his food?
  When his young ones cry unto God, they wander for lack of meat.
  Knowest thou the time when the wild goats of the rock bring forth?
  Or canst thou mark when the hinds do calve?
  Canst thou number the months that they fulfil?
  Or knowest thou the time when they bring forth?
  They bow themselves, they bring forth their young ones,
  They cast out their sorrows.
  Their young ones are in good liking, they grow up with corn;
  They go forth, and return not unto them.
  Who hath sent out the wild ass free?
  Or who hath loosed the bands of the wild ass?
  Whose house I have made the wilderness,
  And the barren land his dwellings.
  He scorneth the multitude of the city,
  Neither regardeth he the crying of the driver.
  The range of the mountains is his pasture,
  And he searcheth after every green thing.

  Canst thou bind the unicorn with his band in the furrow?
  Hast thou given the horse strength?
  Hast thou clothed his neck with thunder?
  Canst thou make him afraid as a grasshopper?
  The glory of his nostrils is terrible.
  He paweth in the valley, and rejoiceth in his strength:
  He goeth on to meet the armed men.
  He mocketh at fear, and is not affrighted;
  Neither turneth he back from the sword.
  The quiver rattleth against him,
  The glittering spear and the shield.
  He swalloweth the ground with fierceness and rage:
  Neither believeth he that it is the sound of the trumpet.
  He saith among the trumpets, 'Ha, ha';

[ 297 ]

*God ends the account
of his magnificence*

And he smelleth the battle afar off,
The thunder of the captains, and the shouting.
Doth the hawk fly by thy wisdom,
And stretch her wings toward the south?
Doth the eagle mount up at thy command,
And make her nest on high?
She dwelleth and abideth on the rock,
Upon the crag of the rock, and the strong place.
From thence she seeketh the prey,
And her eyes behold afar off."

Moreover the Lord answered Job, and said,

"Shall he that contendeth with the Almighty instruct him?
He that reproveth God, let him answer it."

*Job humbles himself
before God*

Then Job answered the Lord, and said,

"Behold, I am vile; what shall I answer thee?
I will lay mine hand upon my mouth.
Once have I spoken; but I will not answer:
Yea, twice; but I will proceed no further."

*God lifts up Job*

Then answered the Lord unto Job out of the whirlwind, and said,

"Gird up thy loins now like a man:
I will demand of thee, and declare thou unto me.
Wilt thou also disannul my judgment?
Wilt thou condemn me, that thou mayest be righteous?
Hast thou an arm like God?
Or canst thou thunder with a voice like him?
Deck thyself now with majesty and excellency;
And array thyself with glory and beauty.
Cast abroad the rage of thy wrath:
And behold every one that is proud, and abase him.
Look on every one that is proud, and bring him low;
And tread down the wicked in their place.
Hide them in the dust together.

[ 298 ]

*JOB CONFESSING HIS PRESUMPTION TO GOD*

Then will I also confess unto thee
That thine own right hand can save thee."

Then Job answered the LORD, and said,

"I know that thou canst do every thing,
And that no thought can be withholden from thee.
Who is he that hideth counsel without knowledge?
Therefore have I uttered that I understood not;
Things too wonderful for me, which I knew not.
Hear, I beseech thee, and I will speak:
I will demand of thee, and declare thou unto me.
I have heard of thee by the hearing of the ear:
But now mine eye seeth thee.
Wherefore I abhor myself, and repent in dust and ashes."

And it was so, that after the LORD had spoken these words unto Job, *The Lord reproves* the LORD said to Eliphaz the Temanite, "My wrath is kindled against thee, *Job's friends* and against thy two friends: for ye have not spoken of me the thing that is right, as my servant Job hath. Therefore take unto you now seven bullocks and seven rams, and go to my servant Job, and offer up for yourselves a burnt offering; and my servant Job shall pray for you: for him will I accept: lest I deal with you after your folly, in that ye have not spoken of me the thing which is right, like my servant Job."

So Eliphaz the Temanite and Bildad the Shuhite and Zophar the Naamathite went, and did according as the LORD commanded them: the LORD also accepted Job. And the LORD turned the captivity of Job, when he prayed for his friends.

The LORD gave Job twice as much as he had before. Then came there *Job's blessings returned* unto him all his brethren, and all his sisters, and all they that had been of his acquaintance before, and did eat bread with him in his house: and they bemoaned him and comforted him over all the evil that the Lord had brought upon him: every man also gave him a piece of money, and every one an earring of gold.

So the LORD blessed the latter end of Job more than the beginning: for he had fourteen thousand sheep, and six thousand camels, and a thousand yoke of oxen, and a thousand she asses. He had also seven sons and

*Job's death*  three daughters. And he called the name of the first, Jemima; and the name of the second, Kezia; and the name of the third, Kerenhappuch. And in all the land were no women found so fair as the daughters of Job: and their father gave them inheritance among their brethren.

After this lived Job an hundred and forty years, and saw his sons, and his sons' sons, even four generations. So Job died, being old and full of days.

## Interpolations in the Book of Job

*Elihu remarks on the inscrutability of God's ways*  And Elihu the son of Barachel the Buzite answered and said,

"I am young, and ye are very old;
Wherefore I was afraid, and durst not shew you mine opinion.
I said, 'Days should speak,
And multitude of years should teach wisdom.'
But there is a spirit in man:
And the inspiration of the Almighty giveth them understanding.
Great men are not always wise:
Neither do the aged understand judgment.
Therefore I said, 'Hearken to me;
I also will shew mine opinion.'

"The spirit of God hath made me,
And the breath of the Almighty hath given me life.
But none saith, 'Where is God my maker,
Who giveth songs in the night;
Who teacheth us more than the beasts of the earth,
And maketh us wiser than the fowls of heaven?'
I will fetch my knowledge from afar,
And will ascribe righteousness to my Maker.
Behold, God is mighty, and despiseth not any:
He is mighty in strength and wisdom.
Behold, God is great, and we know him not,
Neither can the number of his years be searched out.
For he maketh small the drops of water:

They pour down rain according to the vapour thereof:
Which the clouds do drop
And distil upon man abundantly.
Also can any understand the spreadings of the clouds,
Or the noise of his tabernacle?
With clouds he covereth the light;
And commandeth it not to shine by the cloud that cometh betwixt.
The noise thereof sheweth concerning it,
The cattle also concerning the vapour."

"At this also my heart trembleth,
And is moved out of his place.
Hear attentively the noise of his voice,
And the sound that goeth out of his mouth.
He directeth it under the whole heaven,
And his lightning unto the ends of the earth.
After it a voice roareth:
He thundereth with the voice of his excellency;
And he will not stay them when his voice is heard.
God thundereth marvellously with his voice;
Great things doeth he, which we cannot comprehend.
For he saith to the snow, 'Be thou on the earth';
Likewise to the small rain,
And to the great rain of his strength.
He sealeth up the hand of every man;
That all men may know his work.
Then the beasts go into dens,
And remain in their places.
Out of the south cometh the whirlwind:
And cold out of the north.
By the breath of God frost is given:
And the breadth of the waters is straitened.
Also by watering he wearieth the thick cloud:
He scattereth his bright cloud:
And it is turned round about by his counsels:
That they may do whatsoever he commandeth them

*God is to be feared
because of his great
works*

[ 301 ]

*His wisdom is*
*unsearchable in them*

Upon the face of the world in the earth.
He causeth it to come, whether for correction,
Or for his land, or for mercy.
Hearken unto this, O Job:
Stand still, and consider the wondrous works of God.
Dost thou know when God disposed them,
And caused the light of his cloud to shine?
Dost thou know the balancings of the clouds,
The wondrous works of him which is perfect in knowledge?
How thy garments are warm,
When he quieteth the earth by the south wind?
Hast thou with him spread out the sky,
Which is strong, and as a molten looking glass?
Teach us what we shall say unto him;
For we cannot order our speech by reason of darkness.
Shall it be told him that I speak?
If a man speak, surely he shall be swallowed up.
And now men see not the bright light which is in the clouds:
But the wind passeth, and cleanseth them.
Fair weather cometh out of the north:
With God is terrible majesty.
Touching the Almighty, we cannot find him out:
He is excellent in power, and in judgment, and in plenty of justice:
He will not afflict.
Men do therefore fear him:
He respecteth not any that are wise of heart."

Then answered the Lord unto Job, and said,

"Behold now behemoth, which I made with thee;
He eateth grass as an ox.
Lo now, his strength is in his loins,
And his force is in the navel of his belly.
He moveth his tail like a cedar:
The sinews of his stones are wrapped together.
His bones are as strong pieces of brass;
His bones are like bars of iron.

# 15

Can any understand the spreadings of the Clouds
the noise of his Tabernacle

Also by watering he wearieth the thick cloud
He scattereth the bright cloud also it is turned about by his counsels

Of Behemoth he saith. He is the chief of the ways of God
Of Leviathan he saith. He is King over all the Children of Pride

Behold now Behemoth which I made with thee

W Blake inuenit & sculpt.

London Published as the Act directs March 8. 1825 by Will Blake N³ Fountain Court Strand

Proof

He is the chief of the ways of God:
He that made him can make
His sword to approach unto him.
Surely the mountains bring him forth food,
Where all the beasts of the field play.
He lieth under the shady trees,
In the covert of the reed, and fens.
The shady trees cover him with their shadow;
The willows of the brook compass him about.
Behold, he drinketh up a river, and hasteth not:
He trusteth that he can draw up Jordan into his mouth.

"Canst thou draw out leviathan with an hook?
Or his tongue with a cord which thou lettest down?
Canst thou put an hook into his nose?
Or bore his jaw through with a thorn?
Will he make many supplications unto thee?
Will he speak soft words unto thee?
Will he make a covenant with thee?
Wilt thou take him for a servant for ever?
Wilt thou play with him as with a bird?
Or wilt thou bind him for thy maidens?
Shall the companions make a banquet of him?
Shall they part him among the merchants?
Canst thou fill his skin with barbed irons?
Or his head with fish spears?
Lay thine hand upon him,
Remember the battle, do no more.
Who can discover the face of his garment?
Or who can come to him with his double bridle?
Who can open the doors of his face?
His teeth are terrible round about.
His scales are his pride,
Shut up together as with a close seal.
One is so near to another,
That no air can come between them.

*Of behemoth and leviathan*

*Of leviathan*

They are joined one to another,
They stick together, that they cannot be sundered.
By his neesings a light doth shine,
And his eyes are like the eyelids of the morning.
Out of his mouth go burning lamps,
And sparks of fire leap out.
Out of his nostrils goeth smoke,
As out of a seething pot or caldron.
His breath kindleth coals,
And a flame goeth out of his mouth.
In his neck remaineth strength,
And sorrow is turned into joy before him.
The flakes of his flesh are joined together:
They are firm in themselves; they cannot be moved.
His heart is as firm as a stone;
Yea, as hard as a piece of the nether millstone.
When he raiseth up himself, the mighty are afraid:
By reason of breakings they purify themselves.
The sword of him that layeth at him cannot hold:
The spear, the dart, nor the habergeon.
He esteemeth iron as straw,
And brass as rotten wood.
The arrow cannot make him flee:
Slingstones are turned with him into stubble.
Darts are counted as stubble:
He laugheth at the shaking of a spear.
Sharp stones are under him:
He spreadeth sharp pointed things upon the mire.
He maketh the deep to boil like a pot:
He maketh the sea like a pot of ointment.
He maketh a path to shine after him;
One would think the deep to be hoary.
Upon earth there is not his like,
Who is made without fear.
He beholdeth all high things:
He is a king over all the children of pride."

## *Where shall Wisdom be found?*

S URELY there is a vein for the silver,
  And a place for gold where they fine it.
Iron is taken out of the earth,
And brass is molten out of the stone.
He setteth an end to darkness,
And searcheth out all perfection:
The stones of darkness, and the shadow of death.
The flood breaketh out from the inhabitant;
Even the waters forgotten of the foot:
They are dried up, they are gone away from men.
As for the earth, out of it cometh bread:
And under it is turned up as it were fire.
The stones of it are the place of sapphires:
And it hath dust of gold.
There is a path which no fowl knoweth,
And which the vulture's eye hath not seen:
The lion's whelps have not trodden it,
Nor the fierce lion passed by it.
He putteth forth his hand upon the rock;
He overturneth the mountains by the roots.
He cutteth out rivers among the rocks;
And his eye seeth every precious thing.
He bindeth the floods from overflowing;
And the thing that is hid bringeth he forth to light.
But where shall wisdom be found?
And where is the place of understanding?
Man knoweth not the price thereof;
Neither is it found in the land of the living.
The depth saith, It is not in me:
And the sea saith, It is not with me.
It cannot be gotten for gold,
Neither shall silver be weighed for the price thereof.

*Unlike material things, Wisdom has no earthly location*

[ 305 ]

# WISDOM

It cannot be valued with the gold of Ophir,
With the precious onyx, or the sapphire.
The gold and the crystal cannot equal it:
And the exchange of it shall not be for jewels of fine gold.
No mention shall be made of coral, or of pearls:
For the price of wisdom is above rubies.
The topaz of Ethiopia shall not equal it,
Neither shall it be valued with pure gold.
Whence then cometh wisdom?
And where is the place of understanding?
Seeing it is hid from the eyes of all living,
And kept close from the fowls of the air.
Destruction and death say,
We have heard the fame thereof with our ears.
God understandeth the way thereof,
And he knoweth the place thereof.
For he looketh to the ends of the earth,
And seeth under the whole heaven;
To make the weight for the winds;
And he weigheth the waters by measure.
When he made a decree for the rain,
And a way for the lightning of the thunder:
Then did he see it, and declare it;
He prepared it, yea, and searched it out.
And unto man he said, Behold, the fear of the Lord, that is wisdom;
And to depart from evil is understanding.

All wisdom cometh from the Lord,
And is with him for ever.
Who can number the sand of the sea,
And the drops of rain, and the days of eternity?
Who can find out the height of heaven,
And the breadth of the earth, and the deep, and wisdom?

Wisdom hath been created before all things,
And the understanding of prudence from everlasting.

## WISDOM

The word of God most high is the fountain of wisdom;
And her ways are everlasting commandments.
To whom hath the root of wisdom been revealed?
Or who hath known her wise counsels?

The fear of the Lord maketh a merry heart,
And giveth joy, and gladness, and a long life.
The fear of the Lord is a crown of wisdom,
Making peace and perfect health to flourish.
Wisdom raineth down skill and knowledge of understanding,
And exalteth them to honour that hold her fast.
The root of wisdom is to fear the Lord,
And the branches thereof are long life.
The fear of the Lord driveth away sins.

Wisdom shall praise herself,
And shall glory in the midst of her people.
In the congregation of the most High shall she open her mouth,
And triumph before his power.
I came out of the mouth of the most High,
And covered the earth as a cloud.
I dwelt in high places,
And my throne is in a cloudy pillar.
I alone compassed the circuit of heaven,
And walked in the bottom of the deep.
In the waves of the sea, and in all the earth,
And in every people and nation, I got a possession.
With all these I sought rest:
And in whose inheritance shall I abide?

So the Creator of all things gave me a commandment,
And he that made me caused my tabernacle to rest,
And said, Let thy dwelling be in Jacob,
And thine inheritance in Israel.
He created me from the beginning before the world,
And I shall never fail.

*Wisdom brings skill and
gives understanding*

[ 307 ]

# WISDOM

*Praise of wisdom*   In the holy tabernacle I served before him;
And so was I established in Sion.
Likewise in the beloved city he gave me rest,
And in Jerusalem was my power.
And I took root in an honourable people,
Even in the portion of the Lord's inheritance.
I was exalted like a cedar in Libanus,
And as a cypress tree upon the mountains of Hermon.
I was exalted like a palm tree in Engaddi,
And as a rose plant in Jericho,
As a fair olive tree in a pleasant field,
And grew up as a plane tree by the water.

I gave a sweet smell like cinnamon and aspalathus,
And I yielded a pleasant odour like the best myrrh,
As galbanum, and onyx, and sweet storax,
And as the fume of frankincense in the tabernacle.
As the turpentine tree I stretched out my branches,
And my branches are the branches of honour and grace.
As the vine brought I forth pleasant savour,
And my flowers are the fruit of honour and riches.

I am the mother of fair love, and fear, and knowledge, and holy hope;
I therefore, being eternal, am given to all my children which are named
    of him.
Come unto me, all ye that be desirous of me,
And fill yourselves with my fruits.
For my memorial is sweeter than honey,
And mine inheritance than the honeycomb.
They that eat me shall yet be hungry,
And they that drink me shall yet be thirsty.
He that obeyeth me shall never be confounded,
And they that work by me shall not do amiss.

The first man knew her not perfectly:
No more shall the last find her out.
For her thoughts are more than the sea,

## WISDOM

And her counsels profounder than the great deep.　　　　　　　*Wisdom available to*
I also came out as a brook from a river,　　　　　　　　　　　　*all that seek*
And as a conduit into a garden.
I said, I will water my best garden, and will water abundantly my
　　　garden bed:
And, lo, my brook became a river, and my river became a sea.
I will yet make doctrine to shine as the morning,
And will send forth her light afar off.
I will yet pour out doctrine as prophecy,
And leave it to all ages for ever.
Behold that I have not laboured for myself only,
But for all them that seek wisdom.

In three things I was beautified,
And stood up beautiful both before God and men:
The unity of brethren, the love of neighbours,
A man and a wife that agree together.

My son, gather instruction from thy youth up:　　　　　　　　*But it must be sought*
So shalt thou find wisdom till thine old age.　　　　　　　　　*from youth up*
Come unto her as one that ploweth and soweth,
And wait for her good fruits:
For thou shalt not toil much in labouring about her,
But thou shalt eat of her fruits right soon.
For wisdom is according to her name,
And she is not manifest unto many.

Give ear, my son, receive my advice,
And refuse not my counsel,
And put thy feet into her fetters,
And thy neck into her chain.
Bow down thy shoulder, and bear her,
And be not grieved with her bonds.
Come unto her with thy whole heart,
And keep her ways with all thy power.
Search, and seek, and she shall be made known unto thee:

[ 309 ]

## *WISDOM*

*Men are happy who draw near to wisdom*

And when thou hast got hold of her, let her not go.

For at the last thou shalt find her rest,
And that shall be turned to thy joy.
Then shall her fetters be a strong defence for thee,
And her chains a robe of glory.
For there is a golden ornament upon her,
And her bands are purple lace.
Thou shalt put her on as a robe of honour,
And shalt put her about thee as a crown of joy.

Blessed is the man that doth meditate good things in wisdom,
And that reasoneth of holy things by his understanding.
He that considereth her ways in his heart
Shall also have understanding in her secrets.
Go after her as one that traceth,
And lie in wait in her ways.
He that prieth in at her windows
Shall also hearken at her doors.
He that doth lodge near her house
Shall also fasten a pin in her walls.
He shall pitch his tent nigh unto her,
And shall lodge in a lodging where good things are.
He shall set his children under her shelter,
And shall lodge under her branches.
By her he shall be covered from heat,
And in her glory shall he dwell.

My son, if thou wilt, thou shalt be taught:
And if thou wilt apply thy mind, thou shalt be prudent.
If thou love to hear, thou shalt receive understanding:
And if thou bow thine ear, thou shalt be wise.
Stand in the multitude of the elders;
And cleave unto him that is wise.
Be willing to hear every godly discourse;
And let not the parables of understanding escape thee.

[ 310 ]

# WISDOM

And if thou seest a man of understanding, get thee betimes unto him,
And let thy foot wear the steps of his door.
A man of understanding knoweth when he slippeth.
The knowledge of a wise man shall abound like a flood:
And his counsel is like a pure fountain of life.
As timber girt and bound together in a building
Cannot be loosed with shaking:
So the heart that is stablished by advised counsel
Shall fear at no time.
A heart settled upon a thought of understanding
Is as a fair plaistering on the wall of a gallery.

*The wise man's heart stands firm*

Forego not a wise and good woman:
For her grace is above gold.

My son, if thou come to serve the Lord,
Prepare thy soul for temptation.
Set thy heart aright, and constantly endure,
And make not haste in time of trouble.
Cleave unto him, and depart not away,
That thou mayest be increased at thy last end.

Whatsoever is brought upon thee take cheerfully,
And be patient when thou art changed to a low estate.
A patient man will bear for a time,
And afterward joy shall spring up unto him.
For gold is tried in the fire,
And acceptable men in the furnace of adversity.
Believe in him, and he will help thee;
Order thy way aright, and trust in him.
Ye that fear the Lord, wait for his mercy;
And go not aside, lest ye fall.

My son, sow not upon the furrows of unrighteousness,
And thou shalt not reap them sevenfold.
Seek not of the Lord preeminence.

[ 311 ]

Hate not laborious work, neither husbandry, which the Most High
      hath ordained.
Humble thy soul greatly.

My son, hast thou sinned? do so no more,
But ask pardon for thy former sins.
Flee from sin as from the face of a serpent:
For if thou comest too near it, it will bite thee:
The teeth thereof are as the teeth of a lion,
Slaying the souls of men.
He that hateth to be reproved is in the way of sinners:
But he that feareth the Lord will repent from his heart.

Say not thou, It is through the Lord that I fell away:
For thou oughtest not to do the things that he hateth.
Say not thou, He hath caused me to err:
For he hath no need of the sinful man.

The Lord hateth all abomination;
And they that fear God love it not.
He himself made man from the beginning,
And left him in the hand of his counsel;
If thou wilt, to keep the commandments,
And to perform acceptable faithfulness.
He hath set fire and water before thee:
Stretch forth thy hand unto whether thou wilt.

Before man is life and death;
And whether him liketh shall be given him.
For the wisdom of the Lord is great,
And he is mighty in power,
And beholdeth all things:
And his eyes are upon them that fear him,
And he knoweth every work of man.
He hath commanded no man to do wickedly,
Neither hath he given any man licence to sin.

[ 312 ]

## WISDOM

My son, defraud not the poor of his living,
And make not the needy eyes to wait long.
Make not an hungry soul sorrowful;
Neither provoke a man in his distress.
As the wild ass is the lion's prey in the wilderness:
So the rich eat up the poor.
Add not more trouble to an heart that is vexed;
And defer not to give to him that is in need.
Reject not the supplication of the afflicted;
Neither turn away thy face from a poor man.
Let it not grieve thee to bow down thine ear to the poor,
And give him a friendly answer with meekness.

*The poor to be lifted up*

Force not the course of the river,
Strive for the truth unto death,
And the Lord shall fight for thee.
Be not hasty in thy tongue,
And in thy deeds slack and remiss.
Be stedfast in thy understanding;
And let thy word be the same.
Let thy life be sincere.
Be not ignorant of any thing in a great matter or a small.

*Wisdom requires truthful words and a sincere life*

Be in peace with many:
Nevertheless have but one counsellor of a thousand.
If thou wouldest get a friend, prove him first,
And be not hasty to credit him.
For some man is a friend for his own occasion,
And will not abide in the day of thy trouble.
Again, some friend is a companion at the table,
And will not continue in the day of thy affliction.
But in thy prosperity he will be as thyself.
If thou be brought low, he will be against thee,
And will hide himself from thy face.

*The true friend rare*

A faithful friend is a strong defence:

*The faithful friend*
*a treasure*

And he that hath found such an one hath found a treasure.
Nothing doth countervail a faithful friend,
And his excellency is invaluable.
A faithful friend is the medicine of life;
And they that fear the Lord shall find him.
Whoso feareth the Lord shall direct his friendship aright:
For as he is, so shall his neighbour be also.
Change not a friend for any good by no means;
Neither a faithful brother for the gold of Ophir.

*The old friend*
*better than the new*

Forsake not an old friend;
For the new is not comparable to him:
A new friend is as new wine;
When it is old, thou shalt drink it with pleasure.
He that toucheth pitch shall be defiled therewith;
And he that hath fellowship with a proud man shall be like unto him.

*A backbiting tongue*
*destructive*

Curse the whisperer and doubletongued:
For such have destroyed many that were at peace.
A backbiting tongue hath disquieted many,
And driven them from nation to nation:
Strong cities hath it pulled down,
And overthrown the houses of great men.
A backbiting tongue hath cast out virtuous women,
And deprived them of their labours.
Whoso hearkeneth unto it shall never find rest,
And never dwell quietly.

The stroke of the whip maketh marks in the flesh:
But the stroke of the tongue breaketh the bones.
Many have fallen by the edge of the sword:
But not so many as have fallen by the tongue.
Honour and shame is in talk:
And the tongue of man is his fall.
Be not called a whisperer,
And lie not in wait with thy tongue,

# WISDOM

For an evil condemnation is upon the double tongue.                    *Avoid talebearing*

He that can rule his tongue shall live without strife;
And he that hateth babbling shall have less evil.
Rehearse not unto another that which is told unto thee,
And thou shalt fare never the worse.
Whether it be to friend or foe, talk not of other men's lives;
And if thou canst without offence, reveal them not.
If thou hast heard a word, let it die with thee;
And be bold, it will not burst thee.

He that hath small understanding, and feareth God
Is better than one that hath much wisdom, and transgresseth the law
    of the Most High.

Whoso discovereth secrets loseth his credit;                    *Betray not secrets*
And shall never find friend to his mind.
Love thy friend, and be faithful unto him:
But if thou bewrayest his secrets, follow no more after him.
For as a man hath destroyed his enemy;
So hast thou lost the love of thy neighbour.
As one that letteth a bird go out of his hand,
So hast thou let thy neighbour go, and shalt not get him again.
Follow after him no more, for he is too far off;
He is as a roe escaped out of the snare.
As for a wound, it may be bound up;
And after reviling there may be reconcilement:
But he that bewrayeth secrets is without hope.

Forgive thy neighbour the hurt that he hath done unto thee,                    *On forgiveness*
So shall thy sins also be forgiven when thou prayest.
One man beareth hatred against another,
And doth he seek pardon from the Lord?
He sheweth no mercy to a man, which is like himself:
And doth he ask forgiveness of his own sins?
A sinful man disquieteth friends,

*Lying and swearing despicable*

And maketh debate among them that be at peace.

A man's attire, and excessive laughter,
And gait, shew what he is.

A lie is a foul blot in a man,
Yet it is continually in the mouth of the untaught.
The disposition of a liar is dishonourable,
And his shame is ever with him.
Accustom not thy mouth to swearing;
Neither use thyself to the naming of the Holy One.
The talk of him that sweareth much maketh the hair stand upright;
And their brawls make one stop his ears.
Strive not with a man that is full of tongue,
And heap not wood upon his fire.

*Drunkenness also*

Take not pleasure in much good cheer,
Neither be tied to the expence thereof.
A labouring man that is given to drunkenness shall not be rich:
And he that contemneth small things shall fall by little and little.
Wine and women will make men of understanding to fall away.
Better is the life of a poor man in a mean cottage
Than delicate fare in another man's house.

*Health to be preferred above wealth*

Better is the poor, being sound and strong of constitution;
Than a rich man that is afflicted in his body.
Health and good estate of body are above all gold,
And a strong body above infinite wealth.
There is no riches above a sound body,
And no joy above the joy of the heart.

As the clay is in the potter's hand,
To fashion it at his pleasure:
So man is in the hand of him that made him,
To render to them as liketh him best.

# WISDOM

A man that hath travelled knoweth many things;
And he that hath much experience will declare wisdom.
He that hath no experience knoweth little:
But he that hath travelled is full of prudence.
When I travelled, I saw many things;
And I understand more than I can express.

*Wise in experience is
the traveller*

The heart of a man changeth his countenance,
Whether it be for good or evil:
And a merry heart maketh a cheerful countenance.
A cheerful countenance is a token of a heart that is in prosperity.
A man may be known by his look,
And one that hath understanding by his countenance, when thou
    meetest him.
Whether a man be rich or poor, if he have a good heart toward the
    Lord,
He shall at all times rejoice with a cheerful countenance.

*A merry heart makes a
cheerful countenance*

The Lord created man of the earth,
And turned him into it again.
He gave them few days, and a short time,
And power also over the things therein.
He endued them with strength by themselves,
And made them according to his image.
Counsel, and a tongue, and eyes, ears,
And a heart, gave he them to understand.
Withal he filled them with the knowledge of understanding,
And shewed them good and evil.
He set his eye upon their hearts,
That he might shew them the greatness of his works.
He gave them to glory in his marvellous acts for ever,
That they might declare his works with understanding.
Beside this he gave them knowledge,
And the law of life for an heritage.
He made an everlasting covenant with them,
And shewed them his judgments.

*Man created in God's
image*

*Man's life is short*

Their ways are ever before him,
And shall not be hid from his eyes.

When a man hath done, then he beginneth;
And when he leaveth off, then he shall be doubtful.
What is man, and whereto serveth he?
What is his good, and what is evil?
The number of a man's days
At the most are an hundred years.
As a drop of water unto the sea, and a gravelstone in comparison of the
    sand;
So are a thousand years to the days of eternity.
Therefore is God patient with them,
And poureth forth his mercy upon them.
He saw and perceived their end to be evil;
Therefore he multiplied his compassion.
The mercy of man is toward his neighbour;
But the mercy of the Lord is upon all flesh:
He reproveth, and nurtureth, and teacheth,
And bringeth again, as a shepherd his flock.
He hath mercy on them that receive discipline,
And that diligently seek after his judgments.

*The beauty of ripe age*

If thou hast gathered nothing in thy youth,
How canst thou find any thing in thine age?
O how comely a thing is judgment for gray hairs,
And for ancient men to know counsel!
O how comely is the wisdom of old men,
And understanding and counsel to men of honour!
As the clear light is upon the holy candlestick;
So is the beauty of the face in ripe age.
Much experience is the crown of old men,
And the fear of God is their glory.
But the love of the Lord passeth all things for illumination:
He that holdeth it, whereto shall he be likened?
The fear of the Lord is the beginning of his love:

And faith is the beginning of cleaving unto him.

*A loving wife the gift of God*

Well is him that dwelleth with a wife of understanding,
And that hath not slipped with his tongue,
And that hath not served a man more unworthy than himself.

A man that breaketh wedlock,
Saying thus in his heart, Who seeth me?
I am compassed about with darkness,
The walls cover me,
And no body seeth me;
What need I to fear?
The most High will not remember my sins:
Such a man only feareth the eyes of men,
And knoweth not that the eyes of the Lord
Are ten thousand times brighter than the sun,
Beholding all the ways of men,
And considering the most secret parts.
This man shall be punished in the streets of the city,
And where he suspecteth not he shall be taken.
Thus shall it go also with the wife that leaveth her husband.

*The breaker of wedlock seen by the eyes of the Lord*

As the golden pillars are upon the sockets of silver;
So are the fair feet with a constant heart.

My son, keep the flower of thine age sound;
And give not thy strength to strangers.
When thou hast gotten a fruitful possession through all the field,
Sow it with thine own seed, trusting in the goodness of thy stock.
So thy race which thou leavest shall be magnified,
Having the confidence of their good descent.
Have regard to thy name; for that shall continue with thee
Above a thousand great treasures of gold.
A good life hath but few days:
But a good name endureth for ever.

*A good name everlasting*

*The blessing of a good
wife*

Blessed is the man that hath a virtuous wife,
For the number of his days shall be double.
A virtuous woman rejoiceth her husband,
And he shall fulfil the years of his life in peace.
A good wife is a good portion,
Which shall be given in the portion of them that fear the Lord.

Children and the building of a city continue a man's name:
But a blameless wife is counted above them both.
A friend and companion never meet amiss:
But above both is a wife with her husband.
A silent and loving woman is a gift of the Lord;
And there is nothing so much worth as a mind well instructed.
As the sun when it ariseth in the high heaven;
So is the beauty of a good wife in the ordering of her house.
The beauty of a woman cheereth the countenance,
And a man loveth nothing better.
If there be kindness, meekness, and comfort, in her tongue,
Then is not her husband like other men.
He that getteth a wife beginneth a possession,
A help like unto himself, and a pillar of rest.

Where no hedge is, there the possession is spoiled:
And he that hath no wife will wander up and down mourning.
As the climbing up a sandy way is to the feet of the aged,
So is a wife full of words to a quiet man.

*Heed your conscience*

And let the counsel of thine own heart stand:
For there is no man more faithful unto thee than it.
For a man's mind is sometime wont to tell him more than seven
     watchmen,
That sit above in an high tower.
And above all this pray to the most High,
That he will direct thy way in truth.
In all thy works keep to thyself the preeminence;
Leave not a stain in thine honour.

[ 320 ]

## WISDOM

Honour a physician with the honour due unto him for the uses which
     ye may have of him:

For the Lord hath created him.

For of the most High cometh healing.

The skill of the physician shall lift up his head:

And in the sight of great men he shall be in admiration.

The Lord hath created medicines out of the earth;

And he that is wise will not abhor them.

Was not the water made sweet with wood,

That the virtue thereof might be known?

And he hath given men skill,

That he might be honoured in his marvellous works.

With such doth he heal [men,] and taketh away their pains.

Of such doth the apothecary make a confection;

And of his works there is no end;

And from him is peace over all the earth.

My son, in thy sickness be not negligent:

But pray unto the Lord, and he will make thee whole.

Then give place to the physician,

For the Lord hath created him:

Let him not go from thee, for thou hast need of him.

There is a time when in their hands there is good success.

For they shall also pray unto the Lord,

That he would prosper that, which they give for ease

And remedy to prolong life.

*The physician to be held in honour, for the art of healing is God-given*

The wisdom of a learned man cometh by opportunity of leisure:

And he that hath little business shall become wise.

How can he get wisdom that holdeth the plough,

And that glorieth in the goad,

That driveth oxen, and is occupied in their labours,

And whose talk is of bullocks?

He giveth his mind to make furrows;

And is diligent to give the kine fodder.

So every carpenter and workmaster,

That laboureth night and day:

*The wisdom of a learned man*

[ 321 ]

And they that cut and grave seals,
And are diligent to make great variety,
And give themselves to counterfeit imagery,
And watch to finish a work:
The smith also sitting by the anvil,
And considering the iron work,
The vapour of the fire wasteth his flesh,
And he fighteth with the heat of the furnace:
The noise of the hammer and the anvil is ever in his ears,
And his eyes look still upon the pattern of the thing that he maketh;
He setteth his mind to finish his work,
And watcheth to polish it perfectly:
So doth the potter sitting at his work,
And turning the wheel about with his feet,
Who is always carefully set at his work,
And maketh all his work by number;
He fashioneth the clay with his arm,
And boweth down his strength before his feet;
He applieth himself to lead it over:
And he is diligent to make clean the furnace:

All these trust to their hands:
And every one is wise in his work.
Without these cannot a city be inhabited:
And they shall not dwell where they will, nor go up and down:
They shall not be sought for in publick counsel,
Nor sit high in the congregation:
They shall not sit on the judges' seat,
Nor understand the sentence of judgment:
They cannot declare justice and judgment;
And they shall not be found where parables are spoken.
But they will maintain the state of the world,
And [all] their desire is in the work of their craft.

But he that giveth his mind to the law of the most High,
And is occupied in the meditation thereof,

# WISDOM

Will seek out the wisdom of all the ancient,
And be occupied in prophecies.
He will keep the sayings of the renowned men:
And where subtil parables are, he will be there also.
He will seek out the secrets of grave sentences,
And be conversant in dark parables.
He shall serve among great men,
And appear before princes:
He will travel through strange countries;
For he hath tried the good and the evil among men.
He will give his heart to resort early to the Lord that made him,
And will pray before the most High,
And will open his mouth in prayer,
And make supplication for his sins.
When the great Lord will,
He shall be filled with the spirit of understanding:
He shall pour out wise sentences,
And give thanks unto the Lord in his prayer.
He shall direct his counsel and knowledge,
And in his secrets shall he meditate.
He shall shew forth that which he hath learned,
And shall glory in the law of the covenant of the Lord.
Many shall commend his understanding;
And so long as the world endureth, it shall not be blotted out;
His memorial shall not depart away,
And his name shall live from generation to generation.
Nations shall shew forth his wisdom,
And the congregation shall declare his praise.
If he die, he shall leave a greater name than a thousand:
And if he live, he shall increase it.

Yet have I more to say, which I have thought upon;
For I am filled as the moon at the full.
Hearken unto me, ye holy children, and bud forth
As a rose growing by the brook of the field:
And give ye a sweet savour as frankincense,

And flourish as a lily, send forth a smell,
And sing a song of praise,
Bless the Lord in all his works.
Magnify his name,
And shew forth his praise with the songs of your lips,
And with harps, and in praising him ye shall say after this manner:
All the works of the Lord are exceeding good,
And whatsoever he commandeth shall be accomplished in due season.
And none may say, What is this? wherefore is that?
For at time convenient they shall all be sought out:
At his commandment the waters stood as an heap,
And at the words of his mouth the receptacles of waters.
At his commandment is done whatsoever pleaseth him;
And none can hinder, when he will save.
The works of all flesh are before him,
And nothing can be hid from his eyes.
He seeth from everlasting to everlasting;
And there is nothing wonderful before him.
A man need not to say, What is this? wherefore is that?
For he hath made all things for their uses.
His blessing covered the dry land as a river,
And watered it as a flood.
He hath turned the waters into saltness:
His ways are plain unto the holy.
For the good are good things created from the beginning.
The principal things for the whole use of man's life
Are water, fire, iron, and salt,
Flour of wheat, honey, milk,
And the blood of the grape, and oil, and clothing.
All these things are for good to the godly.

There be spirits that are created for vengeance,
Which in their fury lay on sore strokes;
In the time of destruction they pour out their force.
Fire, and hail, and famine, and death,
All these were created for vengeance;

## WISDOM

They shall rejoice in his commandment,
And they shall be ready upon earth, when need is;
And when their time is come, they shall not transgress his word.
Therefore from the beginning I was resolved,
And thought upon these things, and have left them in writing.
All the works of the Lord are good:
And he will give every needful thing in due season.
So that a man cannot say, This is worse than that:
For in time they shall all be well approved.
And therefore praise ye the Lord with the whole heart and mouth,
And bless the name of the Lord.

*All the works of the Lord are good*

When I was yet young, or ever I went abroad,
I desired wisdom openly in my prayer.
I prayed for her before the temple,
And will seek her out even to the end.
Even from the flower till the grape was ripe
Hath my heart delighted in her:
My foot went the right way,
From my youth up sought I after her.
I bowed down mine ear a little, and received her,
And gat much learning.
I profited therein,
Therefore will I ascribe the glory unto him that giveth me wisdom.
For I purposed to do after her,
And earnestly I followed that which is good; so shall I not be con-
      founded.
My soul hath wrestled with her,
And in my doings I was exact:
I stretched forth my hands to the heaven above,
And bewailed my ignorances of her.
I directed my soul unto her,
And I found her in pureness:
I have had my heart joined with her from the beginning,
Therefore shall I not be forsaken.
My heart was troubled in seeking her:

*The search for wisdom*

[ 325 ]

## *WISDOM*

Therefore have I gotten a good possession.
The Lord hath given me a tongue for my reward,
And I will praise him therewith.
Draw near unto me, ye unlearned,
And dwell in the house of learning.
Wherefore are ye slow, and what say ye of these things,
Seeing your souls are very thirsty?
I opened my mouth, and said,
Buy her for yourselves without money.
Put your neck under the yoke,
And let your soul receive instruction:
She is hard at hand to find.
Behold with your eyes, how that I have had but little labour,
And have gotten unto me much rest.
Get learning with a great sum of money,
And get much gold by her.
Let your soul rejoice in his mercy,
And be not ashamed of his praise.
Work your work betimes,
And in his time he will give you your reward.

For the Lord is full of compassion and mercy,
Longsuffering, and very pitiful, and forgiveth sins,
And saveth in time of affliction.
Woe be to fearful hearts, and faint hands,
And the sinner that goeth two ways!
Woe unto him that is fainthearted! for he believeth not;
Therefore shall he not be defended.
Woe unto you that have lost patience!
And what will ye do when the Lord shall visit you?

Love righteousness, ye that be judges of the earth:
Think of the Lord with a good (heart,)
And in simplicity of heart seek him.
For wisdom is a loving spirit;

# WISDOM

And will not acquit a blasphemer of his words:
For God is witness of his reins,
And a true beholder of his heart,
And a hearer of his tongue.
For the Spirit of the Lord filleth the world:
And that which containeth all things hath knowledge of the voice.

*God observes the whole man*

He [Enoch] pleased God, and was beloved of him:
So that living among sinners he was translated.
He, being made perfect in a short time, fulfilled a long time:
For his soul pleased the Lord:
Therefore hasted he to take him away from among the wicked.

*Enoch's reward*

We wearied ourselves in the way of wickedness and destruction:
Yea, we have gone through deserts, where there lay no way:
But as for the way of the Lord, we have not known it.
What hath pride profited us?
Or what good hath riches with our vaunting brought us?
All those things are passed away like a shadow,
And as a post that hasted by;
And as a ship that passeth over the waves of the water,
Which when it is gone by, the trace thereof cannot be found,
Neither the pathway of the keel in the waves;
Or as when a bird hath flown through the air,
There is no token of her way to be found,
But the light air being beaten with the stroke of her wings,
And parted with the violent noise and motion of them, is passed
    through,
And therein afterwards no sign where she went is to be found;
Or like as when an arrow is shot at a mark,
It parteth the air, which immediately cometh together again,
So that a man cannot know where it went through.
Even so we in like manner, as soon as we were born, began to draw to
    our end,
And had no sign of virtue to shew;

*Pride and riches are short-lived*

*God rewards the just with eternal life*

But were consumed in our own wickedness.

For the hope of the ungodly is like dust that is blown away with the wind;

Like a thin froth that is driven away with the storm;

Like as the smoke which is dispersed here and there with a tempest,

And passeth away as the remembrance of a guest that tarrieth but a day.

But the righteous live forevermore;

Their reward also is with the Lord,

And the care of them is with the most High.

Therefore shall they receive a glorious kingdom,

And a beautiful crown from the Lord's hand:

For with his right hand shall he cover them,

And with his arm shall he protect them.

He shall put on righteousness as a breastplate,

And true judgment instead of an helmet.

He shall take holiness for an invincible shield.

*Sovereignty and power are of God*

Hear therefore, O ye kings, and understand;

Learn, ye that be judges of the ends of the earth.

Give ear, ye that rule the people,

And glory in the multitude of nations.

For power is given you of the Lord,

And sovereignty from the Highest,

Who shall try your works, and search out your counsels.

For he which is Lord over all shall fear no man's person,

Neither shall he stand in awe of any man's greatness:

For he hath made the small and great,

And careth for all alike.

But a sore trial shall come upon the mighty.

Unto you therefore, O kings, do I speak,

That ye may learn wisdom, and not fall away.

For they that keep holiness holily shall be judged holy:

And they that have learned such things shall find what to answer.

Wherefore set your affection upon my words;

Desire them, and ye shall be instructed.

## WISDOM

Wisdom is glorious, and never fadeth away:
Yea, she is easily seen of them that love her,
And found of such as seek her.
She preventeth them that desire her, in making herself first known
    unto them.
Whoso seeketh her early shall have no great travail:
For he shall find her sitting at his doors.
To think therefore upon her is perfection of wisdom:
And whoso watcheth for her shall quickly be without care.
For she goeth about seeking such as are worthy of her,
Sheweth herself favourably unto them in the ways,
And meeteth them in every thought.
For the very true beginning of her is the desire of discipline;
And the care of discipline is love;
And love is the keeping of her laws;
And the giving heed unto her laws is the assurance of incorruption;
And incorruption maketh us near unto God.

Wherefore I prayed, and understanding was given me:
I called upon God, and the spirit of wisdom came to me.
I preferred her before sceptres and thrones,
And esteemed riches nothing in comparison of her.
Neither compared I unto her any precious stone,
Because all gold in respect of her is as a little sand,
And silver shall be counted as clay before her.
I loved her above health and beauty,
And chose to have her instead of light:
For the light that cometh from her never goeth out.
All good things together came to me with her,
And innumerable riches in her hands.
And I rejoiced in them all, because wisdom goeth before them:
And I knew not that she was the mother of them.
I learned diligently, and do communicate her liberally:
I do not hide her riches.
For she is a treasure unto men that never faileth:
Which they that use become the friends of God,

[ 329 ]

# WISDOM

Being commended for the gifts that come from learning.

God hath granted me to speak as I would,
And to conceive as is meet for the things that are given me:
Because it is he that leadeth unto wisdom, and directeth the wise.
For in his hand are both we and our words;
All wisdom also, and knowledge of workmanship.
For he hath given me certain knowledge of the things that are,
Namely, to know how the world was made, and the operation of the
        elements:
The beginning, ending, and midst of the times:
The alterations of the turning of the sun, and the change of seasons:
The circuits of years, and the positions of stars:
The natures of living creatures, and the furies of wild beasts:
The violence of winds, and the reasonings of men:
The diversities of plants, and the virtues of roots:
And all such things as are either secret or manifest, them I know.
For wisdom, which is the worker of all things, taught me:
For in her is an understanding spirit, holy,
One only, manifold, subtil, lively, clear,
Undefiled, plain, not subject to hurt,
Loving the thing that is good, quick, which cannot be letted, ready to
        do good,
Kind to man, stedfast,
Sure, free from care,
Having all power, overseeing all things,
And going through all understanding,
Pure, and most subtil, spirits.
For wisdom is more moving than any motion:
She passeth and goeth through all things by reason of her pureness.
For she is the breath of the power of God,
And a pure influence flowing from the glory of the Almighty:
Therefore can no defiled thing fall into her.
For she is the brightness of the everlasting light,
The unspotted mirror of the power of God,
And the image of his goodness.

## WISDOM

And being but one, she can do all things:
And remaining in herself, she maketh all things new:
And in all ages entering into holy souls,
She maketh them friends of God, and prophets.
For God loveth none but him that dwelleth with wisdom.
For she is more beautiful than the sun,
And above all the order of stars:
Being compared with the light, she is found before it.
For after this cometh night:
But vice shall not prevail against wisdom.

*The beauty of wisdom*

Now when I considered these things in myself,
And pondered them in my heart, how that to be allied unto wisdom is
    immortality;
And great pleasure it is to have her friendship;
And in the works of her hands are infinite riches;
And in the exercise of conference with her, prudence;
And in talking with her, a good report;
I went about seeking how to take her to me.
For I was a witty child, and had a good spirit.
Yea, rather, being good, I came into a body undefiled.
Nevertheless, when I perceived that I could not otherwise obtain her,
    except God gave her me;
And that was a point of wisdom also to know whose gift she was;
I prayed unto the Lord, and besought him,
And with my whole heart I said,
O God of my fathers, and Lord of mercy,
Who hast made all things with thy word,
And ordained man through thy wisdom,
That he should have dominion over the creatures which thou hast
    made,
And order the world according to equity and righteousness,
And execute judgment with an upright heart:
Give me wisdom, that sitteth by thy throne;
And reject me not from among thy children:
For I thy servant and son of thine handmaid

*Wisdom an ally unto immortality*

[ 331 ]

# WISDOM

*A prayer for wisdom*

Am a feeble person, and of a short time,
And too young for the understanding of judgment and laws.
O send her out of thy holy heavens,
And from the throne of thy glory,
That being present she may labour with me,
That I may know what is pleasing unto thee.
For she knoweth and understandeth all things,
And she shall lead me soberly in my doings,
And preserve me in her power.
So shall my works be acceptable,
And then shall I judge thy people righteously,
And be worthy to sit in my father's seat.

*God merciful to all his creatures*

For thou canst shew thy great strength at all times when thou wilt;
And who may withstand the power of thine arm?
For the whole world before thee is as a little grain of the balance,
Yea, as a drop of the morning dew that falleth down upon the earth.
But thou hast mercy upon all; for thou canst do all things,
And winkest at the sins of men, because they should amend.
For thou lovest all the things that are,
And abhorrest nothing which thou hast made:
For never wouldest thou have made any thing, if thou hadst hated it.
And how could any thing have endured, if it had not been thy will?
Or been preserved, if not called by thee?
But thou sparest all: for they are thine,
O lord, thou lover of souls.

For thine incorruptible Spirit is in all things.
Therefore chastenest thou them by little and little that offend,
And warnest them by putting them in remembrance wherein they
    have offended,
That leaving their wickedness they may believe on thee, O Lord.

Forsomuch then as thou art righteous thyself, thou orderest all things
    righteously:
Thinking it not agreeable with thy power

## WISDOM

To condemn him that hath not deserved to be punished.
For thy power is the beginning of righteousness,
And because thou art the Lord of all, it maketh thee to be gracious
    unto all.

Surely vain are all men by nature, who are ignorant of God,
And could not out of the good things that are seen know him that is:
Neither by considering the works did they acknowledge the work-
    master;
But deemed either fire, or wind, or the swift air,
Or the circle of the stars, or the violent water, or the lights of heaven,
To be the gods which govern the world.
With whose beauty if they being delighted took them to be gods;
Let them know how much better the Lord of them is:
For the first author of beauty hath created them.
But if they were astonished at their power and virtue,
Let them understand by them, how much mightier he is that made
    them.
For by the greatness and beauty of the creatures
Proportionably the maker of them is seen.

But thou, O God, art gracious and true,
Longsuffering, and in mercy ordering all things.
For if we sin, we are thine, knowing thy power:
But we will not sin, knowing that we are counted thine.
For to know thee is perfect righteousness:
Yea, to know thy power is the root of immortality.

For while all things were in quiet silence,
And that night was in the midst of her swift course,
Thine Almighty word leaped down from heaven out of thy royal
    throne,
As a fierce man of war into the midst of a land of destruction,
And brought thine unfeigned commandment as a sharp sword,
And standing up filled all things with death;
And it touched the heaven, but it stood upon the earth.

Then suddenly visions of horrible dreams troubled them sore,
And terrors came upon them unlooked for.
And one thrown here, and another there, half dead,
Shewed the cause of his death.
For the dreams that troubled them did forshew this,
Lest they should perish, and not know why they were afflicted.
Yea, the tasting of death touched the righteous also,
And there was a destruction of the multitude in the wilderness:
But the wrath endured not long.
For then the blameless man made haste, and stood forth to defend
      them;
And bringing the shield of his proper ministry,
Even prayer, and the propitiation of incense,
Set himself against the wrath,
And so brought the calamity to an end,
Declaring that he was thy servant.
So he overcame the destroyer,
Not with strength of body, nor force of arms,
But with a word subdued he him that punished,
Alleging the oaths and covenants made with the fathers.
For when the dead were now fallen down by heaps one upon another,
Standing between, he stayed the wrath,
And parted the way to the living.
For in the long garment was the whole world,
And in the four rows of the stones was the glory of the fathers graven,
And thy Majesty upon the diadem of his head.

God created man to be immortal,
And made him to be an image of his own eternity.

The souls of the righteous are in the hand of God,
And there shall no torment touch them.
In the sight of the unwise they seemed to die:
And their departure is taken for misery,
And their going from us to be utter destruction:
But they are in peace.

# WISDOM

For though they be punished in the sight of men,
Yet is their hope full of immortality.
And having been a little chastised, they shall be greatly rewarded:
For God proved them, and found them worthy for himself.
As gold in the furnace hath he tried them,
And received them as a burnt offering.
And in the time of their visitation they shall shine,
And run to and fro like sparks among the stubble.
They shall judge the nations, and have dominion over the people,
And their Lord shall reign for ever.
They that put their trust in him shall understand the truth:
And such as be faithful in love shall abide with him:
For grace and mercy is to his saints,
And he hath care for his elect.

*The righteous shall abide with the Lord*

Better it is to have no children, and to have virtue:
For the memorial thereof is immortal:
Because it is known with God, and with men.
When it is present, men take example at it;
And when it is gone, they desire it:
It weareth a crown, and triumpheth for ever,
Having gotten the victory, striving for undefiled rewards.

*Praise of virtue*

For honourable age is not that which standeth in length of time,
Nor that is measured by number of years.
But wisdom is the gray hair unto men,
And an unspotted life is old age.

# VII

# PROVERBS AND ECCLESIASTES, OR
# THE PREACHER

EVERY word of God is pure:
  He is a shield unto them that put their trust in him.
  The fear of the LORD is the beginning of wisdom:
  And the knowledge of the holy is understanding.
  Wisdom crieth without; she uttereth her voice in the streets:
She crieth in the chief places of concourse,
In the openings of the gates:
In the city she uttereth her words, saying,
How long, ye simple ones, will ye love simplicity?
And the scorners delight in their scorning,
And fools hate knowledge?
Turn you at my reproof:
Behold, I will pour out my spirit unto you,
I will make known my words unto you.
But whoso hearkeneth unto me shall dwell safely,
And shall be quiet from fear of evil.
Through wisdom is an house builded;
And by understanding it is established:
And by knowledge shall the chambers be filled
With all precious and pleasant riches.

Doth not wisdom cry?
And understanding put forth her voice?
She standeth in the top of high places,
By the way in the places of the paths.
She crieth at the gates,
At the entry of the city,
At the coming in at the doors.
Unto you, O men, I call;
And my voice is to the sons of man.

## PROVERBS

O ye simple, understand wisdom:
And, ye fools, be ye of an understanding heart.
Hear; for I will speak of excellent things;
And the opening of my lips shall be right things.
For my mouth shall speak truth.
All the words of my mouth are in righteousness.
They are all plain to him that understandeth,
And right to them that find knowledge.
Receive my instruction, and not silver;
And knowledge rather than choice gold.
For wisdom is better than rubies;
And all the things that may be desired are not to be compared to it.
The fear of the LORD is to hate evil:
Pride, and arrogancy, and the evil way,
And the froward mouth, do I hate.
I love them that love me;
And those that seek me early shall find me.
Riches and honour are with me;
Yea, durable riches and righteousness.
My fruit is better than gold, yea, than fine gold;
And my revenue than choice silver.
I lead in the way of righteousness,
In the midst of the paths of judgment:
That I may cause those that love me to inherit substance;
And I will fill their treasures.
The LORD possessed me in the beginning of his way,
Before his works of old.
I was set up from everlasting,
From the beginning,
Or ever the earth was.
When there were no depths, I was brought forth;
When there were no fountains abounding with water.
Before the mountains were settled,
Before the hills was I brought forth:
While as yet he had not made the earth, nor the fields,
Nor the highest part of the dust of the world.

*Discipline of wisdom*

When he prepared the heavens, I was there:
When he set a compass upon the face of the depth:
When he established the clouds above:
When he strengthened the fountains of the deep:
When he gave to the sea his decree,
That the waters should not pass his commandment:
When he appointed the foundations of the earth:
Then I was by him, as one brought up with him:
And I was daily his delight,
Rejoicing always before him;
Rejoicing in the habitable part of his earth;
And my delights were with the sons of men.
Now therefore hearken unto me, O ye children:
For blessed are they that keep my ways.
Hear instruction, and be wise, and refuse it not.
Blessed is the man that heareth me,
Watching daily at my gates,
Waiting at the posts of my doors.
For whoso findeth me findeth life,
And shall obtain favor of the LORD.
But he that sinneth against me wrongeth his own soul:
All they that hate me love death.

Give instruction to a wise man, and he will be yet wiser:
Teach a just man, and he will increase in learning.
A wise man will hear, and will increase learning;
And a man of understanding shall attain unto wise counsels:
To understand a proverb, and the interpretation;
The words of the wise, and their dark sayings.
A fool uttereth all his mind:
But a wise man keepeth it in till afterwards.
A man of understanding is of an excellent spirit.
A man of understanding walketh uprightly.
The fear of the LORD is the instruction of wisdom;
And before honour is humility.
A man's pride shall bring him low:

## PROVERBS

But honour shall uphold the humble in spirit.
A wise man is strong;
Yea, a man of knowledge increaseth strength.
If thou faint in the day of adversity, thy strength is small.
Counsel in the heart of man is like deep water;
But a man of understanding will draw it out.
The just man walketh in his integrity:
His children are blessed after him.
Even a child is known by his doings,
Whether his work be pure,
And whether it be right.
The hearing ear, and the seeing eye,
The Lord hath made even both of them.

The spirit of man is the candle of the Lord,
Searching all the inward parts.
The glory of young men is their strength:
And the beauty of old men is the grey head.

He that goeth about as a talebearer revealeth secrets:
Therefore meddle not with him that flattereth with his lips.

These six things doth the Lord hate:
Yea, seven are an abomination unto him:
A proud look, a lying tongue, and hands that shed innocent blood,
An heart that deviseth wicked imaginations,
Feet that be swift in running to mischief,
A false witness that speaketh lies,
And he that soweth discord among brethren.
He that keepeth the commandment keepeth his own soul.
There are many devices in a man's heart;
Nevertheless the counsel of the Lord, that shall stand.
The fear of the Lord tendeth to life:
And he that hath it shall abide satisfied;
He shall not be visited with evil.
Where there is no vision, the people perish:

[ 339 ]

But he that keepeth the law, happy is he.
The name of the LORD is a strong tower:
The righteous runneth into it, and is safe.

All the ways of a man are clean in his own eyes;
But the LORD weigheth the spirits.
Commit thy works unto the LORD,
And thy thoughts shall be established.
The highway of the upright is to depart from evil:
He that keepeth his way preserveth his soul.
Pride goeth before destruction,
And an haughty spirit before a fall.
Better it is to be of an humble spirit with the lowly,
Than to divide the spoil with the proud.
He that handleth a matter wisely shall find good:
And whoso trusteth in the LORD, happy is he.
The wise in heart shall be called prudent:
And the sweetness of the lips increaseth learning.
Understanding is a wellspring of life
Unto him that hath it.
The hoary head is a crown of glory,
If it be found in the way of righteousness.

He that is slow to anger is better than the mighty;
And he that ruleth his spirit than he that taketh a city.
He that hath no rule over his own spirit
Is like a city that is broken down, and without walls.

The simple believeth every word:
But the prudent man looketh well to his going.
A wise man feareth, and departeth from evil.
In the fear of the LORD is strong confidence:
And his children shall have a place of refuge.
The fear of the LORD is a fountain of life.
He that is slow to wrath is of great understanding.
Better is little with the fear of the LORD

## PROVERBS

Than great treasure and trouble therewith.
Better is a dinner of herbs where love is,
Than a stalled ox and hatred therewith.
The righteous shall never be removed.
The integrity of the upright shall guide them:
But the perverseness of transgressors shall destroy them.
A gracious woman retaineth honour:
And strong men retain riches.
He that trusteth in his riches shall fall:
But the righteous shall flourish as a branch.
The fruit of the righteous is a tree of life;
And he that winneth souls is wise.
A righteous man hateth lying.
Righteousness keepeth him that is upright in the way.
He that walketh with wise men shall be wise.
A good man leaveth an inheritance to his children's children.
He that spareth his rod hateth his son:
But he that loveth him chasteneth him betimes.
Correct thy son, and he shall give thee rest;
Yea, he shall give delight unto thy soul.
Boast not thyself of to morrow;
For thou knowest not what a day may bring forth.
Let another man praise thee, and not thine own mouth;
A stranger, and not thine own lips.
The discretion of a man deferreth his anger;
And it is his glory to pass over a transgression.
The words of a man's mouth are as deep waters,
And the wellspring of wisdom as a flowing brook.
The fear of the LORD is the beginning of knowledge.

My son, hear the instruction of thy father,
And forsake not the law of thy mother:
For they shall be an ornament of grace unto thy head,
And chains about thy neck.
My son, if sinners entice thee,
Consent thou not.

*Moral virtues and
contrary vices*

*Wisdom promises
godliness and safety*

My son, walk not thou in the way with them;
Refrain thy foot from their path:
For their feet run to evil, and make haste to shed blood.
My son, if thou wilt receive my words,
And hide my commandments with thee;
So that thou incline thine ear unto wisdom,
And apply thine heart to understanding;
Yea, if thou criest after knowledge,
And liftest up thy voice for understanding;
If thou seekest her as silver,
And searchest for her as for hid treasures;
Then shalt thou understand the fear of the LORD,
And find the knowledge of God.
For the LORD giveth wisdom:
Out of his mouth cometh knowledge and understanding.
He layeth up sound wisdom for the righteous:
He is a buckler to them that walk uprightly.
He keepeth the paths of judgment,
And preserveth the way of his saints.
Discretion shall preserve thee,
Understanding shall keep thee:
To deliver thee from the way of the evil man,
From the man that speaketh froward things;
Who leave the paths of uprightness,
To walk in the ways of darkness;
Whose ways are crooked:
That thou mayest walk in the way of good men,
And keep the paths of the righteous.
For the upright shall dwell in the land,
And the perfect shall remain in it.

My son, forget not my law;
But let thine heart keep my commandments;
For length of days, and long life, and peace,
Shall they add to thee.
Let not mercy and truth forsake thee:

## PROVERBS

Bind them about thy neck;
Write them upon the table of thine heart:
So shalt thou find favour and good understanding
In the sight of God and man.
Trust in the LORD with all thine heart;
And lean not unto thine own understanding.
In all thy ways acknowledge him,
And he shall direct thy paths.
Happy is the man that findeth wisdom,
And the man that getteth understanding.
For the merchandise of it is better than the merchandise of silver,
And the gain thereof than fine gold.
She is more precious than rubies:
And all the things thou canst desire are not to be compared unto her.
Length of days is in her right hand;
And in her left hand riches and honour.
Her ways are ways of pleasantness,
And all her paths are peace.
She is a tree of life to them that lay hold upon her:
And happy is every one that retaineth her.
Then shalt thou walk in thy way safely,
And thy foot shall not stumble.
When thou liest down, thou shalt not be afraid:
Yea, thou shalt lie down, and thy sleep shall be sweet.

Labour not to be rich:
Cease from thine own wisdom.
For riches certainly make themselves wings;
They fly away as an eagle toward heaven.
For as he thinketh in his heart, so is he.
My son, if thine heart be wise,
My heart shall rejoice, even mine.
Yea, my reins shall rejoice,
When thy lips speak right things.
Let not thine heart envy sinners:
But be thou in the fear of the LORD all the day long.

[ 343 ]

The father of the righteous shall greatly rejoice:
And he that begetteth a wise child shall have joy of him.
Thy father and thy mother shall be glad,
And she that bare thee shall rejoice.
My son, give me thine heart,
And let thine eyes observe my ways.

Be not afraid of sudden fear,
Neither of the desolation of the wicked, when it cometh.
For the LORD shall be thy confidence,
And shall keep thy foot from being taken.
Withhold not good from them to whom it is due,
When it is in the power of thine hand to do it.
Say not unto thy neighbour, Go, and come again,
And tomorrow I will give;
When thou hast it by thee.
Devise not evil against thy neighbour,
Seeing he dwelleth securely by thee.
Strive not with a man without cause,
If he have done thee no harm.
Envy thou not the oppressor,
And choose none of his ways.
For the froward is abomination to the LORD:
But his secret is with the righteous.
He giveth grace unto the lowly.
The wise shall inherit glory.

Hear, ye children, the instruction of a father,
And attend to know understanding.
For I give you good doctrine,
Forsake ye not my law.
For I was my father's son,
Tender and only beloved in the sight of my mother.
He taught me also, and said unto me,
Let thine heart retain my words:
Keep my commandments, and live.

## PROVERBS

Get wisdom, get understanding:
Forget it not;
Neither decline from the words of my mouth.
Forsake her not, and she shall preserve thee:
Love her, and she shall keep thee.
Wisdom is the principal thing;
Therefore get wisdom:
And with all thy getting get understanding.
Exalt her, and she shall promote thee:
She shall bring thee to honour,
When thou dost embrace her.
She shall give to thine head an ornament of grace:
A crown of glory shall she deliver to thee.
Hear, O my son, and receive my sayings;
And the years of thy life shall be many.
I have taught thee in the way of wisdom;
I have led thee in right paths.
When thou goest, thy steps shall not be straitened;
And when thou runnest, thou shalt not stumble.
Take fast hold of instruction;
Let her not go:
Keep her; for she is thy life.

A good name is rather to be chosen than great riches,
And loving favour rather than silver and gold.
The rich and poor meet together:
The LORD is the maker of them all.
By humility and the fear of the LORD are riches, and honour, and life.
Thorns and snares are in the way of the froward:
He that doth keep his soul shall be far from them.
Train up a child in the way he should go:
And when he is old, he will not depart from it.
He that hath a bountiful eye shall be blessed;
For he giveth of his bread to the poor.
He that loveth pureness of heart,
For the grace of his lips the king shall be his friend.

*Importance of
obtaining wisdom*

Bow down thine ear, and hear the words of the wise,
And apply thine heart unto my knowledge.
For it is a pleasant thing if thou keep them within thee;
They shall withal be fitted in thy lips.
That thy trust may be in the LORD,
I have made known to thee this day, even to thee.
Seest thou a man diligent in his business?
He shall stand before kings:
He shall not stand before mean men.


My son, keep my words, and lay up my commandments with thee.
Keep my commandments, and live;
And my law as the apple of thine eye.
Bind them upon thy fingers,
Write them upon the table of thine heart.
Say unto wisdom,
Thou art my sister;
And call understanding thy kinswoman:
That they may keep thee from the strange woman,
From the stranger which flattereth with her words.
Hear me now therefore, O ye children,
And depart not from the words of my mouth.
Remove thy way far from her,
And come not nigh the door of her house:
Lest thou give thine honour unto others,
And thy years unto the cruel:
And thou mourn at the last,
And say, How have I hated instruction,
And my heart despised reproof;
And have not obeyed the voice of my teachers,
Nor inclined mine ear to them that instructed me!
Drink waters out of thine own cistern,
And running waters out of thine own well.
Let thy fountains be dispersed abroad,
And rivers of waters in the streets.
Let them be only thine own,

And not strangers' with thee.
Let thy fountain be blessed:
And rejoice with the wife of thy youth.
Let her be as the loving hind and pleasant roe;
And be thou ravished always with her love.
And why wilt thou, my son, be ravished with a strange woman,
And embrace the bosom of a stranger?
For the ways of man are before the eyes of the LORD,
And he pondereth all his goings.

My son, keep thy father's commandment,
And forsake not the law of thy mother:
Bind them continually upon thine heart,
And tie them about thy neck.
When thou goest, it shall lead thee;
When thou sleepest, it shall keep thee;
And when thou awakest, it shall talk with thee.
For the commandment is a lamp;
And the law is light;
And reproofs of instruction are the way of life:
To keep thee from the evil woman,
From the flattery of the tongue of a strange woman,
Which forsaketh the guide of her youth,
And forgetteth the covenant of her God.
Lust not after her beauty in thine heart;
Neither let her take thee with her eyelids.
A strange woman is a narrow pit.
The adulteress will hunt for the precious life,
And lieth in wait at every corner.
Her house inclineth unto death,
And her paths unto the dead.
None that go unto her return again,
Neither take they hold of the paths of life.
She also lieth in wait as for a prey,
And increaseth the transgressors among men.
Hearken unto me now therefore, O ye children,

*Adultery leads to
destruction*

And attend to the words of my mouth.
Let not thine heart decline to her ways,
Go not astray in her paths.
For she hath cast down many wounded:
Yea, many strong men have been slain by her.
Her house is the way to hell,
Going down to the chambers of death.
Can a man take fire in his bosom,
And his clothes not be burned?
Can one go upon hot coals,
And his feet not be burned?
But whoso committeth adultery with a woman lacketh understanding:
He that doeth it destroyeth his own soul.

*The evil effects of
wine*

Who hath woe? who hath sorrow?
Who hath contentions? who hath babbling?
Who hath wounds without cause?
Who hath redness of eyes?
They that tarry long at the wine;
They that go to seek mixed wine.
Wine is a mocker, strong drink is raging:
And whosoever is deceived thereby is not wise.
Look not thou upon the wine when it is red,
When it giveth his colour in the cup,
When it moveth itself aright.
At the last it biteth like a serpent,
And stingeth like an adder.
Thine eyes shall behold strange women,
And thine heart shall utter perverse things.
Yea, thou shalt be as he that lieth down in the midst of the sea,
Or as he that lieth upon the top of a mast.
They have stricken me, shalt thou say, and I was not sick;
They have beaten me, and I felt it not:
When shall I awake? I will seek it yet again.

Enter not into the path of the wicked,

# PROVERBS

And go not in the way of evil men.
Avoid it, pass not by it,
Turn from it, and pass away.
For they sleep not, except they have done mischief;
And their sleep is taken away, unless they cause some to fall.
For they eat the bread of wickedness,
And drink the wine of violence.
The wicked flee when no man pursueth:
But the righteous are bold as a lion.
The way of the wicked is as darkness:
They know not at what they stumble.

My son, attend to my words;
Incline thine ear unto my sayings.
Let them not depart from thine eyes;
Keep them in the midst of thine heart.
For they are life unto those that find them,
And health to all their flesh.
Keep thy heart with all diligence;
For out of it are the issues of life.
Put away from thee a froward mouth,
And perverse lips put far from thee.
Let thine eyes look right on,
And let thine eyelids look straight before thee.
Ponder the path of thy feet,
And let all thy ways be established.
Turn not to the right hand nor to the left:
Remove thy foot from evil.
The eyes of the LORD are in every place,
Beholding the evil and the good.
The fining pot is for silver,
And the furnace for gold:
But the LORD trieth the hearts.
He that tilleth his land shall have plenty of bread:
But he that followeth after vain persons shall have poverty enough.
If thine enemy be hungry, give him bread to eat;

*Discipline and doctrine*
*of wisdom*

And if he be thirsty, give him water to drink:
For thou shalt heap coals of fire upon his head,
And the LORD shall reward thee.
Take away the dross from the silver,
And there shall come forth a vessel for the finer.
But the path of the just is as the shining light,
That shineth more and more unto the perfect day.

*On friendship*

As cold waters to a thirsty soul,
So is good news from a far country.
A man that hath friends must shew himself friendly:
And there is a friend that sticketh closer than a brother.
A friend loveth at all times.
A merry heart doeth good like a medicine:
But a broken spirit drieth the bones.
A merry heart maketh a cheerful countenance:
But by sorrow of the heart the spirit is broken.
He that is of a merry heart hath a continual feast.
He that followeth after righteousness and mercy
Findeth life, righteousness and honour.
Whoso keepeth his mouth and his tongue
Keepeth his soul from troubles.

*On foolish women*

A foolish woman is clamourous:
She is simple, and knoweth nothing.
For she sitteth at the door of her house,
On a seat in the high places of the city,
To call passengers who go right on their ways:
Whoso is simple, let him turn in hither:
And as for him that wanteth understanding, she saith to him,
Stolen waters are sweet,
And bread eaten in secret is pleasant.
But he knoweth not that the dead are there;
And that her guests are in the depths of hell.
It is better to dwell in a corner of the housetop,
Than with a brawling woman in a wide house.

# PROVERBS

A continual dropping in a very rainy day
And a contentious woman are alike.
It is better to dwell in the wilderness,
Than with a contentious and an angry woman.

Who can find a virtuous woman?
For her price is far above rubies.
The heart of her husband doth safely trust in her,
So that he shall have no need of spoil.
She will do him good and not evil all the days of her life.
She seeketh wool, and flax,
And worketh willingly with her hands.
She is like the merchants' ships;
She bringeth her food from afar.
She riseth also while it is yet night,
And giveth meat to her household,
And a portion to her maidens.
She considereth a field, and buyeth it:
With the fruit of her hands she planteth a vineyard.
She girdeth her loins with strength,
And strengtheneth her arms.
She perceiveth that her merchandise is good:
Her candle goeth not out by night.
She layeth her hands to the spindle,
And her hands hold the distaff.
She stretcheth out her hand to the poor;
Yea, she reacheth forth her hands to the needy.
She is not afraid of the snow for her household:
For all her household are clothed with scarlet.
She maketh herself coverings of tapestry;
Her clothing is silk and purple.
Her husband is known in the gates,
When he sitteth among the elders of the land.
She maketh fine linen, and selleth it;
And delivereth girdles unto the merchant.
Strength and honour are her clothing;

*Praise and properties of a good wife*

*A prudent wife is from
the Lord*

And she shall rejoice in time to come.
She openeth her mouth with wisdom;
And in her tongue is the law of kindness.
She looketh well to the ways of her household,
And eateth not the bread of idleness.
Her children arise up, and call her blessed;
Her husband also, and he praiseth her.
Many daughters have done virtuously,
But thou excellest them all.
Favour is deceitful, and beauty is vain:
But a woman that feareth the LORD,
She shall be praised.
Give her of the fruit of her hands;
And let her own works praise her in the gates.
A prudent wife is from the LORD.

*Four things small but
exceeding wise*

There be four things which are little upon the earth,
But they are exceeding wise:
The ants are a people not strong, yet they prepare their meat in the
    summer;
The conies are but a feeble folk, yet make they their houses in the
    rocks;
The locusts have no king, yet go they forth all of them by bands;
The spider taketh hold with her hands, and is in kings' palaces.

Go to the ant, thou sluggard;
Consider her ways, and be wise:
Which having no guide, overseer, or ruler,
Provideth her meat in the summer,
And gathereth her food in the harvest.
How long wilt thou sleep, O sluggard?
When wilt thou arise out of thy sleep?

I went by the field of the slothful,
And by the vineyard of the man void of understanding;
And, lo, it was all grown over with thorns,

# PROVERBS

And nettles had covered the face thereof,
And the stone wall thereof was broken down.
Then I saw, and considered it well:
I looked upon it, and received instruction.
Yet a little sleep, a little slumber,
A little folding of the hands to sleep:
So shall thy poverty come as one that travelleth:
And thy want as an armed man.
The slothful man saith,
There is a lion in the way; a lion is in the streets.
As the door turneth upon his hinges,
So doth the slothful upon his bed.
The slothful hideth his hand in his bosom;
It grieveth him to bring it again to his mouth.
The sluggard is wiser in his own conceit
Than seven men that can render a reason.
Where no wood is, there the fire goeth out:
So where there is no talebearer, the strife ceaseth.
The sluggard will not plow by reason of the cold;
Therefore shall he beg in harvest, and have nothing.
An idle soul shall suffer hunger.
He also that is slothful in his work is brother
To him that is a great waster.

The heart knoweth his own bitterness;
And a stranger doth not intermeddle with his joy.
A soft answer turneth away wrath:
But grievous words stir up anger.
Prepare thy work without,
And make it fit for thyself in the field;
And afterwards build thine house.
Faithful are the wounds of a friend;
But the kisses of an enemy are deceitful.
The way of the Lord is strength to the upright.
The righteous shall never be removed.

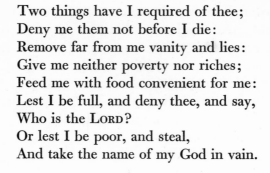

*The marvel of God's creation*

Two things have I required of thee;
Deny me them not before I die:
Remove far from me vanity and lies:
Give me neither poverty nor riches;
Feed me with food convenient for me:
Lest I be full, and deny thee, and say,
Who is the LORD?
Or lest I be poor, and steal,
And take the name of my God in vain.

There be three things which are too wonderful for me, which I know
    not:
The way of an eagle in the air;
The way of a serpent upon a rock;
The way of a ship in the midst of the sea.

If thou sayest, Behold, we knew it not;
Doth not he that pondereth the heart consider it?
And he that keepeth thy soul,
Doth not he know it?
And shall not he render to every man according to his works?
Rejoice not when thine enemy falleth,
And let not thine heart be glad when he stumbleth.
Fret not thyself because of evil men.

## The Words of the Preacher

*A time for everything* ONE generation passeth away, and another generation cometh: but the
earth abideth for ever. To every thing there is a season, and a time
to every purpose under the heaven: a time to be born, and a time to die;
a time to plant, and a time to pluck up that which is planted; a time to kill,
and a time to heal; a time to break down, and a time to build up; a time
to weep, and a time to laugh; a time to mourn, and a time to dance; a

time to cast away stones, and a time to gather stones together; a time to *The way of wisdom* embrace, and a time to refrain from embracing; a time to get, and a time to lose; a time to keep, and a time to cast away; a time to rend, and a time to sew; a time to keep silence, and a time to speak; a time to love, and a time to hate; a time of war, and a time of peace. What profit hath he that worketh in that wherein he laboureth? I have seen the travail, which God hath given to the sons of men to be exercised in it. He hath made every thing beautiful in his time: also he hath set the world in their heart, so that no man can find out the work that God maketh from the beginning to the end.

Better is an handful with quietness, than both the hands full with travail and vexation of spirit. He that loveth silver shall not be satisfied with silver; nor he that loveth abundance with increase; this is also vanity. The sleep of a labouring man is sweet, whether he eat little or much: but the abundance of the rich will not suffer him to sleep. There is a sore evil which I have seen under the sun, namely, riches kept for the owners thereof to their hurt.

Every man also to whom God hath given riches and wealth, and hath given him power to eat thereof, and to take his portion, and to rejoice in his labour; this is the gift of God. For he shall not much remember the days of his life; because God answereth him in the joy of his heart.

A good name is better than precious ointment. Better is the end of a thing than the beginning thereof: and the patient in spirit is better than the proud in spirit. Be not hasty in thy spirit to be angry: for anger resteth in the bosom of fools. Wisdom strengtheneth the wise more than ten mighty men which are in the city.

Lo, this only have I found, that God hath made man upright.

Who is as the wise man? and who knoweth the interpretation of a thing? a man's wisdom maketh his face to shine. When I applied mine heart to know wisdom, and to see the business that is done upon the earth: (for also there is that neither day nor night seeth sleep with his eyes:) then I beheld all the work of God, that a man cannot find out the work that is done under the sun: because though a man labour to seek it out, yet he shall not find it; yea farther; though a wise man think to know it, yet shall he not be able to find it.

I returned, and saw under the sun, that the race is not to the swift, nor the battle to the strong, neither yet bread to the wise, nor yet riches to men of understanding, nor yet favour to men of skill; but time and chance happeneth to them all. Whatsoever thy hand findeth to do, do it with thy might.

Wisdom is better than strength; wisdom is better than weapons of war; nevertheless wisdom is despised: one sinner destroyeth much good.

As thou knowest not what is the way of the spirit, nor how the bones do grow in the womb of her that is with child: even so thou knowest not the works of God who maketh all. A bird of the air shall carry the voice, and that which hath wings shall tell the matter. Cast thy bread upon the waters: for thou shalt find it after many days.

Truly the light is sweet, and a pleasant thing it is for the eyes to behold the sun.

Remember now thy Creator in the days of thy youth, while the evil days come not, nor the years draw nigh, when thou shalt say, I have no pleasure in them; while the sun, or the light, or the moon, or the stars, be not darkened, nor the clouds return after the rain: in the day when the keepers of the house shall tremble, and the strong men shall bow themselves, and the grinders cease because they are few, and those that look out of the windows be darkened, and the doors shall be shut in the streets, when the sound of the grinding is low, and he shall rise up at the voice of the bird, and all the daughters of musick shall be brought low; also when they shall be afraid of that which is high, and fears shall be in the way, and the almond tree shall flourish, and the grasshopper shall be a burden, and desire shall fail: because man goeth to his long home, and the mourners go about the streets: or ever the silver cord be loosed, or the golden bowl be broken, or the pitcher be broken at the fountain, or the wheel broken at the cistern.

Then shall the dust return to the earth as it was: and the spirit shall return unto God who gave it.

# VIII

# JONAH

NOW the word of the LORD came unto Jonah the son of Amittai, saying, "Arise, go to Nineveh, that great city, and cry against it; for their wickedness is come up before me."

*Jonah sent to Nineveh*

But Jonah rose up to flee unto Tarshish from the presence of the LORD, and went down to Joppa; and he found a ship going to Tarshish: so he paid the fare thereof and went down into it, to go with them unto Tarshish from the presence of the LORD.

But the LORD sent out a great wind into the sea, and there was a mighty tempest in the sea, so that the ship was like to be broken. Then the mariners were afraid, and cried every man unto his god, and cast forth the wares that were in the ship into the sea, to lighten it of them. But Jonah was gone down into the sides of the ship; and he lay, and was fast asleep.

So the shipmaster came to him, and said unto him, "What meanest thou, O sleeper? arise, call upon thy God, if so be that God will think upon us, that we perish not."

And they said every one to his fellow, "Come, and let us cast lots, that we may know for whose cause this evil is upon us." So they cast lots, and the lot fell upon Jonah.

Then said they unto him, "Tell us, we pray thee, for whose cause this evil is upon us; What is thine occupation? and whence comest thou? what is thy country? and of what people art thou?"

And he said unto them, "I am an Hebrew; and I fear the LORD, the God of heaven, which hath made the sea and the dry land."

Then were the men exceedingly afraid, and said unto him, "Why hast thou done this?" For the men knew that he fled from the presence of the LORD, because he had told them. Then said they unto him, "What shall we do unto thee, that the sea may be calm unto us?" for the sea wrought, and was tempestuous.

And he said unto them, "Take me up, and cast me forth into the sea; so shall the sea be calm unto you: for I know that for my sake this great tempest is upon you."

# JONAH

*Jonah cast into the sea*

Nevertheless the men rowed hard to bring it to the land; but they could not: for the sea wrought, and was tempestuous against them. Wherefore they cried unto the LORD, and said, "We beseech thee, O LORD, we beseech thee, let us not perish for this man's life, and lay not upon us innocent blood: for thou, O LORD, hast done as it pleased thee."

So they took up Jonah, and cast him forth into the sea: and the sea ceased from her raging. Then the men feared the LORD exceedingly, and offered a sacrifice unto the LORD, and made vows.

Now the LORD had prepared a great fish to swallow up Jonah. And Jonah was in the belly of the fish three days and three nights. Then Jonah prayed unto the LORD his God out of the fish's belly, and said,

*Jonah's prayer*

I cried by reason of mine affliction unto the LORD,
And he heard me;
Out of the belly of hell cried I,
And thou heardest my voice.
For thou hadst cast me into the deep,
In the midst of the seas;
And the floods compassed me about:
All thy billows and thy waves passed over me.
Then I said, "I am cast out of thy sight;
Yet I will look again toward thy holy temple."
The waters compassed me about, even to the soul:
The depth closed me round about,
The weeds were wrapped about my head.
I went down to the bottoms of the mountains;
The earth with her bars was about me for ever:
Yet hast thou brought up my life from corruption, O LORD my God.
When my soul fainted within me I remembered the LORD:
And my prayer came in unto thee,
Into thine holy temple.
They that observe lying vanities forsake their own mercy.
But I will sacrifice unto thee with the voice of thanksgiving;
I will pay that that I have vowed.
Salvation is of the LORD.

# JONAH

And the LORD spake unto the fish, and it vomited out Jonah upon the dry land.

And the word of the LORD came unto Jonah the second time, saying, "Arise, go unto Nineveh, that great city, and preach unto it the preaching that I bid thee."

So Jonah arose, and went unto Nineveh, according to the word of the LORD. Now Nineveh was an exceeding great city of three days' journey. And Jonah began to enter into the city a day's journey, and he cried, and said, "Yet forty days, and Nineveh shall be overthrown."

So the people of Nineveh believed God, and proclaimed a fast, and put on sackcloth, from the greatest of them even to the least of them. For word came unto the king of Nineveh, and he arose from his throne, and he laid his robe from him, and covered him with sackcloth, and sat in ashes. And he caused it to be proclaimed and published through Nineveh by the decree of the king and his nobles, saying, "Let neither man nor beast, herd nor flock, taste any thing: let them not feed, nor drink water: but let man and beast be covered with sackcloth, and cry mightily unto God: yea, let them turn every one from his evil way, and from the violence that is in their hands. Who can tell if God will turn and repent, and turn away from his fierce anger, that we perish not?"

And God saw their works, that they turned from their evil way; and God repented of the evil, that he had said that he would do unto them; and he did it not.

But it displeased Jonah exceedingly, and he was very angry. And he prayed unto the LORD, and said, "I pray thee, O LORD, was not this my saying, when I was yet in my country? Therefore I fled before unto Tarshish: for I knew that thou art a gracious God, and merciful, slow to anger, and of great kindness, and repentest thee of the evil. Therefore now, O LORD, take, I beseech thee, my life from me; for it is better for me to die than to live."

Then said the LORD, "Doest thou well to be angry?"

So Jonah went out of the city, and sat on the east side of the city, and there made him a booth, and sat under it in the shadow, till he might see what would become of the city.

And the LORD God prepared a gourd, and made it to come up over Jonah, that it might be a shadow over his head, to deliver him from his grief. So Jonah was exceeding glad of the gourd. But God prepared a worm when the morning rose the next day, and it smote the gourd that it withered.

And it came to pass, when the sun did arise, that God prepared a vehement east wind; and the sun beat upon the head of Jonah, that he fainted, and wished in himself to die, and said, "It is better for me to die than to live."

And God said to Jonah, "Doest thou well to be angry for the gourd?"

And he said, "I do well to be angry, even unto death."

Then said the LORD, "Thou hast had pity on the gourd, for the which thou hast not laboured, neither madest it grow; which came up in a night, and perished in a night: And should not I spare Nineveh, that great city, wherein are more than sixscore thousand persons that cannot discern between their right hand and their left hand; and also much cattle?"

# THE COMMANDMENTS

KEEP my commandments, and live; write them on the table of thine heart. *The ten commandments*

He that keepeth the commandment keepeth his own soul.

## *Commandments given to Moses*

And God spake all these words, saying, I am the LORD thy God.

### I

Thou shalt have no other gods before me.

### II

Thou shalt not make unto thee any graven image, or any likeness of any thing that is in heaven above, or that is in the earth beneath, or that is in the water under the earth: thou shalt not bow down thyself to them, nor serve them: for I the LORD thy God am a jealous God, visiting the iniquity of the fathers upon the children unto the third and fourth generation of them that hate me; and shewing mercy unto thousands of them that love me, and keep my commandments.

### III

Thou shalt not take the name of the LORD thy God in vain; for the LORD will not hold him guiltless that taketh his name in vain.

### IV

Remember the sabbath day, to keep it holy. Six days shalt thou labour, and do all thy work: but the seventh day is the sabbath of the LORD thy God: in it thou shalt not do any work, thou, nor thy son, nor thy daughter, thy manservant, nor thy maidservant, nor thy cattle, nor thy stranger that is within thy gates: for in six days the LORD made heaven and earth, the sea, and all that in them is, and rested the seventh day: wherefore the LORD blessed the sabbath day, and hallowed it.

### V

Honour thy father and thy mother: that thy days may be long upon the land which the LORD thy God giveth thee.

### VI

Thou shalt not kill.

### VII

Thou shalt not commit adultery.

### VIII

Thou shalt not steal.

### IX

Thou shalt not bear false witness against thy neighbour.

### X

Thou shalt not covet thy neighbour's house, thou shalt not covet thy neighbour's wife, nor his manservant, nor his maidservant, nor his ox, nor his ass, nor any thing that is thy neighbour's.

Now these are the commandments, which the LORD your God commanded to teach you, that thou mightest fear the LORD thy God, to keep all his statutes and his commandments, thou, and thy son, and thy son's son, all the days of thy life.

And these words, which I command thee this day, shall be in thine heart: and thou shalt teach them diligently unto thy children, and shalt talk of them when thou sittest in thine house, and when thou walkest by the way, and when thou liest down, and when thou risest up. And thou shalt bind them for a sign upon thine hand, and they shall be as frontlets between thine eyes. And thou shalt write them upon the posts of thy house, and on thy gates.

The LORD our God is one LORD: and thou shalt love the LORD thy God with all thine heart, and with all thy soul, and with all thy might.

Ye shall walk after the LORD your God, and fear him, and keep his commandments, and obey his voice, and ye shall serve him, and cleave unto him. Ye are the children of the LORD your God.

## Commandments of Jesus

THINK not that I am come to destroy the law, or the prophets: I am not *The sermon on the* come to destroy, but to fulfil. For verily I say unto you, Till heaven *mount* and earth pass, one jot or one tittle shall in no wise pass from the law, till all be fulfilled. I am come that they might have life, and that they might have it more abundantly.

If thou wilt enter into life, keep the commandments.

Ye have heard that it was said by them of old time, "Thou shalt not kill"; and "whosoever shall kill shall be in danger of the judgment": but I say unto you, that whosoever is angry with his brother without a cause shall be in danger of the judgment. Therefore if thou bring thy gift to the altar, and there rememberest that thy brother hath ought against thee; leave there thy gift before the altar, and go thy way; first be reconciled to thy brother, and then come and offer thy gift.

Ye have heard that it was said by them of old time, "Thou shalt not commit adultery": but I say unto you, that whosoever looketh on a woman to lust after her hath committed adultery with her already in his heart.

Again, ye have heard that it hath been said by them of old time, "Thou shalt not forswear thyself, but shalt perform unto the Lord thine oaths": but I say unto you, Swear not at all; neither by heaven; for it is God's throne: nor by the earth; for it is his footstool: neither by Jerusalem; for it is the city of the great King. Neither shalt thou swear by thy head, because thou canst not make one hair white or black.

Ye have heard that it hath been said, "An eye for an eye, and a tooth for a tooth": but I say unto you, that ye resist not evil: but whosoever shall smite thee on thy right cheek, turn to him the other also.

And if any man will sue thee at the law, and take away thy coat, let him have thy cloke also. And whosoever shall compel thee to go a mile,

*The commandments of Love*

go with him twain. Give to him that asketh thee, and from him that would borrow of thee turn not thou away.

Ye have heard that it hath been said, "Thou shalt love thy neighbour, and hate thine enemy." But I say unto you, Love your enemies, bless them that curse you, do good to them that hate you, and pray for them which despitefully use you, and persecute you; that ye may be the children of your Father which is in heaven: for he maketh his sun to rise on the evil and on the good, and sendeth rain on the just and on the unjust. For if ye love them which love you, what reward have ye? And if ye salute your brethren only, what do ye more than others? Be ye therefore perfect, even as your Father which is in heaven is perfect.

A new commandment I give unto you, that ye love one another; as I have loved you. By this shall all men know that ye are my disciples, if ye have love one to another.

As the Father hath loved me, so have I loved you: continue ye in my love.

Ask, and it shall be given you; seek, and ye shall find; knock, and it shall be opened unto you: for every one that asketh receiveth; and he that seeketh findeth; and to him that knocketh it shall be opened.

Therefore all things whatsoever ye would that men should do to you, do ye even so to them: for this is the law and the prophets.

"Thou shalt love the Lord thy God with all thy heart, and with all thy soul, and with all thy mind." This is the first and great commandment. And the second is like unto it, "Thou shalt love thy neighbour as thyself." On these two commandments hang all the law and the prophets.

# The Lord's Prayer

THOU, when thou prayest, enter into thy closet, and when thou hast *The manner of praying* shut thy door, pray to thy Father which is in secret; and thy Father which seeth in secret shall reward thee openly. For your Father knoweth what things ye have need of, before ye ask him. After this manner therefore pray ye:

> Our Father which art in heaven,
> Hallowed be thy name.
> Thy kingdom come.
> Thy will be done
> In earth, as it is in heaven.
> Give us this day
> Our daily bread.
> And forgive us our debts,
> As we forgive our debtors.
> And lead us not into temptation,
> But deliver us from evil:
> For thine is the kingdom,
> And the power,
> And the glory,
> For ever. Amen.

# X

# COVENANTS AND HOLY COMMUNION

THE secret of the LORD is with them that fear him; and he will shew them his covenant.

Incline your ear, and come unto me: hear, and your soul shall live; and I will make an everlasting covenant with you.

*Covenant with Noah*

And God spake unto Noah, and to his sons with him, saying, "And I, behold, I establish my covenant with you, and with your seed after you; and with every living creature that is with you, of the fowl, of the cattle, and of every beast of the earth with you; from all that go out of the ark, to every beast of the earth. And I will establish my covenant with you; neither shall all flesh be cut off any more by the waters of a flood; neither shall there any more be a flood to destroy the earth."

And God said, "This is the token of the covenant which I make between me and you, and every living creature that is with you, for perpetual generations: I do set my bow in the cloud, and it shall be for a token of a covenant between me and the earth. And it shall come to pass, when I bring a cloud over the earth, that the bow shall be seen in the cloud: and I will remember my covenant, which is between me and you and every living creature of all flesh; and the waters shall no more become a flood to destroy all flesh. And the bow shall be in the cloud; and I will look upon it, that I may remember the everlasting covenant between God and every living creature of all flesh that is upon the earth."

*Covenant with Moses*

And God spake unto Moses, and said unto him, "I am the LORD: and I appeared unto Abraham, unto Isaac, and unto Jacob, by the name of God Almighty, but by my name JEHOVAH was I not known to them. And I have also established my covenant with them, to give them the land of Canaan, the land of their pilgrimage, wherein they were strangers. And I have also heard the groaning of the children of Israel, whom the Egyptians keep in bondage; and I have remembered my covenant. Wherefore say unto the children of Israel, 'I am the LORD, and I will bring you out from under the burdens of the Egyptians, and I will rid you out of

their bondage, and I will redeem you with a stretched out arm, and with
great judgments: and I will take you to me for a people, and I will be to
you a God: and ye shall know that I am the LORD your God, which
bringeth you out from under the burdens of the Egyptians.'

"Speak thou also unto the children of Israel, saying, Verily my sabbaths ye shall keep: for it is a sign between me and you throughout your
generations; that ye may know that I am the LORD that doth sanctify you.
Ye shall keep the sabbath therefore; for it is holy unto you."

"Behold, the days come," saith the LORD, "that I will make a new
covenant with the house of Israel, and with the house of Judah: not according to the covenant that I made with their fathers in the day that I
took them by the hand to bring them out of the land of Egypt; which my
covenant they brake, although I was an husband unto them," saith the
LORD: "But this shall be the covenant that I will make with the house of
Israel; After those days," saith the LORD, "I will put my law in their inward parts, and write it in their hearts; and will be their God, and they
shall be my people. And they shall teach no more every man his neighbour, and every man his brother, saying, 'Know the LORD': for they shall
all know me, from the least of them unto the greatest of them," saith the
LORD: "for I will forgive their iniquity, and I will remember their sin no
more." Thus saith the LORD, which giveth the sun for a light by day, and
the ordinances of the moon and of the stars for a light by night, which
divideth the sea when the waves thereof roar; The LORD of hosts is his
name.

The word of the LORD came unto me, saying, "Behold, all souls are
mine. If a man hath walked in my statutes, and hath kept my judgments,
to deal truly; he is just, he shall surely live. Have I any pleasure at all
that the wicked should die?" saith the Lord GOD: "and not that he
should return from his ways, and live? Yet ye say, The way of the Lord is
not equal. Hear now, O house of Israel; Is not my way equal? are not
your ways unequal? Therefore I will judge you, O house of Israel, every
one according to his ways," saith the Lord GOD. "Repent, and turn yourselves from all your transgressions; so iniquity shall not be your ruin.
Cast away from you all your transgressions, whereby ye have trans-

*The Covenant of Peace* gressed; and make you a new heart and a new spirit: for why will ye die, O house of Israel? For I have no pleasure in the death of him that dieth," saith the Lord GOD: "wherefore turn yourselves, and live ye.

"Moreover I will make a covenant of peace with them; it shall be an everlasting covenant with them: and I will place them, and multiply them, and will set my sanctuary in the midst of them for evermore.

"As for me, this is my covenant," saith the LORD that hath mercy on thee: "The mountains shall depart, and the hills be removed; but my kindness shall not depart from thee, neither shall the covenant of my peace be removed. My spirit that is upon thee, and my words which I have put in thy mouth, shall not depart out of thy mouth, nor out of the mouth of thy seed, nor out of the mouth of thy seed's seed, from henceforth and for ever."

*The Lord's Covenant is fast* "My covenant will I not break, nor alter the thing that is gone out of my lips. Now therefore, if ye will obey my voice indeed, and keep my covenant, then ye shall be a peculiar treasure unto me above all people: for all the earth is mine."

He hath remembered his covenant for ever, the word which he commanded to a thousand generations.

## *Holy Communion*

THE cup of blessing which we bless, is it not the communion of the *The Lord's Supper* blood of Christ? The bread which we break, is it not the communion of the body of Christ?

For I have received of the Lord that which also I delivered unto you, that the Lord Jesus the same night in which he was betrayed took bread: and when he had given thanks, he brake it, and said, "Take, eat: this is my body, which is broken for you: this do in remembrance of me."

After the same manner also he took the cup, when he had supped, saying, "This cup is the new testament in my blood: this do ye, as oft as ye drink it, in remembrance of me."

For as often as ye eat this bread, and drink this cup, ye do shew the Lord's death till he come.

But let a man examine himself, and so let him eat of that bread, and drink of that cup.

# XI

# THE REVELATION OF ST. JOHN THE DIVINE

T HE Revelation of Jesus Christ, which God gave unto him, to shew unto his servants things which must shortly come to pass; and he sent and signified it by his angel unto his servant John: who bare record of the word of God, and of the testimony of Jesus Christ, and of all things that he saw.

"I am Alpha and Omega, the beginning and the ending," saith the Lord, which is, and which was, and which is to come, the Almighty.

I John, who also am your brother, and companion in tribulation, and in the kingdom and patience of Jesus Christ, was in the isle that is called Patmos, for the word of God, and for the testimony of Jesus Christ.

I was in the Spirit on the Lord's day, and heard behind me a great voice, as of a trumpet, saying, "I am Alpha and Omega, the first and the last": and, "What thou seest, write in a book, and send it unto the seven churches which are in Asia; unto Ephesus, and unto Smyrna, and unto Pergamos, and unto Thyatira, and unto Sardis, and unto Philadelphia, and unto Laodicea."

And I turned to see the voice that spake with me. And being turned, I saw seven golden candlesticks; and in the midst of the seven candlesticks one like unto the Son of man, clothed with a garment down to the foot, and girt about the paps with a golden girdle. His head and his hairs were white like wool, as white as snow; and his eyes were as a flame of fire; and his feet like unto fine brass, as if they burned in a furnace; and his voice as the sound of many waters. And he had in his right hand seven stars: and out of his mouth went a sharp twoedged sword: and his countenance was as the sun shineth in his strength.

And when I saw him, I fell at his feet as dead. And he laid his right hand upon me, saying unto me, "Fear not; I am the first and the last: I am he that liveth, and was dead; and, behold, I am alive for evermore, Amen; and have the keys of hell and of death. Write the things which thou hast seen, and the things which are, and the things which shall be hereafter; the mystery of the seven stars which thou sawest in my right hand, and the seven golden candlesticks. The seven stars are the angels of the seven churches: and the seven candlesticks which thou sawest are the seven churches.

"He that hath an ear, let him hear what the Spirit saith unto the churches; 'To him that overcometh will I give to eat of the tree of life, which is in the midst of the paradise of God.' He that hath an ear, let him hear what the Spirit saith unto the churches; 'To him that over-cometh will I give to eat of the hidden manna, and will give him a white stone, and in the stone a new name written, which no man knoweth saving he that receiveth it. And I will give unto every one of you according to your works. And he that overcometh, and keepeth my works unto the end, to him will I give power over the nations; and I will give him the morning star.

" 'Be watchful, and strengthen the things which remain, that are ready to die: for I have not found thy works perfect before God. Remember therefore how thou hast received and heard, and hold fast, and repent. He that overcometh, the same shall be clothed in white raiment; and I will not blot out his name out of the book of life, but I will confess his name be-fore my Father, and before his angels. I know thy works: behold, I have set before thee an open door, and no man can shut it; for thou hast a little strength, and hast kept my word, and hast not denied my name. Because thou hast kept the word of my patience, I also will keep thee from the hour of temptation, which shall come upon all the world, to try them that dwell upon the earth.

" 'Behold, I come quickly: hold that fast which thou hast, that no man take thy crown. Him that overcometh will I make a pillar in the temple of my God, and he shall go no more out: and I will write upon him the name of my God, and the name of the city of my God, which is new Jerusalem, which cometh down out of heaven from my God: and I will write upon him my new name. As many as I love, I rebuke and chasten: be zealous therefore, and repent.

" 'Behold, I stand at the door, and knock: if any man hear my voice, and open the door, I will come in to him, and will sup with him, and he with me. To him that overcometh will I grant to sit with me in my throne, even as I also overcame, and am set down with my Father in his throne.'

He that hath an ear, let him hear what the Spirit saith unto the churches."

Thou art worthy, O Lord, to receive glory and honour and power: for thou hast created all things, and for thy pleasure they are and were created.

And I beheld, and, lo, in the midst of the throne and of the four beasts, and in the midst of the elders, stood a Lamb as it had been slain, having seven horns and seven eyes, which are the seven Spirits of God sent forth into all the earth. And he came and took the book out of the right hand of him that sat upon the throne. And I beheld, and I heard the voice of many angels round about the throne and the beasts and the elders: and the number of them was ten thousand times ten thousand, and thousands of thousands; saying with a loud voice, "Worthy is the Lamb that was slain to receive power, and riches, and wisdom, and strength, and honour, and glory, and blessing."

And every creature which is in heaven, and on the earth, and under the earth, and such as are in the sea, and all that are in them, heard I saying, "Blessing, and honour, and glory, and power, be unto him that sitteth upon the throne, and unto the Lamb for ever and ever."

And the stars of heaven fell unto the earth, even as a fig tree casteth her untimely figs, when she is shaken of a mighty wind.

After this I beheld, and, lo, a great multitude, which no man could number, of all nations, and kindreds, and people, and tongues, stood before the throne, and before the Lamb, clothed with white robes, and palms in their hands; and cried with a loud voice, saying, "Salvation to our God which sitteth upon the throne, and unto the Lamb."

And all the angels worshipped God, saying, "Blessing, and glory, and wisdom, and thanksgiving, and honour, and power, and might, be unto our God for ever and ever. Amen."

And one of the elders answered, saying unto me, "What are these which are arrayed in white robes? and whence came they?"

And I said unto him, "Sir, thou knowest."

And he said to me, "These are they which came out of great tribulation, and have washed their robes, and made them white in the blood of the Lamb. Therefore are they before the throne of God, and serve him day and night in his temple: and he that sitteth on the throne shall dwell among them. They shall hunger no more, neither thirst any more; neither shall the sun light on them, nor any heat. For the Lamb which is in the midst of the throne shall feed them, and shall lead them unto living fountains of waters: and God shall wipe away all tears from their eyes."

And the seventh angel sounded; and there were great voices in heaven, saying, "The kingdoms of this world are become the kingdoms of our Lord, and of his Christ; and he shall reign for ever and ever."

And I heard a loud voice saying in heaven, "Now is come salvation, and strength, and the kingdom of our God, and the power of his Christ."

> If any man have an ear, let him hear.
> He that leadeth into captivity
> Shall go into captivity:
> He that killeth with the sword
> Must be killed with the sword.
> Here is the patience and the faith of the saints.

And I saw another angel fly in the midst of heaven, having the everlasting gospel to preach unto them that dwell on the earth, and to every nation, and kindred, and tongue, and people, saying with a loud voice, "Fear God, and give glory to him; for the hour of his judgment is come: and worship him that made heaven, and earth, and the sea, and the fountains of waters."

Here is the patience of the saints: here are they that keep the commandments of God, and the faith of Jesus.

And I heard a voice from heaven saying unto me, "Write, 'Blessed are the dead which die in the Lord from henceforth: Yea, saith the Spirit, that they may rest from their labours; and their works do follow them.' "

And they sing the song of Moses the servant of God, and the song of the Lamb, saying,

> Great and marvellous are thy works, Lord God Almighty;
> Just and true are thy ways, thou King of saints.
> Who shall not fear thee, O Lord,
> And glorify thy name?
> For thou only art holy:

For all nations shall come and worship before thee;
For thy judgments are made manifest.

And after these things I heard a great voice of much people in heaven, saying, "Alleluia; Salvation, and glory, and honour, and power, unto the Lord our God." And a voice came out of the throne, saying, "Praise our God, all ye his servants, and ye that fear him, both small and great."

And I heard as it were the voice of a great multitude, and as the voice of many waters, and as the voice of mighty thunderings, saying, "Alleluia: for the Lord God omnipotent reigneth."

And I fell at his feet to worship him. And he said unto me, "See thou do it not: I am thy fellowservant, and of thy brethren that have the testimony of Jesus: worship God: for the testimony of Jesus is the spirit of prophecy."

And I saw heaven opened, and behold a white horse; and he that sat upon him was called Faithful and True, and in righteousness he doth judge and make war. And I saw a new heaven and a new earth: for the first heaven and the first earth were passed away; and there was no more sea. And I John saw the holy city, new Jerusalem, coming down from God out of heaven, prepared as a bride adorned for her husband. And I heard a great voice out of heaven saying, "Behold, the tabernacle of God is with men, and he will dwell with them, and they shall be his people, and God himself shall be with them, and be their God. And God shall wipe away all tears from their eyes; and there shall be no more death, neither sorrow, nor crying, neither shall there be any more pain: for the former things are passed away."

And he that sat upon the throne said, "Behold, I make all things new." And he said unto me, "Write: for these words are true and faithful."

And he said unto me, "It is done. I am Alpha and Omega, the beginning and the end. I will give unto him that is athirst of the fountain of the water of life freely. He that overcometh shall inherit all things; and I will be his God, and he shall be my son."

And he carried me away in the spirit to a great and high mountain, and shewed me that great city, the holy Jerusalem, descending out of heaven from God.

And I saw no temple therein: for the Lord God Almighty and the *The new Jerusalem* Lamb are the temple of it. And the city had no need of the sun, neither of the moon, to shine in it: for the glory of God did lighten it, and the Lamb is the light thereof. And the nations of them which are saved shall walk in the light of it: and the kings of the earth do bring their glory and honour into it. And the gates of it shall not be shut at all by day: for there shall be no night there. And they shall bring the glory and honour of the nations into it. And there shall in no wise enter into it any thing that defileth, neither whatsoever worketh abomination, or maketh a lie: but they which are written in the Lamb's book of life.

And he shewed me a pure river of water of life, clear as crystal, proceeding out of the throne of God and of the Lamb. In the midst of the street of it, and on either side of the river, was there the tree of life, which bare twelve manner of fruits, and yielded her fruit every month: and the leaves of the tree were for the healing of the nations.

And there shall be no more curse: but the throne of God and of the Lamb shall be in it; and his servants shall serve him: and they shall see his face; and his name shall be in their foreheads. And there shall be no night there; and they need no candle, neither light of the sun; for the Lord God giveth them light: and they shall reign for ever and ever.

And he said unto me, "These sayings are faithful and true: and the Lord God of the holy prophets sent his angel to shew unto his servants the things which must shortly be done. Behold, I come quickly: blessed is he that keepeth the sayings of the prophecy of this book."

And I John saw these things, and heard them. And when I had heard and seen, I fell down to worship before the feet of the angel which shewed me these things.

And he saith unto me, "Seal not the sayings of the prophecy of this book: for the time is at hand. And, behold, I come quickly: and my reward is with me, to give every man according as his work shall be. I am Alpha and Omega, the beginning and the end, the first and the last. Blessed are they that do his commandments, that they may have right to the tree of life, and may enter in through the gates into the city.

"I Jesus have sent mine angel to testify unto you these things in the churches. I am the root and the offspring of David, and the bright and morning star. And the Spirit and the bride say, 'Come.' And let him that heareth say, 'Come.' And let him that is athirst come. And whosoever will, let him take the water of life freely."

He which testifieth these things, saith, "Surely I come quickly." Amen. Even so, come, Lord Jesus.

## *Benediction*

Now unto him that is able to keep you from falling, and to present you faultless before the presence of his glory with exceeding joy, to the only wise God our Saviour, be glory and majesty, dominion and power, both now and ever. Amen.

THE grace of the Lord Jesus Christ, and the love of God, and
the communion of the Holy Ghost, be with you all. Amen.

# INDEX TO PART I

*[References to the Apocrypha are in Italics]*

# INDEX TO PART I

# INDEX TO PART I

[ 379 ]

# INDEX TO PART I

# INDEX TO PART I

# INDEX TO PART I

# INDEX TO PART II

*[References to the Apocrypha are in Italics]*

# INDEX TO PART II

[ 385 ]

# INDEX TO PART II

# INDEX TO PART II

## INDEX TO PART II

# INDEX TO PART II

[ 391 ]

# INDEX TO PART II

COMPOSITION BY THE UNIVERSITY PRESS, INC.

UNDER THE SUPERVISION OF

JOHN BIANCHI OF THE MERRYMOUNT PRESS

PRINTING AND BINDING BY

THE HADDON CRAFTSMEN, INC.

PUBLISHED BY HARPER & BROTHERS

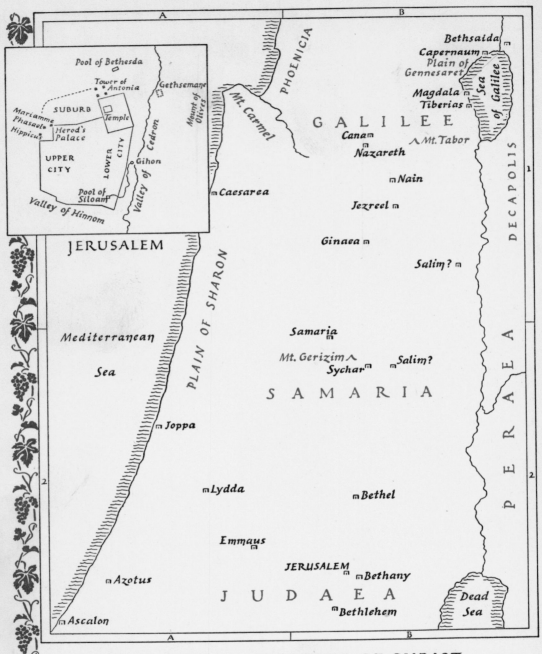

PALESTINE AT THE TIME OF CHRIST